I0729509

THE REAL DEAL

FIELD NOTES FROM THE LIFE OF A WORKING PHOTOGRAPHER

JOE McNALLY

The Real Deal: Field Notes from the Life of a Working Photographer
Joe McNally

www.joemcnally.com

Project editor: Ted Waitt
Project manager: Lisa Brazieal
Interior and cover design: Aren Straiger
Interior layout: Kim Scott, Bumpy Design
Indexer: James Minkin

ISBN: 978-1-68198-801-6
1st Edition (1st printing, December 2021)
© 2022 Joe McNally

All images © Joe McNally except as follows: photo of Joe on front cover (top left) by Michael Quinones; photo of Joe and Annie on page v by Jayna Hedges; photo of Joe and Bill Douthitt on page ix by unknown assistant; double-exposure Polaroid of Joe on page 87 by Garth Vaughan; photo of Joe on bridge on page 104 by unknown bridge worker; behind-the-scenes photos on pages 196, 277, 278, and 287–291 by Anne Cahill; behind-the-scenes photo on page 280 and photos of Joe on pages 312 and 313 by Andrew Tomasino; photo of Rita Perrault on page 301 by Michael Keel; photo of Joe on page 330 by Dennis McDonald.

Rocky Nook Inc.
1010 B Street, Suite 350
San Rafael, CA 94901
USA

www.rockynook.com

Distributed in the UK and Europe by Publishers Group UK
Distributed in the U.S. and all other territories by Ingram Publisher Services

Library of Congress Control Number: 2021937328

I imagined a life.
And then I took pictures of it.

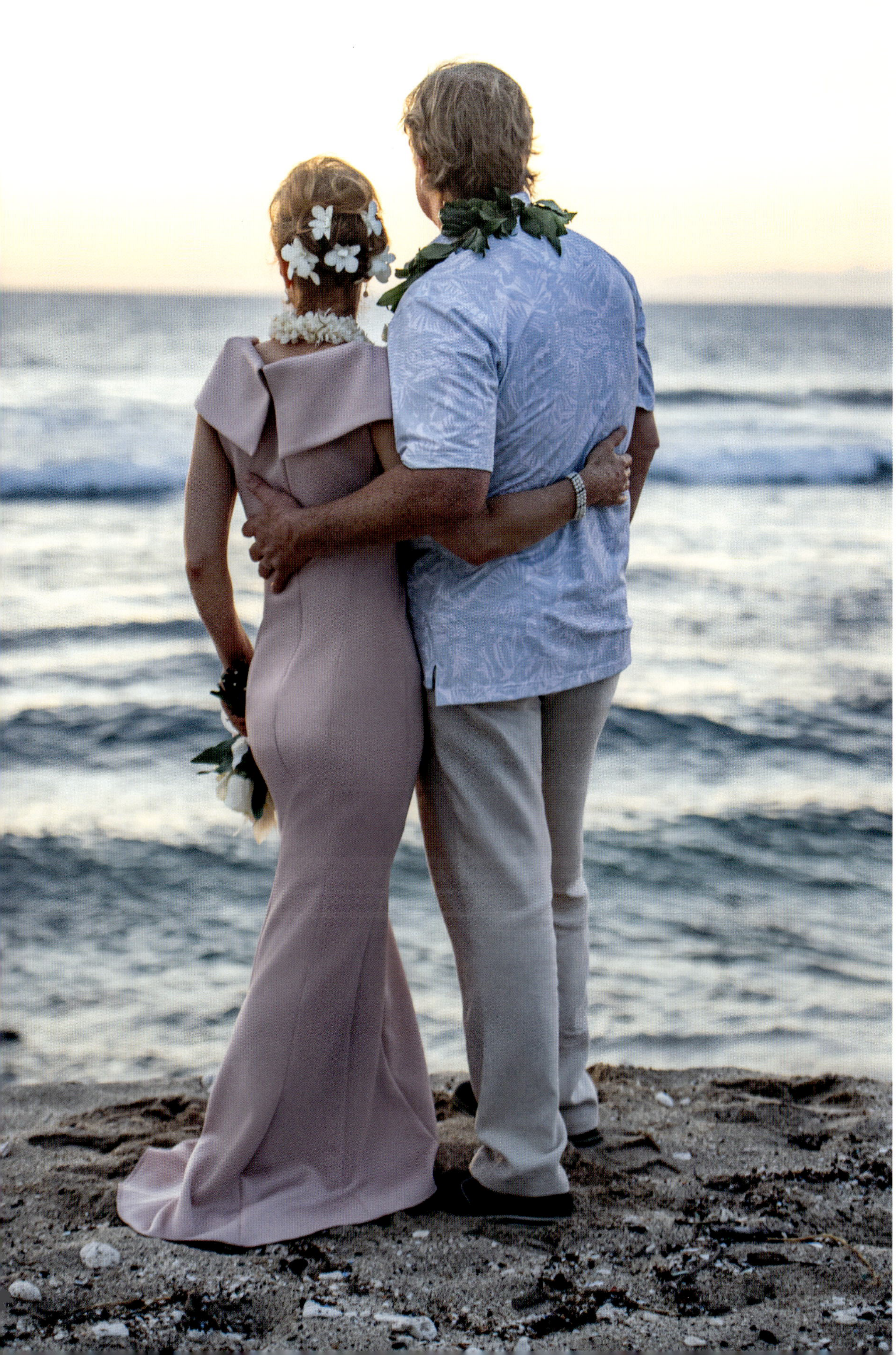

To Annie . . .

Years ago, I saw you for the first time, and you took my breath away. I've never gotten it back. My love, my love. With you, I will always look to the horizon . . .

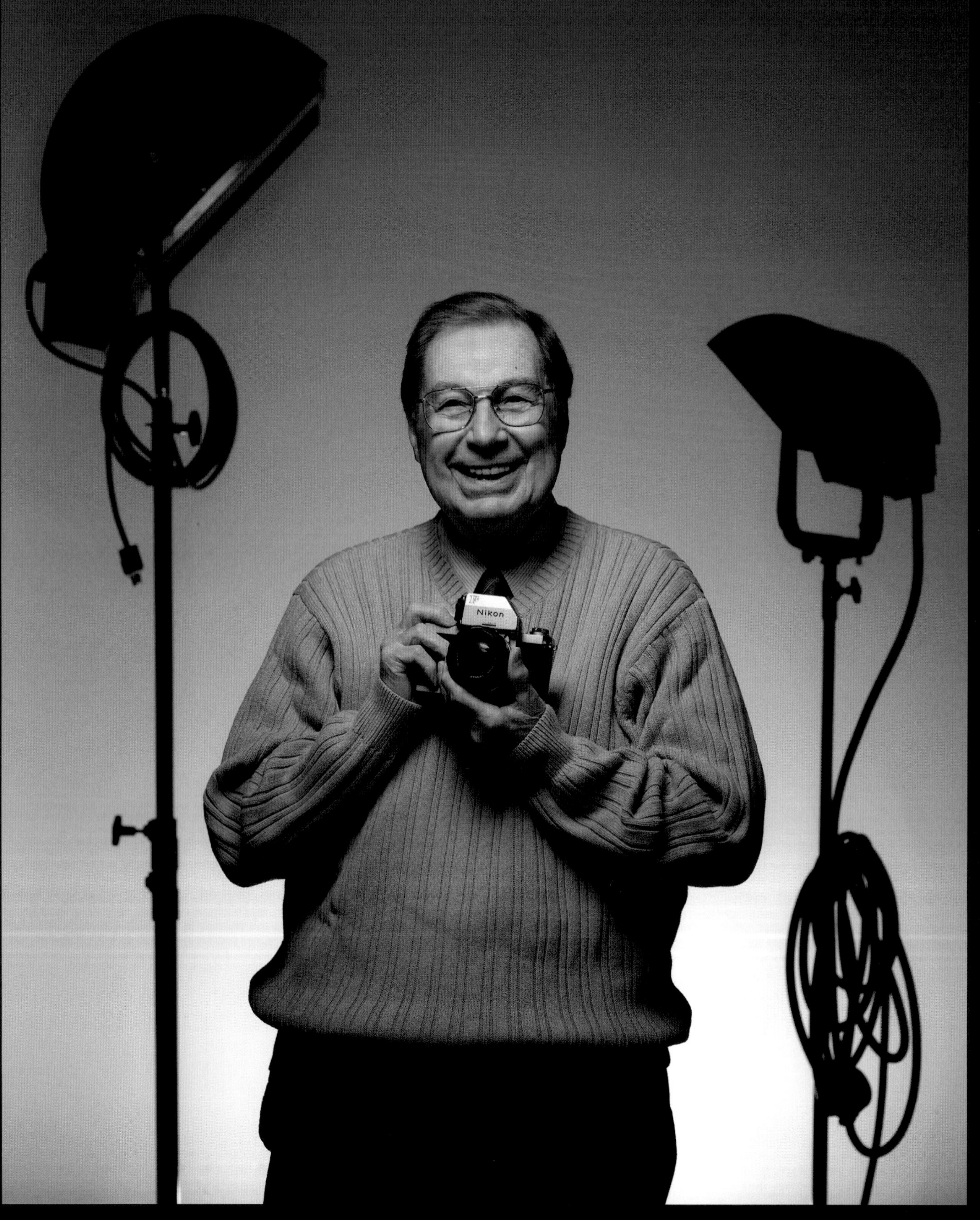

Acknowledgments

Whenever your life intersects with a good teacher, a pathfinder, it's a momentous and powerful occasion. For me, Professor Fred Demarest of the Newhouse School photography program was that intersection. He was calm, wise, and lucid, and possessed a bubbling chuckle that still reverberates in my memory. He was not charismatic or dashing—rather, the opposite. He was a bit on the fuddy-duddy side of things, leading him to be called "Uncle Fred" amongst us students. But it was that very avuncular, considerate demeanor which was perfect to channel the unknowing, hubristic, inexperienced, raging id of one certain graduate student in his program, back long ago.

I was a writing major, thus not allowed by rule to take any of the upper-level photo classes. Fred made exceptions and created a path that, were it up to others, would have been denied me. He admitted me to the graduate level program when there was no real photographic evidence that such an admission would ultimately prove fruitful.

He channeled and redirected disorganized student-level ideas and impulses so effectively that I would leave his office with new direction and purpose, and pat myself on the back. "Glad I thought of that!"

He was direct and calm in his criticism. He understood the creation of bad work was necessary to find the way to good work, and he would weed wack through the thickets of my ineptitude to find evidence of potential that he could nurture and encourage. He didn't tear you down. He reassured. He would tell you it would be okay.

That was Fred. When I visited him in hospice, we had a good talk. He told me, "Joe, I'm not afraid. I'll be okay, until I'm not okay." His words.

I made this picture of him (opposite) as he neared the end of his life. It was an infinitely small way to thank him. He taught me about f-stops and shutter speeds, but he also taught me much about being calm and kind and patient. (It took many years for those lessons to really take root.) I miss him. He was my teacher. He was my friend. His forbearance is the reason this book exists.

Fred (I suspect quite happily) passed me, and ultimately the entire photo program, onto Tony Golden, another fine teacher, in Fred's mold. Like Fred, he tolerated, channeled, inquired, and informed. He went on to run the department for many years, and it thrived under his guidance. We became family, and his boundless passion for photography and teaching stays with me to this day.

All of my schooling, youthful angst, and fiery misdirection landed me in New York City, camera in hand, eager eyes at the ready. A lifetime of mentors awaited. Too many to mention all told, but significantly, blessedly, I bumped up against formidable talents, so assured and confident of their own skills they were open and easy about sharing.

Danny Farrell (below). "Thousand at 11, kid!"

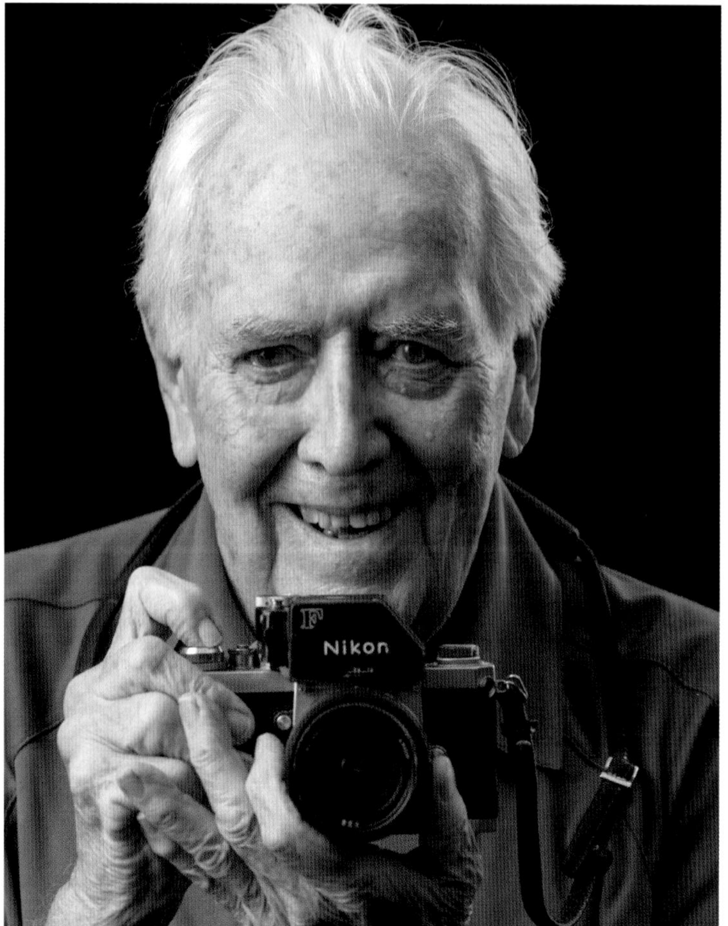

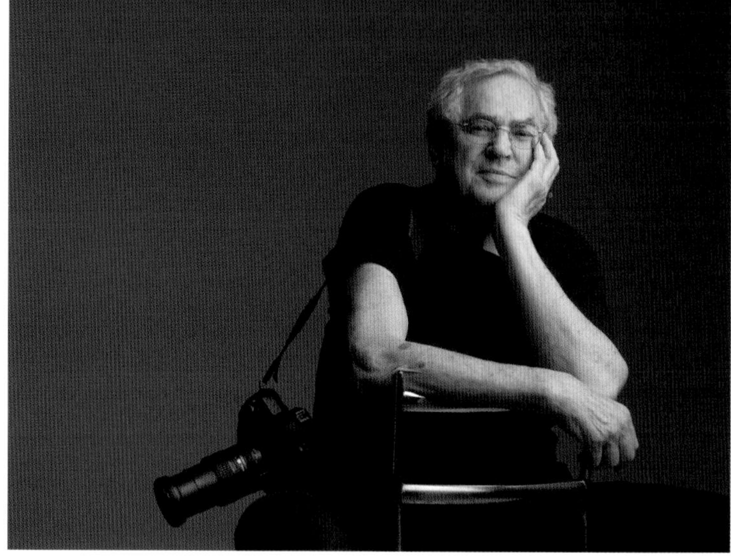

Jay Maisel (above). "Light, gesture, color." Pretty much covers it.

So many others! Carl Mydans, Gordon Parks, Eddie Adams, Mary Ellen Mark, Paul Fusco, Dave Burnett, Maggie Steber, Wally McNamee, John White, Bill Eppridge, Mark Kettenhofen, Ari Espay, Neil Leifer, Hank Morgan, Carol Guzy, Matthew Jordan Smith, Dennis McDonald, Ami Vitale, Brian Lanker, Deanne Fitzmaurice, Bill Frakes, Bob Martin, Yunghi Kim, Heinz Kluetmeier . . . all possessed astonishing skills and a willingness to share them.

Picture editors. Theirs is the often unnoticed and thankless task of giving you the right job at the right moment, and then shepherding the resulting pictures into the public eye. Guiding, critiquing, pushing, demanding, and, hopefully only occasionally, being clear about the nature of their disappointment. Dispassion is a requisite for a good picture editor. You might have gone through hell and back for a photo, but their job is to put your travails aside and bear down on the essential question of whether you infused that photo with emotion, impact, information, and graphical order. In other words, yes, you went through a lot in the field to bring this back, but does it work?

Editors who were excellent at isolating that crucial issue and asking that question have been formative for me. Larry DeSantis, Eliane Laffont, John Loengard, Mel Scott, Bobbi Burrows, Gen Umei, and Tom Kennedy were extraordinary at pushing a photographer to the next level and finding the unexpected eloquence of a take. They not only opened doors, but they also turned on the lights in the hallway of your next passage.

Jimmy Colton especially. "Uncle Jimmy" to many a beleaguered photog, he is never forgetful of the drafty, isolating, unforgiving nature of freelancing, and has always been there for the photographer in the field. He was the editor on one of my first big international assignments for *Newsweek*, the return of Pope John Paul II to his native Poland in the very early '80s. He remains my editor today; as I write this, I am packing up to shoot the Tokyo Olympics for Zuma Press.

And then there's Bill. Bill Douthitt, formerly of the *National Geographic.* We had many adventures, and did good work, but also made a concerted effort to not take things too seriously, which was a bit of an outlier attitude within the yellow border, where, at least back then, everything needed to be treated seriously, with grave intent, as the task at hand was for the ages.

Hence, preparing a coverage about the human brain, we left word at NGS headquarters that we had gone to the research library at the National Institute of Mental Health, when in actuality we went to the very first show (10 a.m.) of the very first day of the very first *Jurassic Park* movie. Bill blanched upon returning to the office, where he found a slew of angry messages from the boss, who was demanding to know his whereabouts in angrier and angrier terms. The editor at the time was the impatient sort, especially after lunch. But the NIMH research library trip was our story, and we stuck to it.

The picture here (above right) does not show a sense of collaboration, but it was done in jest. Bill always allowed me a voice and listened to it well. But blessedly, he was undeterred by our friendship and unswayed by my madcap descriptions of the importance of a particular frame. He did not hesitate to read me the riot act or dismiss pictures I quixotically had a fondness for. We shot, edited, and produced 11 coverages for *Nat Geo* in our time together there, amongst them being the first all-digital coverage ever in the magazine's history, which was a highly pressurized project that had many eyes on it. My wonderful friend, and a great editor.

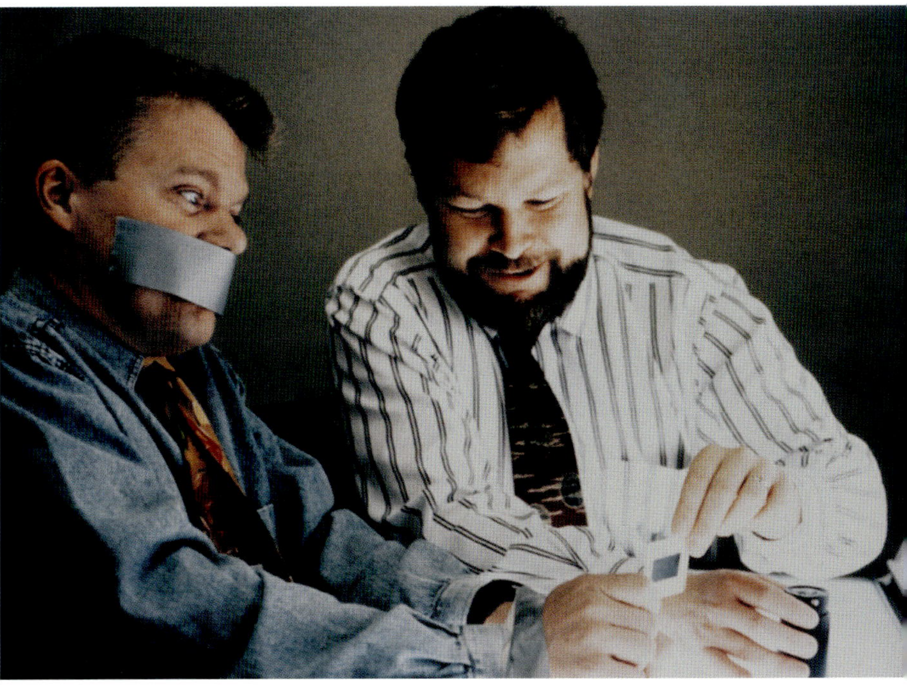

Every year in December, for many years, Lynn DelMastro, dearest of friends and our studio manager since forever, has hosted "Abbondanza" at her home. Literally translated as "abundance," it's a time for studio friends and family to literally exhale and celebrate another year of successfully balancing on the tightrope called freelancing . . . and making it, yet again. Never a certain proposition.

And we are a family. Lynn steers the ship in stalwart fashion, with love, confidence, unerring business savvy, and life wisdom. She has kept McNally Photography on track and moving forward, despite the roadblocks and headwinds of this nutty business, and she has done so with kindness and patience. Annie shepherds our social media and marketing efforts with boundless creativity and an eye for coherence of message. Together, they have saved me from my more lunatic imaginings so often it defies memory. And the "lost boys," as we refer to them, even though they move onto other things, remain forever a part of our hearts. Cali, who over 10 years progressed from intern to crew chief, is seeking a path apart from photography. Brad Moore, Drew Gurian, Jon Cospito, Mike Grippi, and Andrew Tomasino have all gone onto bright futures as visual storytellers. And they never call! And they never write!

Kidding. We all remain close. Photography involves heart, mind, and spirit, in addition to blood, sweat, and tears. We remain a family. How could we not?

Speaking of families, I have two sisters, Kathy and Rosemary, who I remain incredibly close to, and are a blessing in my life. I also have three blood brothers—Mike Corrado and Lindsay Silverman of Nikon are two of them. We've been part of the Nikon family basically since birth. And then there's the big guy, Jeff Snyder. Been buying my cameras from Jeff since forever. They have always been there for me, as brothers, as fellow photogs, and as camera and flash consiglieri. They remain so to this day. We've had many an adventure.

I have a family in the photographic teaching community as well. So many workshop participants over the years stay in touch, and have become dear friends. And at the heart of that family are Liza Politi and Ari Espay—Fancy Girl, Street Boy. Sums it up well.

And Sid and Michelle Monroe, of the Monroe Gallery in Santa Fe, are also dear friends and fierce defenders of photography. So proud to be a part of their gallery.

This photo business is basically a small town, filled with supportive, passionate people and companies, without which the photographer would be lost. I'm fortunate to have many friends at Nikon, Nikon UK, Lastolite, Manfrotto, Gitzo, Profoto, Capture One, Maha, Tether Tools, Adorama, Grays of Westminster, and Printique to put names to this wonderful support system. Without their advice, counsel, and products, it would be infinitely harder to make pictures and forge ahead. These photo enterprises also do an excellent job at fostering young talent.

Daniel Norton, Todd Owyoung, Seth Miranda, Charmi Peña, Elly Russell, M.D. Welch, and Audrey Woulard are great examples of wonderful young photographers being nurtured by our small, supportive community.

And the editor of this book, Ted Waitt at Rocky Nook. The contract to do this was actually signed years ago, and Ted was content to let it ride while I roamed the earth, promising to someday come to a keyboard with stamina and intent. He has the patience of a saint and the serenity of a monk. And the sense of humor of . . . well, you'll have to read on. A great editor and a great friend.

And Annie, my wife. Happiness entered my life with Annie. As a photographer, you have to live, breathe, see, photograph, teach, and write from the heart, and I know my heart is safe with her . . . always.

Table of Contents

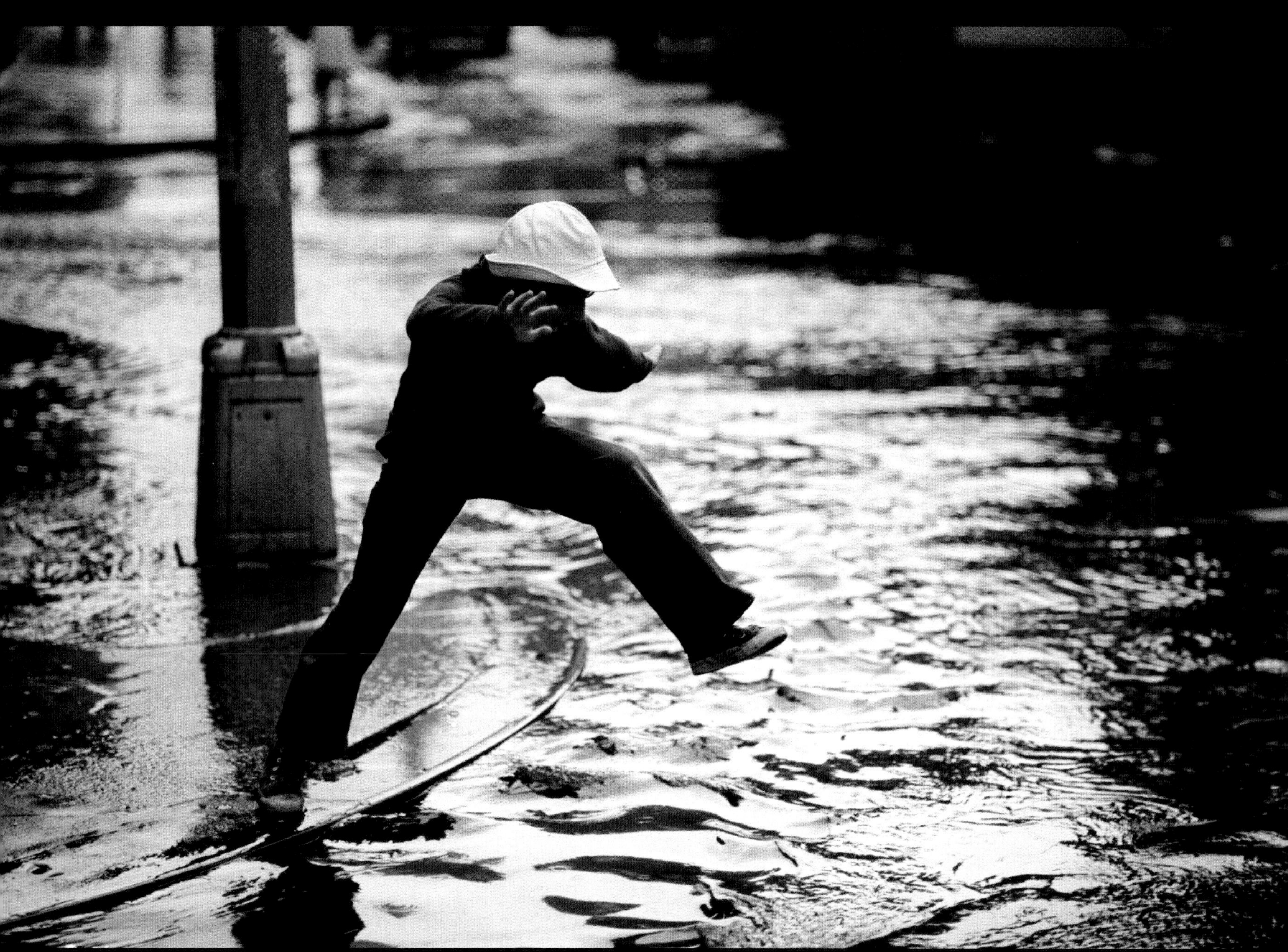

A Leap of Faith

Funny how a career in this flimsy, vexingly whimsical profession can turn on the simplest of things. A tick, a tock, a time, and a place. A question. A conversation. At the camera, a lucky sliver of a second when head, heart, eye, and right index finger really do click. "Random" doesn't begin to describe it. But I can't think of a better term, so let's go with it.

In 1976 I went to New York to become a professional photographer. In the typically hubristic, arrogant fashion of know-nothing youth, I thought the combination of my engaging personality, my woeful and totally preliminary skill set as a shooter, and a ton of sheer drive and enthusiasm would be welcomed, yea, even embraced.

It wasn't.

I headed south on Route 17, another would-be photojournalist duly minted by the Newhouse School in Syracuse, New York, determined to make a go of being a photographer in New York City. I had no real use for small town America. For me, the city was it. Maybe it was the movies I was raised on, like *The French Connection* and *Serpico*, but I wanted the grit, the concrete, the lights, and the 24-hour hum of the city. Without ever living there, I knew it was the only place I wanted to live. I couldn't wait to pound the concrete with a camera in hand and have a regular coffee shop I went to. I loved the idea of going to sleep with traffic snarl as my lullaby. Even the squeal of subway brakes was music. There, in NYC, I could be alone with my inner drive, my angst, and my insecurities, and I could concentrate, push the camera, and walk the talk. Trust me, if you want to be alone, the big city, as teeming as an ant hill with humanity, is the place to do it.

There was this problem of making a living.

I was so green upon arrival in New York, I might as well have been a bushel of lettuce arriving in the pre-dawn chill at the famed Hunts Point Market, the entry point for most of the country-grown produce that makes its way into the big city.

I was raw, untutored, and unknowing. The scope of what I did not know about life, and lens, was boundless. All that stuff in the movies was, well, the movies. The truth? I was scared.

I moved into my mom's house, in Eastchester, NY, a commuter suburb north of the city, and started going into the city every day to look for work. I knew her house was not a long-term deal. I mentioned how expensive rents were downtown, and she looked at me with her usual mix of disapproval and steely love and said, "Don't think you're living here."

One of the first stops on the hunt for work was Sygma Photo News, up on West 72nd Street. Sygma was an international photo news agency run by Eliane Laffont, the dragon lady of the business. She was tough, whip-smart, and connected. I had gotten an audience with her by communing briefly with Sean Callahan, also a Syracuse grad. Sean was a writer, editor, some-time photographer, full-time entrepreneur, and spinner of tall tales. He was manic, and helpful, and a perennial way station for woebegone Syracuse grads arriving in the city. He gave me a few names and numbers, Eliane's among them. I showed her my standard, regulation 11x14 black and white bleed mounted

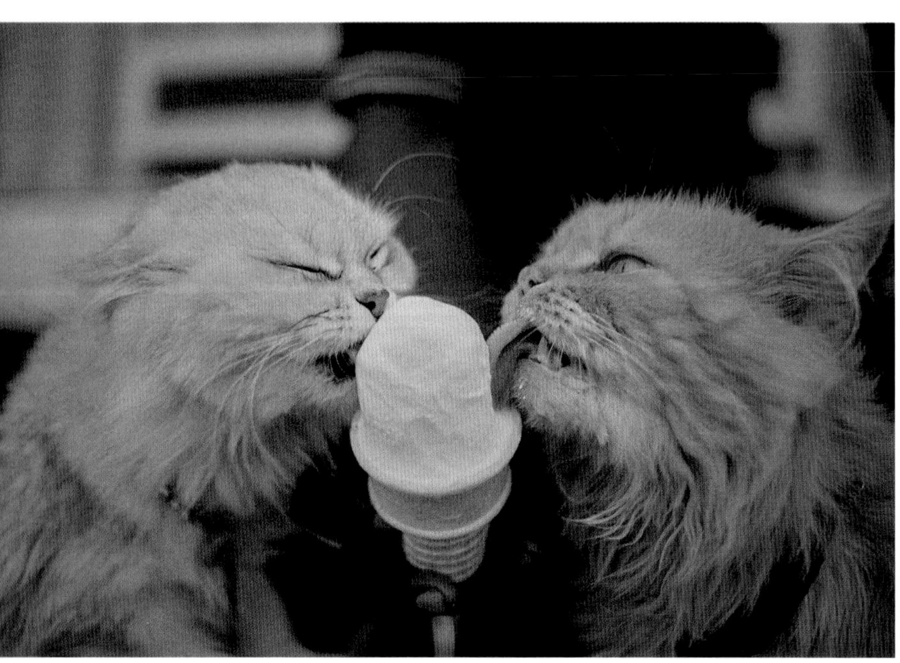

portfolio. She eyed me across the desk like I was an under-cooked meal that needed seasoning and a lot longer in the oven. "If you come to New York, I will use you." So intimidated was I that, stupidly, I never went back.

(At least, not immediately. Much, much later in my career, I actually did join Sygma, still run by Eliane, who was even more formidable by that time. Sygma had moved to much larger offices on West 57th Street, across from the famed [and fright-fully expensive] Russian Tea Room. Ever the rube, I asked Eliane to lunch and was determined to impress her by buying her the meal. I asked the waiter for the check, confident and assured of my worldly status and know-how. Eliane laughed and told me it was already taken care of. "Darling, don't worry about the bill. I have an account here." Sigh.)

But, circa 1976, I couldn't have afforded a dog and a Coke at a street vendor. Things weren't going well. My mother's thread-bare patience was running thin with the ongoing presence of her returned package of a child. I needed something that would produce a paycheck. And then I remembered my mom's neighbor, Chuck, had spent his whole career at the New York *Daily News*.

I never viewed Chuck Klinefelter as someone who was going to be important in my life. To me, moving in next door to him as I commenced the eighth grade, he was just the elderly, mildly grouchy next-door neighbor who pissed my mother off because his roses were more luscious and vibrant than hers.

We had moved next to him as my mother continued her des-perate migratory efforts to find a house she liked that had a dry basement and a living room big enough to fit her oriental rugs, which she prized more than her children. My father changed jobs a fair bit, and we moved from place to place, school sys-tem to school system. Eighth grade was the final pit stop of my grammar school career, which had spanned five different schools, and five different orders of nuns.

If moods were plotted with, say, a pressure gauge, all this mov-ing had pretty much pushed mom's needle sort of permanently into the red zone. She was always ready to blow a gasket, and

Chuck's roses just tightened her valves further. Me, I was just dealing with being the new kid yet again. Surprisingly, it was our last house. Mom stayed there for many years, and I finished all my schooling while she remained at that address, experimenting with Miracle-Gro and eggshells.

I got along with Chuck okay. I didn't hit my ball into his yard all that often, and I would occasionally dig him out of a winter snow as a freebie. All these years later, I went next door and asked him about the press biz in NYC, and he said, "Go see Eddie Quinn."

Sitting across from Ed Quinn, the editorial department manager at the New York *Daily News*, the largest tabloid paper in the Big Apple, I was a ball of nerves. Seemed like a natural fit—get a job at "New York's Picture Newspaper." Except I really didn't know how to get a job, and pretty much didn't know how to shoot much of a picture, either. Plus, I was timid. I still had that deep, abiding fear of the teacher that had leached into my bones, courtesy of generations of ruler-wielding nuns, habit-clad and as fierce and unforgiving as a horde of Huns. I called everybody "sir." Afraid to fail, even more afraid to offend.

I was also too dumb to understand that he was trying to sell me on taking the job and joining the *News*. He was schooled in the old ways, of course, but he was observant enough to know the future of newspapering was not going to remain in the hands of trench-coated, fedora-wearing, Speed Graphic–toting, flash-bulb-blasting one-exposure-and-done types of photogs. The public was demanding more nuanced coverage, celebrity and style stuff, done pretty and well, and picture stories that moved and shook the reader. Cheesecake and dead bodies on the subway platforms, always the grist of tabloids, were no longer necessarily the order of the day (though of course they still ran).

Stammering and uncertain, I turned down his offer of a copyboy job at the paper. Beneath me, I thought. I wanted to be a photographer! I'm a goddamn college graduate! (I was also too dumb to know my attitude was arrogant.) Ed, Irish to the core, grizzled and wise after 40 years in the New York newspaper game,

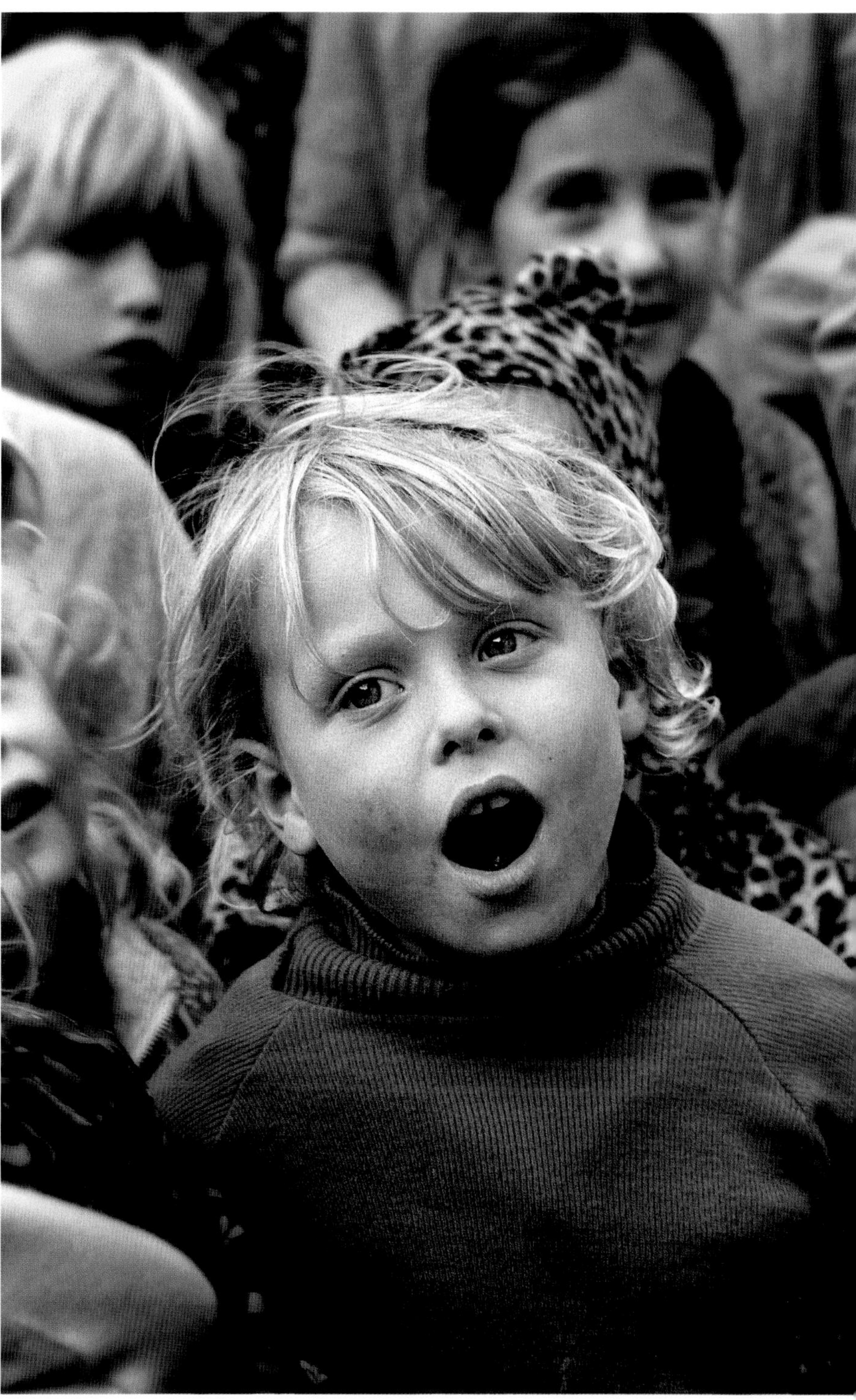

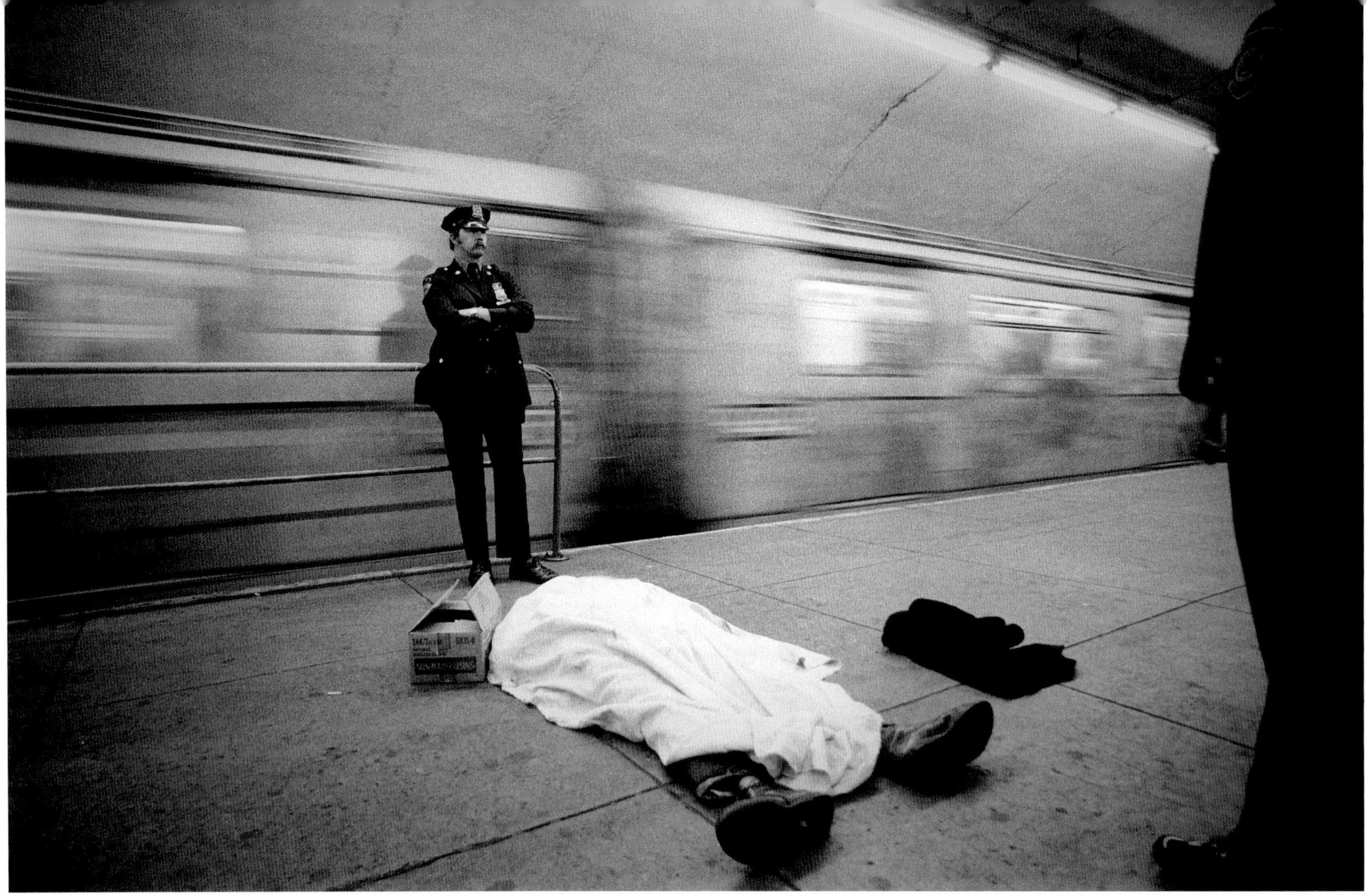

cocked his head, and looked at me with a weary, knowing glint in his eye.

He casually asked one of those pivotal questions. He inquired if I had read the latest issue of *Editor & Publisher*, the monthly bible of the newspaper industry. It had a "Positions Available" section in the back. Like a lawyer who knows the answer to his question before he asks it, Ed serenely perused the job offerings. "Let's see, Joe," he said. "Photographer wanted, Kankakee, Illinois."

He put down the magazine and peered over his wire rims at me with a look that pretty much said, "You want a job like that, you know-it-all little sumbitch? You want to work in some East Bejesus backwater and shoot pictures of PTA meetings, ribbon cuttings, and Mrs. McGillicutty's latest, best cornbread recipe?"

Instead, he was more polite. He simply said, "Joe, do you want to work in Kankakee?"

I started the following week.

I moved into a quite scruffy place at that time, The Beacon, on Broadway and 74th Street on the Upper West Side of Manhattan. My apartment was a narrow, small room with one window, directly overlooking the Beacon Theatre roof, which had a thick, silvery paint job, typical of old roofing. I'm sure it kept most of the rain out of the theater. What it did for my apartment was bounce the sun right through my window. Remember when you were a kid and, on a hot summer day, you would take a magnifying glass and focus the sun's rays down to a scorching little beam that would burn up a leaf? My apartment was the leaf.

Honestly, I remember that little place with a measure of fondness. My dad and I painted it, and it was the last time we worked together on something. A lifetime of smoking unfiltered Camels caught up to him shortly thereafter. And, truth be told, for the opportunity to work at the *News*, and actually be in New York with a crack at being a photog, I would have slept on the sidewalk.

Which, on certain nights, might have been an upgrade. I would lay there in the superheated blackness, window wide open, with my bed pulsing to the beat of whatever live act was onstage at the theater below. There were nights when, getting up to pee, my feet would hit the floor with a crunch. Which meant I hadn't hit the threadbare carpet, I had landed on a limousine-sized cockroach scuttling about in the darkness.

The music wasn't the only thing that kept me awake. I was woken up one night by the rhythmic oomphing of highly penetrative sex at my door. Or, rather, on my door. A couple were evidently going at it in the hallway and using my apartment door as a vertical mattress. A New York version of the knee trembler! I didn't have the heart to shout to them and interrupt the festivities.

The hotel location was handy. There was a coffee shop on the ground floor, which had cheap, delicious chocolate donuts. And a McDonald's down the block. At that point, a Big Mac was about a buck, fries were 50 cents, and a soda was maybe a quarter. Calzones were super cheap, and very filling. The fabled 72nd Street subway stop was a short two blocks away, albeit right through Needle Park, at that time the main port of call for a great deal of the heroin flooding the city. If you made it through there unscathed, the subway cost half a buck. And 72nd Street was an express stop! I could zoom to Times Square and hop on the shuttle over to Grand Central, which was a couple blocks from the storied New York News Building, workplace of Lois Lane, Clark Kent, and Jimmy Olsen.

And home to the lobby's famous globe, which is an art deco masterpiece—huge, glowing, and silently rotating, 24/7, in the middle of the lobby, to this day. That wonderful globe, a tourist attraction for many years, has been used as a photo prop, according to *News* legend. Charged with making some sort of illustration photo (not their strong point) depicting the Russian launching of a dog into space orbit aboard Sputnik, the two old school *News* photogs assigned to this task started ruminating, which meant of course getting knee-walking drunk at a local establishment, where they evidently struck up a conversation with two airline stewardesses. These ladies lived in Tudor City, next door to the News Building, and as tradition had it back then, shared a small apartment with numerous other stews. (The term "stewardess" was the vernacular of the day.) This group of roomies had a puppy, and some goldfish. One of the photographers had a fishing pole and tackle in his trunk. It was not long before the puppy, stashed in the fishbowl, was flying over the earth, held aloft by a photog on a ladder, wielding his fishing pole. I'm sure the photo was not memorable, but points given for improvisation.

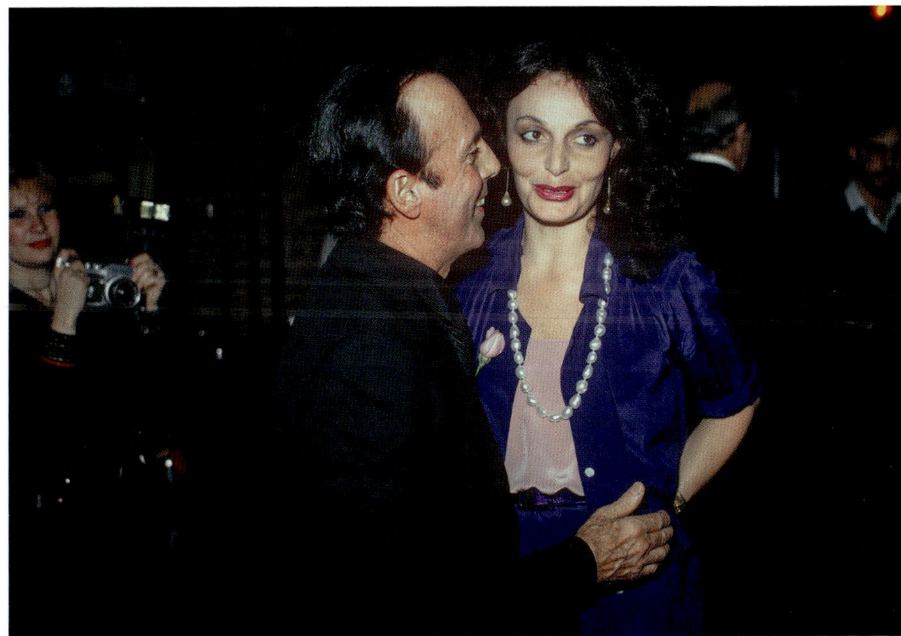

If I was working the afternoon shift, I would get out late enough to grab the after-10 p.m. discount, when subway and bus fares went to half price. I'd hop on the 104 bus, which had a stop in front of the *News*, and another right in front of my apartment building. The whole ride cost a quarter. Which was important, given the math of my survival in that first year. I was making $150 a week, which for some reason I remember came out to $109 total, after the feds, the state, and the city got done with you.

I preferred above-ground transit home at night, not for safety reasons, but just for the sheer theater of it. Ever go to the movies for a quarter? That was what it was like, when the bus I was on got jammed up in traffic crossing through Times Square. The long block of 42nd Street between 7th Avenue and 8th Avenue was the epicenter of the raucous, steamy, filthy, dangerous theater that was the city in the seventies. The street people, hookers, flashers with oversized raincoats, the scammers with lookouts, staging "find the pea" games on discarded boxes, fleecing tourists—all sweaty and glistening in the sickly green of the streetlights and the hot neon of the movie marquees showing fare such as *The Devil in Miss Jones*. I was drawn to it, fascinated by it, and scared of it all at once.

It was the time of *Taxi Driver*, and Travis Bickle saying, accurately, that "this city here is like an open sewer." Crumbling streets, garbage everywhere. Steam venting from ancient subways, running intermittently at best, just below your feet. And then President Gerry Ford, telling the bankrupt city to "Drop Dead," as the *Daily News* famously screamed on its front page.

Understand this was all before the go-go eighties, when Wall Street became the financial North Star of the city, and woke it up with the beautiful, deadly kiss of unbridled avarice. The Elysium that is the current version of Manhattan is unrecognizable relative to the tawdry 1970s mess. Yet that version of the city, as messy and dangerous and crime-ridden as it was, had desperate energy to it, like a bunch of folks engaged in sweaty, gyrating, vulgar, dirty dancing the night before the bombs drop. It wasn't a dry, observed experience one could safely have from the leather-clad confines of an Uber. It was decidedly wet

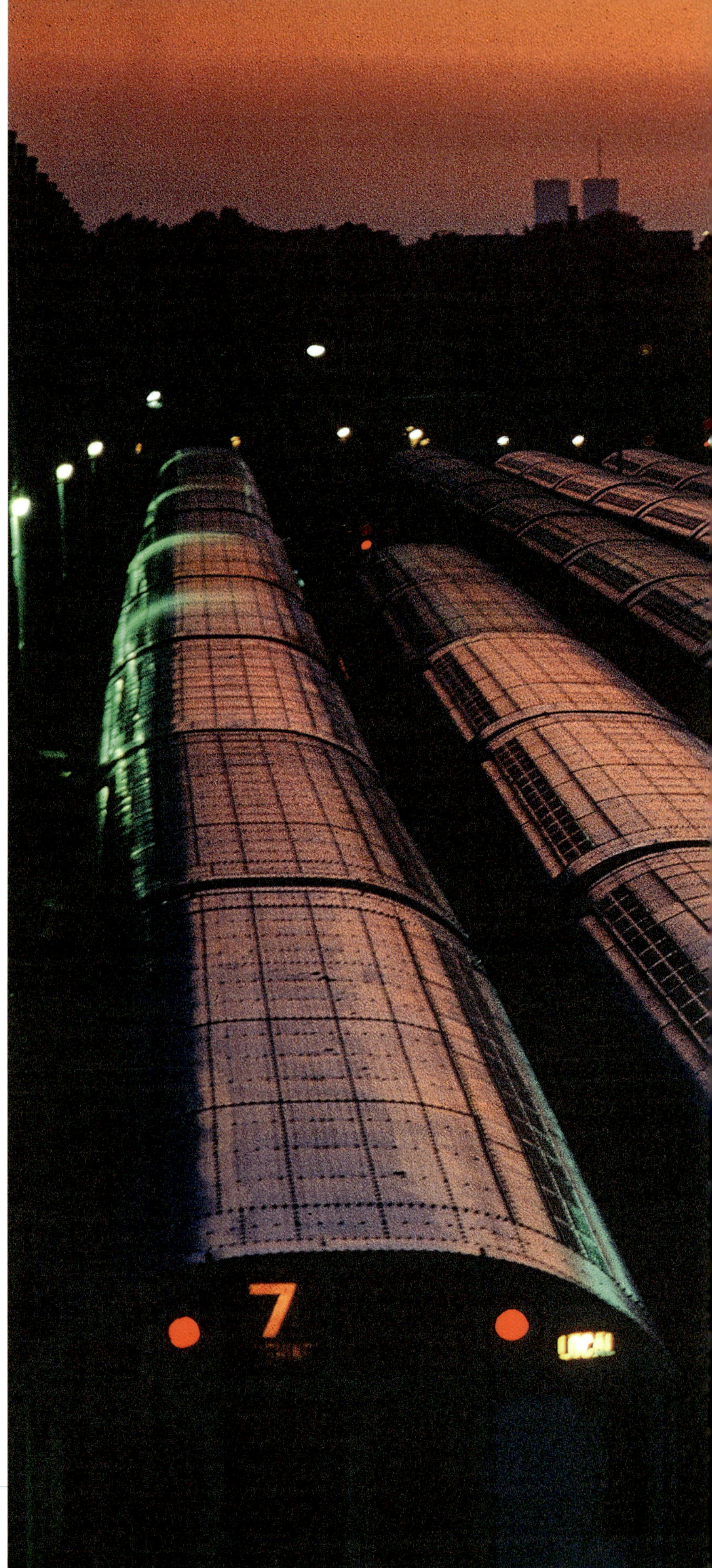

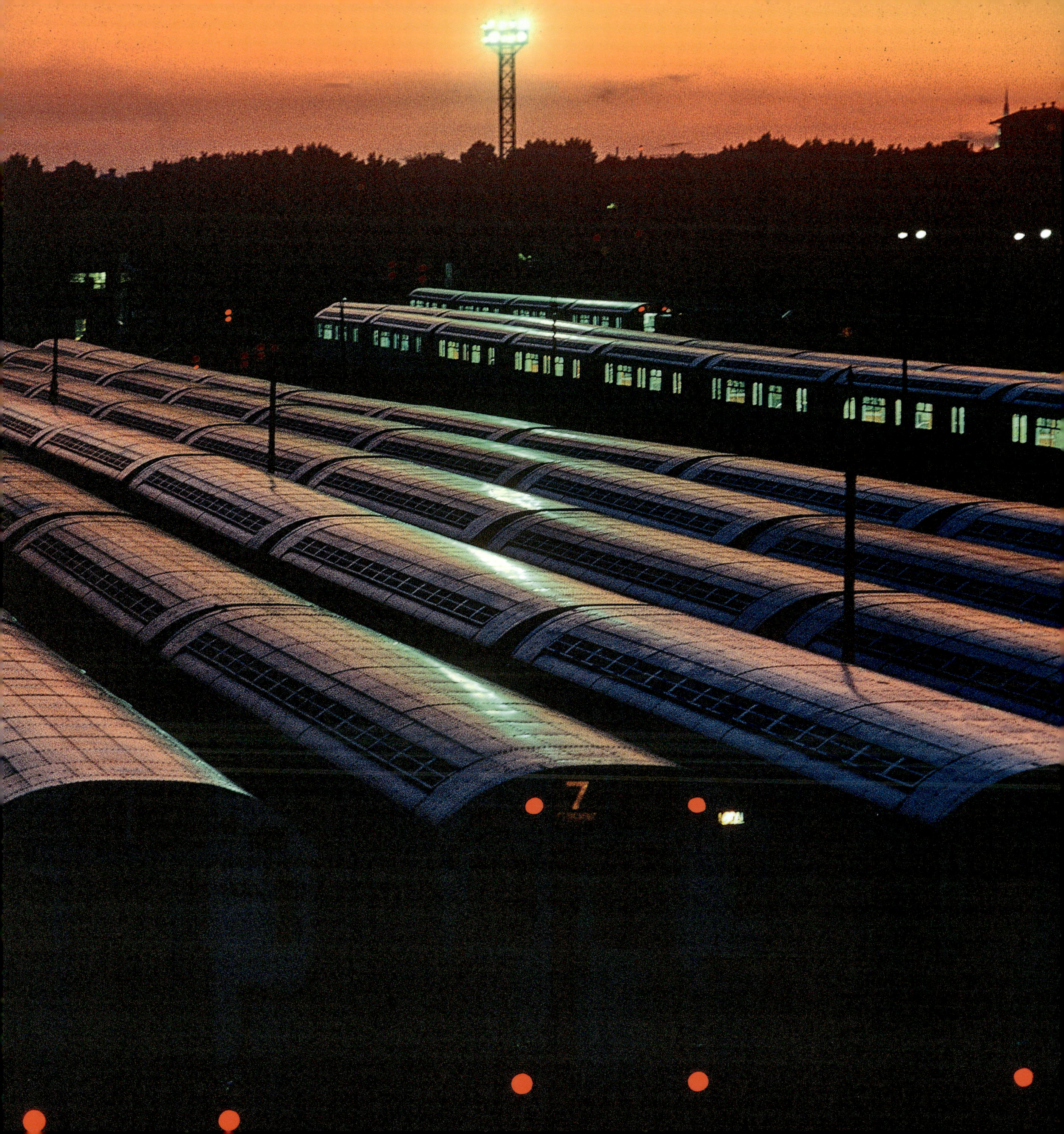

and sloppy and random and raunchy. But as desperate as the city was, I thrived on the cracked concrete, and loved the sheer grime and lurking menace of the place.

Most of the time. There were nights, though, as the lurid cacophony of Times Square faded, and the bus I was riding headed north on 8th Avenue into the bleak, broken Upper West Side, when I would retreat to the dark and the heat of my hole in the wall, and I would sit on my bed and weep. Ed Quinn's words would rise up in my head. "Do you want to work in Kankakee?"

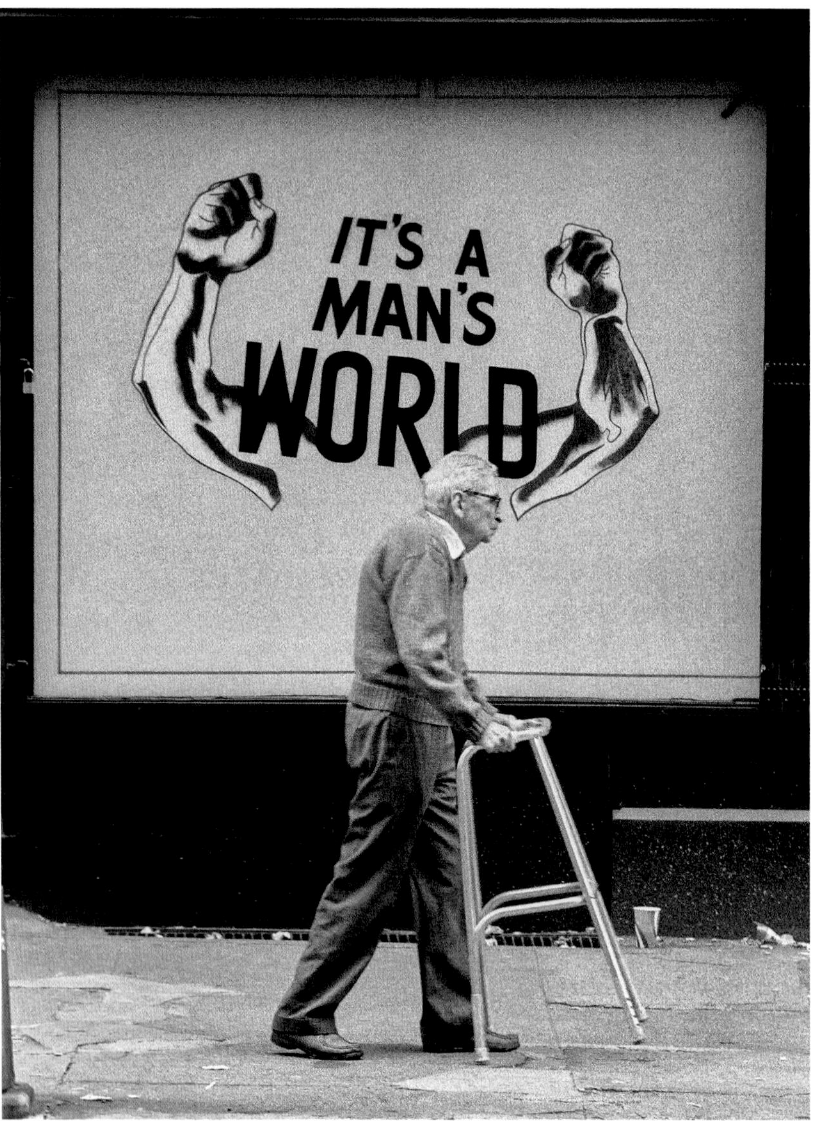

It Certainly Wasn't Kankakee

A copyboy sits on "the bench." Like taxis in a queue, you wait for the next call. It might be a raspy "Copy!" from an ossified editor on "the rim," which was slang for the copy desk. Some would just shout, "Boy!"

Life was not easy for the copyboy. You were at the beck and call of a lot of old-timey newspaper men who were determined to make you suffer just the way they did upon their entry into the business, when they were reporting the casualties of the Battle of Bull Run. They also looked enviously and resentfully at you and your youth, and your flat belly, and had fanciful imaginings about your voluminous sex life in NYC, 1970s, pre-AIDS.

For most of them, their hard-ons had gone south sometime around the Kennedy administration, and they were resigned to a life being hectored by editors in their workday, and I suspect not much different upon arrival home. If they ever engaged in an argument with one of their peers in the newsroom, the ultimate closing insult was, invariably, "Well at least I can still see my prick."

The shouts of "Copy!" would come from all over the newsroom, increasingly shrill and strained as deadline approached, and there would be various benches geographically situated in the cacophonous sprawl of desks to service the barking scribes. Your job on deadline would be to move copy from place to place, grabbing pages from an editor's "slot" and moving them to "the rim," literally a half-moon-shaped table where copy editors, pencils sharpened for the task, would correct for grammar, misspellings, and general usage of the language. The edited stories would make their way to the sixth floor composing room and be forged into lead, married to ink, and thus become a page in tomorrow's paper.

They would also be responsible for writing headlines.

Which was a fraught task to give to what was essentially a group of (mostly) dirty old men. Copy editors, necessarily sly in the use of words, lived to slide something filthy into the paper, undetected. I tapped into this unique skill set at one point, submitting to the gentlemen of the rim a story sent to me by a photog friend with whom I'd graduated school. He'd done the sensible thing and gone to a small market, and that burst of common sense was rewarded with a full-time job as a staff photographer, right out of the gate, albeit in rural New Jersey. He would send me clips he had published, and the occasional pithy story of life in the country.

One particular story he sent was a short piece, headlined "Sodomy Charged." It seems a local farmer suspected someone was "tampering with" (I'll always remember that phrase) one of his cows. I guess Bessie must have cut a fine figure out there in the barnyard, as she had attracted the amorous intentions of a neighbor. The farmer called the police, who initiated a stakeout, and caught the assaulter in the process of his bovine debauchery. The arrest was made and a trial date set, all properly reported in colorless, straightforward fashion, using no salacious language or florid descriptions. It was a decidedly non-lurid, prosaic account of bestiality, duly noted in the paper. The folks on the copy desk refused to let such an opportunity pass, and made quick work of the story, returning it to me with the headline changed from "Sodomy Charged" to "Cowpoke Arrested."

This fast and loose sport was not limited to the word merchants, of course. Jerry Schlamp, one of the notably colorful cartoonists, would regularly draw something salacious into his artwork. Once he showed me a soon-to-be-published cartoon depicting a New York personality who was being publicly persecuted for some foible or frailty. The cartoon showed the character tied to a stake, being burned alive, surrounded by an angry, axe-toting mob. At the base of the stake was, of course, a pile of small sticks starting to smolder and catch fire. He showed it to me and barked, "Find the dick!"

Other calls would just demand coffee: "Light and sweet and a soft roll, kid." You'd go to the cafeteria to grab the order, then place it, and the change, on their desk. Sometimes they would say nothing, continuing to furiously peck away at their typewriter. Occasionally, as you were walking away, you might get

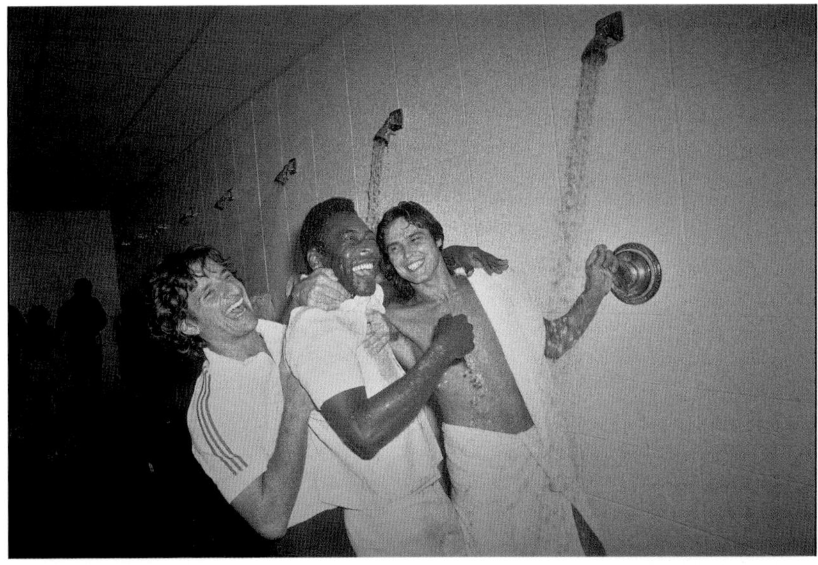

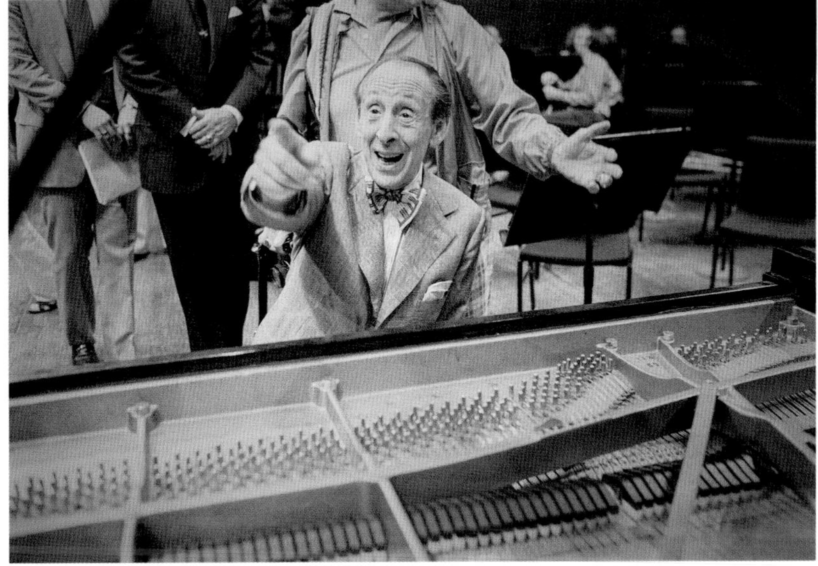

a quick, "Hey, kid!" You would return to their desk, and they would slide a nickel over to you. "That's for you." Such were finances in those days, I took the nickel. I could introduce a little snide humor here about this preparing me for photography day rates, but that comes later, dear reader.

Other tasks were more adventuresome, like getting in a radio car and heading out to grab a film bag from a photog on deadline. The *Daily News*, at that time, had nearly 60 photographers

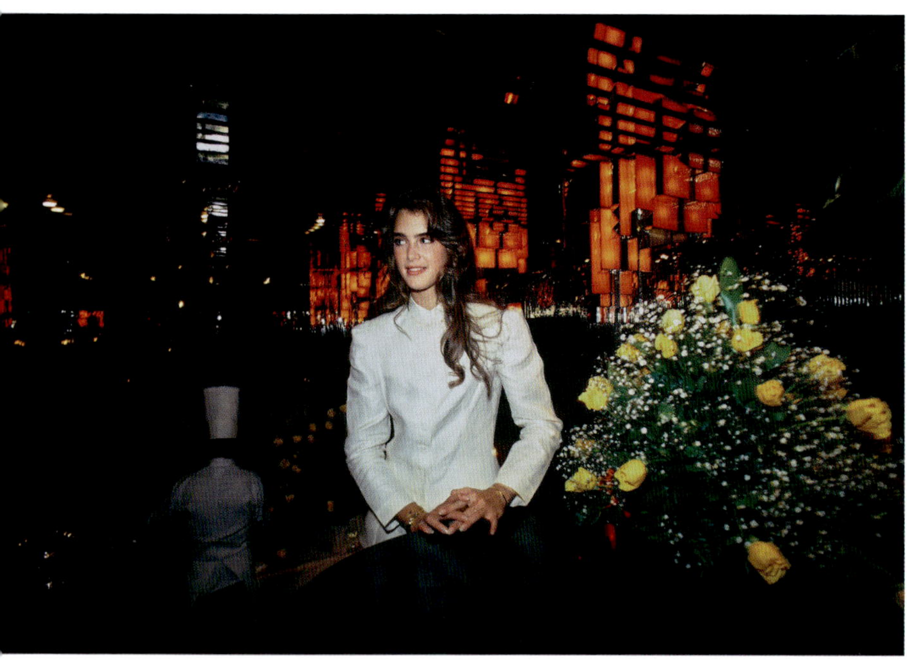

on staff and a huge number of vehicles, all radio-equipped, to move those shooters around. Those were the fun calls, listening to the chatter on the scanner, sometimes running lights, chasing a deadline. I would take my extra days and ride with photogs, just to learn. I got an education, to be sure.

I was riding once with Jimmy McGrath, a fine young shooter who died tragically, early in his career, and he started really booking on a call about a jumper in the 60's off Park Avenue. He was pushing it, taking crazy chances in the traffic, running red lights, cutting people off, horns blaring everywhere. I asked, "Why, man, are you jamming on this one so hard?" The answer came back: "Park Ave in the 60's, man, could be somebody rich!"

An early lesson in the metrics of tabloid journalism. The richer, the stranger, the more delectable the details, the more dire and dirty the backstory, the more likely the story would be page one. Which did not happen on that day. Jimmy's pix of the incident did not run. We screamed up the block, and there was, in fact, a poor soul who was so desperately despondent that he pitched himself off a six-story brownstone onto the unforgiving sidewalk. Though still moving, the cops didn't even put a rush on

the ambulance, as this individual had clearly accomplished his task and was beyond saving. It was my first dead body, and the gruesome splatter of it was a bit much. I had to walk away.

News of my squeamishness circulated, of course, in a newsroom as unforgiving as that sidewalk. Another photog came up to me. "Hey kid, we're going for lunch. Wanna come? I feel like a nice, juicy hamburger, man, nice and raw." It was brutal at times.

Other copyboy tasks would be just plain odd. "Go get Kay Gardella's groceries at the D'Agostino's on Third and bring them to her apartment." Seriously. She was the overlarge TV critic, and quite well known, so she had the juice to have a copy kid deliver the cause of her immobility. Bags of it. I actually liked that call. She would give me a dollar.

The best, for me, was being assigned to go to Yankee Stadium to pick up the photographers' film, especially if it was a big game in the Bronx. I'd hop the 4 train in Grand Central, and bomb up to 161st Street, which was the stadium stop. What a grand, graying repository of history that stadium was, even as it edged toward decrepitude in the '70s. It was there I got to know Danny Farrell a bit better. He was the dean of NYC press photography at the time, even though there were other photogs who pounded their chests a lot harder than Danny did. Danny let his pictures speak. Tough, competitive, and savvy, Danny just never got beat.

He would pull me aside and give me pointers. He shot an F2 and a Nikkor 400mm f/5.6 for baseball, and he had home plate and second base gaffer-tape-marked on the focus barrel. (Think of this as early AF.) Occasionally, because he was so confident in himself and his knowledge of the game, he would let me shoot a batter or two. He once saw me playing with the focus for second base, and I was off his mark. He quickly asked, "Kid, are you sharp right now?" I was not, I explained, just playing with the throw of the lens, which was new to me. He nodded. "Okay, because I saw you off my mark, and I was thinking, you know, you got those young eyes." I didn't completely understand until years later.

Going to Yankee Stadium, especially for day games, was a plum copyboy task. You would have to wait for something

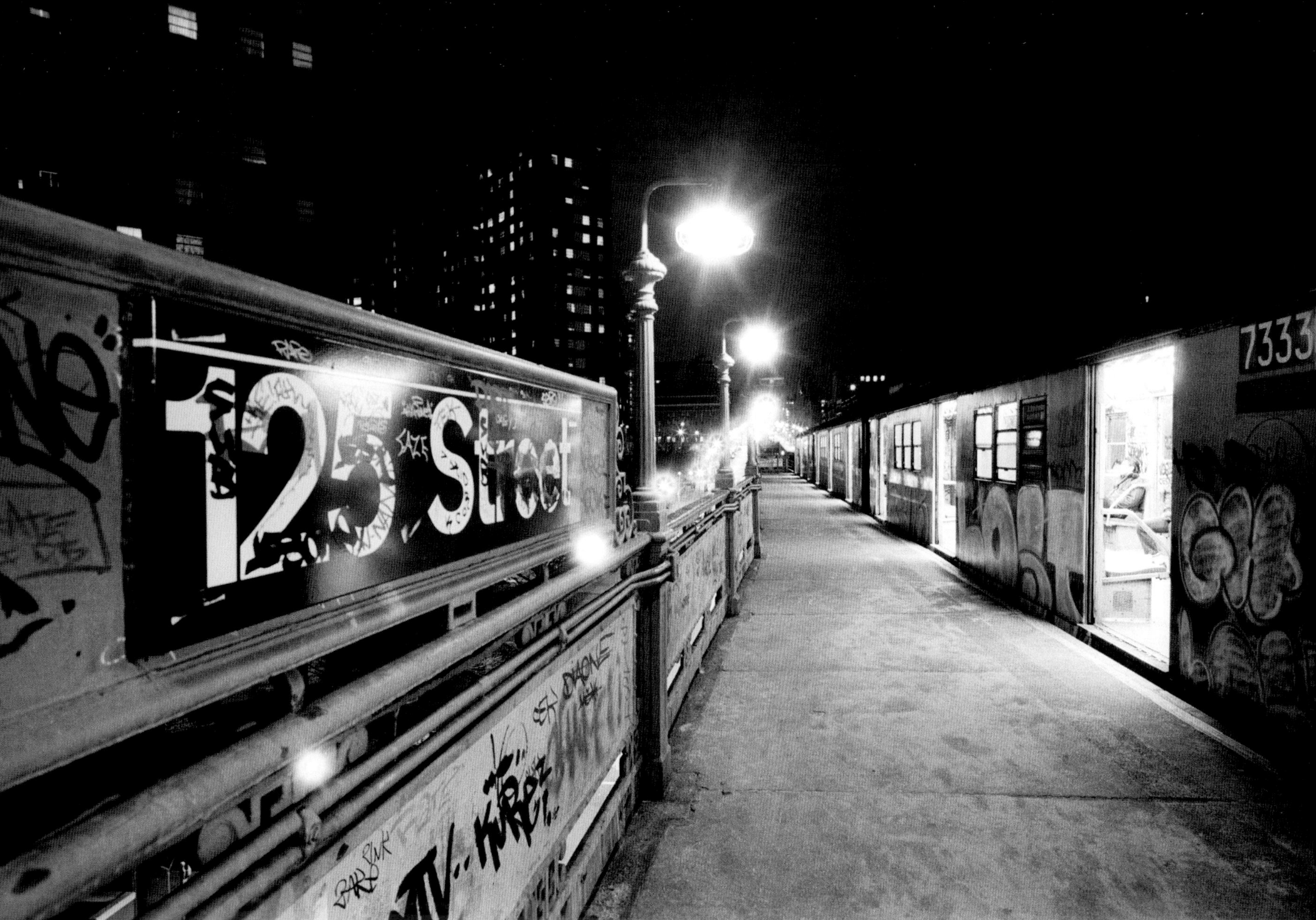

significant to happen—which in a baseball game can take, you know, a while—before the photog would bag up their Tri-X, jot out caption notes, and hand it off for the subway run back to the paper. That meant you could hit the press bar for a dog and a Coke, then sit behind the shooters and drink in the sounds, smells, and sights of big-league baseball. The crack of the bat would reverberate, accompanied by that quick, barely perceptible intake of breath from the whole crowd, that beat, measured in milliseconds, where thousands of people's eyes pop, heads crane, and lungs stop while they see where the ball goes. Then, as is so often the case in baseball, nothing happens, as the ball goes foul and the crowd settles back into the hum of the in-between, and the bark of "Hey, beer heah!" resumes and resounds. I loved going to the ball games.

It wasn't always leisurely. For big games, the *News*, having the photo resources, would attack: a shooter on both foul lines, one in dead center field, and one up top, for "God's View," the overhead coverage position made famous by Ernie Sisto of the *New York Times*. He was legendary for managing Big Bertha, the long lens monster camera from the 4x5 press days, swinging that beast around from his vantage point like the massive piece of artillery from which it derived its nickname. Those games were a non-stop, high-speed marathon for the copyboy, as you had to race to all the camera positions, gather the film bags, and then meet a courier, who was often on a motorcycle, to make the trip to the lab. It was a far cry from today's sports coverage, where the editors, sitting at terminals linked by ethernet cable to the photographer on the field, are literally seeing the images as they are being shot.

The maestro of the center field position was Vinny Riehl, last name pronounced "real"—which was unfortunate for him, as the whole staff would look at him as he recounted a story and tilt their heads quizzically and say, "Seriously, Vinny? For real?" It was lonely out there, under the scoreboards and bleachers. And the task was unenviable, indeed. The photog would be working a 1000mm lens, max aperture of f/11, and was charged with making a picture of every single swing. Yep, every swing. Because every swing could be a homer and decide the game. It was the baseball equivalent of covering a committee meeting for C-SPAN. You had to stay alert through all the droning unimportance of it, and shoot it for the record, but understand it would only get interesting if the committee chairperson, irate

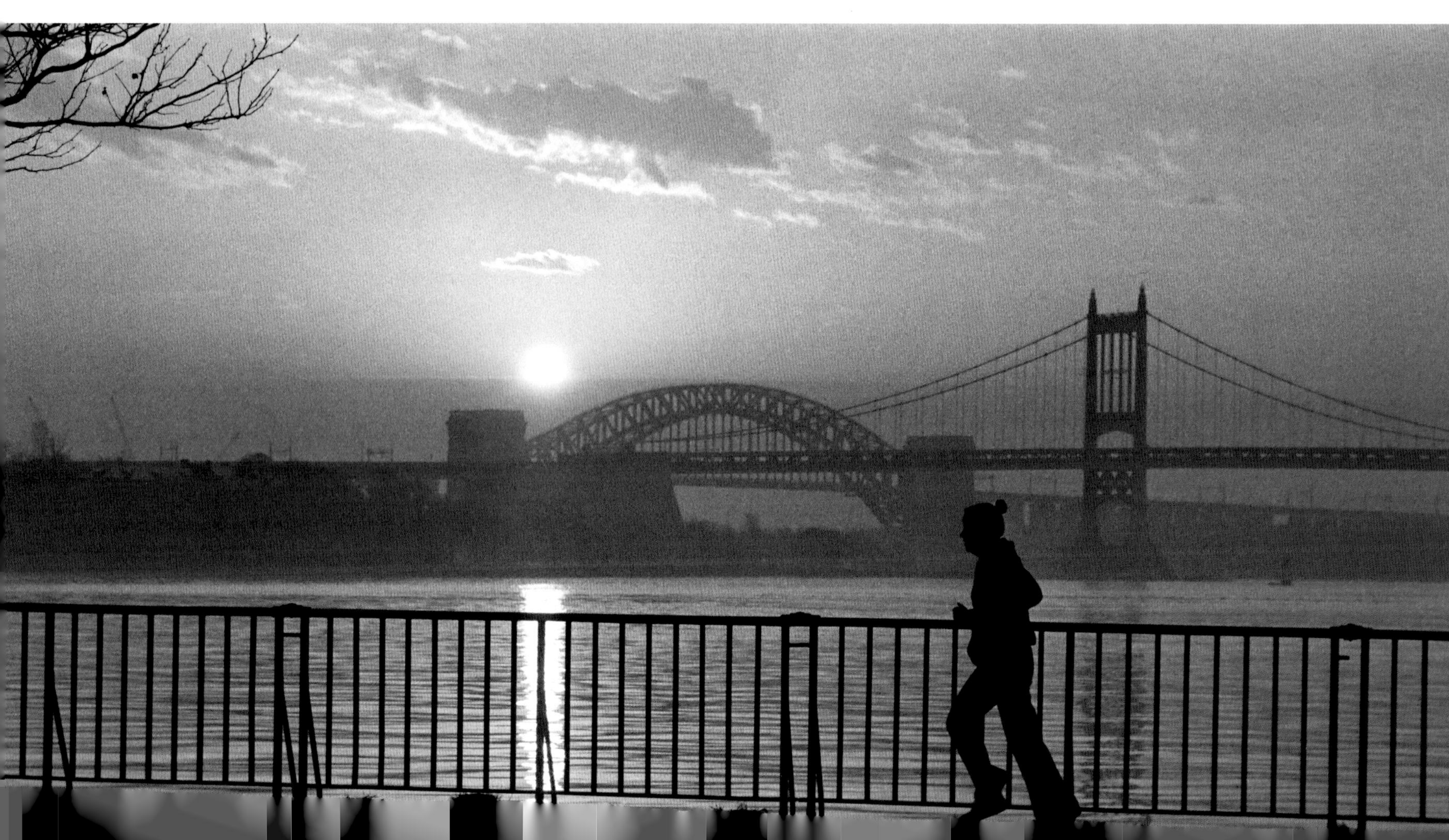

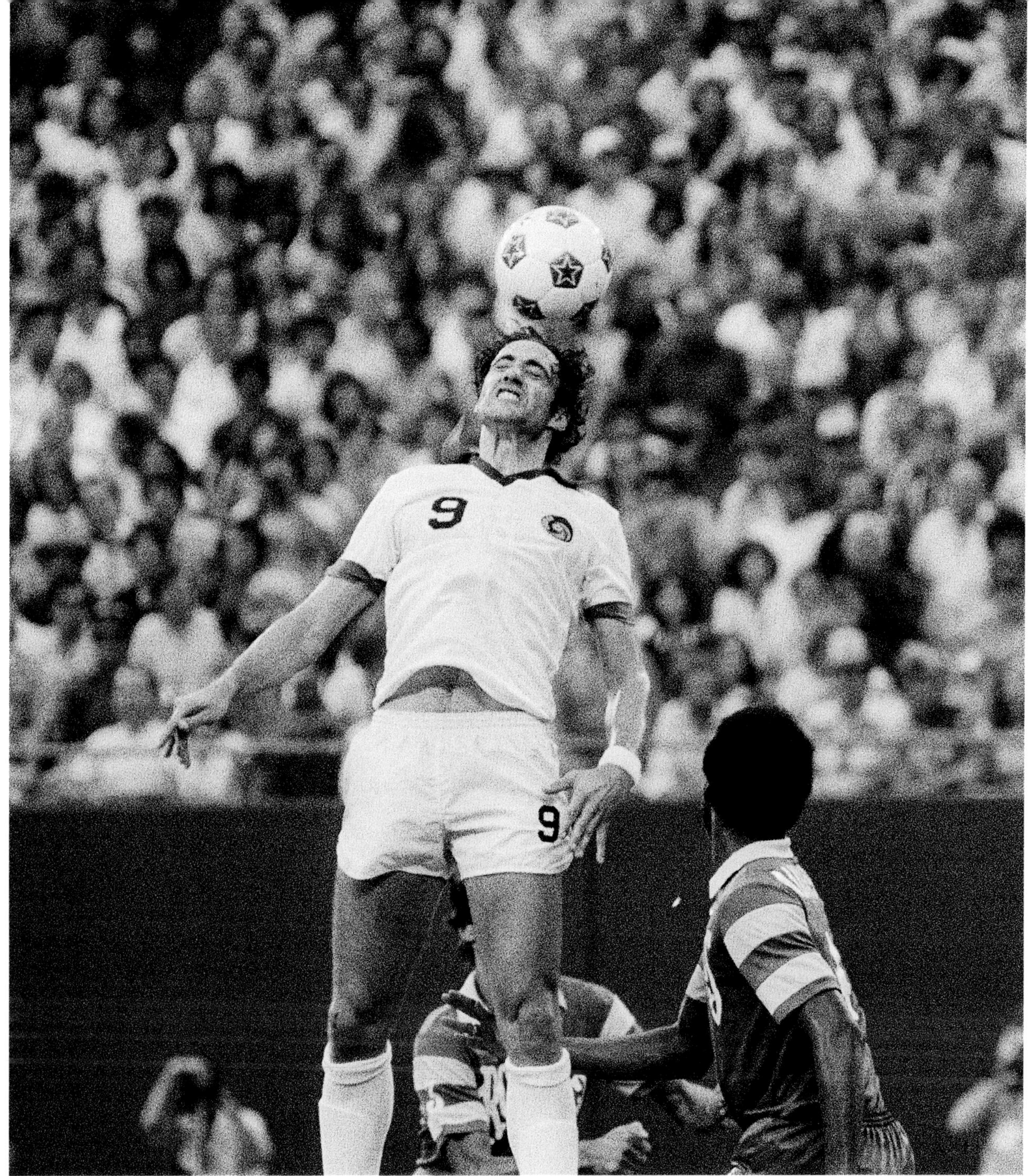

over the impertinent views being espoused, leaped over the desk and punched out a witness.

It was also hard manual labor. Vinnie had to haul that bloody great lens out there, along with a monster tripod. In those days, lens construction was hardly the advanced art it is now, with lighter composite materials making a big piece of glass quite totable. Back then, a 1000mm lens was like carrying a bag of bricks. The photogs who were assigned to this position knew the drill and would leave a chain and cinder blocks in those vacant spaces under the scoreboard where no one would tread or notice, season to season. They would hook the chain to the tripod, hanging the cinder block on it for lens and tripod stability.

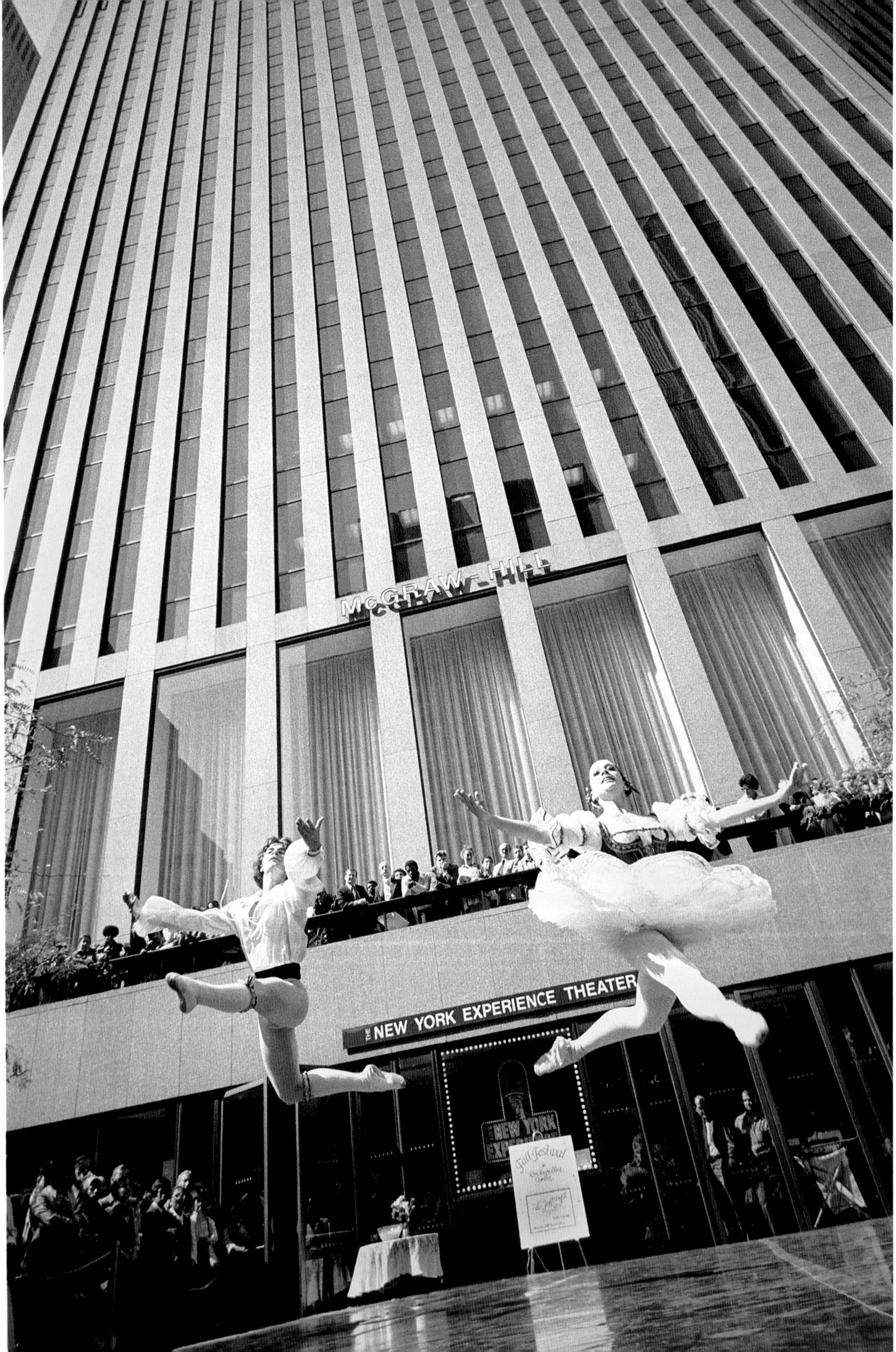

McGRAW-HILL
THE NEW YORK EXPERIENCE THEATER
NEW YORK EXPE
Fall Festival

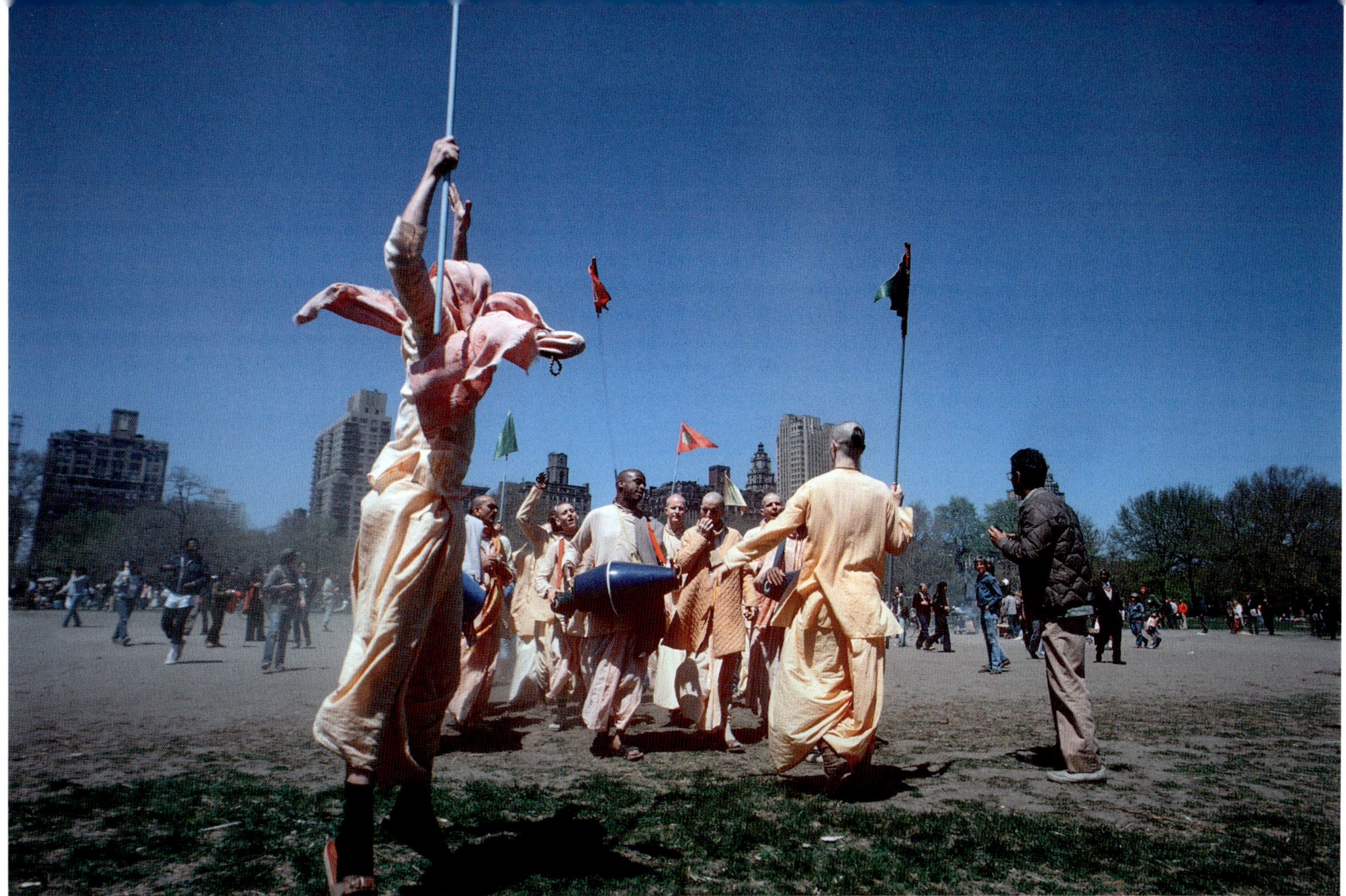

But the rewards for getting that home run swing, back in the time of Mr. October, Reggie Jackson, were great. His dinger histrionics at the old stadium, in the glare of the lights and the pressure, were the stuff of legend. Every camera in the stadium was banging away like crazy, every time Reggie touched a bat.

Danny, of course, thrived under the pressure of those big games, while never losing his humor or the relentless drive among newspaper shooters to give each other shit. As I gathered Danny's film bags, at one point during a World Series contest, he winked at me and told me on my next run out to center field, "Tell Riehl the office called. His stuff's fantastic."

But those were the high moments for the lowly copy kid. Mostly, it was drudge work, moving paper, running errands, and sitting on the bench with fellow runners, bemoaning the lack of upward movement at a paper like the *News*. It was a classic union shop. Before you moved up, somebody had to move out.

Many of my mates on the bench were waiting for writing opportunities, a chance to be a reporter. I was waiting impatiently for an opening in what was called the studio. It was the photo lab, where three Versamat processing machines could take a roll of exposed Tri-X from inside the film cassette to finished, fixed black and white negatives in about four or five minutes. Dry to dry processing. No time to soup film and hang it and dry it and make contact sheets. The editors were excellent at reading the negs right out of the machines, essentially reading in reverse. It was fast. The *News* lab could go from an exposed, unprocessed roll to a series of finished, captioned prints in under 10 minutes.

After the film would come out of the Versamat, which was the hoped-for result (and never guaranteed, as they were not called "film mulchers" for nothing), it would be stripped into long glassines and brought to the projection room. Editors would project the negatives, large, on screens. It was an excellent, immediate way of ascertaining quality and sharpness. Frame numbers would be called out and written down, and then the whole kit and caboodle would be passed through light-tight boxes into the printing room. The wizard of the editing room was Phil Stanziola, one of the kindest men I ever met. He loved pictures, finding oddities that appealed to him that you were never aware of when you were shooting, and doing it at lightning speed. I once presented him with a Central Park summer picture of a group of bike riders pedaling away from me on one of the park's curvy streets. I didn't think much of it, but he enjoyed it. He said, "Look at them all on the bike seats. Look at all the different size asses!" I confess that was not my original motivation to put the camera to my eye.

Even as a copyboy, I was regularly bringing in my own film. The paper could almost always use a street feature, often called a "weather rop" (pronounced "rope"), which stood for "run of paper." Useful art, something to fill a hole. At many papers this was called "wild art" or "enterprise," where a photog, sans assignment, would go shoot what they could find. In my world, storms and snow were welcome events. Also heat, springtime blossoms, you name it. I was desperate to get a pic in the paper, and not just for reputational purposes. Because I was not a staff photog, my film was regarded as freelance imagery, and even though I worked full-time at the paper, they would pay me $25 a shot. Given my regular weekly pay was just over $100, a pic in the paper could mean a movie ticket or an extra couple of beers at Louie's East.

I got a super nice weather pic once, which made the paper, of an overlarge woman on a park bench, feeding pigeons. She had a bag of seed, and she was leaning over toward the ground, feeding the birds by hand. It was a hot day, and the flimsy material of the sundress she was wearing was literally being overwhelmed by massive breasts that were well and truly responding to the mandate of gravity as she bent over. The dress was simply not structurally engineered for the task at hand.

When the picture passed the desk of Joe Kovacs, the news editor, he started laughing outright. I happened to be working his

slot that night. He saw the credit and, holding the picture aloft, cried, "Joe, this isn't a weather shot! It's a whether or not shot!"

Desperate as I was, I never stooped to the extremes some of the old school shooters would occasionally deploy. Once there was a lovely spring picture, heading for page one, of skaters on Wollman Rink at the southern end of Central Park. It was shot wide angle, through a branch of budding cherry blossoms, just opening in the newfound warmth of the season. Lovely, as I say. Until someone pointed out that the only cherry trees in Manhattan existed over at the UN Plaza, just off 42nd Street over by the East River. Under questioning, the photog admitted going over to the UN and surreptitiously sawing off a branch, bringing it to Central Park, and holding it in one hand while he shot wide glass through it, looking at the frolicking skaters.

It was a nice photo, it just wasn't real, and the *News* did the responsible thing and didn't publish it. It was such a nice photo, it really made you want to publish it, which reminded me of an old journalistic adage, when confronted with a story that was so sensational, lovely, or heart-wrenching you desperately wished for it to be true: "Some facts are too good to check."

But the studio, where the film was processed and the prints were made, was my goal. I had to wait. As a copyboy, I was definitely a boy. And as a studio apprentice, I would also be a boy. You didn't become a man until you went on the street, camera in hand, as a full-blown staffer. It was a very old school process, and not based on talent. You hooked on, signed up for the seniority system, and got in line. It produced some amazing talent out there on the streets of New York. Danny, Keith Torie, Michael Lipack, Jimmy Garrett—wonderful shooters all. But, predictably, it also produced a veritable legion of duds. There were guys who would go out into a radio car and actually shut the radio off, hit a watering hole, or duck under the elevated areas of the FDR Drive near the East River bridges and nap.

It was these kinds of photogs that bosses on the photo desk would occasionally demand a "real estate" from. This was a picture of the building or street where the job was supposed to be taking place. Historically, if a photog didn't want to make the effort, they could report back that the job was refused. The picture desk would counter with, "Make a real estate." This would ensure that the shooter in question actually *went* to the job, and wasn't calling in from a dark, quiet bar.

In many ways, there was a historical precedent operating here. All the bosses who did the hiring at the paper were writers. To them, photography was a dark art, not completely understandable, but necessary. They valued the written word much more highly than the photo, even though the moniker of the paper was, "New York's Picture Newspaper." To be a reporter, you had

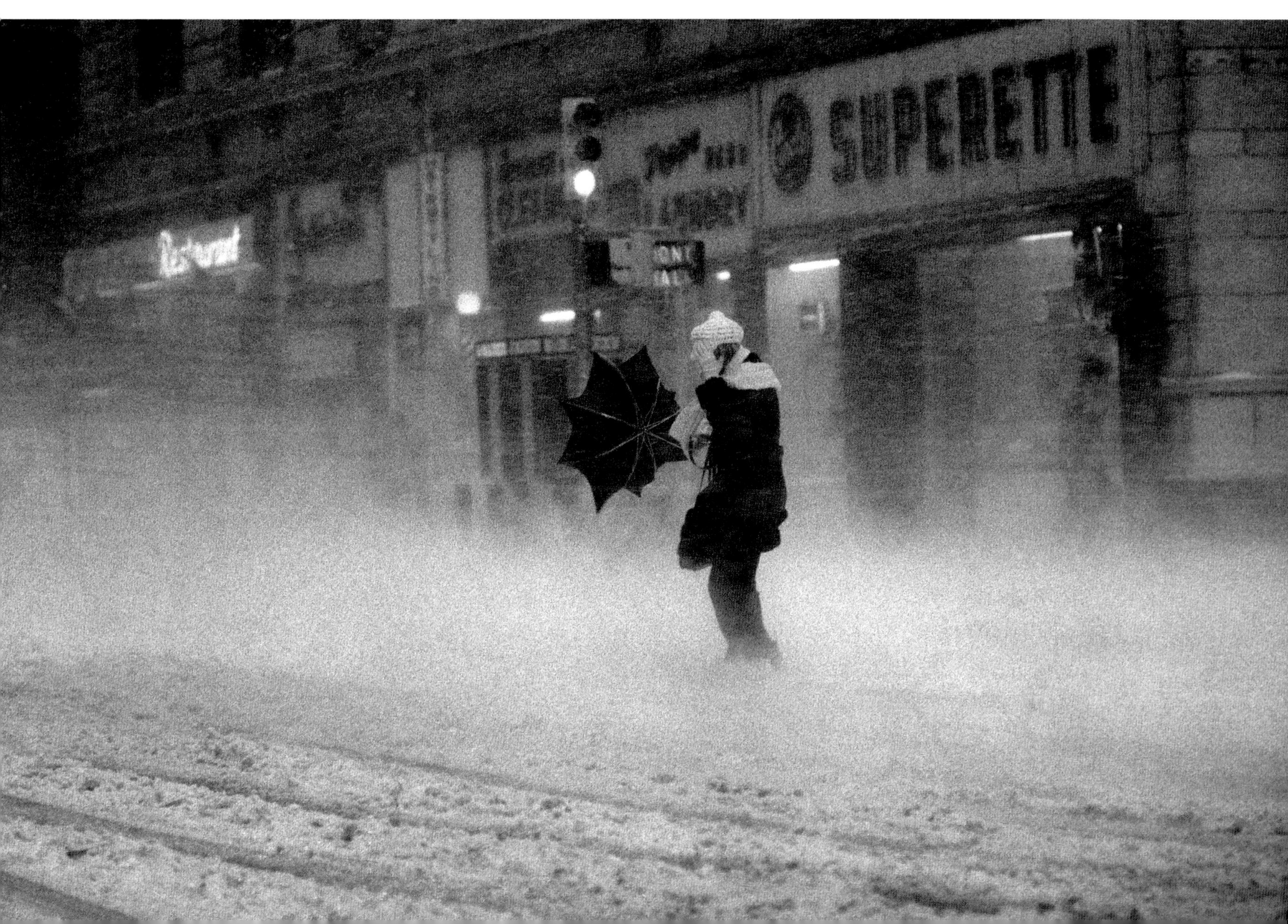

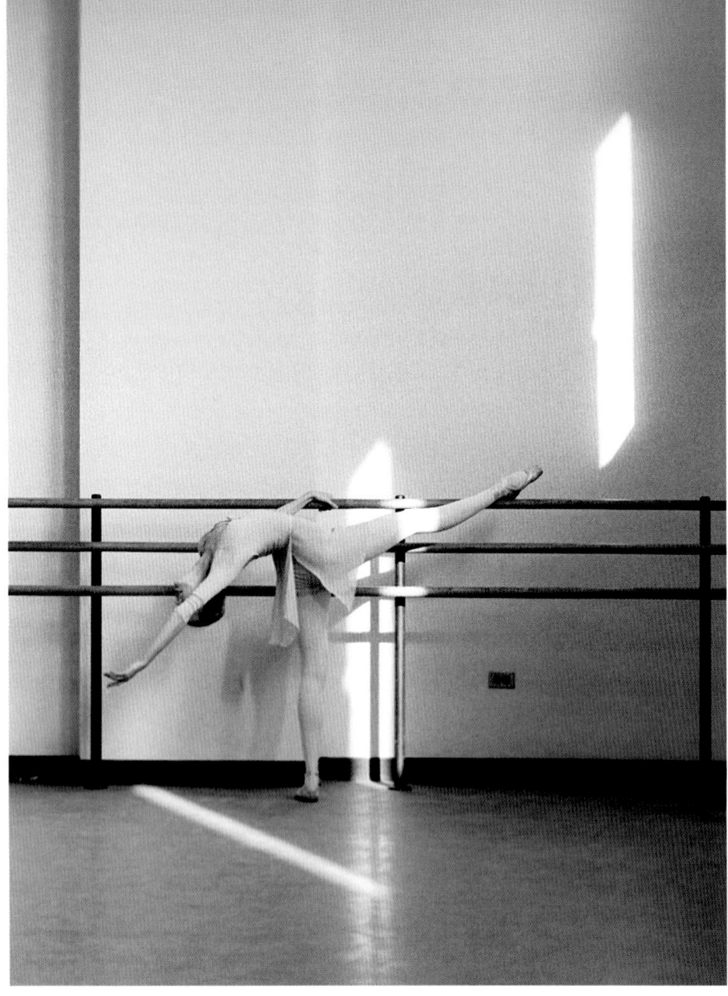

on the studio bulletin board, and we would pore over it, straining to see who might have called in sick. "He's sick? Really? How bad?"

I wanted to be a photog so awful I don't recall even feeling that bad that I wanted somebody to die. Or suffer major impairment.

Actually, I was temporarily content at the studio, and I dug in and learned the ropes. I learned how to pop the film cassettes in complete darkness and tape the leader to a broad piece of acetate to feed into the waiting jaws of a Versamat. From its entry point, the roll would snake its way over many rollers and through the various baths of developer, stop solution, fixer, and wash. The process had a certain kinship with doing your laundry. Film speed was referred to as ASA at that point, and whatever ASA was shot would determine if the machine would run at a normal speed, or whether you needed to slow it down so the black and white negs could cook a little longer.

I learned how to decipher the rushed shorthand of photogs who would jot caption notes and frame numbers on their film bags, transposing the scribble onto a caption sheet that would be affixed with rubber cement to the back of a print. The 8x10 prints would then get rolled up, put into a plexiglass tube, and shot out to the assignment desk via a pneumatic air system. Seriously. You would place the tube at the mouth of the pipe, which led into the ceiling. Hit the button and a rush of air would suck it, at great speed, out to waiting editors, sweating out a deadline.

This air-based system was, of course, an invitation to mayhem. Many inappropriate items flew throughout the News Building in those pipes. Once, fellow apprentice Johnny Roca and I collaborated on a mildly elaborate scheme, which we thought would just be some lighthearted fun. One staffer was the epitome of a dirty old man. He was also, perhaps, on the verge of being legally blind. His eyes were pretty shot. And, he wore a not particularly well-designed or cared-for toupee. He was a walking, talking, target-rich environment. And, for Johnny and me, this was the perfect storm of practical joke possibilities. We cut a small photo out of a girlie magazine and taped it down

to be able to write, to find a story. You needed smarts and you were valued. As Danny once told me, "If you could write, they made you a reporter. If you had a driver's license, they made you a photographer." A motley photo work force resulted from this practice, and hence, the occasional need for a real estate.

Moving Up

Finally, my ascension occurred. Michael Lipack, then a boy in the studio, got put on the street as a photog, creating that precious open spot I so coveted.

I thought my life was set. I was on track. Spend some time in the studio, and then, when there was an opening, go out on the street as a shooter and become a man. That was the goal of all the apprentices in the studio. Our impatience with this process was thinly veiled. The staff photog schedule was always posted just under the air tube in the lab. We lured him over to the desk where, as the picture was so small, he had to take off his glasses and get his head down near the desk to focus. With his head hovering just below the tube, Johnny hit the button. His rug lifted right off his head and was heading for the newsroom when he reacted and slapped his noggin, trapping a few sturdy strands of hair and preventing the complete disappearance of this hairball into the piping. Lord knows what might have ensued if that thing had screamed out of the tube and landed on the picture assignment desk.

Retribution was afoot, of course. That staffer's brother, nicknamed Cheech, was a printer in the studio, and eventually the printers, as a group, cornered Johnny, picked him up, and dumped him in the print wash basin, fully clothed. I managed to escape punishment, for whatever reason of luck or schedule.

It was a wonderful time. I got to know the photogs, and I went to school on how they handled a job, which was readily apparent as you watched their rolls get projected and picked. I hung out in that room, listening to Stanziola or, more affectionately, Stanzi. When not on deadline, he would take the time to teach. Some shooters' film was a lesson plan in classic coverage. Good exposures, variance of lens and scale, thorough captions, emotion, empathy, and information, all there in 36-exposure rolls. But, conversely, sometimes I could see his frustration boiling over when a photog in the field zigged when he obviously should have zagged. How the laziness of a coverage just screamed at you in black and white, projected right there on the wall. He was a newspaper man, and he took the job of making pictures for New York's Picture Newspaper seriously.

The big news for me was that I had access to a darkroom again, as well as printing paper, and I lived, once again, in the smell of a photo lab, one of the early, seductive delights of photography that I had been introduced to in school. I had community there, in the studio. I joined the Photo Studio Bowling League, and we would bowl at the lanes at Madison Square Garden every Thursday night.

I was all of a sudden making $250 a week, which meant I could leave the bump and grind of the Beacon and find a place to live that didn't come with a nightly soundtrack. Which I did, moving to a wonderful studio apartment on West 65th Street just off Columbus Ave. It was a palace by comparison to my previous digs. It had a bit of room, northern light, and a fire escape I could picnic on. And it cost $250 a month. Seriously. Rent-controlled, $250 every 30 days. Apologies to anyone who might be reading this who is currently renting an apartment in Manhattan. Please don't go near the windows. Think of your three roommates with whom you are currently splitting the $5,000 rent for the broom closet you all share just over the loading dock with a view of the dumpster. If you give in to despair and off yourself, you'll leave them in the lurch for next month's payment, and they might end up having to sell their blood, or worse.

Unfortunately, that apartment was a move up that I did not make fast enough. On one of those Thursday bowling nights, my place at the Beacon was broken into. It wasn't a hard thing for a thief to pull off, as my cubby had a simple door key lock and not a throw bolt. (I did tell you I was pretty green when I moved into the big city, didn't I?) All my rudimentary camera gear was stolen. It happened the same week I lost my dad. News of my tough go circulated in the studio, they passed the hat, and when I came back in to work after my union-allotted three days of bereavement, there was an envelope in my locker with $500 cash in it. I used that dough to buy a Leica M4, with a 35mm Summicron f/2 lens. I have it to this day. Newspaper folks pull together and look after their own.

So, the studio was cool. Good people, enough money to live, a real—if somewhat removed—connection to what I wanted to do, and the beginnings of a social life that did not revolve around getting a Big Mac and eating it on a park bench. I had a life! It was going to be great!

It was early in my career, so the photo gods had not yet buggered me senseless with the sheer, confounding, ongoing, incessant reversals that occur throughout a career in photography. I was still a babe, swaddled in unblunted hopes, cooing and burbling with the magic of it all, keen for the decisive moments yet to come. But, as Deadpool once said, "Life is an endless series of train wrecks with only brief, commercial-like breaks of happiness."

The great newspaper strike of 1977 happened, and all bets were off. The paper tried to publish, but it was a shadow effort. It was back when the unions had some measure of power left. I remember the strike went on for 88 days.

I had just started to make a living, and all of a sudden I was out of work. But, in those desperate clouds, there were streaks of light. Several strike newspapers cropped up, powered by out-of-work guild members. One paper, the *City News*, hired Dan Farrell as the sole member of the photo department. I called Danny. He said, "Kid, I need anything. I got no library, no archive. I got nothing. Bring me something, I'll pay you fifty bucks a picture."

I left my apartment, Domke bag slung, and basically didn't come back for about three days, stopping by only to grab a couple hours rack time and a quick shower. I shot everything I saw. Kids on swings. Horse-drawn carriages in the park. Halston and Warhol at Studio 54. I kept running my film in to Danny. At the end of the first week of the paper's existence, he owed me almost $500. He looked at me and said, "Kid, I'm gonna put you on staff. I can pay you $250."

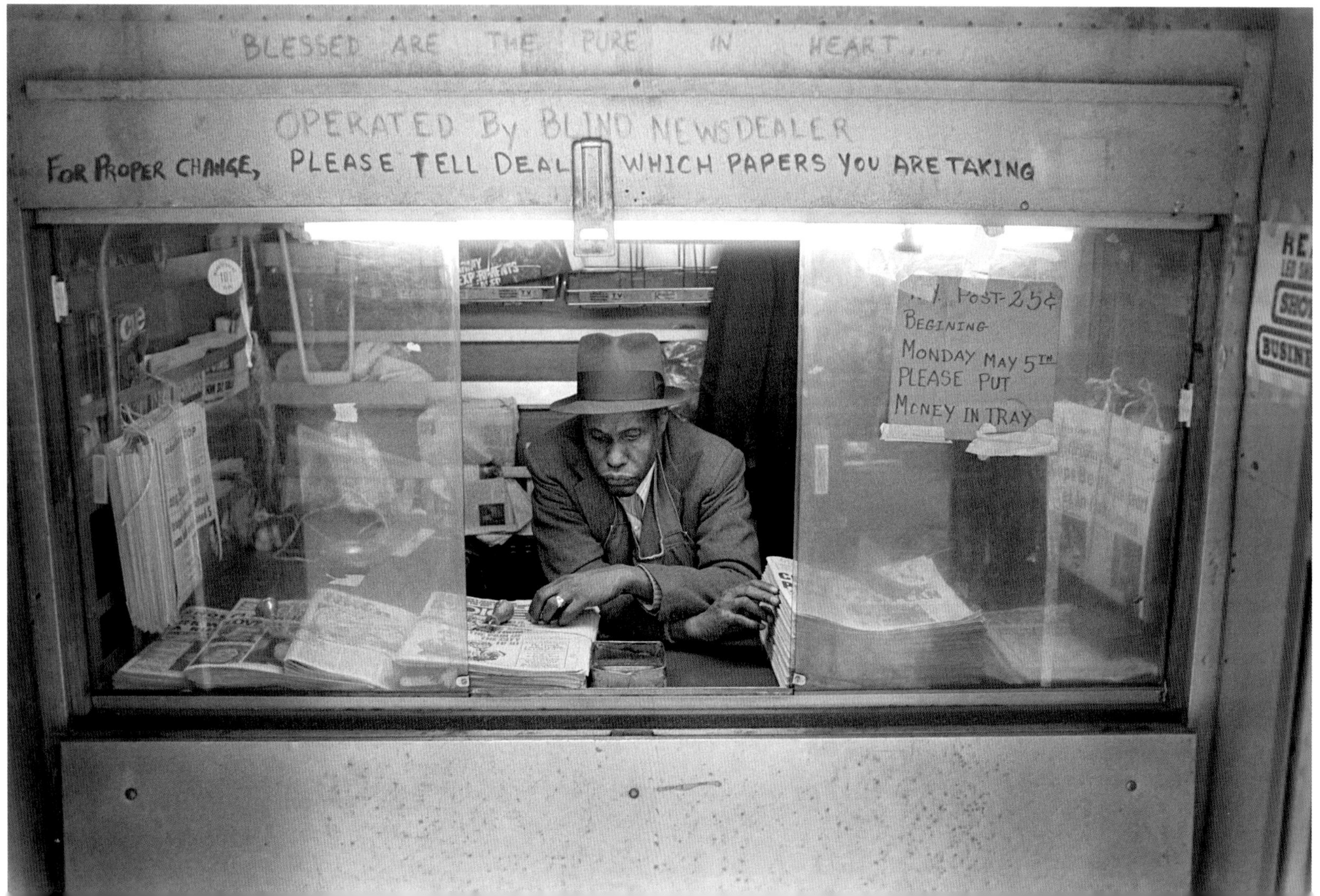

On the Street

With that sentence, I realized I had just been cannon shot from copyboy to studio apprentice to staff photographer at a publishing NYC daily newspaper. I got a NYC press pass, what they called a "reserve card," which gave me all the access the regular press received, though the pass did not have my picture on it, acknowledging the temporary nature of it. I also got one of the most highly prized pieces of paper in the city, a press parking card, which meant I could roll up onto a news scene and leave my battered VW bus just about anywhere. It was heady stuff, and scary. Time to sink or swim.

I got all those precious press docs courtesy of the *City News* editor, Bill Federici, who was a legendary reporter/editor at the *News*. Nominated for a Pulitzer three times, Federici was connected. He was the reporter who recovered the DeLong Star Ruby in the fabled Murph the Surf gem heist. The 100-carat gem was stolen from the American Museum of Natural History in 1964. An unidentified third person, seeking a ransom payment, contacted Federici, and told him to go to a phone booth in Palm Beach, FL. The phone rang and the caller told him, "Turn around and face the door. Reach up and you'll feel the ruby." A famous *Daily News* page one shot showing Federici pulling the gem out of the phone booth ceiling and handing it to John D. MacArthur, the famed philanthropist who agreed to pay the ransom, was made by, you guessed it, Danny Farrell. This was tough-guy, connected, NYC gangster stuff. This was the world I stumbled into.

We had no access to the *Daily News* studio, of course, and thus no way to process film. I had a small darkroom setup in my apartment, but it was next to useless for deadline stuff. Danny fixed that daunting problem by making a deal with Larry DeSantis, the UPI (United Press International) managing editor for news pictures in New York. UPI was the poor cousin to the AP (Associated Press). It was the scrappy, under-resourced wire service always competing at a disadvantage with the more well-financed, well-oiled machine of the AP. Danny gave them our staff's output for use on the UPI wire. In return, UPI would process and print our stuff for the newspaper. Mind you, it was a

staff of three—Danny, Jimmy Garrett, and me, but we instantly almost doubled their regular NY staff numbers.

All of a sudden, I was covering the Giants, the Yankees, the World Series, politics, features, and who knows what else.

Well, I do know what else. As a for instance, I was sent to one of the residence apartments at the Waldorf Astoria, a really tony address. A particularly zaftig lady had her highly valuable jewelry heisted. Now, seeing that this lady's sole reason for being in said apartment and sporting such shiny finery was her ample bosom and hips that must have been a never-ending source of comfort for whomever was buying all that jewelry for her, this was definitely tabloid news.

She came out in a slinky negligee and posed in curvy fashion on an inviting sofa. I was professional and stupidly Catholic about the whole thing, and just made pictures and left. Later, as our ramshackle little rag made its way into print, my picture, stamped with my caption, passed through the copy desk and came to Federici's attention. He came up to me, holding the picture. He said to me, quietly, off to the side, "I don't care about the picture. It's fine. What I want to know, did you get a blow job?"

It didn't stop there. The head of copy, Tommy Shields, didn't even look up from the desk as he continued to red pencil grammatical errors in the stories flying by his eyes. He held my picture aloft and shouted to the whole newsroom, "Who got the blow job?"

Such was newspaper life in the '70s, when human resources meant how many people you had on staff.

It was a heady stint, for sure. I prayed the strike would just keep going. It was an impromptu little paper, but it sold well on the streets to New Yorkers for whom getting on the subway without a daily newspaper in hand was like going to work having forgotten to put on their pants. It featured what was called the "double truck," a centerfold spread of photos, just like the *News*. Danny would lay it out, calling a big vertical an "el deepo" and a spacious horizontal an "el wido." It was surely from him that I gathered my preference, true to this day, of using bigger, fewer pictures. As he said to me, "Kid, you'd be surprised at how much shit you can hang off of one good picture."

And it's true. It's not something you aspire to, for sure, to shoot only one significant picture. But it solidified in my head the importance of that lead photo, the big pic, the one you can hang your hat on and, when played right upon publication, will gobsmack the eyeballs of the readers.

But, like Cinderella, I was doomed. The strike ended, and I went back into the studio as an apprentice, and not a happy one. I had made the jump. I was behind the lens, making pictures! Now I was stuck back at the ass end of a Versamat, coaxing it to ingest another photog's film.

Salvation came in the predictably bad financial news the paper received after the strike. Ed Quinn, the head of the editorial department, called me in and told me they were laying off a staffer, pulling him back into the studio, which then, given the union logic of the place, meant that I would, as he said to me, "Go back to being a copyboy." I quit on the spot.

I had made a small name for myself during the strike, and sure enough, I hit the streets and the wires and the *New York Times* came calling. Can you do this? Can you do that? Why, yes I can! News, sports, and features came my way. Single-day assignments, mind you, nothing grand. But in those snippets of jobs, there was a living to be had. And more lessons to be learned.

UPI used me a lot. Which was necessary, as their jobs paid just $50. That was it. The *Times* was high rent at about $125 a pop. AP was somewhere in between. But, given my rent was $250, you could make a living if you stacked up enough of these in a week. And I did. I was voracious. It was not unusual for me to shoot a job for UPI in the morning, knock back an AP job after lunch, and bounce out at night to shoot a celeb at Studio 54 to score another $50 at the UPI. It was non-stop, feverish, and fun.

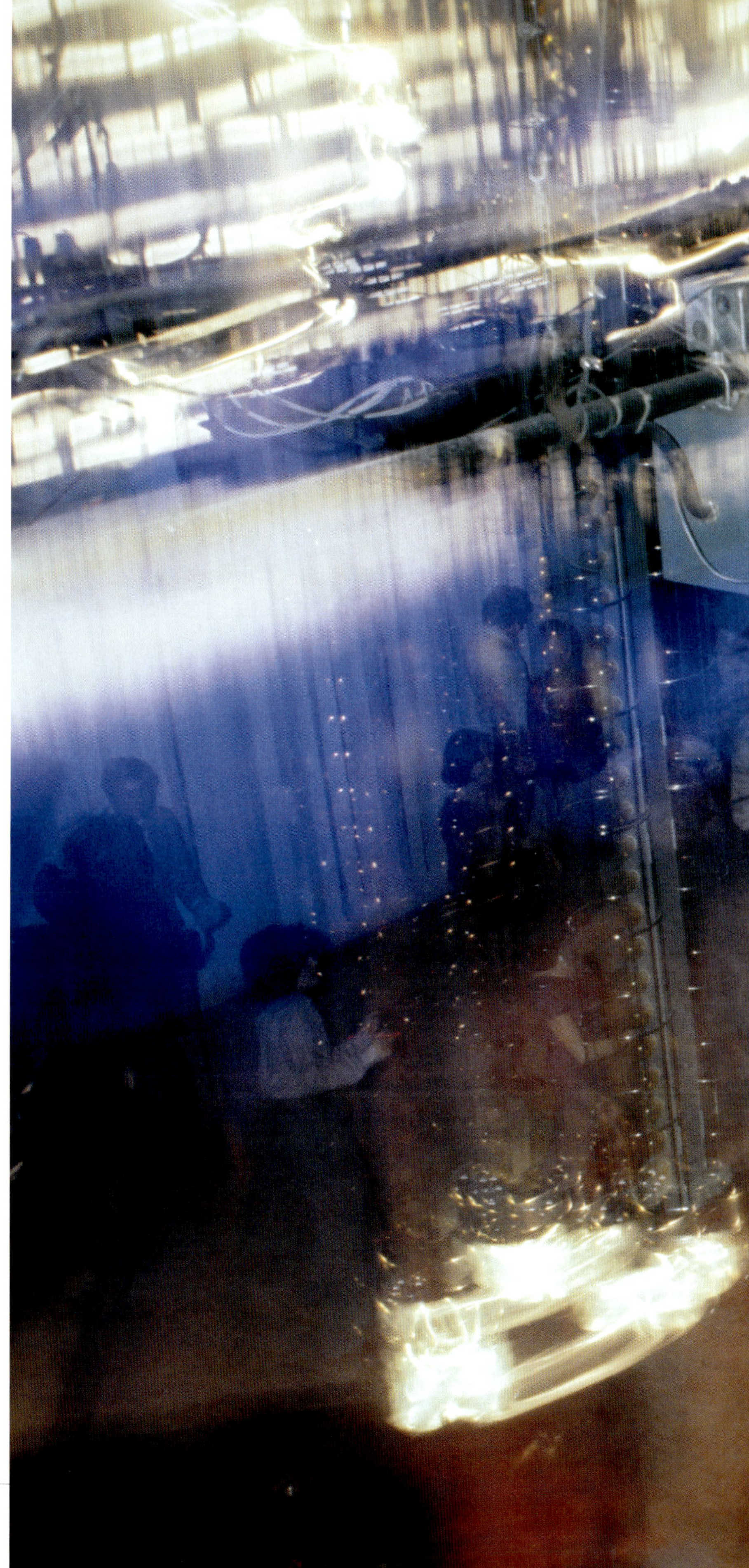

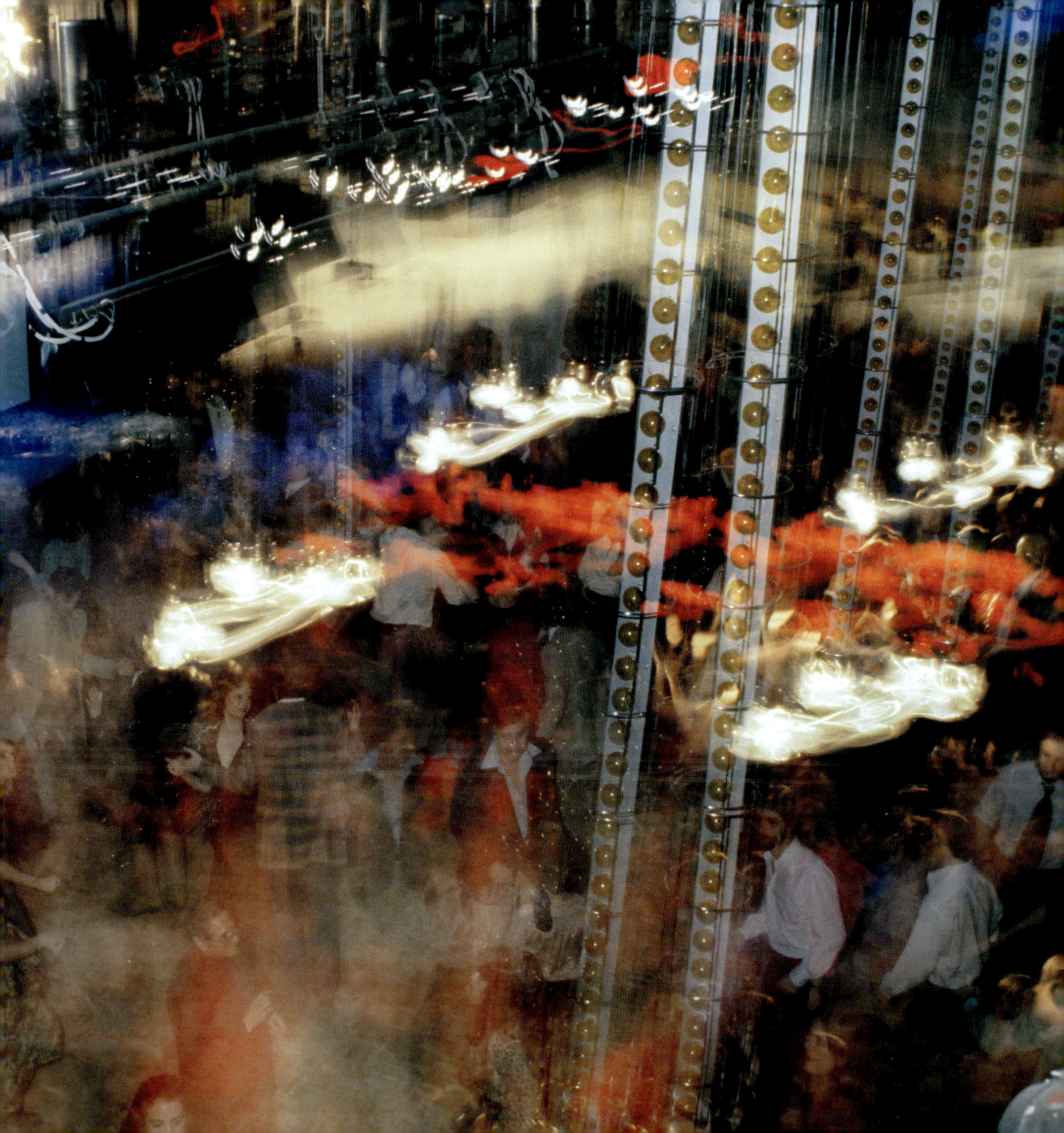

It was a dream fulfilled. The angels chorused, and my heart sang a song of delight.

No, it didn't.

The realization that I had climbed my own small, personal mountain wasn't attended to by a gaggle of accolades for a magnificently rendered cover story, or an invitation to join Magnum, or, really, anything at all. I still didn't have a legit, full-time job as a photog. I was an itty-bitty freelancer, a wire service stringer, the guy they called when the grown folks were all too busy with the real jobs. What I did was look around and realize I was paying all my bills by getting checks sent to me by people who had employed me to shoot pictures for them. Those little jobs added up. Fifty bucks here, a hundred there. I was making a living as a photographer in NYC. I think I might have tilted my head a bit, and said, "Huh. Cool."

But, you know, I was still a boy. A freelancer. An itinerant vendor with a beeper and a Domke bag. Sure, I was a working photog, but I had yet to punch the ticket of a full-time staffer. That was a border yet to be crossed.

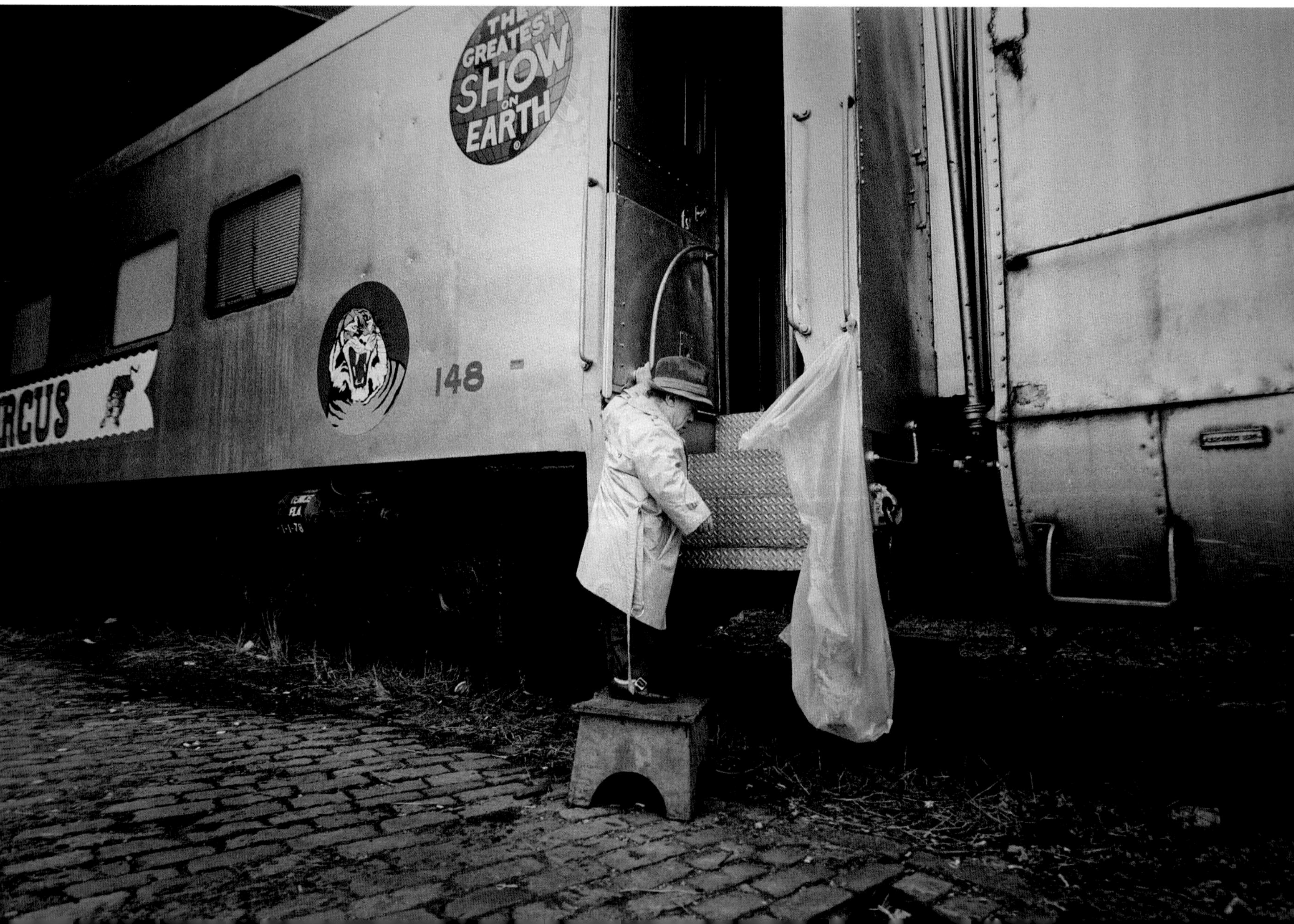

And here's where random intersects yet again with the path of a photog. Tom Orr, the photo director at *Newsweek*, shared a flight with Rick Giacalone, the veep of communications at ABC television network. Rick mentioned he was looking for a photog and Tom, a kindly man I had showed my work to in my early days in the city, told him about me.

I got a call. Or, this being 1979, I got a beep on my pager. It was Giacalone. He offered me to do a test for the job, giving me two days to shoot three different concepts. He said he would pay me $250 a day! I damn near keeled over. He cautioned me, though, that he was offering the same deal to two other photogs. Nothing was certain. I knocked out those jobs, as well as a couple other gigs, during those two days. I was used to shooting multiple assignments in rapid fire. Evidently, the two other freelancers he had tapped for the test were not. They did not finish and turned in incomplete work.

I got the gig. When my pager buzzed with the news, I was on a job for the AP covering the end of a three-month tugboat strike that had crippled the New York harbor and led to the city being literally awash in garbage. The tugboats are essential to disposing the tons of garbage and human detritus the Big Apple generates daily. People don't like to think about this much, of course, but the tugs customarily tow a lot of that stuff out to sea. Barges of it. I've been on those boats, and trust me, you want the captain to crank up the engine so your nose stays in the wind, ahead of the steaming mess you are towing. The tugs get to a certain mileage limit and open the drains, and what just went down the toilets in New York pours into the sea and becomes brunch for the fish.

Which then get caught and end up on the plates of society swells paying fifty bucks a plate for haddock, steamed in a zesty mélange of vinegar and chives, served with a topping of roasted almonds and accompanied by a pea puree. There's an irony in there that is just as delicious as the fish.

The strike was done and the tugboat crews were celebrating the conclusion of the negotiations over at the Waldorf. My competition on the job was a former mate at the *News*, a photog whose incompetence was legendary. I had processed his film in the studio, and it was generally memorable for all the wrong reasons.

I remember him once getting chewed out by the photo assignment desk, which on that day was manned by Danny Farrell. Given his preeminence, Danny occasionally stayed inside and ran the show, dispensing the visual chores of the day to the *News* photogs. He had assigned this woebegone lensman to a grip-and-grin in the lobby of the News Building, which was precisely seven floors down from the newsroom. He missed it. He told Danny, by way of excuse, "I couldn't get an elevator." True story.

So, here he was at the celebratory conclusion of the strike, and he was kicking my ass. I had ducked out to receive that momentous call (no cell phones back then, only pay phone booths) and came back in to see him, up on a chair, surrounded by cheering tugboat pilots. He was egging them on and shouting at them to goose the enthusiasm. I lifted my camera over my head and made a series of hopeless Hail Marys, totally outflanked and out shot.

So, on the day I got my first job as a photographer, I blew the job I was shooting. I should have taken that as a sign, perhaps. A warning. Failure will be with you always, grasshopper!

But I was so elated by the phone call, I recall not caring. I had a job as a professional photographer in New York City.

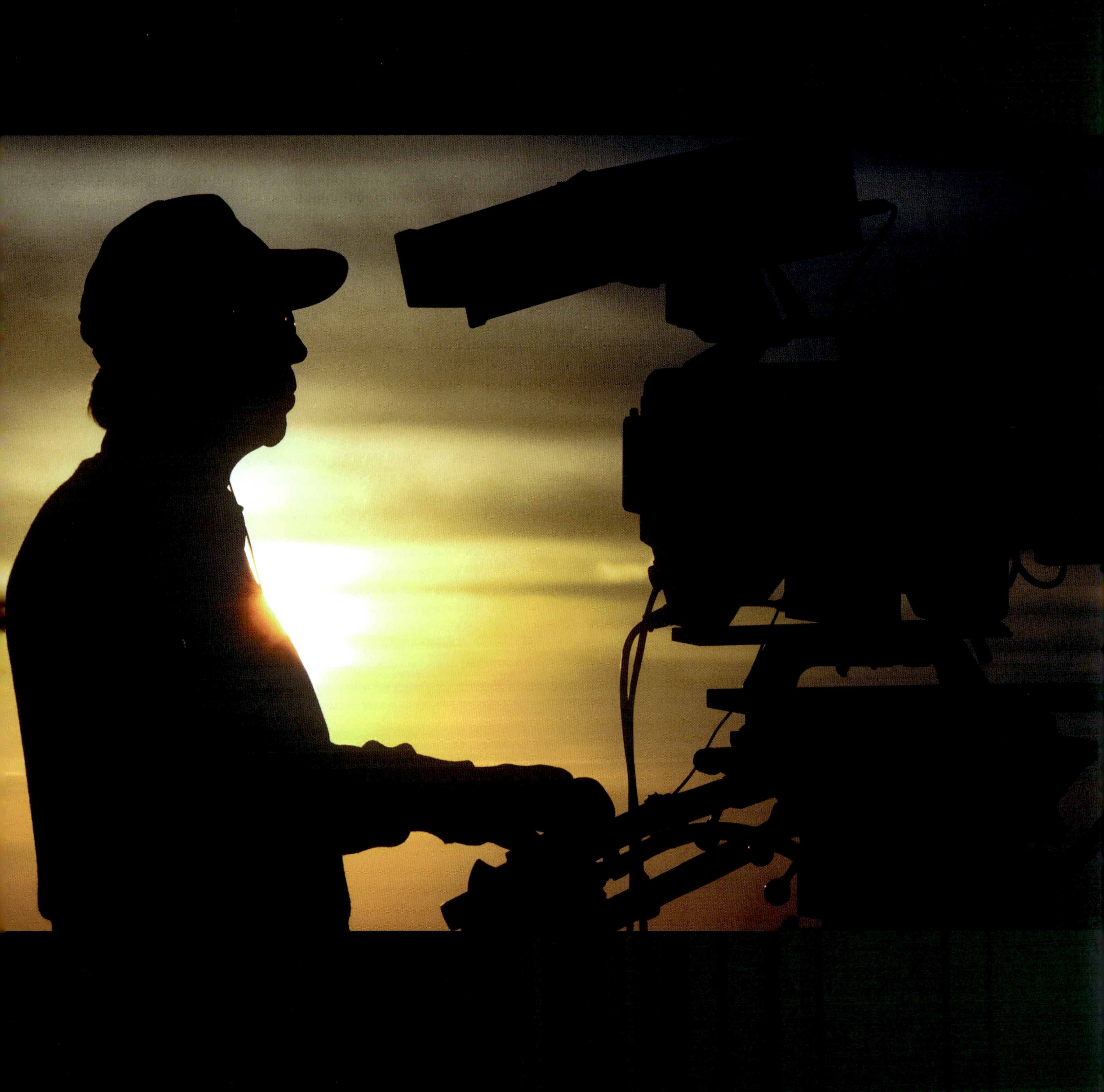

Learning the ABCs

I left the beeper-driven, happenstance life of a wire service stringer and took the job ABC Television offered me. A staff job, an island of assurance, if you will, in the dangerous waters of never knowing where your next paycheck might come from. It turned out to be only a brief respite from the turbulent seas of the freelance life, however. I lasted 18 months and quit. Even in that short stint, a sameness was setting in, and it turned out that I was more onboard with uncertainty than I was with shooting cast pictures on the soaps.

I was assigned to the public relations department, because that's what we did. We pictorially spread the gospel of all things ABC. I was off to the races with my first staff photography job! I had a business card, benefits, a steady paycheck, gear for the using in the camera locker, a small studio at my disposal, and a newcomer to my camera bag: color transparency film. Strange stuff, not completely foreign, but certainly not overly familiar. Unseen mysteries in a yellow box. Questions to be answered, spooling out of a canister.

One of the mandates of the job, continuously in place, was to shoot color and black and white, horizontal and vertical, of everything I was assigned to. I had to cover the bases in a broadly utilitarian way, the reason being the usage of my photos was quite diverse. They would be published by newspapers, which were most often, at that time, printed in monochrome. Or they might run as the cover of the TV section, embedded in the newspaper, which demanded a color vertical. Or, they might possibly be used by the news magazines, if ABC had the inside track on a coveted, news-of-the-moment guest. The job of the network photographer was to cover the show, the action, the guests, and the on-air talent, and then also show the behind-the-scenes involvement of the camera people, the control room machinations, and literally follow everything that had an ABC logo on it. It was not an odd week to shoot *Monday Night Football*, then a studio still life of an Emmy statue, then report early to *Good Morning America* for a political figure or movie star, then zap down to Washington, D.C., to cover a nightly anchor behind the desk, and then back up to New York to shoot headshots of the new character on a soap opera. All in color and black and white, horizontal and vertical. Variety was the order of the day.

Given that directive, I had to get quick off the mark computing f-stops appropriate for the various ISO ratings (then called ASA) I had in my film cameras. And carry similar glass, or zooms, as I had to switch cameras quickly without changing lenses. And then, of course, manually focus everything. I was often out there with three or four motor-driven SLR cameras slung off my shoulders. As maddening as it could be, it was also great training, hopscotching my way through the cameras, lenses, ISOs, and f-stops. Throw in the fact that I had to also learn to use flash, quickly and well, and I became, for that brief time, a hothouse plant. Forced to grow and learn, though not necessarily always thrive. Being a photographer for a television network felt like being one of the cans on a string attached to the bumper of the fancy car the newlyweds drive away in. You were along for the ride, with no control over your fate. You often got literally minutes to work with the talent or step in front of the TV cameras to get your own angle. Sometimes you got no time at all.

Thankfully, my immediate superiors knew the challenges, and were pleasantly surprised when a good coverage was turned in. They tended to expect failure, and I routinely delivered on that expectation. But, as has been famously said, failure is a form of progress. I made a lot of progress.

I did, however, get really good at the thirty-second portrait session.

Those successes were countered by some tough moments trying to precisely expose chrome film. I wished I hadn't had one of those when Ronald Reagan accepted the Republican presidential nomination. Sheesh.

One particular trial was control rooms. Confronting a wall of TV monitors, I recall just, you know, giving up. Take a look at Ted Koppel, shot in the Washington, D.C., control room around the time that he became the anchor of the famed *Nightline* ABC news program. Ted's a helluva journalist and a very decent guy

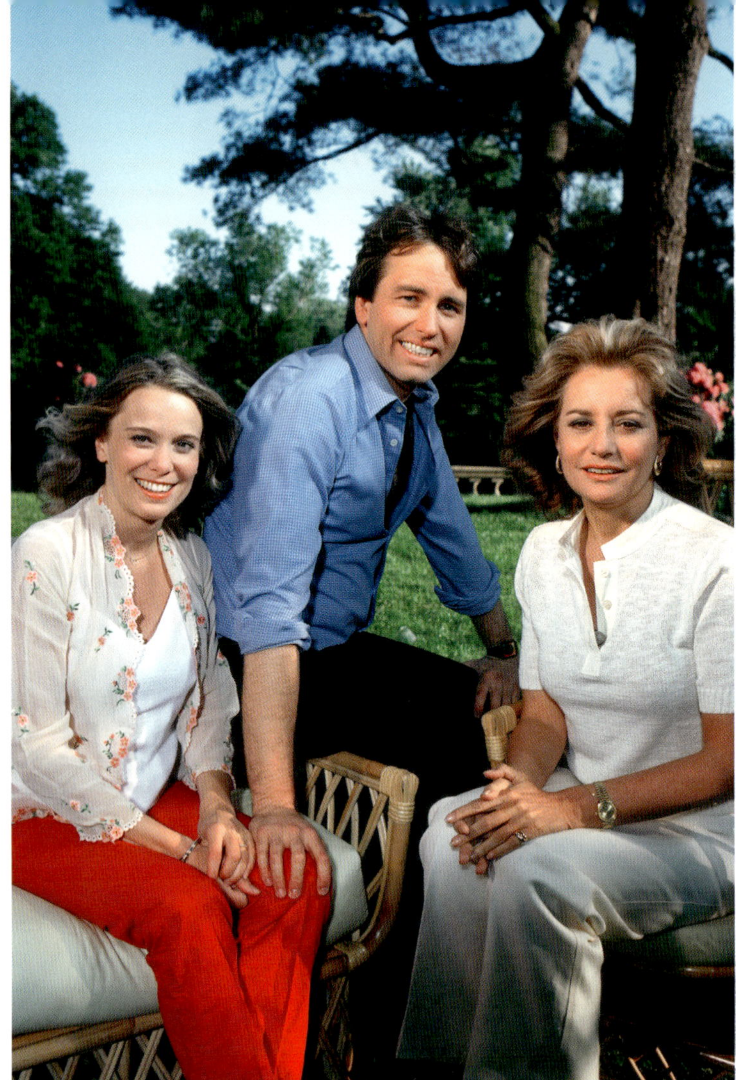

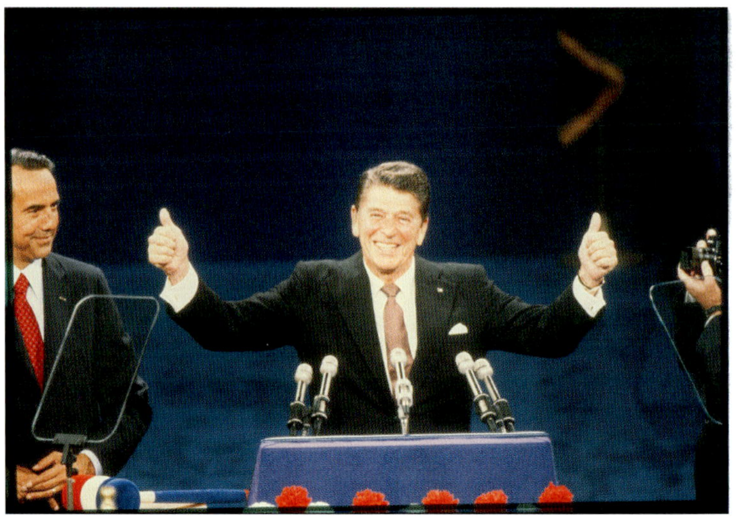

to work with. He bore with me while I stumbled around creating strobe hits in virtually every monitor, eventually producing this photo (right), which got extremely wide play, as the show was very popular.

There are two versions of this shot: the original chrome, scanned but unretouched. I did my best at the time, and this picture was also a lesson for me in how a photo, however technically or otherwise flawed, can still have a purpose, and impact. Then there's the cleaned up, retouched version, scanned and worked on, circa 2021. This, of course, shows that some of my mistakes have an unrelenting, proud durability to them, defying even the wizardry of modern post-production.

Oh, those first, uncertain adventures in lighting. When I took the job, my new boss, Rick, looked at me and said, "We shoot Kodachrome, and we light things." This turned out to be no idle threat.

Terror-struck, I went out and bought a set of Dynalites, which were the workhorse location flashes of that era. It was back in the day when power packs were about a dollar a watt-second. In other words, my shiny new Dynalite 800 pack was about 800 bucks, and I think the two heads I got were maybe an additional 300–400 bucks? I got a case, a couple stands, a couple of umbrellas (didn't even know what a softbox was), and maybe, maybe a honeycomb grid. A couple of warming gels. Spent my own money, quietly. That might have been due to my embarrassment at not owning the gear already, and my consequent lack of proficiency. Which was a small thing given the much larger embarrassment of what I produced when I started to use it. I barely knew how to plug these things in.

Given my insecurities at the time, I was quite nervous and too utterly unassured of my skill set to ask the questions I should have, like, "How do you use that Polaroid camera in the gear locker? You know, the one where you can tell what your strobes are doing before you start shooting film?" There was another photog at ABC who had been on staff for awhile. Great guy, but I was intimidated by both his technical knowledge and the fact that he could walk on sets like *Good Morning America*

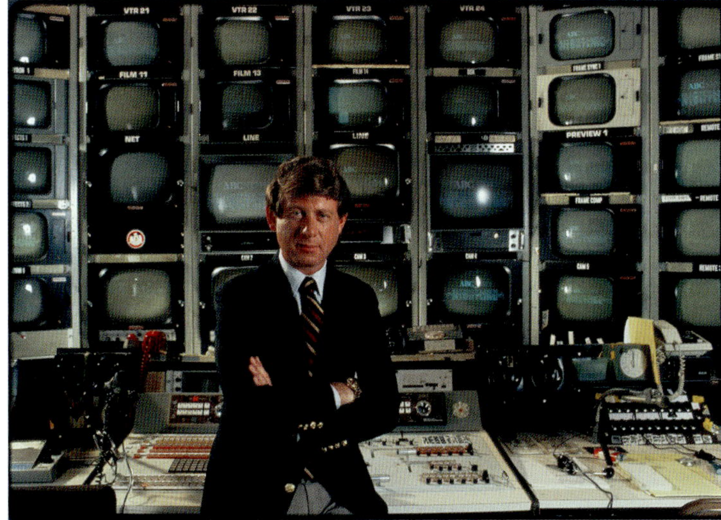

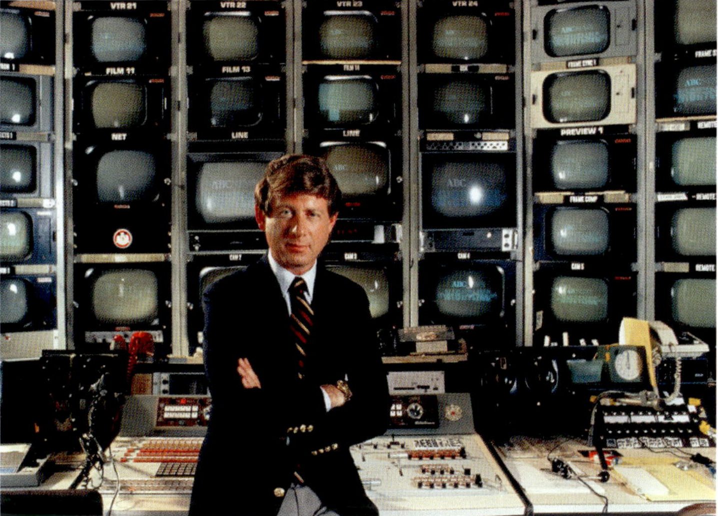

and everybody knew him already. So I bluffed my way through things, and plunged into my own maelstrom of trial and error. And error, and more error. Mistakes are great teachers, but if they come at you with the numbers and frequency with which I was committing them, you can feel like you're fleeing some intergalactic bad guys in a high-speed chase through an asteroid field.

But in that error-strewn landscape of failure, as stern and unsparing as the desert, there were oases of learning, and little by little, a chrome or two would return from the lab that actually looked a bit like what I had intended. Amazing. Progress. I turned a corner in my head. Those strobes sitting there in the lighting case, growling at me like junkyard dogs, could be tamed. The path of the light could be known.

One of my first tasks at the network was to be the photographer of record for the informational program known as *FYI*. These were 60-second spots, aired three times a day during daytime television, and hosted by the avuncular, affable Hal Linden, who starred in the extremely popular TV cop show *Barney Miller*. The spots were designed to offer helpful health and lifestyle advice, parenting tips, and the like. It also responded to viewers'

questions about all manner of stuff, from how to discuss sensitive subjects with your kids to psychology to germs in the bathroom to cooking natural.

I had to learn how to light open, clean, and commercial. Like for a photo of a woman in a kitchen with freshly baked bread.

Or light a twofer, as a couple of models acted out being a concerned mom and son, post boo-boo.

The *FYI* program was also a first toe dip in the waters of conceptual photography, as in, go illustrate how drinking a glass of milk before going to bed can make for a better night's sleep. There was some office brainstorming, as I recall, and I was

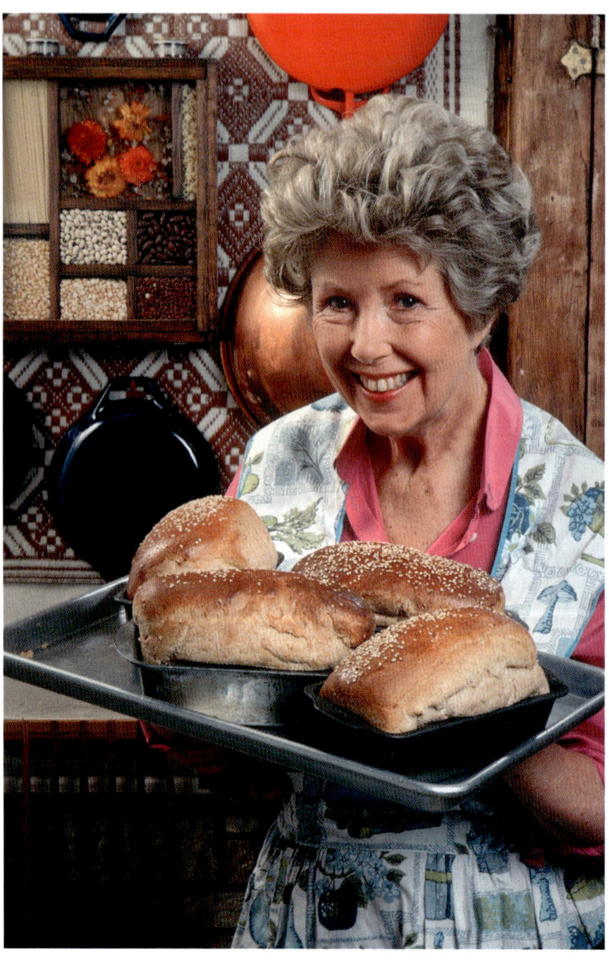
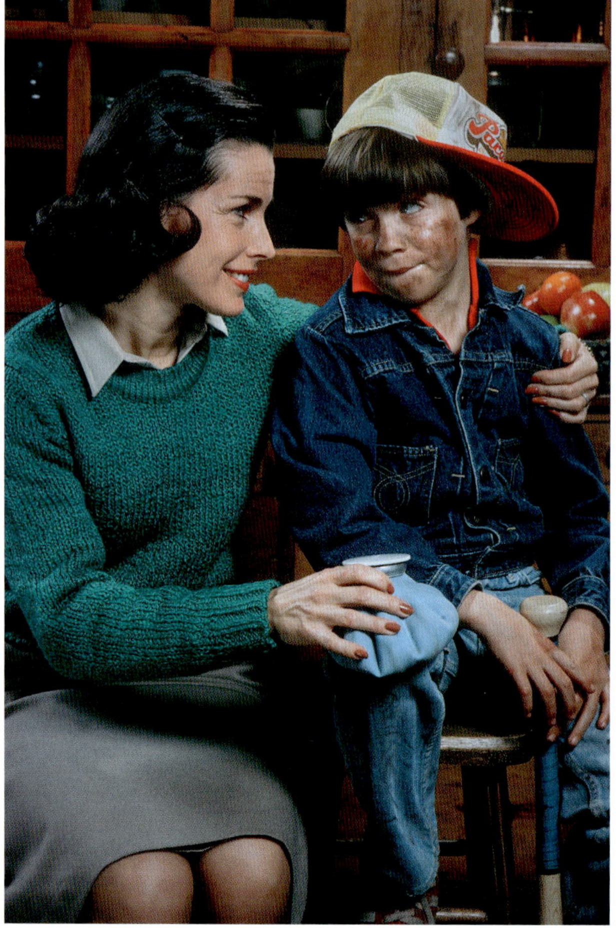

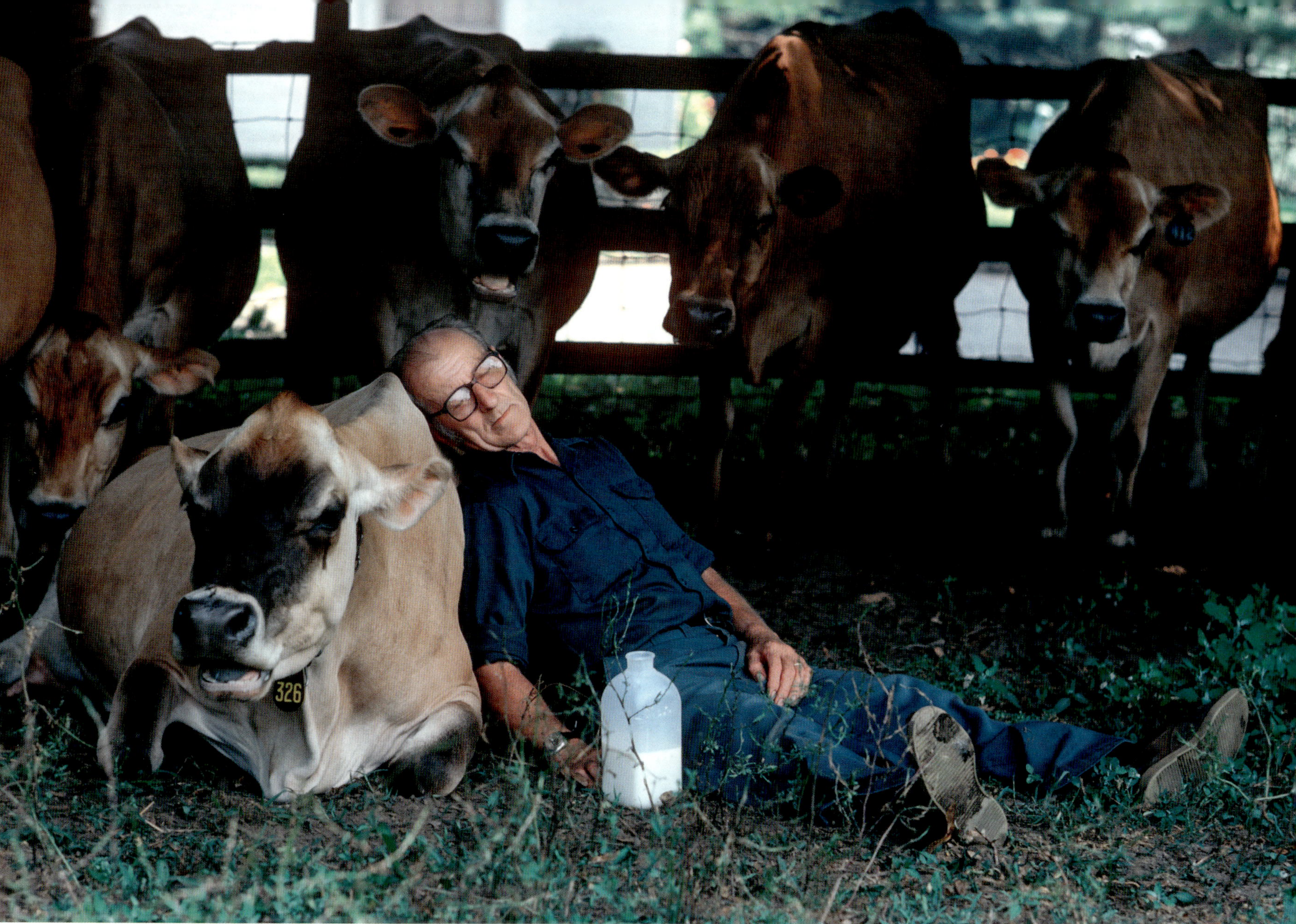

dispatched to a dairy farm on Long Island to sort out how to get a sleeping somebody near a cow. The farmer was a very decent man and was completely bemused by my lack of cow knowledge. I recall him chuckling and shaking his head. He then picked up the container of milk we had brought, walked over and feigned sleep, using one of his cows as a backrest. It was effortless, and fun.

I was so grateful to him! I looked through the lens and knew immediately that this was the picture. It fit the bill. Did the trick. Illustrated the idea. How do you smack the viewer in the eyes with a picture that speaks to the idea of the story or discussion at hand? Get a farmer to sleep on one of his cows! This picture opened a door in my head, and made me unafraid of picture ideas, however apparently outlandish they might be. A lesson that stayed with me.

The pictures shown here could have happened in an average month or so.

The lovely Brooke Shields, a teenager at the time, in her dressing room doing homework, prior to a shoot with Scavullo, which was being filmed by ABC.

David Hartman, then host of *Good Morning America*, with heavyweight boxer Ken Norton, comparing fists. Near Norton's training camp in upstate New York.

Geoffrey Holder (below), playing the role of Jupiter in an ABC afterschool special based on Edgar Allan Poe's "The Gold-Bug."

ABC was a tenant of the antenna tower atop the north tower of the World Trade Centers, so I used that as a wedge to initiate permission to climb the tower. I don't even recall signing a waiver to do this. I just went up with the technicians.

The gentleman in this shot (opposite, top right), I recall, was Johnny, aka "Spiderman." Which you pretty much needed to be up there, as you see the work being done at great height, with nothing but a simple safety belt. No elaborate harnesses back then. Just a rope and a belt. Go climb.

Publicity still with Danny Aiello for ABC's *Afterschool Special* series (opposite, bottom right).

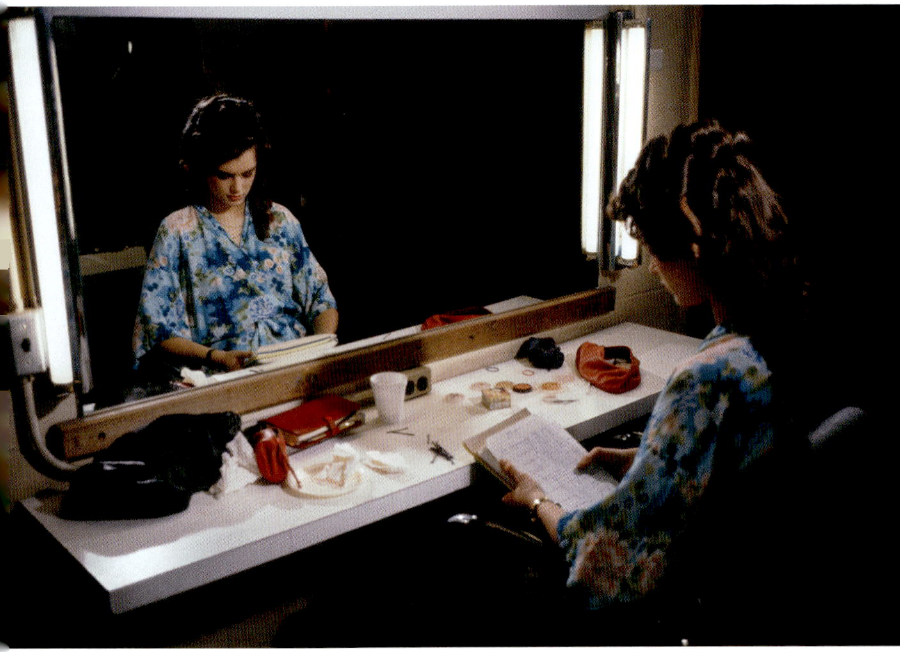

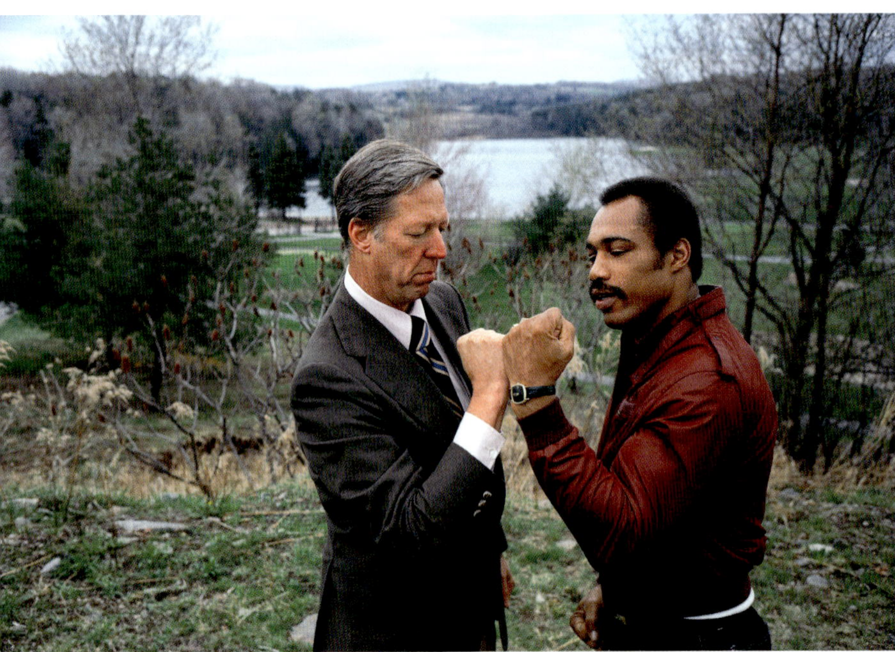

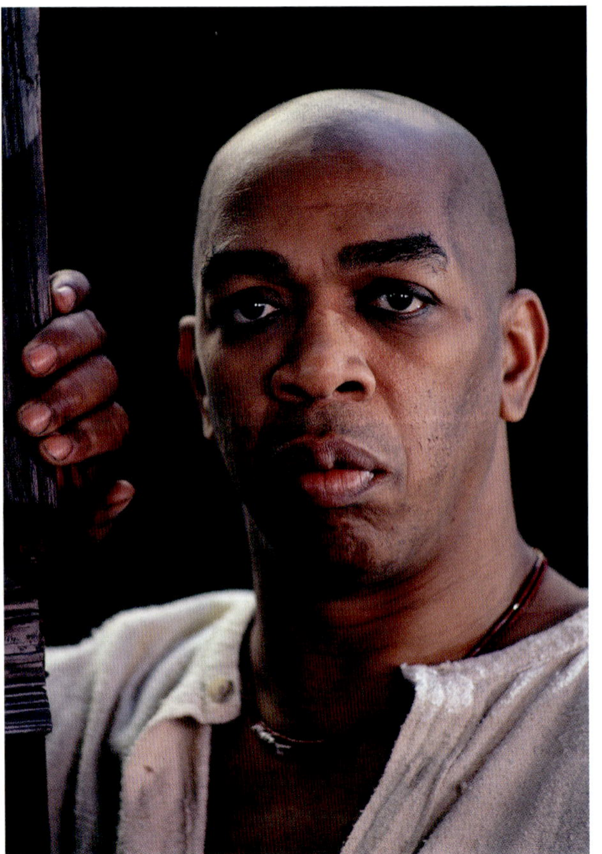

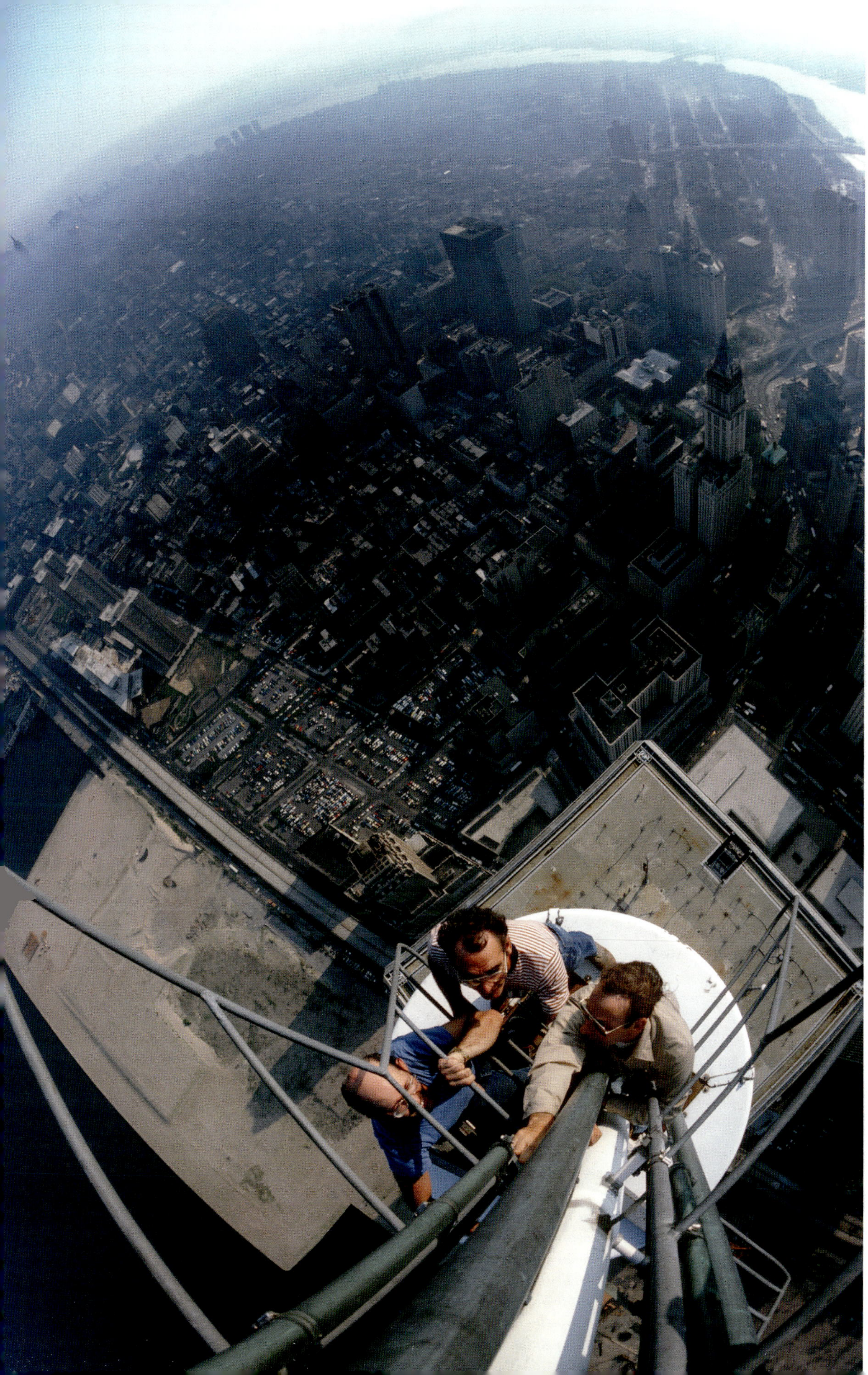

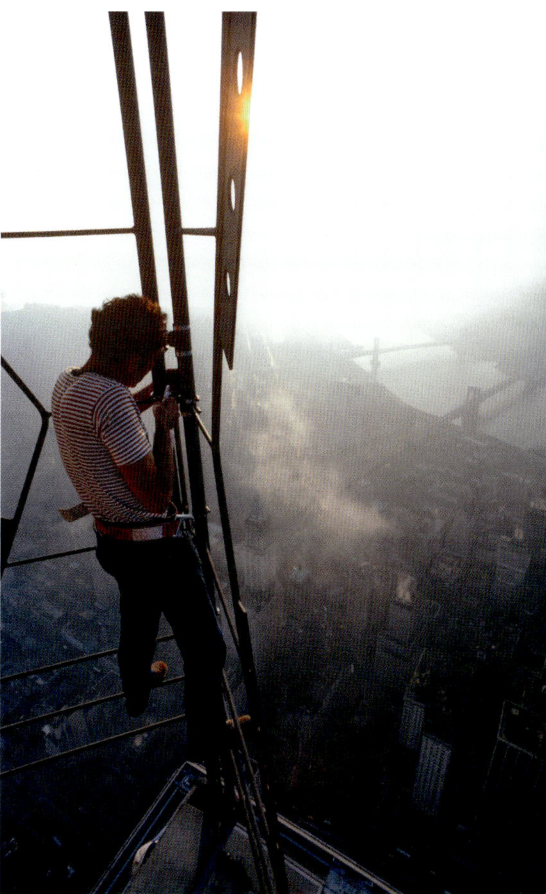
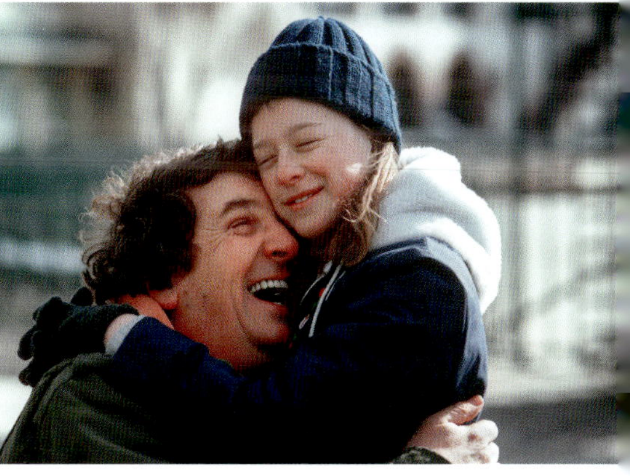

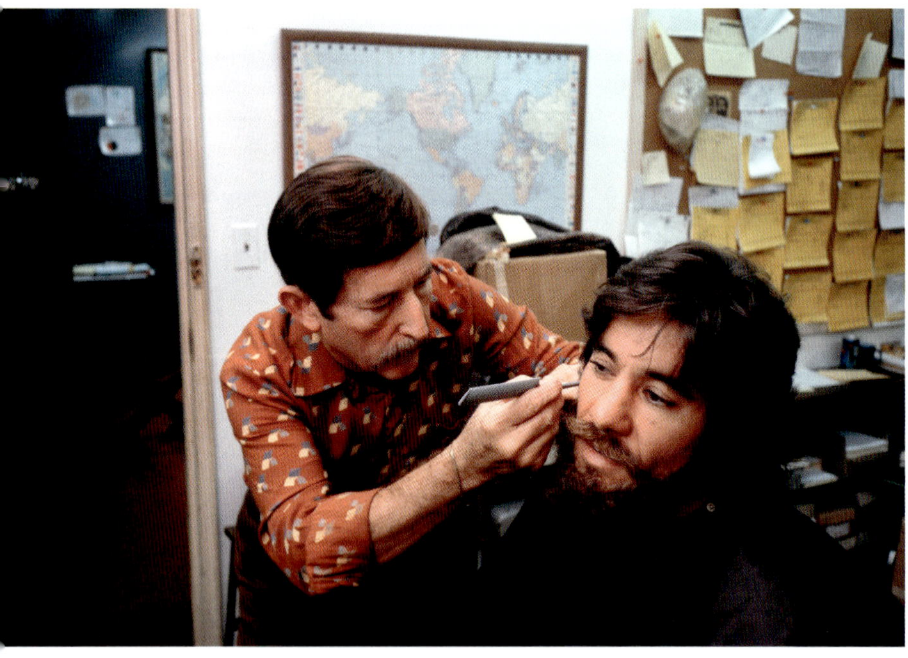

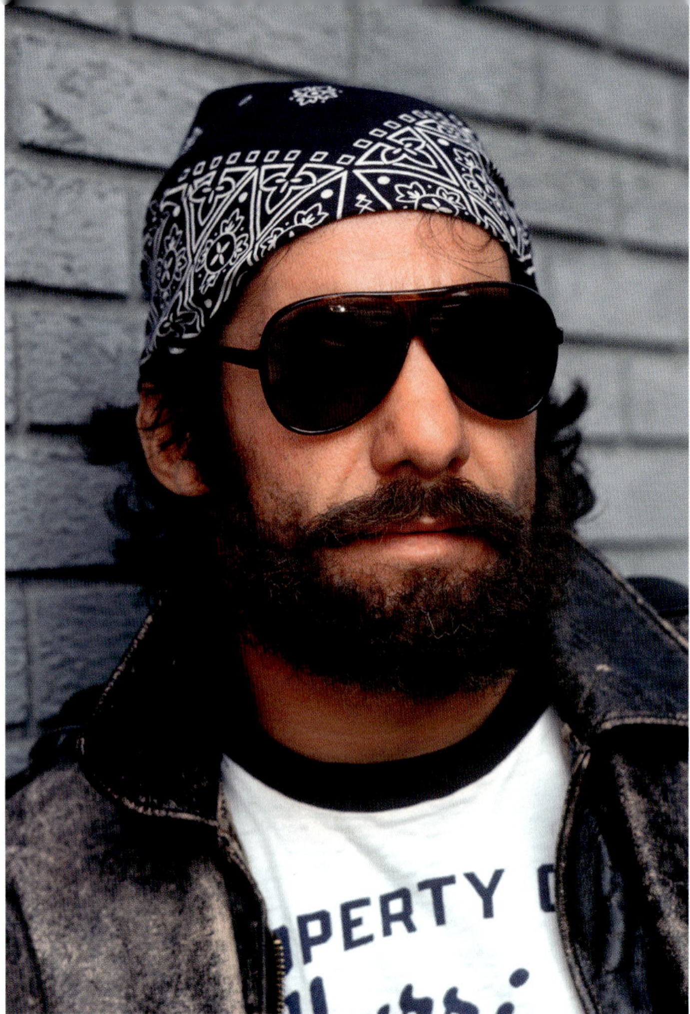

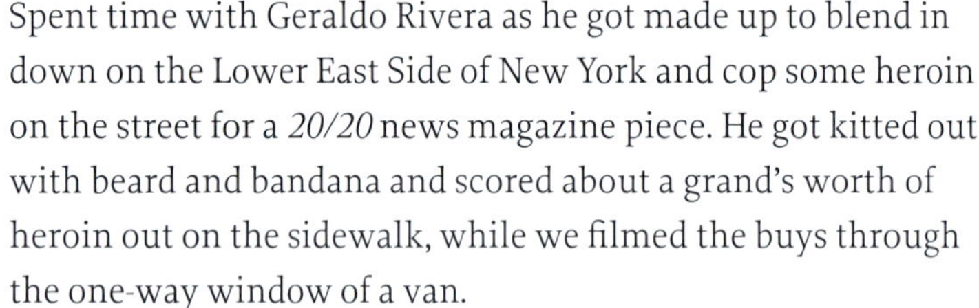

Spent time with Geraldo Rivera as he got made up to blend in down on the Lower East Side of New York and cop some heroin on the street for a *20/20* news magazine piece. He got kitted out with beard and bandana and scored about a grand's worth of heroin out on the sidewalk, while we filmed the buys through the one-way window of a van.

On the set with Susan Lucci and David Canary of *All My Children*. As opposed to Erica Kane, her villainous television alter ego, Susan was an absolute delight to photograph. The overhead TV set lighting was harsh and unforgiving for publicity stills, so she was always thankful if you brought lights and an umbrella for a quick, graceful fill light. A good, early lesson in going the extra mile for the portrait, and the appreciation and goodwill that can spool up in your subject.

The test firing of the very first Space Shuttle's engines in February, 1981. The shuttle Columbia sitting on the launch pad in the Florida moonlight.

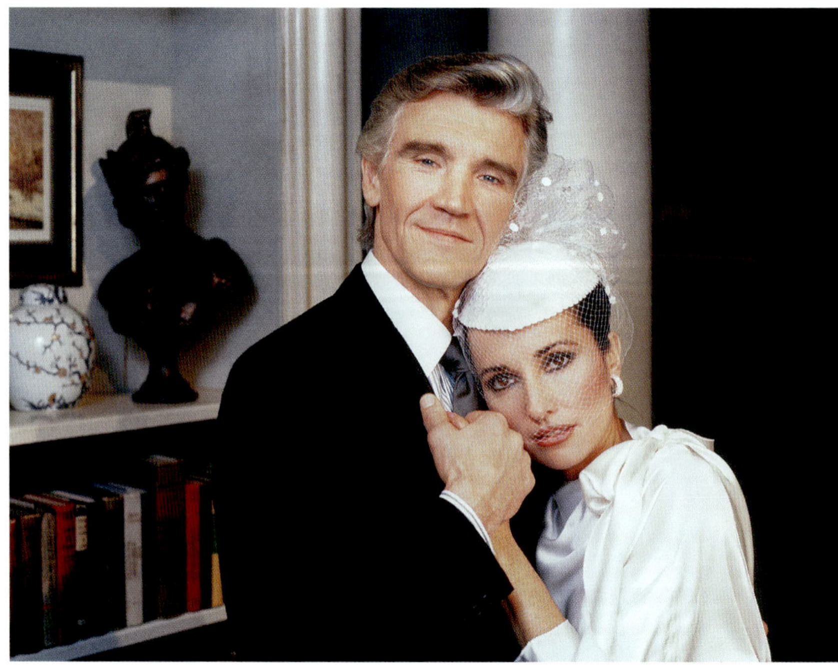

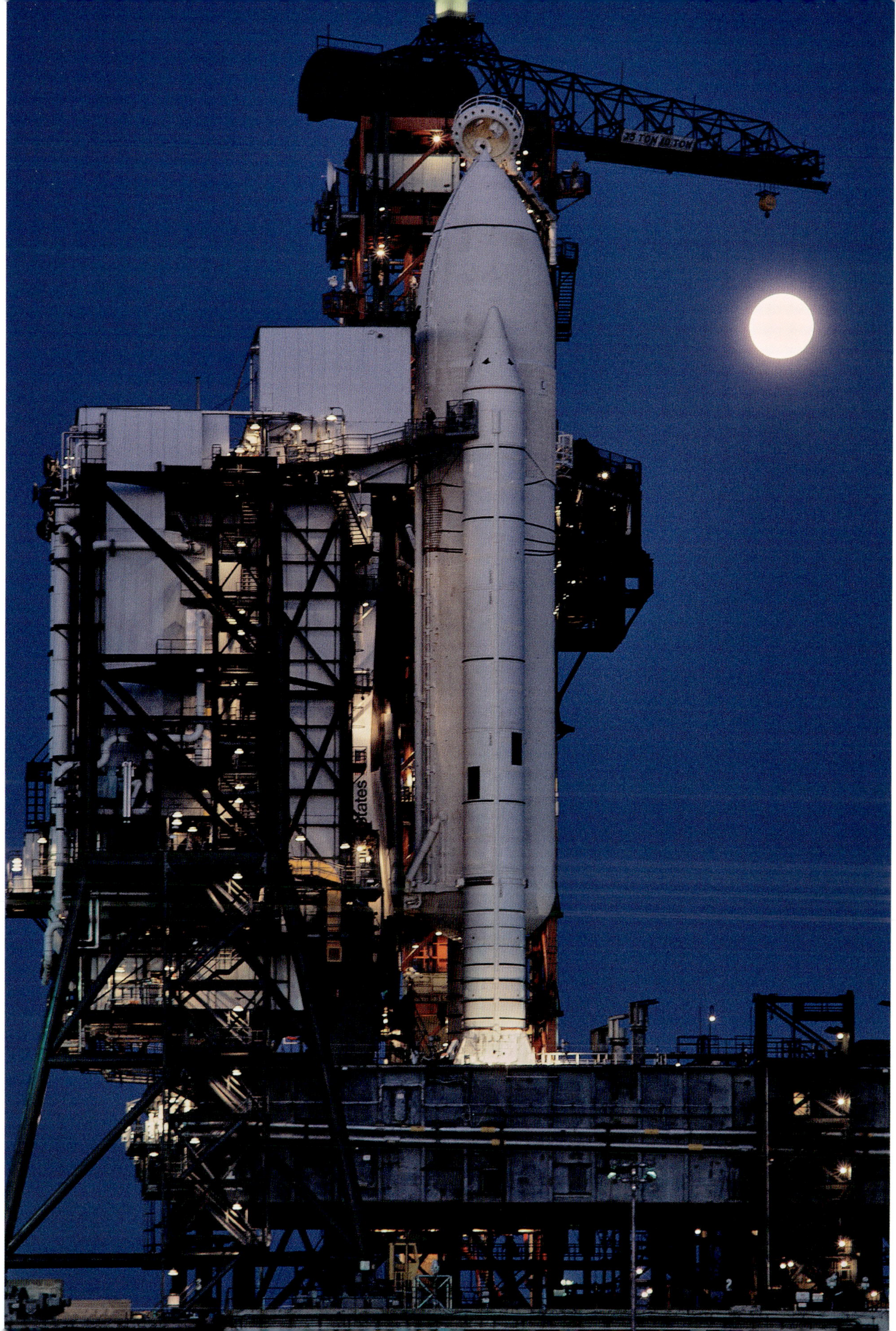

The 1980 Republican Convention was held in Detroit. I learned a lot during the brief stint I had covering politics around this time. One was to be careful on the photo stands! Nestled into a compact structure with a couple dozen other photogs, all sporting multiple cameras bearing long glass, one must make sure things are locked down. A colleague, just a row below me, thought he had bolted his 600mm lens to his tripod, and abandoned it to crouch and reach into his camera bag. It wasn't secured. Extremely front-heavy, this lens came off the tripod head and did a full gainer with a twist onto the head of the TV cameraman setting up on the row below him. It just about split the guy's skull. Not a good beginning, in terms of camaraderie amongst a bunch of already keyed-up assignment photographers who were destined to be cramped in together for three tension-filled days.

We all photographed Barry Goldwater from the vantage point of that stand. He gave a typically fiery speech which we were shooting intermittently until he paused and pulled out a hanky. It was

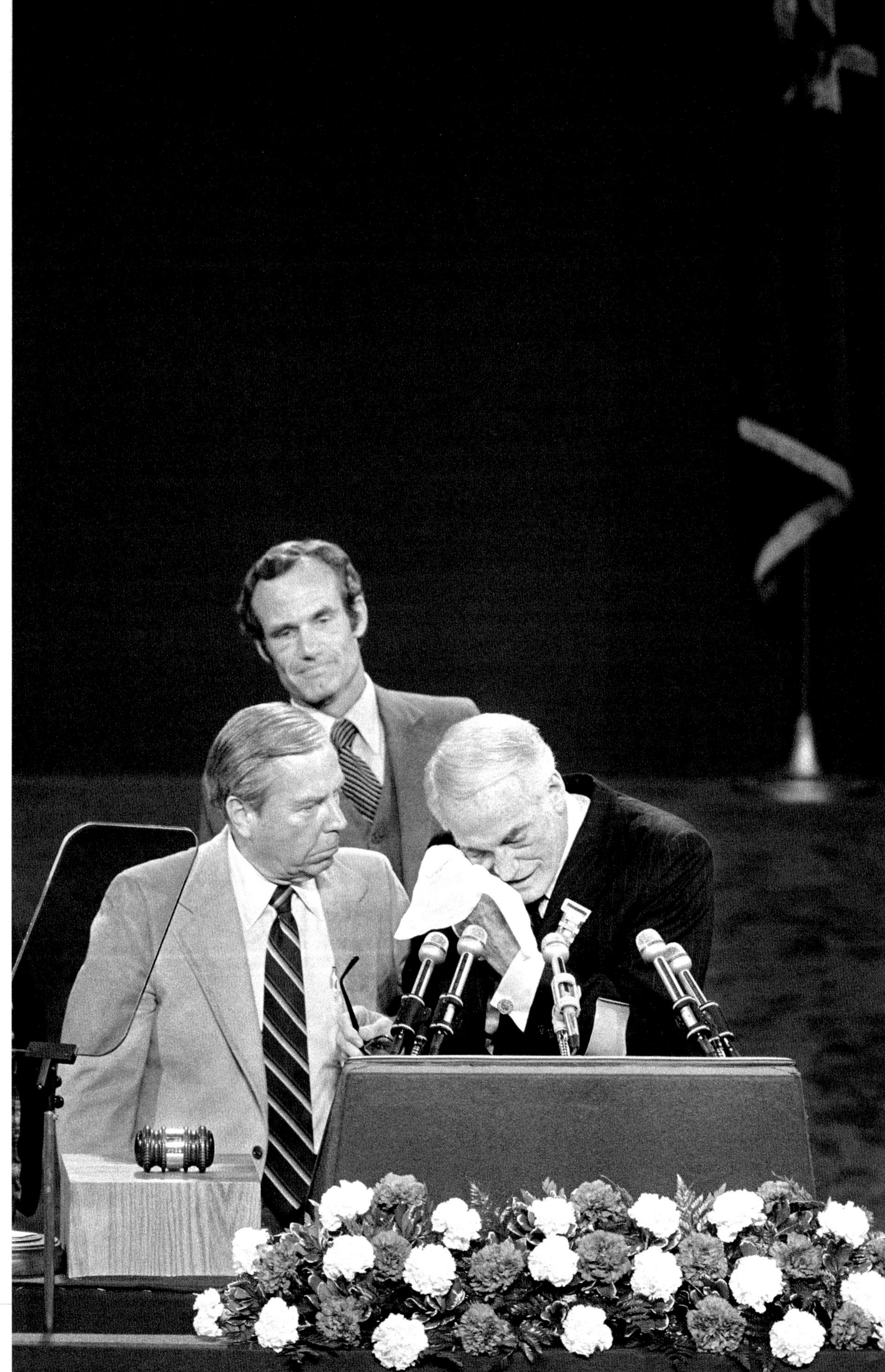

unclear if he was cleaning his glasses or overcome with emotion. Pause for cleaning glasses? The picture never sees ink. Weeping on the podium? Page one. You got to be on this and shoot the bejesus out of it. Questions come later. And it did turn out to be emotion. As Sally Quinn of *The Washington Post* wrote at the time, "They could not get enough of him and the hall shook with their cries of 'We want Barry!' until he had to quiet them himself, close to tears in the emotion of the moment."

It was at this convention that I pulled off a great scam on behalf of my colleague. Peter Murray was a terrific guy, a good picture editor, and a great boss. He was also wonderfully devoted to his wife, and the convention's time frame crossed over her birthday. He came to me and said, "Joe, I'm gonna fly home tonight, and be there for my wife for her birthday through tomorrow. Think you can cover for me?" Wink and a nod. Yes. Gotcha covered.

You see, it wasn't a matter of me going double-time and doing his work. Just doing that would have been easy breezy. The real deal was that all of the big ABC honchos were out there in Detroit, supervising this huge effort by the network, and it was all hands on deck for 18–20 hours a day. If Peter had asked his superiors to leave for his wife's birthday, he would have received derision and a somewhat incredulous "No." You'd have to be bleeding from the ears to get cut some slack from a convention coverage, and even then the bosses would most likely only give you 20 minutes in the break room for a sit-down and a donut.

So, for 36 hours I played find the pea with the big bosses. They'd come charging into the edit room looking for Peter, and I'd be like, "Oh man, you just missed him! He was here but I think he went out to the convention floor." In the hallways: "Where's Peter?!" I'd reply, "Wow! You didn't see him? You musta just walked right past him, 'cause he headed that direction you just came from!" Then I'd lay it on thick, and stand on tiptoes, craning my neck, trying to see if I could see him in the distance.

It was a convention, after all. Lots of room to move, and lots of places you could have been. Lots of people. Crowds to get lost in. The time of life before cell phones and GPS. You could pull off stuff like that.

As noted earlier, these pictures could easily have been made within a month or so. It was never dull, as the network was always doing something. Good training, good job. But I yearned for the world of magazines and those glossy pages. I lasted about 18 months as a staffer at ABC and quit.

My first day of freelance life was the day Reagan was shot in Washington, March 30, 1981. My old boss, Peter, he of the political convention disappearing act, was desperate to get somebody behind the scenes in the New York–based control rooms, someone who knew the ropes and could document the legendary Roone Arledge directing the coverage, but do so quietly, without getting screamed at. (Tensions often ran high in the control rooms, and distractions such as a pushy, less than quiet photographer were not welcome.) He beeped me, and I shot the job and turned in the film. He paid me the standard day rate of that time, $250, plus subway fare. Which was almost as much as my staff take-home pay for a whole week of work, after taxes. This was an interesting awakening.

> *You got to be on this and shoot the bejesus out of it. Questions come later.*

I resolutely stepped out on the tightrope of freelancing and have pretty much stayed out there for 40 years. What follows in this book are stories of balancing, wobbling, learning, laughing, and, occasionally, hanging on for dear life.

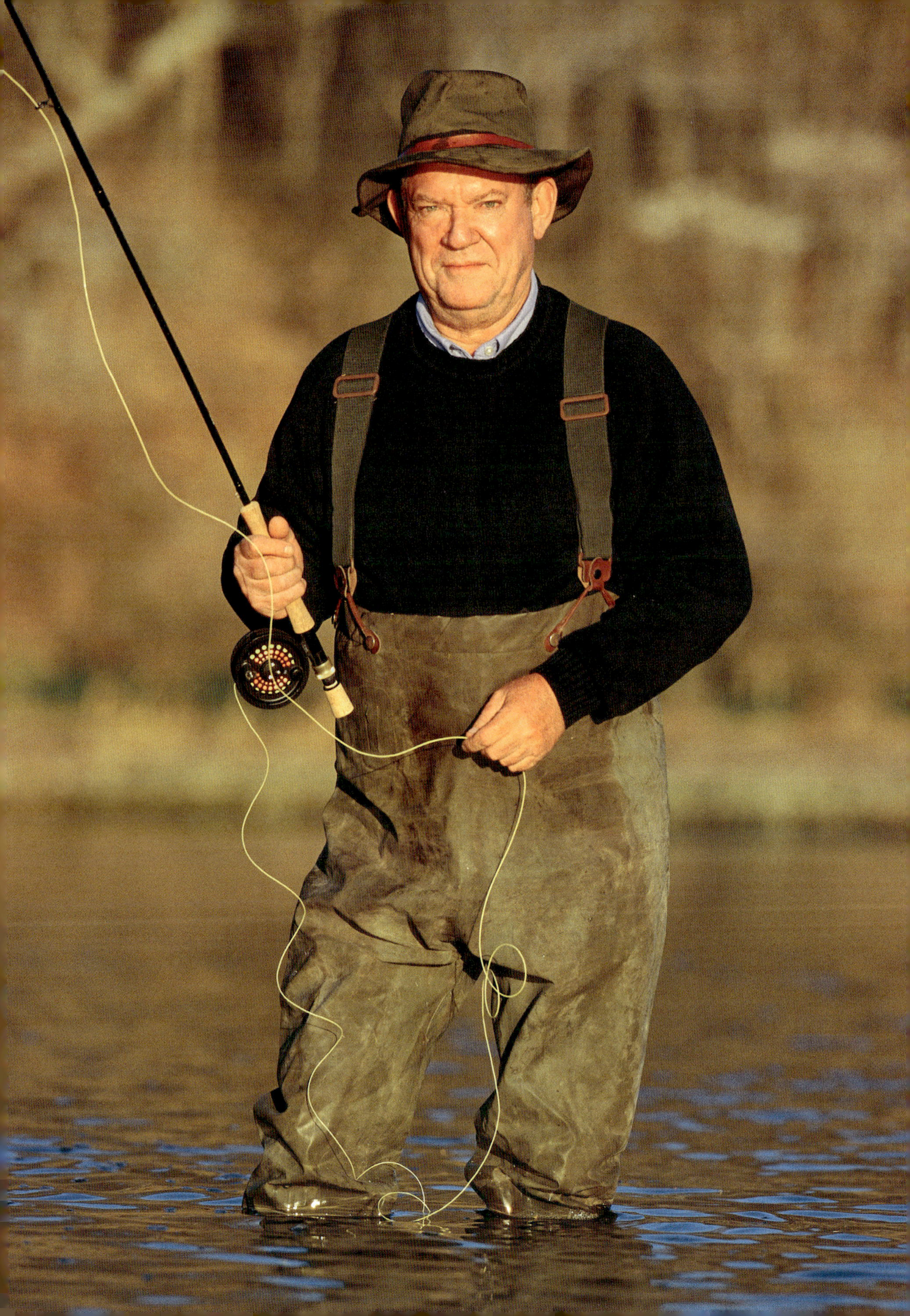

A Jerk on One End…

…is the title of a book about fishing, written by noteworthy art critic Robert Hughes, an Aussie who possessed a gruff demeanor, an acerbic wit, and an ever-active twinkle in his eye that indicated he had guessed the punchline of the joke long before you did. Such was his smarts.

He's deceased now, but at the height of his fame, he wrote and presented a TV series, and a book, called *The Shock of the New*, which was highly acclaimed and led to him being described in the *New York Times* as "the most famous art critic in the world." Part of his notoriety was his willingness to tweak the art world endlessly. He wrote, "The new job of art is to sit on the wall and get more expensive." Such commentary did not endear him to the high and mighty art establishment. I was sent out to photograph him when he followed on in his voluminous career with a humorous trifle of a book about fishing. The pictures were destined to be used for the book jacket and press releases.

In a way, the title of his book, *A Jerk on One End: Reflections of a Mediocre Fisherman*, could easily have been the title of this book, if you replace the fishing pole with a camera. So many missteps on my end of the lens! A veritable avalanche of ineptitude, at least periodically. So many pictures where, in fishing parlance, I cast in the wrong place. It haunts me, when I allow it to, and I give those feelings allowance quite often. It's always worst on the morning of the shoot, really, when I desperately hope, at least occasionally, that the client will call at the last moment and cancel everything. Then I won't have to go in once again and summon "it," and be cool, be wise, be funny, direct the action, make decisions, rig up the camera, and peer at the world through a rectangle. I rummage through the equipment cases on those days, searching not for a lens or a light stand, but for something much more elusive: confidence. Or, perhaps, a way out. Maybe no one will notice if I just, you know, leave?

(Maybe that's why landscape photography is so appealing to so many photographers? The rocks and the trees don't give a shit if you leave or stay, if you bumble or stumble. The birds and mountains have no expectations of you.)

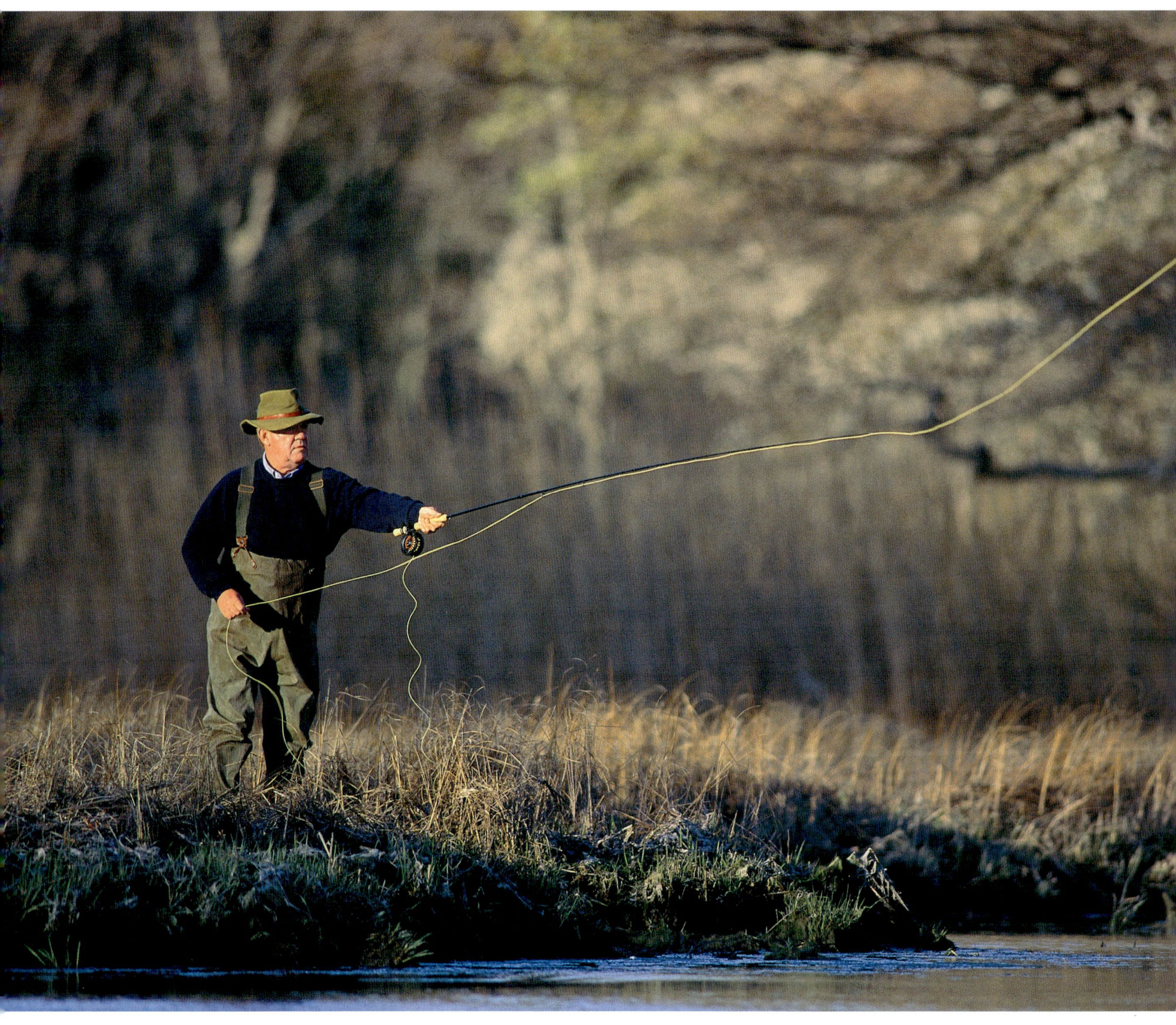

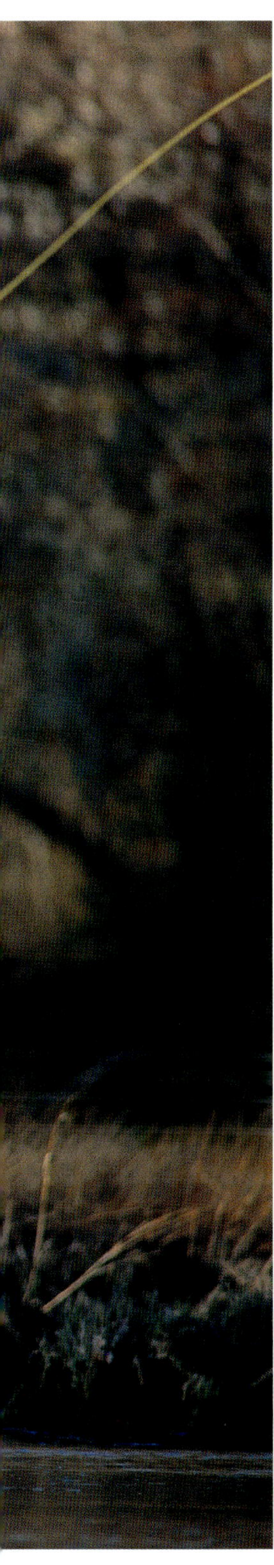

So, it was a random, wonderfully apt pairing when I was sent to photograph Mr. Hughes, who had a place on Shelter Island out near the eastmost tip of Long Island. In terms of creative insecurities, he wrote at one point, "The greater the artist, the greater the doubt. Perfect confidence is granted to the less talented as a consolation prize."

So, there we were, matched up. A couple of guys, outwardly assured of themselves, but inwardly seething with self-doubt. And, in his case, loneliness. He was between marriages, rattling around on his island estate, and insisted that myself and my assistant stay for dinner. We had traveled to his place the day before, so we could rise at 4 a.m. for the early morning fishing adventure. He made a really good carbonara, as I recall. We had little in common, and I'm sure, for him, conversation with us was like driving the Ferrari of his intellect through the Holland Tunnel during the bump and grind of rush hour. But at that point in his life, company was company. We filled empty chairs at his table.

Ever notice, on a sunrise shoot, when the sun peaks over the horizon and curling tendrils of light, tentative at first, then more forceful and insistent in their loveliness, make the ordinary magical, and your doubts at camera disappear? Forget about canceling the assignment! What was I thinking? The breathless anxieties about the whole deal are replaced with a breathless urgency to photograph. The sun inexorably rises, and your head and heart race. Eye in the camera! Shoot! Move fast. The light fills you with confidence. Frames rattle away. No need to wait for a flash to recycle; you've got a million watt-seconds in the sky! Go to consecutive high and shoot. Shoot! The rising of the sun at that hour warms your face and your heart and immediately transports you from "Why am I doing this?" to "How could I ever do anything else?"

Backed up by light like this, you can do no wrong at the camera. What were you doing awake last night, in the darkness, worrying?

> *What were you doing awake last night, in the darkness, worrying?*

Effortless shoots like this—with the gestures of fishing needing no direction, with your subject wonderfully absorbed in his own world, and you chose the right lens (in this case, a 200–400mm), and the sun loves you—make all the dry well adventures worth it. It's not a shoot where you labor mightily to resuscitate the patient (your attempt at a picture), all the while realizing that no matter what you do, you won't be able to confer upon those frames what they might call in a medical scenario a "good quality of life."

Just like fishing, this is a good catch. One you can remember fondly, a morning where it all just worked.

Until, of course, the next job, when the clouds gather again and the pesky demons of uncertainty natter about in your head and heart. I'd like to tell you they go away with time and experience, but they don't, dear reader. If you are involved in this uncertain adventure, it will always be thus.

Fun, huh?

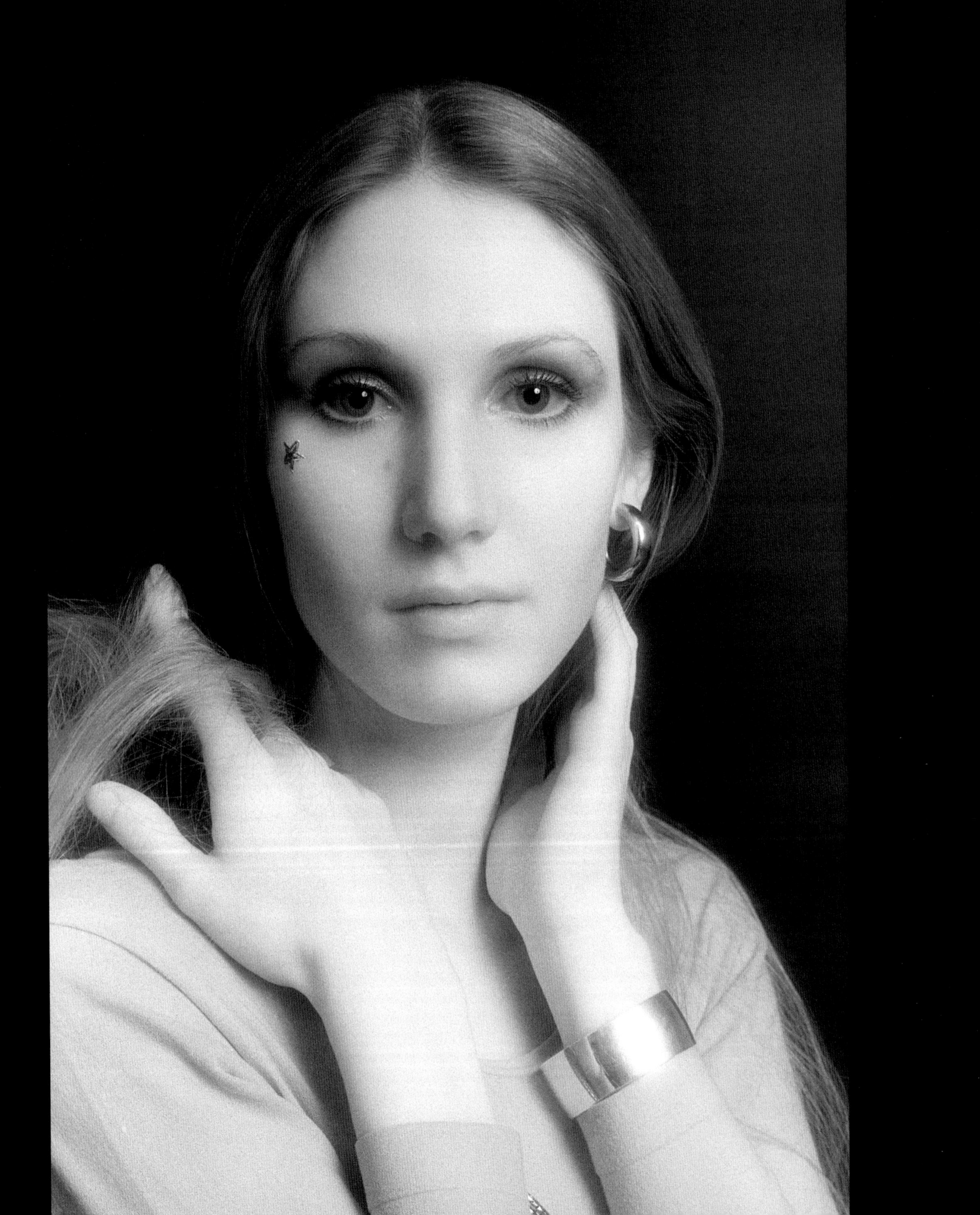

Trust the Machine

I started experimenting with flash back in college. We had, as I remember, anvil-like Ascor powerpacks that were blocky and weighty, and not particularly hot swappable—as in, if you weren't careful on the electrical front, the pack could easily arc, and blow you and/or your model across the room. Tough to reestablish confidence in your subject when you just melted the power box and you look like a cartoon character who just peed on an electric fence. But the idea of controlling light and the look of it was drumming in my head. I was training to be a newspaper photog, run and gun, but at the same time I was poring over the work of Avedon, Penn, Helmut Newton, and Guy Bourdin. The image shown here (opposite) was perhaps the one lonesome success I produced in the Newhouse School photo studio.

The subject is my good bud (still in touch on Facebook) Nancy Barnes. She was a drama student and lovely in front of the camera. Not content to just mess unknowingly with lights, I shot this on B&W infrared film, essentially copying the work of another friend and fellow student, Dennis McDonald. He went on to be an incredibly fine newspaper photographer in his native South Jersey. He was messing with infrared, and I loved the look. (Dennis also shot the final pic in this book, way up on the Verrazzano Bridge.)

Nancy sat for me patiently, and beautifully, as I worked out this unknown terrain. The extent of our "styling" was the sticky silver star affixed to her cheek. Styling on a student budget!

I continued to play with cumbersome flashes when I hit the *Daily News*. Eddie Peters, a stellar, long-time staffer who had gone inside as a boss, gave me his old case of potato mashers, powered by wet cell battery packs. Crude, no controls, and heavy. With one of them, an umbrella, and a guess of an f-stop, I made a picture of Prince Paul, the Ringling Brothers Circus clown (following page).

John Loengard, the DOP at *LIFE*, and a mentor, liked the picture. To him, it was "peculiar." He also said it was a bit of a window into the interior of a performer's life, as the powdering and makeup process looked, in his words, "painful." Some of the

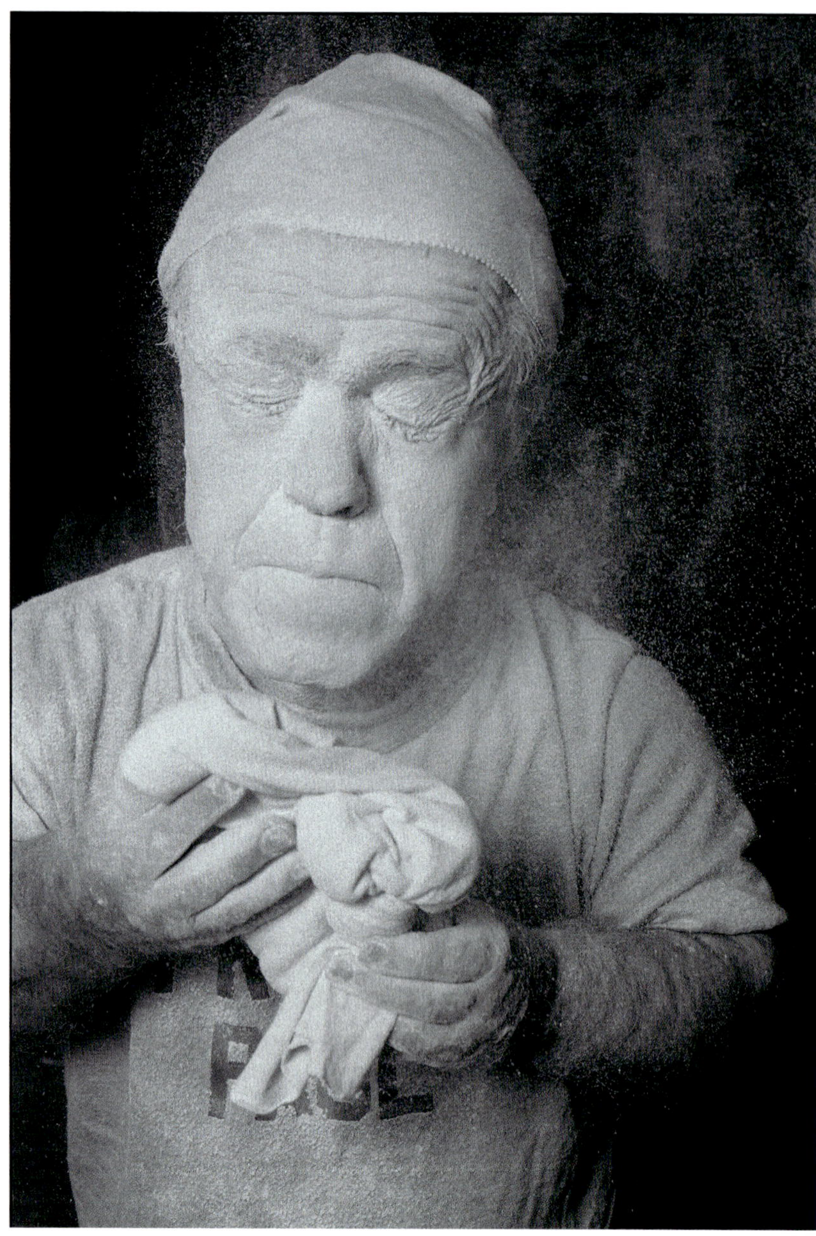

then, not exactly "smart." It was like when you go into the parent-teacher meeting, and teach says your sixth grader has "great potential."

I was able to put away the long division of guide numbers and camera-to-subject distance! Not that I used the formulas very much. I made gut calls, thumb in the air, nose to the sky. Now, I had a partner in making those calls! This will be easy!

And comparatively, it was. However, easy is not to be confused with dependable. TTL (through the lens) flash photography has been much decried over the years as being error-prone and unknowable, a dark, magic brew possessed of fearfully uncertain powers. Shakespeare, when he penned *Macbeth*, might well have been describing TTL flash, an alchemy that's akin to a witch's spell, mixing parts of snakes, bats, lizards, and the like. "For a charm of powerful trouble, / Like a hell-broth boil and bubble."

And then, with a cackle and a pre-flash, see if the exposure corresponds to your chosen f-stop. And don't forget to wear a pointy hat.

The thing is, back then, it didn't correspond all that often. About as precise as a thrown hand grenade, these flashes were the roulette wheel of exposure. They performed, or not, in whimsically vexing fashion.

In one instance, it would give you perfection.

And then, in the next, blowout. All within minutes, or seconds, as you shot your way through a job. I like the term "blowout." It's perfect to describe TTL losing it. You're cruising down the highway, going like sixty, as they say, and then . . . *blowout!* The wheel wrenches in your hands, and you scrape sideways across the highway. Out of control. In the ditch.

oddity here comes from the formidable flash, freezing all the powder in the air around the Prince. At that point, I had no real understanding of why, but I was fevered with flash, and the possibilities.

One can imagine what a gift a Speedlight seemed to be! Having toted bulky, undependable lights for years, I was looking at something light, controllable, and smart. Well, okay, back

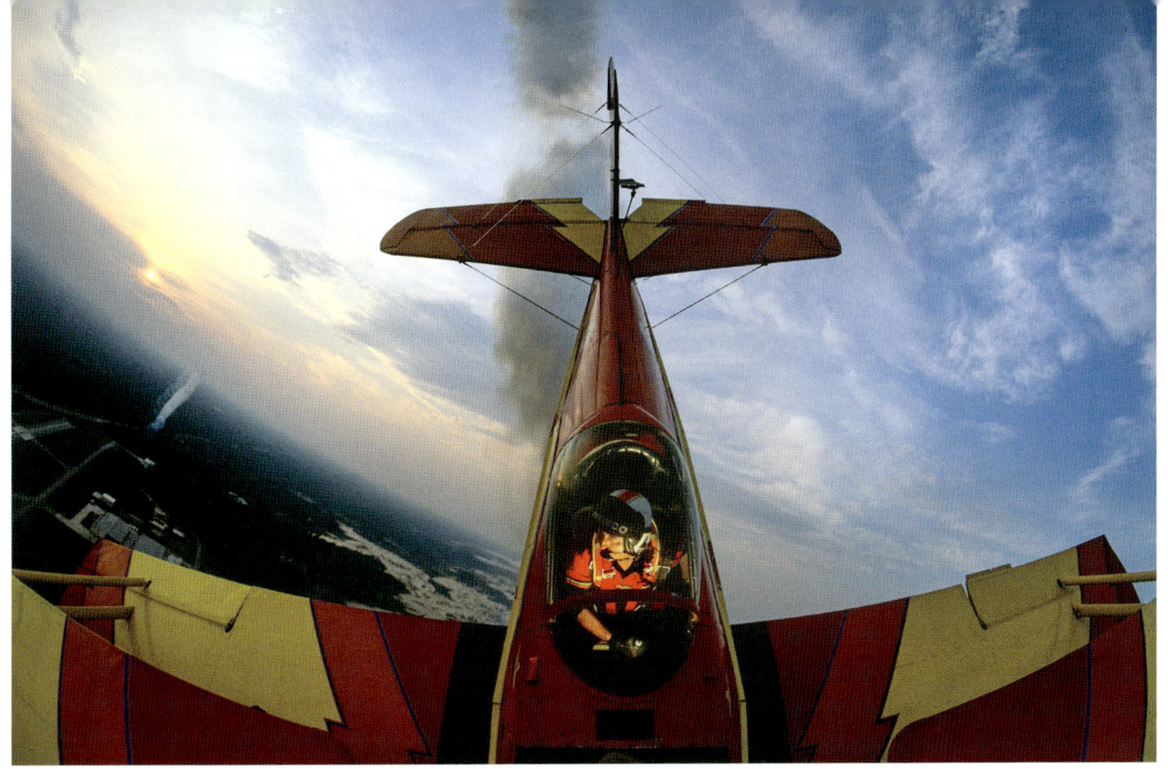

Encroaching darkness, backgrounds, closeness of your subject, color of their garments—all could create an exposure fracas. For instance, while this biplane was zooming along and there was light in the sky, i.e., information for the camera/flash tandem to chew on, you'd be okay.

But let darkness take its course, and the flash would respond. *Blowout!*

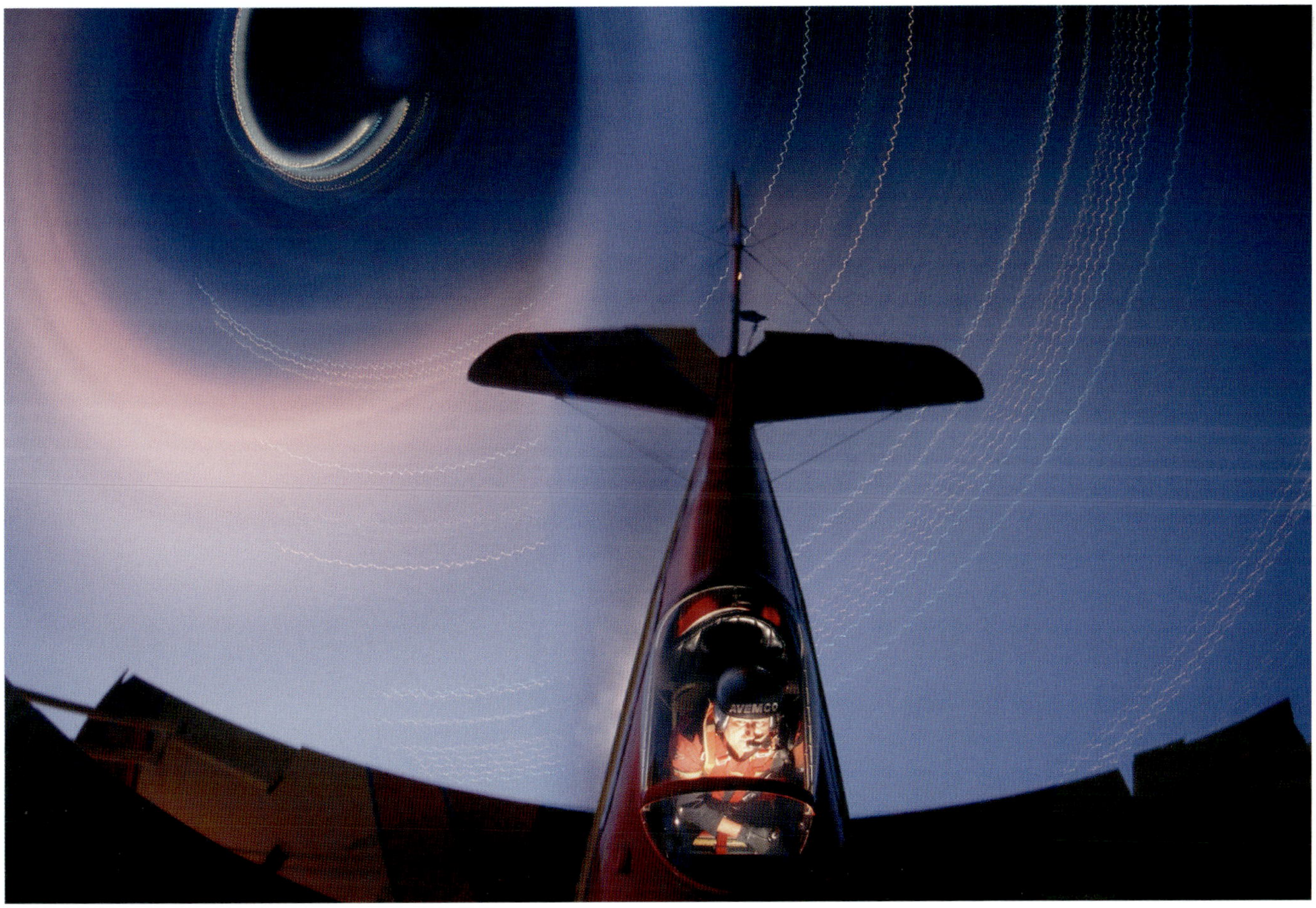

I kept at it. Having no other choice is a great motivator. The path my imagination was leading me, even back then, was toward a world that I would need to parse out with the application of light. I was shooting for magazines that demanded high gloss and big color. Film was unforgiving and had serious limits in the realm of pushability. ISO 50,000 was not even a shimmering mirage, far ahead in the desert. The fault line for getting an assignment often swung on whether the photog could use a flash well. I wanted to work.

I plunged into the uncharted swamp of TTL flash. I had many failures, but failures are great teachers. I learned the value of risk, as well as the rewards that trusting the tech and pushing the system can bring. I have always said that flash photography is a lifelong series of experiments, which I continue to engage in, and those adventures alternately lift my heart or crush my spirit.

My level of determination was an exasperation to those around me. Everyone was a target for a TTL portrait session! My oldest daughter, Caitlin, went for a while to an Isadora Duncan dance class, she of the veils and the dreamlike moves. Not one to let an opportunity pass, I took her instructor out to the Brooklyn beaches (right). Just me, my subject, one stand, and one flash. Hard flash. No assistant, so no putting up an umbrella on the windswept shores of the Rockaways. It was probably my first inkling that these little Speedlights—fragile as they were, teetering on the edge of uncertainty—held great promise for effective lighting solutions, done with minimal gear and maximum mobility.

It's the way of this life as a photographer. Nothing is certain, really, when you venture with a camera, and then especially when you add the mystical component of flash. When you let the camera decide certain things for you, some describe it as irresponsible, and they raise questions about your judgement at the lens. "Why don't you use manual?" is a question I hear often. I do use manual, in relentless fashion.

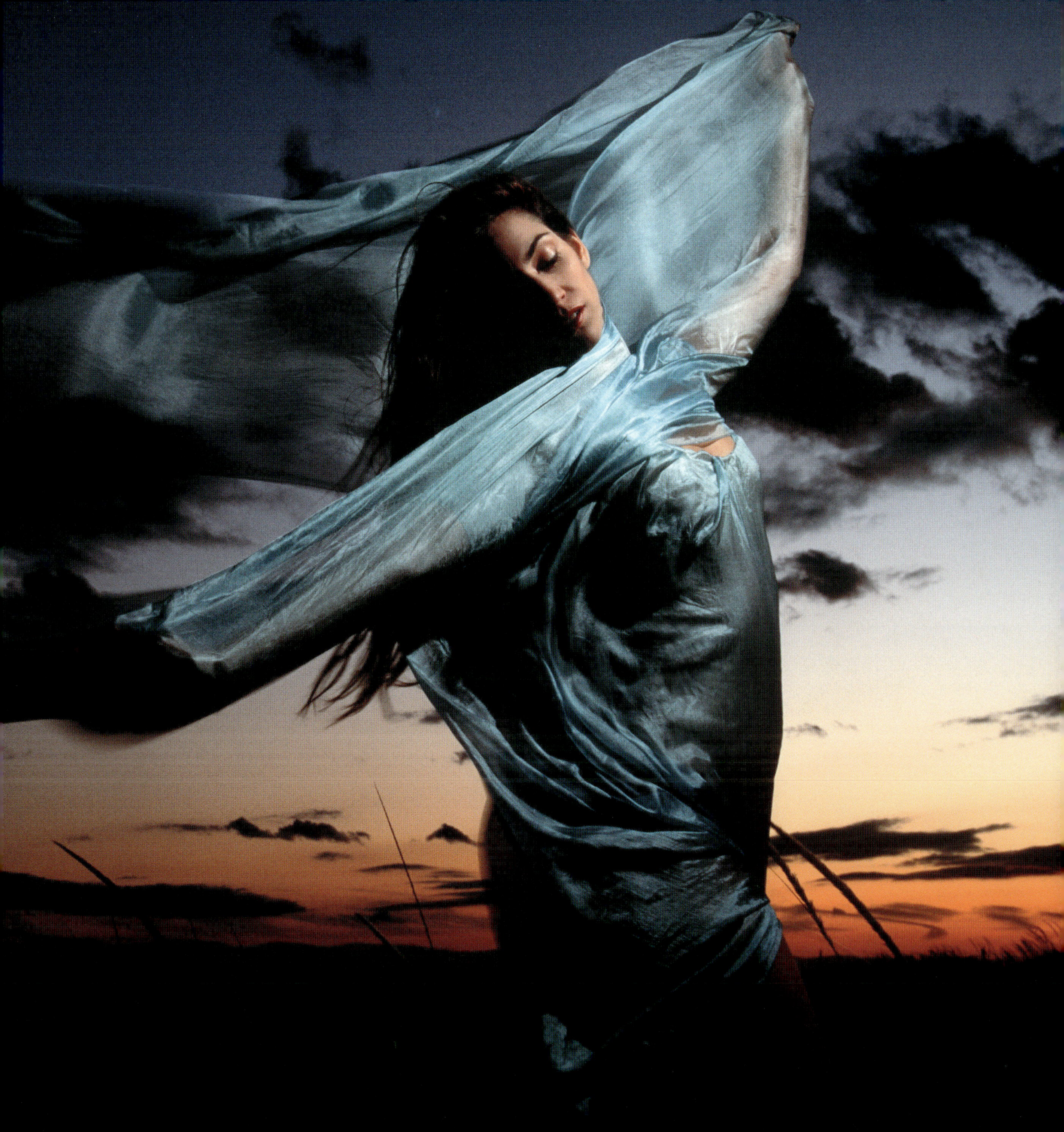

I use TTL as well, and view it as a helpful pathfinder in certain scenarios. It's the blazing headpiece atop the Staff of Ra, helping Indy find the Ark. The path TTL nimbly leads you down can easily result in a manual solution that you then dial in with certainty, like the sturdy dock where you tie off the bobbing boat. Or, nowadays, given the dependability of this technology, you can let it ride in through-the-lens mode, and just closely monitor the camera as it makes its decisions. You can feel it at the camera when all is working; your head is close-in to the machinery, and with the flashes nearby, there's an intuitive connection between you, the camera, and the flash system. You can also tell if it's confused, as you listen to the shutter drag, for instance, if you are in Aperture Priority. Or you hear (and feel) as the TTL misreads and dumps full power on your subject, turning them

Grab one flash. Don't confuse the issue. Just one.

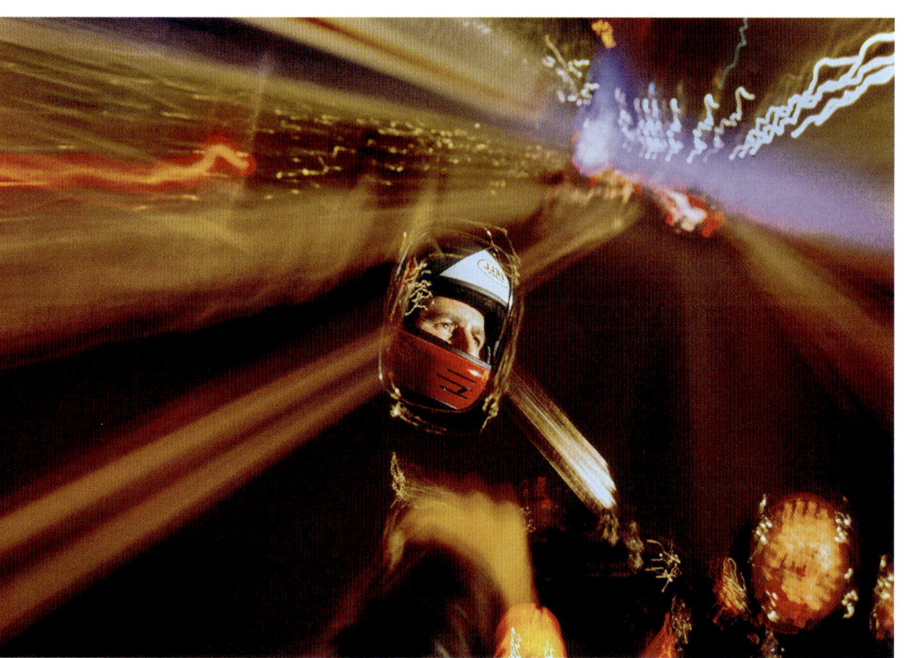

into a glowing fuel rod right there on your LCD. A full-power thunk from the Speedlight! *Blowout!*

You can also pick up the relative power of your exposure, which is why I always have instant replay turned on. With your eye jammed into the eyepiece, there's a certainty you can feel when the picture just made dupes into the LCD. Right? Too bright? Too dark? You can read it, feel it, right there in the lower quadrant of your eye. Now, with EVF and mirrorless becoming the standard, all the info is automatically right there in your electronic viewfinder as you shoot.

So, take a plunge. As they say, what could go wrong? It's just a bunch of pixels! If you are in the mood for experimentation, grab one flash. Don't confuse the issue. Just one. Read the manual! What a novel idea!

Then take it and mess around. *And I mean, mess around!*

I don't recommend this, 'cause it's nuts, but I put one on the handles of a motorcycle, wrapped two SC-17 cords around the biker to the camera's hot shoe, and then half stood in the back seat of the bike as it whizzed through the Lincoln Tunnel in NYC (left). Pulled a focus on the driver's eyes and worked the TTL prayer beads. Nowadays, in this world of radio TTL, SC-17 cords are unnecessary. And, given current technology, if exposures are looking slightly wonky, you can change the flash power while the bike is zooming along. Great evolutions in the world of TTL hotshoe flash. Not possible for me, tipping around on this bike.

The tunnel's interior gave the flash some measure of constant light level, which was a great thing to offer these TTL small flashes, still in their infancy. I did runs on TTL, and runs on manual, as that made good sense, because the biker stayed at the same distance relative to the flash. If he had made any radical changes in distance, we would've both had much more to worry about than flash exposure.

By contrast, what would bedevil early TTL was in-and-out changing light levels, such as in . . . Times Square! When Sam, who was a phenomenal athlete, and at the time making a living

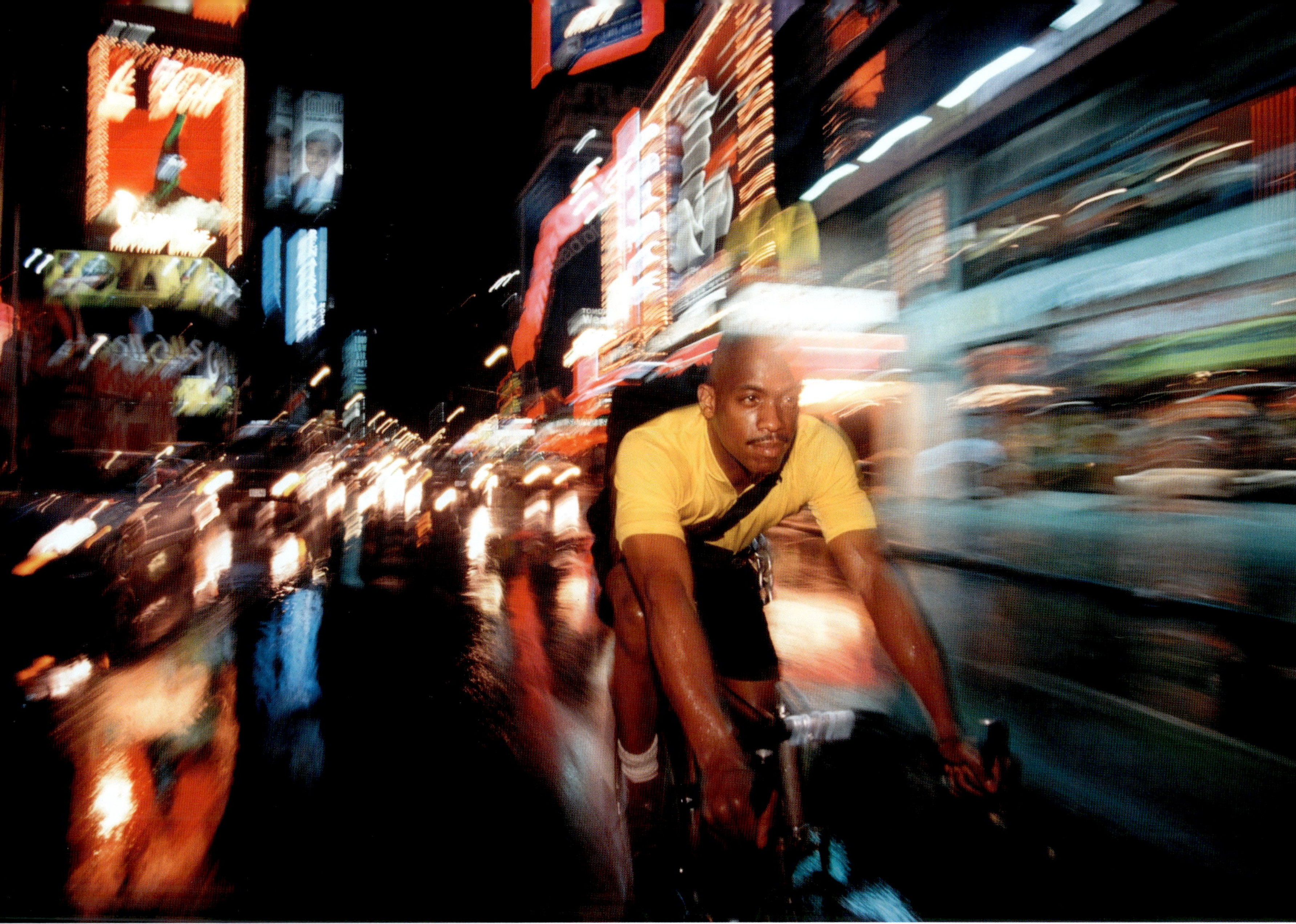

as a bike messenger, rolled through that maelstrom of blinking and flickering display neon, I had a lot of failure, and was lucky to get a decent shot (above).

I shot Sam out of the back of a minivan, hatch door up. This was shot in the mid-'90s or so.

Fast forward to much, much better TTL, and in 2010 I am, again, hanging out of the back of a van, this time in Vancouver (following page). Some things don't change.

Here, the concert performance of the camera is truly approaching symphony-like levels. I'm using AF and Aperture Priority mode at camera. I've rigged the minivan with an upper main light and a light off camera, to the right, for fill and some directionality. I'm speaking to the flashes via line-of-sight commands at the camera, which is a lock, of course, as the flashes are right next to me. The piece of this puzzle that constantly varies is not the exposure; we were shooting in the Pacific Northwest, with its seemingly infinite cloud canopy.

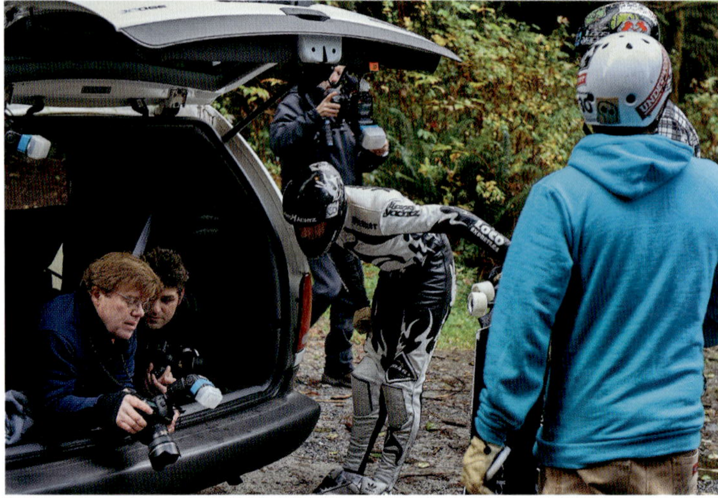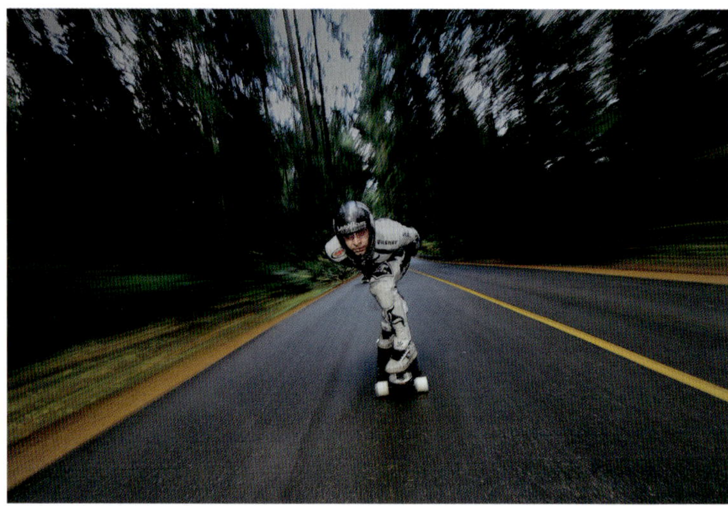

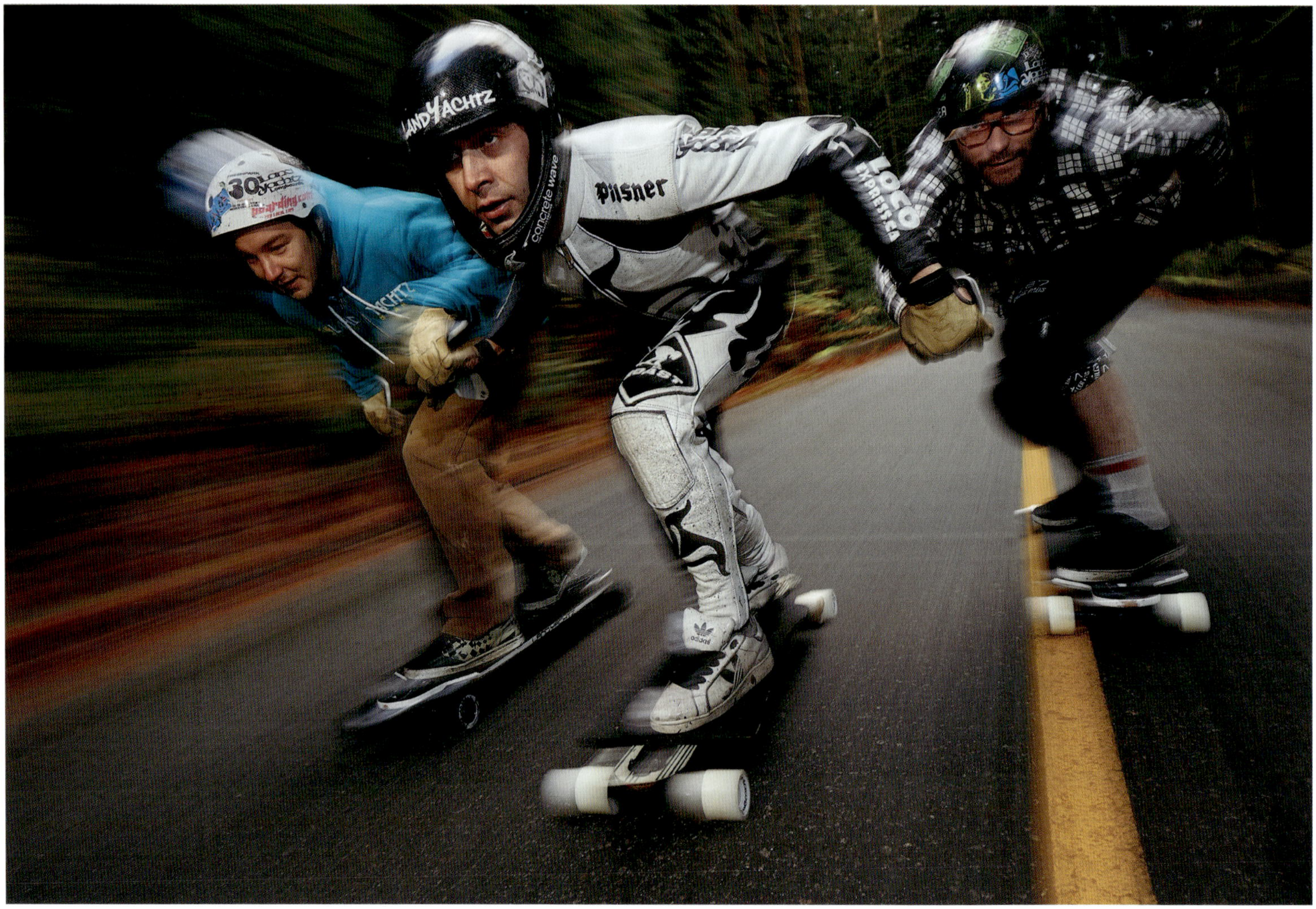

The big variant was the distance the skateboarders maintained with the vehicle.

We'd have one situation, where they were right on the bumper.

And then another, when a drift would occur.

The flash kept pace and made exposure adjustments, dealing with the deep surrounding greenery and not blowing out the banging-white skating leathers of the lead longboarder. Moving fast like this, with everything fluid, reliance on the machine allows you, at camera, to concentrate on what's important, such as framing, and holding your camera as steady as possible. The frame of the single skateboarder is 1/6th of a second, handheld. That's enough to worry about, right there.

You could get a bunch of mirrors, and just one Speedlight (below). Years ago, out on a Florida beach, there were a bunch of retirees conducting their late day walk. They stopped and tilted their heads while we frantically dug these mirrors into the sand, racing the falling light. I swear I heard one of them say, in a beautiful southern drawl, something to the effect of, "Look at that fella over there with all those mirrors. He surely does like himself!"

One raw flash, camera left. The mirrors were by far the hard part.

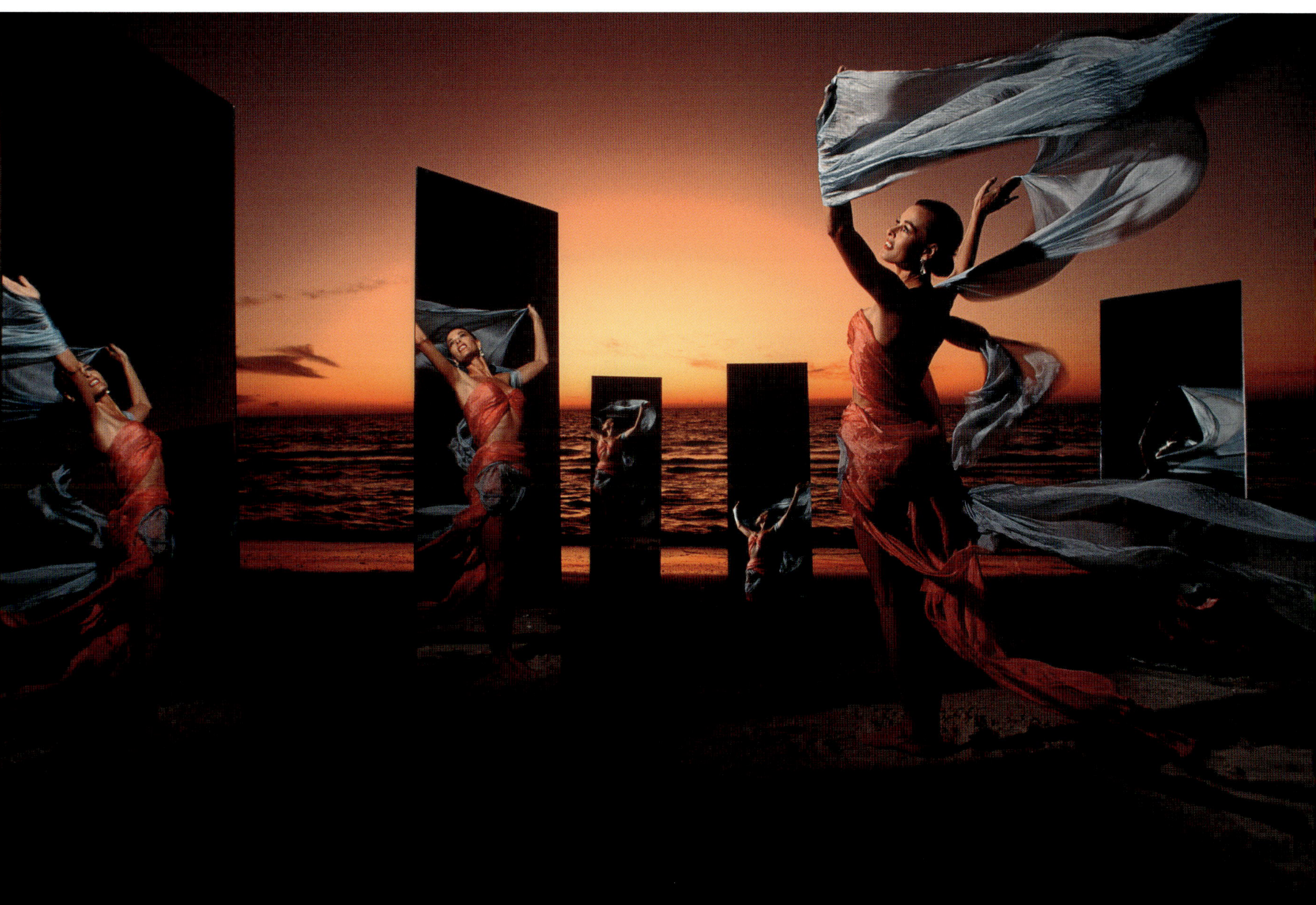

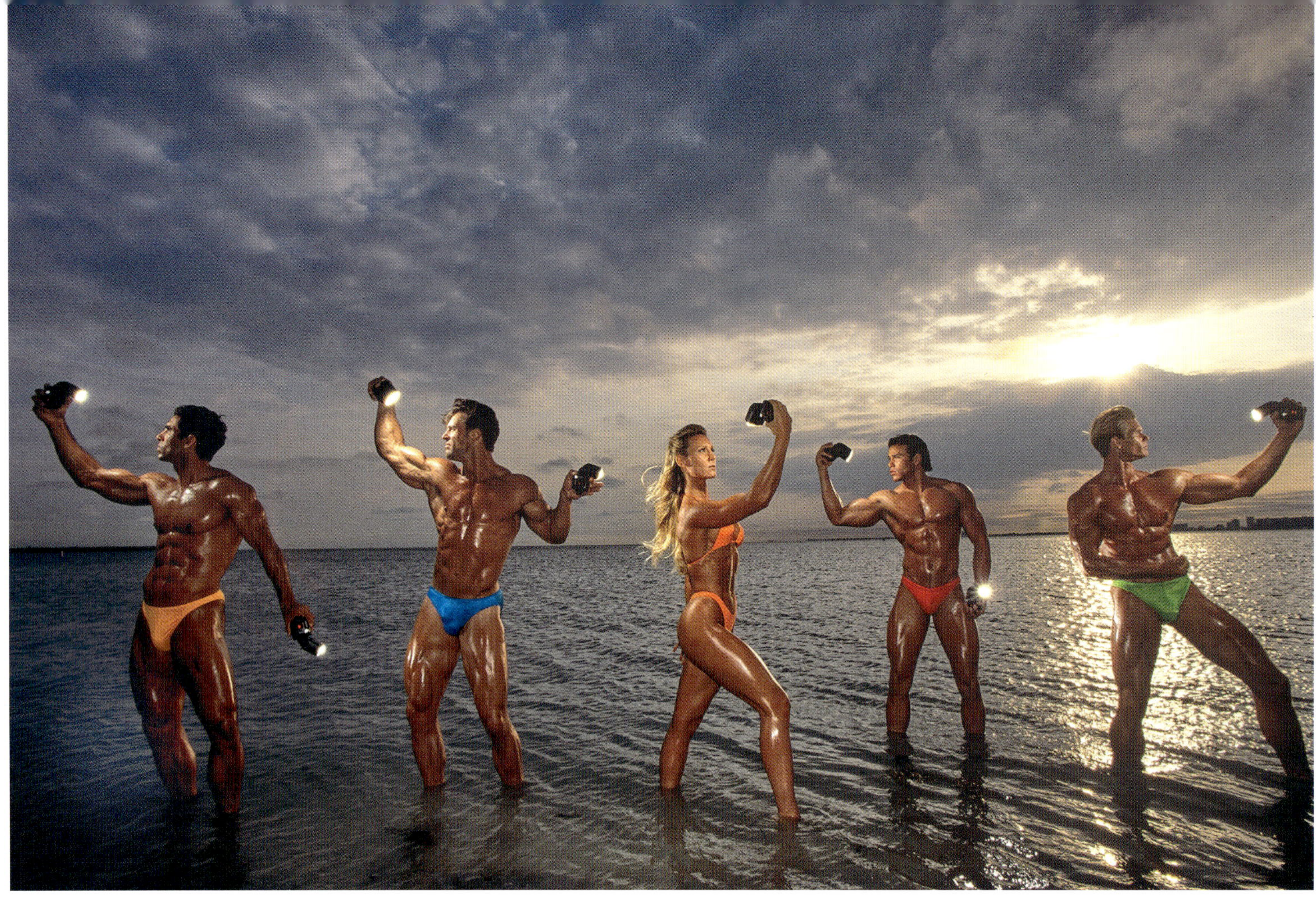

I've tried flashes on a beach with a bunch of body builders (above). Manual settings on all these flashes, which were SB-26 units, which had a built-in optical eye, an important step on this tortuous path to TTL dependability and Speedlight sophistication.

I used these units to create my favorite cover I ever shot for *Nat Geo* (opposite, left). SB-26 units, popping through a bed sheet in Mumbai, India. Continued steps to more knowledge. I enlarged my thinking of what might be possible. Shot on Kodachrome 64. No LCD. No confirmation. No do-overs. Trust the machine.

I dragged a line-of-sight Speedlight into a swamp at one point (opposite, top right). Put it on a C-stand extension arm with a warming gel, got up at 3:00 a.m., donned a heavy wetsuit, and jumped into the mucky end of a lake in Connecticut in the winter! Scott, my assistant at the time, was straight out of Florida, and grew up running a swamp boat, so he was cool about the murky water, holding the light. He was relaxed. As he said to me, "No alligators in Connecticut." Sigh of relief there.

The flash was the only thing warm that morning. This was shot on a major job for a huge company. Simulated special forces scenario. It all hung on one battery-operated Speedlight.

But it's just light. Push it, pull it, prod it. Like the look, or don't. Keep moving. Keep cooking. Get one flash sorted out. Make it your friend. It's just one light! Simple. None of the lighting solutions in these pictures so far (i.e., "experiments throughout the years") derived their look from the use of a light shaper. No umbrellas, no softboxes. Just raw light, blasting away. (Okay, well, in one instance, into a bed sheet.)

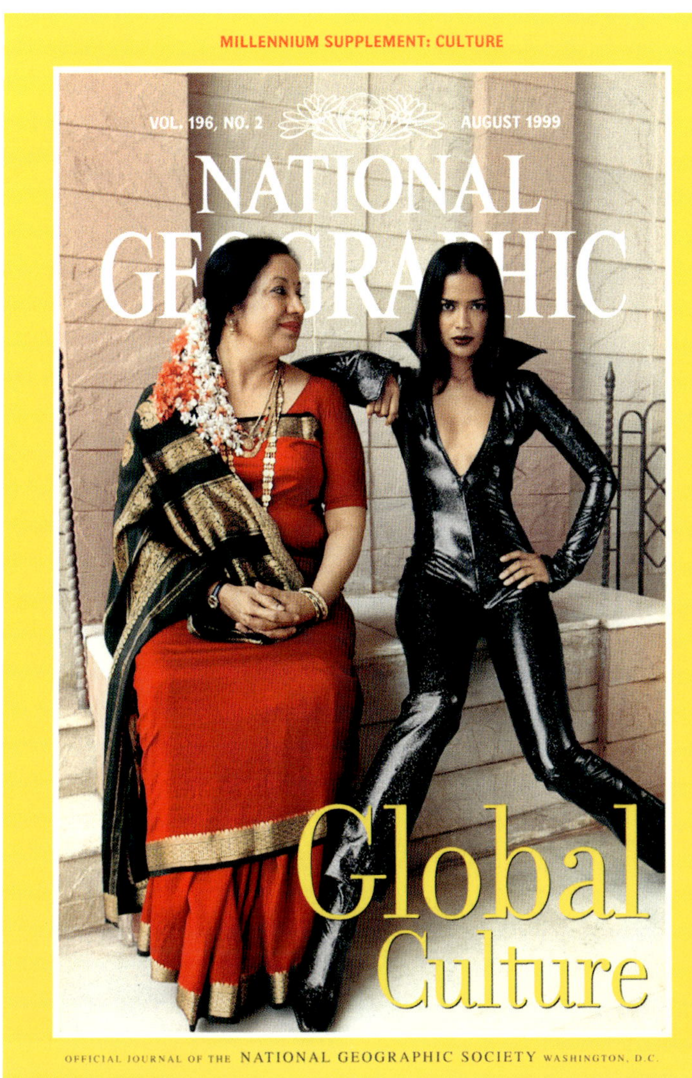

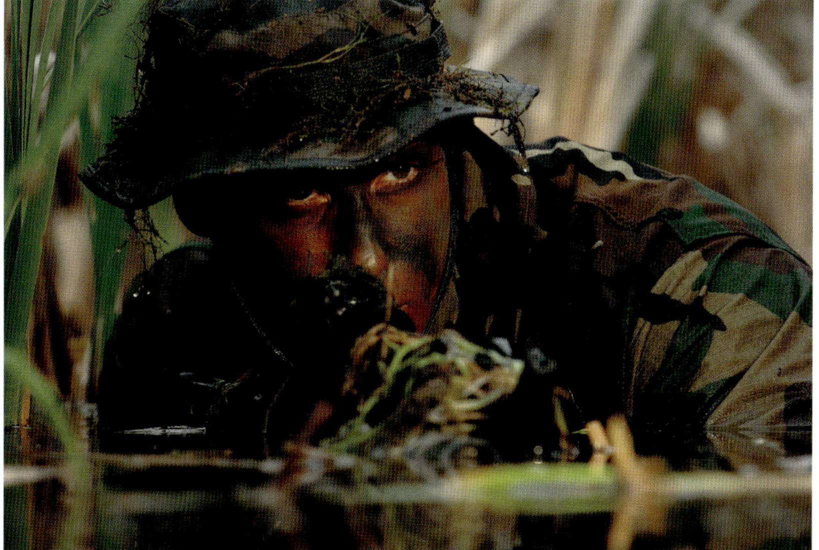

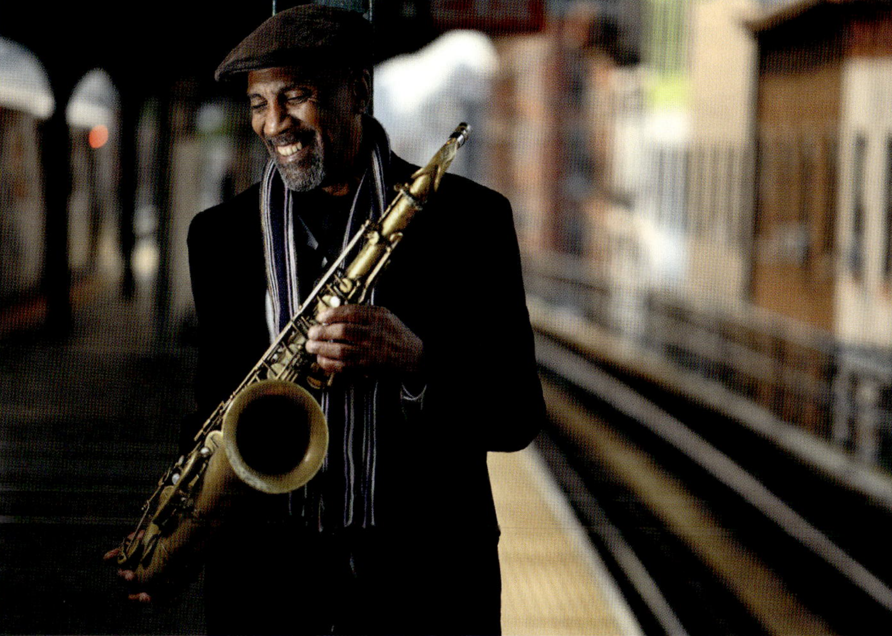

So much mystery is gone! Here's a recent image (right, bottom), made with new SB-5000 units and a new radio controller. In this instance, finally, I used light shapers, but the simplest of shapers, the kind you can stuff in a camera bag. Two Speedlite Two Plus softboxes, designed by yours truly. My friend Les was down the platform in Brooklyn, and I was shooting an 85mm at f/1.8 with a Z 7II mirrorless camera. Mirrorless tech. Improved metering. Improved flash connectivity. Fast, sharp lens. Beautiful LCD. Instant knowing. Touch-screen adjustments. Infinitely adjustable white balance. Pinpoint, accurate autofocus.

I mean, you take this stuff out on location, with all the attendant bells and whistles, and it's a bit like Christmas.

Try it. Use a flash. Banish the darkness. As Bane said to the doctor when the plane was falling from the sky, "Now is not the time for fear! That comes later!"

How's That for Random?

Remember, at the very beginning, I said a photo career spins on randomness?

I'll take a stab and say this guy's name was Jerry. He was a Resident Advisor in DellPlain Hall at Syracuse, the same hall where I had lived as an underclassman for three years, as I recall. I don't know for sure. It's a tough one to remember, seeing as I shot this picture in the fall of 1973. I was a photo student, sitting in the stands of a Syracuse football game, with my Nikkormat camera, fitted with a 135mm f/2.8 lens. I turned just as he started screaming encouragement, ridicule, referee-centric abuse—choose one—toward the field of play. He went full throated, as you can see. I put my camera to my eye and, for the first time I can ever remember, my timing on the shutter and my spin of the focus barrel was in perfect concert. I shot one frame on the single-shot Nikkormat. Click.

And I remember turning away and sitting, looking at the camera, which was glowing like a talisman in my hands. I could almost feel the heat radiating from it, I had done so well. It felt good, so good it actually had a kinship with the first time my high school girlfriend reached over in the darkness of the F-85 Oldsmobile and undid my belt and unzipped my fly. There was a disturbance in my force, a ripple. I processed the film, and the neg was as sharp as I remembered. It was even well exposed, which was something of a rarity for me in those learning days. I printed it powerfully. At that time, I was going to school on the W. Eugene Smith print method—deep, dark blacks, burned corners, moody like crazy.

It went on exhibit in the Newhouse Lobby, along with the work of my other classmates. Quietly, as I went through the lobby, I would stare at it, there behind the glass. And, more importantly, it became the lead pic in the portfolio that I needed to present to the photo admins who would determine whether I, as a non-photo major, could continue my studies and go on to the next, more advanced class. (It was highly unusual, and against

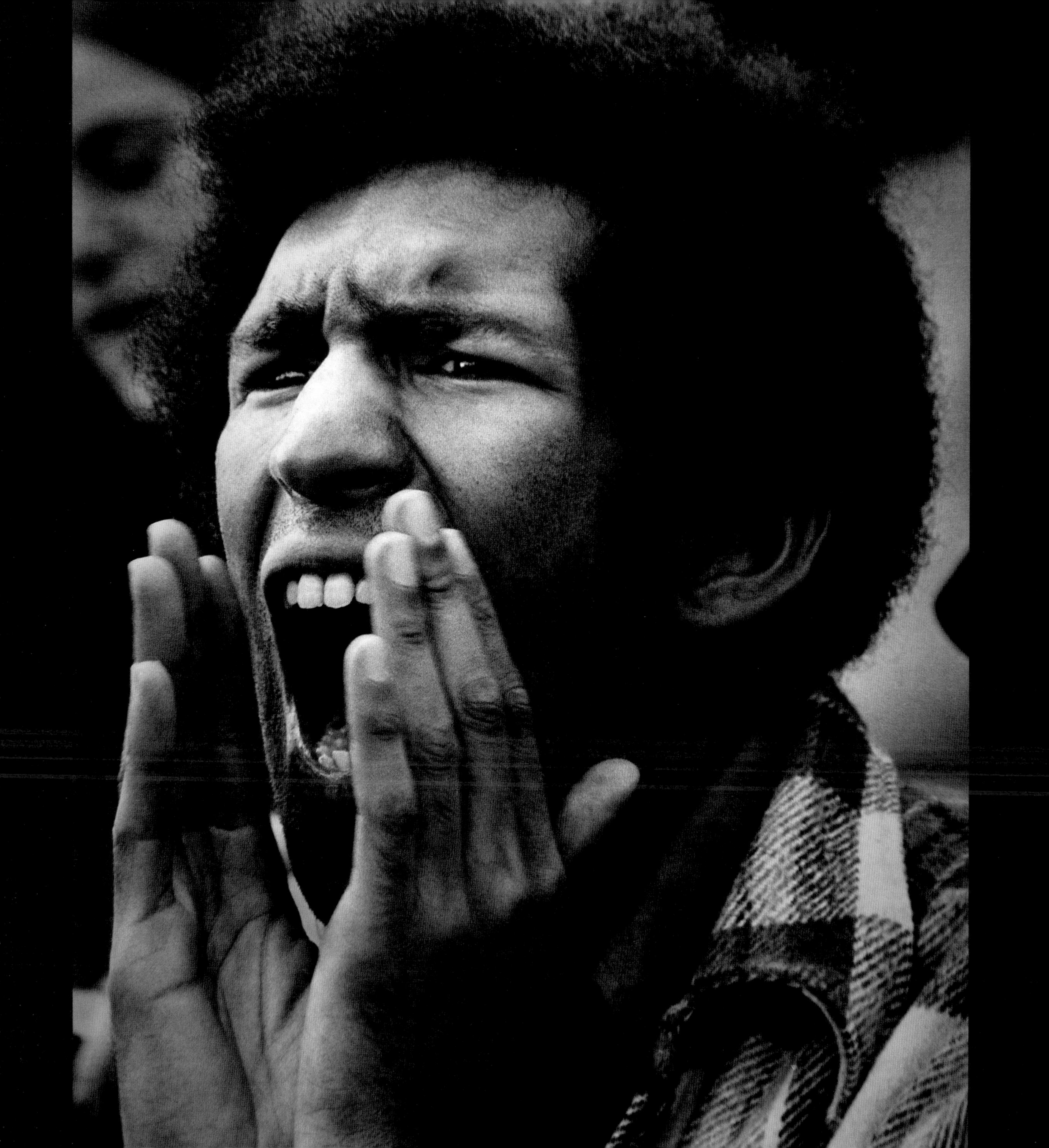

normal policy, to allow anyone not majoring in photography to advance to the upper-level photo courses. I was a writing major who discovered photography late in my academic career, so I was always subject to scrutiny and gateways.)

A graduate student in the Syracuse photo program, Red McLendon, who went on to a stellar career with the AP, gave me the news. I was accepted. He told me that most of my portfolio was just okay, mild grumbles here and there, but that photo of Jerry cheering? He said, "Joe, they looked at that and went, 'Ahhhhhhh.'" I was in.

I have to imagine—being at a football game, high up in uncovered stands, under the gray skies of Syracuse, with Tri-X loaded—that my shutter speed on this picture was probably around 1/500th of a second. 1/500th of a second: I get in. I don't get in. I continue, or I am shut down.

A successful, random 1/500th of a second, occurring in a sea of other hundredths of seconds that failed so miserably, opened the gates to a lifetime of pictures.

How's that for random?

The image running with this story is not from the original negative, which fell off the itinerant, horse-drawn covered wagon known as McNally Photography long ago. It's a scan from an 11x14 bleed-mounted print I made in 1973. Thankfully, I made a decent print, hence the presence of the photo in this book.

That print, that picture, allowed me to take more advanced photo courses into my senior year, which paved the way to graduate school and a Master's degree in photojournalism. I grew up steeped in the photographic legend and lore of Steichen, Stieglitz, Eisenstaedt, and the durable, painfully beautiful images of the FSA. I spent my days shooting, shooting. Whatever I could see. At night, I lived in the darkroom, breathing Dektol fumes like they were the pungent, aromatic vapors of excellent Lebanese hashish. The rest of my studies went to shit, and I just barely graduated. The camera had become the road to the world, the windows of the classrooms I stared off into, when I should have been listening to the lecturer.

As I wrote about earlier, with this education in tow, I hit the very reality-based world of tabloid journalism in the company of the New York *Daily News* staff—longtime photogs, grizzled and worn, hitting the pavement every day, clicking for a living, shooting everything from subway murders to high society. No frills. Don't dwell. Shoot it and ship it, head for the bar. Tomorrow, another newspaper rolls off the presses. Nothing as stale as yesterday's news. (It does keep your feet on the ground when you realize your work on any given day is papering someone's birdcage the next.) Mention Steichen or Stieglitz to them, and they would've thought you were an uppity little prick talking about imported beer. I remember speaking with Danny Godfrey, great guy, rock-solid shooter, New York tough, brass balls. He asked me how I learned to shoot, and I mentioned my education. He looked at me in disbelief. "You went to school to learn this craft?" He looked at me quizzically, shook his head, and walked away.

On the Versatility of Tools of the Trade

The old school 8x Agfa Loupe was always a quick and dirty, unfancy but excellent eyeball used to edit your chromes. Sling it in your camera bag, have it at the ready for a field test. Keep it on the light table, bang through your images. Not expensive, no moving parts.

Historically speaking, though, the Agfa Loupe had other uses.

Like, for those shoots when you've looked at the whole take and there's not a damn picture in there worthy of calling a select. Those jobs where you sat back at the light table, numbed by your ineptitude, staring at stacks of yellow boxes filled with dozens or even hundreds of little lifeless squares testifying, in color, to your lack of expertise and acumen. Those jobs where you shrugged and hoped the client might be dumb enough to like it. Those jobs where you hoped the magazine would publish the picture(s) without a credit, so you could remain anonymous, and hide in the cloistered shadows of your abject failure.

At that point, you take that loupe, turn it over, pour yourself a shot of Irish whiskey, and call it a day.

"Historically speaking, though, the Agfa Loupe had other uses."

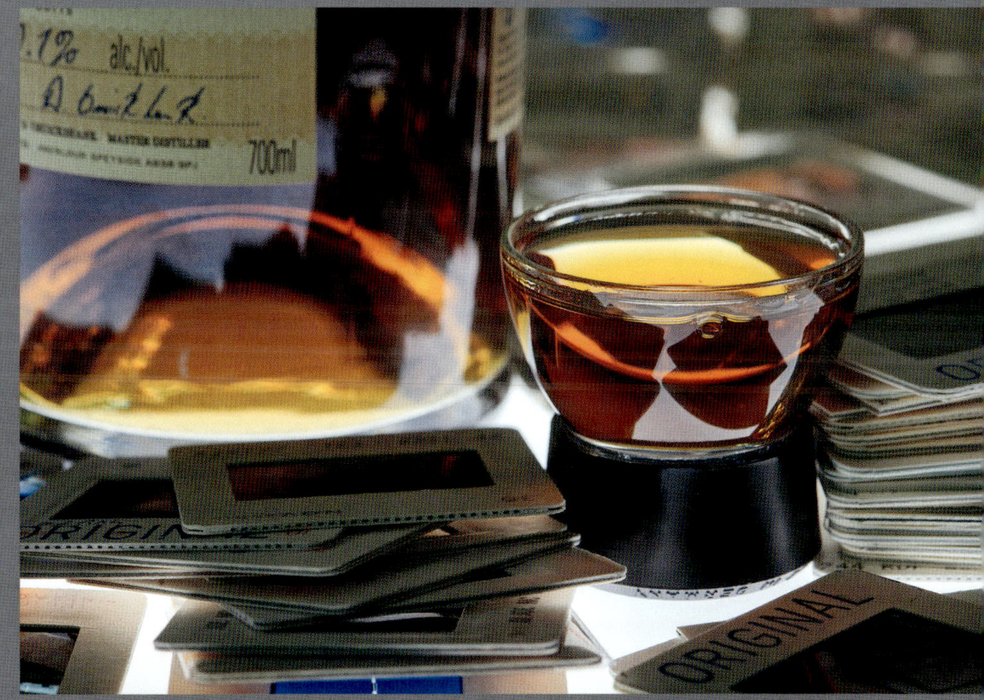

The Window in Your Dreams

Sometimes I see better when my eyes are closed.

In the depth and darkness of a late night in a hotel room, the dream of a picture will bubble to the surface. You remember frames and travels, things you missed, photos never realized, and pictures that call you back for unfinished business. Things that must be returned to and seen again. The feel of failure that must be assuaged.

Years ago, at the very end of 1985, prior to Super Bowl XX in New Orleans, *Sports Illustrated* dispatched me there to create a mood piece, a visual poem, to that grand, beautiful mess of a city. In magazine parlance, it's referred to as a "walk-up," a set of pictures that establishes the mood and flavor of the place where the big game was to be played out. It would perhaps run in the issue before the game coverage ensued. A visual teaser, something to whet the appetite of the reader (and fill some pages) before the serious business of "hut one, hut two" commenced. I learned many lessons shooting this and made the best picture of the job 25 years later. Let me explain.

I have always loved making pictures in the Big Easy. Color and characters abound. That's not to say it's easy. It's definitely not. Tourists are there by the boatload, and much of the city's character has been compartmentalized, tour-ified, regulated, ticketed, charged for, and thus offered by rote to smartphone-toting gawkers. The surface is there for all to see and visually pluck at will. Pictures of ubiquitous buskers, the de rigueur images of the horse-drawn carriage and steamboat, the must-have snap of jazz performances in the clubs—all are ready to add to the album, pictorial mementos as dependably available as chewing gum from the vending machine. And, given the internet-driven crush of foodie bloggers, lest I forget that the pic of the gumbo to end all gumbos, the one that enters and exits your system like a four-alarm fire, is a must. All are there for the taking and the paying for. Like a cunning thespian, the city offers a convincing pop-up facsimile of its own self, onstage and on the street every night and day.

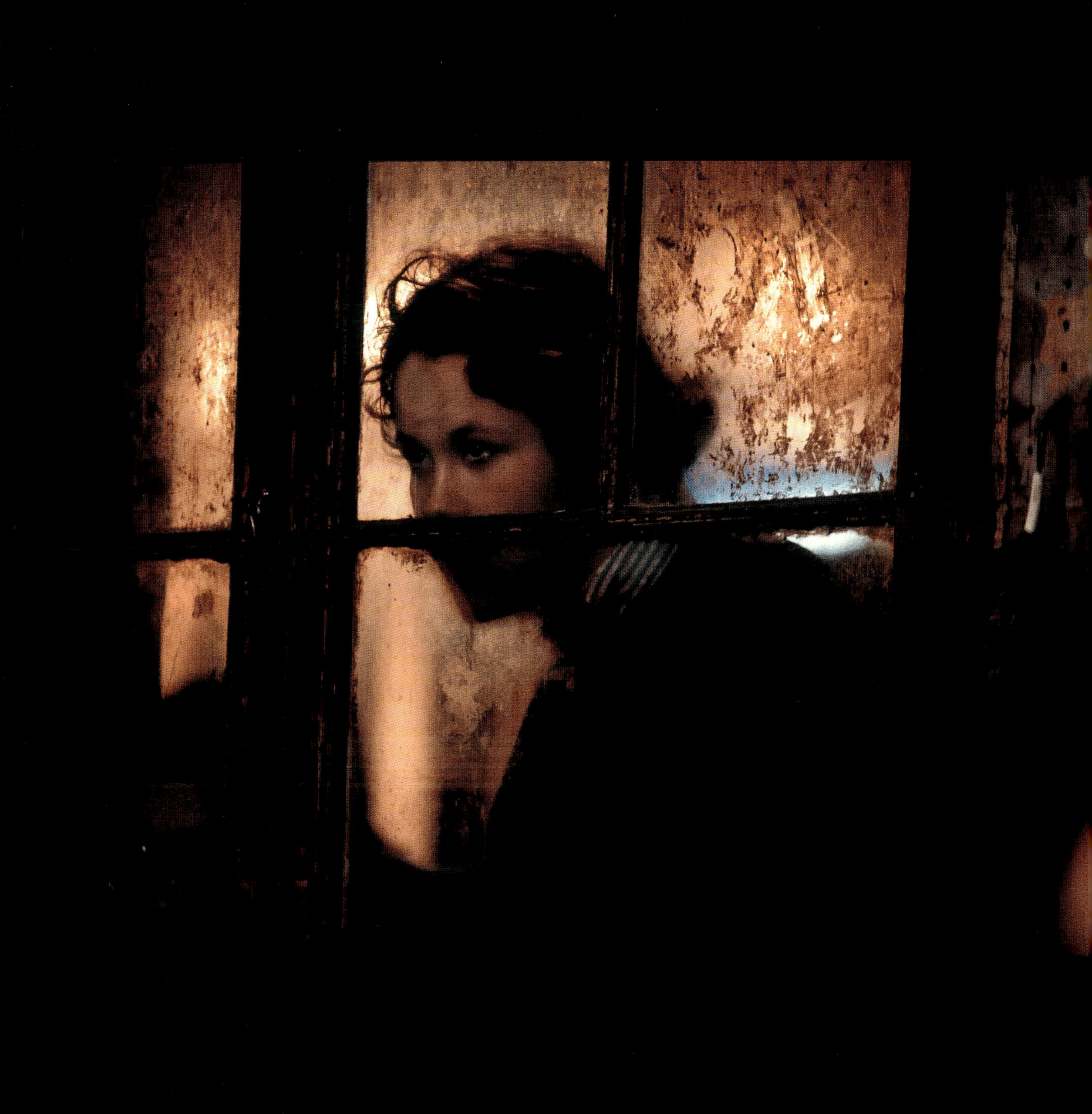

Meanwhile, the real city waits and watches in the wings for those who might risk and seek it out. It doesn't take reservations or politely seat you by the window per your request.

In other words, it's pretty much like every other super fascinating damn place in the world you might fancy going to with a camera and an eager eye. It's overrun, and its soul has run to the shadows.

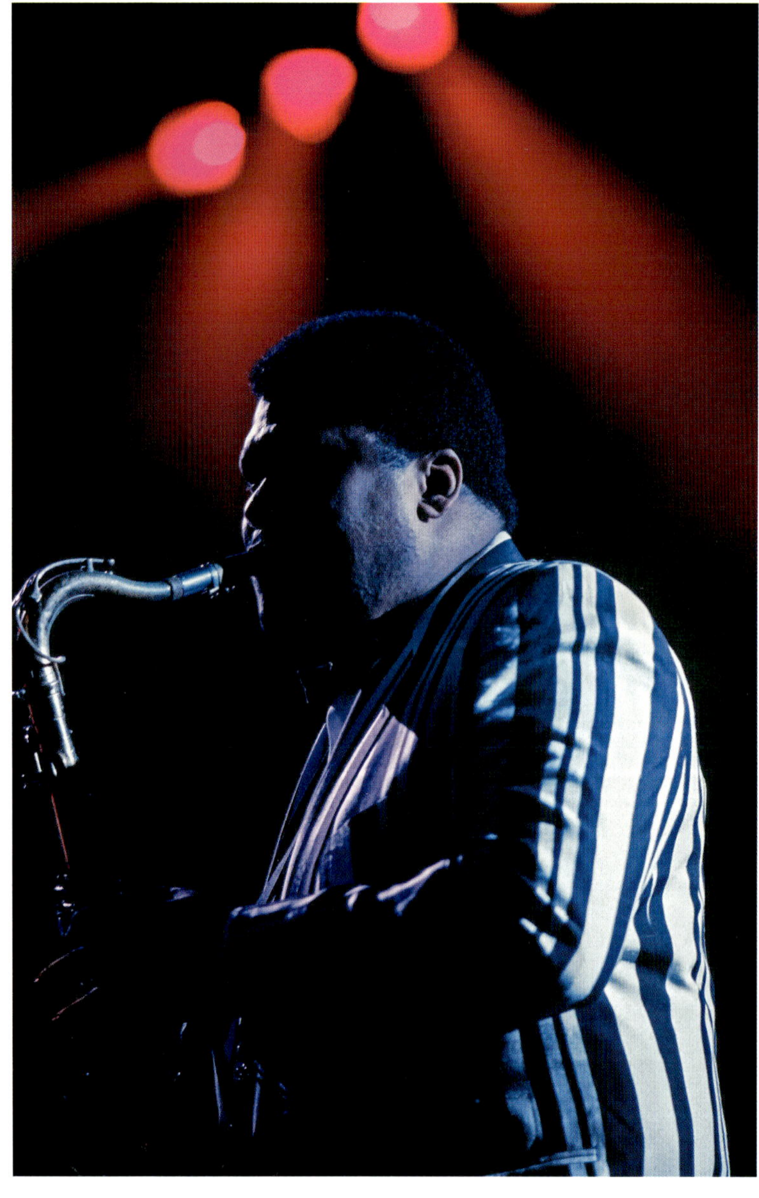

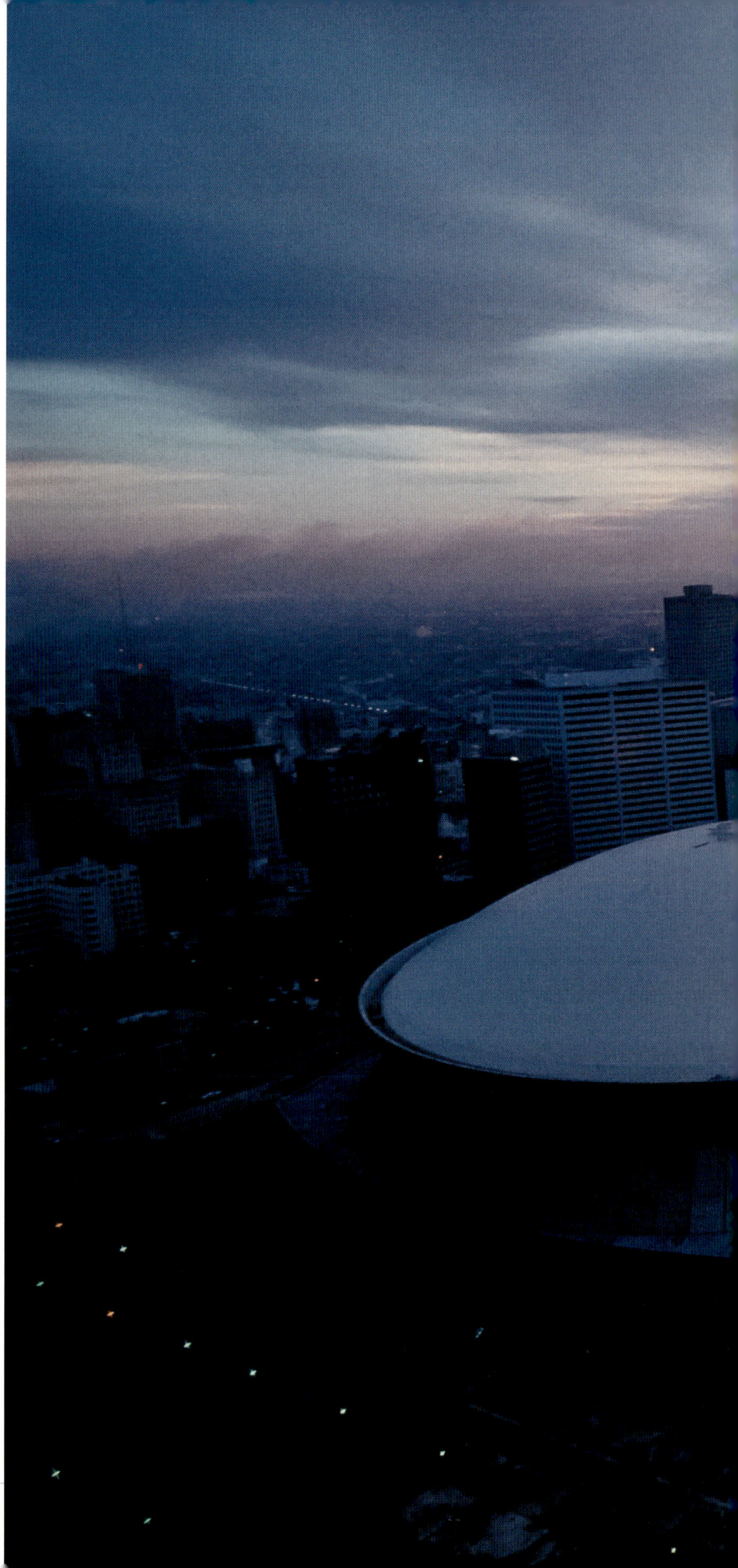

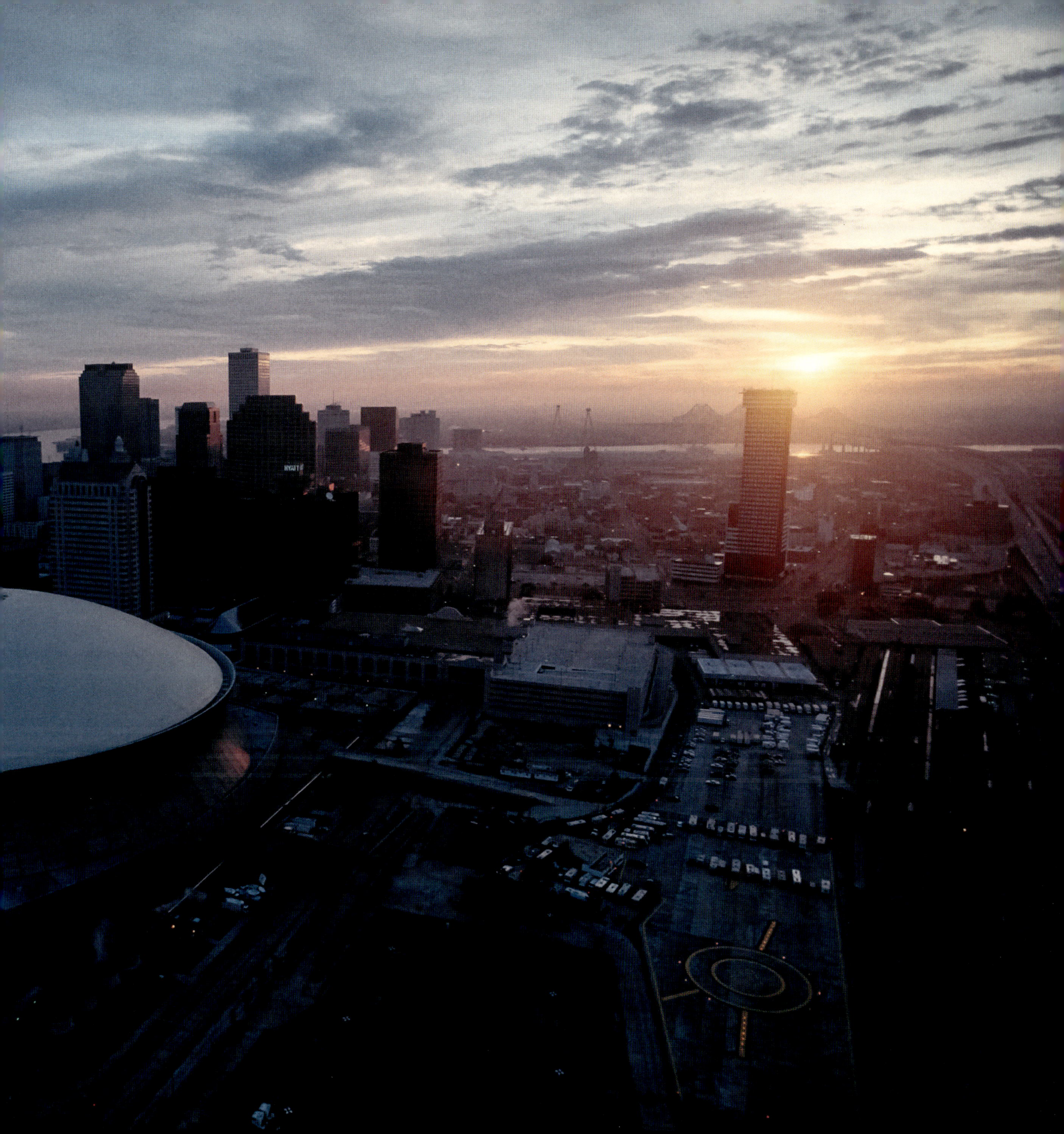

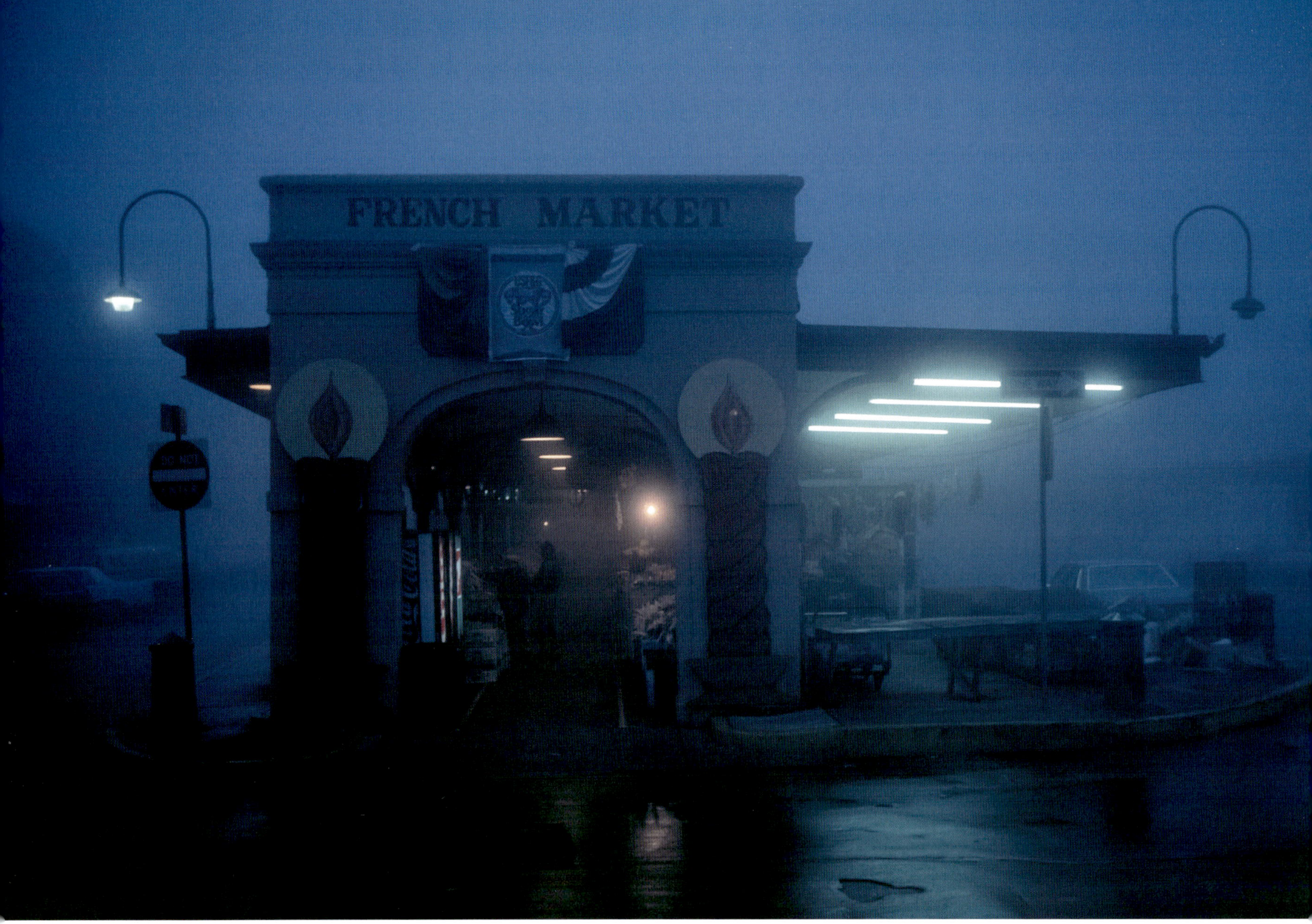

I was charged with seeing it differently, capturing a mood, finding a beat, something, anything that connected to the spirit of the city and offered the magazine's readership a feel, a look, or a yen to visit one day. A colorful postcard that had a measure of truth and punch to it but wasn't overly shiny. An impossible mission, really. You could live in a complex city like New Orleans your whole life and never really get it "right" in pictures. I had a few days.

But it was fun to try, alternately maddening and heartening, as all days with a camera are, and I felt good about my pictures, until I got back to the magazine and my editor told me she felt I had swung and missed. The stuff never ran. I worked big and small, late and early, and, in her eyes, never turned the corner.

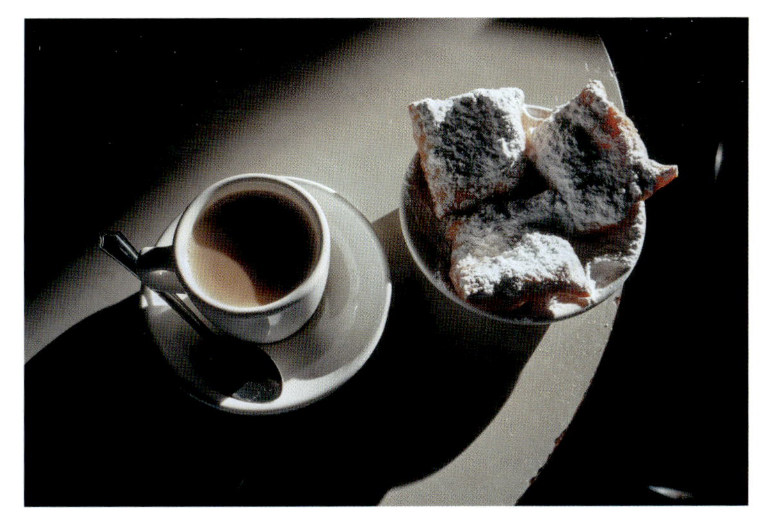
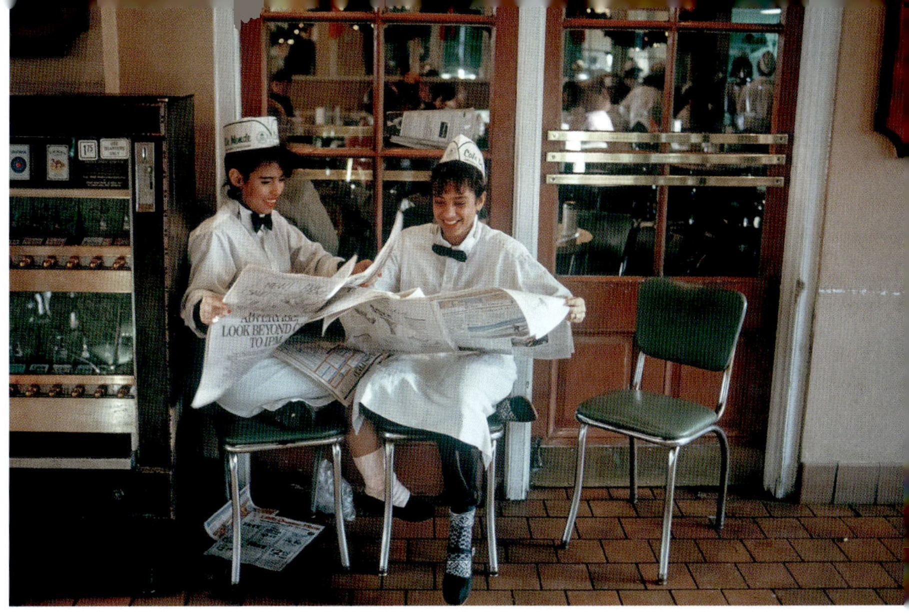

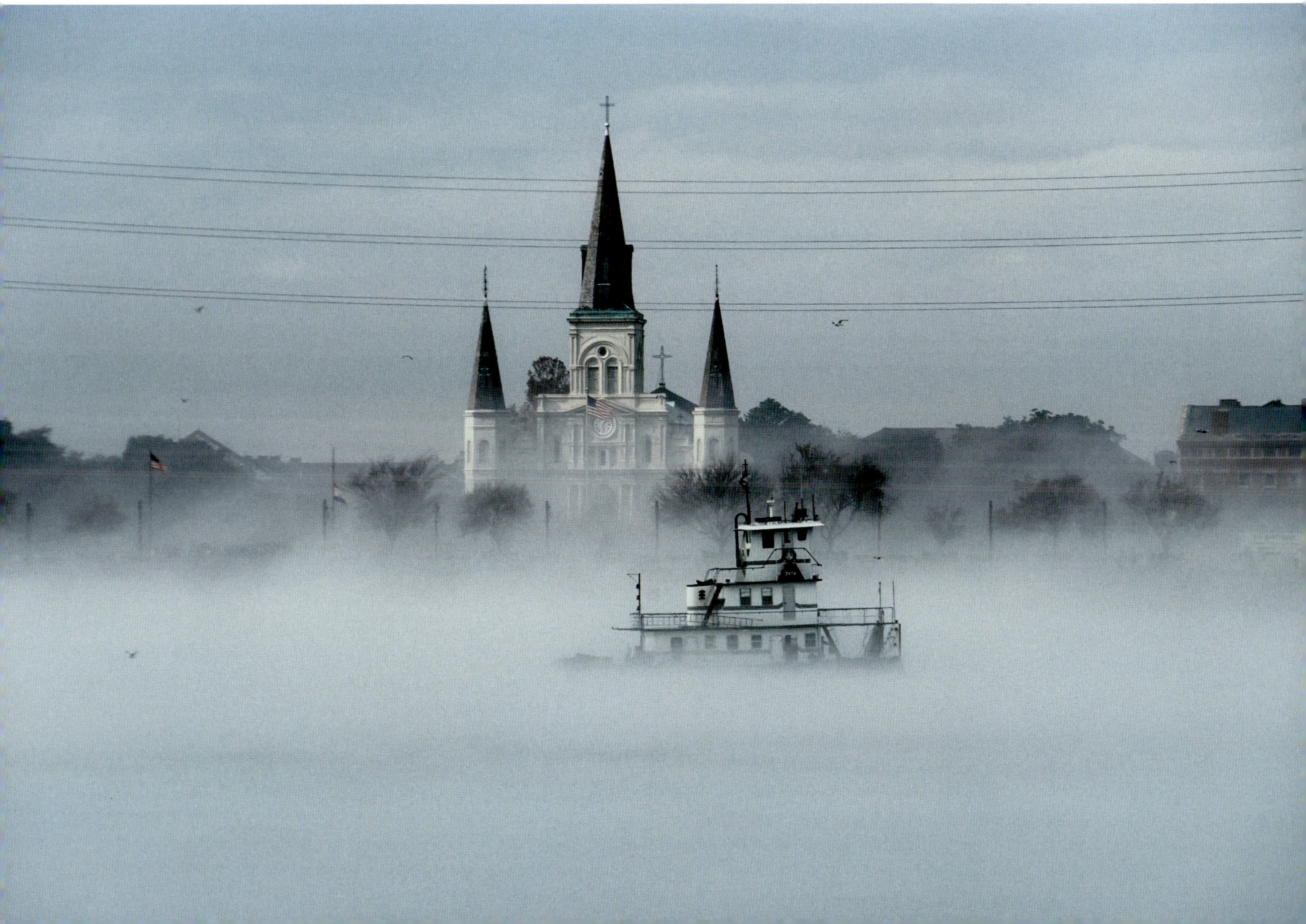

The craziest thing about being there was spending New Year's Eve on Bourbon Street. My bud and fixer, Billy Sanchez, a Big Easy firefighter, took me into the mayhem, ladder in hand, and basically became a human sandbag, weighting the ladder as the crowd broke over me like a Nor'easter driving a wave at the seawall. In the photo on Bourbon Street (below), I've always been fond of the hand on the light pole, the only sharp human element in the image. "Krazy Korner" pretty much says it all. I clung to my oversized Gitzo tripod for dear life, leaning on it for stability. Billy was like a big offensive tackle down on the street level, trying to keep me from getting sacked by the madding revelers.

You can't depart New Orleans without making pictures at Preservation Hall, if you can get access. Special arrangements have to be made, as the place, out of a very reasonable concern for "the old men"—the musicians who play there regularly—doesn't allow photography. They don't want people selling photos of these accomplished artists without compensation returning to them. Fair enough. The place fairly defies photography anyway, truth be told. At least back then it did. The whole joint was basically lit by a 60-watt bulb in the ceiling. I exaggerate, but not overmuch. It was dark and dingy, and I was shooting chrome in the days before ISO ran to five figures.

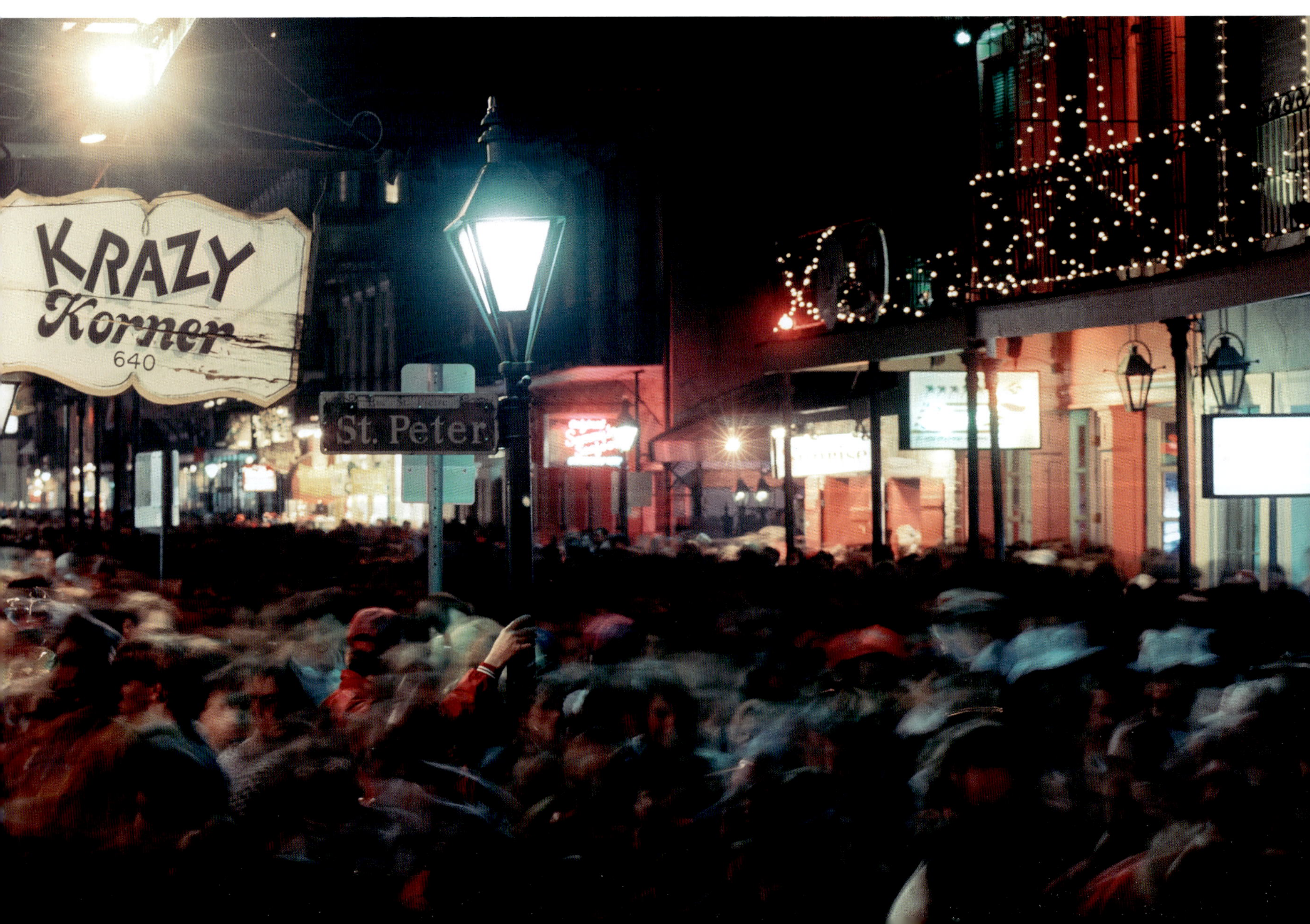

I went to see the admin at the Hall, and given the weight of *Sports Illustrated*, they put it over to the artists. Could *SI* shoot pictures? One night only. And could the photog put a single Norman 200B flash up in the ceiling? They said okay.

Not much resulted from my efforts that night, but I was able to carve some pictures into reluctant, intractable transparency material. Compared to the sleek digital tools at hand now, I was cave painting.

My favorite shot of the night was not of the musicians. I took a flying guess at an exposure of someone peering through the ancient windows, rendered almost opaque by years of accumulated grunge. It was never published. From the perspective of the editor/magazine, why would you? It had nothing to do with jazz, and certainly not football. The pages of *Sports Illustrated* were valuable real estate, fiercely vied for by competing stories, words, pictures, headlines. No time or consideration for an obscure frame in the hurly burly of going to press. This trifle of a photo, which leads this story, has been unpublished until now.

I have always remembered the peering and the window and the character of it. Like the yellowed smoke stains on those panes of glass, it stuck with me.

Fast forward to 2011, when I, along with other photogs, shot the Nikon D4 campaign. I had made some good frames during this job, even some sparkly ones, but it's never enough, right? When you are cranking on a big job, one that has the potential of visibility and the concomitant rendering of internet judgement, you push. Money, and reputation, are on the line. What else to do? Where to go? You are an unfillable pit of yearning, anxiety, and self-doubt. You sleep with the job, shower with it. Like an especially tough piece of jerky, you chew relentlessly on the damn thing. You are not just shooting it, you're conceptualizing it, designing it in your head, running the camera, directing the lighting, selecting the talent.

An assignment is like a big, wet dog, laying on your chest in the middle of the night, panting in your face with bad breath. You

are unable to ignore it or shoo it away, and it renders rest an impossibility. One night, as the job was in progress, I woke, bolt upright. That window. There's a picture there. I had to go back to Preservation Hall. A pictorial imperative, a dreamscape with a 3:2 aspect ratio, flying through my head. The uneasy sleep of a photographer who remembers an unpublished frame, 25 years downstream. Don't we all? Or am I just especially screwed?

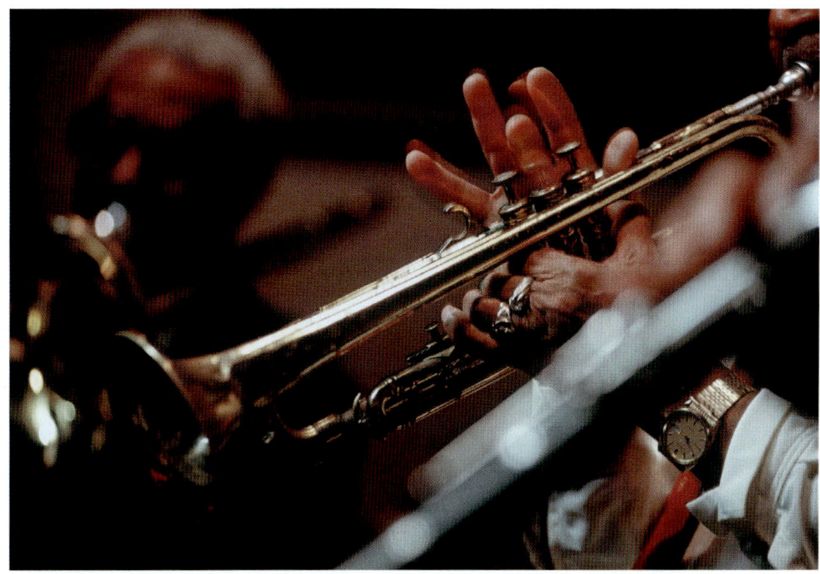

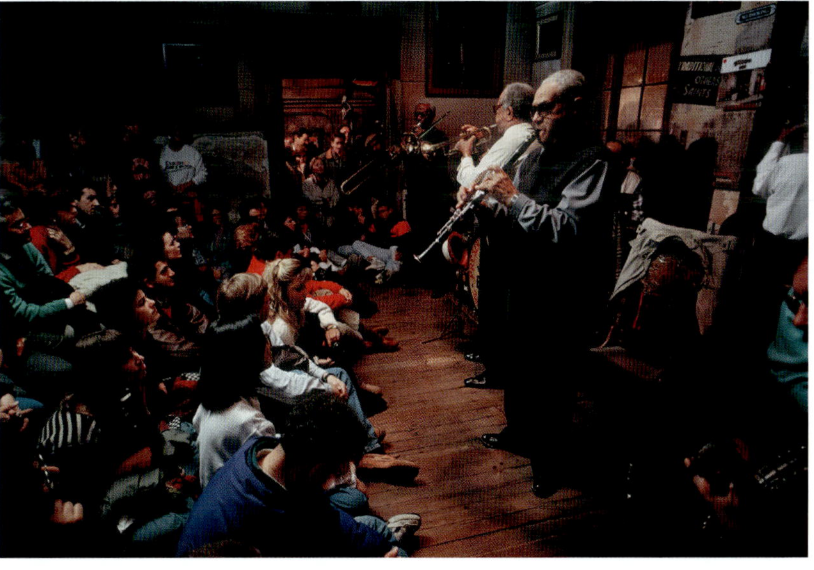

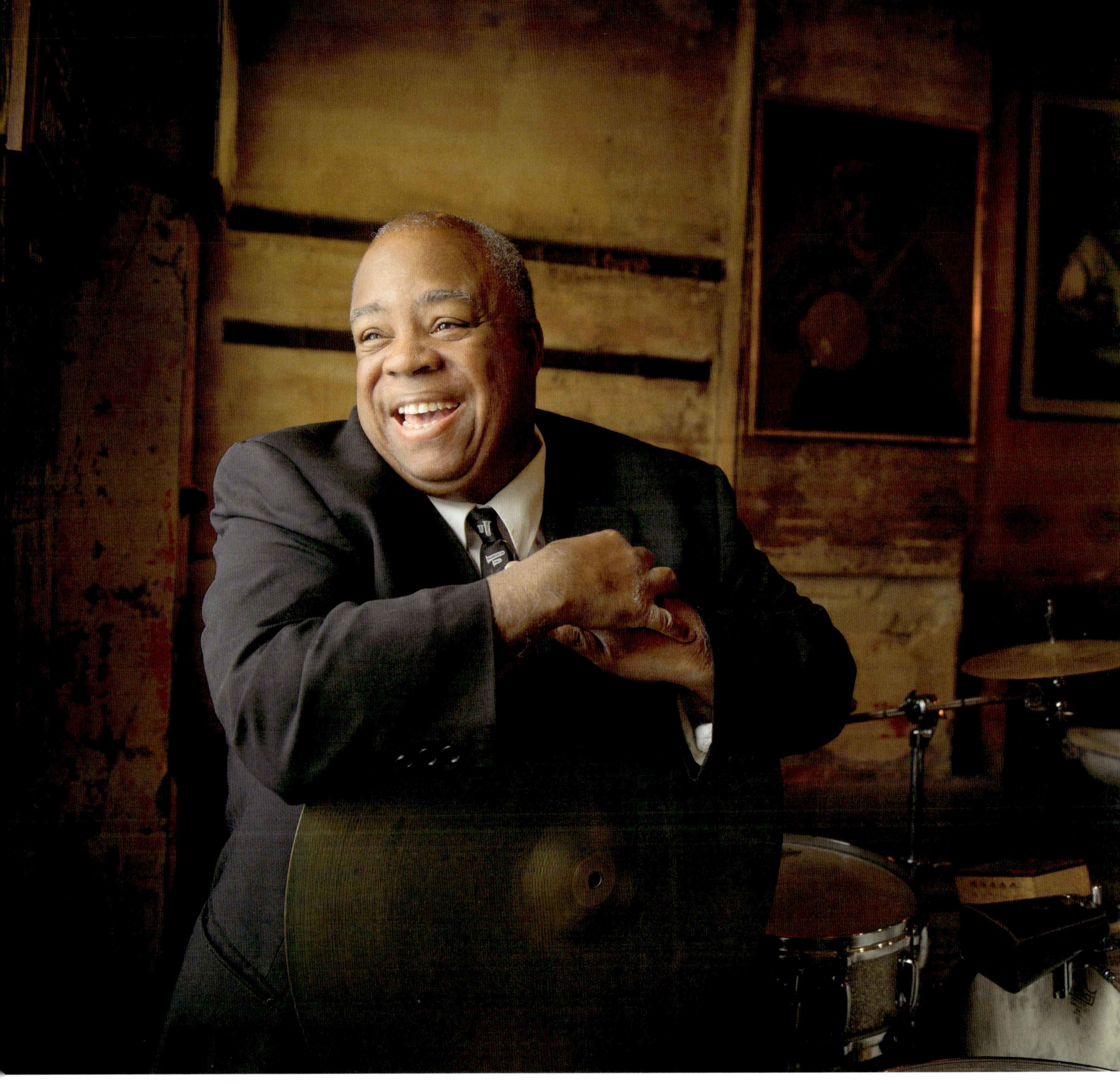

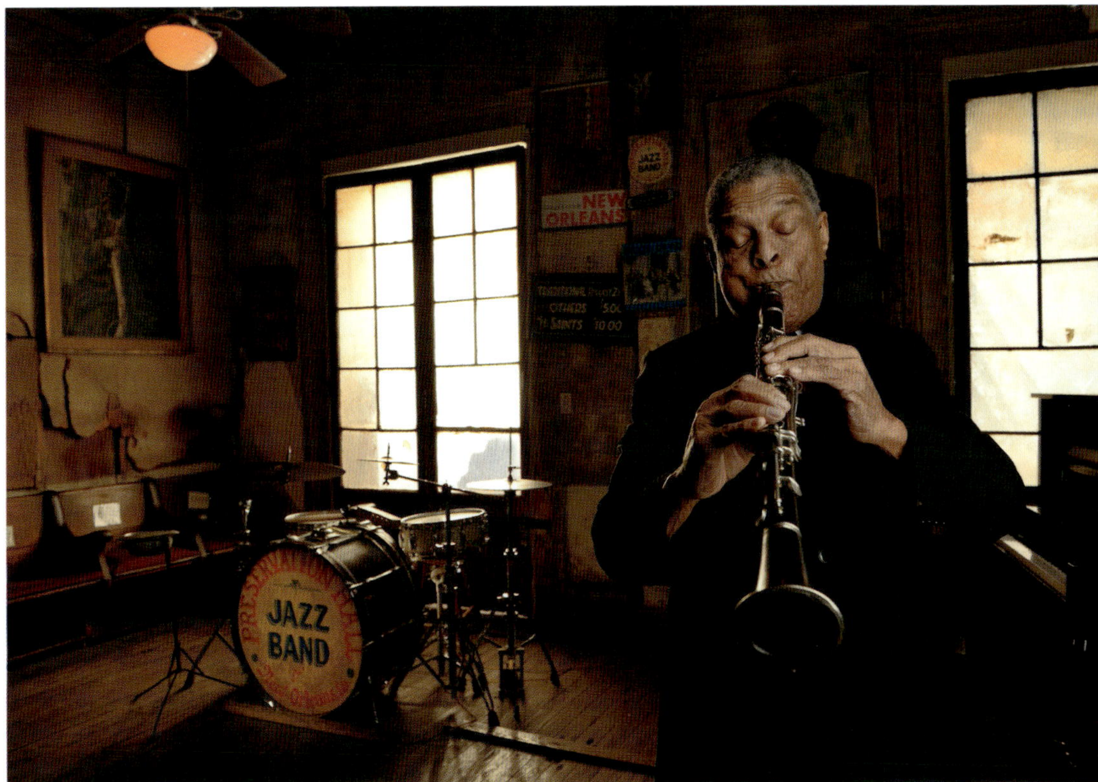

I called Lynn, our marvelous producer, studio manager, and solver of all problems (at a reasonable time the next morning) and said, no matter what, get me into Preservation Hall. Don't know how hard it will be. We still had time and budget. Needs to happen.

And it did, through her tireless efforts and production magic. Tenacious phone calls, fees, insurance, travel, crew, equipment . . . all to return to the window I had seen a quarter century earlier. I had not set foot in Preservation Hall since that Super Bowl time. But when the angst is that strong, and the possibilities of the picture in your head that vivid, you pursue. Face it, you won't sleep unless you do.

I worked with Joe Lastie (left) and Charlie Gabriel (above), two of the nonpareil resident musicians in the Preservation Hall Jazz Band. Speedlights were in the street, bed sheets over those old windows.

When I made the picture of Joe by his drum set, and I looked at it on the LCD, there was peace. A circle completed. A picture made, a term paper, started long ago, that I finally handed in.

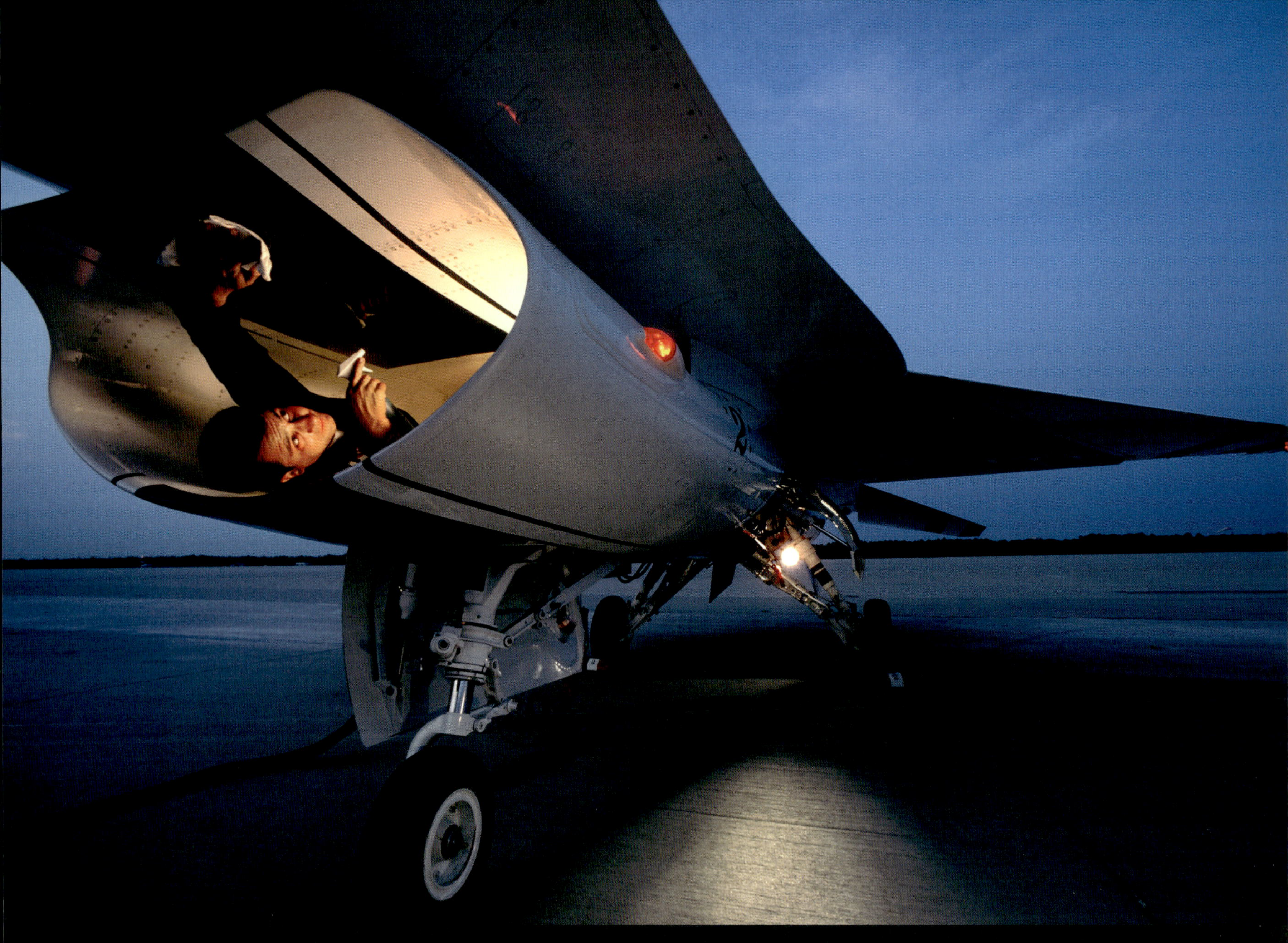

Stashing Flash!

Upon perusal, having written the headline for this story, it has a somewhat, you know, pornographic tilt? Or is it my mind, spinning into those areas Sister Mary Consolata warned me about in the sixth grade? Poor woman, it was already too late.

Sorry, nothing particularly racy ensues here, unless a measure of excitement can be derived from the mundane task of numbering your flashes with colorful tape, thus sparking the unrelenting black plastic construction of these little boxes of lightning, making the tracking and accounting for them at the end of a day in the field a tad easier.

It's wise to number your flashes, should you use multiple units, and habitually stash them in unlikely places. 'Nuff said. The last thing you want to do is leave one of your flashes behind in the intake of an F-16 (opposite).

Or, in the cockpit of an F-15 (right).

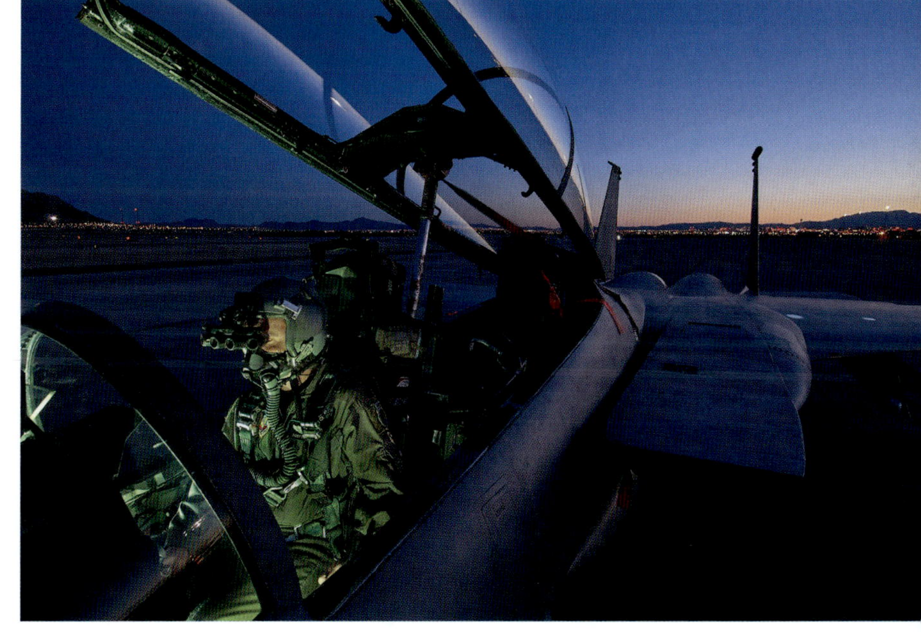

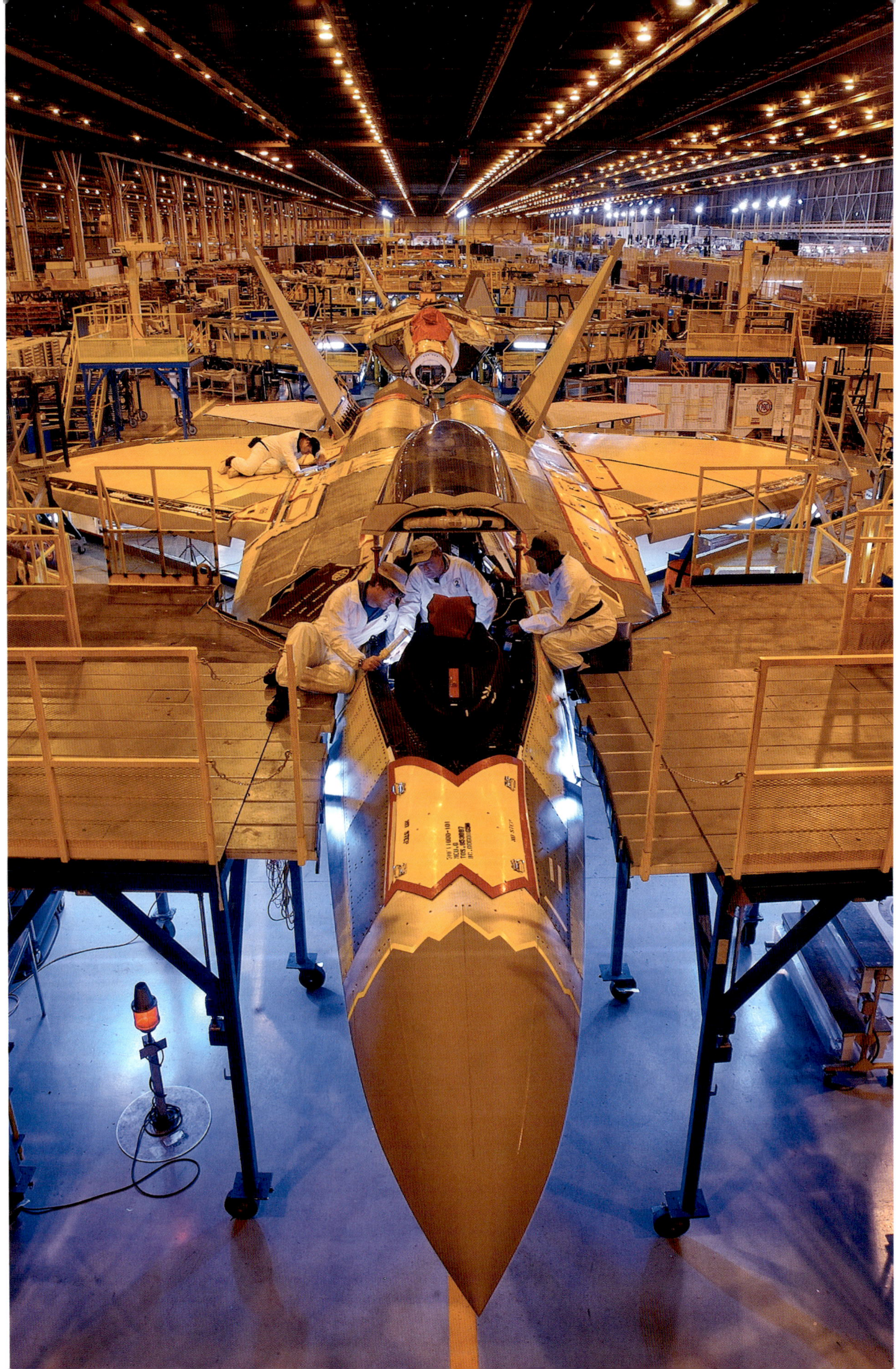

Or, perhaps even worse, in an F-22 on the assembly line (opposite).

And certainly not in the fan jet of a Boeing 777 (below).

In the rush to pack, often in the accumulating darkness, those compact, stubby little sons of guns, no longer flashing and thus announcing their position, can easily go missing. Best to liven up the Speedlights' lack-of-color scheme with some tape, and number them, and their respective cases, lest mayhem occur, post picture. It's easier to ask, "Where'd you put number six?" than to ask yourself or your assistant, as you drive away, "All the flashes get packed?" The answer comes back, "Uh, I think so."

Bad feeling.

"FAA DECLARES PHOTO SPEEDLIGHT TO BE CAUSE OF AIR DISASTER. PHOTOGRAPHER SOUGHT FOR QUESTIONING."

Not a good headline.

Number them, remember them, and, like children at the end of a long play date outdoors, make sure they get home and tucked away safely. This is super simple to do. Just use colored tape and a marker. No need for imagination and intricacy, unless you are so inclined. One prominent photographer I know—the Strobist himself, David Hobby, known possessor of numerous Speedlights—used to go beyond identifying his flashes and actually named his batteries. He's a pretty precise guy, and he would batch his batteries according to age and use, and give each batch the name of one of his old girlfriends.

When he married, I believe he stopped doing that.

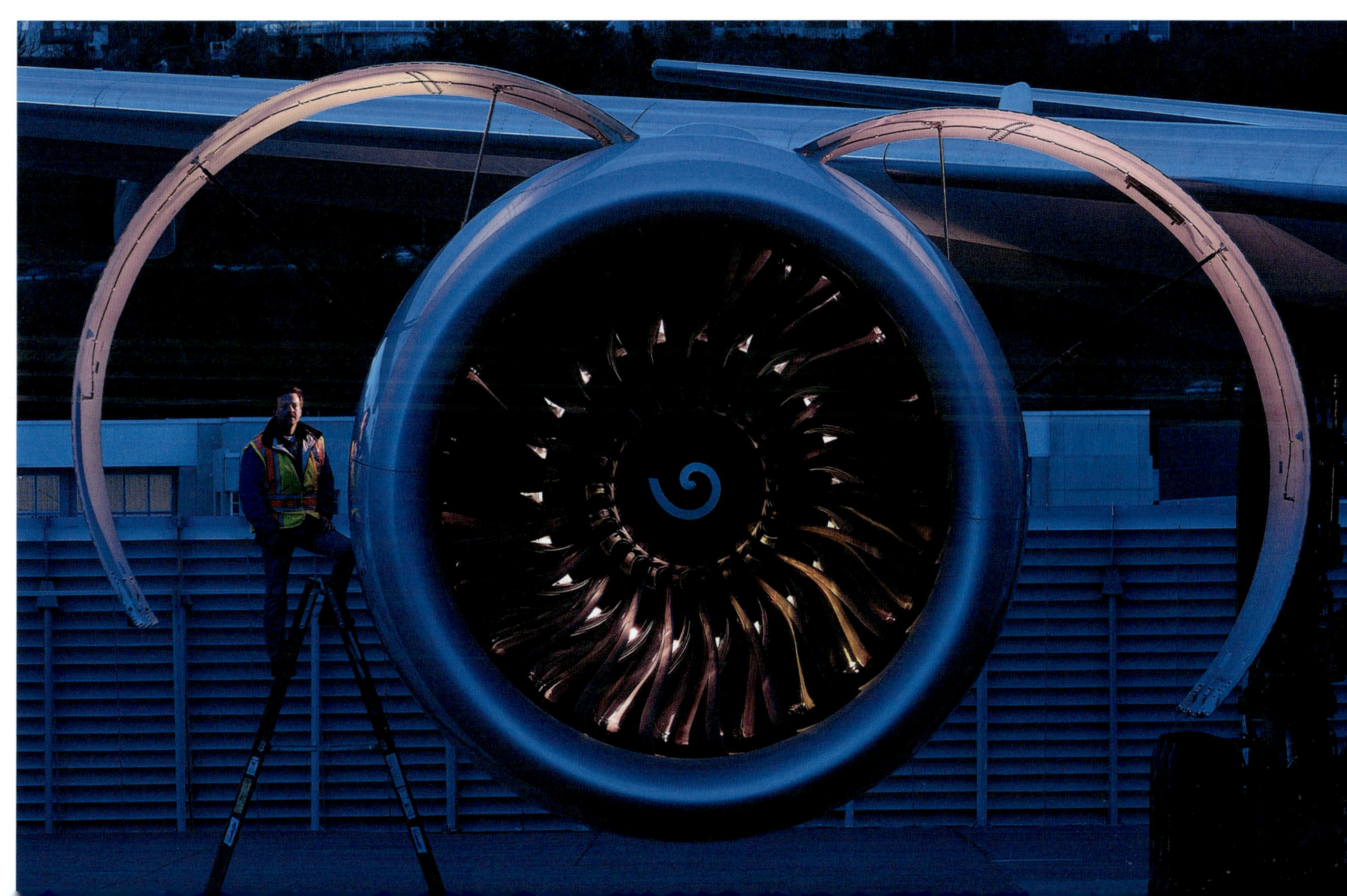

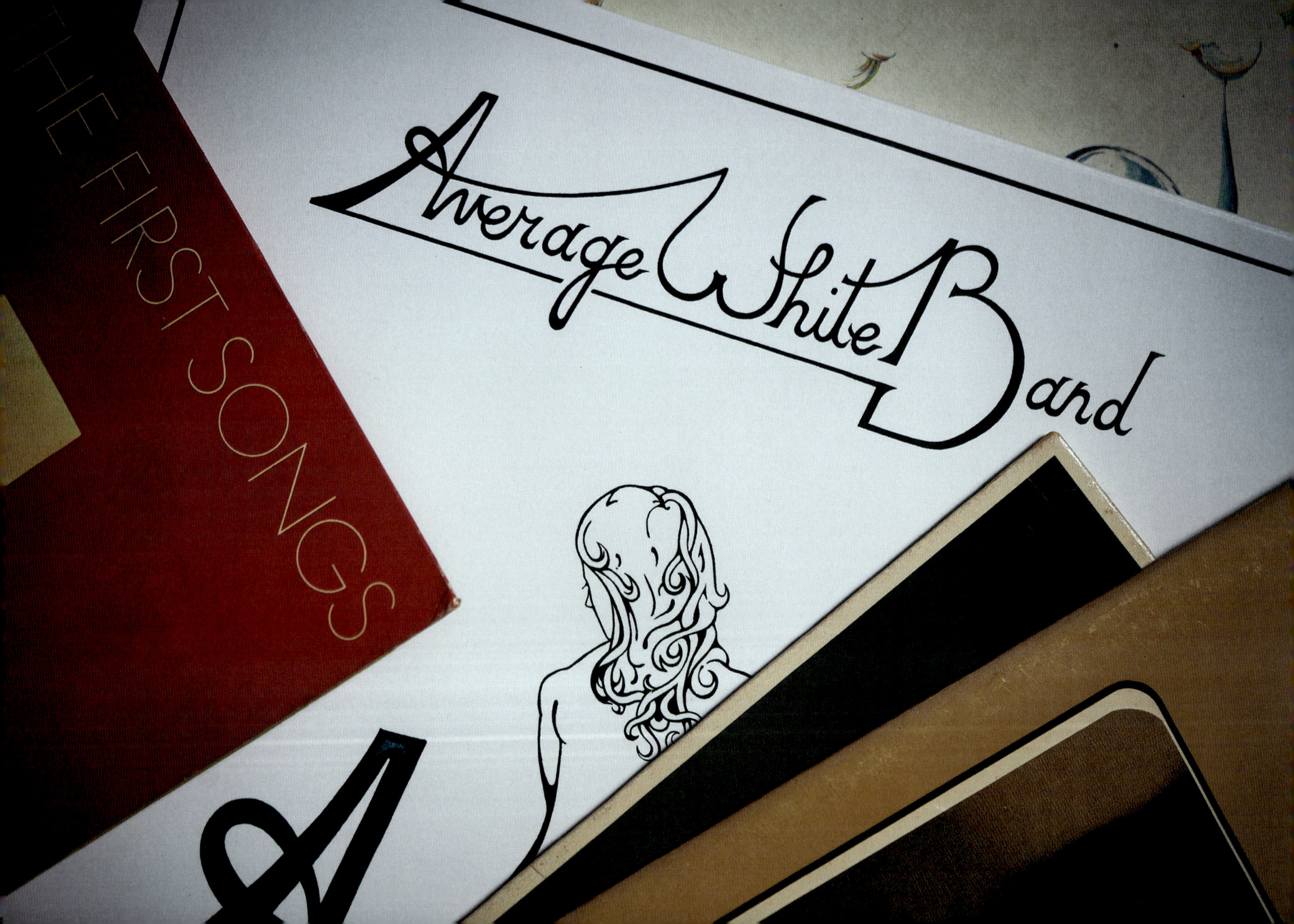
THE FIRST SONGS
Average White Band

Remember When AWB Was a Band?

If you're a younger photographer, you probably do not know what I'm talking about. But the Average White Band, or AWB, originating in Scotland, was huge in the '70s, and they still perform. I bought a couple of their albums long ago. Their big hit, "Pick Up the Pieces," was an R&B/soul standard. And it lives on! It was part of the Biden–Harris Official Inaugural Playlist.

Now, in camera parlance, AWB is Auto White Balance, and it's one of the smartest, most efficient tools in any photographer's bag. AWB is my go-to mode of balance, at least to start the shoot. It gives me the weather report for the coloration of the location, be it indoors or out. I assess the camera's AWB opinion and go from there. You can drag white balance from the auto mode into a whole variety of fixed categories, depending on the light. And you can further customize it in camera by pulling the color response of a certain balance further into a desired area of the spectrum. Want some more blue or red? Use the command dial and push your white balance any which way you choose. Or dial in a Kelvin temperature. Infinite color choices await, all with the flick of a button.

What you see here (below) used to be the white balance controls available to the photographer.

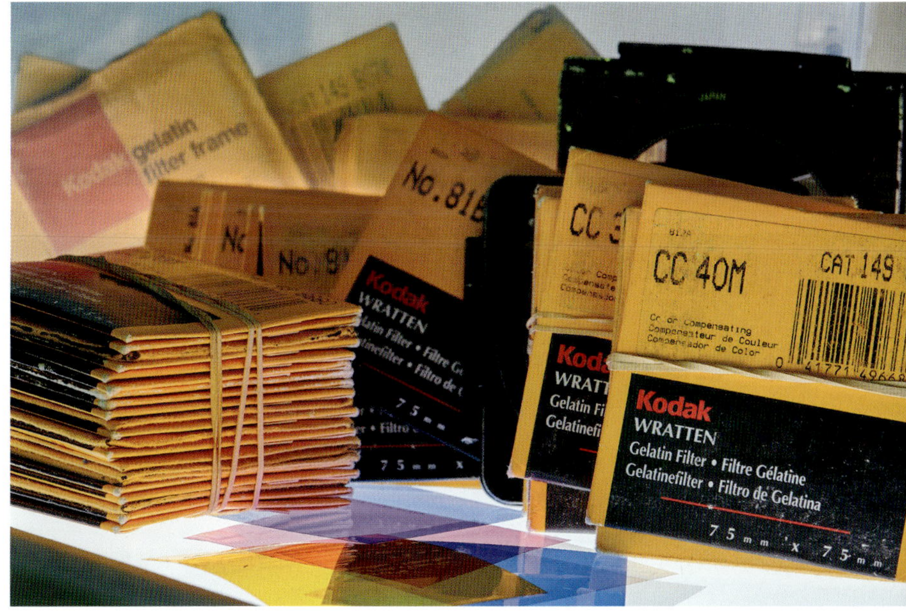

There was no metadata attached to the chromes, obviously. You had to test and make notes. The photo below is of my long ago slide page of different films, bundled with different combos of filtration, noting whether flash was used, and if so, noting the gel needed on the flash.

This was numbing, repetitive work, and hardly precise work at that. On location, moving fast, the best I could produce after all this would be considered good only in the ballpark sense of the word. If I could get within spitting distance of a good skin tone, I figured that was a win.

It was, indeed, the bad old days. A good thing about the bad old days was that there wasn't the acute sense of restriction on what you could do and where you could go that abounds today. For example, I could position myself overhead of the trading floor, during trading hours, with a motor-driven Mamiya RZ Pro II with a winder and a bulbous fisheye lens. The whole rig weighed a ridiculous amount, and I safety rigged it, but a slip would have meant certain death for anyone below. But they wanted these pictures, and I was allowed to shoot up there, looking down on the frenzy.

Here is my favorite frame from that position (opposite, top). This is an unretouched scan of the original chrome. It was never published, and I submitted a different select to the client. Reason being is the tears in the chrome itself, which you can see in the far right of the image. White splotches, and cracks in the emulsion.

These tears meant that this chrome got snagged up as part of the "snip test," or "clip test," that would be run through the chemistry at the lab to determine if the overall roll needed a push or a pull. On a big job, you would run these tests with a couple of frames, and not simply drop the whole roll or, more likely, a batch of rolls into the chemistry. You would risk potentially destroying a couple of frames to ensure a truly proper exposure for the take. This frame was a victim. It was not the lab tech's fault. Those folks were actually amazing, measuring out a small stretch of film in the dark, then attaching it to a clip and running it through the soup. This was just bad luck. The tears you see are from the metal clips the film got hooked to.

I had the chrome fixed for this book. Repaired, but not color corrected, it's shown here (opposite, bottom).

And finally, a retouched, color corrected version (page 78). As you can see, the New York Stock Exchange still proves unruly and not easily subdued, color-wise, even with today's prodigious color correction tools.

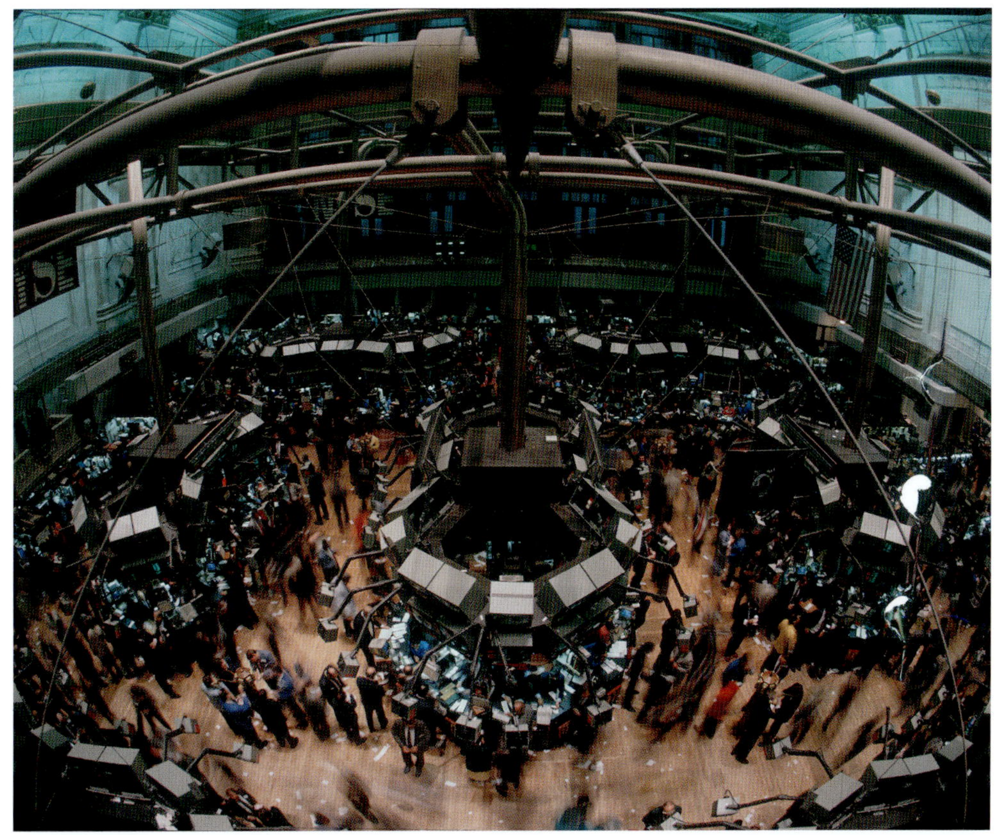

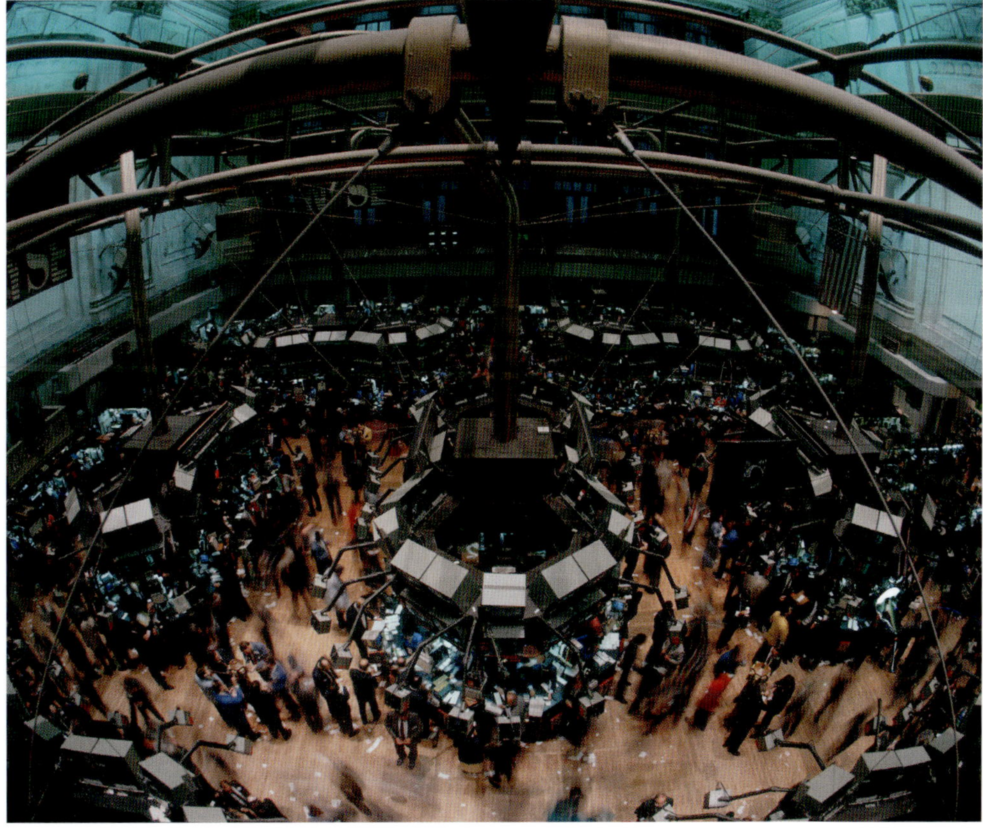

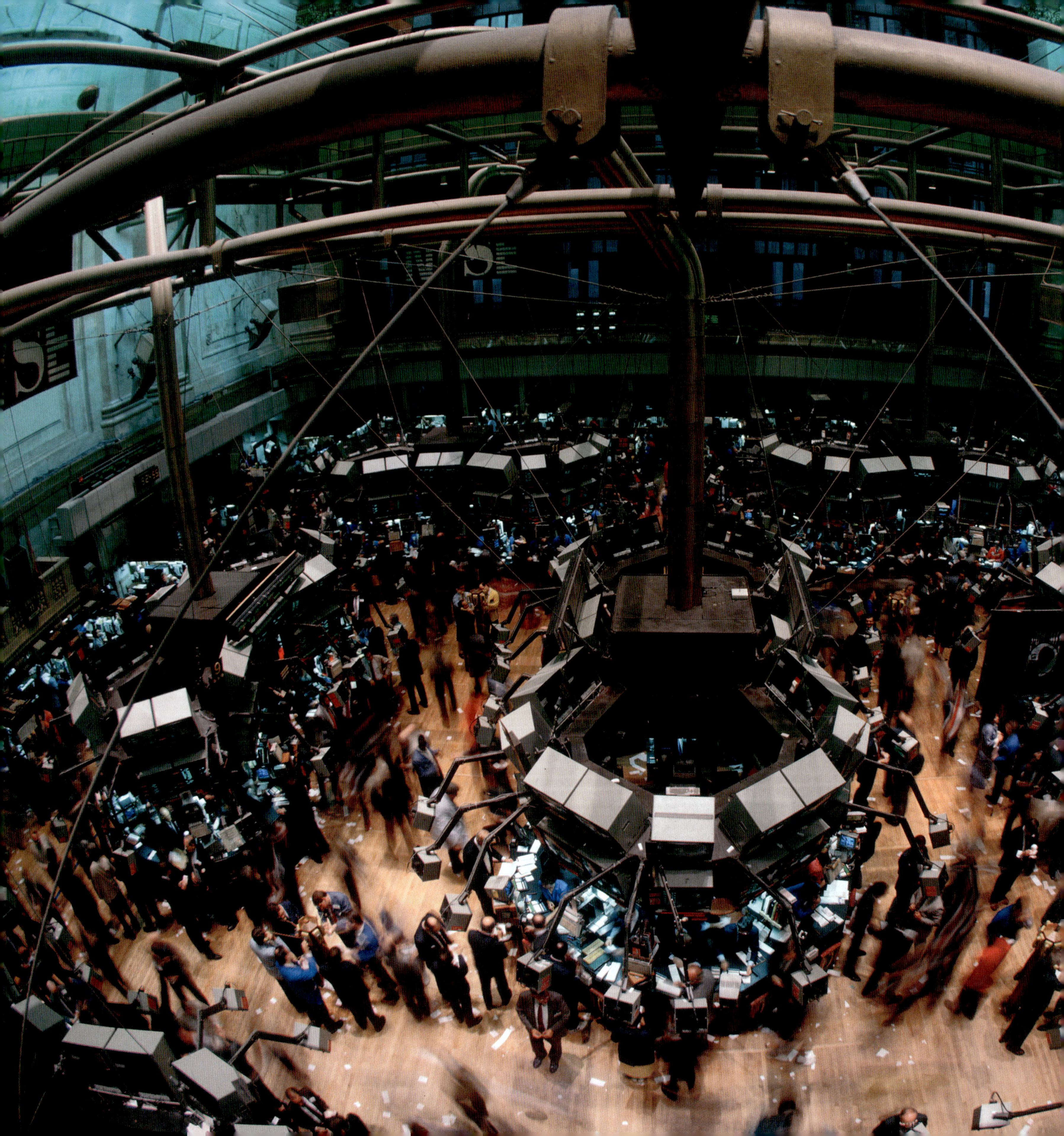

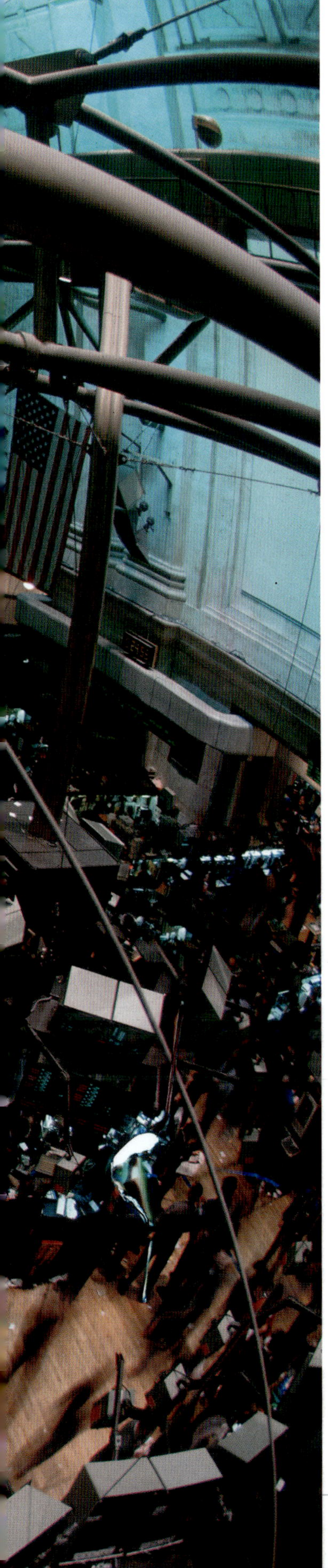

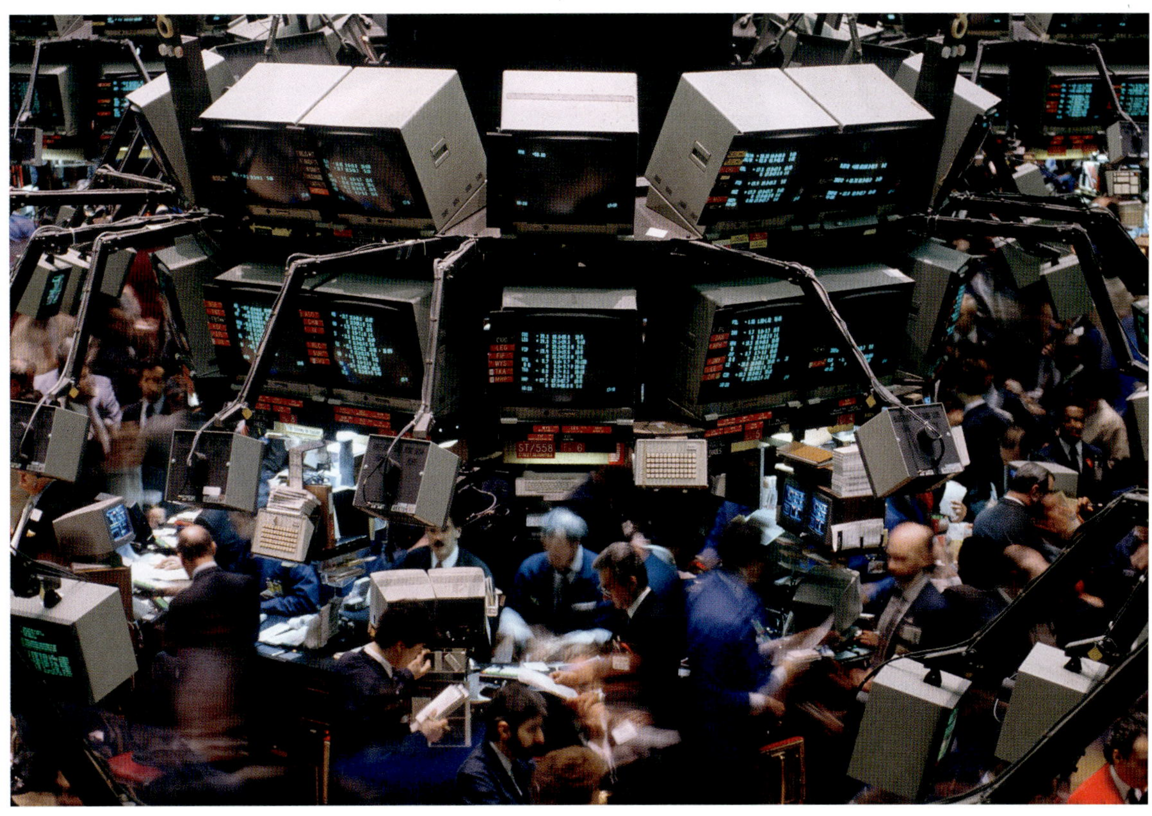

As far as the mishap with that image, I also shot panorama 617 images, which, blessedly, the NYSE felt more strongly about, choosing to run something along the lines of this frame (above).

Many variables! From the filtration and the light and the exposure and the expressions to the sharp little teeth on the clip test bracket. And was the lab running hot that day? Was the chemistry nearing the end of its run, and your film was being sunk in a developer batch that was the equivalent of yesterday's french fry oil at McDonald's? Or was it tuned up, fresh, and ready?

Always best to test.

On top of that, your film was a physical object, or bag of objects. A very valuable bag. No backups, no duping as you shot. No simultaneous wireless transmission to a computer, manned by a digital tech, who was automatically backing up imagery on three separate hard drives. It was a pretty simple equation: Lose the bag, lose the job. It was easy and calm on a local job like the stock exchange. You would go from Wall Street to the lab. No real tension there, except perhaps on the subway ride.

> *Was your film being sunk in a developer batch that was the equivalent of yesterday's french fry oil at McDonald's?*

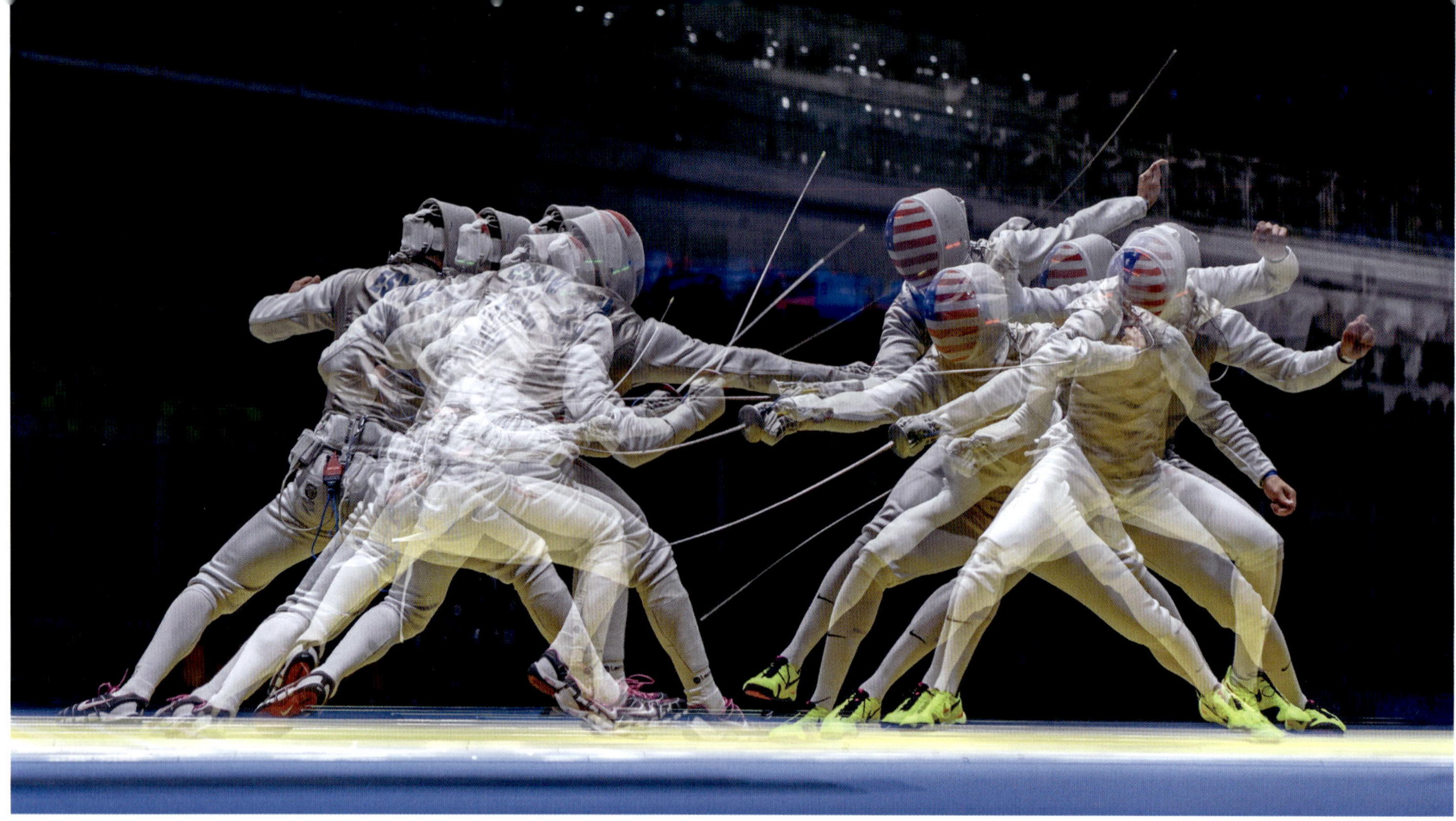

But on location you would often just have to suck it up and ship it. After spending three weeks in India shooting for the *Geographic*, I took the 300 rolls of Kodachrome I shot, boxed it, and shipped it via FedEx out of Mumbai to Washington, D.C. And waited three days for the confirmation of its arrival. All of my work for three weeks was in that box. And much more, too. All the costs of the job were in there. Airfares to India. Twenty-two nights in hotels, food, cars and drivers and fixers. In that box, rattling around on a roll of K64 was also, as I discuss in "Trust the Machine," the favorite cover I ever shot for *Nat Geo* (page 53).

Bye bye! Kiss for luck! This is perhaps why I am relatively calm about the great memory card slot furor of nowadays. It's super nice to have a second slot, and I guess it's essential in today's frenzied digital zeitgeist. But I don't lose sleep over the slots, or the number of pixels, or their shape. Rather, I choose to revel in what's possible now.

An off-the-cuff, hand-held multiple exposure of world class fencers (above).

A flying dancer, mirrorless technology, autofocus, instantaneous confirmation of getting the shot, and on-the-fly, push-button adjustments at the ready (opposite, bottom left).

Lightning fast frames per second (opposite, bottom right).

Radio TTL flash technology, obviously, at distance (opposite, top).

And color response that Kodachrome never dreamed of (page 82).

You might see why, given the above, I have little patience for petulant screamers on the photo blogs and podcasts nowadays, where complaining about the missing pixel or two of this or that camera is apparently a desirable way of gathering an audience. Exactly how much are you expecting that camera over your shoulder to do for you? In addition to solving white balance issues with a couple of ticks of a button, it also autofocuses, auto exposes, talks to automatic flashes, gives you resolution options and framing options, and supports storage cards that hold so many pictures that they're the photo equivalent of ocean-going oil tankers. It can shoot silent, fast, or slow.

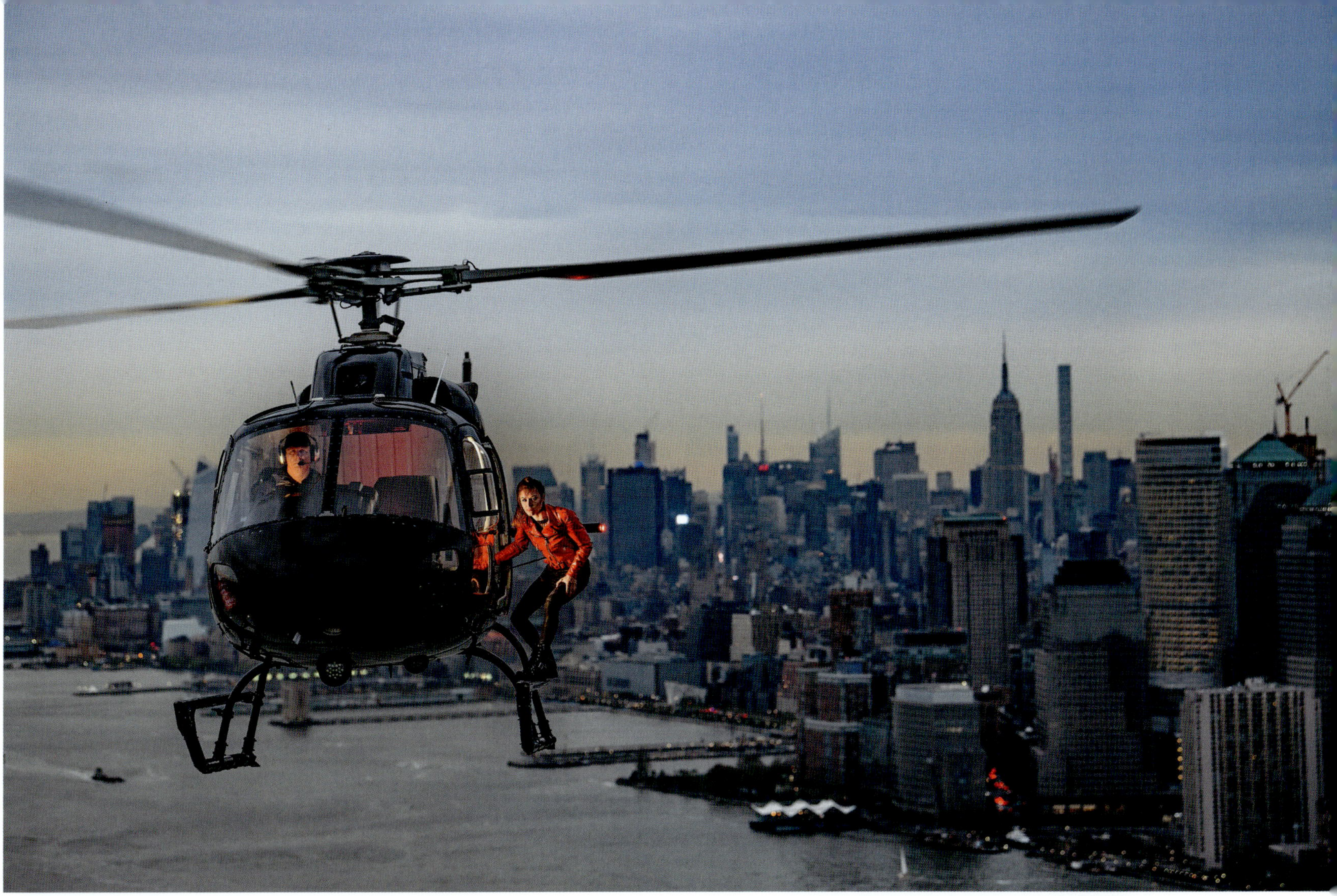

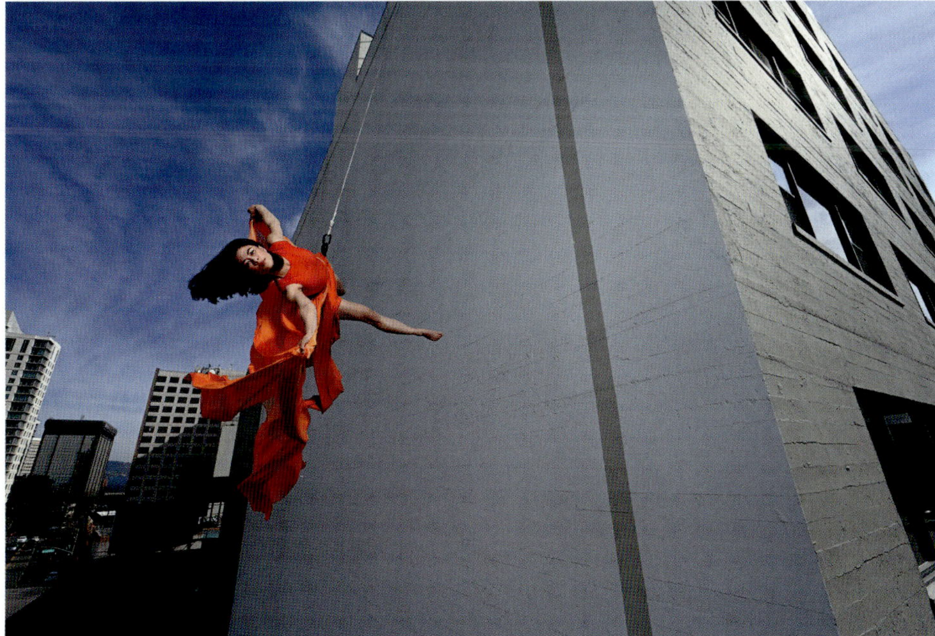

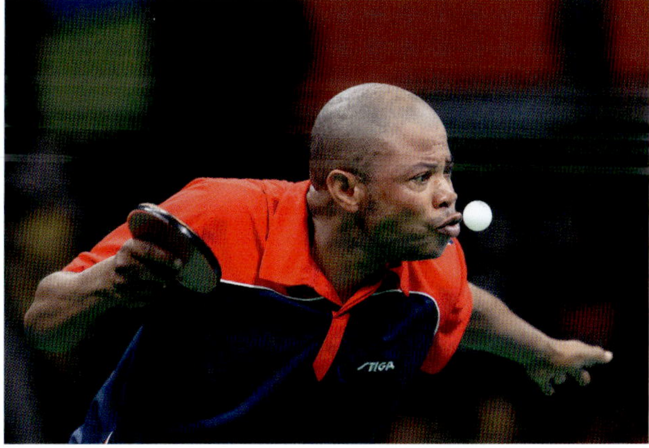

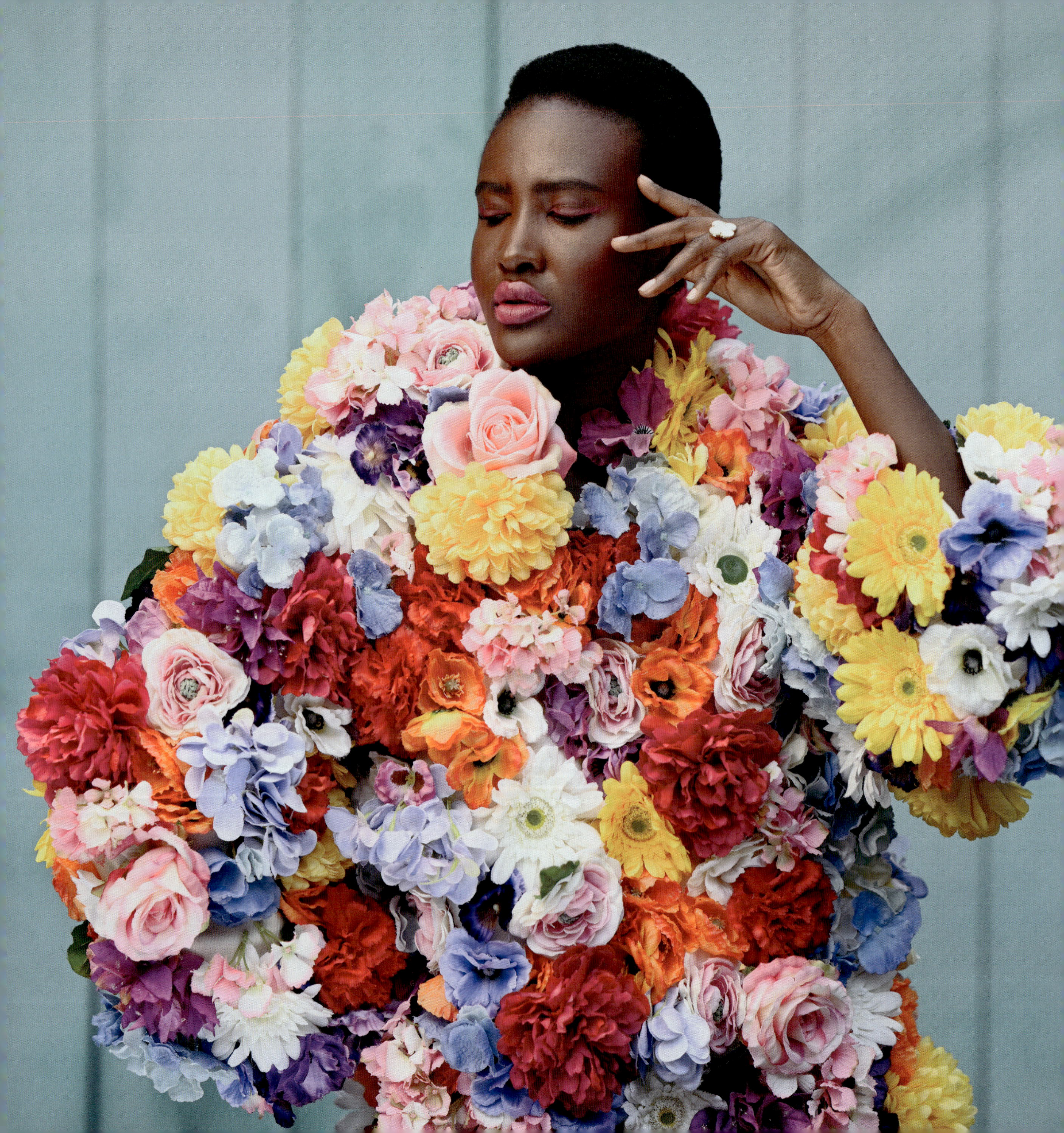

It gives birth to a raw file that you can put into post-production programs and hothouse it from larva to chrysalis to hopefully resplendent adult.

And if the plain and simple goosing of color or smoothing of blemishes isn't enough, there are galaxies of software plugins out there. These programs are quick fixes, the Amazon one-click of photo alteration. The picture becomes a frozen dinner thrown in the microwave as opposed to homemade soup simmering over the flame. I browsed a few current plugins while writing this book, and there are some doozies out there that can turn summer into fall, enable you to grab someone else's photo for free, and of course replace buildings and skies. And then there are those … *other* plugins. Let's call them the Timothy Leary suite. Take your picture on an acid trip. "Abandon all hope, ye who enter here."

And yes, there are the sane ones that make perfect sense and are damn handy in the best of worlds and uses—say, for a photog who shoots portraits for the local little league and has to deliver hundreds of finished images quickly.

The lenses of our current time are fast and excellent. ISO is off the charts. Take a gander at those test chromes that are pictured. Look at the notations. See the shutter speeds? Reason they're so slow is that I'm bumping up against the ISO ceiling of that time. If I had pushed the hell out of an indoor Ektachrome to gain quickness of shutter, the film structure would have exploded into a loosely connected bunch of dots. Delivering an impressionist painting when the client was expecting a sharp, well-defined photo of the business at hand would have quickly resulted in a lack of work.

Here's a detail shot of wrestlers at the Rio Olympics in 2016 (right). Indoors, with an 800mm lens. Autofocus. ISO 6400. Years ago, this was simply not a possible shot.

Given the amazing machines that are today's cameras and lenses, combined with the infinite options of post-processing, do you really feel something is egregious and amiss that merits invective? Hey, if you're looking for stuff that falls short of expectations, try looking hard at your own pictures. That's what I do. What might be missing there? Form and content, perhaps? It's easy to hide in the dense underbrush of the pixel forest and yip, hoot, and grunt about how the underperformance of the camera's buffer short-circuits the magnificence of your vision. It's much harder to get naked and step into the hot spotlight of delivering a job under scrutiny, clinging to the camera like a life preserver in a rough ocean, and project confidence, all while the fact that you're a month behind on the mortgage is gnawing at your gut.

Get in the ring. Risk. Chase the comet of your imagination and see where it takes you. Feel the haymaker of failure. Get your bell rung. Fall short. Taste the canvas, laced with blood and sweat. And then get back up and get your eye back in the camera, because at the end of the day it's about how you see and whether anybody actually gives a damn about that.

Okay, okay, I'll stop. At this point I feel like I'm channeling my mom at her most hectoring. "You want something to complain about, mister? Huh? I'll give you something to complain about!" All the while brandishing whatever kitchen utensil might have been handy.

Just go shoot.

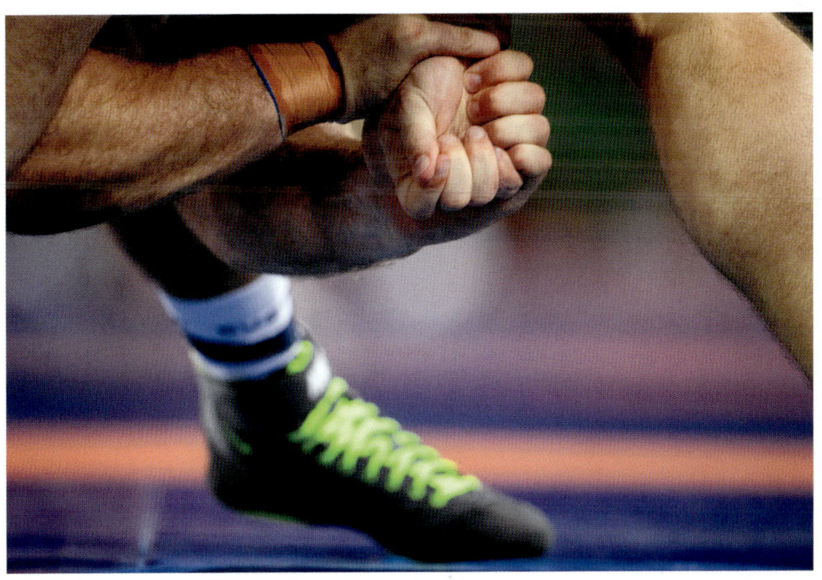

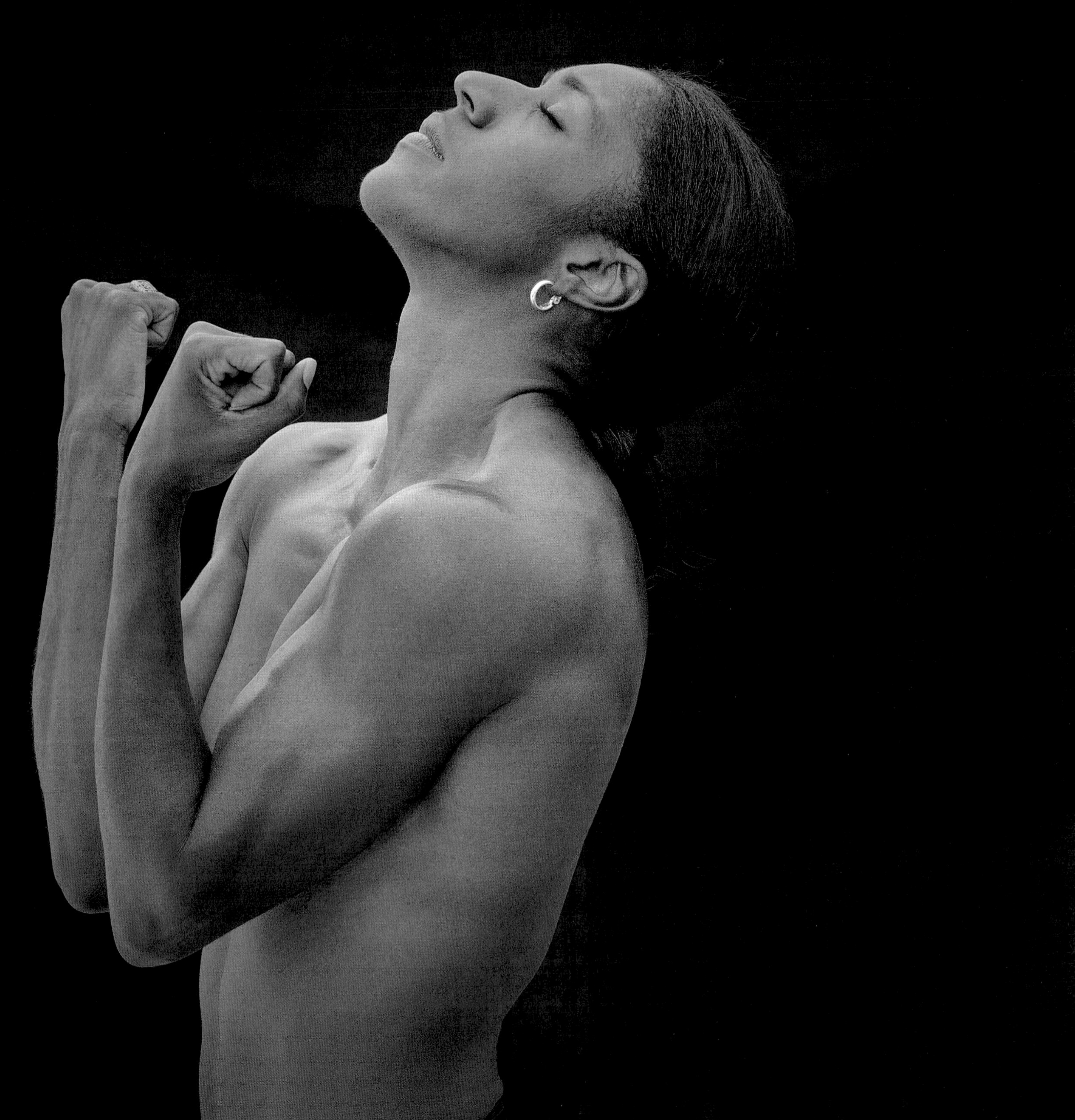

Photographing Excellence

I've said it many times: One of the truly beautiful things about being a photographer is that you are often called to be a witness to excellence. You're sent to photograph someone, somewhere, because of the uniqueness of their persona or the powerful pitch of their skills, intellect, physicality, or grace. Because of the richness of their knowledge and acumen, the hyper drive of their talents. You go because the ferocity of their gifts, often honed and polished by years of dedicated drive, awaits your camera, humming and crackling like high-voltage power lines. They have pitched their tent at a place where we can only call to from afar, in hopes they'll lower a rope.

Approach with caution and respect. Care must be taken. When you are working with or observing someone in their creative flow, no matter what form that takes, it's best to remember what famed author Joyce Carol Oates is fond of saying: "Interruption is the enemy of creativity." Remember, too, your subject is not an ATM or a pinball machine. You can't drop in a quarter and start hitting the flippers. Just because they're exceedingly

excellent at something or other doesn't mean it's easy. They still must summon it, with their face, body, mind, and gesture. Foreign noises, distractions that pierce their space, aimless chatter, hitting the shutter to produce endless frames, constant timeouts for LCD consultation—all are disturbances that kill creation.

I photographed Moses Pendleton (following page), one of the originators of the famed Pilobolus Dance Company, for a TV dance special years ago. He's a marvelous subject who provided me with an early lesson in photographing artists. They are tuned up and their senses, all of them, are often running at a pitch unfamiliar to the rest of us. The crew was filming, and I was behind the video cameras shooting quietly with a Leica M4. Something went wrong with my camera, nothing major, but under my breath (or so I thought) I muttered, "Shit."

Pendleton abruptly stopped performing. He looked at the director and asked what was wrong. The director said, "Nothing, why did you stop?" He said he heard somebody say "Shit," and he thought things were off the rails, so he stopped. I froze in the

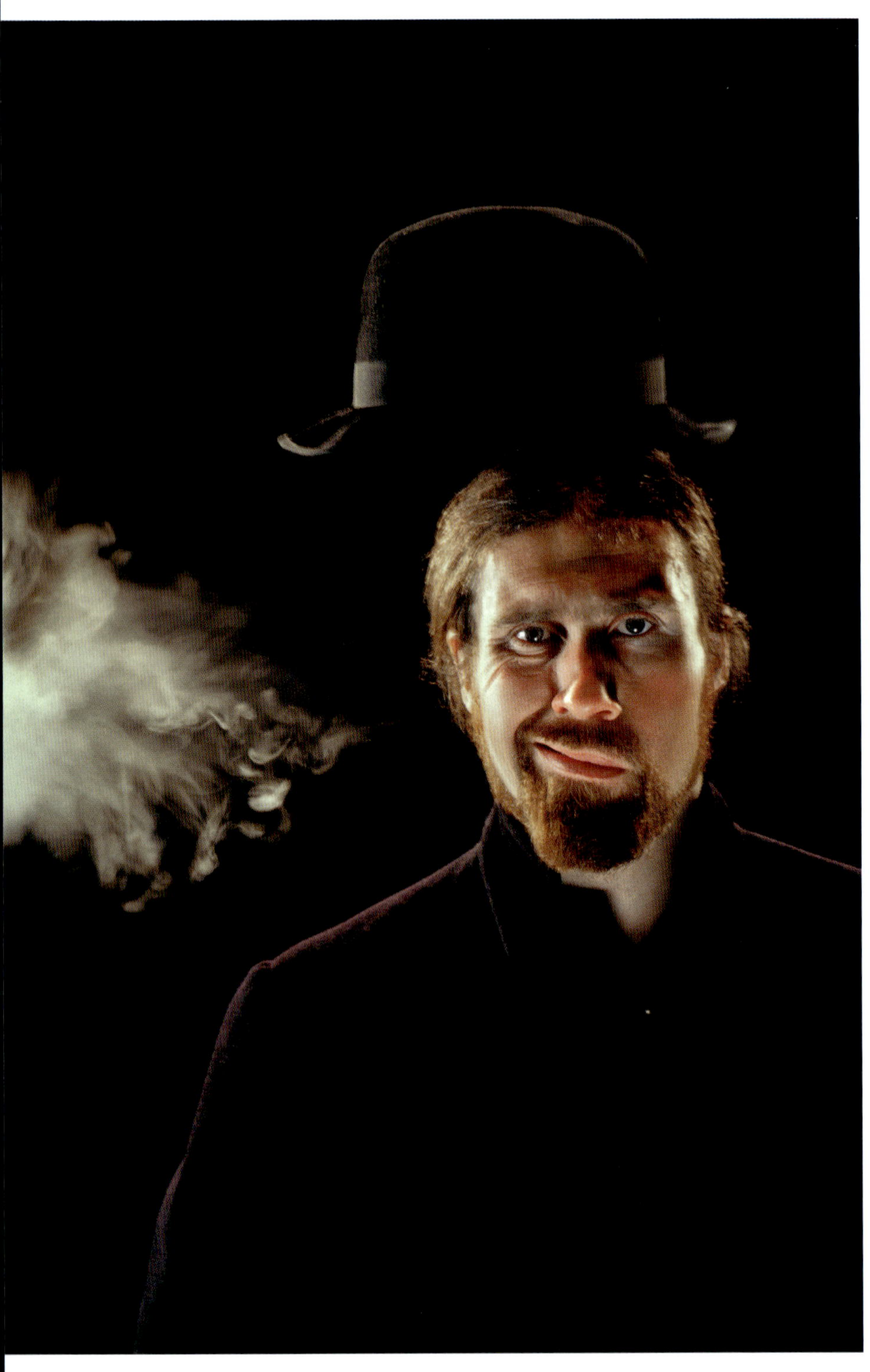

darkness off camera. No one—no one—on the crew, who were much, much closer to me than Moses was, heard anything. The moment passed and filming resumed. Ever since then, when an artist, actor, or dancer is evolving a mood or a move in front of the lens, I try to stay quiet at camera, physically and verbally. The space they create in their head and heart is not to be pierced, as best as can be managed.

Now, a photo session is by definition a distraction, and you're underfoot just by being there. The old photographic saw of "I spent a few minutes with the family, gaining their trust, then I became invisible, and touched nothing except with my eyes" is often self-serving hogwash. Trust takes time, and that is often what we lack in the field, under deadline. You go in, make requests, ask questions, ascertain what is possible, and then point a lens at those things mutually agreed upon. High-powered people, artists of note, transcendent humans, rarely (read: almost never) have the time to allow extensive relationships to build and photographs to proceed at ever-increasing levels of intimacy, resulting in a body of work with true depth and richness, a set of pictures as flavorful as a resplendently cured ham.

That's not to say photographers over time have not produced nuanced, deep, beautiful, true work. Witness Sam Abell's coverage in *National Geographic* of Newfoundland. Take a deep dive into Bill Allard's essays, such as his work on Faulkner's Mississippi. David Douglas Duncan became an intimate friend of Picasso, and the resulting work is a treasure. Ami Vitale has photographed the Reteti Elephant Sanctuary in Kenya for over a decade. These photogs, and many others, have invested huge chunks of their time and photographic lives in the passionate pursuit of a story or stories that reverberate in their hearts, stories that need telling. What sustains these efforts is fierce tenacity on their part, and often a patchwork quilt of support from publications, grants, donations, and their own bank account. It's work that enriches all, save the photographer who creates it. A labor of love, distinctly not one of commerce.

The one commodity that unites all photographers who engage in long-form work and establish true trust with the people or community they are photographing is time spent. And time is precious indeed, a gift rarely given to the photographer by any publication or assigning entity at this point in the arc of this industry. The first thing you hear about, literally, from almost any editor, anywhere, is budget. Or schedule. As it relates to budget. Or travel. As it relates to budget. Or your fee. As it relates to budget. Or the fact that there is no money. As it relates to budget.

Hence, we are often in the position of doing our research, prepping as well as we can, going in and meeting a subject, making things happen, and then being done. But the cursory intensity of that process doesn't preclude giving your subject time and space and respect. It doesn't preclude the presenting of ideas, borne out of your research, that might engage, incite, or galvanize the mind and body of the person who will be in front of the camera, resulting in pictures that are vibrant, fun, insightful, yea, even memorable. Or at least something the client will like.

A picture that has stuck with me over time is a multiple exposure I did of the famed actor and comic Steve Martin. I've mentioned elsewhere that when you encounter Steve, which I did only briefly, you are not hanging with a "wild and crazy guy." You're dealing with a highly intelligent, somewhat shy individual who only grudgingly offers up his time to do, as they call it in Hollywood, "publicity."

I had four hours with him for *LIFE* magazine. I desperately needed the lead, the big pic, the one that sets off the story. True to form, I did my homework, watching his movies and appearances. During one talk show stint, back on Johnny Carson's *The Tonight Show*, he and Johnny were bantering about Steve's humor, and Steve mentioned the phrase, in jest, that he had the audience "laughing through their tears." I seized on that, as there has always been an element of pain, awkwardness, reticence, of dry, detached observation—call it what you will—in Martin's comedy. Enter the notion of the multiple exposure, and the tragi-comic masks.

In the hotel the night before, my assistant Garth and I did a series of multiples on my Mamiya RZ67 Pro II. It had a clutch button that, when depressed, retained the same frame of film in place, but allowed you to advance the shutter. This made the physicality of creating a double exposure "easy." We shot sample Polaroids, and marked out the placement of the lights, the power, and the positioning of the light shapers. The next morning we headed to Martin's home, which was sort of bunker-like, and made of colorless cement walls. I thought, *Hmmm, the home reflects the man.*

I showed him the Polaroid.

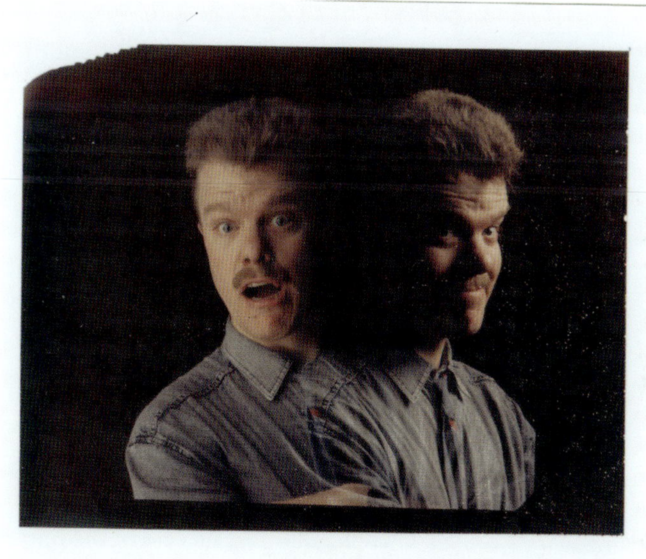

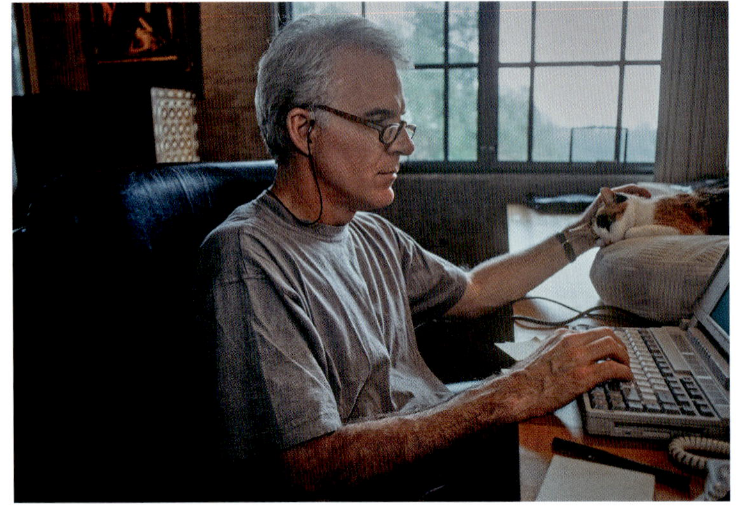

rested entirely on his considerably mobile face and what he could project with it. I did not interrupt that process.

When working with folks of a certain stature or caliber, you move the mountain to them, not the other way around. Be it reasons of schedule, logistics, or simply their need to be in a familiar place and avoid undue interruption, you go to them, you pack what you need to make it work . . . for them. Because when they're comfortable, balanced, and feel accommodated, they breathe better, relaxing in the knowledge that they're being cared for. And that works . . . for you. You create a comfortable approach and space, they give you back better photos. It's simple.

He looked at the 'roid, as we called them, and pondered, while I spewed, seeking his engagement. He was onboard. One, it was a concept, which tweaked his considerable intellect. Two, it gave him the chance to act, and not just sit there and look pretty for the camera. I told him I needed two things. A dark space to work, and for him to wear a black shirt. All good. Garth and I went to the basement with our tech sketch from the night before and found a suitable spot. Garth, who was a wonderful photog and friend, now, sadly, deceased, started moving and shaking with the lights and grip gear, leaving me to wander with Steve, shooting available light, while he ambled about the spacious, high-ceilinged abode. Work at the computer, strum the guitar, wander by the windows, which were blessedly big.

Then, Garth called up from the basement. We were set.

First tests, all done on Polaroid (opposite, top left).

Move fast. Make sure the frame allows enough room for Steve to shift his head position, and start cranking film. I had six pages of *LIFE* to fill, and four hours to do it. I shut up at the camera and let the session play out. I could tell he was intensively creating in his head, thinking of mood, nuance, and gesture. He had no dialogue to utilize, no lines to say. No overlay of music. Just him, in a black shirt, on a black background. The success of the photo

I've worked with lots of athletes over time, and Olympians, especially as a Games approaches (which, sadly, is the only time the world and the press pay a lot of attention to many of these magnificent artisans), get really, understandably, tight about what they will do and what they won't. When I shot naked Olympic athletes prior to the '96 Games, Gwen Torrence, one of the best female sprinters in the world, based in Atlanta, was high on the "get" list. Would she pose? Would she pose nude?

The answer was yes, but the catch was this: she was so devoted to her training routine that she wouldn't leave the Emory University track stadium. She would pose for me, right by the track. At noon. In the middle of gaggles of other folks running, training, and eating lunch.

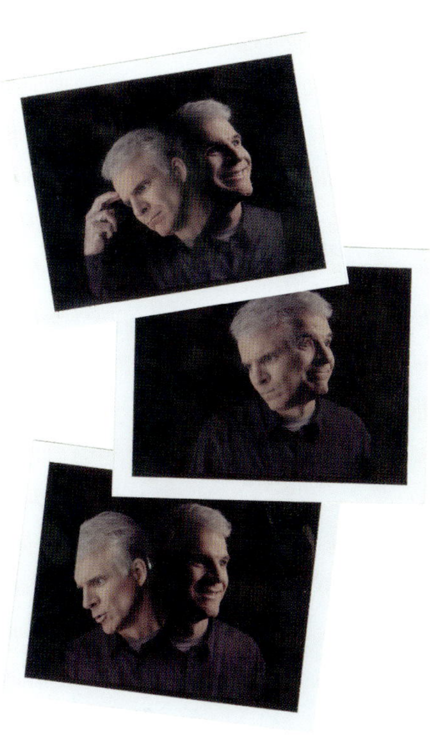

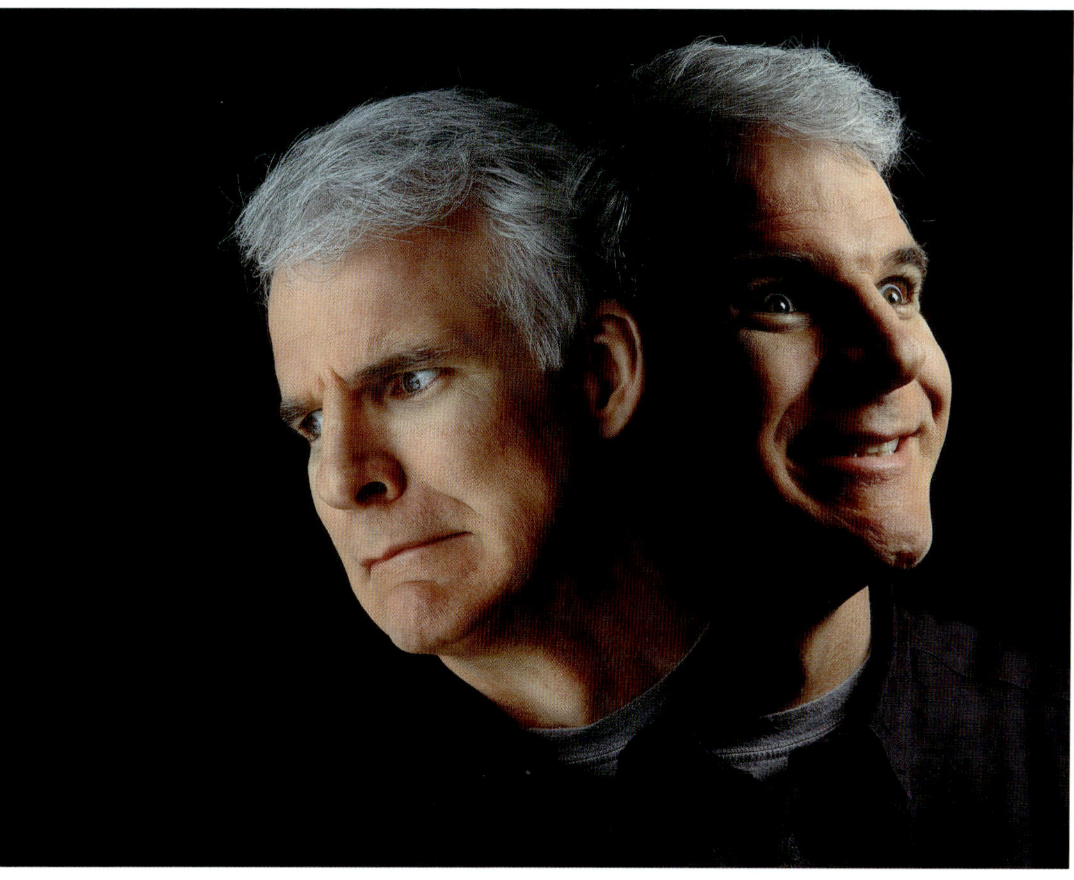

I brought in stands and yards of Duvetyne cloth and created a black box for her right there in the stands. I threw a silk overhead of the box, goosed the softness with a tiny bit of large, soft flash. It wasn't perfect. There were sections of our "studio" that were wide open to the public. But she didn't care. She was not going to go to a fancy downtown photo studio and sip a latte while we prepared a private shoot. Her training schedule was her life force at that point. No diverting of her pace, timing, and intensity would be acceptable to her. Like Moses on stage, she was tuned to a rarified level of intensity.

She disrobed right there, and immediately, comfortably got in front of the camera. And owned it with a look. Such a talented, beautiful woman! I flew through frames while she disregarded the laughs and hoots from her track teammates. She gazed at the camera with power and serenity.

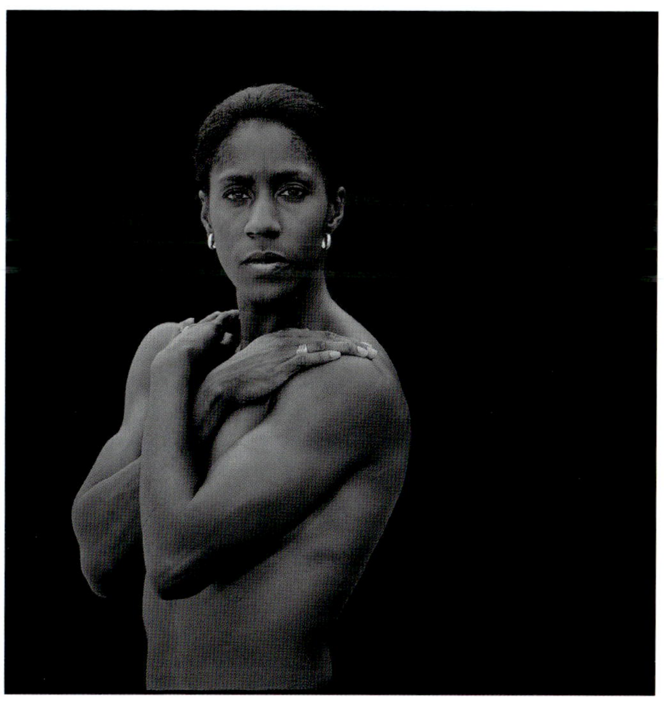

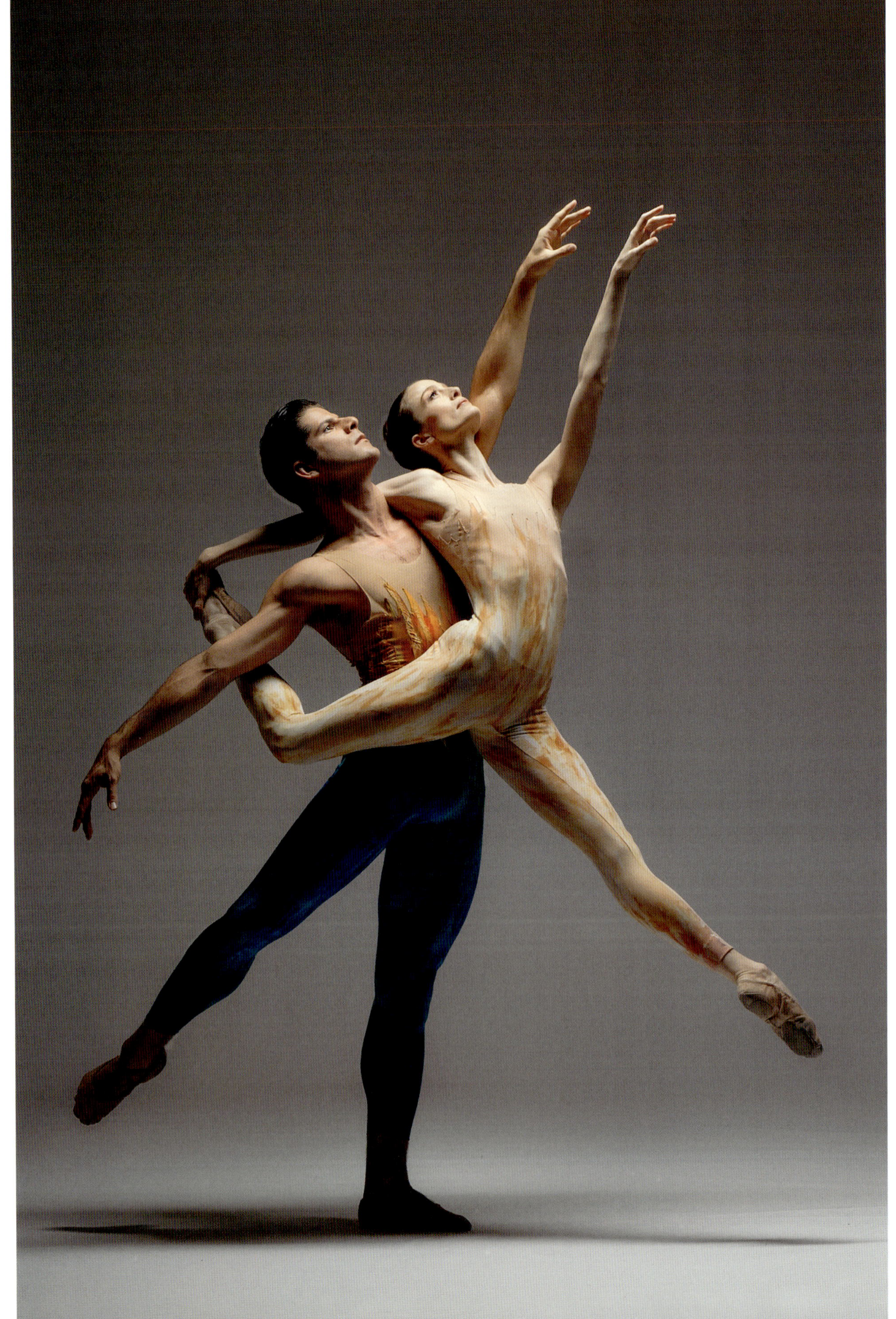

When someone's certainty of mind and purpose is at this pitch, all your skills, determination, and camera work simply stand in service to them. They are operating in a space few of us ever realize is possible.

Likewise, I brought the studio to the American Ballet Theatre, which, oddly, was harder to do than setting up in a track stadium. Long hallways to trundle gear down, lots of rules about what could and couldn't be done. A very long day in the field.

And when Julie Kent and Marcelo Gomes effortlessly wound themselves around each other and struck a dance pose with utter perfection, down to the matching of the gestures of their fingers, I was as nervous as I think I have ever been behind the camera. They were striving for perfection and the originator of the piece, choreographer Lar Lubovitch, was completely strident and unyielding in his direction. I remained utterly mute at camera, actually hoping I could simply disappear should this picture not go well. This was not something to be treated lightly. Asking them to do this over again because of a screwup at camera, well, the response would be unforgiving. I had my finger on the shutter, as tense as I might have been listening to the countdown for a shuttle launch.

And, like a launch, the moment was fleeting, not to be repeated. The flashes fired, and this became a much-used photo over time of one of the brilliant collaborations of Kent and Gomes, two legendary dancers.

This kind of excellence is a rare gift in front of your lens.

Respect it. Photograph it. Don't interrupt it.

And try not to screw it up.

These days, bringing the mountain to your subject is much easier than it used to be. Speed of delivery, and comfort factor for the subject, are paramount. Clients now want the images delivered almost as soon they come out of the camera, and the ever-packed and over-committed nature of those we wish to photograph forces narrow, super quick windows of opportunity. The industry has responded by creating a veritable forest of collapsible, bagged, lightweight, click-it-together solutions that are

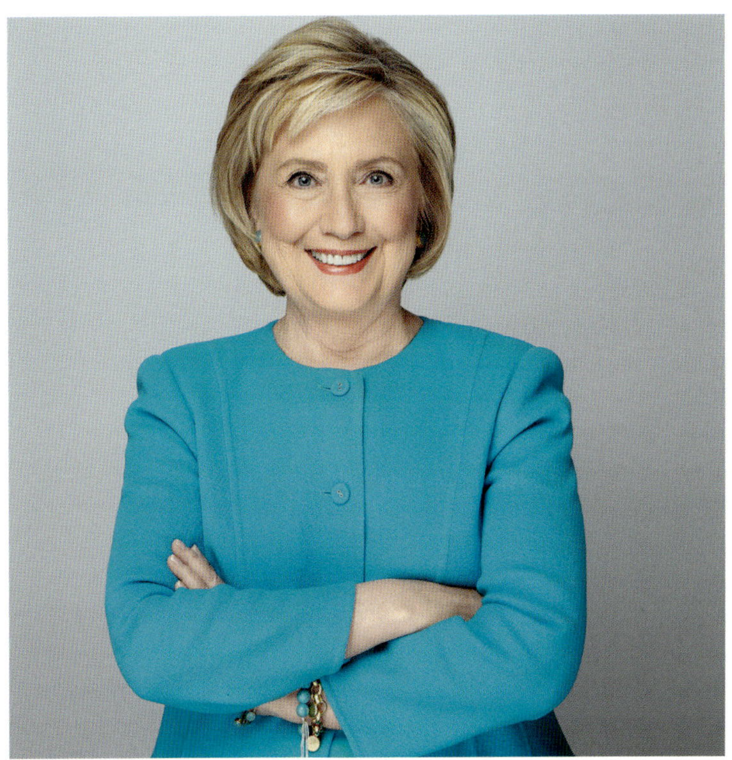

totable, even by a one-person army. These make it easy—okay, easier—to go to your subject and meet them in their comfort zone, their power sphere. The materials of yore, by comparison, required a mule team to haul about. Now, pop-up backdrops abound, as do small but powerful lights. Will you require electricity? Nope, we've got battery-contained power! There exists a huge variety of light shapers that are lightweight, efficient, and illuminate beautifully. Flash packs are easily controlled and adjusted: +1 on the main, −2 on the background, all done by radio. No wires to gaffer-tape down to the carpet. Tripods come in all sorts of strong but featherweight (by comparison) materials.

Makes it less formidable when photographing, for instance, Hillary Clinton. Let's face it, she's not coming to you. You are going to her. She is time-lined and busy, and she and her staff maintain strict control of the pace of her world. I shot this for her (above), and she's used it now for two book jackets, and has tweeted her fondness of the frame. Happy for that, because, as

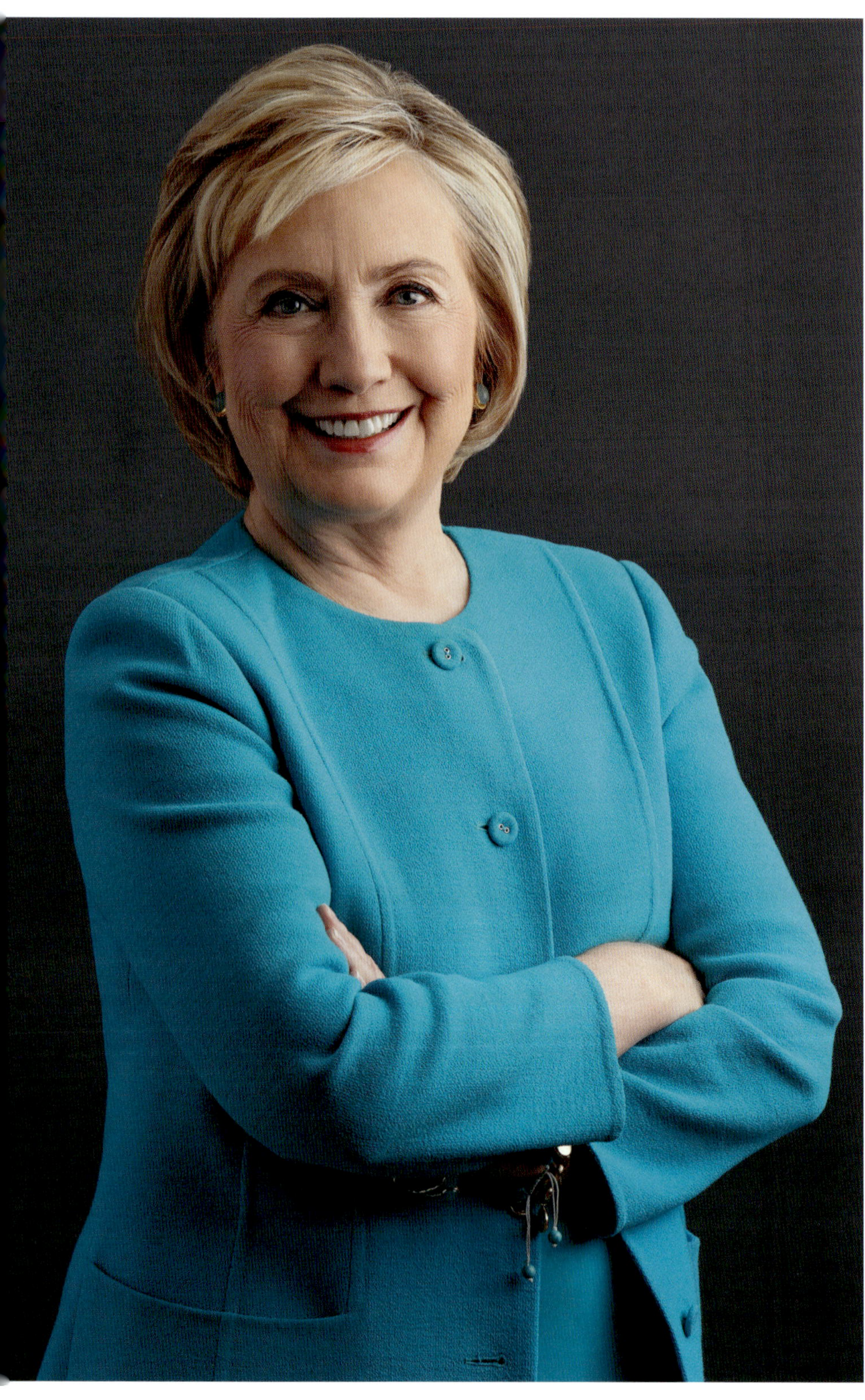

always, you want to please the client. And I think the relaxed and ready nature of her expressions derived at least in part from the fact that she could take a call, write an email, and walk 10 feet to my "studio" which was just outside her office door.

Backdrops and lights at the ready. Don't overplay it; shoot effectively and let her go. Create two sets if you can, for different looks. Be gracious and prepared. Do the research. Know the premise of the book you are shooting this for. Remember the names of her grandkids. Share a story, in self-deprecating fashion, about the time you photographed Bill Clinton being fed space food by John Glenn down at NASA Houston. Lets her know you have visited the halls of power before and are comfortable amongst the titans. Also lets her know this is not your first rodeo and you will not waste her time.

Madam Secretary was, as you would expect, smart, funny, and personable. Kibitzed a bit with staff and my crew. I showed her a frame or two on the LCD, and she was super pleased. She pointed to the fill board I had put out for her, which always produces lovely light, especially for a female subject. She was very fond of this device, asking, "Could I walk around with this all day?"

Laughter and comfort on the set are important. Do the prep, and bring the studio to them, along with good light and humor. A honed set of skills allows you to project easygoing confidence, which in turn gives them confidence in the process. If you bring crew, you all work together with lots of courtesy displayed, and thank yous given and received. Everybody breathes easy. You're remembered well when you leave. Which might mean you'll get called back.

Because all the above means the pictures will be good. Simple. It's not about the machinery. It's very human. Make a connection. Create a good space for your subject. And bring a fill board.

How Stock Photography Sales Are Going

Over the course of time, I've received smaller and smaller checks as the stock photography market races to the bottom. Some have been ridiculously small, barely worth the paper they're printed on.

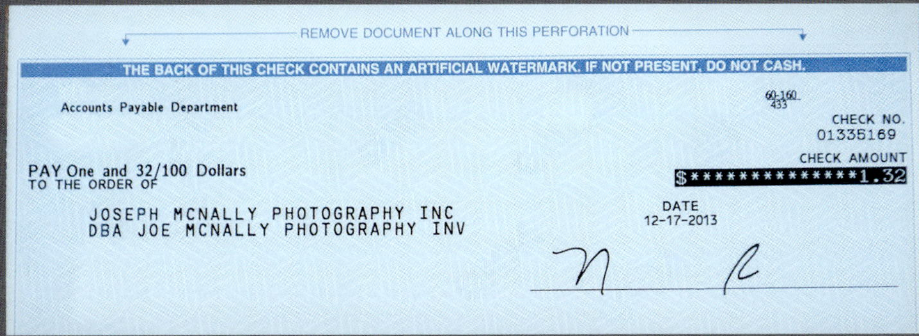

Sorry to say, but things have been trending downwards.

At the end of 2020, my agency sent through the $0.17 payment. Thank goodness, it had been a tight year.

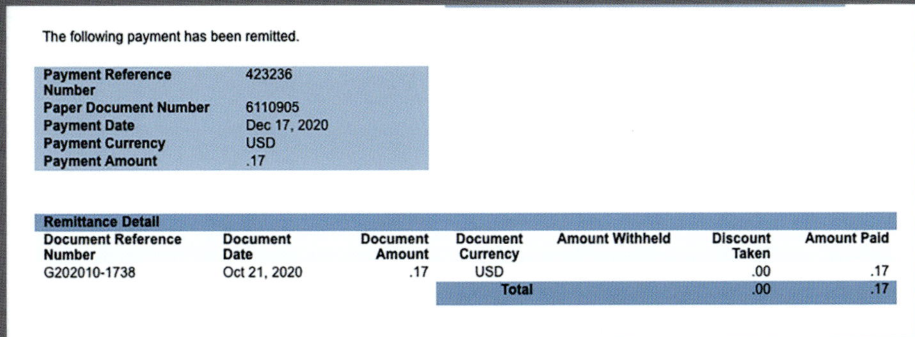

Payment Reference Number	423236
Paper Document Number	6110905
Payment Date	Dec 17, 2020
Payment Currency	USD
Payment Amount	.17

Remittance Detail

Document Reference Number	Document Date	Document Amount	Document Currency	Amount Withheld	Discount Taken	Amount Paid
G202010-1738	Oct 21, 2020	.17	USD		.00	.17
				Total	.00	.17

Look on the bright side. At least it's direct deposit.

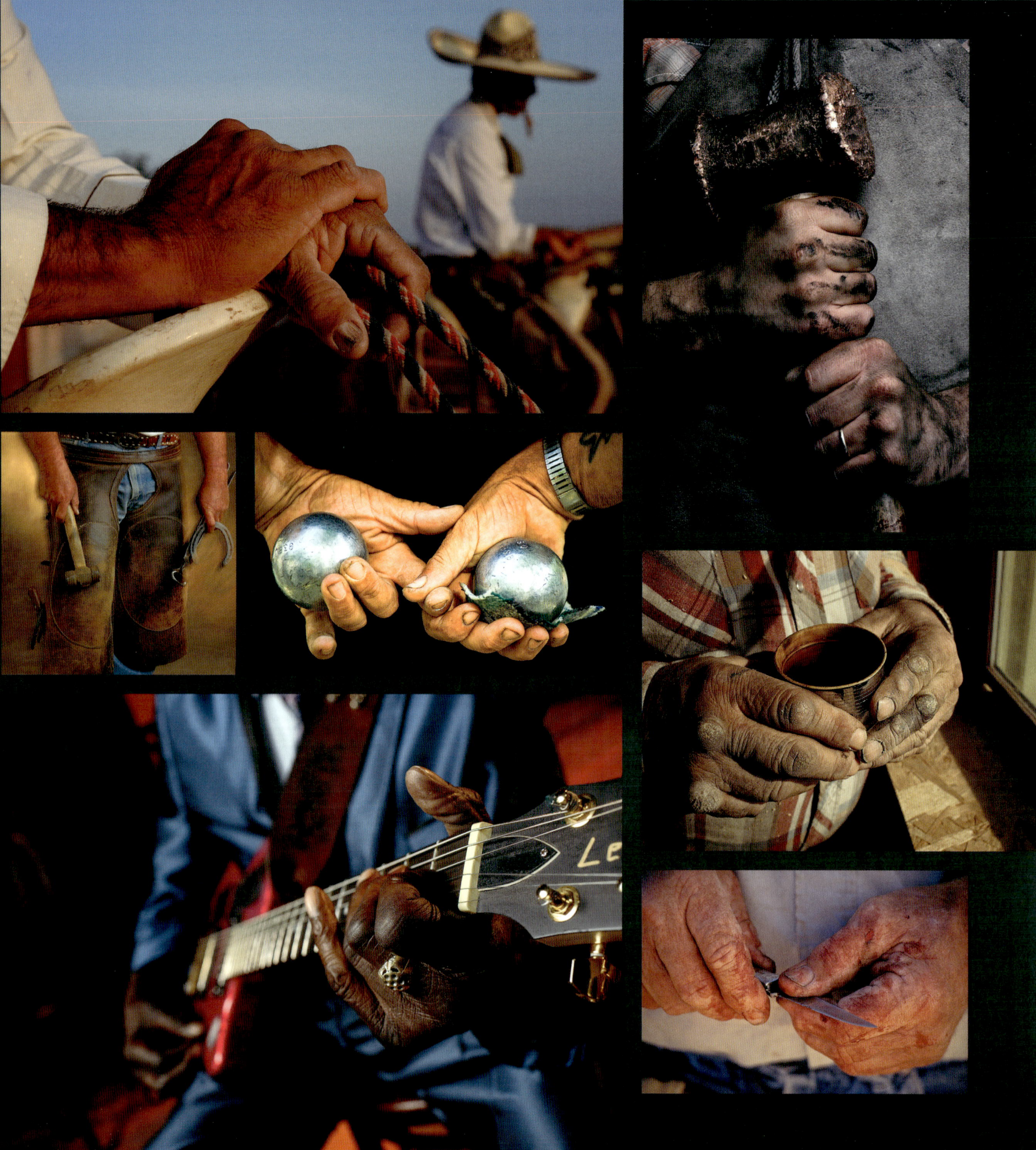

Remember the Hands

Famed *LIFE* photog John Loengard shot hands throughout his career. Later, as DOP, he would counsel assigned photographers to make sure hands were on the list of things to check out, and potentially, photograph.

I shot on assignment for John many times, and to this day, that advice has stuck with me like a good meal. I find hands fascinating. They're very revealing. They are often the roadmap to someone's life and to what they do, which is often inextricable from who they are. When conjoined with someone's tools of their trade—familiar things that are comfortable in their hands (because they work with them every day)—the impact can be powerful. Hands are possessed of language. They have history. They tell stories.

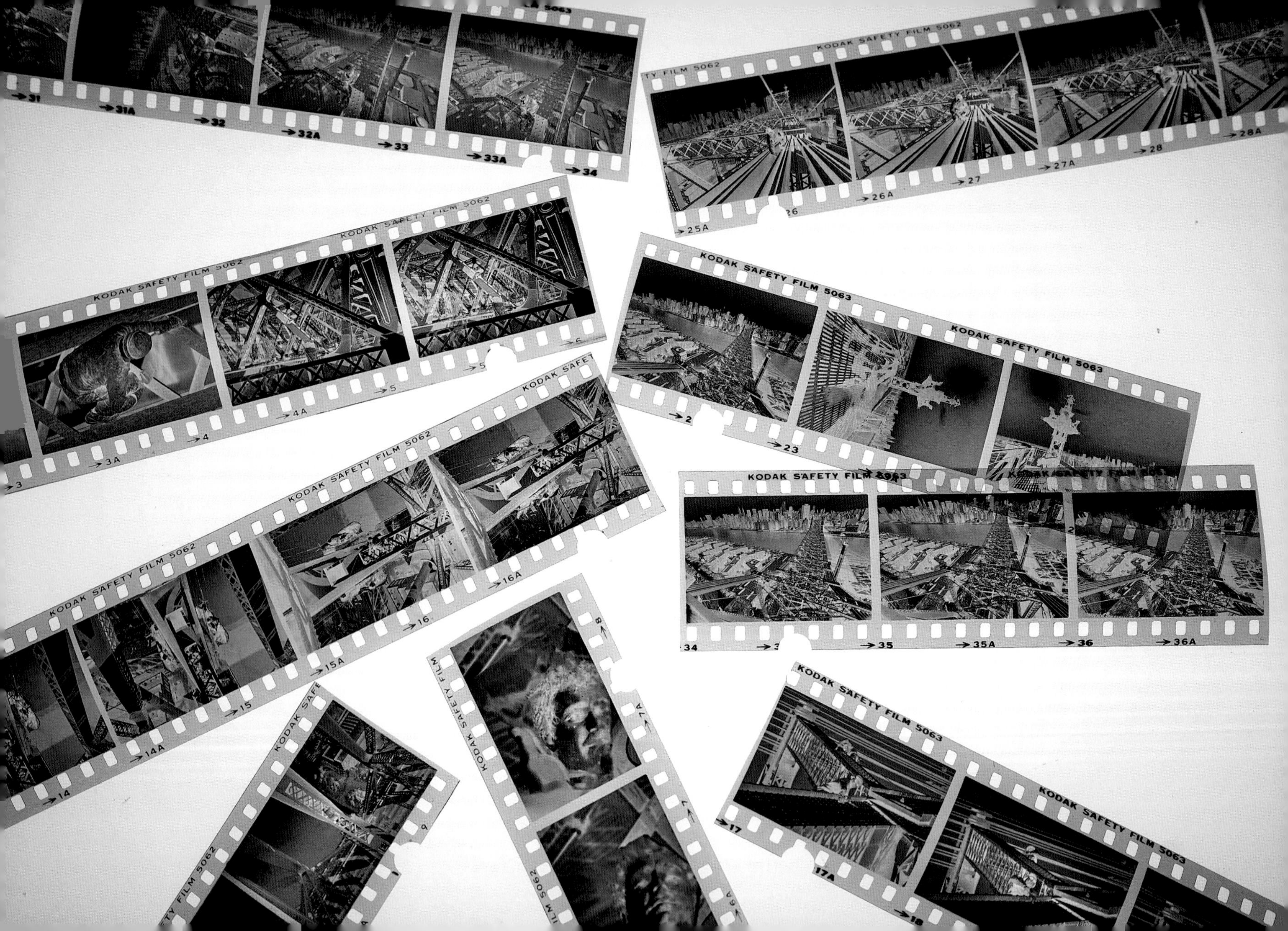

What's Easier Now, and What's Not

Assignment: The repainting of the Queensboro Bridge, 1977. The hole-punched negs are the five stars. Client: United Press International (UPI).

Editing, when shooting transparencies or negatives, historically meant selecting the best one. Punch it, print it.

Editing now has a whole different connotation. The editing process is way past mere selection and involves an entire Gaussian galaxy of sliders, colors, sharpeners, plug-ins, beezelbops, and whoop-de-do's. Editing is an industry unto its own, called post-production. It's what we do after we "browse." It's fast, and sleek.

On balance, this is a good thing. Click and move, drag and drop. Launch the photo into an editing program and tweak the observed reality into something resembling what the photographer had in "their mind's eye." Which is a catchphrase photographers tend to use when the picture they're displaying is a distant cousin, thrice removed, from the original frame.

Which is fine. A lot of photographers out there are doing formative, fascinating work, and for them, the click of the shutter button is just the start of the process, not the end of it. The simple click, or series of clicks, in the studio or in the field can initiate hours' or days' long efforts in the editing suite, assembling, montaging, colorizing, and turbocharging pixels collected from the world into another view or consciousness. It's cool.

And there are legions of other photographers, representing hugely divergent styles, observing, reporting, covering, and portraying the range of events of the natural world and the people therein, and they use post-production tools to seamlessly do the basic darkroom work that used to consume hours in a wet lab. Going from in-camera capture to computer to contrast, saturation, sharpening, tagging, keywording, and launching into the Internet biosphere is a matter of minutes, sometimes even less. The iPhone snap made in Tucson that gets run through a smartphone editing app and posted to an Instagram account where it's viewed by someone in Mumbai happens in a matter of seconds. No time in this digital age for a leisurely stop at the Dektol watering hole and the print drying rack.

Needless to say, none of the above involves a hole puncher. Or an Agfa loupe. Or an irascible, cigar-chomping, pissed-off wire service editor who is apparently offended by your very existence.

Again—for the most part, this is a good thing. The infinitely excellent partnership of the camera and the computer has enhanced the abilities of photographers everywhere to do what they do and create what they always wished for. It's allowed the photog to be their own army of one. The sky's the limit now in the imaging world, and the lone photographer can craft their own Internet-based pipeline to their audience, regardless of their stature or geography. No longer do we stuff film canisters into a large envelope and wait for a motorcycle messenger, then check in with the office hours later to see how it all went and what measure of our humble efforts was deemed worthy of use.

Neither do we have to court, beg, cajole, or otherwise induce a publication, agency, or art director to run our stuff, use our story, consider our pictures. We can create our own world of coverage, our own sphere of visual influence, and speak directly to a tribe, independently of the publication world, which is now vastly reduced in power, and diffuse and tentative in its outreach. Back in the days when magazines, awash in money, wielded vast authority and control, I would shuffle humbly into the Time-Life Building on Sixth Avenue in NYC, clutching my slide pages, clad in comparative rags, as a young photographer. It had the trappings of a penitent pilgrimage, minus the self-flagellation. Do not look the great editor in the eye! Step aside and mumble thanks as they briskly walk to the elevators and thence to their regular table at Elaine's. Now Time Inc. doesn't even exist. Photographers, in this brave (relatively) new digital world, mostly make their own future.

And we have magnificent tools to do so. Shooting, exposing, editing, and publishing are all "easy."

What's not easy—actually, it's damn near impossible these days—is climbing the bridge.

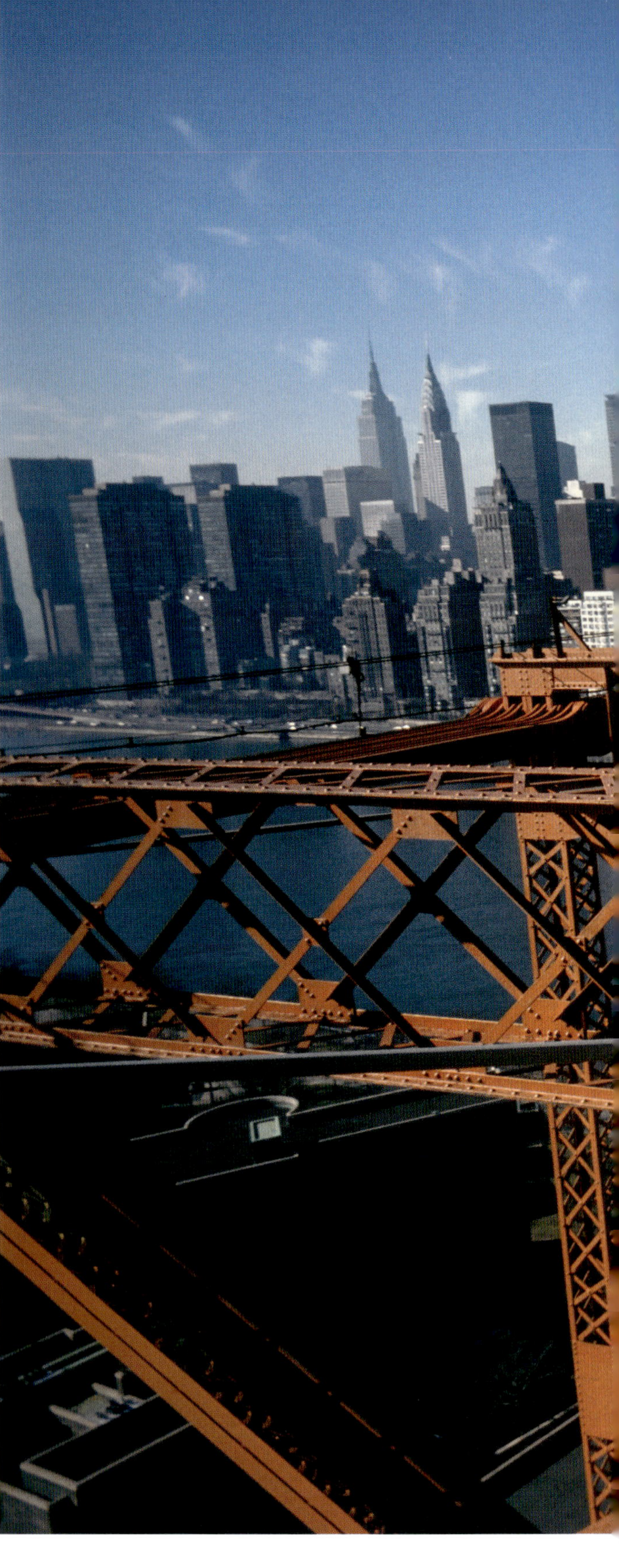

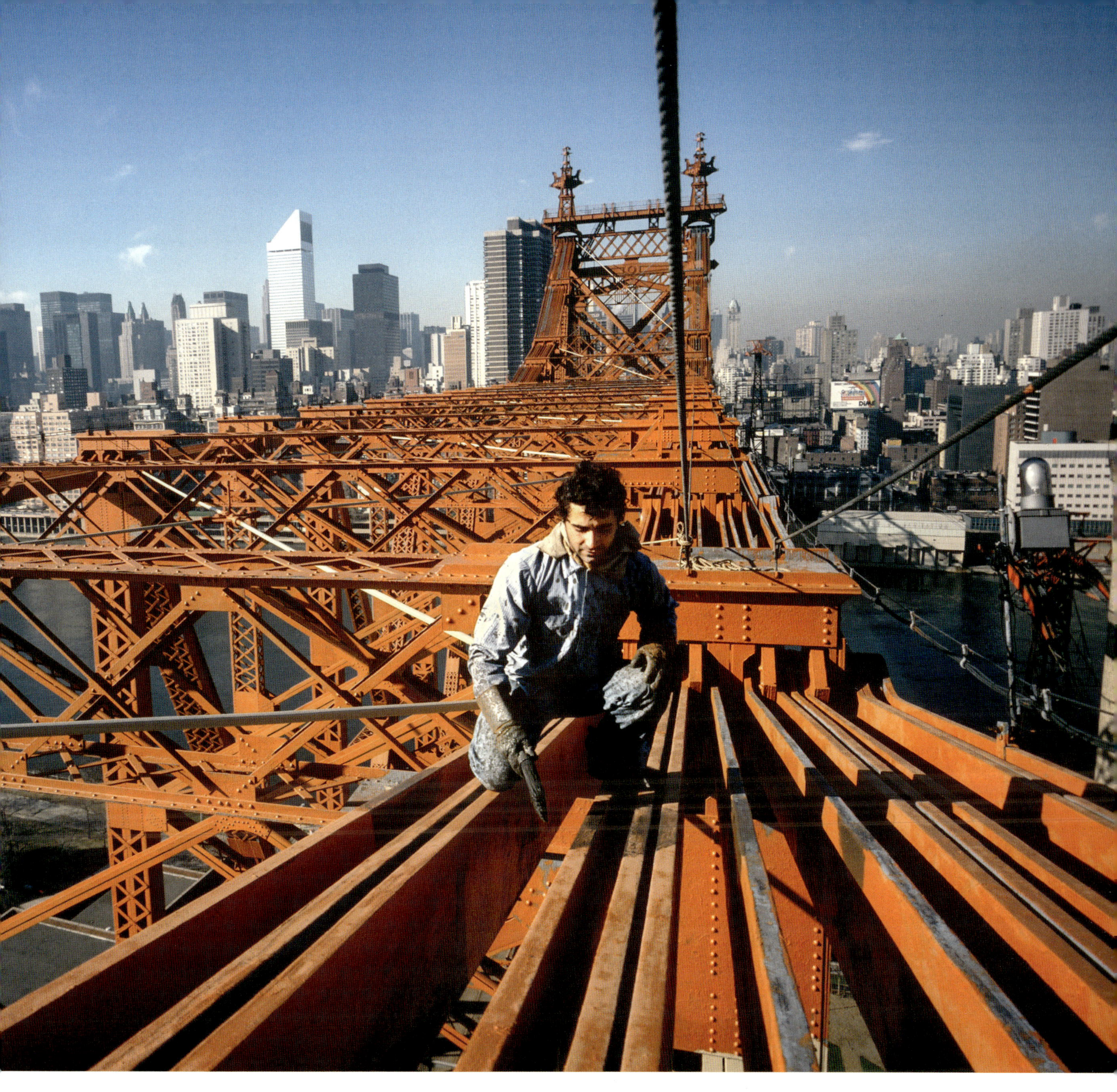

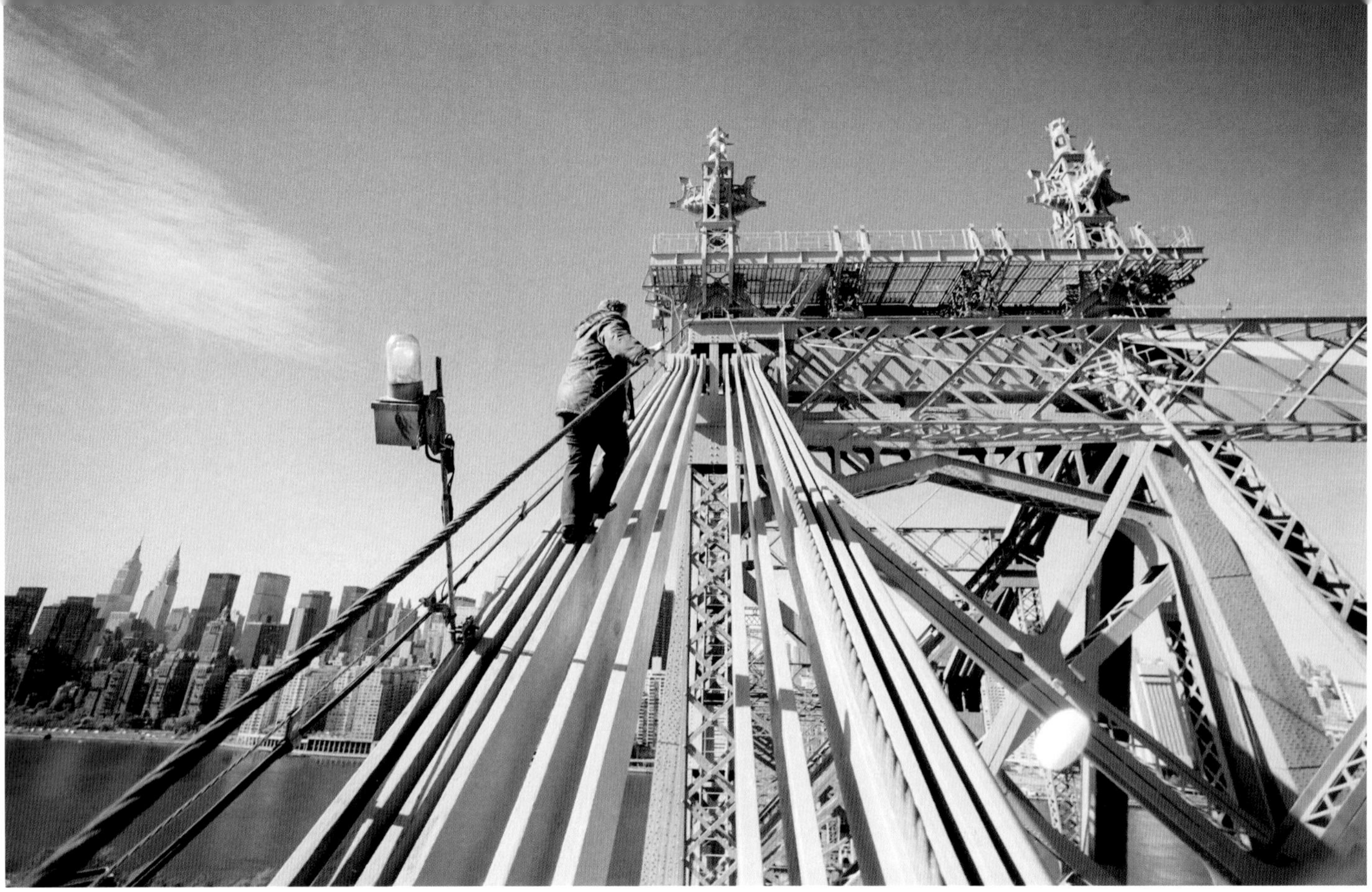

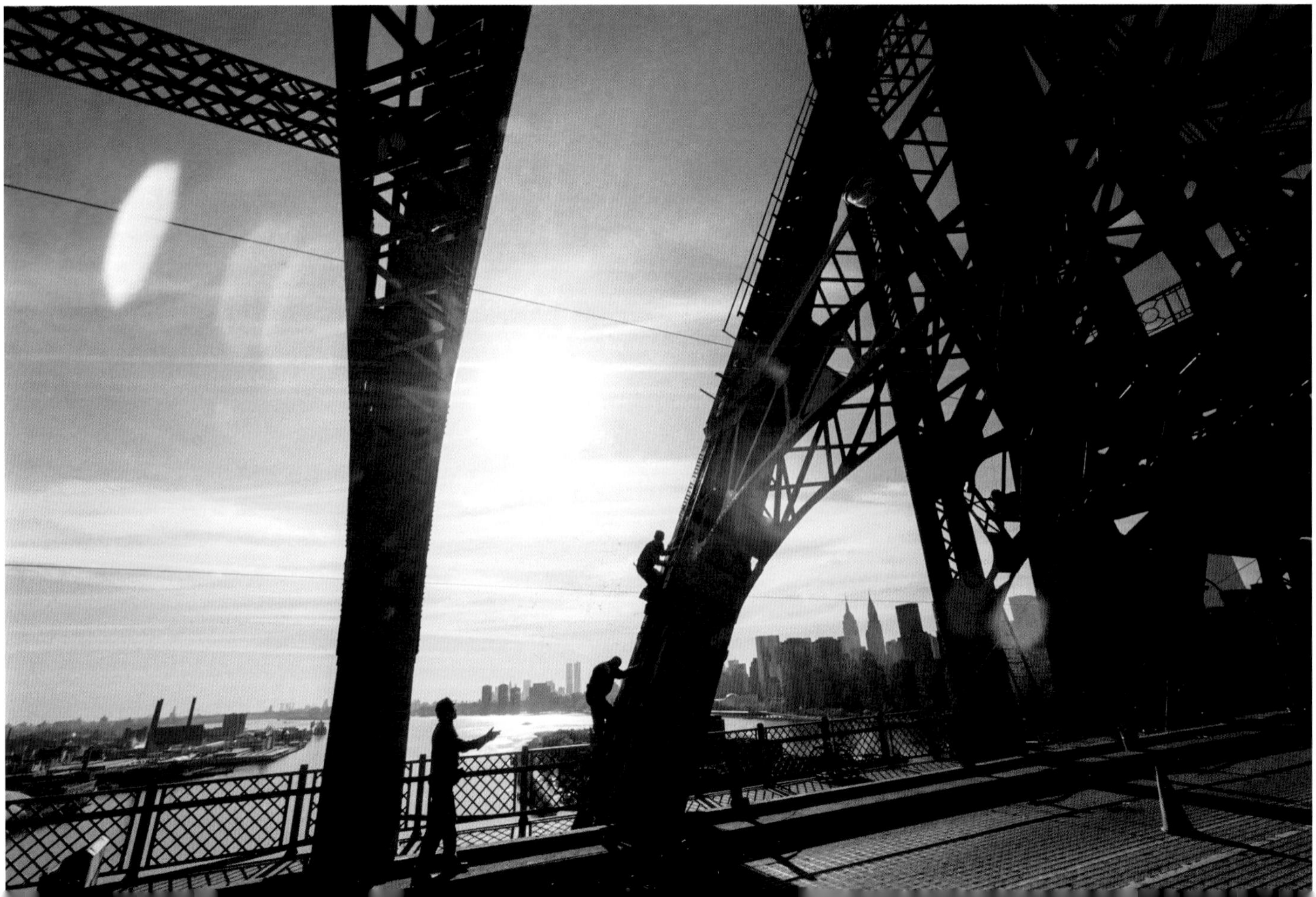

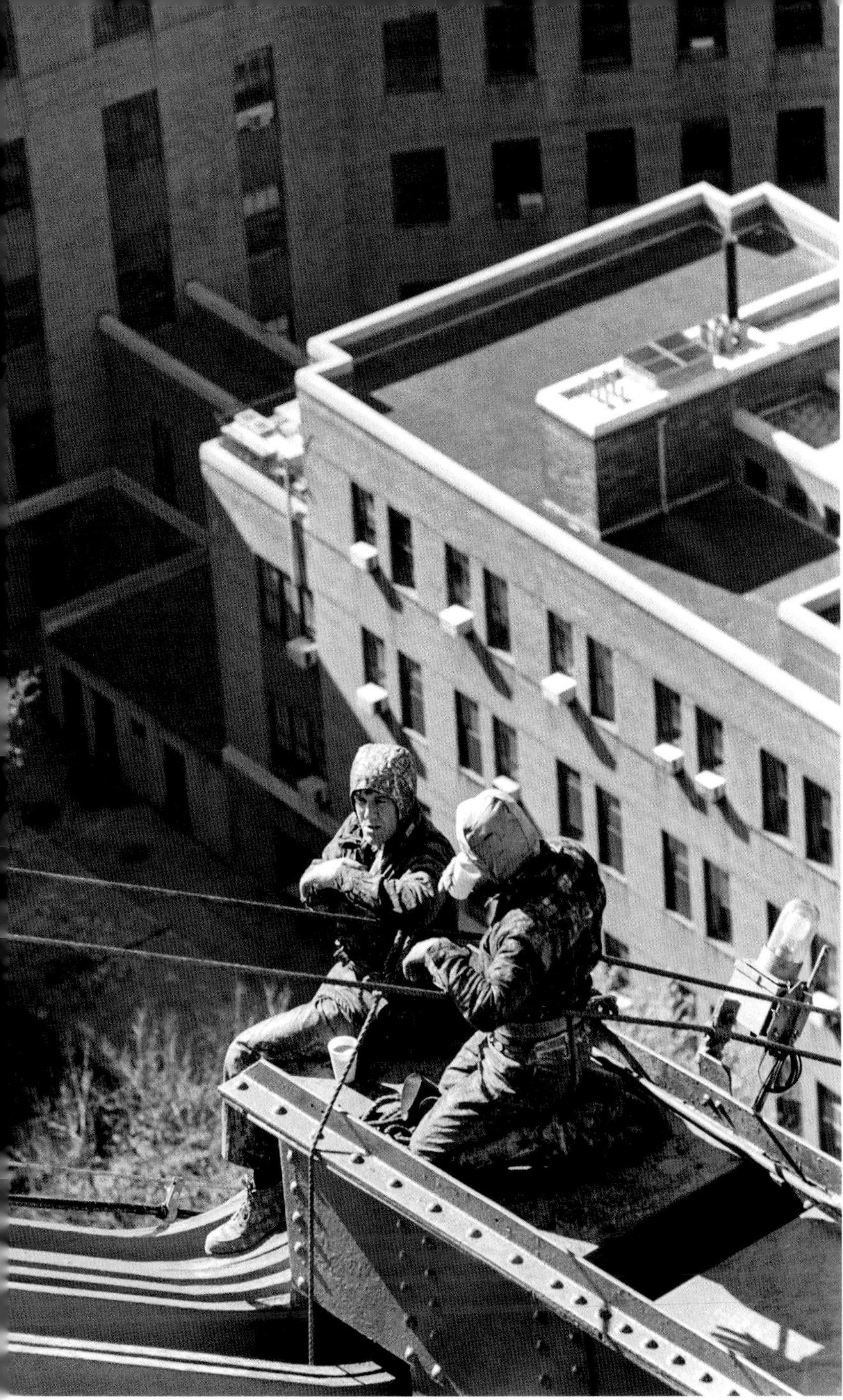

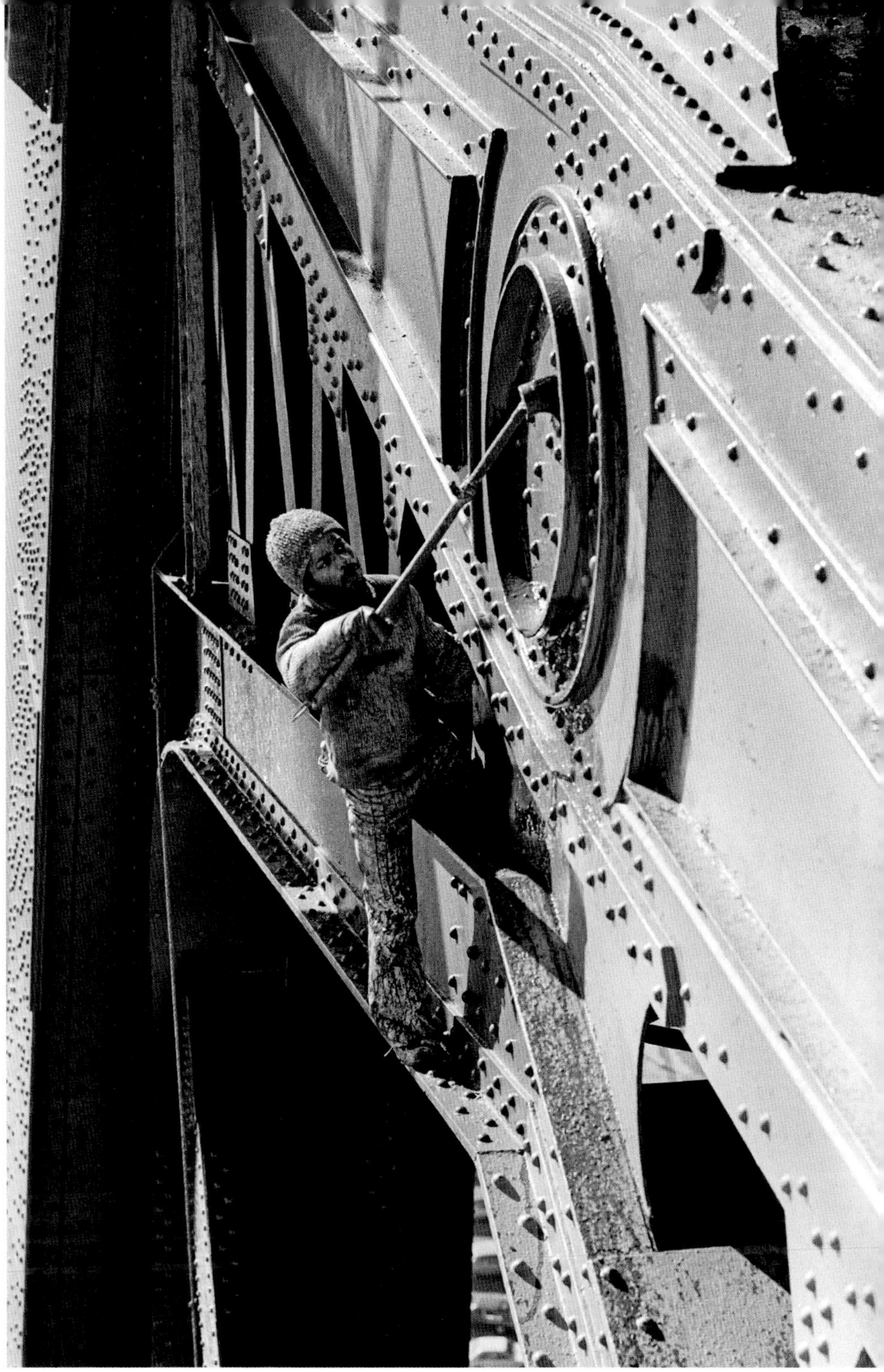

Sheer, cussed competitiveness drove me up the Queensboro Bridge on that day, many years ago. I knew they were painting the bridge, and there was a photographer in New York at that time who was doing a lot of high building work. I was determined not to allow him to own the sky. I was still a studio apprentice at the New York *Daily News*. A true nobody. My life's work at that moment was processing other photographers' film and doing their captions. The only thing notable about me was a near keening interior desperation to shoot some pictures somebody might notice. Which, of course, was yet another aspect of my life that nobody gave a shit about.

On my day off, a beautiful fall day, I shouldered my Domke bag and walked up on the bridge. I met the foreman, shook his hand, and told him I was with the *Daily News*. Truth. And that I had an assignment that had been worked out to climb the bridge and shoot a story about the painters. Lie. He shrugged and called one of his older guys over. "This guy's with the *News*. Take him up."

We started climbing. No safety belts. I climbed outside of the cables on the steel, wet and slick with new paint. Two steps up, one slide back. Orange paint all over me. No gloves. No safety helmet. Wouldn't have mattered; next stop, the East River. My guy was complaining. "Wish they had given us some notice you were coming!"

Nobody called, sir, 'cause nobody knew.

I spent the day up there, sliding around the paint surfaces, climbing steel, hanging out, shooting B&W and color. UPI ran the story, a sequence of six pictures or so out on the wire. The punch holes you see in my negs in the lead pic of this story were made by the legendary Larry DeSantis, UPI picture chief, who I loved, in the way a Marine recruit loves and respects the Drill Instructor who kicks his ass every day, trying to teach him lessons that might save his life later on.

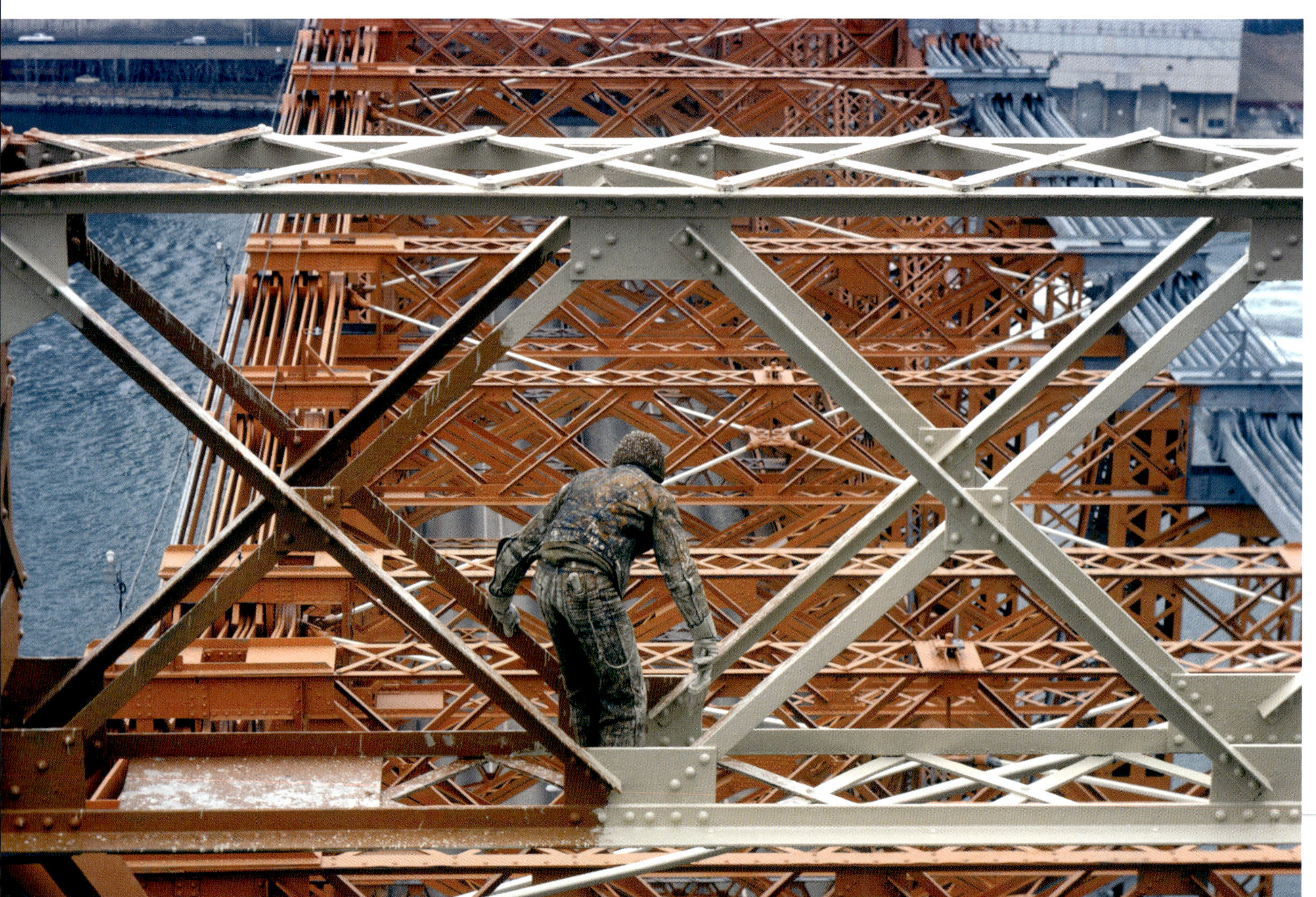

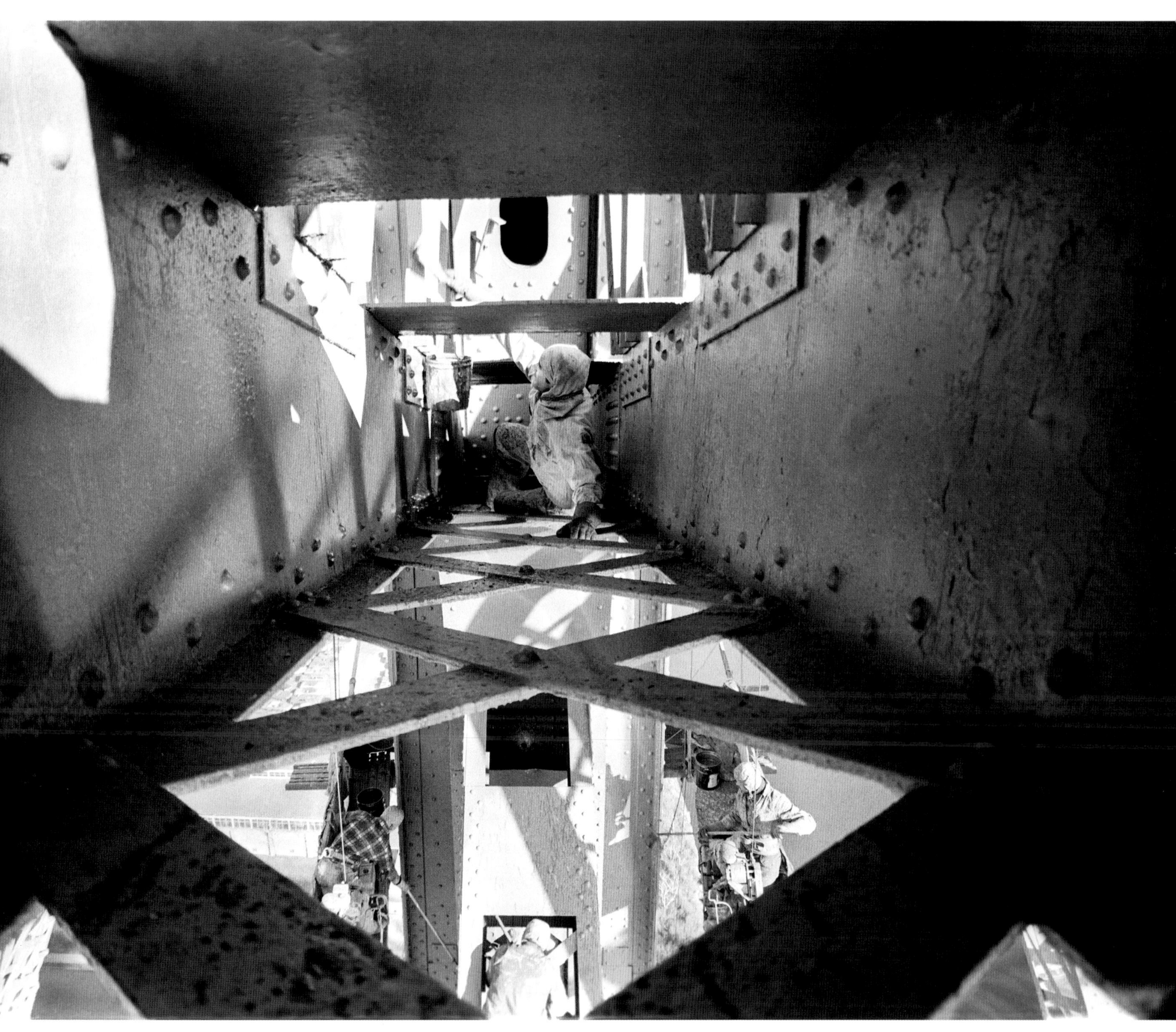

It was 1977. I just walked up the bridge, said hi, produced no identification, documents, or proof of anything, and climbed that friggin' bridge. Try that now.

It was, as they say, a different time.

Now, the reams of paperwork, the insurance, the city officials needed to engage and sign off, the restrictions on the usage of the images afterwards, the filing of requests with the myriad agencies and governing bodies who undoubtedly have overlapping jurisdictions over the bridge—it would be an impenetrable jungle from which you might never return. The bridge connects the boroughs of Manhattan and Queens, so you would most likely be dealing with duplicate or competing sets of rule makers, shot blockers, and bureaucrats who live to crush art and dreams. Representation from a publication would, in this instance, in fact be helpful. The *National Geographic* magazine still reaches more people than your average photographer's blog. (Last time I checked, anyway.) But even that magazine would approach this as a supplicant. They no longer rule.

In fact, the chances of climbing a structure like this are pretty much nil nowadays. The best you can likely do is shoot it from a distance, at sunrise or sunset, maybe with a long lens, from a sidewalk on a street with a good angle on the bridge.

From there, it's easy, as has been noted. You can transfer the files, dupe them, sort them, make selects, and assign star ratings. You can tweak the colors and saturate the sky and make it into a popular Instagram or Facebook banner for your page. Then sit back and watch the likes roll in.

All that you can do with ease. No hole punch, no editor, no darkroom required. From your desktop to the world.

What you can't do is climb the bridge.

Oh, about that picture of the bridge you might make from the sidewalk vantage point with a long lens: If you want to put down a tripod, technically you need to apply for a permit.

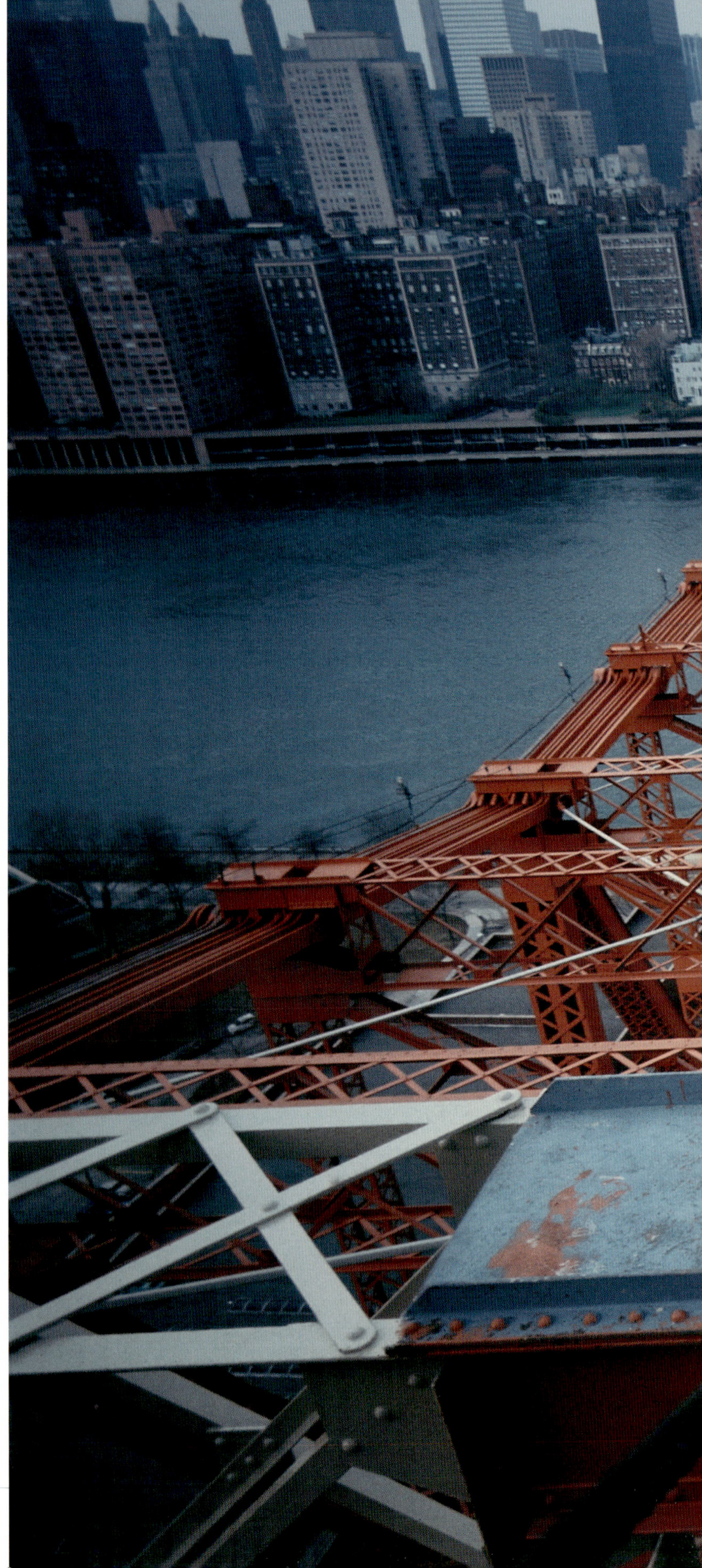

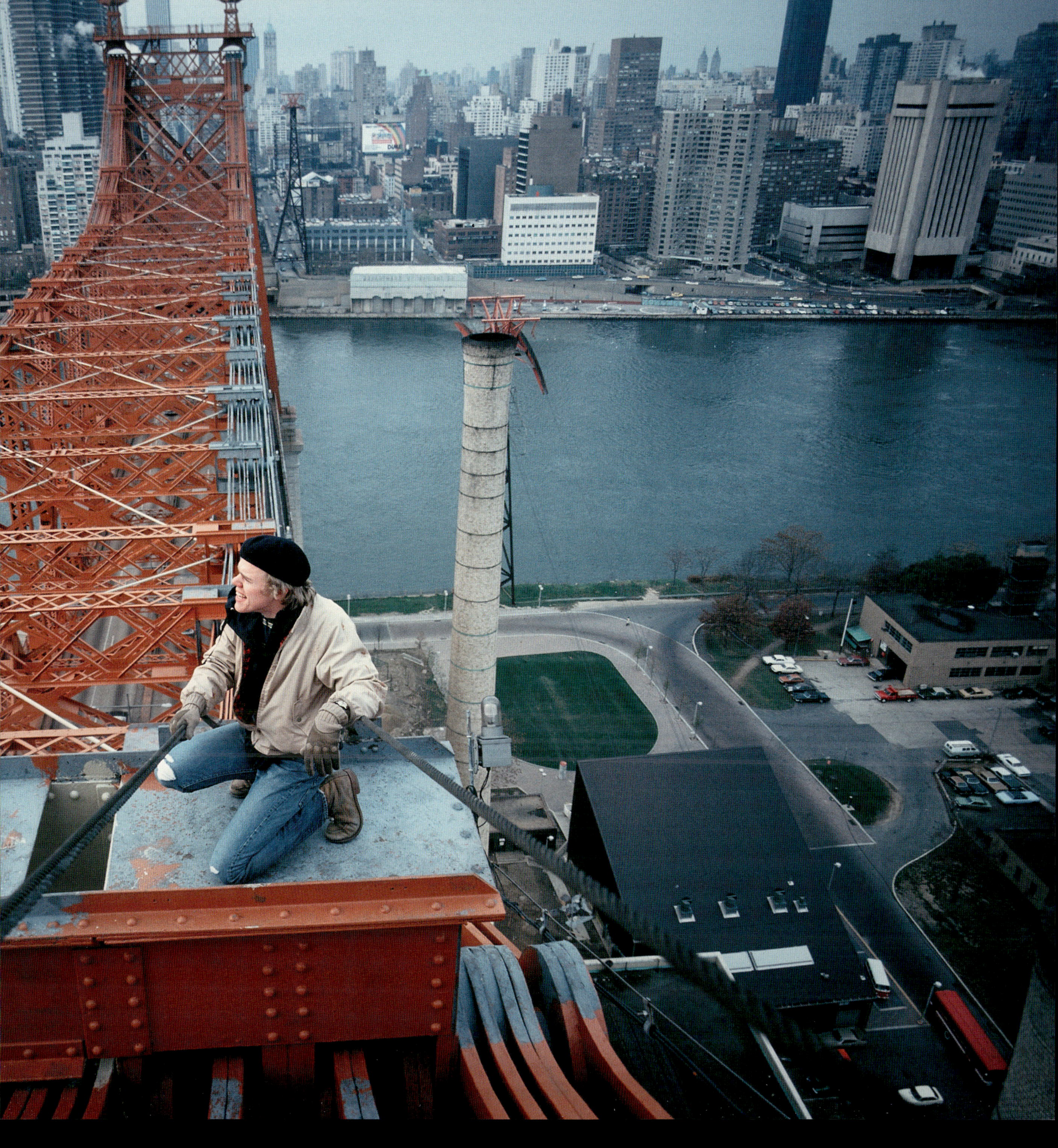

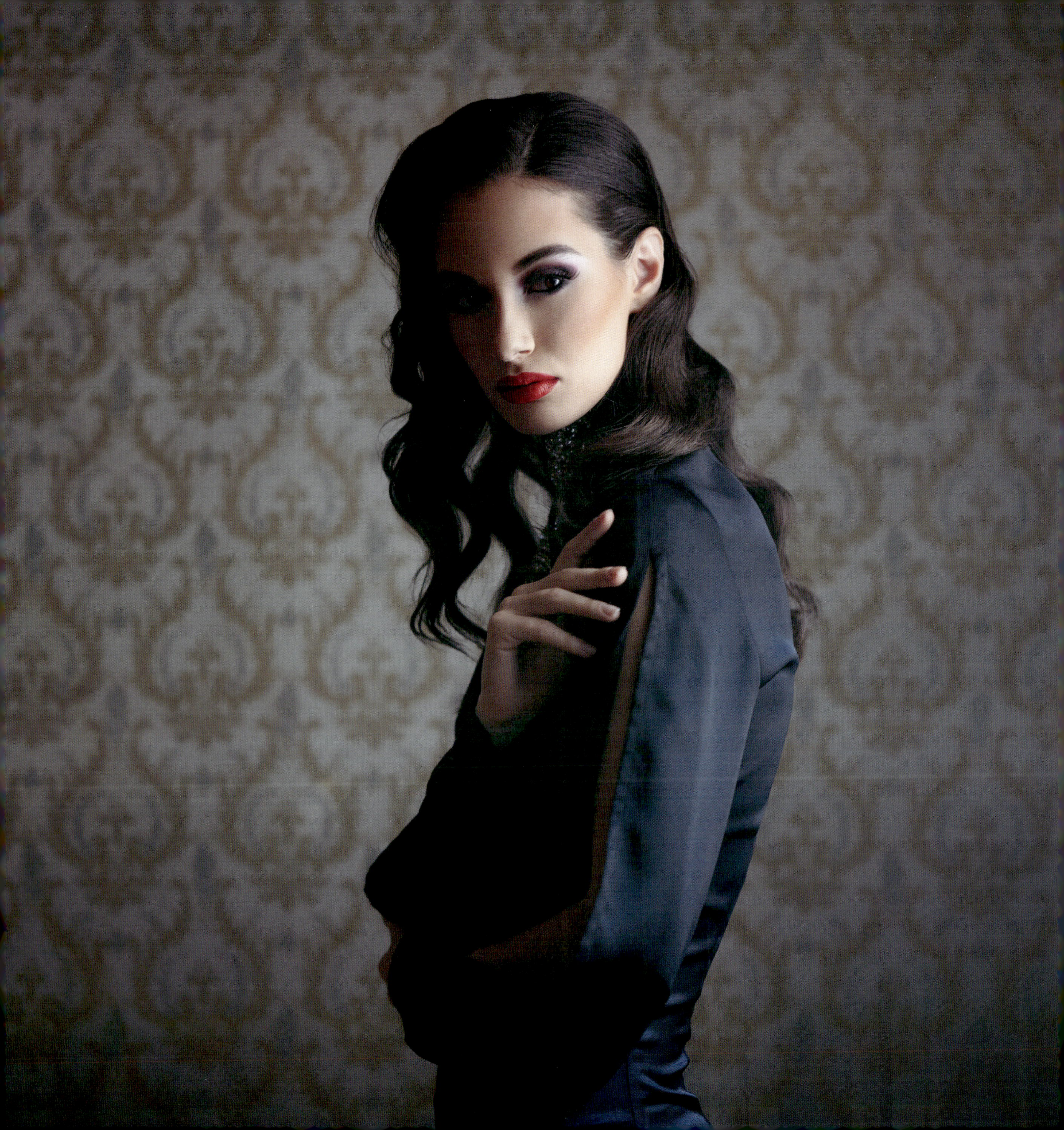

Work the Window!

Granted, the window here is a big, big window.

But it does what all windows do, hopefully—give light. And also hope to the photographer. Window light can't be generally lumped into one class or type. The sun will do what it does, and windows react accordingly. But there is something about being in a place, especially a place with charisma and character, where the window transforms the light into a fairy tale, warbling it, cropping it, or shaping it so it bounces off a floor or a wall. Outside, in naked, harsh sunlight, you point your lens at a sun-blasted scene and the light that enters the lens fries the coatings on the elements and becomes a death ray for your pixels. But go inside in those same conditions, and those harsh beams can bounce, ramble, and skitter up the walls, off the ceiling, and fly around in the most interesting of angles and ways. The shape of a window corrals wild sunlight into patterns that can be put to use.

It also does what your softbox can't. It changes, almost minute to minute. Clouds will fly by. The angle of approach will rotate, as its celestial source moves across the sky. It will perhaps hit uneven drapery, which curates the beams in a strange and compelling way. If there is a part in those drapes, it screams through there like a horde of orcs, slicing harsh patterns across whatever it hits. Dust and dirt clinging to the surfaces of the panes can render tints and colors with shades of subtlety, or intensity. Variable, in other words. Infinitely interesting. Unpredictable nuance. Window light puts an umbrella and all of its lovely, boring dependability to shame.

Look at the windows. Then look at them again during your stay on location. The sun keeps moving, so that kitchen window that was once dull and lifeless is, in a few hours, as sprightly as a cheerleading squad. It can be flat-out lovely, as in, put the portrait subject in there right friggin' now, or it can present a beautiful opportunity once it is tweaked and tamed. I spent about an hour and a half, according to my picture metadata, working this huge window with ancient draping. Sometimes I shaped it, other times I let it be.

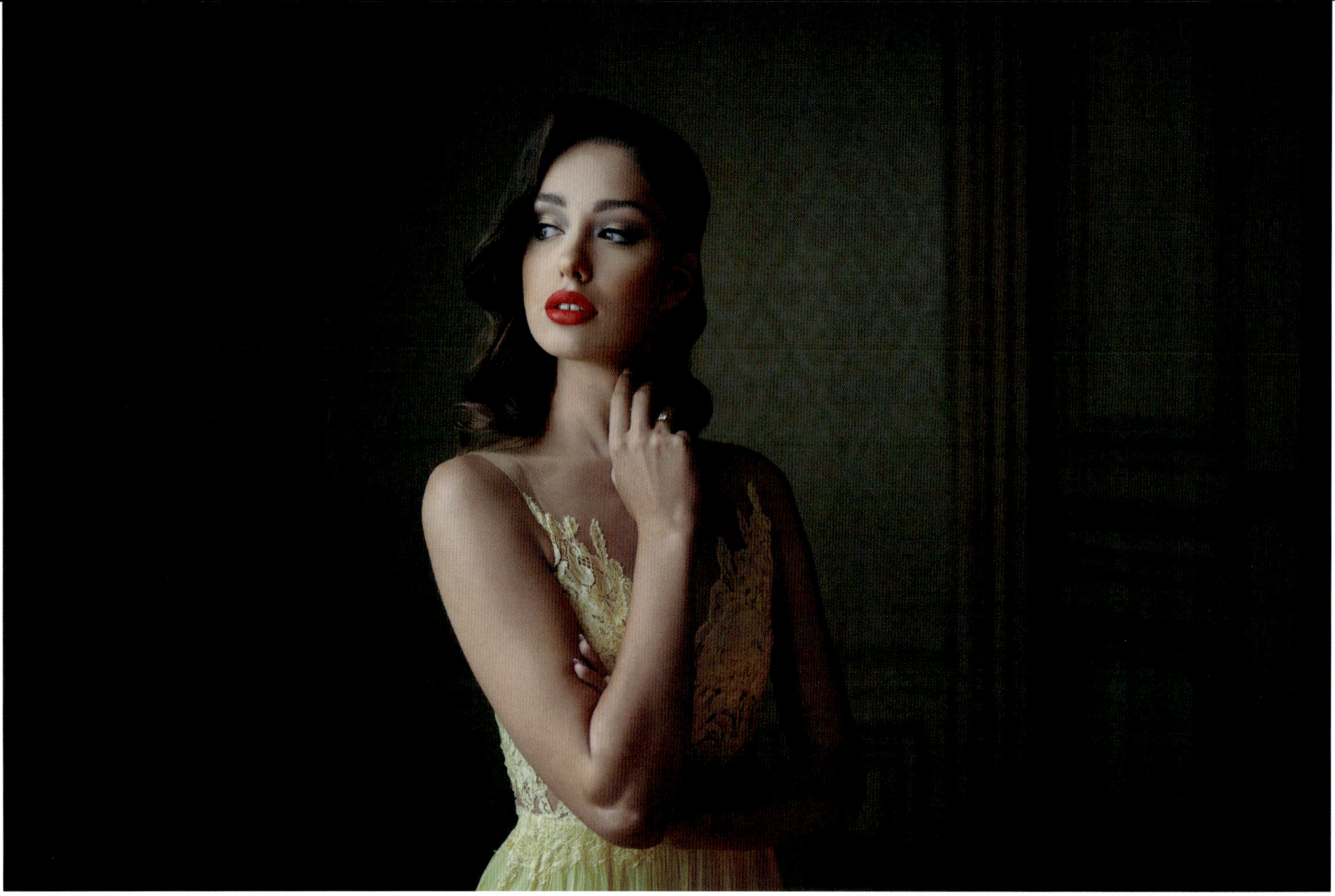

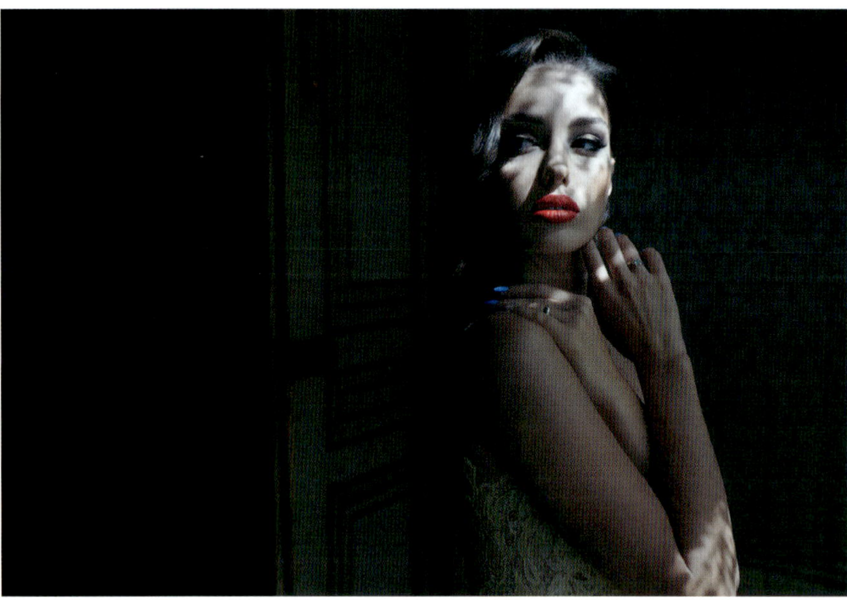

First frames. The select here was shot at 10:10 a.m. (above). The subject is placed in shadow, where she is safe from the screaming hardness of the light but is glowing in the bounce of light off the floor. And the bounce of light off a fill board, just lightly played. She throws an appropriately pensive look at the camera. The lens is a 35mm at f/1.8, and I am shooting a mirrorless camera, the Nikon Z 7. The background fades in rich fashion.

At 10:19 I shot this (left). Placing her directly in the raw sun, with its attendant hard, lacy shadows, was worth a try. But exposing for the highlight here forsakes the shadows, which tumble rapidly toward black. The way to combat this is of course to light the background, i.e., the room. Which had 30-foot ceilings of hand-carved wood. The walls offered nothing in the way of bounce possibilities.

Which would have meant dragging out a softbox, or umbrella, and perhaps even a multiplicity of lights to pump some context into the chamber, and perhaps cast a rim light that would give her more dimension. It might mean a strip with a fabric grid for her hair and shoulders. And then up high, camera left, a soft, biggish umbrella. Which of course might scatter light every-where, requiring another stand bearing a large flag or cutter to shape it. Heavy lifting. Gotta get the crew involved. Lunch break is looming. The other model is almost ready to come out of hair and makeup. Spend the time? Labor over this situation, when other, fruitier possibilities will apparently be effortless?

One could argue that the swaddling darkness in the frame emphasizes the black widow aspects of the look, making her appear beautifully dangerous. At least that's the rationale I would offer to a picture editor peering at me over his or her glasses, wondering why this frame was in the selects. But envi-ronment is important information, and some measure of addi-tional lighting as I have detailed would be needed here to make this incomplete photo something approaching a whole cloth. I looked at the LCD at my early returns, shot less than 70 frames, and moved on.

One of the most powerful tools in the photographer's kit bag is the ability to quickly discern when you are shooting useless shit.

I shot this next select at 10:45 (top right). She is roughly in the same place as the first soft, shaded picture, but now I am pulled back, shooting with a 14–30mm lens. Here the window is a huge player in the frame, glowing in planetary fashion, streaming powerfully right at my camera position. Without assistance in the realm of exposure, she will be lost. If I light her with flash, as I have been known to do, it will be noticed and out of place in the midst of the beams of natural light cascading through the curtains. They take those beamy shapes because of a deli-cate haze of smoke that I have sent drifting through the frame. (It has to be delicate, almost invisible to the eye, or your sub-ject will appear soft as smoke engulfs your lens and snuffs its contrast—and, possibly, your autofocus. Be careful! When the set is hazed, thread the needle with an AF cursor right to your subject's eyes.)

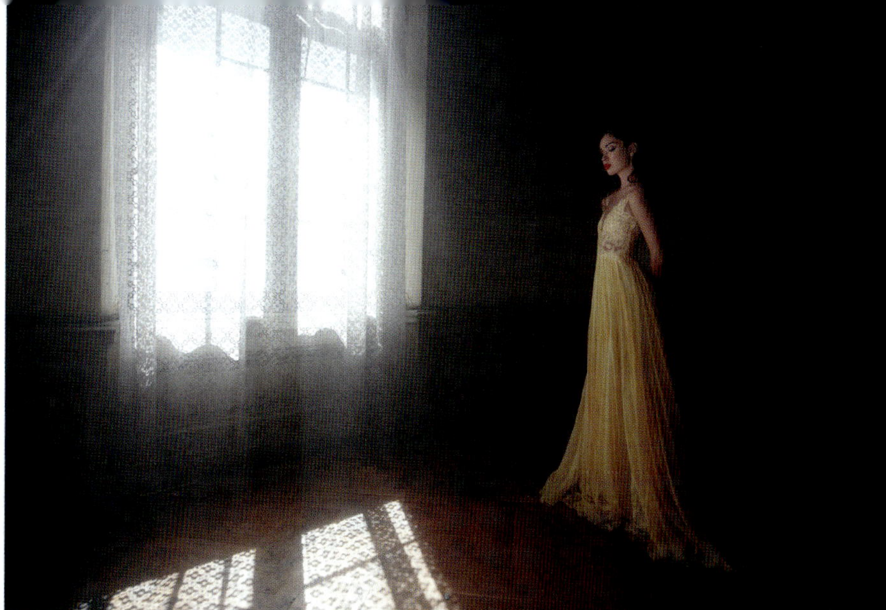

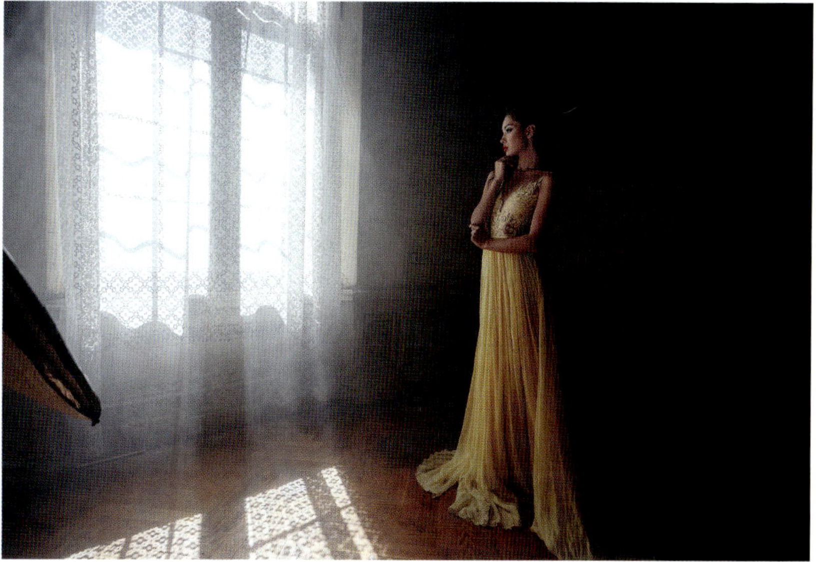

An addition of light here is necessary, as your subject is really a bystander as the light screams past her. But it has to be done with a feather, not a sledgehammer. Best to go with the flow of the purely natural, grass-fed, hormone-free light pouring in the window and try to delicately push it to your advantage. It needs a nudge, not an all-out strobe-based counterattack. Which is what I did, as you can see here (above, bottom). My assistant is holding one of my ever-faithful TriGrips just off camera left. Well, at least most of the time it was off camera. With a 14–30mm lens, operating at the wide end of things, stuff will creep in the edges that you have to be continually aware of, as, at times, I am classically not.

What you are seeing there in the frame represents the only "applied" light in the photo. Catch the window light and play it back gently on your subject. Move it around. Find the sweet spot. Vary it. Shoot whilst varying. If you are working alone, plant the model, and grab a stand and a flexible clamp and arm arrangement to get the reflective surface of the board right where you want, then shoot like mad, because the sun moves infernally fast, and the clouds can conspire against you.

A note. Working alone as I describe, tripod use looms as important. You set the shot, set the model, render your lines straight as you can, spike the tripod, and that becomes your reference point, or at the very least, your starting point. It's tough to run over to adjust a reflecting board or light, and then race back and grab your camera up off the floor. Hand-held, you have to, again, find your spot, re-zoom the lens, level your lines, check the edges of the frame, and calm your scattered brain. You need a tranquil, discerning eye in the camera, and the tripod is a soothing balm for your picture frenzy. Think of it as a deep, luxuriant toke of nice, mellow weed. Whoah, cool! The camera's in, like, the same place I left it. I don't even have to pick it up! Rad. Tripod. Cool. Let's shoot.

Then flip it. Pull a 180 with the camera and look back the other way. This is partially forced by the movement of the sun, with its concomitant highlight patterns, which are now heading toward the wall I've had at my back, and that angle of working is getting tinier by the minute. My assistant holding the bounce, Cali, is a pretty big guy, and can make himself only so small. So, take a breath and move. I say to take a breath advisedly, and that is really what I do. I exhaust the locale, and I kind of exhaust myself. I wring that towel dry, squeezing what I can out of it. If the number of images you crank out for a situation is any sort of applause meter, I must have seriously enjoyed these two angles. Between the 35mm lens view and the 14–30mm wide view, I shot roughly 800 frames.

Excessive? Sure. Ill-advised? Possibly, but then, not really. Here's my thinking, and this actively transports through my head quite regularly on location: I will never be here again, in this room, with this light, with this subject, ever. This is a one-time intersection. I do myself and my client wrong if I don't tear at this like a hyena ripping up an impala carcass.

Here is the flipped, 180-degree opposite view (right). I shot this picture at 11:20.

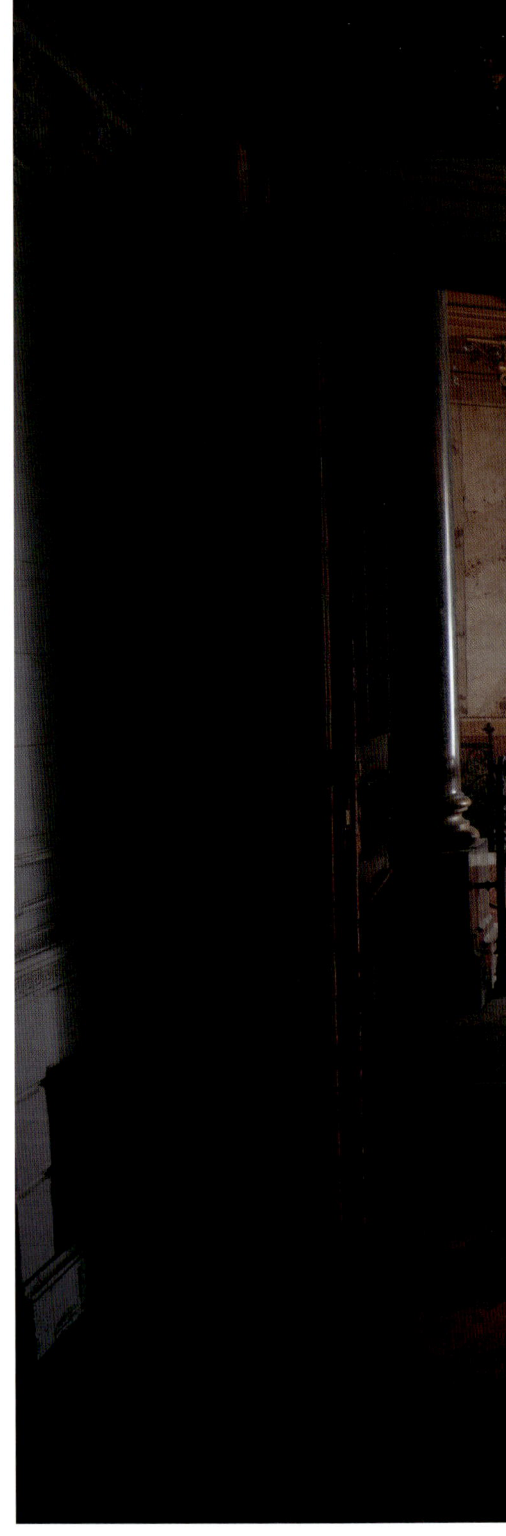

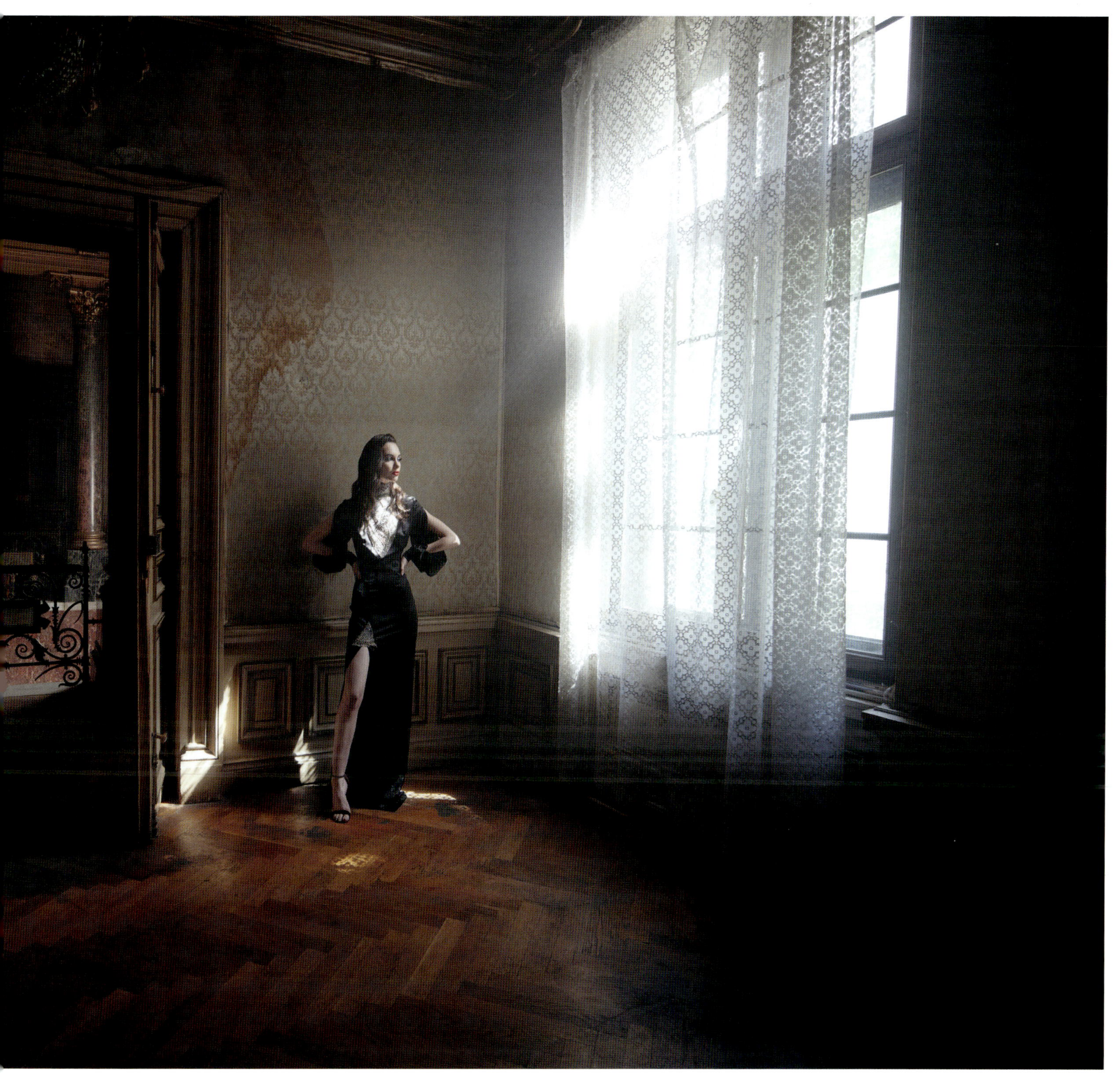

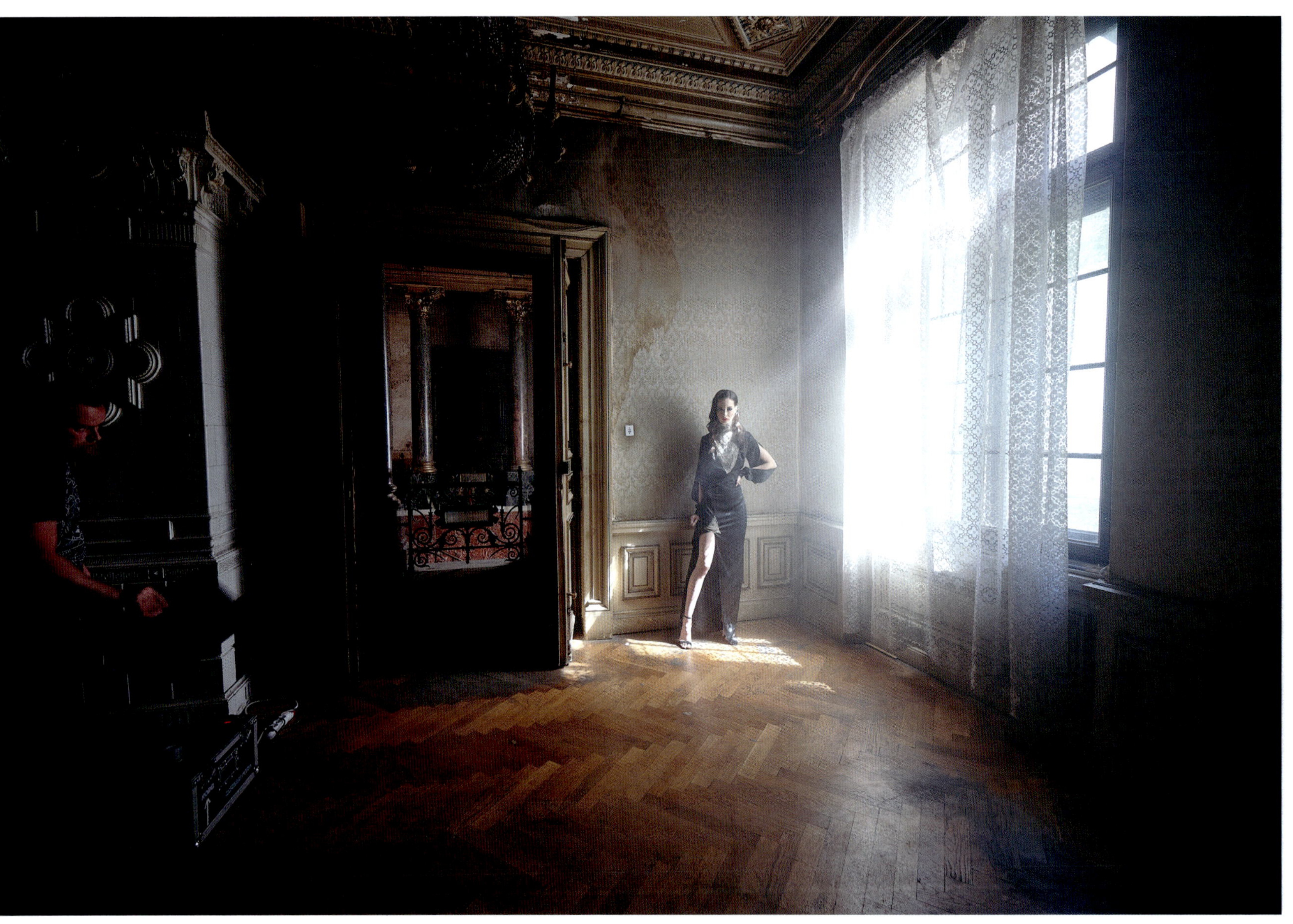

And here is what can happen when you load in too much smoke (above). It becomes its own light source, hanging like a bright lantern in the frame. Let the vapor settle down and dissipate. Rack through some bracketed exposures. See where the fine line is that exposes the scene and model well, but also holds some detail in the window. It's a bit of an eye-of-the-needle thing, because, effectively, you've got your light source in the photo. The blinking highlights feature available in most digital cameras can help here. If there are small, crackling bleached spots, no worries. But if that window area is a big, blaring, seizure-inducing blowout, you got a problem. And of course, if the camera remains static, you could shoot some plates of various exposures and then drop one in later via post-processing. Then go to confession.

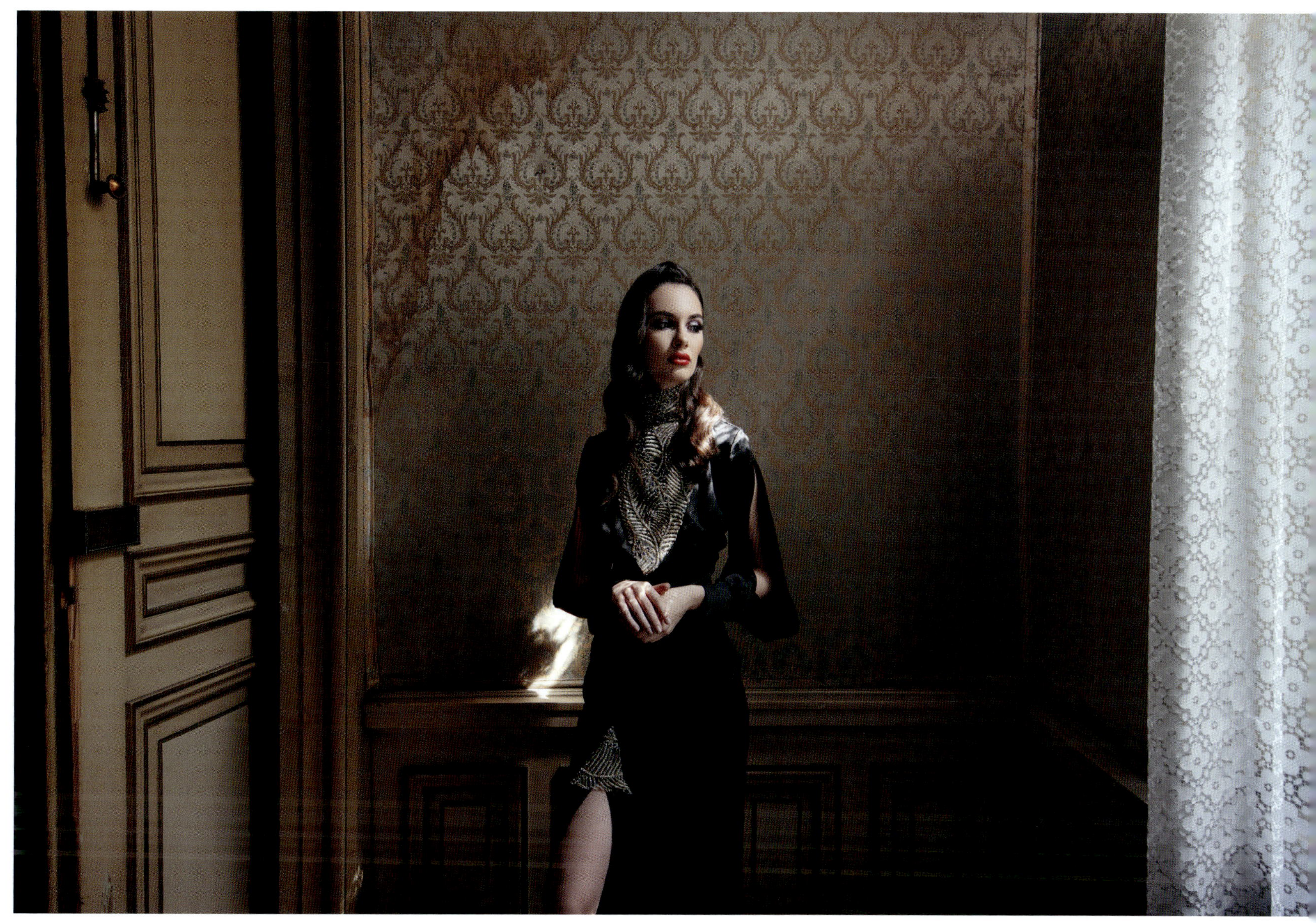

(Joshing you here, dear reader. On a commercial fashion shoot such as this, all bets are off. Do what you need to do for the revenue source, i.e., the client. They are not looking for the pure of spirit. They are looking for somebody who will deliver.)

By 11:24 I was tighter, minimizing the window glow (above). The sun is still pretty nuclear out there, as you can see in the bright splash just behind her right elbow. But the grace of the curtain prevailed for the rest of the frame. The metadata on this pic says I was shooting a 21.5mm lens, which was obviously my zoom throw on the 24–70mm. I don't have a 21.5mm. Sheesh . . . the precision of the new digital mirrorless cameras is much appreciated but, in my case, more than I really need to know.

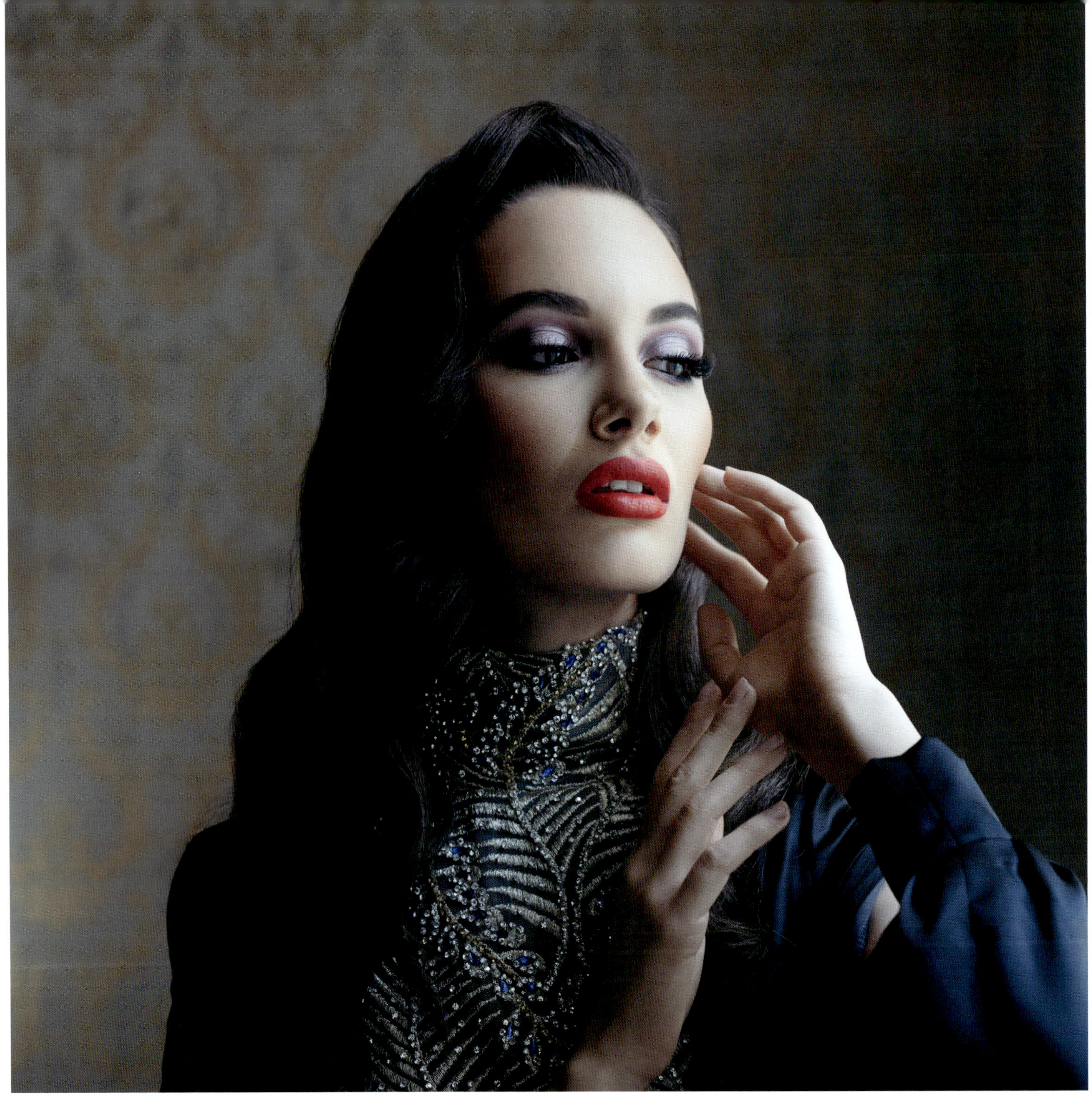

And by 11:34 I was here (above). The sun was changing the attitude of the scene, so I kept moving the model and switching up my lenses in response. This is an 85mm at f/2.8. Flick of the button to shoot in square format.

The only thing that didn't really change was the attitude of the model. She was dead bang beautiful but her go-to expression was somewhere between a bored sneer and outright menace. Which was fine. The camera gobbled it up. Her lovely, aloof

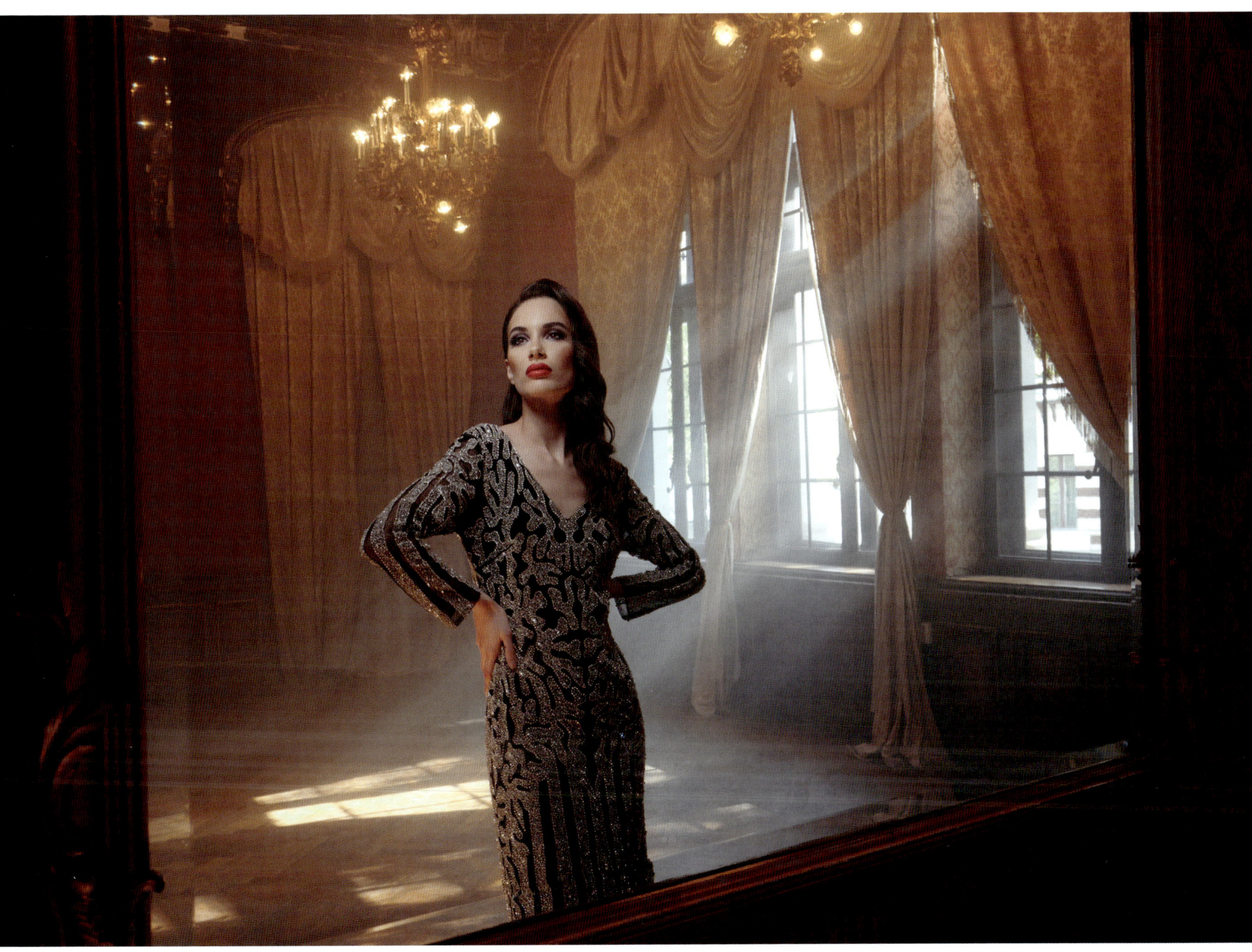

disdain, coupled with the elegant decrepitude of the mansion, really lent itself to kind of a David Bowie, Catherine Deneuve in "The Hunger" type of vibe. Scary, but cool.

Later on, I photographed her reflected in a mirror (above), just to be sure. We were, after all, in Romania.

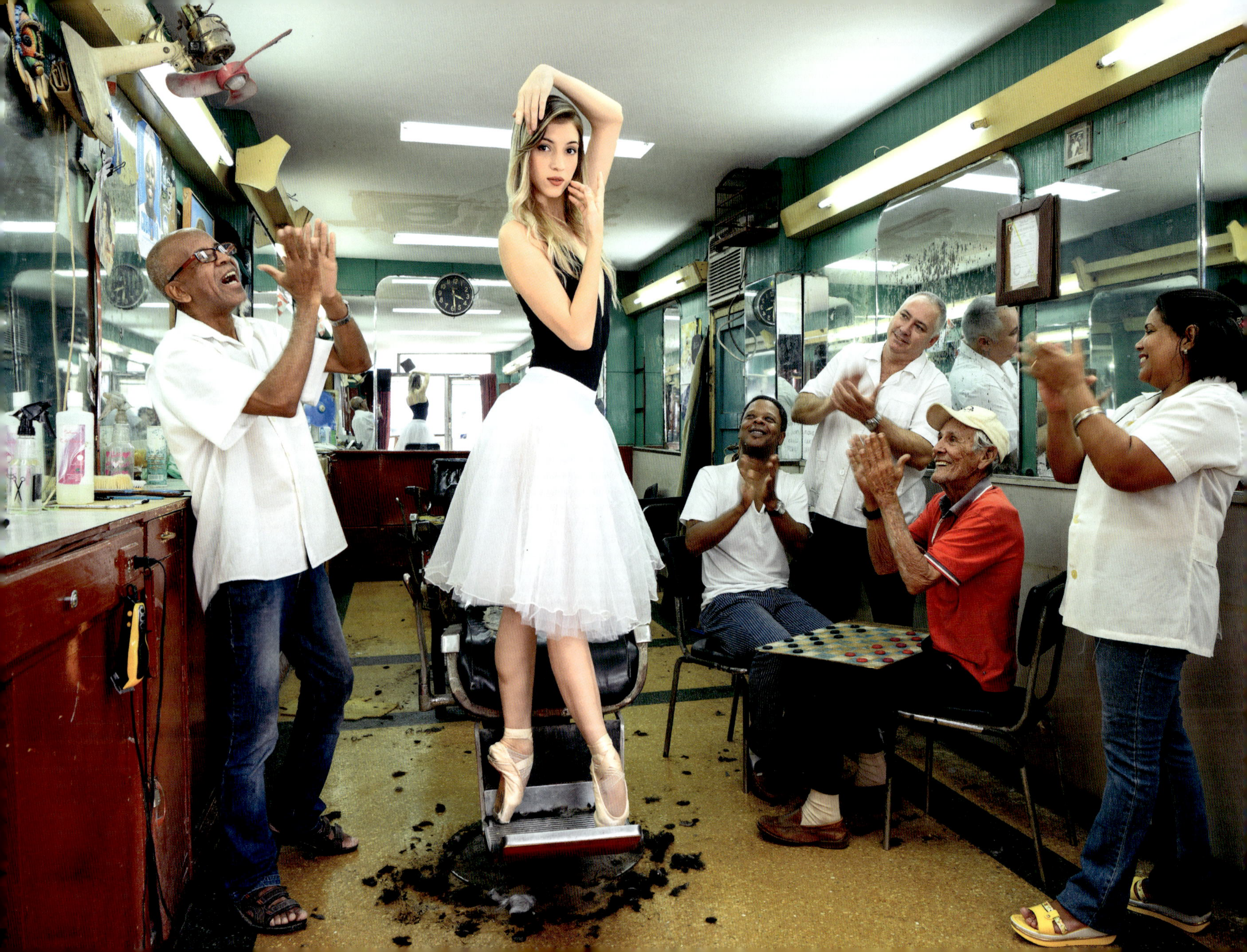

Access Is Everything

In the story of working in New Orleans ("The Window in Your Dreams"), I mentioned Billy, a local firefighter who helped me hold fast on Bourbon Street during the drunken, frenetic revelry of New Year's Eve on one of the most raucous strips of blacktop in America. If you go out there by yourself, you are dependent on the "kindness of strangers." On that eve, strangers were abundant. Kindness, not so much.

Hurly burly is a mild way of putting it. Drunks, screamers, flashers, gropers, perverts, stoners, and football fans just out of the bars flood the pathway, mixing with fearful, awestruck, wide-eyed tourists not smart enough to stay in their hotel rooms. Mean-spirited macho dudes churn through the crowds, fairly frothing in the potent grip of rotgut liquor and testosterone, and uniformly wearing wisely purchased t-shirts bearing questions like, "Did You Get Yours Today?" Near keening for a fight, these guys guzzle Huge Ass beers, neutering their few remaining synapses with alcohol, clouding even further an already almost totally absent sense of judgement. It's not an encounter you seek.

If you're out there with expensive cameras, and God forbid on a ladder, and you don't have help, preferably local help, you're potentially in for a rough night. Vantage points are tough to come by, and somebody who is connected has to get you in a back door and up on a roof. Or guard you while you're on a ladder in the middle of a crowd that started the evening with an already deflated I.Q. and seems determined to squash it even further as the night progresses.

The person you need to come out on an adventure like this with you is known as a fixer. A fixer. Sometimes they might be called a guide, but that title has all the panache of "accounts manager." Fixer. Somebody with juice, somebody who knows the back doors, knows who to bribe, and how much, knows where the light might be relative to the riverbank at dawn, and even better, knows that old riverman with a skiff who will take you out on the water before the sun is up. They know the doorman at the club, and can get you in with a wink and a nod. He or she has the permit office on speed dial, can work an angle for you, is pleasant but persistent on your behalf, and in short, *gets you in.*

I have worked with many fixers over the years, especially when on assignment for *National Geographic.* Over time, some fixers acquired a near-legendary status in the photo world. Resolute, improvisational, determined, undaunted by inconvenience or the first blush of the word "no," they are on your side (you are paying them, after all) and essay mightily to make the picture happen. For example, I once knew a *Geographic* photographer on assignment who was pursuing an exceptionally difficult ask, and his fixer was bargaining with officials in the native language, incomprehensible to the photographer. Even though he did not understand the words, it was utterly apparent the conversation was not going well.

His fixer turned to him and said, referring to the official, "He says absolutely no forever." Pause. "This is very promising."

It's this attitude that must be struck in pursuit of a photo. Energy and determination. A willingness to take the long way around to the destination if the more direct, official channels are closed to you. A positive attitude undimmed by obstacle. Politely bullheaded, obstinate perseverance. Nothing special in the way of a photo out there comes effortlessly nowadays.

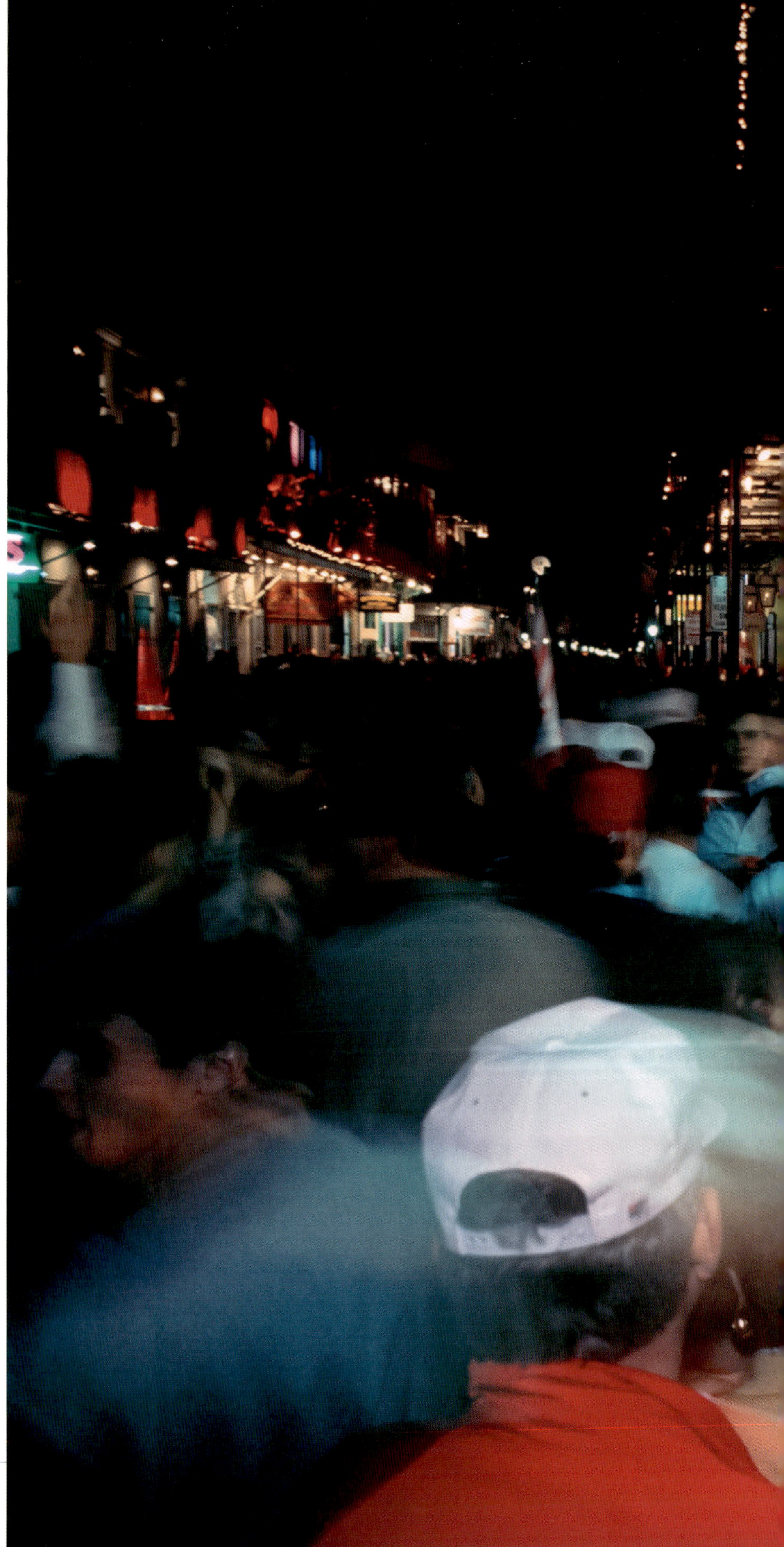

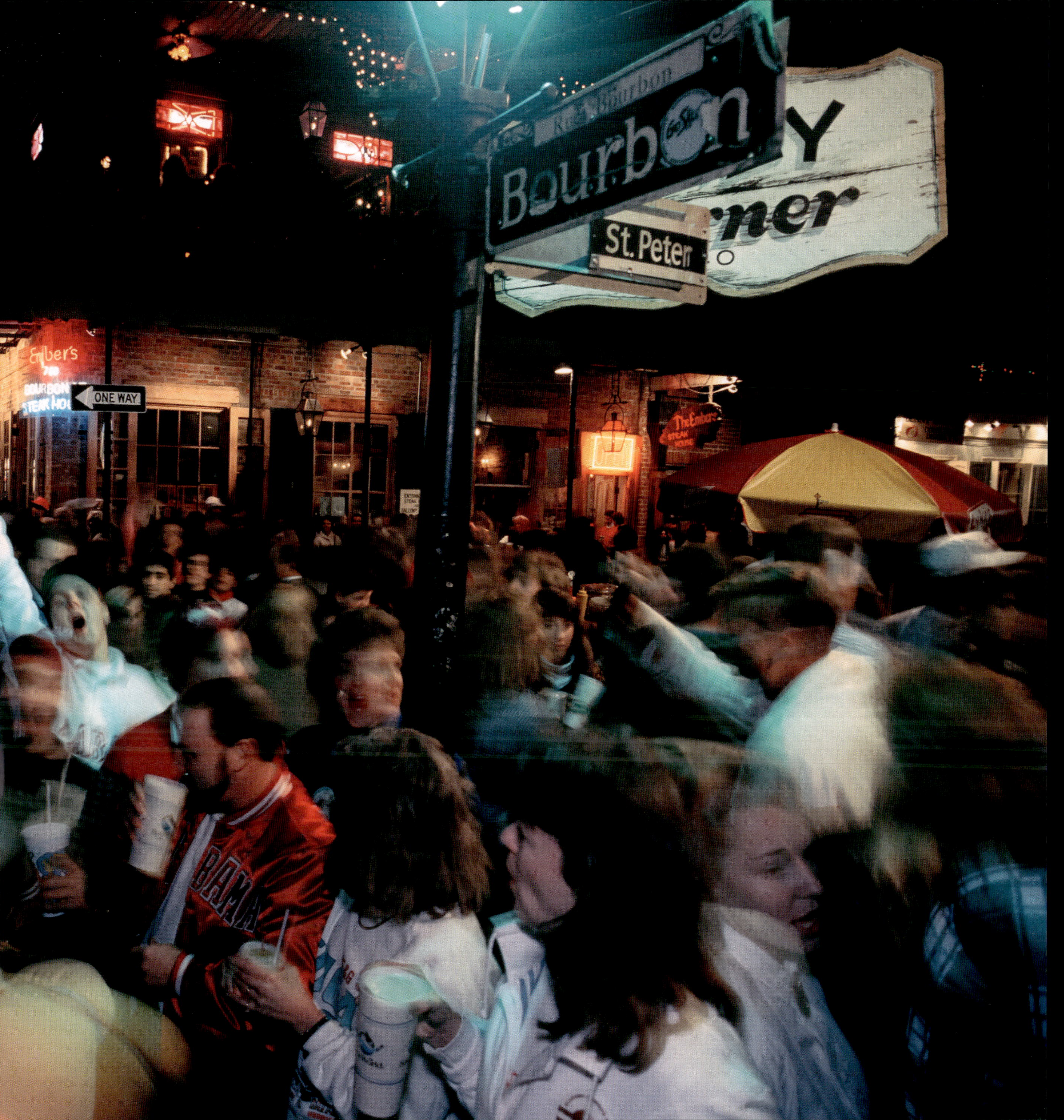
Rue Bourbon
Bourbon
St. Peter
Ember's
BOURBON
STEAK HOUSE
ONE WAY
The Embers
STEAK HOUSE
ALABAMA

I photographed Nadia Grachova, a principal dancer with the Bolshoi Ballet, up on the roof of the GUM department store, located in the heart of Moscow's Red Square on my second try. On the first attempt, I was pulled off the roof by security forces who claimed my camera could see through the windows of the Kremlin (the yellow building in the distance) and copy documents. Okay. Nikon optics are good, they're not that good. But there was no arguing. I was escorted off the roof, despite our paperwork assuring all was approved.

My fixer made a concerted run at the authorities, emphasizing Nadia's fame. He also wisely enlisted the help of her husband, a well-connected Moscow doctor. (You use any connection available to you in these circumstances. It's definitely an extended version of the old "This guy knows a guy who knows a guy" tactic.)

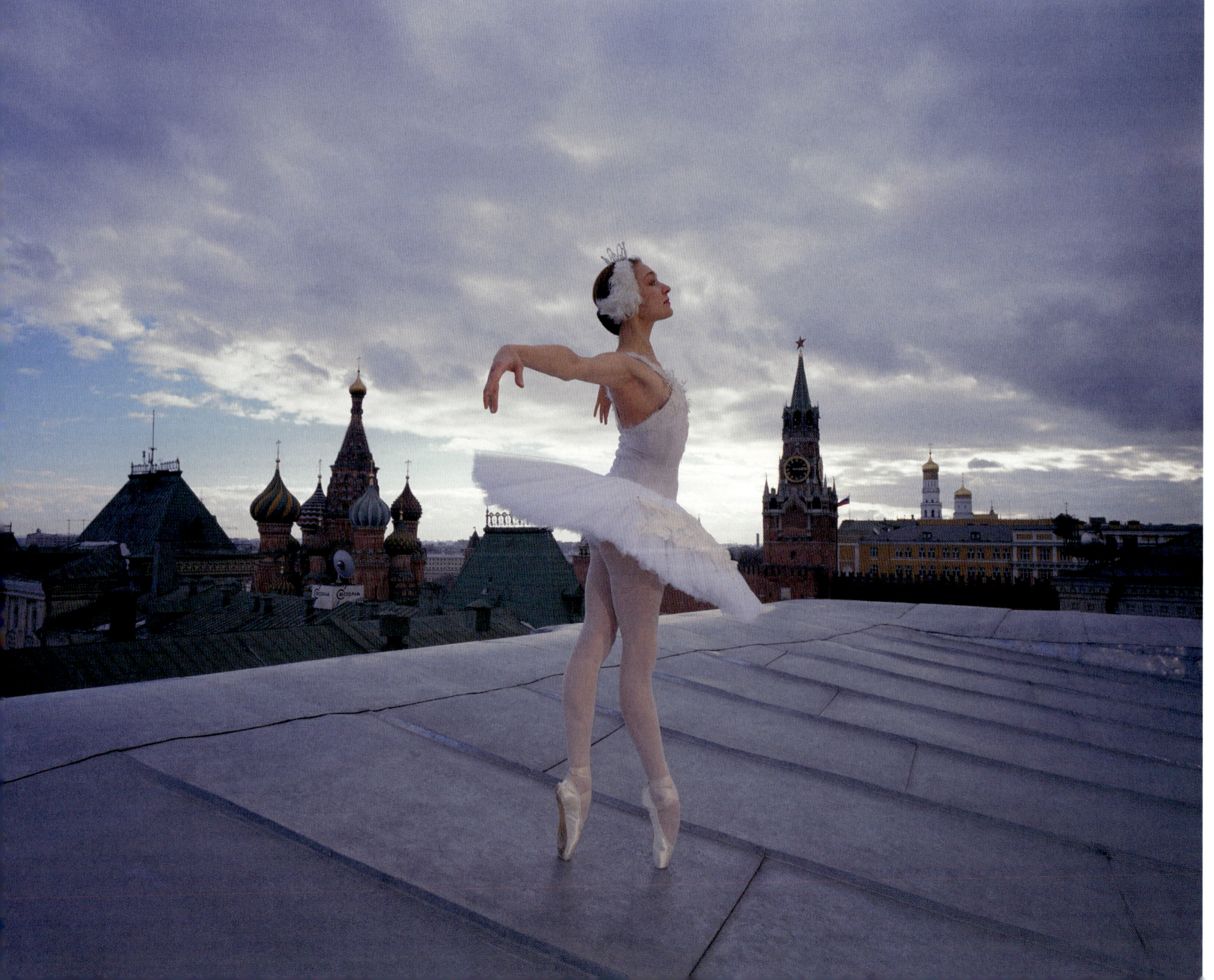

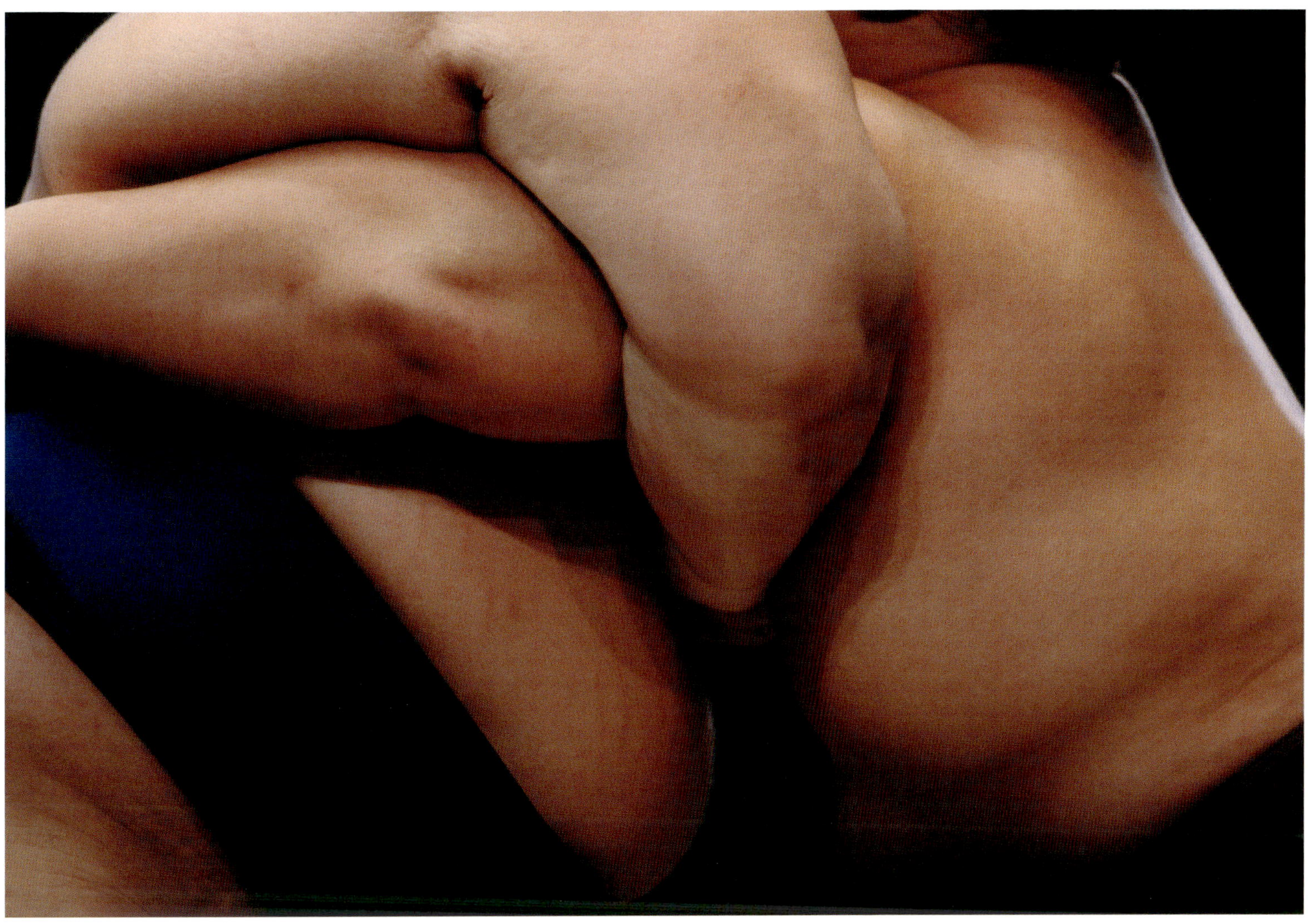

This sumo picture was definitely fixer-driven. I found myself in Japan at the time of the Sumo championships. The sold-out Sumo championships. I implored my fixer to seek a path for access. He came back to me with the plan. Roughly speaking, he told me the next morning we would wait in the lobby of the hotel. I would have an envelope with $500 in it. At the prescribed time, a gentleman bearing my ticket would come in. No words would be exchanged.

In the lobby, precisely on time, an enormous individual, wearing a black suit, white shirt, and black tie walked in. He had no neck. It looked as if, as they say, he'd have to unbutton his shirt to blow his nose. His head seemed ready to burst from the pressure of his closed collar and tied tie. His eyes were heavy-lidded and cruel, and his mouth a short gash in the vast expanse of his jowls. There was no greeting, no pleasantries. I gave him the money. He stuffed the ticket in my hand, turned, and walked away. Fifth row back from ringside. I turned to my fixer with a renewed sense of appreciation, fear, and wonder.

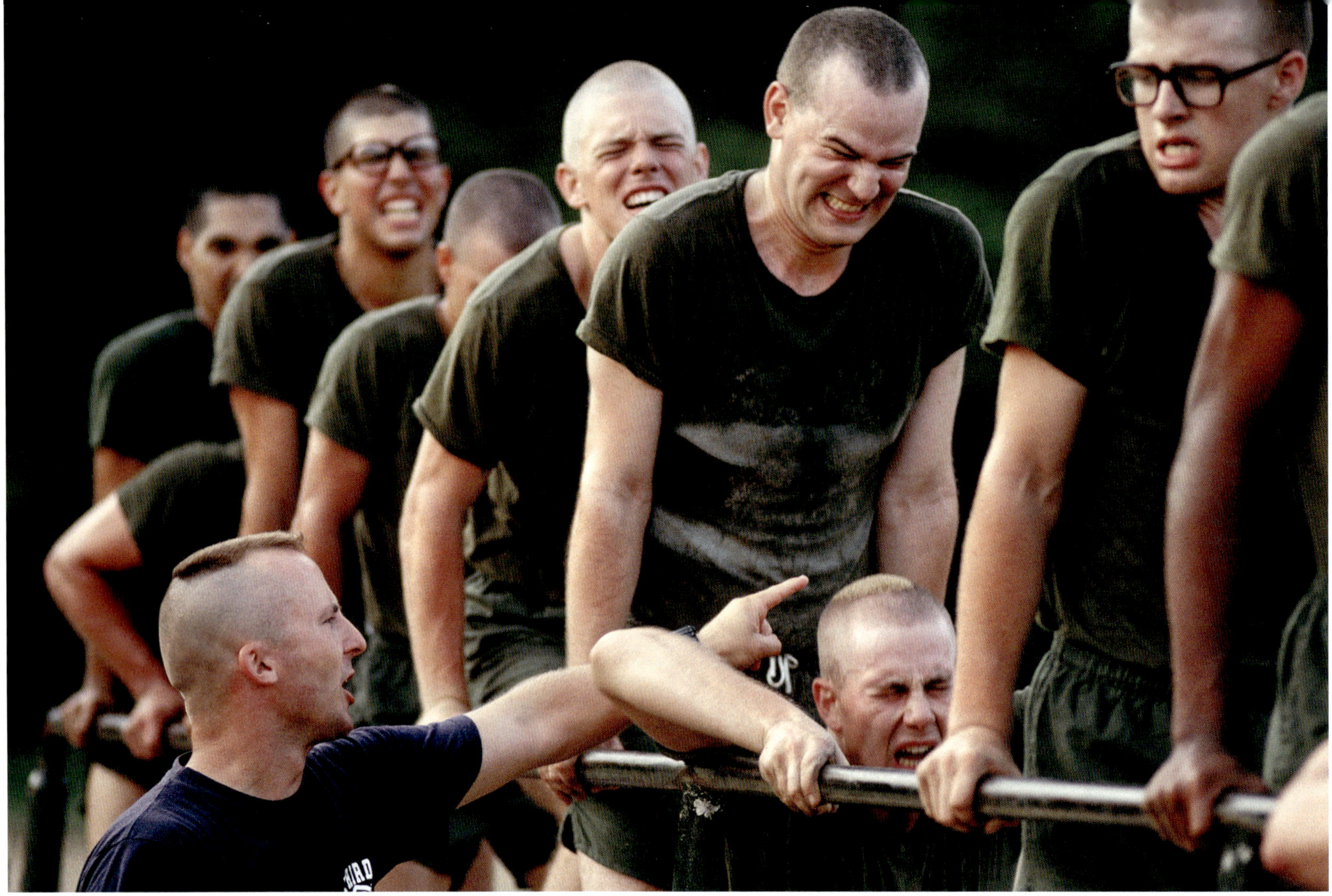

Working with the military, the PAO (Public Affairs Officer) is your fixer, and though it's all very official, the respect your PAO commands among the soldiers you are photographing can elevate your coverage and soften, if not outright bend, some rules. The more your PAO knows, and the more he or she gets out of the office and mixes it up in field with troop activities, the better your pictures will be. At Parris Island, I spent a week with a new class, and my PAO was great. He was with me all the way through, sometimes literally shouting encouragement at me and guiding me through the process. He knew where the pictures would happen during this class's training routine. He knew where the emotion and physical stress would be most evident.

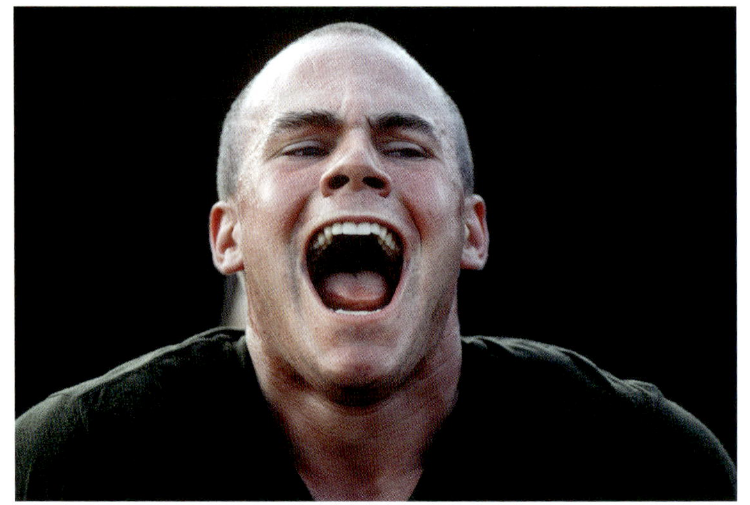

The fixer is the answer to a number of frequently asked questions: How can I make my travel pictures different, better, vital? Maybe even approaching, yikes, that holy grail of "unseen"? How can I get under the skin of somewhere? How can I be allowed in to see places that are at least somewhat unseen? How can I gain the feeling of intimacy for my pictures, a sense that I am quietly observing someone who does not simultaneously have 20 or 30 other cameras pointed at them while they do their weaving, or hand wrap a cigar?

A fixer can ensure you are by yourself, in Parma, Italy, famed for its cheese. Where does all that marvelous cheese come from? That's an excellent first question. Curiosity drives difference at the camera. A fixer can put you in a position to make a photo that answers the question.

"Difference" is tough to capture, in this overseen, over-documented world. Impossible, honestly, in the compressed atmosphere or time frame of a tour, hopping off the bus and spending 20 minutes at the overview, photographing the

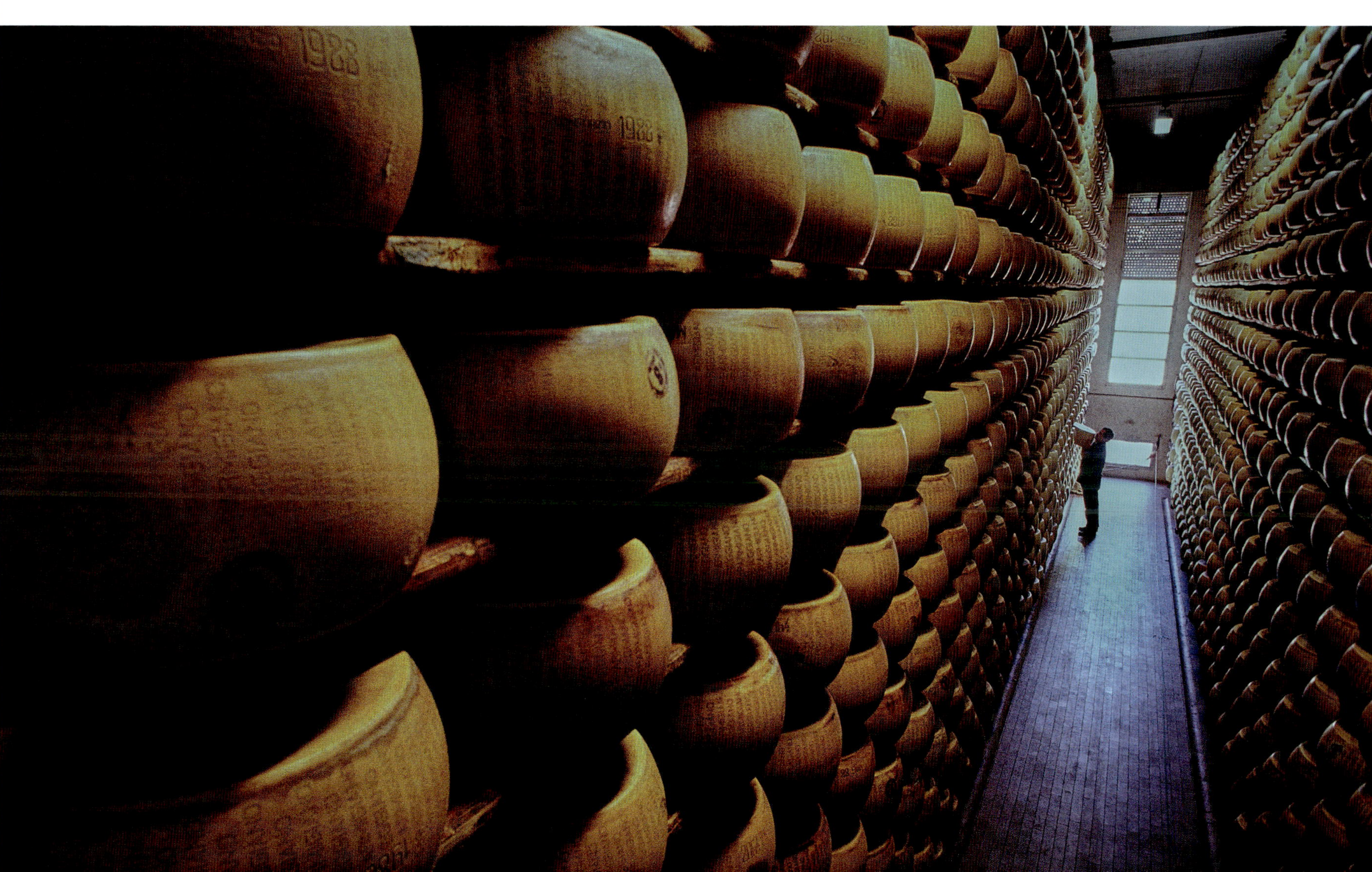

familiar. Slow meander time with the family is wonderful and painful. "Dad's taking pictures again!" Vibrant travel pictures, photos from afar that you return home with like glowing talismans that arrest the eye, make your neighbor jealous, and sing true of the place are generally a process of discovery, not orchestration. Enter the fixer.

To make something adventurously unique happen, you need to be free of encumberment, having done your research and made the arrangements. In the company of your fixer, you need to walk and seek without a timetable or a must-go dinner reservation. And when you walk, you should walk, per noted street photographer and New York denizen Jay Maisel's advice, slowly.

These fixer folks are not overly difficult to find, but it does require some planning and research. First off, it's important to identify your areas of interest. They should go beyond and be more specific than "the farmer's market." Where does the produce for the farmer's market come from? Big industrial farms or small family farms? If the latter, is it possible to visit one of the small farms? Before sunrise, when milking is done? Will you be in the country at harvest time, and for what crops? If so, are those crops voluminous, colorful, accessible? Can you witness the real work of farming, as opposed to showing up in bad light at the city center produce market and trying to photograph irritable vendors who are nestled with their tomatoes under canopies that cut the light to f/2.8 and will just wave you off with a petulant flick of their hand? Exposing for those faces in the tented shade will most likely ensure the background of your photo will go nuclear. Not an exposure game you are likely to win. You can charm the heart of a vendor by buying their fruit or vegetables as a preamble to making a picture or two, but then, how much produce do you want to haul back to your hotel room?

Getting to the source of the food, the real work out there in the earth, as opposed to wandering over to the local marketplace, is the difference between buying a ticket and sitting comfortably in the audience, and getting backstage where the performers are doing makeup and costuming.

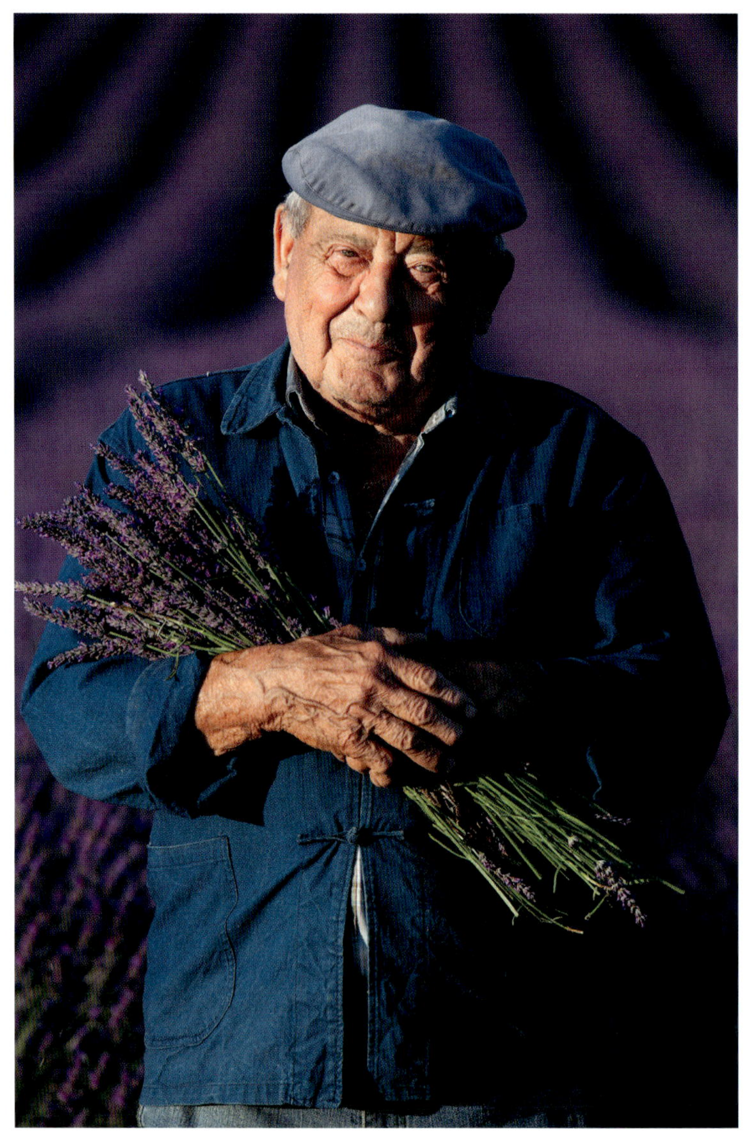

How much produce do you want to haul back to your hotel room?

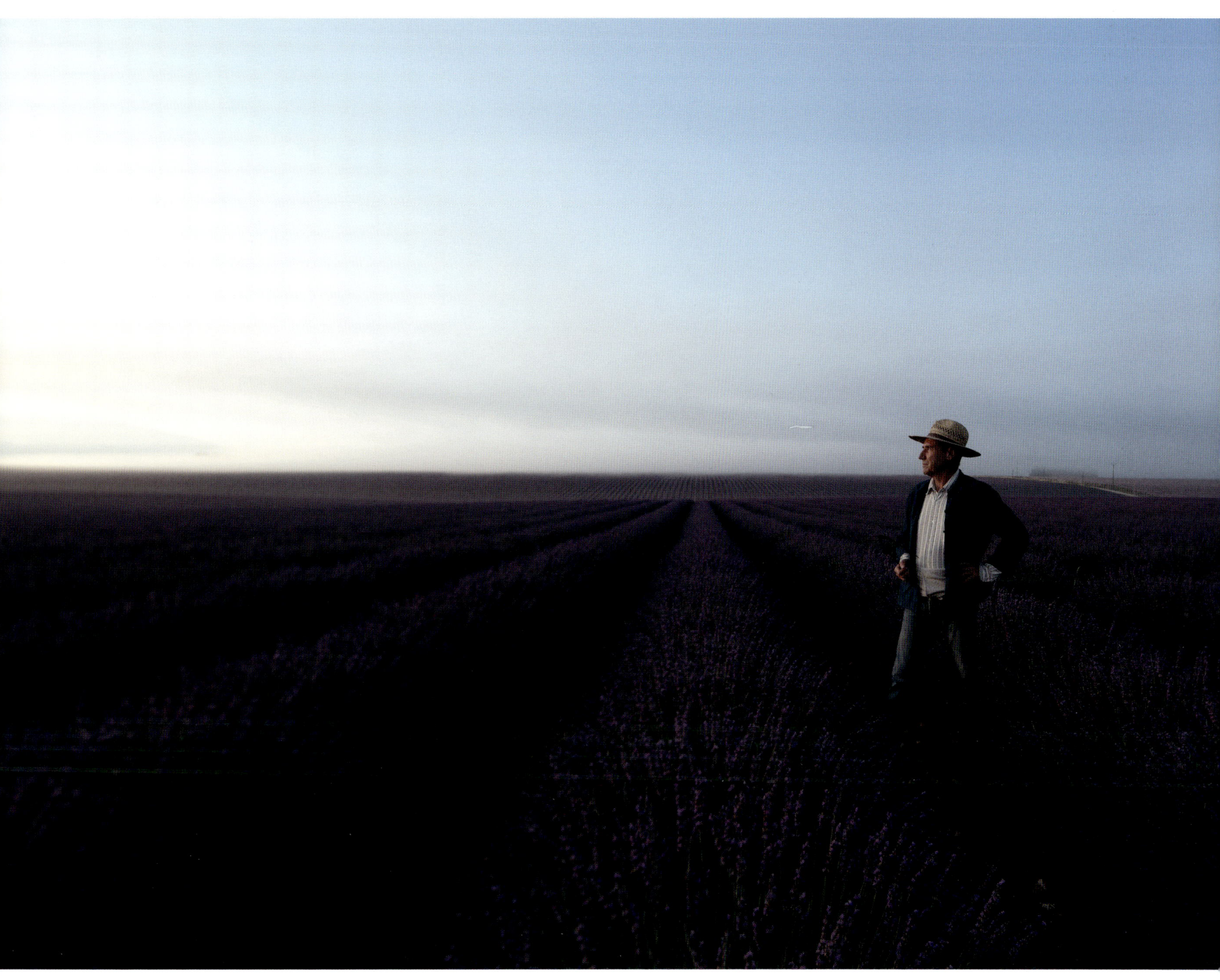

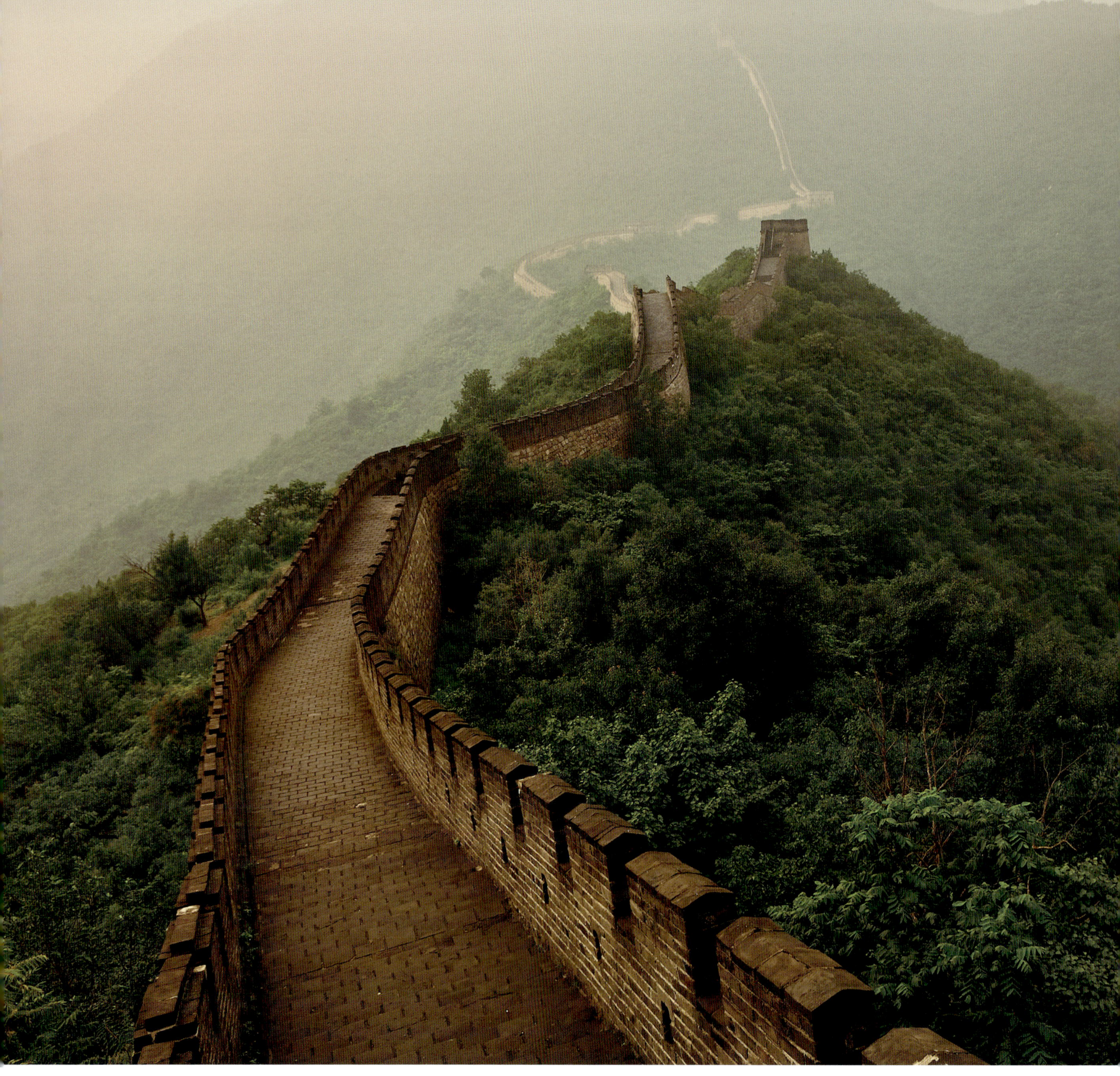

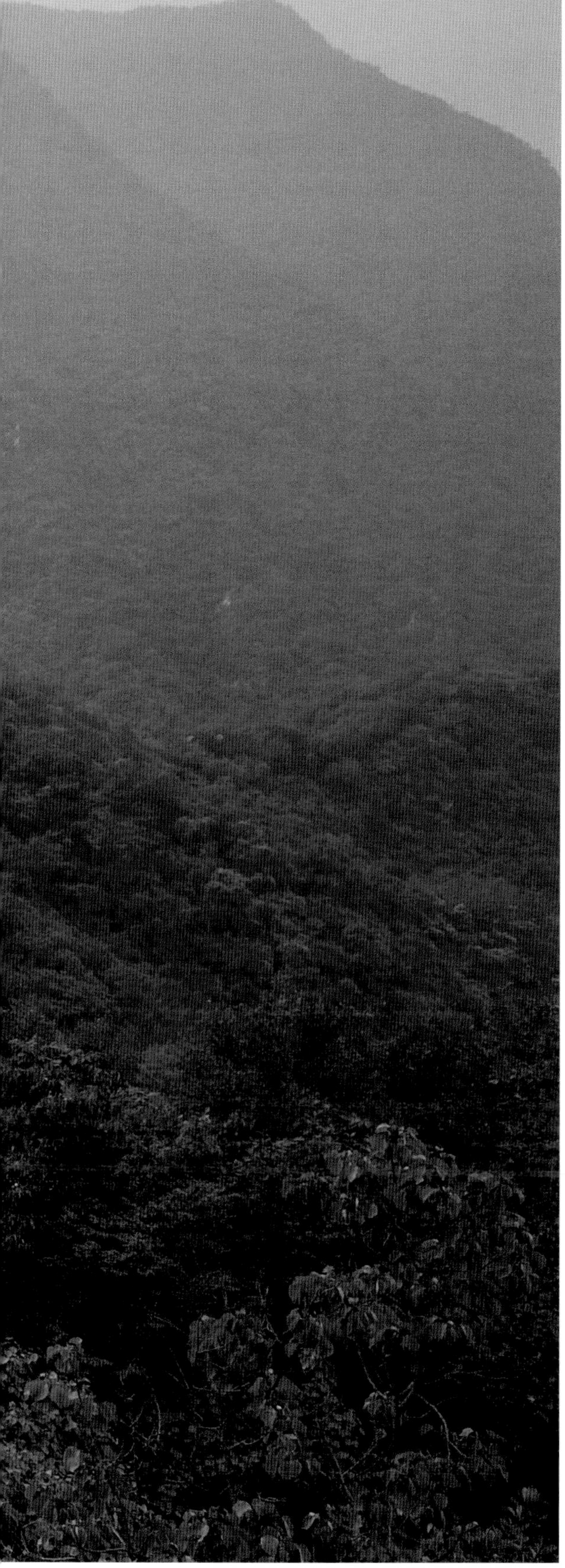

You can even ask for something as hugely familiar as The Great Wall because, well, you just have to go there. It's a must for visitors to China, as it is a stirring, astonishing place, even though it is generally an anthill of tourists and you are the billionth person with a camera up there that week alone. Try to shape the request. Where on The Great Wall? Can you get to areas generally unvisited, or less populated? Is there a back door? (Always exists in China.) Will a long, out-of-the-way drive to a remote section of the wall enable good, or at least better, pictures? Will going during a weekday at a certain time lessen the crowds? Make projections for the weather and direction of light and the time of day so there exists a chance, however infinitely small, to come up with something beautiful, something that looks different from the postcards on the racks at the airport.

This shot of the Great Wall doesn't possess that once-in-a-lifetime weather one might have wished for, but it's a view of the Great Wall that is unusual in that it's devoid of people.

And if you have a particular interest in mind, such as a dancer or gymnast or other equivalently interesting portrait subject, a fixer can potentially make that happen, and help bring all the puzzle pieces together.

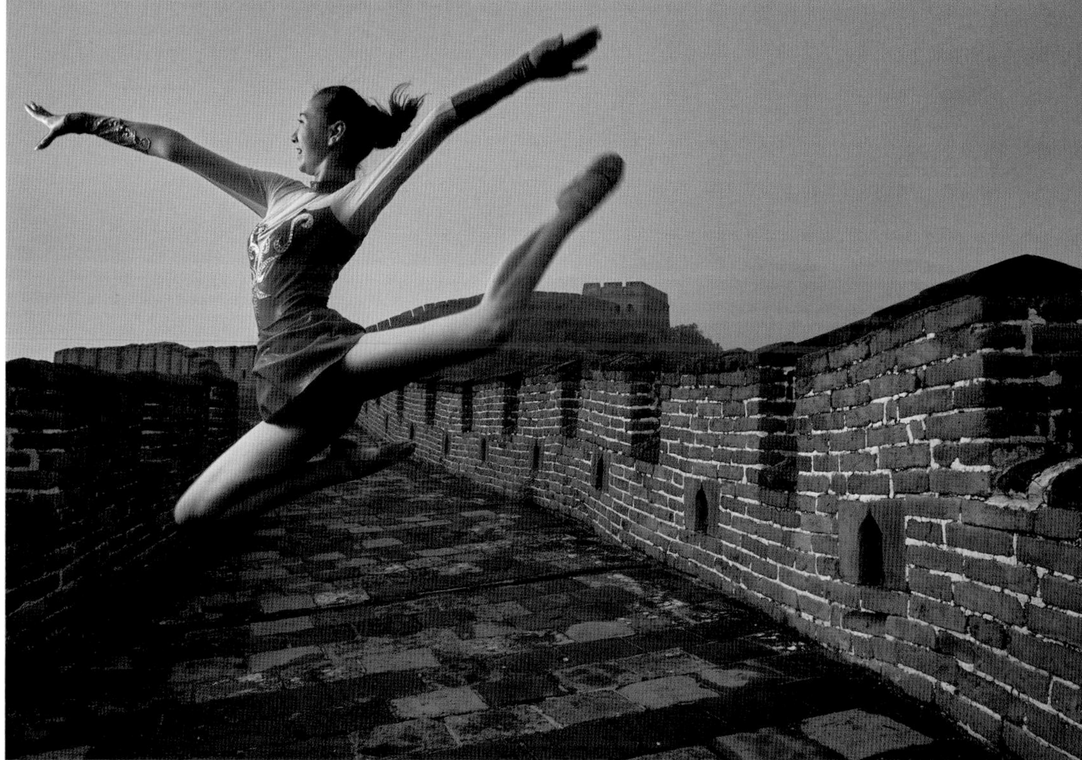

Have a direction in mind. And then reach out, well prior to arrival. A good resource for fixers is often the picture assignment desk of the local newspaper or wire service. Call or message the desk at these places, explain your intentions, and ask if there is anyone they recommend and what their rates might be. Those rates can run from quite reasonable to outright pricey, depending on the area of the world and the nature of your ask. You can also research local photographers and inquire. I have found local photogs to be very giving and helpful. Occasionally, given the competitive nature of this industry, you might be rebuffed, as they could view you as competition and they would be potentially chary of sharing their hard-won knowledge and resources. But most are helpful.

Travel companies can also be a resource, but be mindful that a travel company or tour guide service has the brochure, the spiel, the fixed cost, and they will profit by bringing more people along on an "exclusive" tour. Tour guides might know the date when the battle happened on the site, but they are often clueless when it comes to knowing what a photographer really needs.

Getting good travel pictures in the compressed amount of time you will be in a country is a tall order. The odds are against you. Time, budget, weather, family commitments, and the announced itinerary—which looked so glossy in the brochure and has you rattling to five cities in seven days—all conspire against producing virtuoso results at the camera. But the fixer helps level the playing field. He or she can push back against the odds on your behalf, and coach you along, leading you to photographic water, if you will. They'll cut through red tape, cajole a security guard, and place some coin in appropriately useful pockets. The thing you need to do is *allow that to happen.*

By that I mean you need to take your foot off the vacation gas pedal and sink into photographic mode, which is necessarily slower and more reflective. Vacation mode is great fun, and necessary! But pictures beckon. Good travel pictures don't generally happen poolside. View it this way: You take a vacation to the islands, and spend frenetically fun days going to Carnivale, drinking colorfully potent tropical beverages, dancing at the clubs, dining at luscious buffets. But then, you disappear and go, for instance, scuba diving. You sink beneath the waves, and all the shore-bound noise is gone. Quiet beauty awaits. Time slows down. No cell phone. No appointments. The pace is languid, reflection is possible. It's another world. It's time you give yourself.

Which is what the camera demands. Time you give yourself. Time you selfishly carve out to be absent from the rush and the kids and the rides and the pizza, and pursue a picture. The fixer can help you frame this time, isolate it, and turbocharge its usefulness by cutting to the chase and bringing you to a place or places where pictures might live.

Following the nose of a good fixer often requires you to lose some of your inhibitions and sense of what is traditionally safe. I spent a week in Saigon on the back of my fixer's scooter. Being on a scooter in those streets at that time was a bit akin to a motorized version of broken field running, but it led to pictures.

A couple of women passed us on their scooter, clad in traditional Vietnamese dress, quite beautiful and formal. I inquired as we dodge-balled after them in traffic. My fixer told me over his shoulder that he suspected they were going to a wedding. He pointed to one very large vehicle ahead in the road. "That's the wedding car," he pointed out. "Do you want to go?" I blanched. "We can't just go to somebody's wedding!"

He shook his head and waived off my naturally reticent sensibilities. Maneuvering the scooter next to the limo, he had a rapid-fire conversation with, presumably, the bride's father, and explained our situation. He dropped back in traffic to follow the car. "We're invited," he tossed back at me.

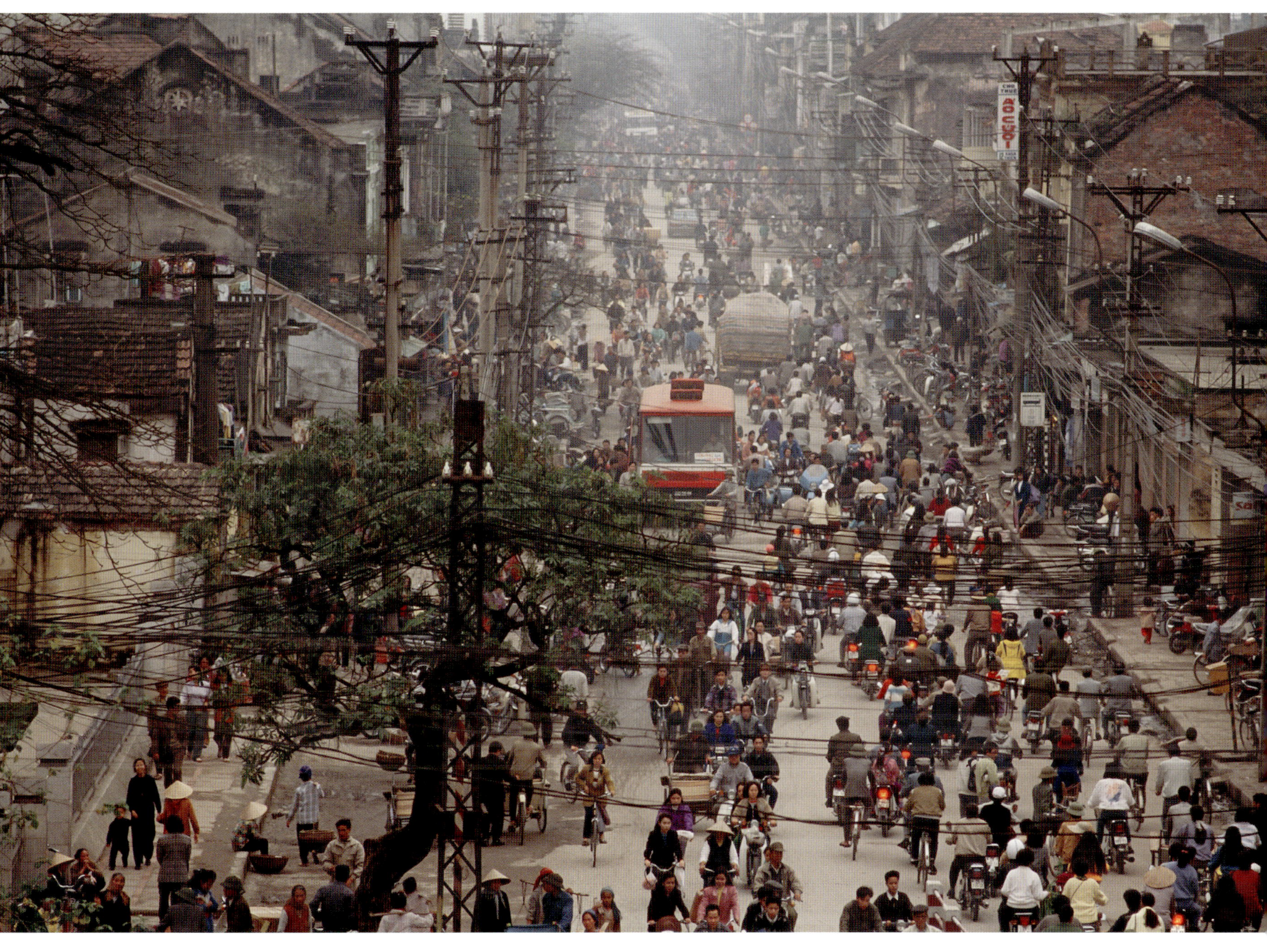

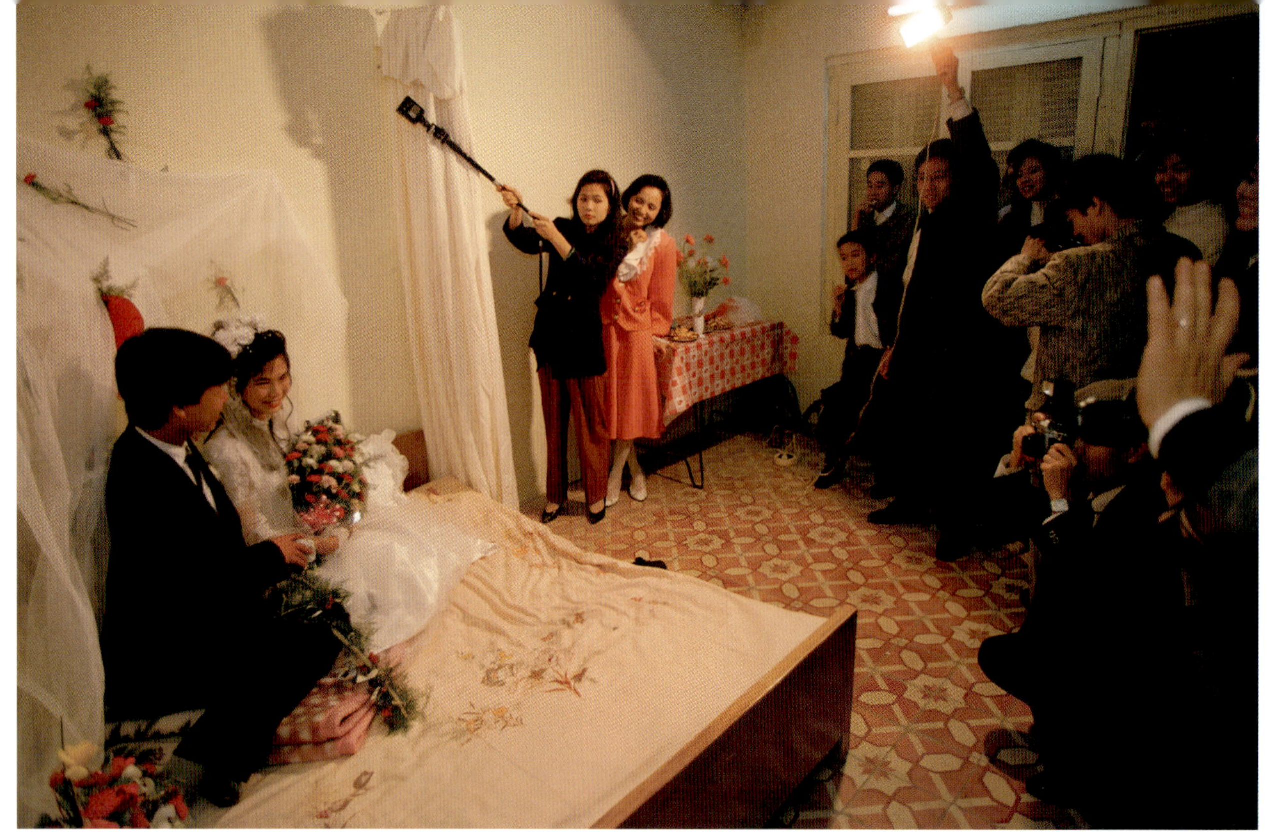

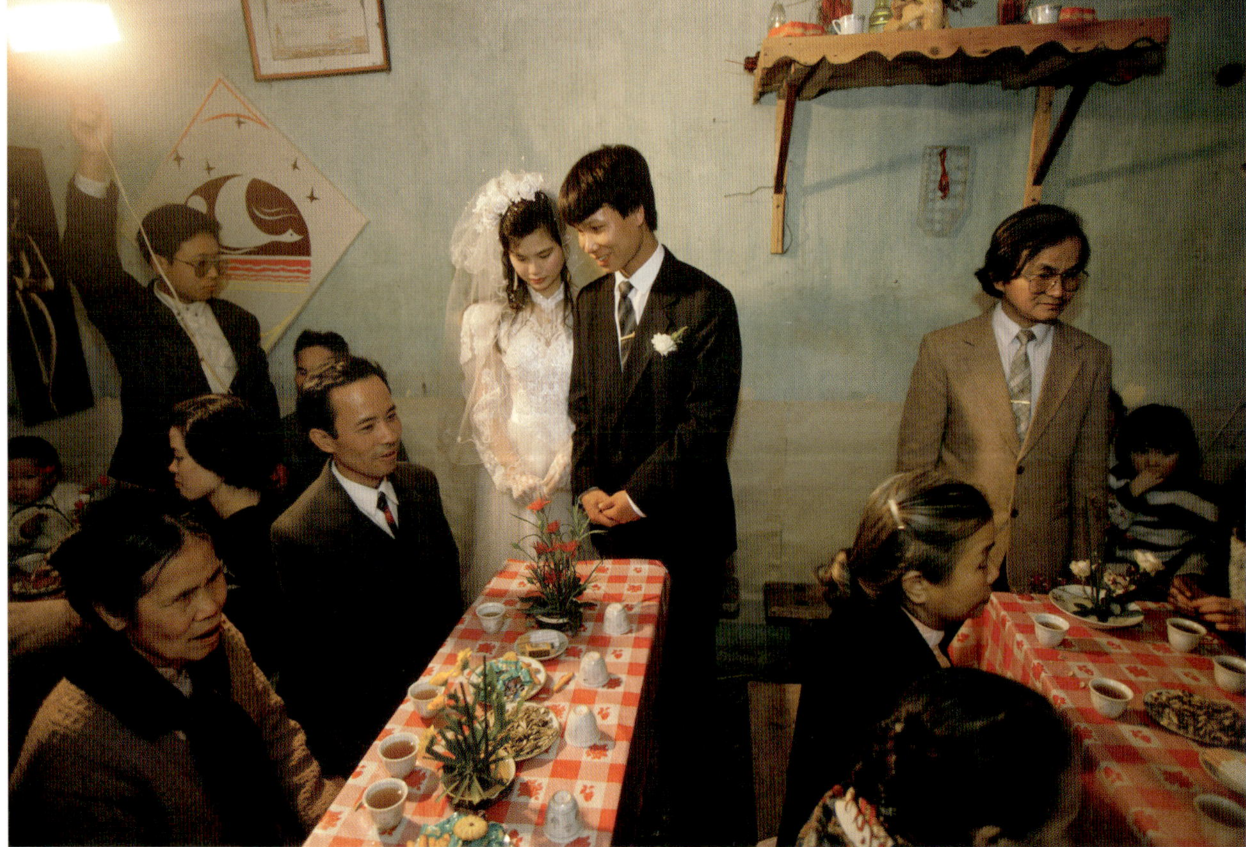

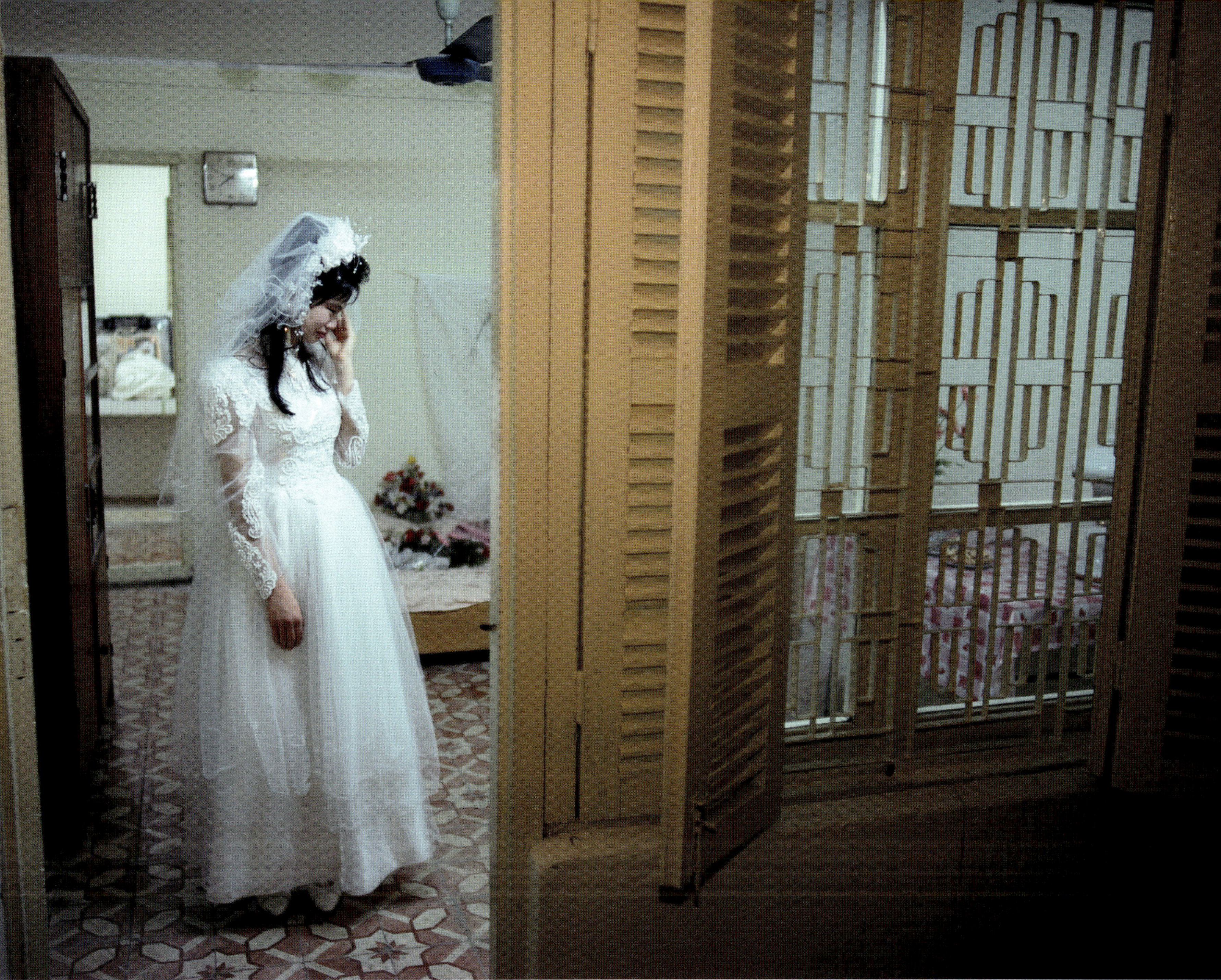

As a stranger, I have never been received more graciously than at this lovely, well documented wedding. Amazing. Food, smiles, embraces for the overbig American. My heart went out to the bride. She was quite young, as was the groom. She was about to spend the first night of her life away from her family's home, and here's this American photographer, flashing away. I was the last person there that night with the couple. I turned and made this picture as I left (above). I hope the couple is well.

Do a test. If you see a wedding vehicle in, say, Manhattan, pull up alongside at a stoplight and ask if you can come to the reception, camera in hand. See how that goes.

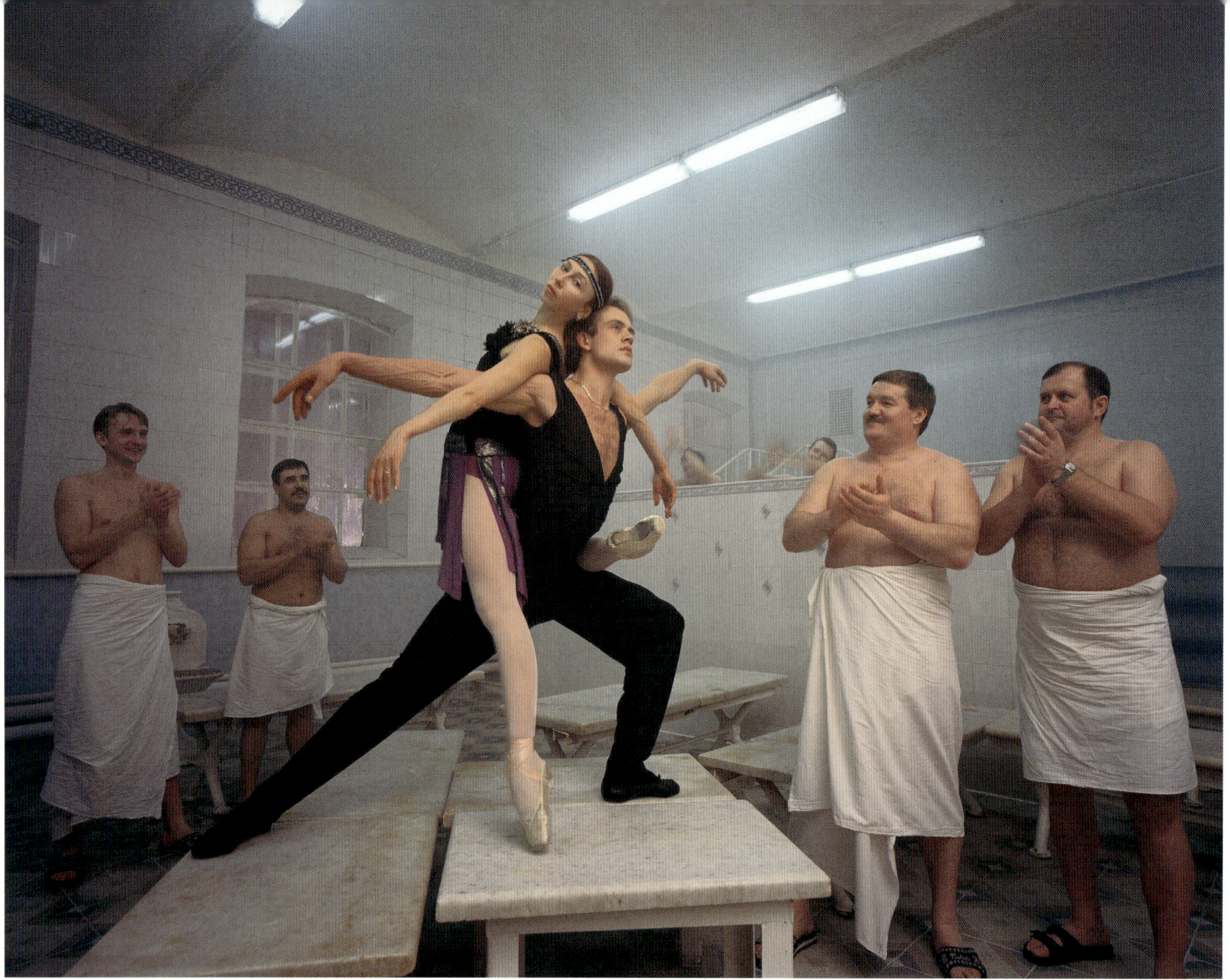

Fixers can also play the role of procurer. As in, do you need something to make this picture? A ladder? A rooftop? A smoke machine?

These astonishing dancers, husband and wife, principals with the Bolshoi, agreed to pose for me in the famed Sanduny bath house in Moscow. As noted earlier with the photo of Nadia Grachova, I was working with the dancers of the historically illustrious company, staging them around the city, trying to use the arts as a window into a city and culture in flux. I needed my fixer to get me a smoke machine to simulate steam. He made a yeoman-like effort, but at that time in turbulent Moscow, apparently no smoke machines were to be had. He conjured what looked to be a paint can filled with a sticky, tarry substance that he would light on fire, extinguish, and then run around the bathhouse ladling smoke out of it via the very imprecise regulating mechanism of the can's lid. "Joe!" exclaimed the irrepressible Igor. "I have found you the smoggy machine!"

Fixers come in all shapes, sizes, and backgrounds. The commonality they share is intimacy with a place, a district, a neighborhood, a "scene," and potentially a permitting structure or political system. They know the turf and how far to push it.

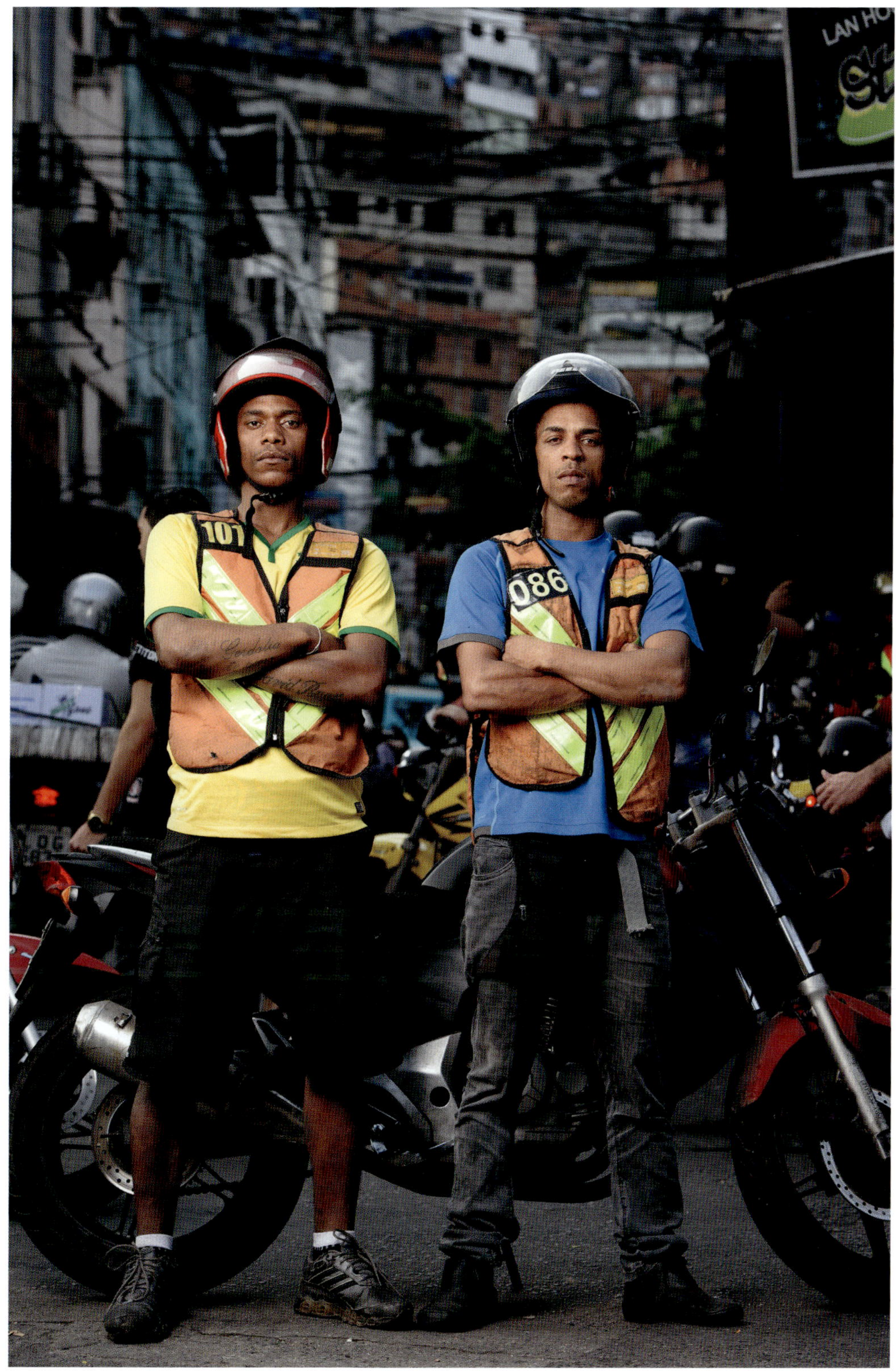

During the 2016 Olympics, I worked in the favelas of Rio, where I could not go with any reasonable expectation of success or safety without a fixer. Or, in this instance, fixers. I met a pair of brothers (introduced by the guy who knows a guy who knows a guy) who both run their own moto-taxi business. We worked out a financial deal. They told me flat-out, "We were born here, and lived here all our lives. We know everybody. Stay with us, and you'll be safe."

They were perfect, combining knowledge and local juice with a means of transport. I stripped down my gear, and my translator and I spent a couple days on the backs of their motor scooters, zipping about the incredibly narrow, twisting streets of this huge neighborhood perched on a hill. The favelas are islands unto themselves and have their own set of laws and practices. If you are an unannounced and unattended stranger, especially one with a camera, you are greeted with suspicion, and very likely a powerful message that you should leave, coming in the form of a gun to your head through the window of your car.

But with the stamp of approval from these gregarious brothers, I could go literally anywhere and photograph. It was Rio at the time of the Olympics. People could not have been more gracious.

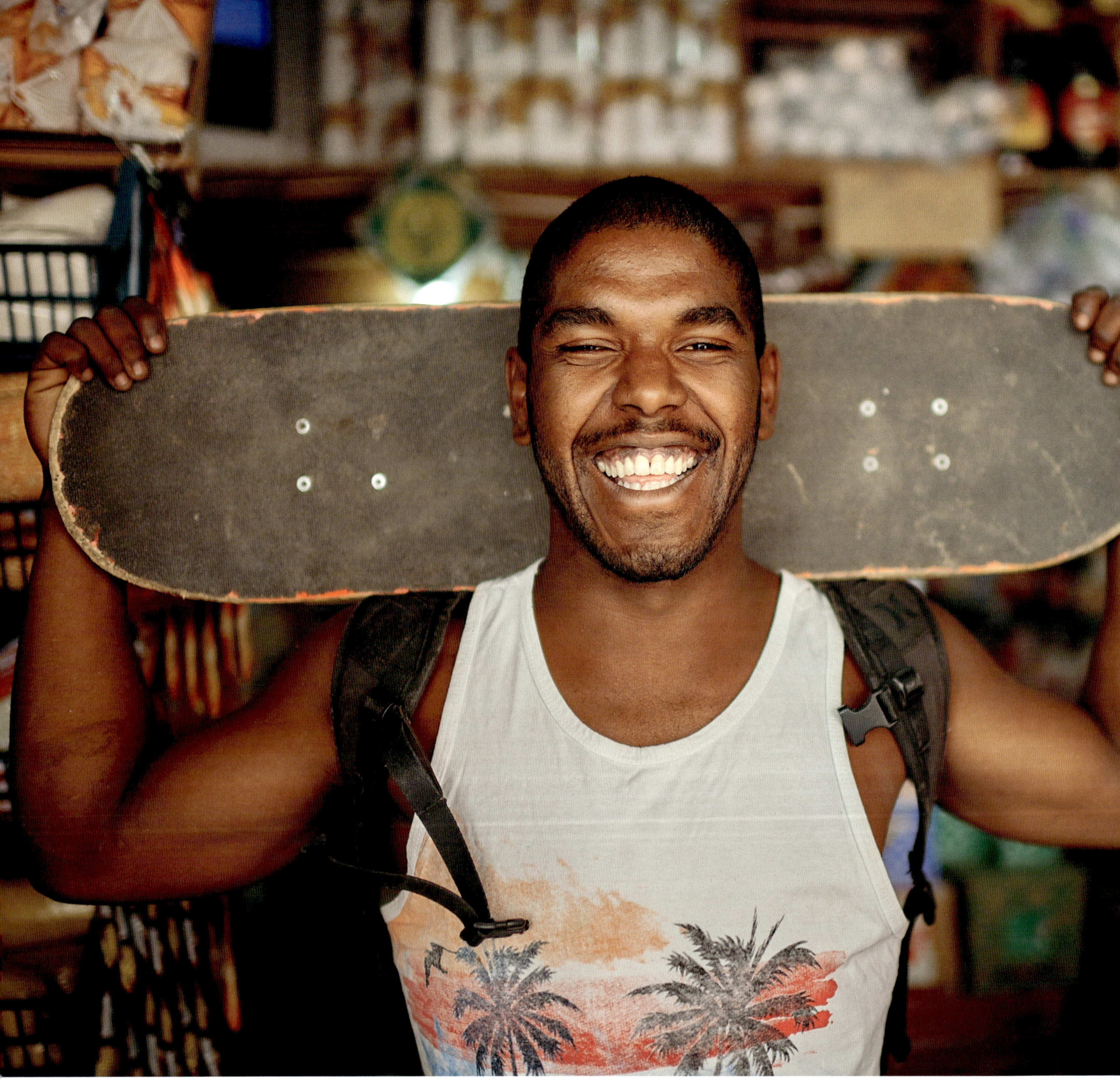

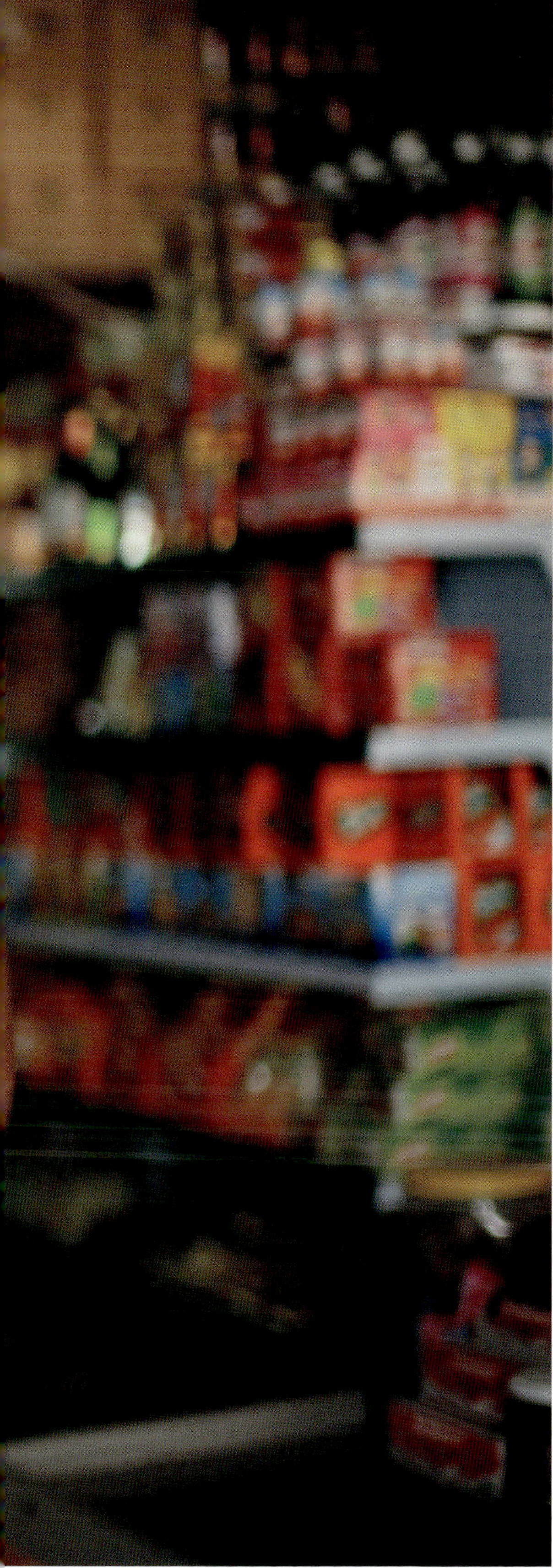

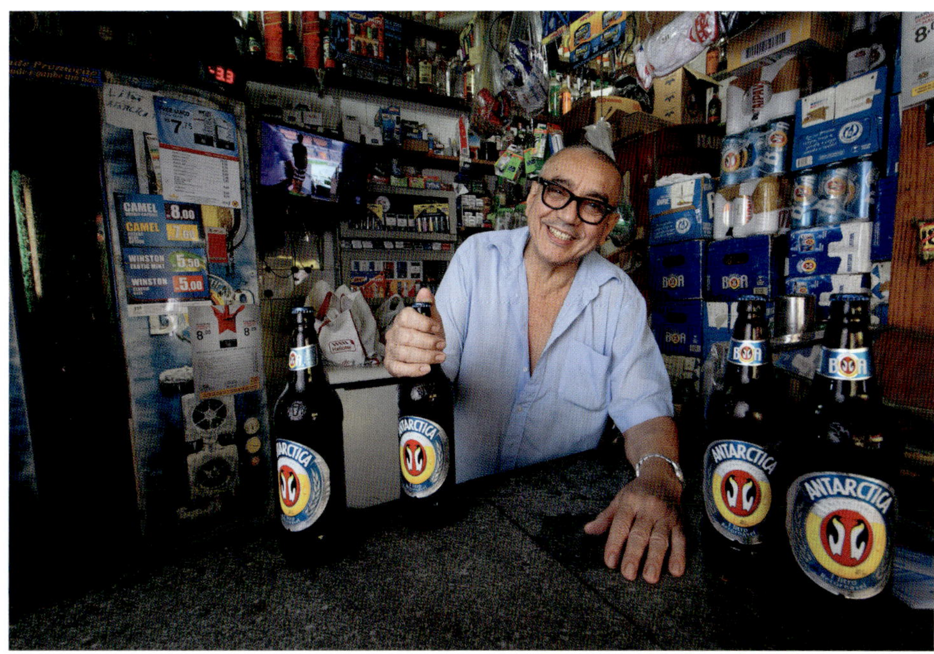

Be prepared to drink, by the way. Get with the program. Be social, lose your inhibitions, and realize the giant beer at midday is just grease on the wheels, and allows you to keep photographing.

And seize a smile like this!

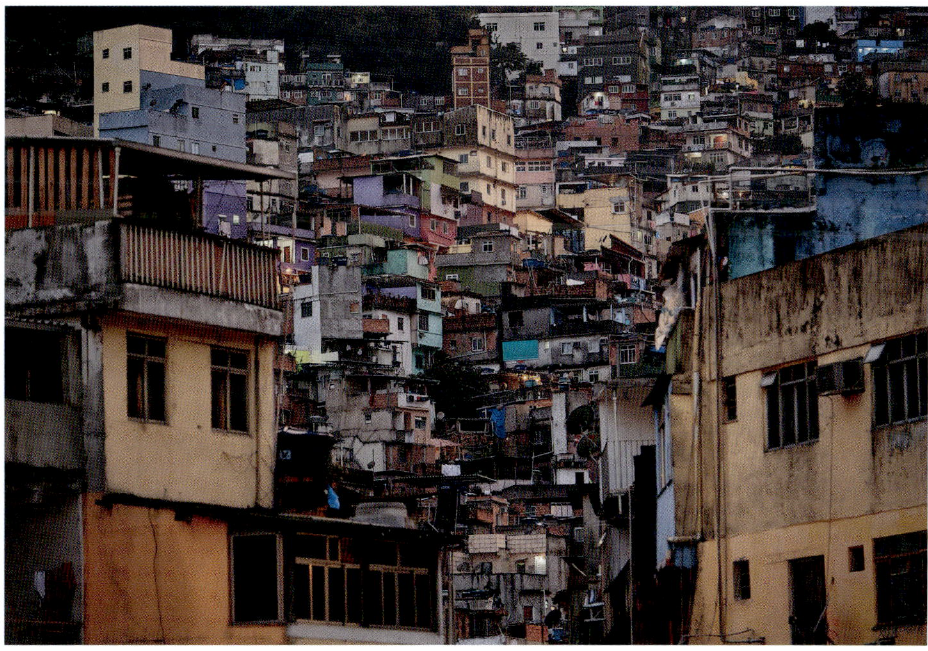

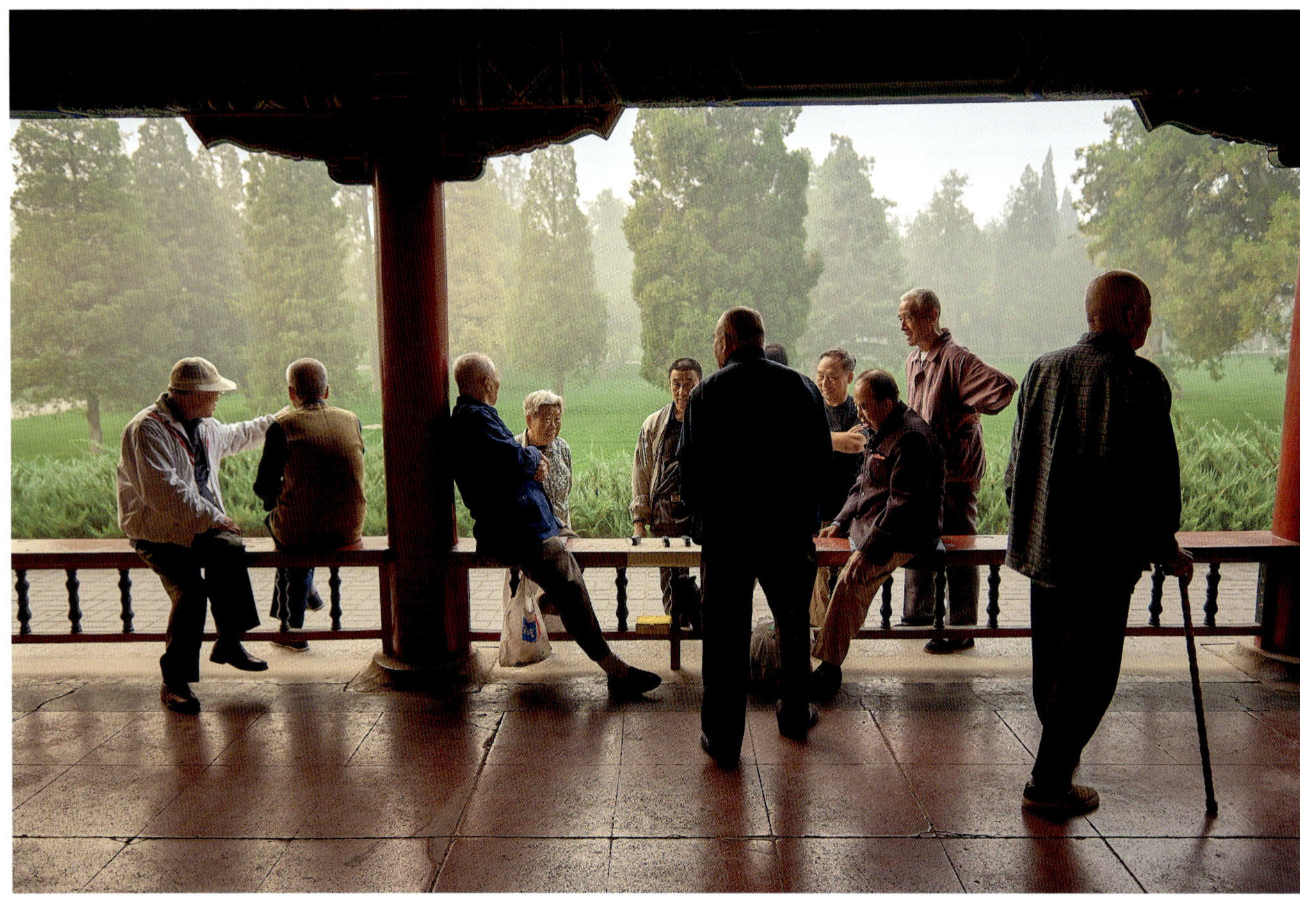

Do your research. You have to realize where you are, which is a ridiculously obvious thing to say. But China, for instance, is not Rio. Chinese fixers have a set of parameters, and they themselves are watched and licensed by the government. What you can get away with in the favelas with a smile, a fist bump, and a twenty-dollar bill is regulated in China by, potentially, reams of paperwork, a polite set of refusals, and then perhaps a measure of allowance in terms of your activity. Wandering the streets making snaps is not a big issue, generally speaking. But something special, something unusual, something you don't buy a ticket for and stand in line to view with thousands of other tourists, is governed and observed. You must recognize this and realize your fixer lives there and will potentially face consequences. You get to leave. They have to live with your mistakes, or the lingering aftermath of any aggressive behavior. Always be gracious and understanding. All they can do in highly regulated societies is make the ask.

I have been to China many times, but never as a tourist or simply a traveler sans agenda. I always have carried the weight, and the advantages, of an assignment. My first visit there was for *Sports Illustrated*, and it had the benefit of being thoroughly blessed by the Chinese government. The whole article was about China's emergence as a world athletic power. I traveled there in 1987, and it was years and many visits back before I completely understood how extraordinary it had been to gain access to an average Chinese person's life, education, and home at that time. My piece of the magazine's whole-issue coverage revolved around a tiny gymnast in training. I had access to her at school, in the gym, and at home in her neighborhood.

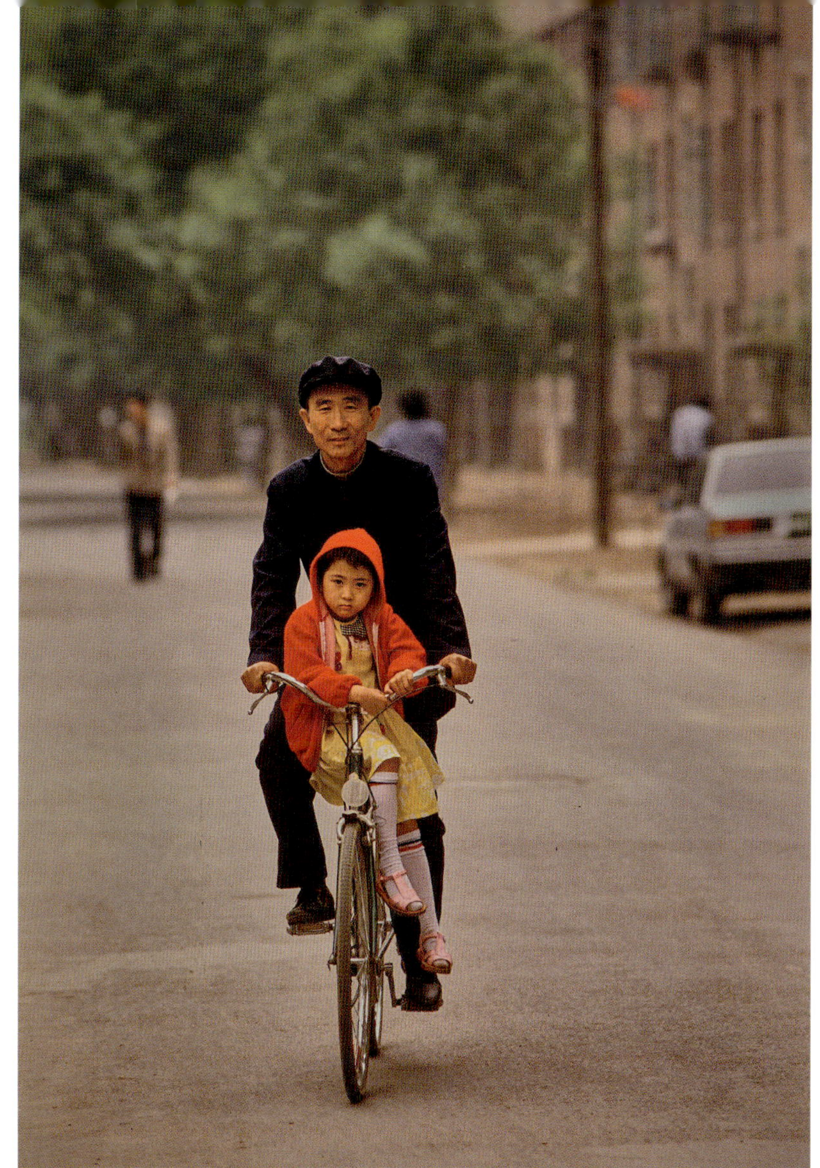

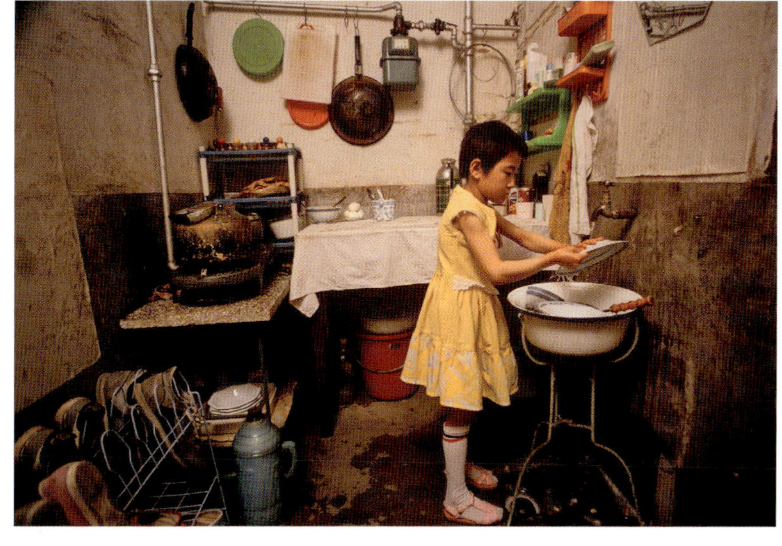

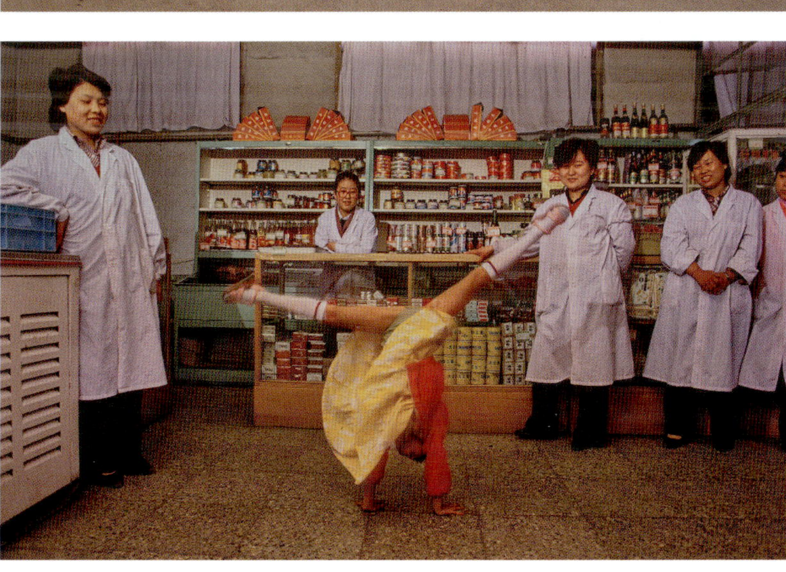

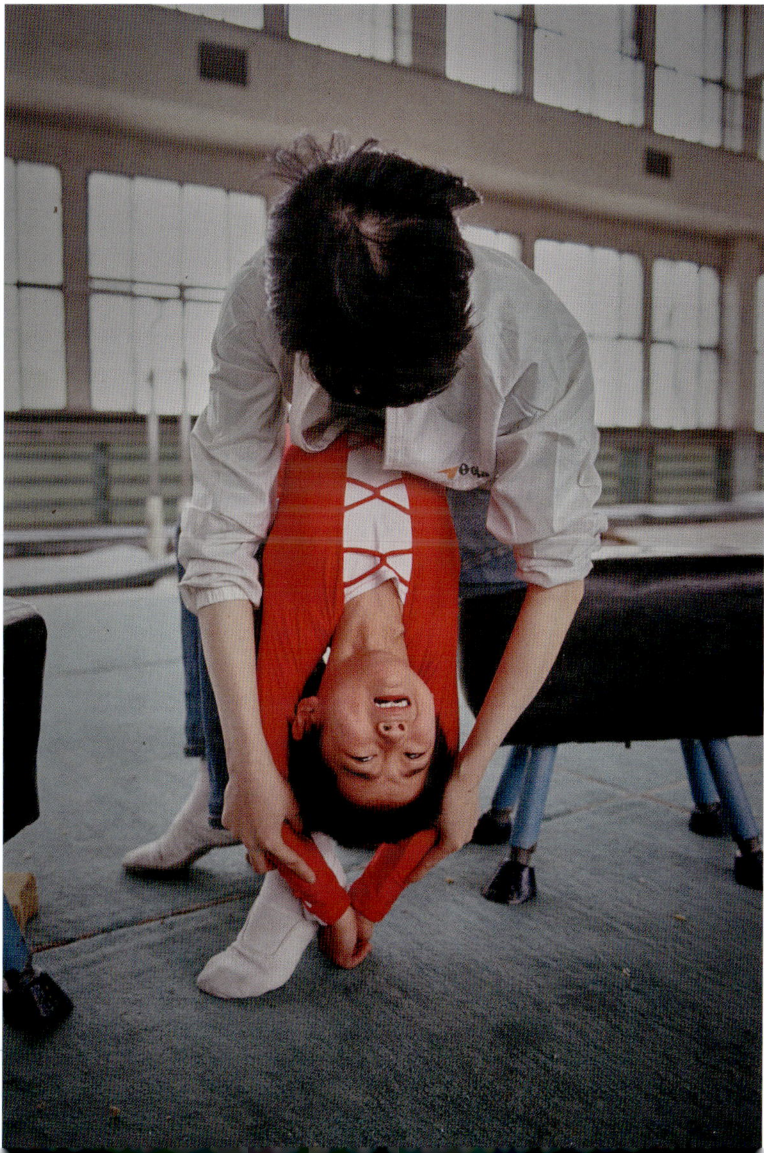

Probably couldn't shoot that final picture now (previous page, bottom right). As a Western journalist in '87, I was regarded as an oddity, and because the pictures I was shooting potentially served the greater good (the public relations desires of the Chinese government), I was allowed to shoot in a reasonably unfettered way. The fierce instructors of these young national-team-in-waiting tykes would no longer allow you to freely shoot their methods as they bend these kids into pretzels. They have become media savvy over time and realize the repercussions and potential negative backlash stemming from a picture of a crying child. At this point, though, I was new, and strange, and thus allowed.

Time and place. The fixer can help you make sure you are at the right place, at the right time. As always, luck plays a huge role in the success of a day in the field, but working with a fixer is a way to make good luck happen. John Loengard, my DOP at *LIFE*, said to me straight up, "I don't care if it's only five minutes, as long as it's the right five minutes." A good fixer can engineer that slice of time where it all works. And those few frames where it all works are well worth the millions of useless pixels spent to get there, at that moment, when the gods of light, color, and gesture smile on you. At times like this, I am always reminded of what my high school basketball coach would say after I made a good move or had a good game: "McNally, the sun doesn't shine on a dog's rear end too much, but right now it's shining on yours." When you get what you came for in your pictures, it makes you want to wiggle your butt and rub your tummy. Privately, of course. Back at the hotel. After the images are triple backed up and you know they're sharp.

Those few frames where it all works are well worth the millions of useless pixels spent to get there, at that moment, when the gods of light, color, and gesture smile on you.

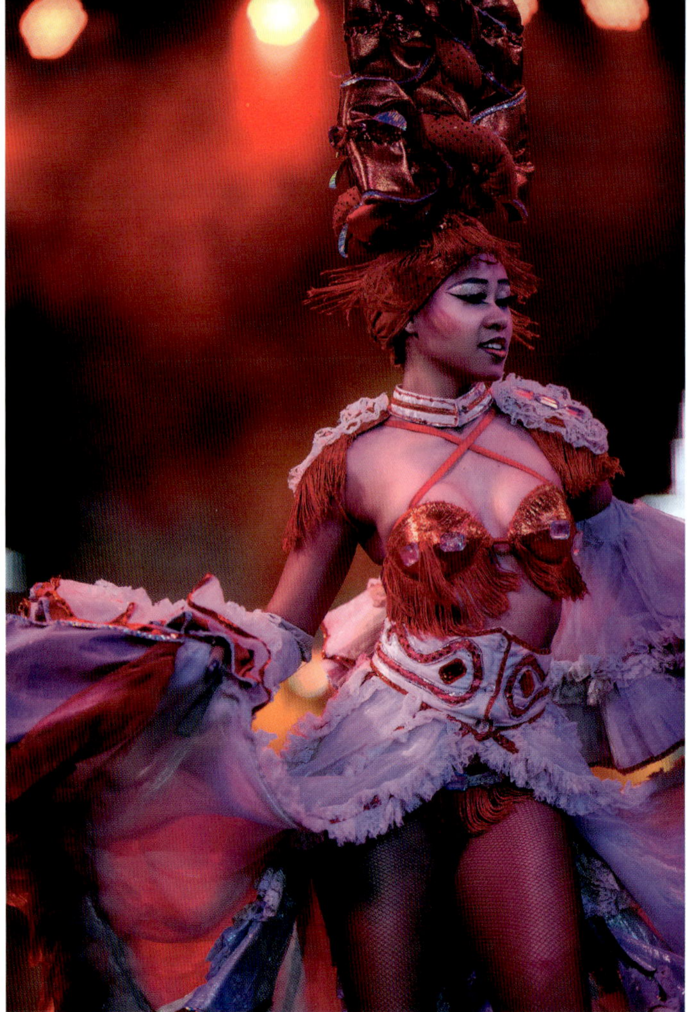

Fixers know the local price of eggs. They can take the burden off of you as the interface, certainly in terms of the nuance of language but, importantly, also in the realm of dollars. You want the picture so badly you are not a good negotiator. You should remain off to the side, out of the fray, the artist who seeks to create. The business happens apart from you. Money is exchanged, and paperwork, if needed, is signed off. What's left is the picture. The decks are clear at that point. No more fussing, except in the choice of scene, shutter speed, f-stop, location, light, lens, expression, and gesture. In other words, you have enough to think about. The fixer is a temporary umbrella for you in the pelting rainstorm of location work.

Your fixer can make sure you have a front row seat at a famed cabaret.

They can walk over to a Havana driver and know a good starting point for the ever-important discussion about the dough. Extra to stand on the hood, of course.

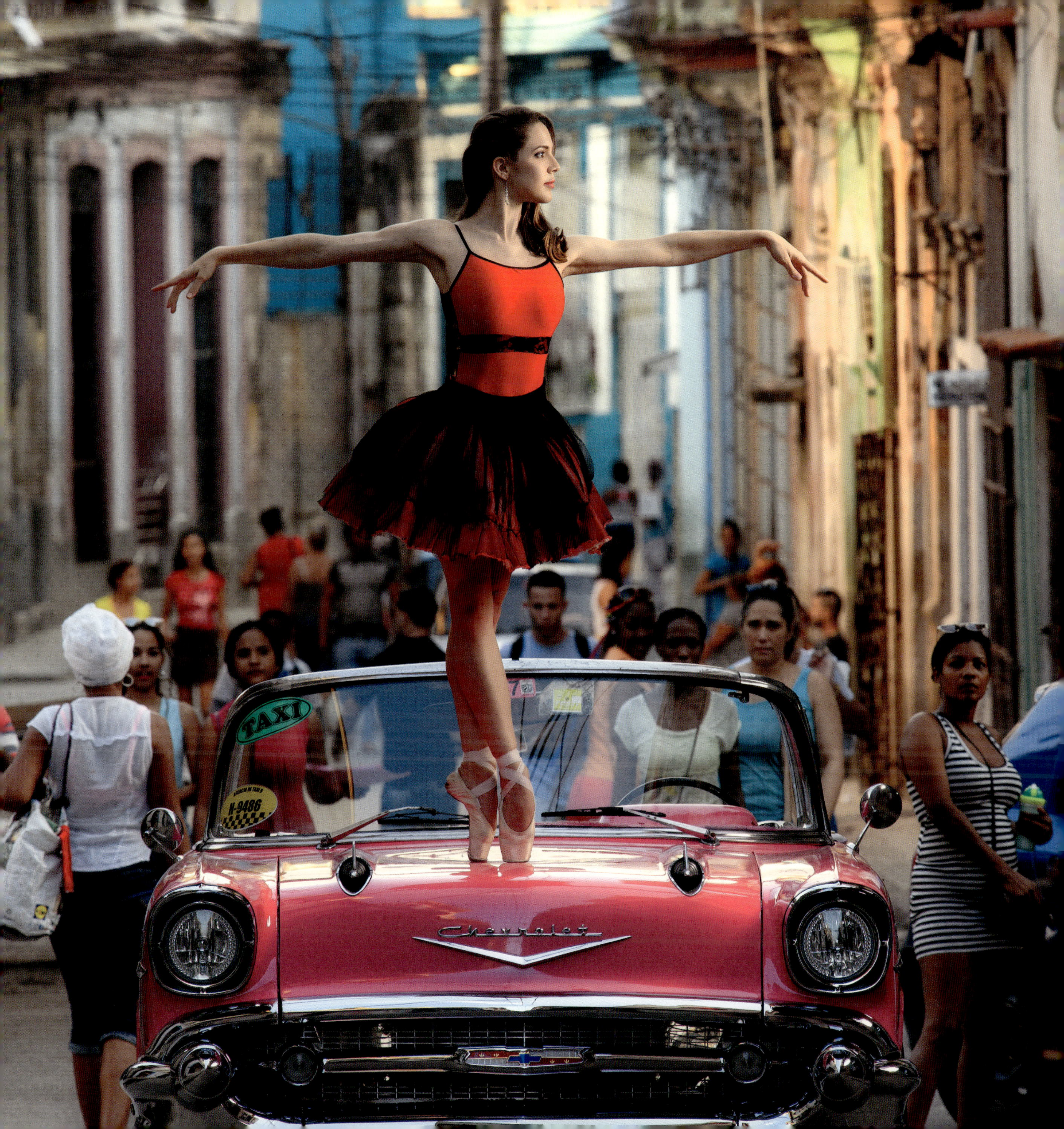

TAXI
H-9486
Chevrolet

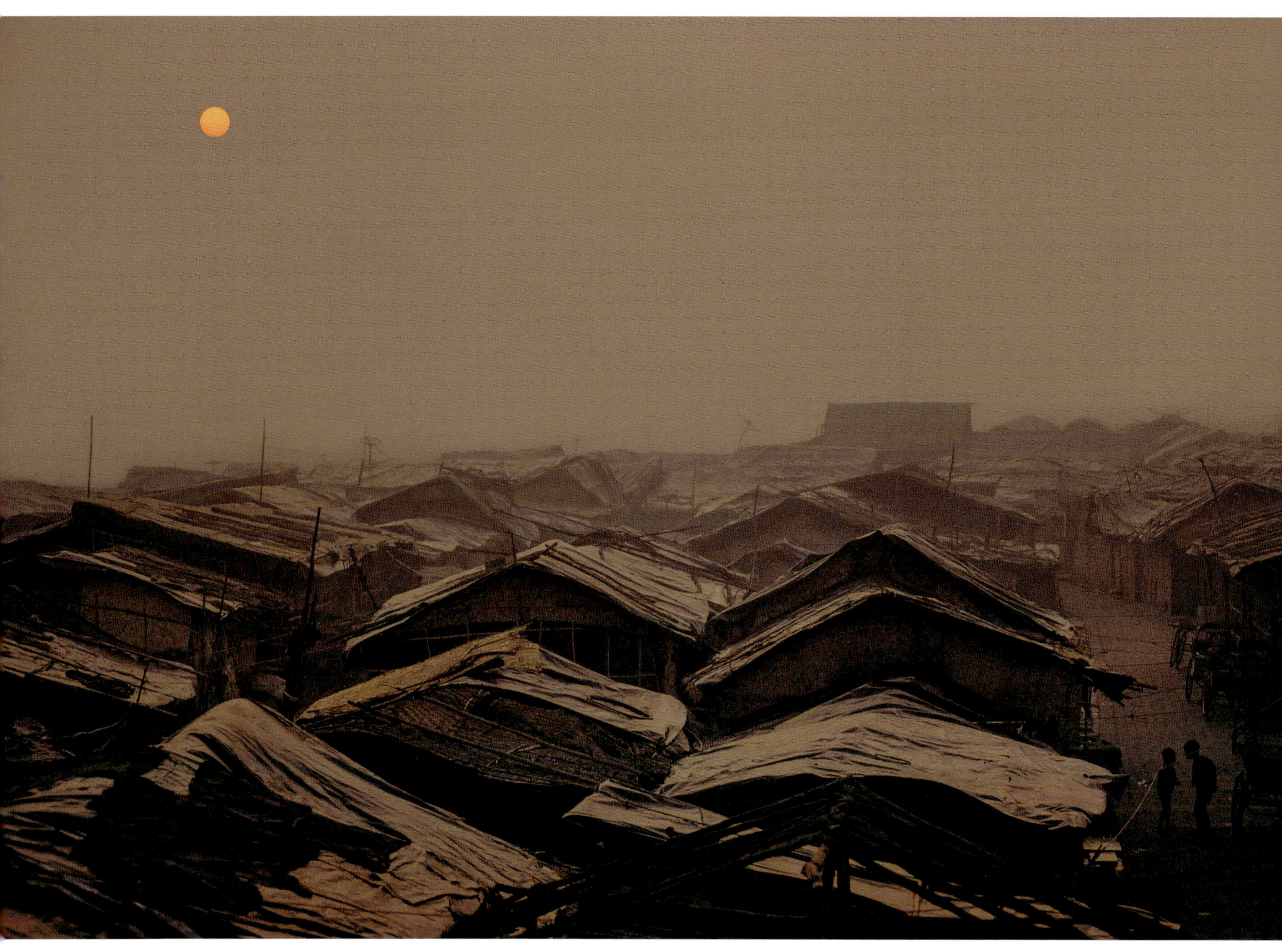

They can navigate a huge New Delhi slum, introduce you to people, and instruct you so that you can make a gift to their local school, and thus be allowed atop a neighborhood house for a sunrise view of the hazy vastness of Delhi.

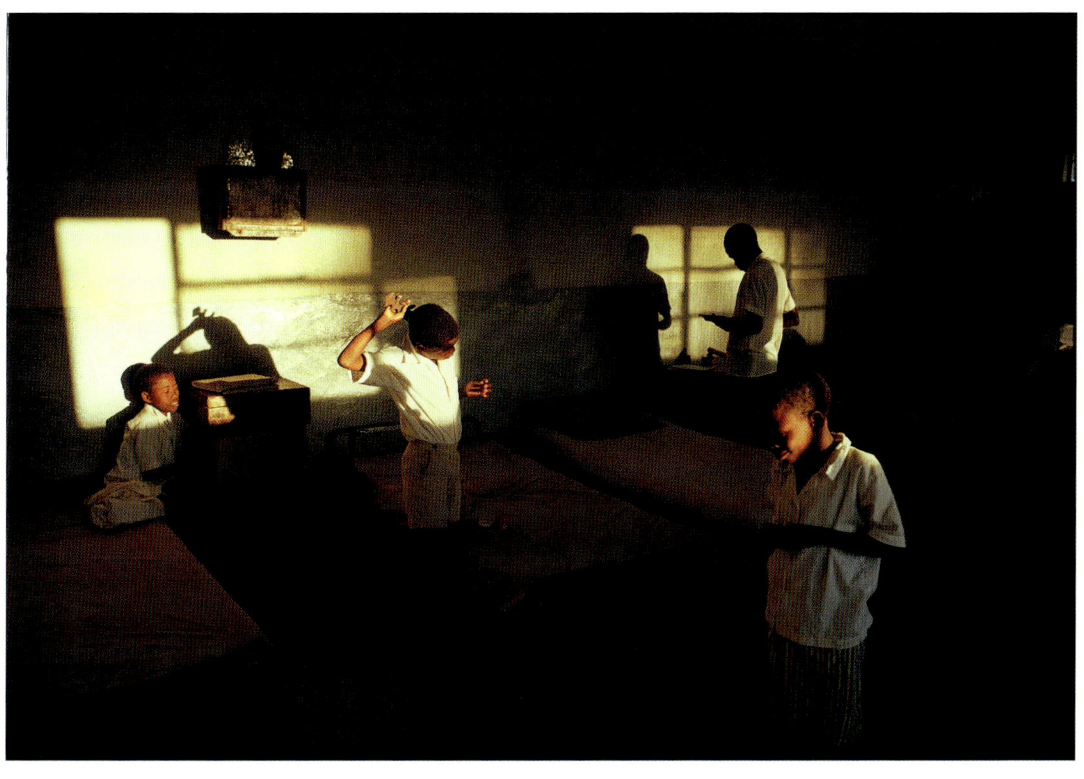

They can broker your entry, as the sun comes up, to a school in Africa for the visually impaired, where you can make a picture of blind children, summoning the astonishing courage and grit to greet another day without their sight, as they live with the devastating aftermath of trachoma.

I made these frames for *National Geographic*, pursuing a story on the human eye, and witnessed beautiful fortitude. I could not have gained entry, and the freedom to work, without my fixer arranging meetings with multiple local people who saw the advantage in getting the word out about this awful disease, an enemy of sight that is very preventable.

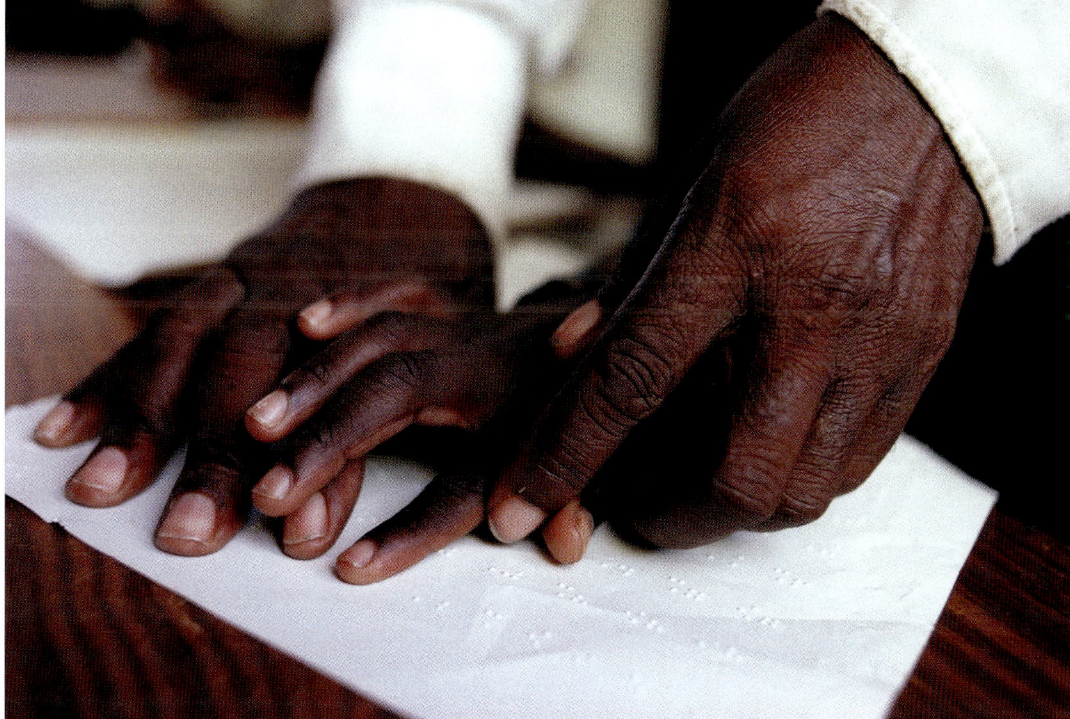

They can persuade the instructors at a Japanese sumo school to allow you to photograph a workout session where young girls are being trained in the traditionally male sport of sumo.

They can negotiate the literal roadblocks (in the form of giant stones in the roads) when seeking out the reclusive Tarahumara Indians in the vast canyons and high sierras of the interior of Chihuahua. The indigenous tribes there don't necessarily welcome visitors, historically, so going there in a solitary, unobtrusive way is best. Again, drinking might be involved. Their native brew is a beer made from corn, called Tesguino.

Here's the deal. There are no guarantees that, with a fixer, you'll find great pictures, or that anything at all will work out in your favor. The warranties that came with your camera do not apply to the results of your using it. Your fixer can't make the sun rise, but they can make sure you get up on a roof in Havana to see if it will.

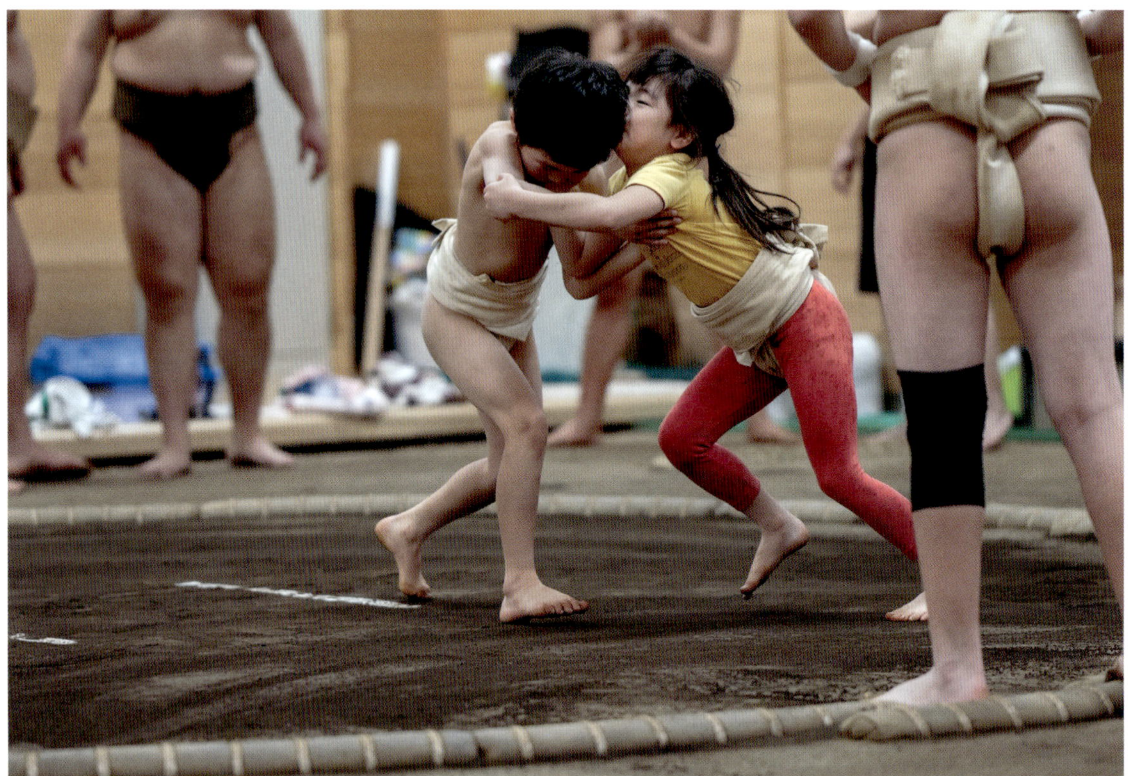

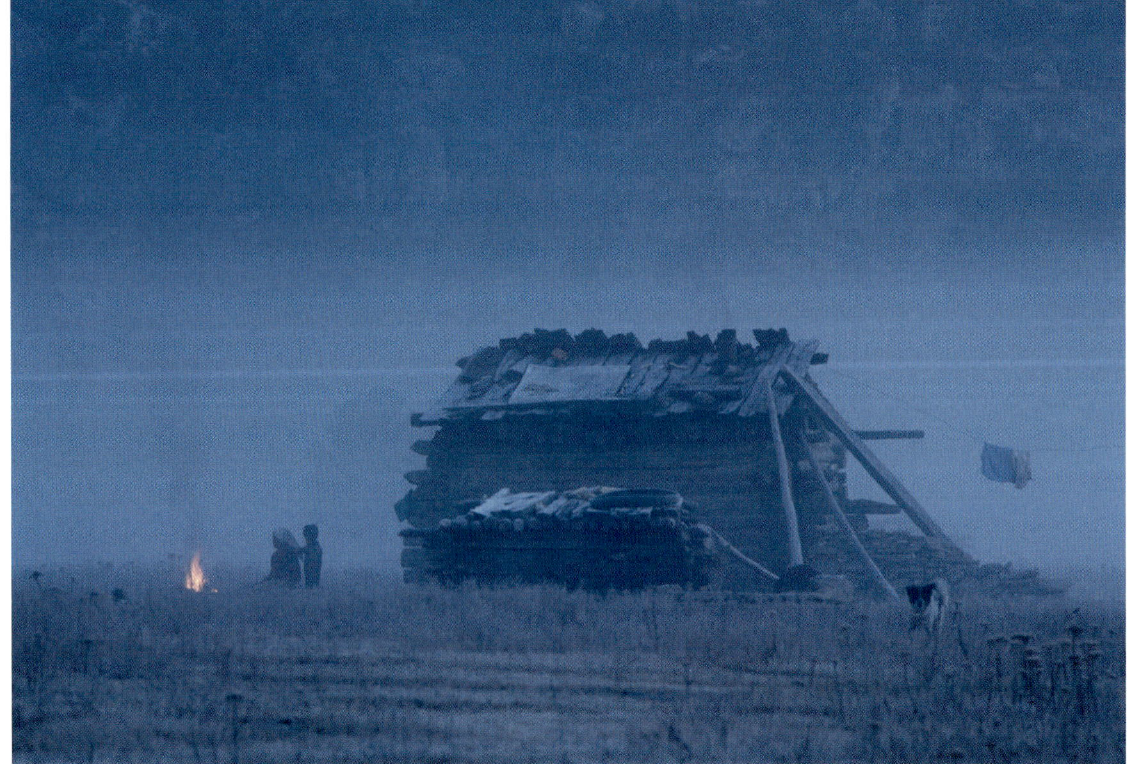

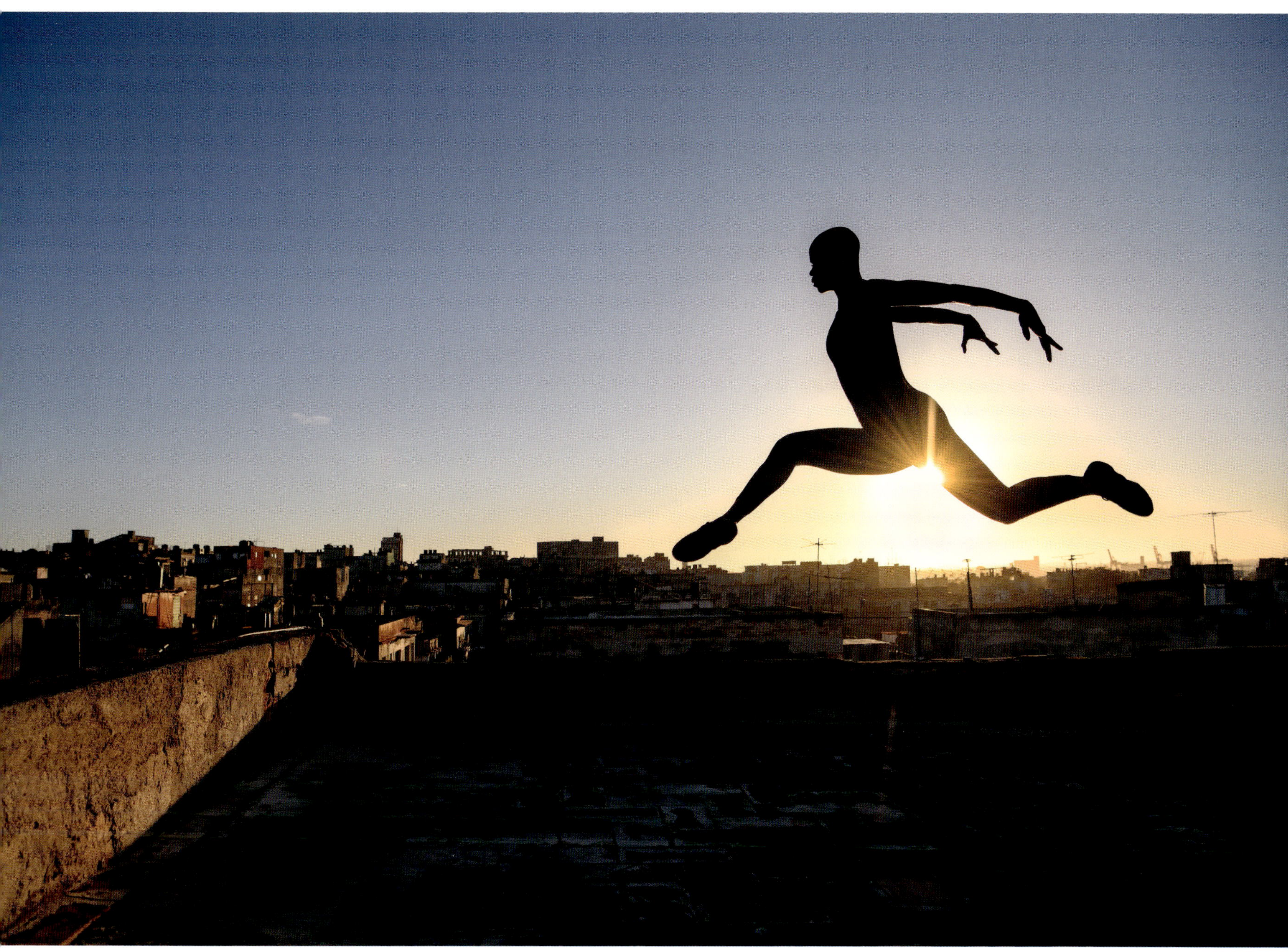

I'd rather be on a roof than a bus any day. Nothing wrong with the tour, or the bus, or the postcard overview, or the company of other photogs. It can be a wonderfully engaging experience and give you the gift of mobility inside a culture where you wouldn't have the resources to create your own, entirely custom week-long adventure. Photo travel workshops are terrific, as the group atmosphere accelerates the learning and enrichens everyone's photography.

But carve out a day for yourself. Find a fixer. Find a path apart.

The Luck
of the Click!

Ever get a shot that you feel really gets somebody? You know, captures their personality?

Eric Lindros, when he was at the top of his game, played for the Philadelphia Flyers. Good scorer, dominating player, feared on the ice. Great guy. We had a hoot in the little impromptu photo booth I set up next to the practice ice. Probably because I was not on the opposing team.

I mean, would you want to see this guy, 6'4", 240, bearing down on you on the ice, flying on skates, with a stick in his hands?

"Ha ha ha! Die opposing team sumbitch! I will beat you with my stick and slash you with my blades, all the while laughing maniacally at your discomfort!"

Sometimes, the camera in your hands sings the truth in whimsical ways. You get lucky. You have fun. Split seconds, frozen forever. Like those Jurassic Park mosquitos, trapped in amber, causing trouble, millions of years later.

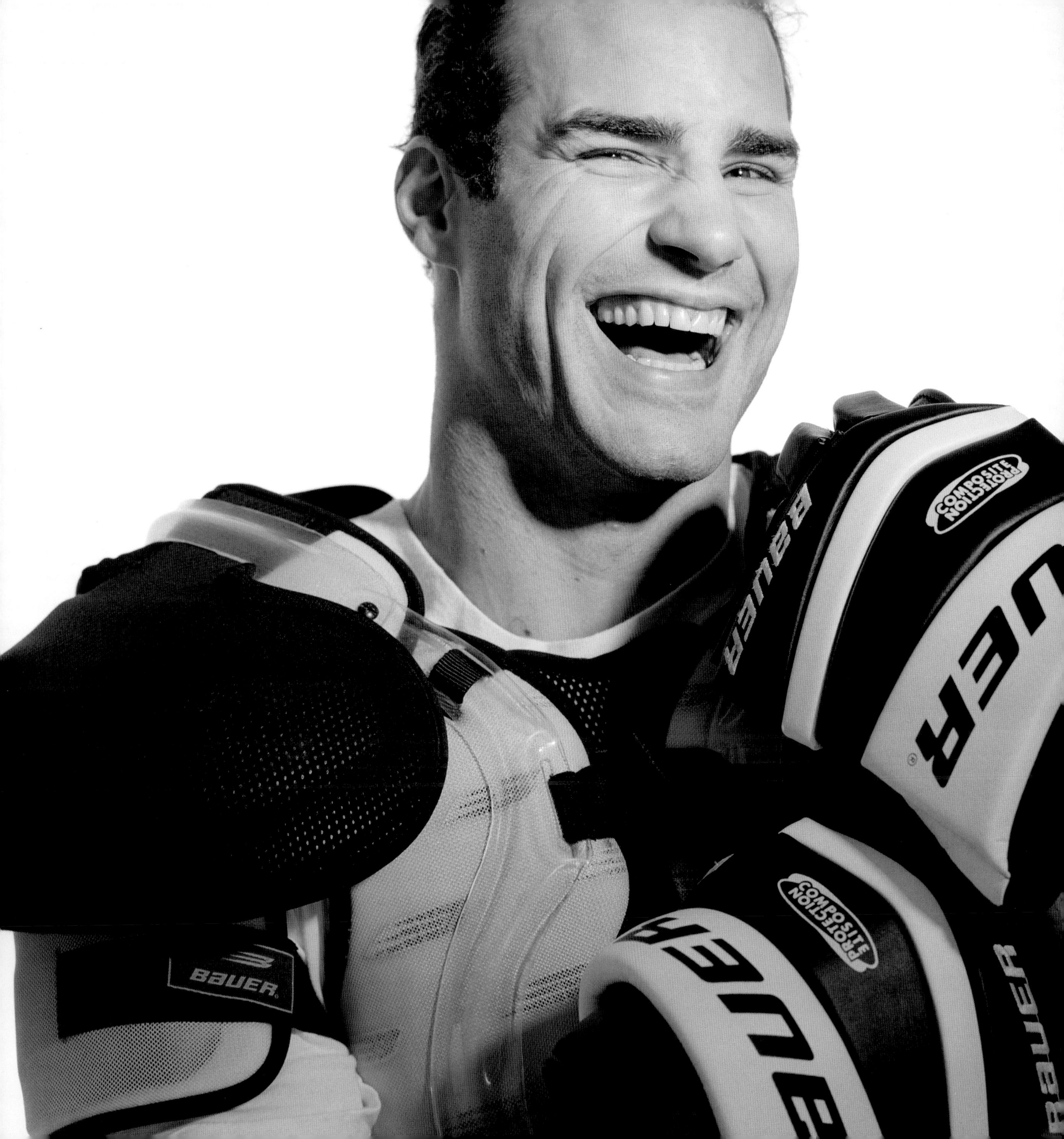

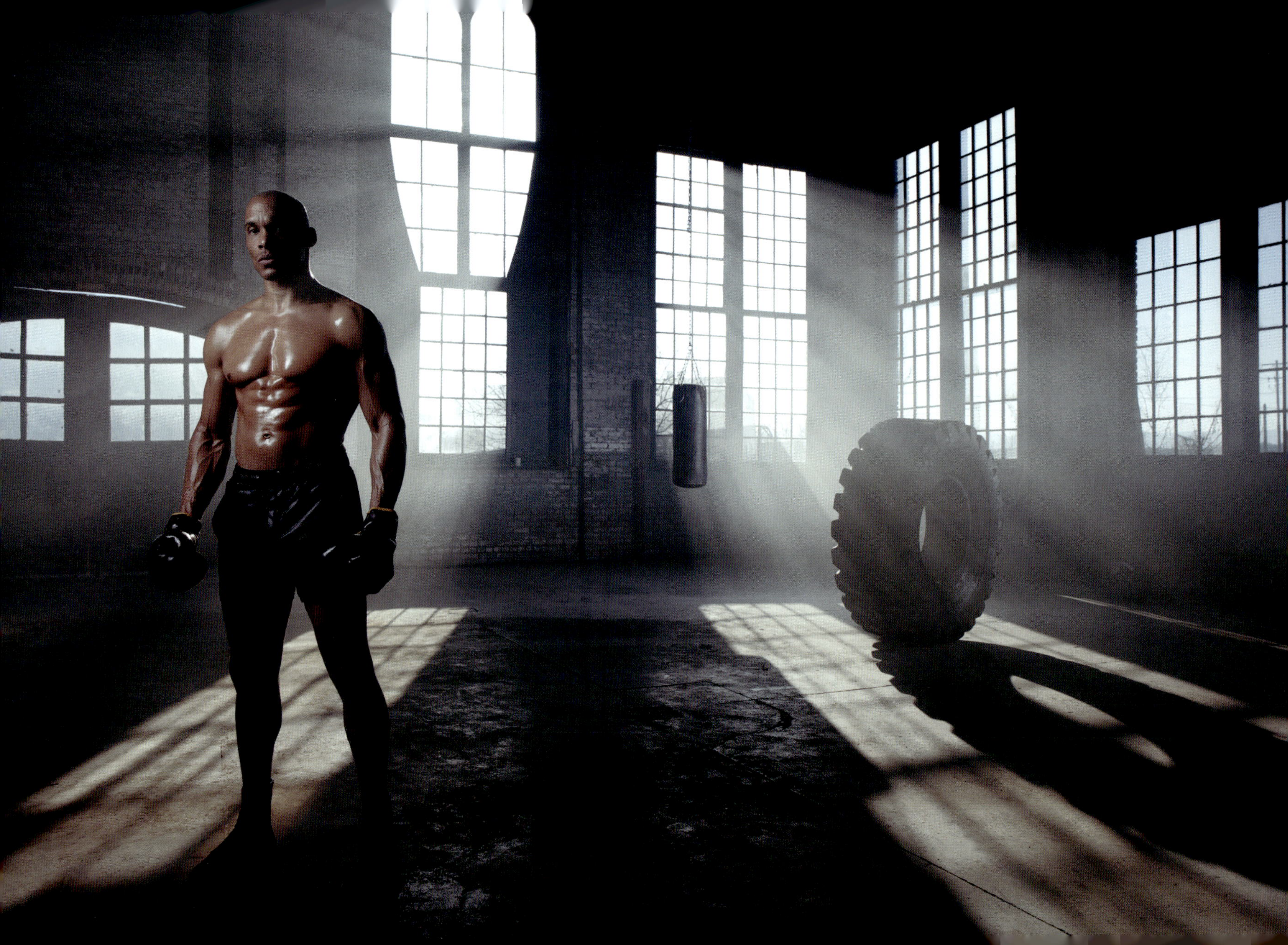

Bullet Points from a Day in the Field

Time and light. They move fast.

Photographers have to move with the light, surely as animals migrate with the seasons. The sun moves relentlessly, and gives you various gifts throughout the day—angling, bouncing, and careening around a location. Look for those gifts, be flexible, and stand ready to grab them at camera. They may be simply splendid on their own, and all you need to do is frame and shoot. Or, as is stated on many gifts, some assembly may be required. An adjustment here and there.

And as the day closes and the sun plummets for the horizon, get ready to race it.

One sun, one old warehouse.

First successful frame (right). 11:05 a.m. The sun is high, hard, and colorless. But the angularity of the light matches the geometry of the location. Be careful to place your subject, and shoot. Outside, this light is an unmitigated disaster. Inside, the windows frame it and shape it to your advantage.

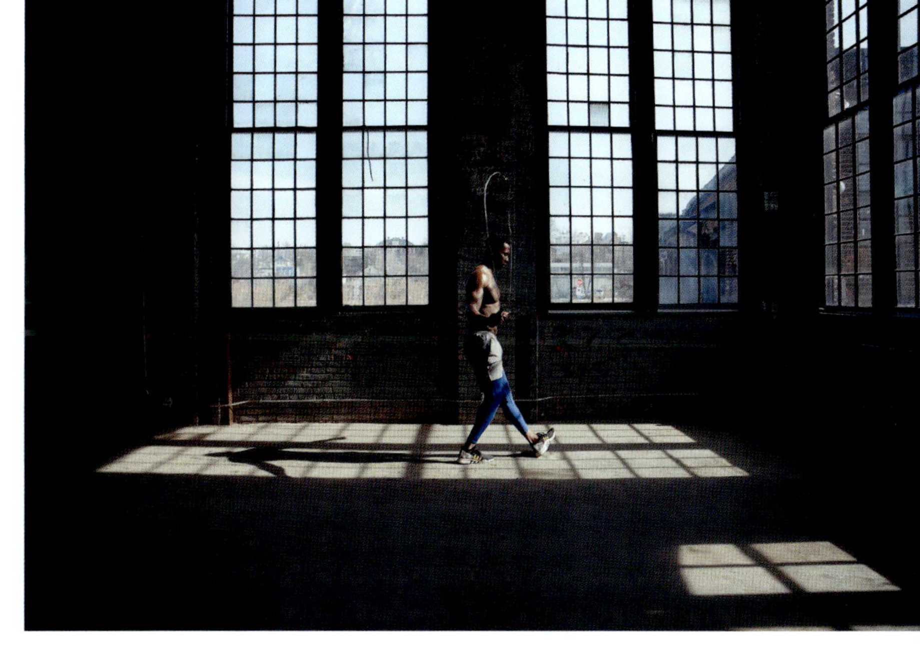

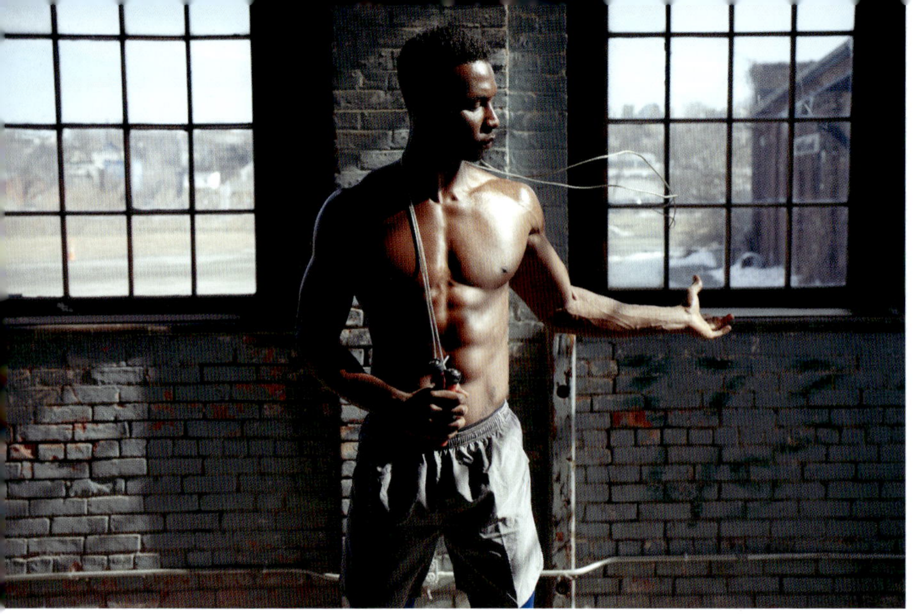

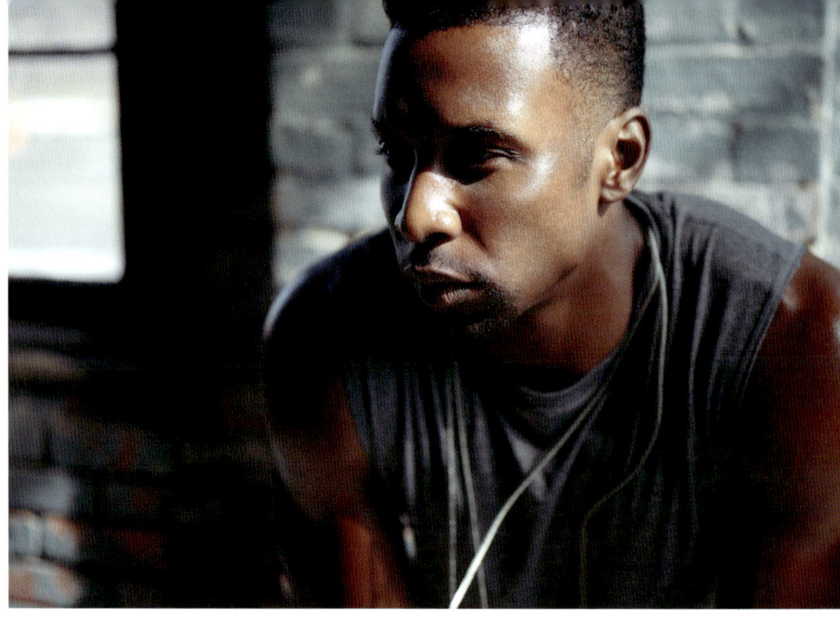

Change your frame. Go with the geometry. Take pieces of it. 11:15 a.m.

Peel the onion! Get closer. Not great portrait light, at all. But it works. 11:41 a.m.

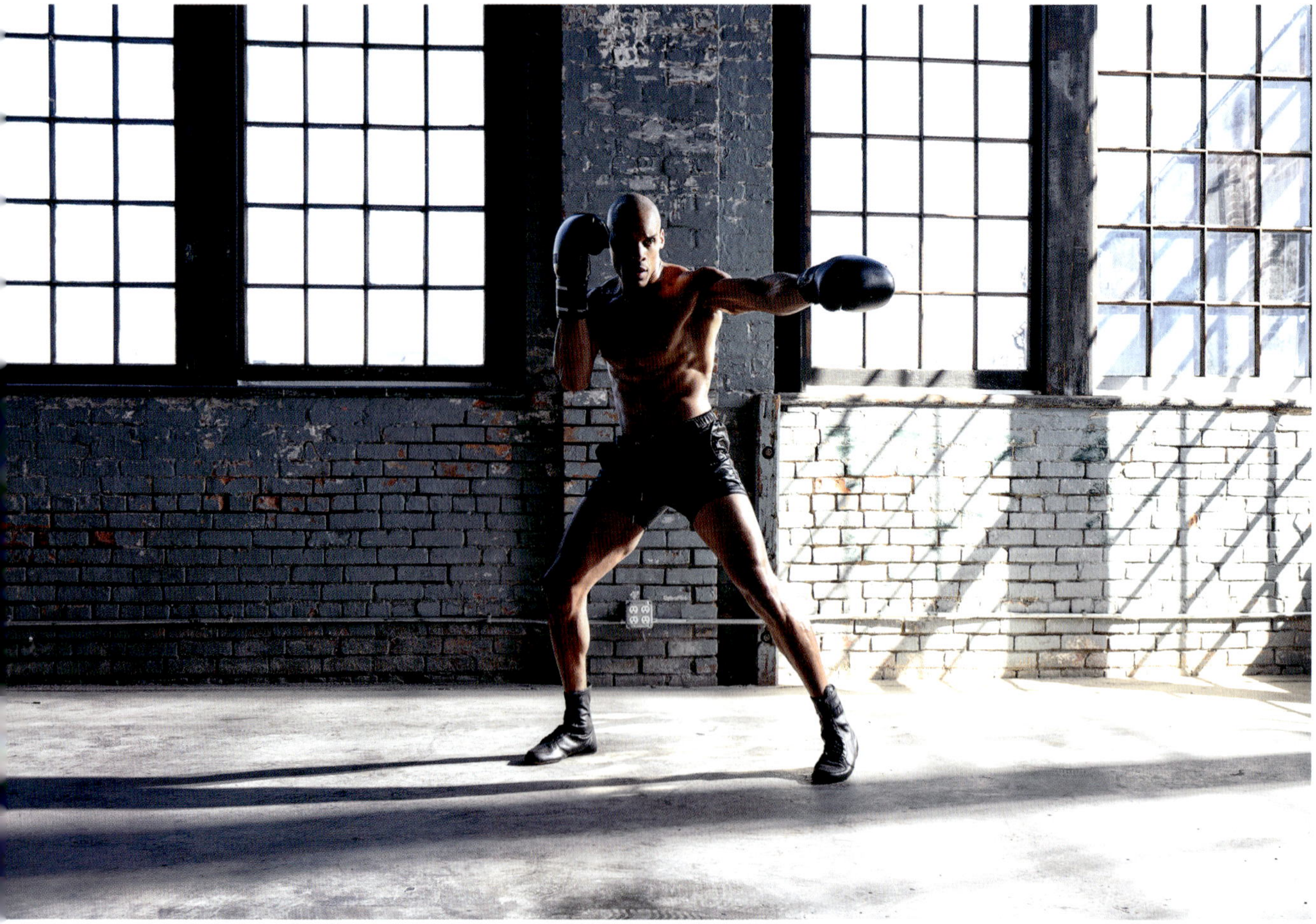

The fierceness of the light, the slashing angularity of it, speaks to gesture. Accommodate with an appropriate subject. 11:51 a.m.

Lunch.

Clear the decks as best you can in this old, cavernous space. Follow the light, now on the other side of the building, heating up different windows, slashing through the skylights. Still high and hard.

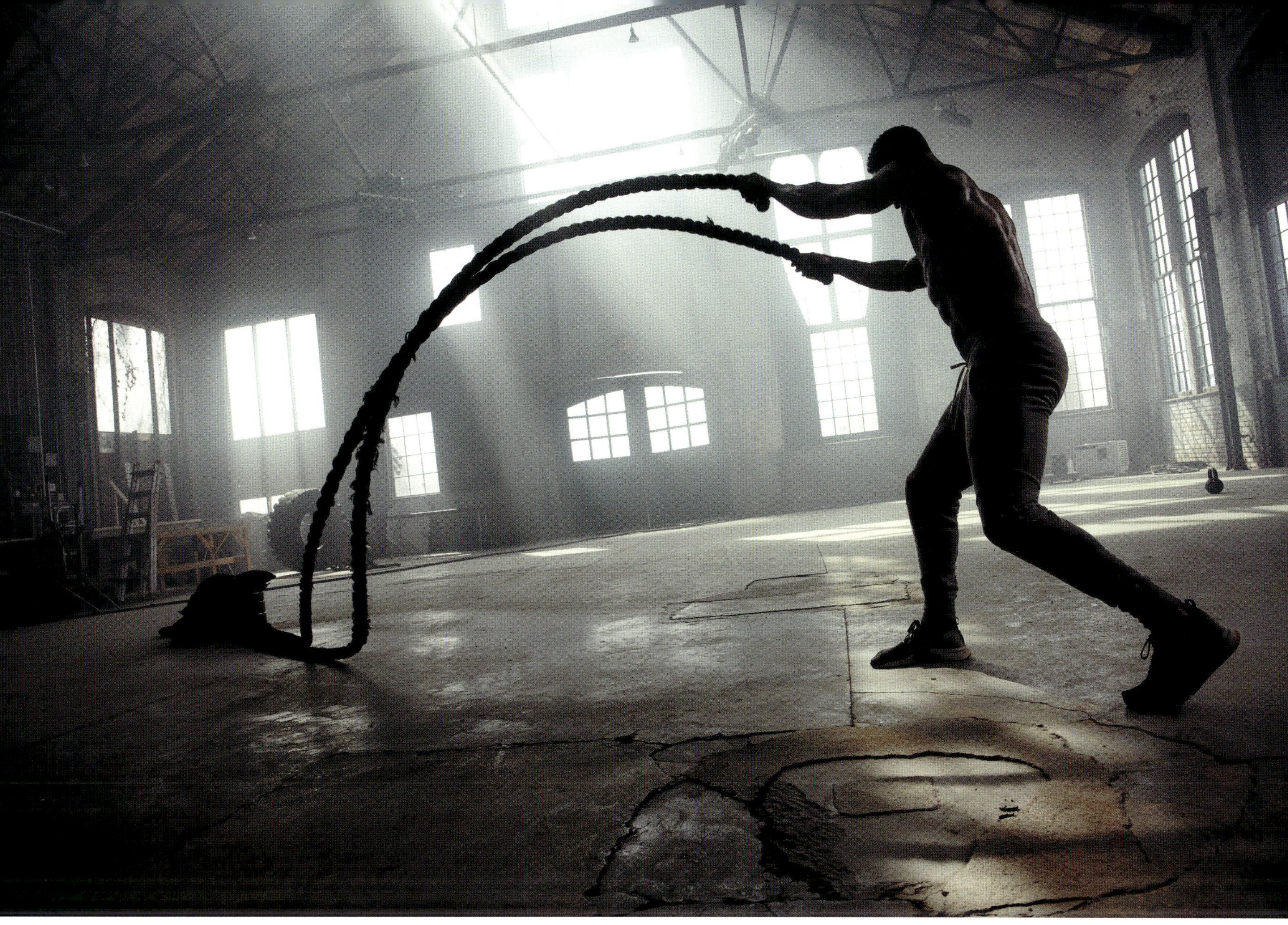

1:56 p.m. Joshua Cummings goes off on the battle ropes, and I do nothing but smoke up the light and place him graphically. Well, almost nothing. He is largely silhouetted, as you would expect. Overt, overplayed, noticeable flash kills this picture. But detail, however slight, is important. Off to camera right is a 1x6 strip softbox, vertically arrayed, and controlled by a fabric grid. This low power source produces an angle of incidence skip off of the musculature of his back. Tiny bit of highlight on his backside and legs. Thread the needle. Don't go by the numbers on the power pack. Go by your eye and your gut. Just enough is already almost too much.

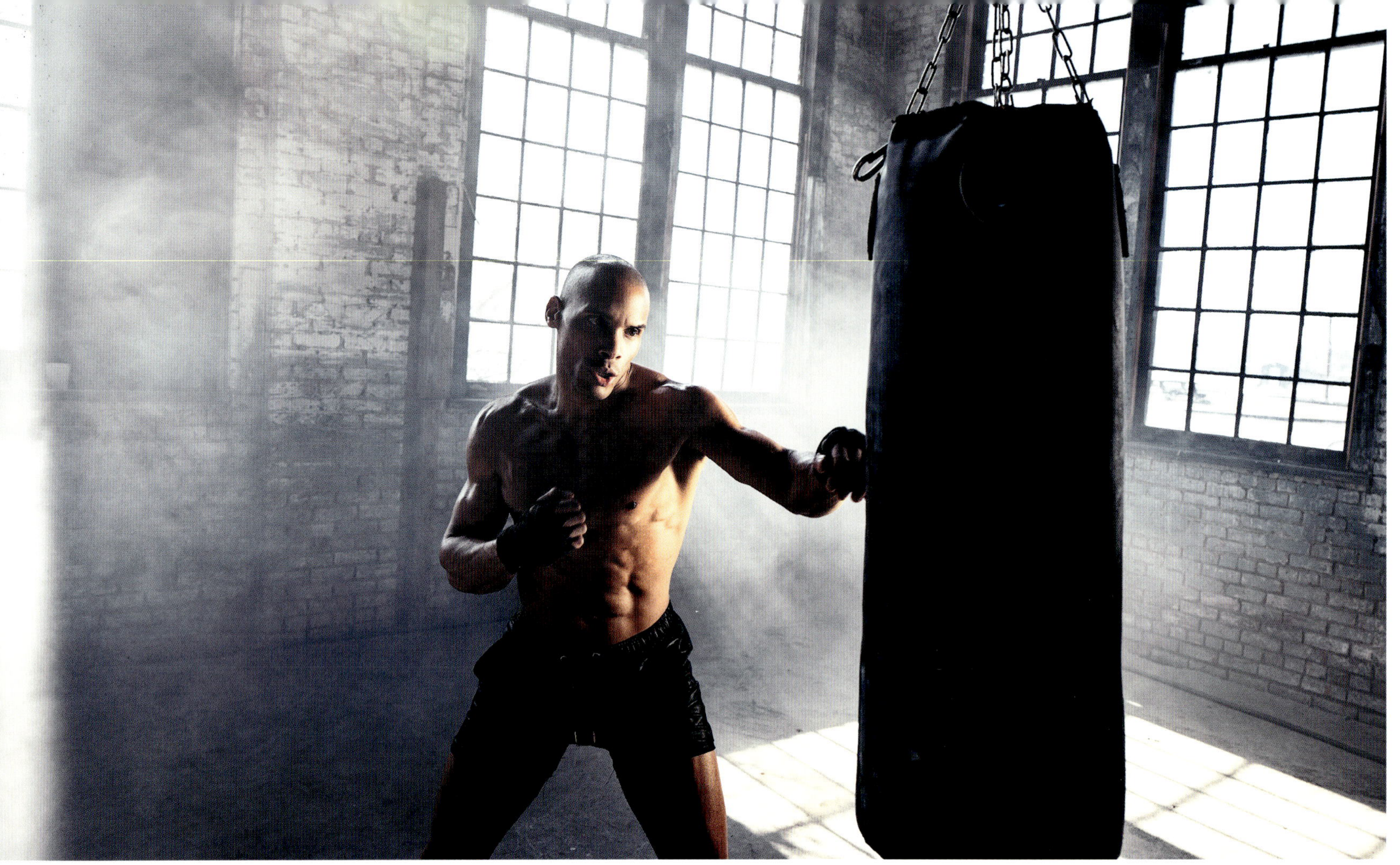

Rig a heavy bag. The sun keeps moving, and fast. Now high-lighting different windows. Shift the angle for the camera and the action.

The screaming light is a perfect backdrop for the chiseled Ray James, who is in the martial arts hall of fame. It's now 4:05 p.m. The day's home stretch begins. He works the bag, and again, I choose to tweak this scene in a minimal but essential way. The light is so hard, all you need is a reflector. One of our crew grabs a small, silvery source—a TriGrip—which can be angled and continuously redirected quickly as our subject beats the living daylights out of the bag. Silvery light matches the colorless sun, still shy of golden hour. Andrew, on our crew, shimmers the

light at Ray, moving it with him. There's real variance here, as the reflected light is not static. It misses, and hits, bobbing and weaving like an opponent in the ring. The erratic nature of the light is a rich vein to mine at the camera. The light wobbles, glancing and flaring. The here-and-there nature of it can be mad-dening, and many frames will be wasted. But the ones that hit in unexpectedly beautiful ways . . . in boxing parlance, a knockout.

4:12 p.m. Angle the reflector low, so the light comes up and emphasizes the fierce nature of the subject. The board here (opposite, top left) has been shifted from silver to a "sunfire" color, where gold banding runs across the silver source, warm-ing the light and breaking up its mirrorlike hardness.

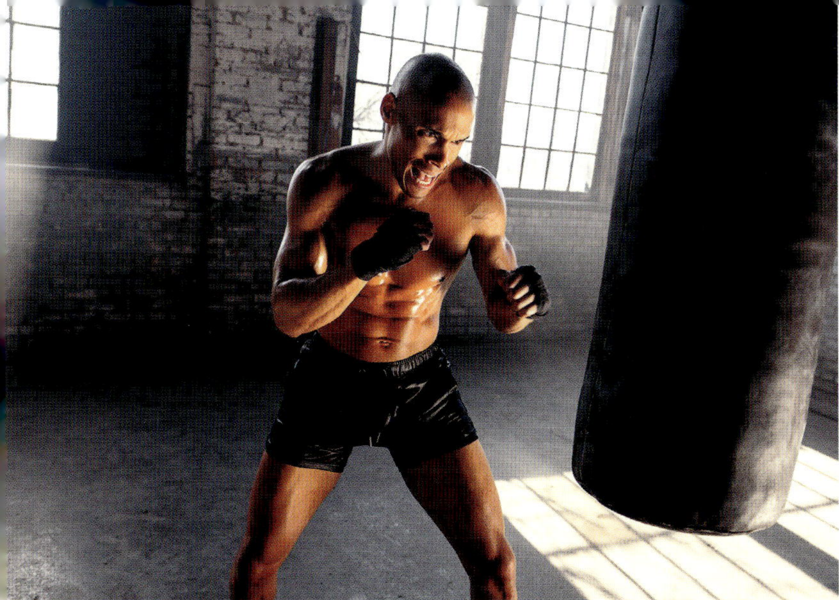

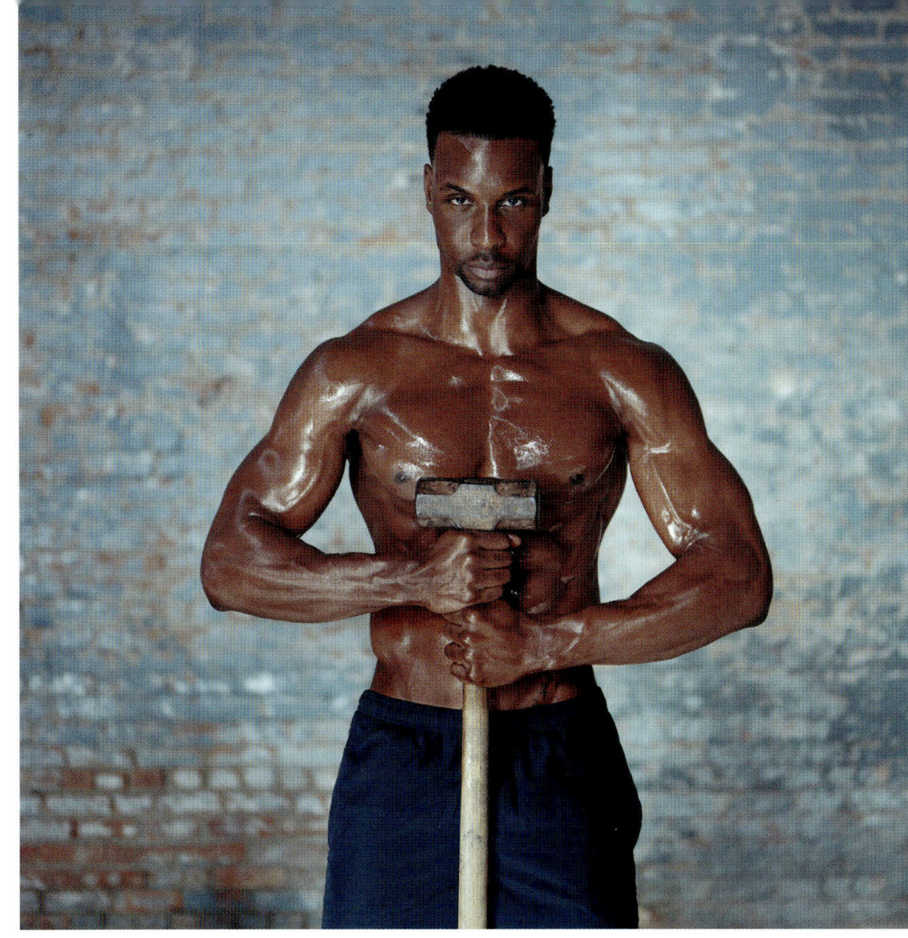

4:53 p.m. Look for the migration patterns of the light. While you can, grab a wall, illuminated by the bouncing highlights off the warehouse floor. Natural late afternoon light. Add oil and a sledgehammer.

5:09 p.m. Scramble. Roll in the truck tire. The shadows grow long. I moved Ray into an appropriate space, and here is the first time I actually lit one of my subjects all day. In the interest of saving time, I grabbed the 1x6 strip softbox, already set up, and pushed it hard to camera left, radical enough to shadow and define his superstructure, and steep enough to let one side of his face go into shadow, emphasizing the menacing determination. The fabric grid in the light source helps with this, as it corrals the light output and directs it. A quick survey of the scene alerted me to the one thing that went blank, drab, and needed explaining for the viewer: The black heavy bag back by the windows was blob-like, a giant, silhouetted Tylenol. I took a Profoto B4 head and fixed it with a ten-degree spot grid and fired it at the bag. The light spread over that distance, of course, but in the general heat of the beaming sun, that bit of scatter is not noticeable. But what it did was highlight the bag. All you need. Define the background. It richens and enlivens the story the picture is telling.

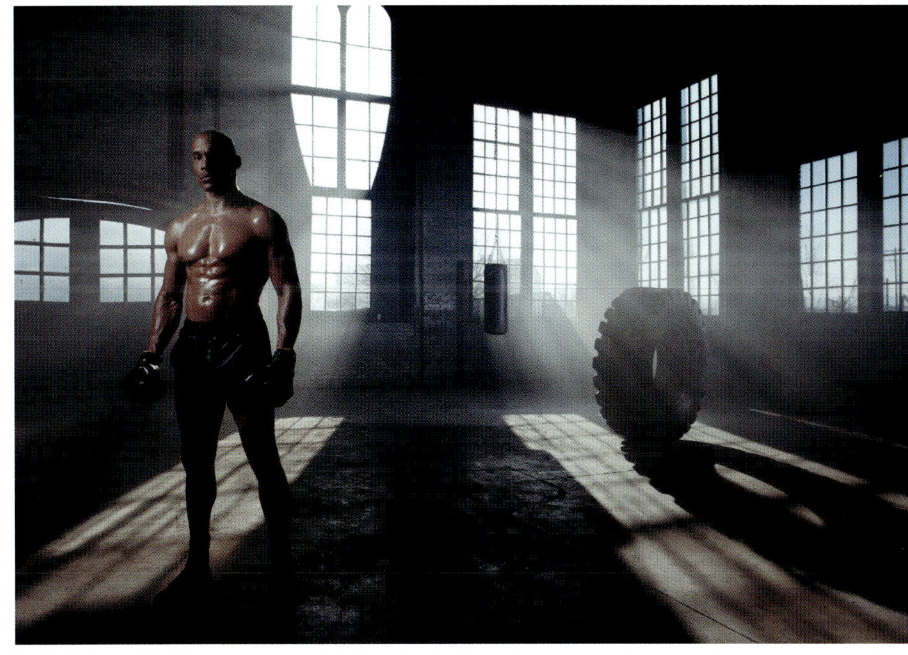

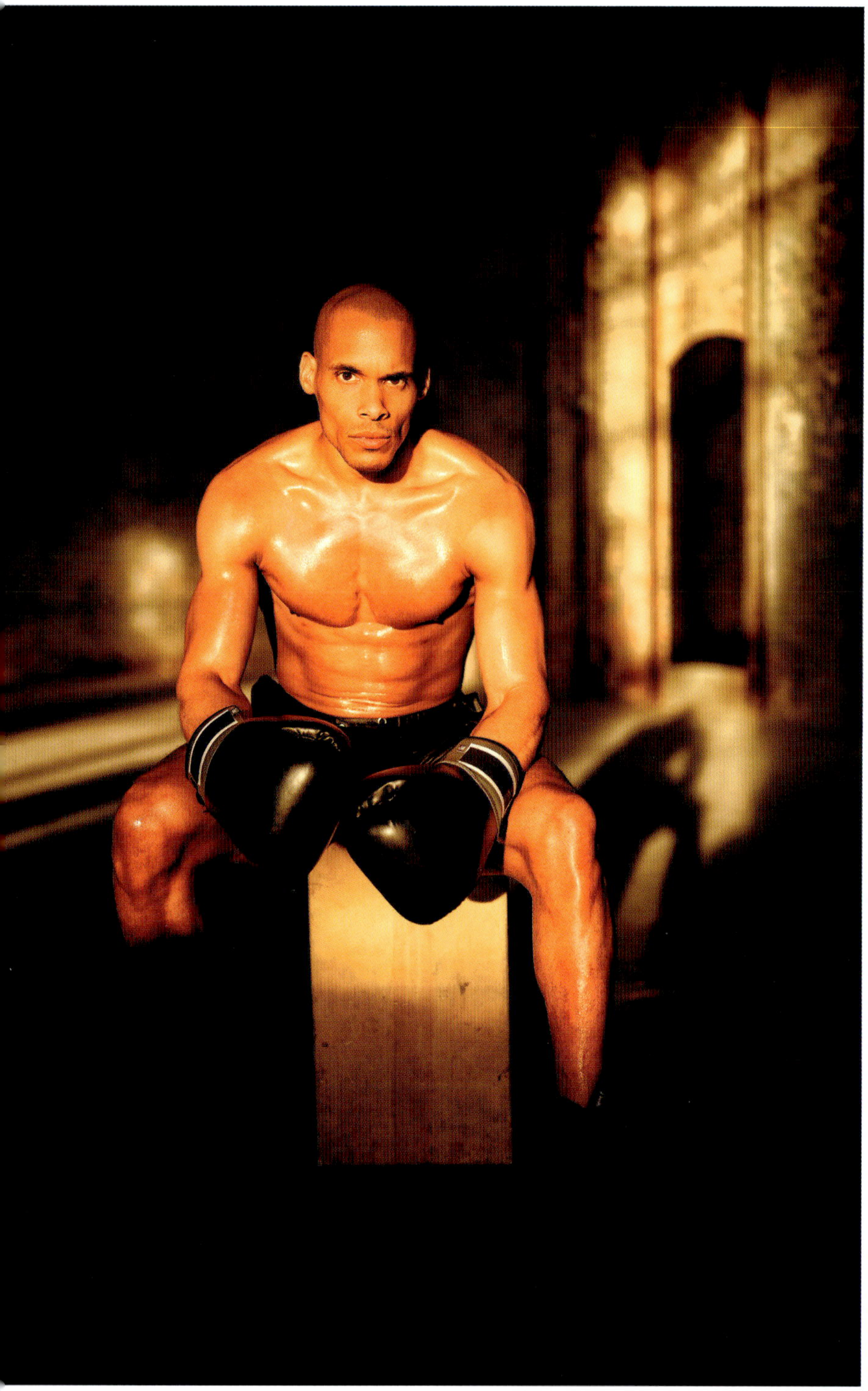

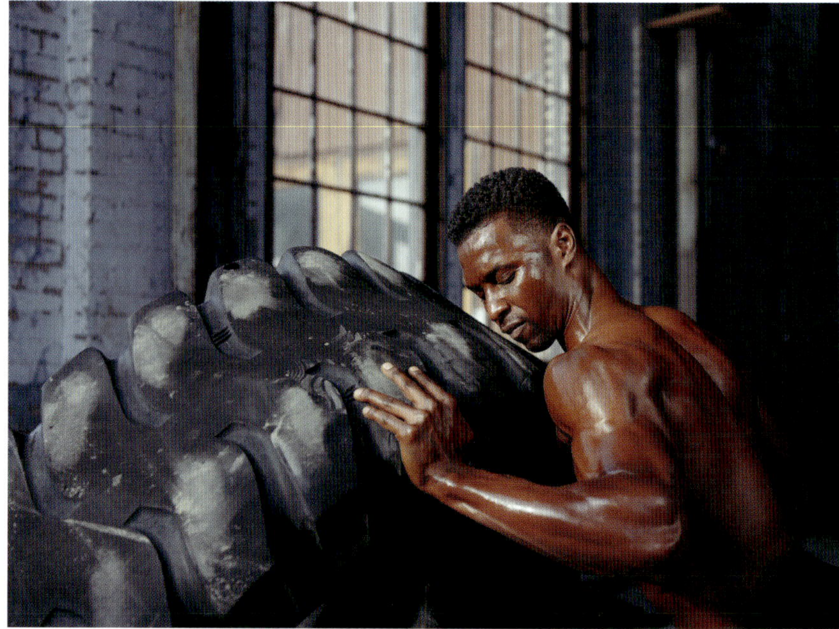

6:15 p.m. The race is just about over. The light is low and golden. Not much to do but sit Ray in its path. He owns the camera, even in repose. Long lens for the power of compression, low angle to emphasize strength and authority.

Fade to black.

If I were to grade my efforts on this day, I'd go in at about an A−. Good pictures. Good crew camaraderie. Treated my subjects well, and Ray James has become a friend. My downside, right there at camera with me, as always, is the need to control. I like light that is rich and beautiful. I like to baffle it, shape it, push it, and pull it. I had to stuff that tendency back down my own throat, follow the sun, and take what it gave me. A couple times in the day, I slowed, and over-directed, and the action got stilted (above).

But thankfully, it was a momentary relapse. Don't overthink. Feel it, shoot it.

The Aging Photographer

Age is like a heavily laden, slow-moving freight train backing up over your private parts while you lay strapped down to the tracks by time. It's relentless in its bumping, lurching, screeching, wheezing, grinding progress. No matter how loud you scream and protest, it drowns you out, and the one thing you know for absolute certain is that the conductor is up there in the cozy cab having a coffee and a ham sandwich and cannot hear you.

After a lifetime in photography, hauling gear, hauling ass, lifting cases, crammed in planes, 3 a.m. calls, and the dreary backstory that accompanies almost every decent photo assignment, my trainer at the gym describes every exercise he gives me to do as "corrective."

Photographers. We spend a lot of time with both our face, literally, and our butt, figuratively, in the breeze. This leaves a rich patina of destruction over what was once a shining visage, radiating with the joy of anticipated decisive moments. I went for a facial not long ago, prior to a public speaking gig, the theory being that even an old, dented car looks better when it's polished. The technician looked over the lunar landscape of my face through a magnifier and recounted the damage. "Well, you have pitted pores over here, and you have blackheads on your nose, and there are exploded capillaries on your nose and chin. Also, up here on your forehead, you have a permanent frown." She said

that last sentence while tracing this line of sadness with her gloved finger.

"Chrissie, bring me the big knife!"

(Many thanks to Nic Cage, who famously uttered the above line in his role as the devastated baker in *Moonstruck*. It was the first thing that came to mind as I finished this note.)

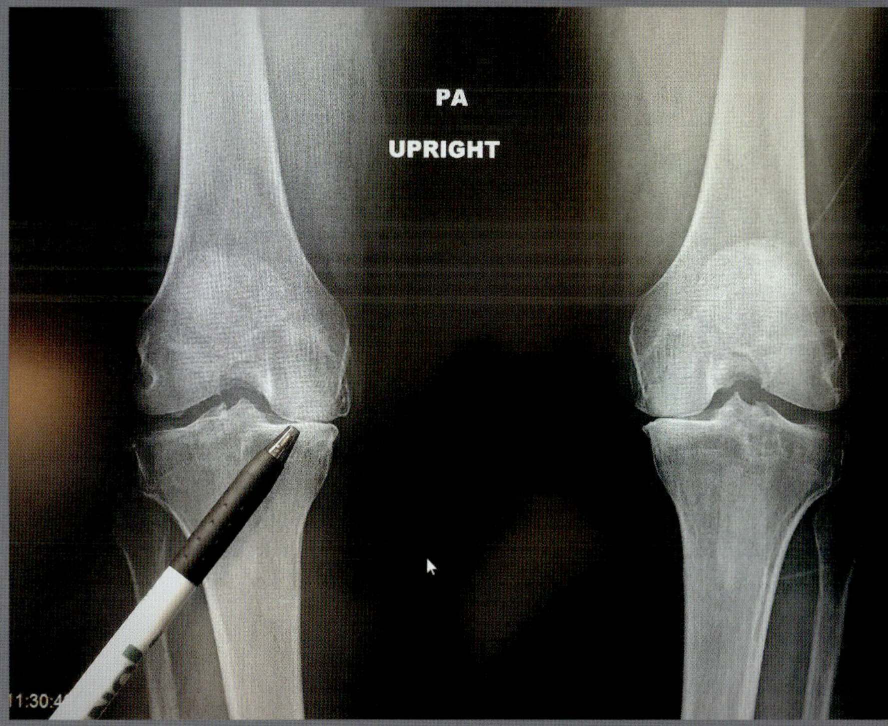

When Hubris Meets Stupid

To be clear, the title of this story is about me.

As a freelance photographer, this is an intersection you wish to avoid. One of the tenets you might want to observe as you conduct business comes straight to you, as they say, "Live from Las Vegas!"

The house always wins.

We can be emotional creatures, us photogs. Hell, we have to be. It's a job requirement just like those you see on government job postings, demanding the potential applicant have "excellent communication skills" or "the ability to work as a team member." For photographers, required skills might include "the ability to improvise quickly in an ever-changing, fluid situation" or "the ability to relate to diverse groups of people and personalities" and, certainly, the much-needed "ability to communicate with empathy and understanding." Somewhere on that list might also be "the ability to react poorly to authority and behave like an ego-driven asshole."

As preeminent photographer Bill Allard has said, "You cannot do superior work if you are indifferent." Very true. But this passionate involvement, this requisite emotionalism, while mandatory at the camera, should be dropped like a hot brick when it comes to business and billing. When you do business from an emotional place, trouble is sure to follow.

TIME magazine sent me out to photograph Phil Sokolof, the "Cholesterol Crusader." Phil grew wealthy in the construction business and, as a hard-charging businessman, suffered a heart attack at the age of 43. He was a non-smoker and not overweight. He became convinced that high-fat foods were the culprit and, using his personal fortune, began a one-man crusade targeting the high-fat content offered by fast food chains, particularly McDonald's. A crucial element of his campaign was huge, full-page ads in prominent newspapers, screaming in bold caps, "The Poisoning of America!" and "McDonald's, Your Hamburgers Have Too Much Fat!"

It worked. He pretty much single-handedly made the fast food industry react and offer healthier options, with less use of tropical oils and less fat across the board. He made a difference in America's diet at the drive thru.

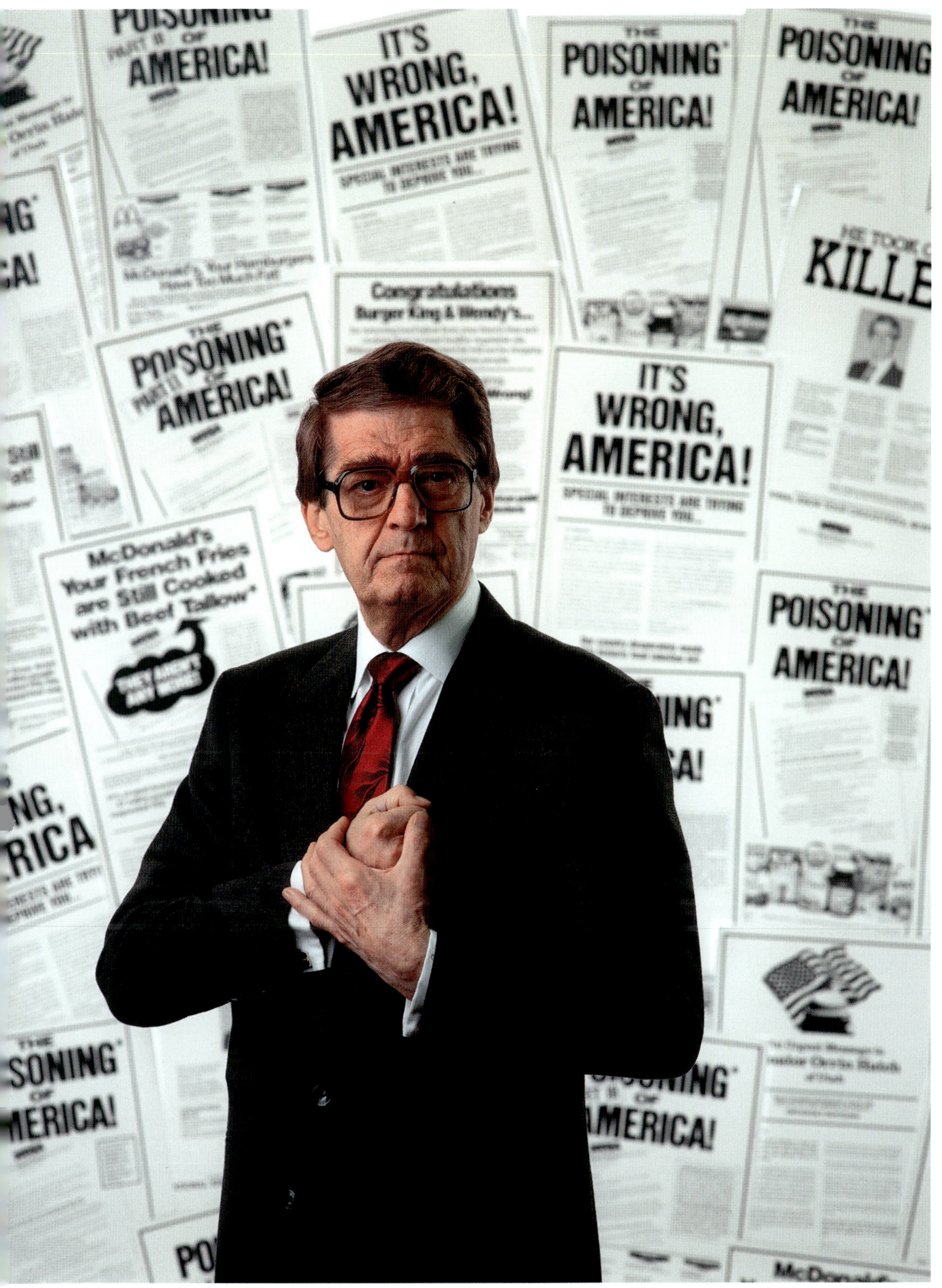

I headed out to meet with Phil, a native of Omaha. We got along okay, though he was quite the art director and used to getting his way. My graphic solution was to concentrate on the newspaper ads, which were the engine of his mission's success. I got Phil to give me page proofs of his ad layouts. Then my assistant and I used spray fixative to adhere these proofs to a really big sheet of milk plexiglass. I rented a studio, braced the plexi upright, and then backlit the living daylights out of it with flash. It filled the frame with black and white punch. Then, of course, I put Phil—and his nearly-impossible-to-light car windshield glasses—in front of the display. I asked him to make a gesture suggesting his heart. Boom.

I also, being the good magazine photog that I am, ever mindful of the mission at hand, and that a magazine like *TIME* needs options, brought Phil at dusk to an intersection with a Mickey D's in the background. This was classic, sunset, old school, medium format, transparency protocol. Full green fluorescent filter on the light, 30 magenta filter on the 90mm Mamiya lens: clean up the ambient green spectrum of the city lights, and pop the sunset. Again, boom.

I remember that, as I was shooting this, Phil was telling me that he was "married" to the studio shot. He didn't like being out there on the road, with the direct connection to the restaurant. I persevered and shot the image (following page), despite his grousing.

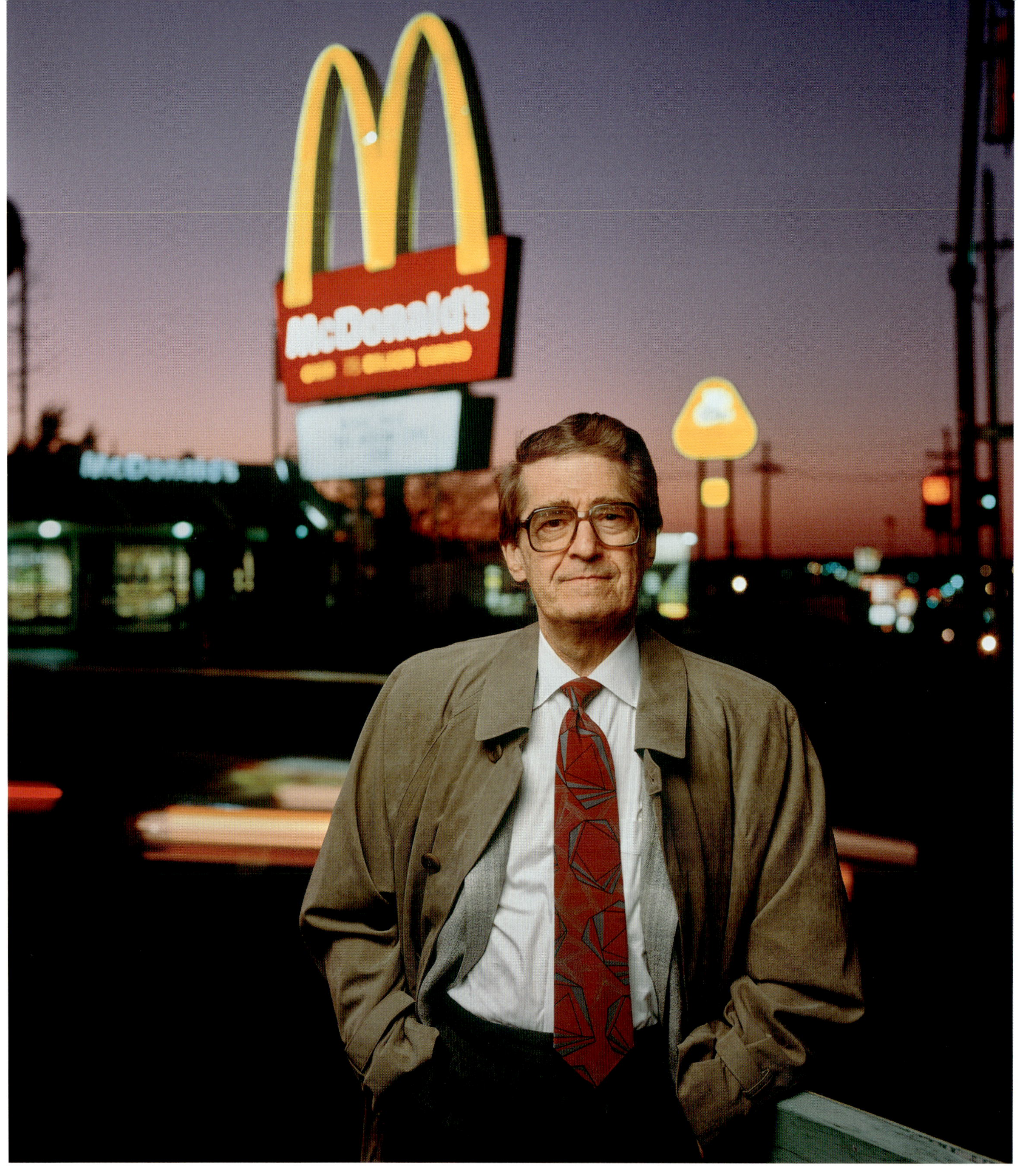

McDonald's

I don't even recall what went on out there in Omaha, but the job extended. Phil's schedule, maybe? Can't remember exactly, but Phil's antics were the heart and soul of extending my time in the field, and I had no control over it. I also bought plexiglass, and rented a studio and additional lighting, all in the blithely passionate, budget-be-damned pursuit of the pictures.

Which *TIME* loved. Until they got my bill. That's when the flying fecal matter hit the quickly rotating metal blades. Lots of splatter, in other words. Serious questions about how the hell did I spend this much? I got blamed for busting the budget on the job. Which was not my doing, at least not all of it. I billed the job in accordance with expenses incurred, and I expected to be compensated for my time spent on location. I didn't even ask for a double day rate for being in Omaha.

TIME didn't see it that way. This was very early in the long, downhill slide of the magazine industry. The budget drums had grown ever louder, signaling the approach of the enemy horde just over the hillside. Quickly! Gather the livestock, crops, and children, and get inside the gates of the fortress! But for the magazine photographer, there was no fortress to run to. No gate we could hide behind. All we had were pictures, and the rights thereto. They were our armor, now effectively stripped.

Magazines had started to routinely expect things from the photographer, like, hey, maybe you could scout the location, you know, for free? Upping the day rate was no longer even discussed. The ravaging of rights was revving up. As an editor friend told me, at his shop, they just wanted the photographer to go off into a corner and be screwed quietly. No pushback.

Well, I pushed back on multiple fronts. In particular, on Phil, who I viewed as the root cause of my extended trip and its resultant costs. He loved the newspaper ad photo and wanted to buy it from my agent, Sygma. I called Eliane Laffont, who ran Sygma, and told her to price the living daylights out of it. Phil objected. Implored. Called the magazine to see if they would give it to him. He was close with a major editor in the Time Life corporate structure and pleaded with him, who in turn pleaded with me. I folded my arms in a petulant huff. No deal. I was angry and emotional, and sadly convinced of my own unique worth.

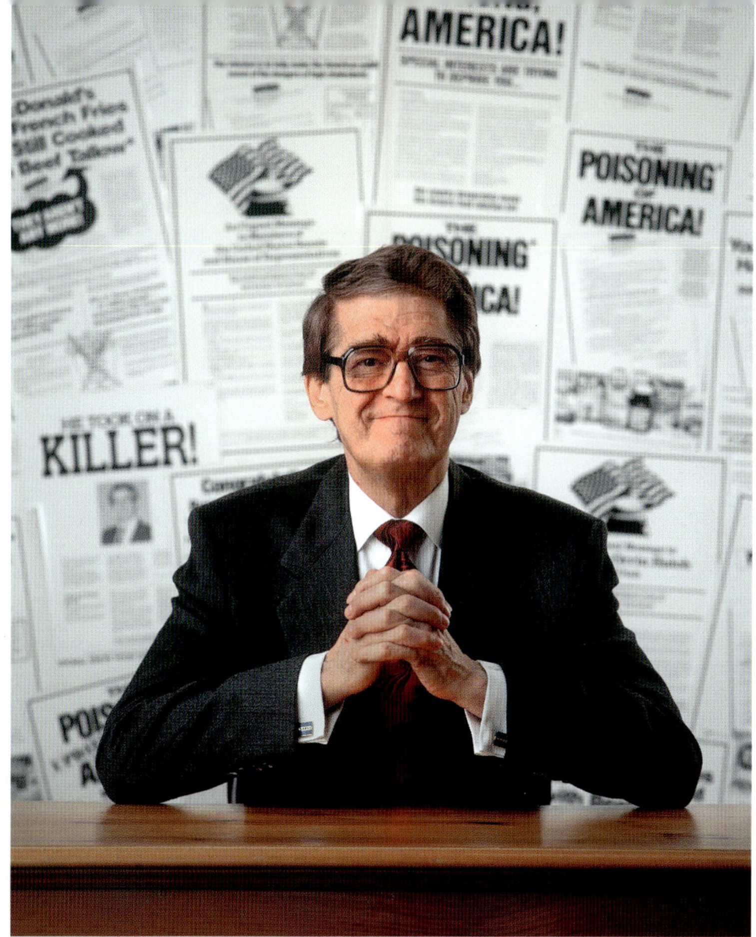

Goddamnit, they can't do this to me! I'll show them who they're messing with!

It was stupid, and less than gracious. I should have just let go and let them do whatever they wanted, because, you know, they were going to anyway, ultimately. I damaged my relationship with *TIME*, who proved they could get along just fine without me and continued to publish, to my astonishment. And I was rude and unfair to my subject, post shoot.

Now, of course, I'm more mature. Or is it resigned? I mean, as photogs, we live in a time when a major Director of Photography of an important publication, in a widely circulated interview, came right out and said that if one wants to pursue photojournalism, it's advisable to have a trust fund. At least now they're up front about the fact that they essentially want you to pay them.

Grading this, I would give myself an A for the photos, but a D– on the business front.

Pick your battles. And remember, the house always wins.

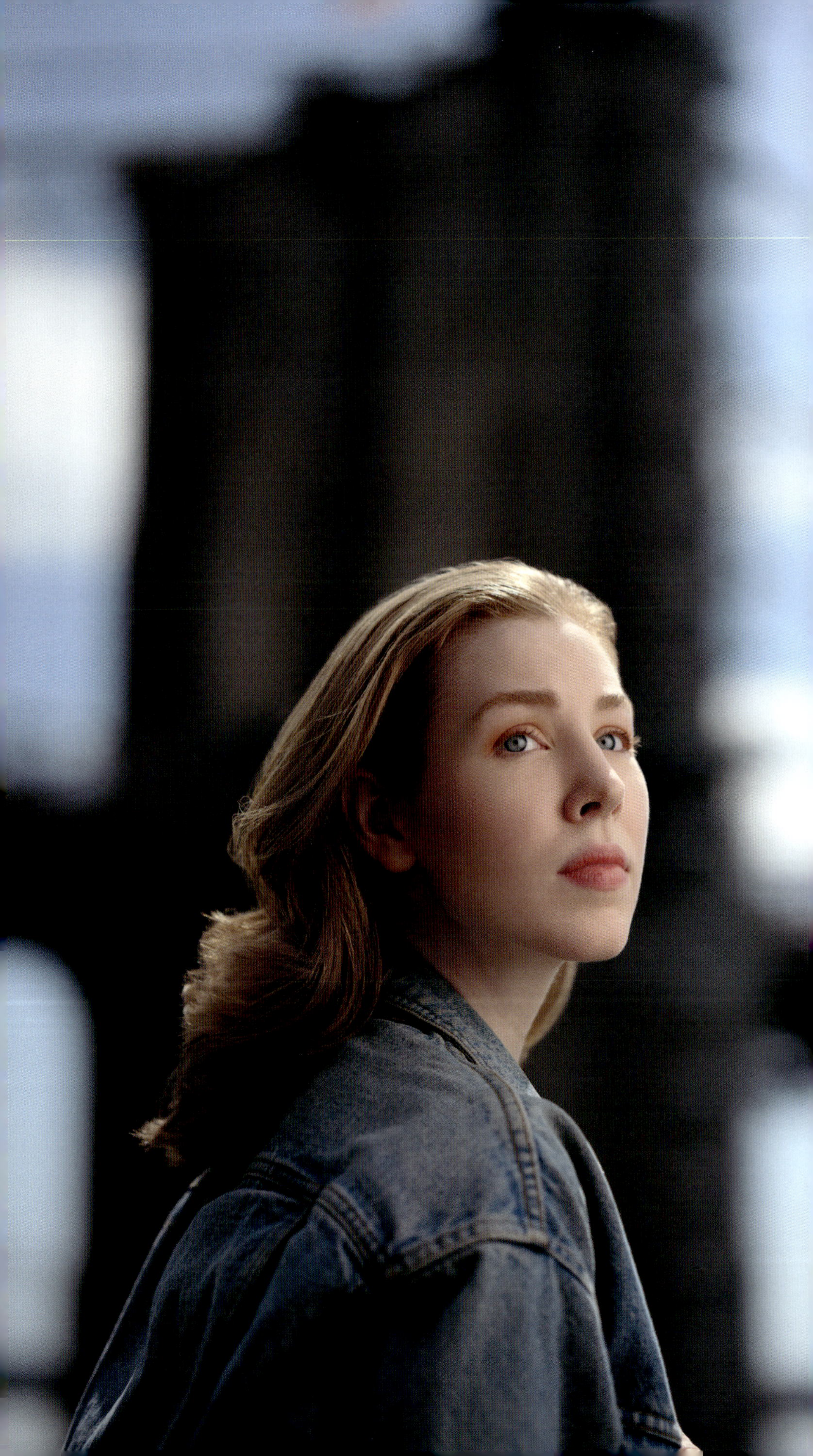

On Taking Shortcuts

As in, why do I need to carry all this gear? Why do I have to set up a light? Why is this such a painstakingly difficult craft to grab a hold of? Right on the box the damn camera came in it says it's all automatic and has 45 million pixels. Aren't they like fairy dust? You sprinkle them on the picture, and it opens like a resplendent flower, dripping with enchantment, yea, even rapture, not to mention saturated colors. And I just go "click"? No assembly required!

Shortcuts. The easy way. When you're driving to location, try one. Might save you time. Call in the coffee order on the app so you can spin in and out of the Starbucks with a Vente Cinnamon Dolce Latte in double-time. In post-production, hit the action key and process a batch of pix whilst sipping yet another latte, or something stronger, depending on the day.

But when it comes to lighting your subject, caring for them, and paying attention to the details and their desire to look good, there are no shortcuts. Just like crying in baseball, you just don't do it.

I recently did a lighting demo at a NYC-based workshop, out on the street. It was fun to do, and my friend Marisa Roper, a talented actress, was the subject, so that part was dead bang easy. It was a bright, sunny day, and I started by posing to the class the question that can confound lots of folks dipping their toes in the lighting waters. Why flash outside? There's so much light! Why do you need "extra"?

A point I've made a couple thousand times while teaching is that quantity of light and quality of light are two distinctly separate things. There was light aplenty that day, verging toward the midday hour, and virtually all of it was bad. Now you can certainly wander on these hot light days, and find open shade, bouncing light, light reflected off buildings, and do just fine. Not a bad way to work if you are mobile and your subject is willing to ramble. But if you have a setting, a location where you are working, and the light from the heavens is cursing your fortunes, you need to step up and take control. You need to wrestle with the photons. The raw sun, shorn of cloud cover, will not

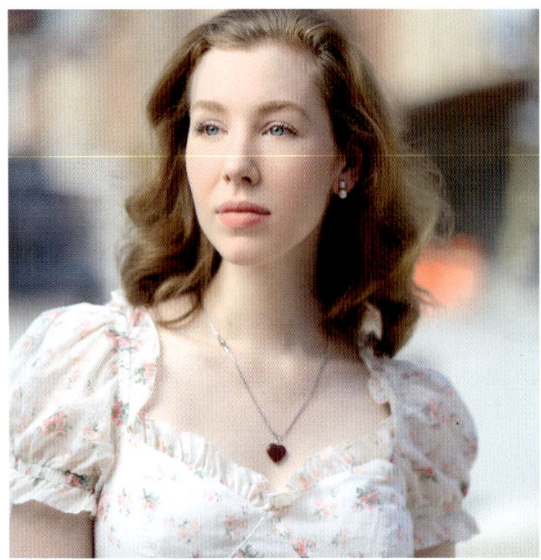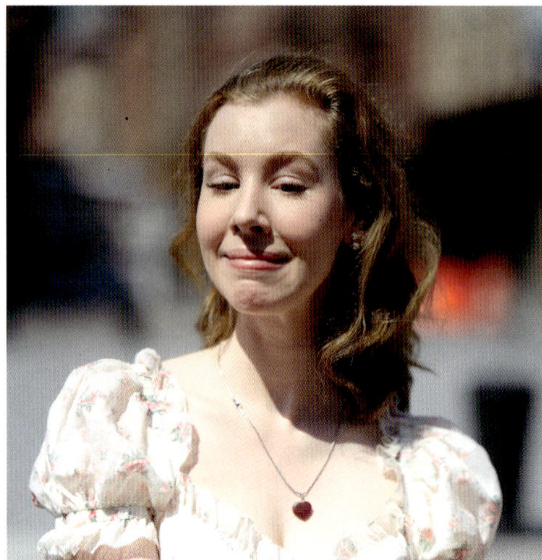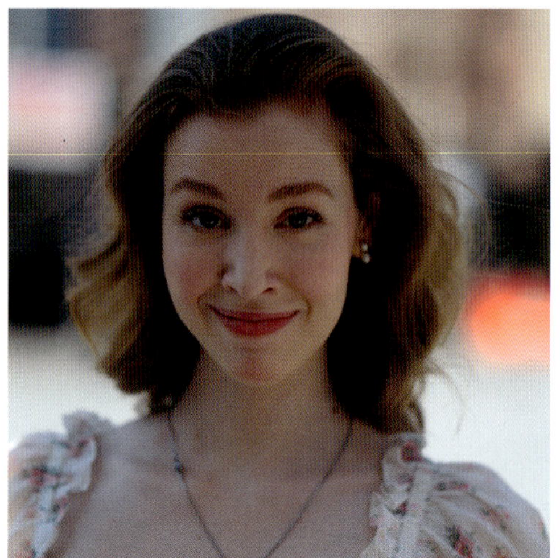

succumb to your wishes in completely subservient fashion, but you can influence, bend, tweak, moderate, mollify, and otherwise cajole the situation to your advantage. You can't simply surrender and take what the sun gives you. That's abdication. Your job is to customize, to push back, to realize vision, and to employ knowledge of craft. Like a tailor, you trim and stitch the light to fit your subject.

I showed the class an example of doing this. To be precise, I used a Nikon Z 7II camera, with an 85mm f/1.8 lens, two Profoto A10 flashes, controlled with the Profoto Air Remote, hot-shoed to the camera. The shaper was a Lastolite Medium Pro Octa softbox, perched on an extender pole slightly to camera left. This is a quick, relatively simple approach, at least for someone like me, who is not unused to trundling a steamer trunk of lights with me everywhere I go.

But at one point a workshop member chipped in with something along the lines of "Why do you have to do this? I mean, can't you get good results without all this stuff?" The unspoken tonal subtext was, "This is an awful lot of work just to get a picture."

I told him that, in this instance, I could get results, but they wouldn't be of comparable quality. He looked at me and said, "Show me."

Game on! The questioner was a good friend, a very smart physician who was in the thick of vaccine development during the pandemic, so my hat is off to him. Remarkable guy, with a good eye for pictures. He had switched on the clinician side of his brain, and he wanted proof in precise fashion. I joked with him on site, asking him if this was a photographic version of a vaccine trial, and I was a control group.

I had shot this (above, left), as a flashed example. ISO 100, 1/2500, f/1.8. All manual, including the flashes, max power.

Okay, this won't get mentioned in dispatches, but it's a nice enough photo. I was then asked to figure out this exact spot without flash. Strip away the fuss and the math and the gear and just shoot it. Marisa complemented the awful light with one of her patented goofy looks. I don't blame her, as I was in the process of making a terrible photo of her (above, middle).

ISO 100, 1/6400, f/1.8.

This was acknowledged as a poor effort. Let's go to the shade! I shifted my position a bit, and shot within the context of a foreground shadow, which hid her from the more violent aspects of the bleached-out street (above, right).

ISO 100, 1/2500, f/1.8.

Flat city. No spark. If you brighten the face, you nuke the background. You can work it in post, but it's so much easier, by my lights, to do the heavy lifting in the field. To look at the LCD and know you got what you come for. To show your portrait subject the results while in the field and have them get buoyed up because they know they look good, and their confidence grows, and the session gets better and better. There's no better boost for the person in front of the camera than to feel strongly that the person behind it knows how to drive.

Flash up close, fighting off the sun, at portrait/headshot distance, is not too much of a problem, given high speed sync, powerful battery-operated flashes, fast lenses, and all the technology advantages we have nowadays. But what about full-length framing? What do you do when the flashes can't be close?

ISO 100, 1/6400, f/2.5. Softbox came off. No light shapers. Raw light from two Profoto A10s.

This picture (right) reflects the continuous adjustments and compromises we make on location with the sun. Backing my flashes off to shoot full length, I lose leverage while using the softbox. That light shaper soaks up at least one stop, maybe even two stops. Which means those flashes, sleek as they are, won't have the juice, from a distance, to push through the softbox and squash the sun. A good, middle-of-the-road maneuver is to take off the shaper. Go with raw light. Blast away. It fits because that's exactly what the sun is doing at that moment. Blasting away. You mimic the look of what's already there. It's not as soft and subtle as an in-your-face big light source, but it gets

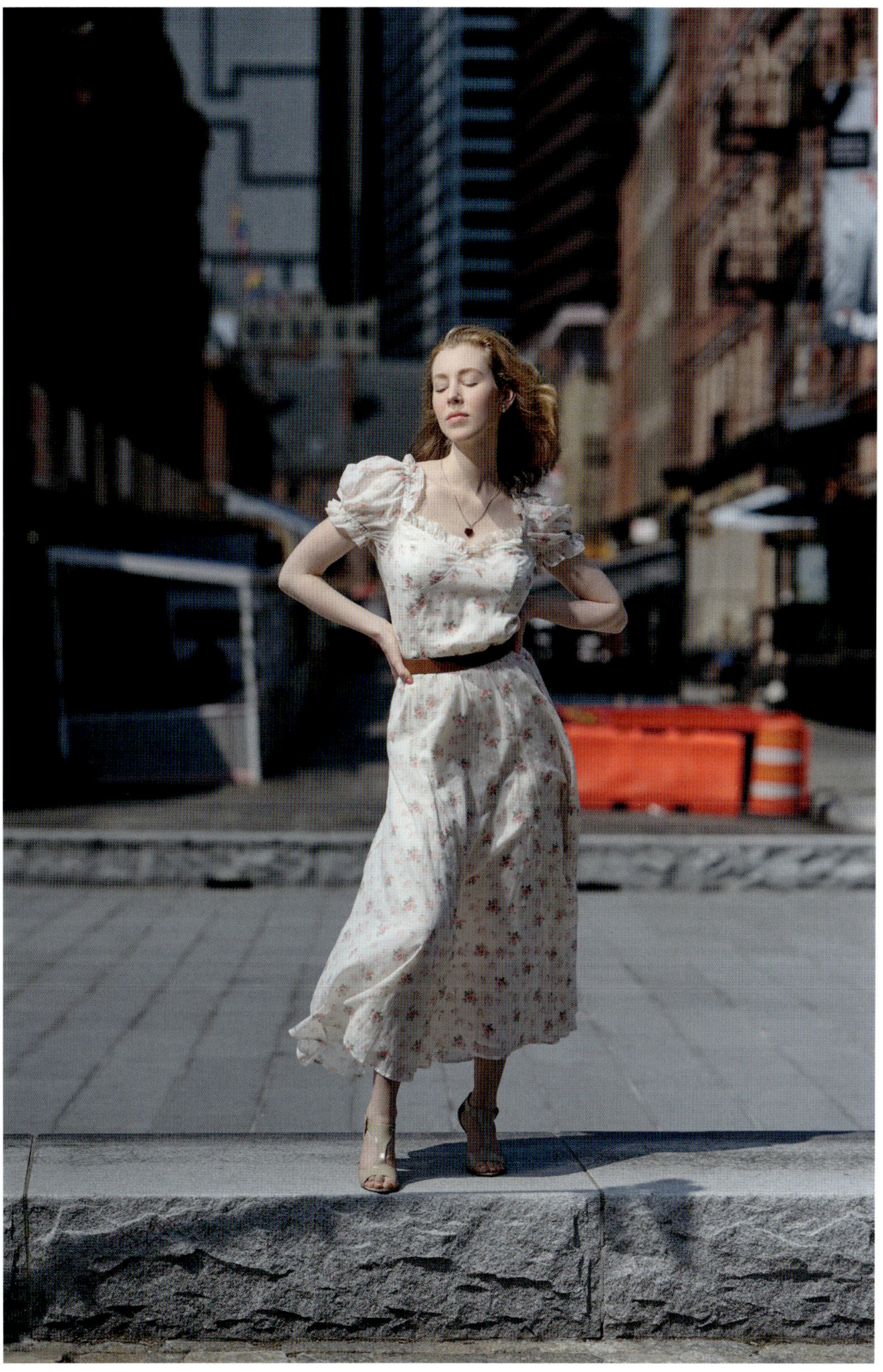

the job done, and again, it puts you back in the driver's seat, at least to a degree. And that's what you are looking for—an edge, however small.

On those glorious days when the natural light is lovely and workable, accept that gift. But when the chips are down, the light is bad, and money is changing hands, you must step in and step up. Carry the gear. Set it up. Work it. Craft a look. That's what folks are presumably paying you for. Like those TV commercials say, "Just okay is not okay."

You must make an investment in excellence, and support that with an investment in the tools. Can you make a beauty dish out of a Tupperware salad bowl? Sure. Is it professional, or preferable? No.

What I had on location was a Z 7II and an 85mm lens. The two Profoto A10 units and the air remote are a dependable, if pricey, combo. The softbox, the backpack to carry it all, the extender pole, and the spare batteries all ramp up the load to carry, both physically and on your bank account. Couple other lenses, for variety's sake, are standard operating procedure. It's a lot to think about, and a lot to accumulate. The ongoing investment in your craft. Knowledge, effort, wisdom—and funding. Ahh, the continuous *ka-ching* of being a photographer. Trust me, it's our soundtrack.

But doing well on the job? The afterglow of a good set of pictures? Priceless.

There's that old phrase, "In for a penny, in for a pound," which is a good summation of the photographic enterprise in general, and it certainly applies to being on location. Once you are there, with your subject, you have jumped out of the plane and pulled the ripcord. No going back. Look up and back, and that plane is receding in the distance, becoming a flyspeck in the sky. You must deal with the onrushing, upcoming ground, and do whatever you have to do.

I have said often on assignment, to my clock-watching subject, who might be anxious to truncate our session, not do another setup, and pull chocks in precipitous fashion, "You and I will never be here together again, in the history of all time. So, give me a few more minutes, and we'll make pictures that will more fully realize our visual ambitions."

In other words, you impatient dufus, give me a chance to do my job and you'll look better.

Time, gear, expense. No shortcuts. Gotta go the distance.

The 300mm Lens Is Actually a Diagnostic Tool

Years ago, I was sent to photograph a Liberace concert. Liberace was not called "Mr. Showmanship" for nothing. He gave an over-the-top, entertaining show, complete with changes of his famed wardrobe, each outfit starrier than the last. At one point he came onstage in his famed chinchilla fur coat and offered the audience the opportunity to come to the edge of the stage and literally feel his garment. The audience, largely ladies of a certain age, as they say, rushed the stage in feverish delight. This enormous coat was made from the fur of many chinchillas and, as he said that night, "It took forever to find them!"

In the dark of the theater, I hunkered down, out of everyone's sight line, which is advisable at concerts, especially if your credentials are potentially not up to snuff. I began to work. At one point, to get tight, I shifted to a manual focus 300mm f/2.8, which was very desirable fast glass back in 1980. I was shooting EPT, an Ektachrome balanced for interior lights, or stage lights. Obviously, this was *waaayyyy* before auto white balance. Load the film and place your bets.

For this shot, I was just about directly under him, a position concert photographers refer to as the pit. He was in full cry, and I banged a focus pull and shot. Didn't think anything of it. Mostly because a few minutes later I became preoccupied with two not particularly gentlemanly individuals who took my business card and escorted me out. (I was legit, and had an assignment and a credential, but

they had no record of it, and my explanations fell on deaf ears.)

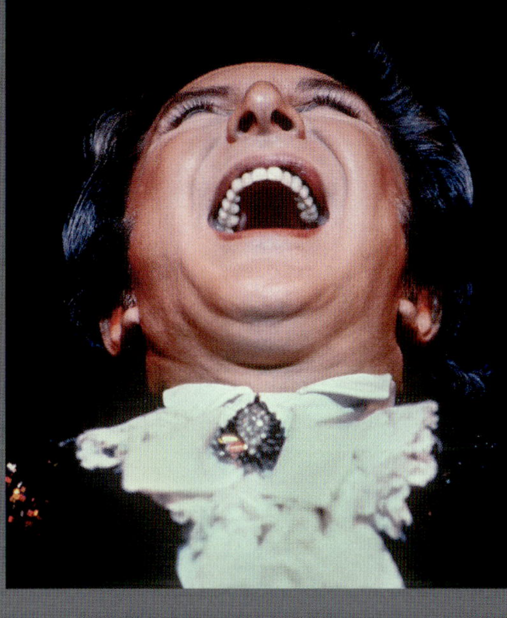

Later, louping my film, I marveled at the condition of his teeth. And now, all these years later, as I publish this picture, I wanted to get the story straight, so I sent a note to my dentist.

Hi Doc:

This is a little nuts, but I'm writing a new book and compiling stories behind some of the photos. This was made long ago at a Liberace concert, low angle, long lens. Got a surprising view of his teeth, which I might riff on a bit. But I wanted to ask your opinion: If I said these were caps, would that be accurate? Any help you can offer so I make sure I get it right would be very helpful.

All the best! And see you soon . . . Joe

He came back with this:

Hi Joe,

They are all caps except for the last tooth on the upper right. You were very accurate with your observation.

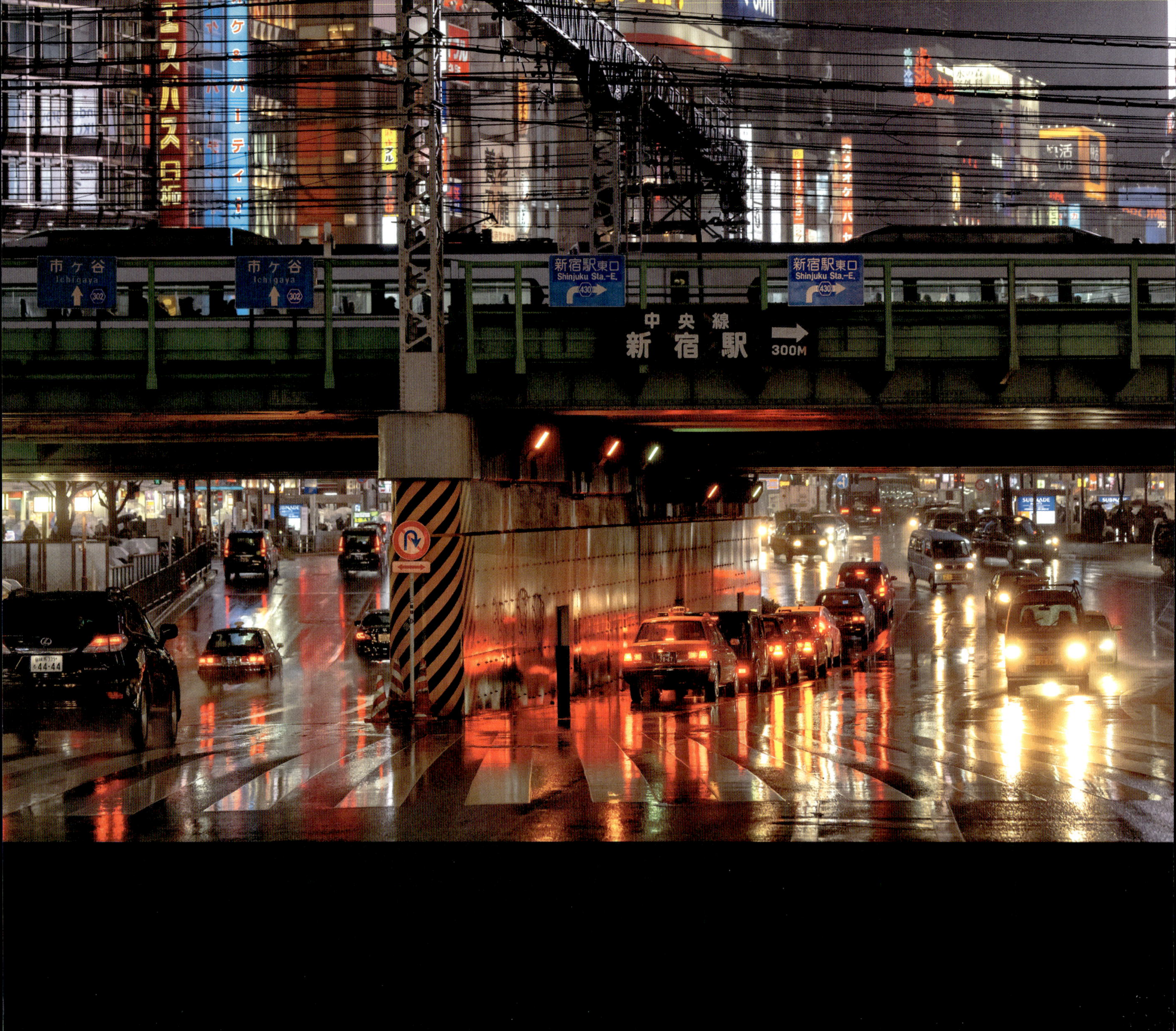

市ヶ谷
Ichigaya
302
市ヶ谷
Ichigaya
302
新宿駅東口
Shinjuku Sta.-E.
430
新宿駅東口
Shinjuku Sta.-E.
430
中央線
新宿駅 →
300M

Let It Rain!

Sounds like a strange directive, given that this whole career could be construed as a search for good light. But I love the rain and have written about the benefits of getting wet while shooting before. I visit it again here because, well, the rain rocks.

Take a cool urban environment, like Tokyo, and mix in a good rainstorm, and you've got *Blade Runner* (opposite).

It can be uncomfortable, but when is the pursuit of good pictures comfortable? The rain transforms drab concrete into a slickly reflective, visual playground.

This is a personal preference, of course, but to me, the rain calls for long glass. Doesn't mean super rain pics have never been shot with wide angles, but for me, using long glass in a full-throated, hardy rainstorm is transformative. In Rio, this image (right) would have been yet another hurdle race were it not for the rain. The density of the rain is multiplied by the millimeters, of course, as the drops get visually compressed and stacked upon each other. The hurdlers were shot with an 800mm, which is a lot of millimeters; that long glass amps the intensity of the storm.

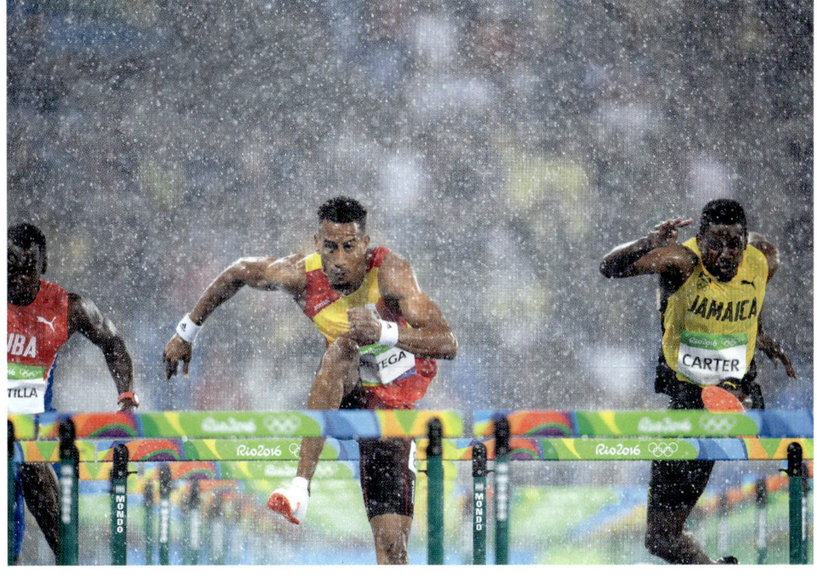

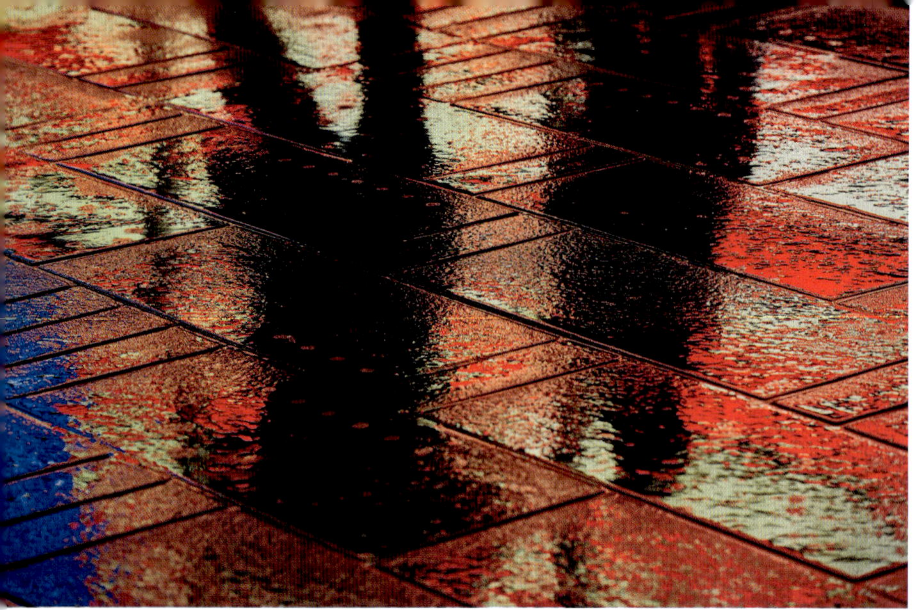

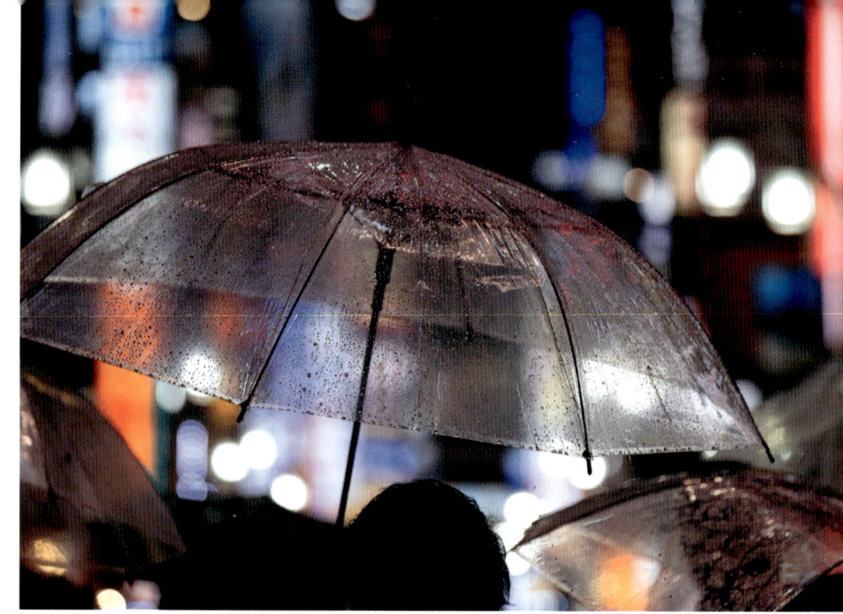

Be careful with your AF mode in a big shower! If you are grouping points or going with a wide area "dynamic" autofocus mode, you may get a picture of sharp raindrops. Best to go with a single cursor or, at most, a small, localized group of AF points. (Obviously AF modes vary camera to camera.) But for the hurdle image, I have a single cursor and dynamic AF on the lead runner. With street scenes, pick a bright reflection spot that is in your crucial field of focus, and push the AF cursor there. If it is a static highlighted area, you can go with a single-point, AF-S type of focus, and bypass the dynamic options. But you have to slide that point to the heart of the matter and, as the old song goes, dance between the raindrops.

Rain pops color and brightens the otherwise drab. In lighting classes, I always bring this up. Why do you think big-time moviemakers bring a water truck through the streets they are shooting, just prior to shouting, "Action!"? The street comes alive, literally drenched in potential visual delights. A black, lifeless hole in the background of the frame becomes a color player, redolent with highlights and reflections.

The mundane can become lovely and visually intriguing, adorned by rain drops.

And a long-ago concert would have largely been forgotten had it not been for a legendary storm. Diana Ross, in Central Park, in 1983. Huge crowd, huge star, huge storm.

From Wikipedia: "That evening, 2.26 inches of rain fell, two-thirds of that month's total precipitation. Winds of nearly 50 mph were reported, and electrical power was disrupted for nearly 40,000 homes throughout the NYC metropolitan area during the storm."

I was unprepared.

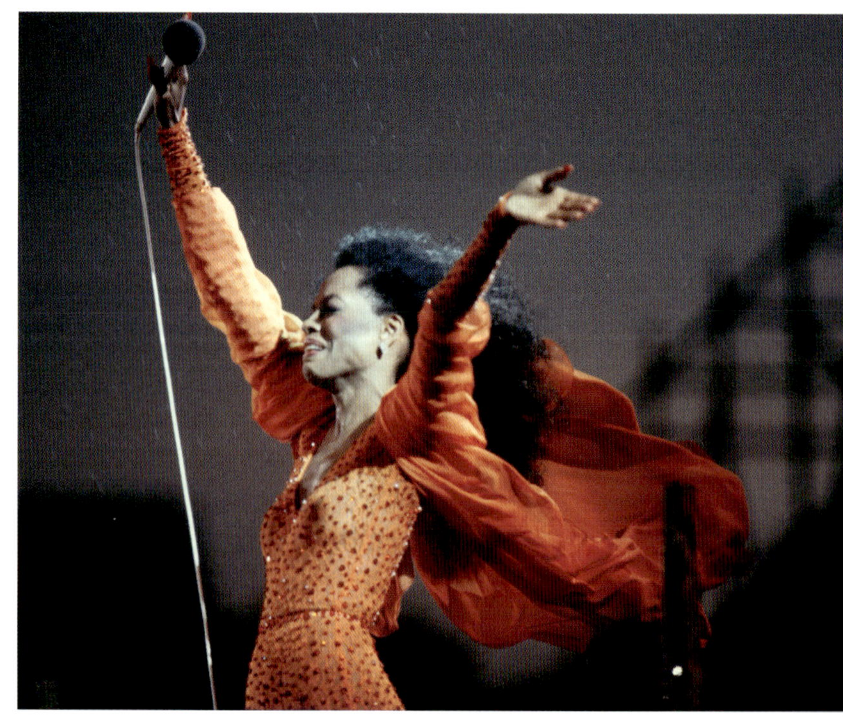

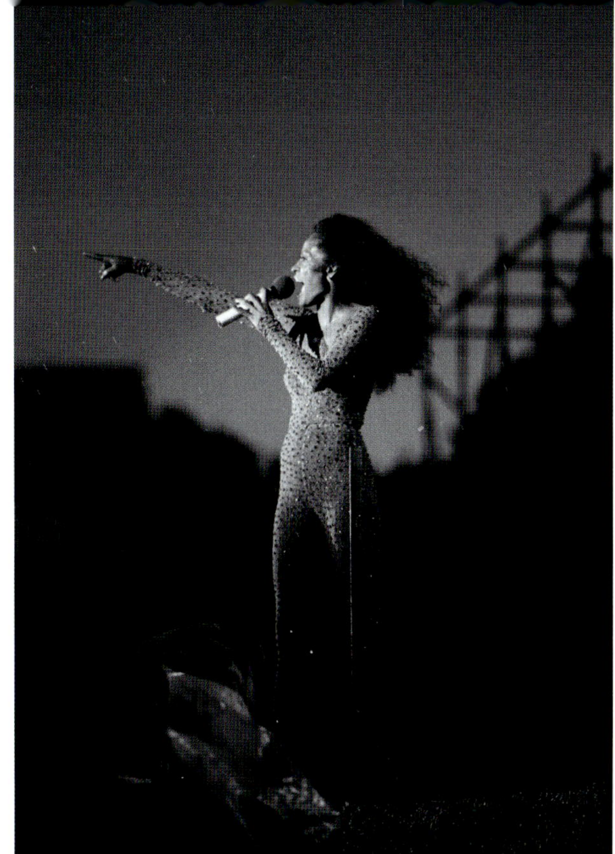

I learned a lot that night, shooting in that fierce rain for *People* magazine. I had not listened to the weather reports and brought nothing in the way of protective gear for me or my cameras. Not that it would have done much, as the wind was actually driving the rain sideways.

Ross braved the storm for as long as she could, in a skin-tight, beaded bodysuit. I had to stick with it, despite the damage that was being done to my gear. I'm glad I did. Those cameras are long-forgotten, discarded metal and glass, left behind in the bleak junkyard of my photo trek. As you shoot, always remember: What you are accumulating inside that machine is far more valuable than the machine itself. Some images have remained with me to this day, and I still occasionally even show them. (Not at universities, where the youngish audiences are likely to ask, "Who's Diana Ross?") The film survived, just barely. Here's a scan of an original B&W I shot that night (right, middle).

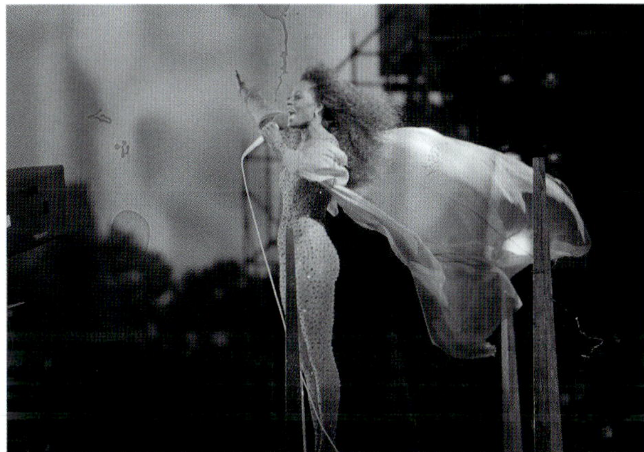

My cameras were basically underwater. Rain was sluicing into them like they were an open drain. Remember, this is 1983, and cameras had nowhere near the weather sealing they have now. I shot through it, wiping my lenses with soaked clothing and peering through a viewfinder speckled with water drops. It made manual focusing long glass an adventure, to be sure. The shot film took a beating. My bad. Young photog, full of beans, light on experience. No plastic bags, no rain protection for anything, no umbrella (though the wind would have destroyed it immediately). The rain-driven carnage was pretty complete. I was using an old school Domke bag for my gear and it was soaked through; the lens compartments started to fill with water. There was nowhere to run, and nowhere to hide.

Thank goodness, now, for modern retouching tools (right, bottom).

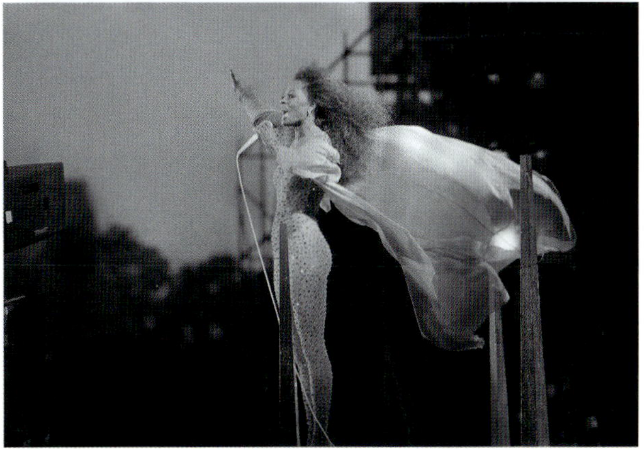

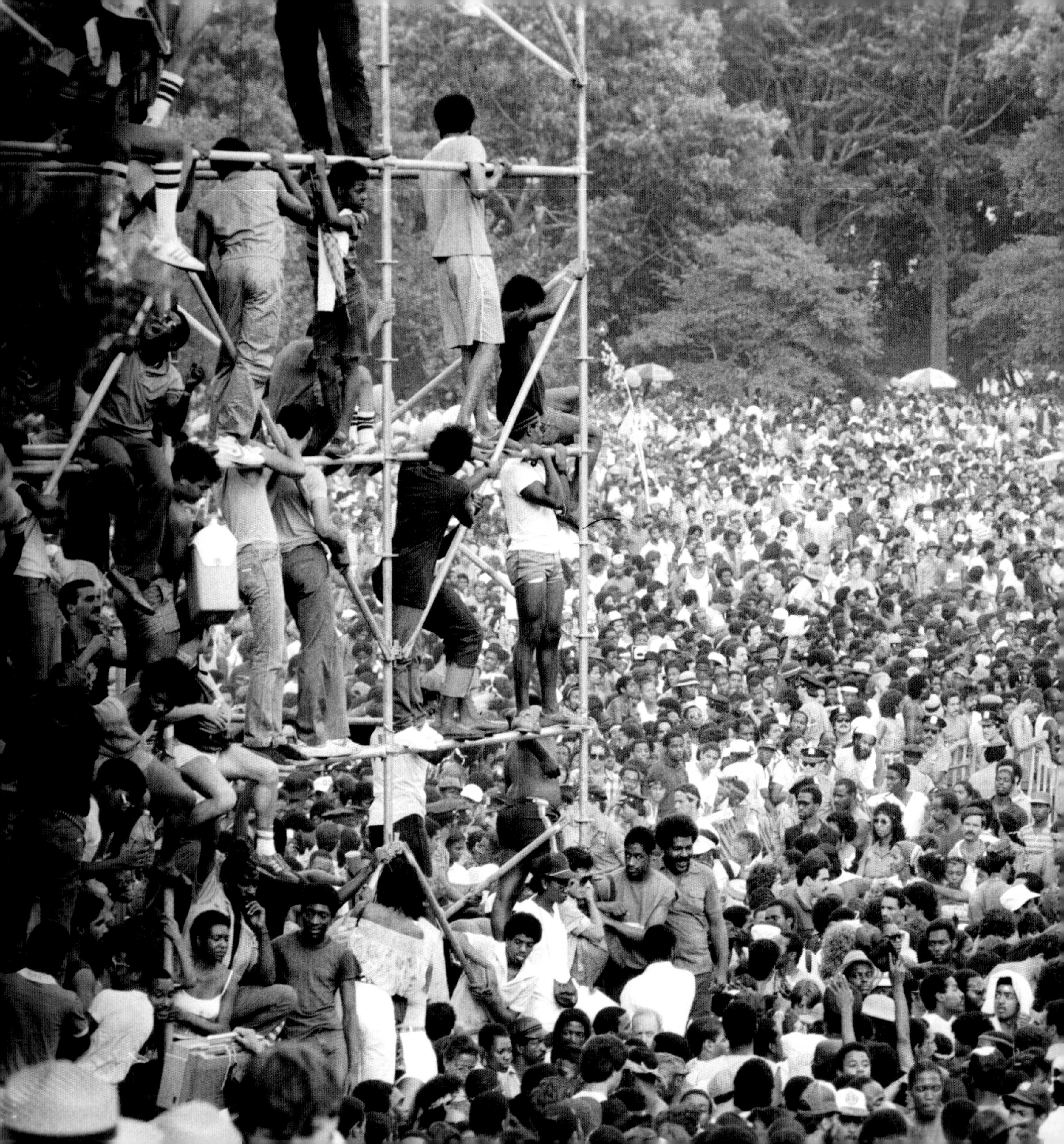

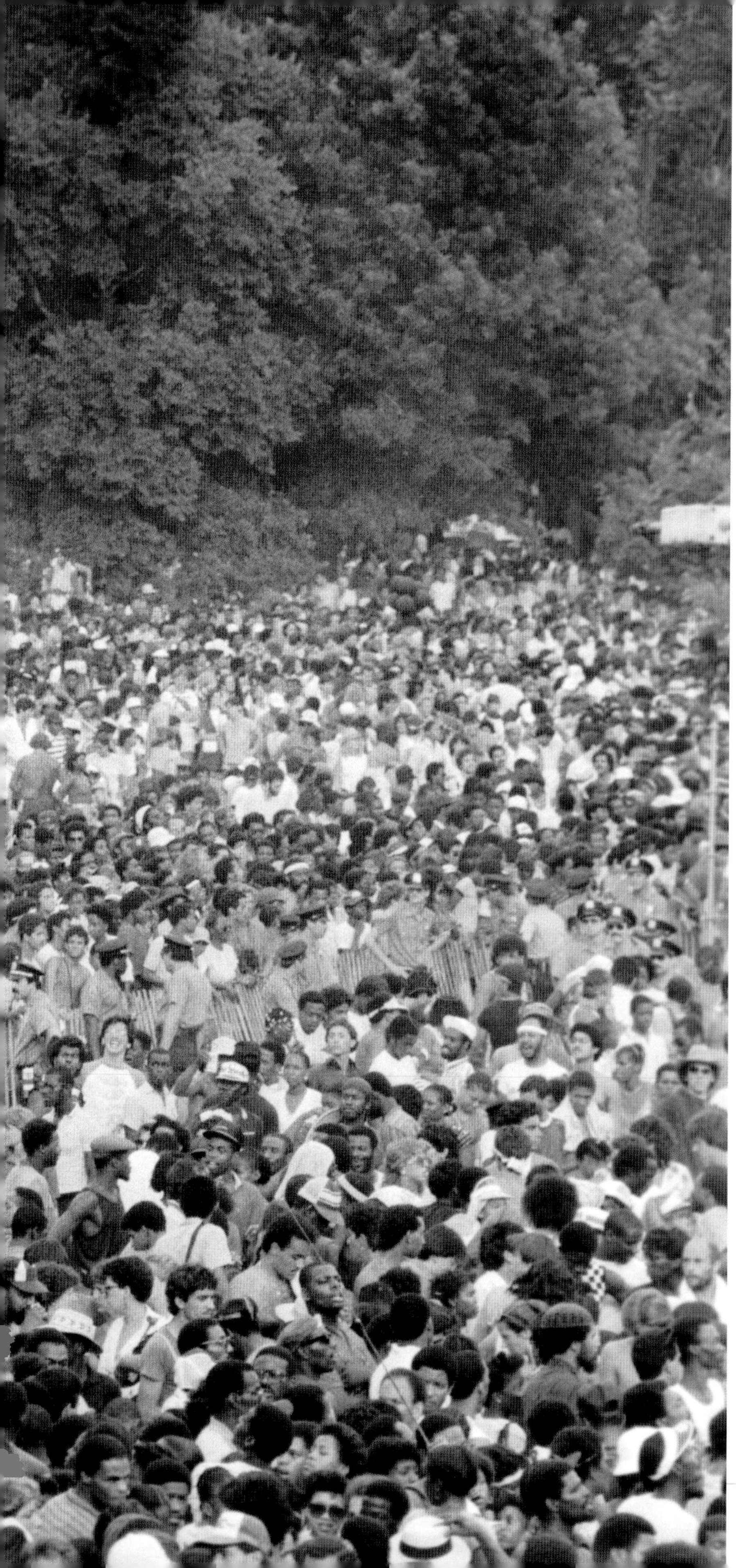

Diana was one tough performer. Talk about singing in the rain. She tried her best as the wind knocked her about.

She tried to coax people down from the light towers, where they had climbed for a better view. She encouraged calm as the organizers shut the show down. It was a dodgy moment, as people were stacked on top of one another.

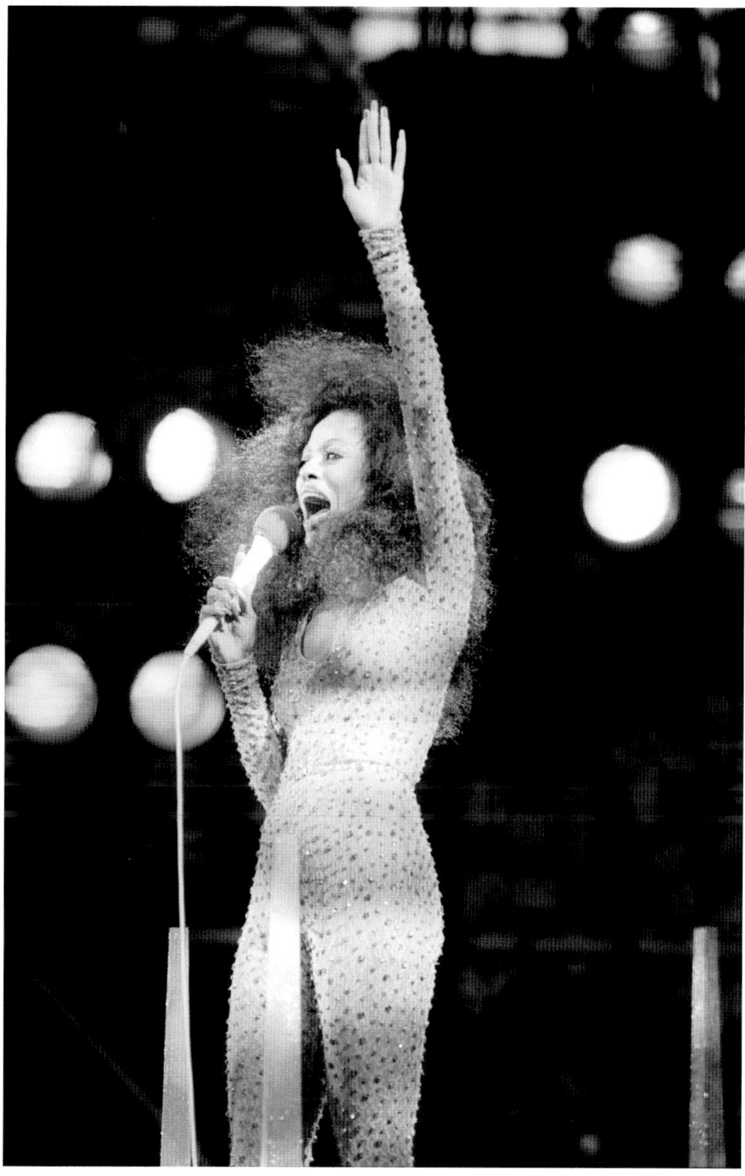

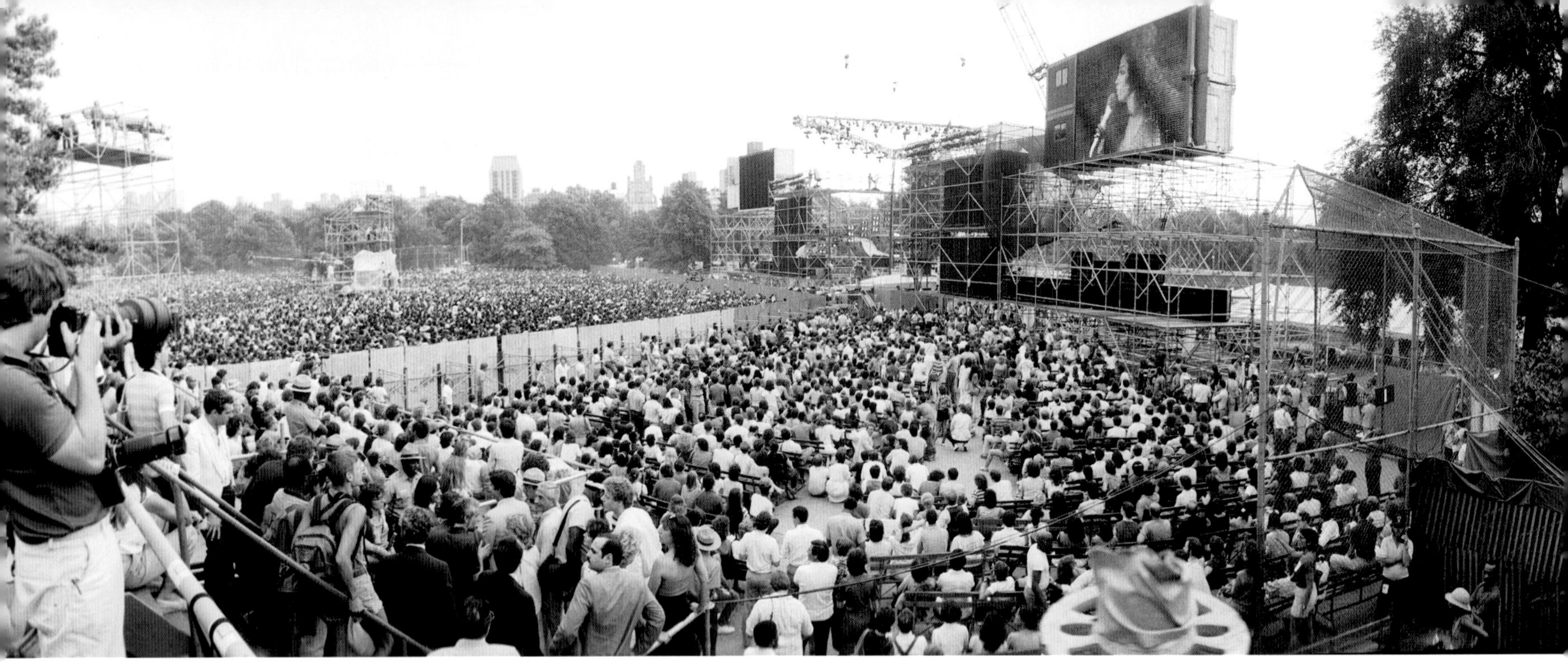

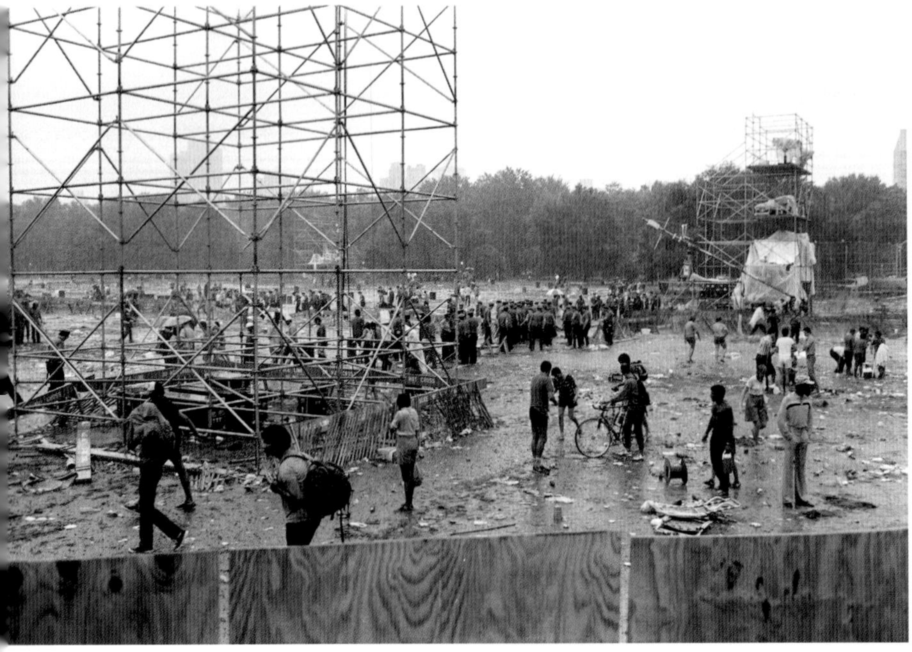

Quite rapidly, with fierce, unrelenting power, the storm turned a normal concert and orderly audience into a bit of post-show havoc.

Personal upshot? The editors at *People* were ripped at me. They had assigned me to shoot it as a cover and felt I had ignored their directive and didn't provide them with a good color cover image. The concert was rescheduled immediately and the editors at *People* (who I adored working for) wanted me to go again and make good. I couldn't, having taken an assignment for the *Daily News* Sunday magazine to photograph a bus tour to Atlantic City. Couldn't get out of it. I had given a commitment. I stayed the course and got on the bus with a bunch of feverish, casino-bound old folks (opposite, right).

The ongoing life of a freelancer. You're the pinball, and the flippers of life and assignments and weather and schedules and personalities and bipolar picture editors and god-knows-what-else careen you around the playfield, where you go dinging, bumping, and slingshotting every which way, desperately trying to avoid the dreaded drain and the end of the game when the lights go out.

This scenario was lose, lose, lose for me: I got a great client pissed off at me, I had extraordinary and expensive damage to my gear, and I honored my commitment to a client who never used me again. Total financial return to me in terms of editorial day rates? For both jobs? All together? $550.

I am rich in memories of a shoot where I actively paid the price for my idiocy but kept shooting, obstinate in my dumb determination, like a cow who digs his heels in and refuses to get on the truck 'cause he's never seen any of his buddies ever come back from that ride. I stayed to the last. Central Park turned into a mini-Woodstock as the crowd dispersed.

So what do you do in a rainstorm? I have no bulletproof solutions for you. No tried-and-true magic that no one else has discovered. Here I find myself in the same position that a very famous photog once found himself, at the podium at a big photographic convention in the UK. He's not just well known, he's seriously famous. And he has vast experience shooting in inclement conditions.

He was showing pictures and offering vague advice to all of us in the audience, raptly receiving his wisdom. One of his "tip" slides about shooting in the rain came up, with the printed admonishment to "Bring an Umbrella" next to a picture of said photographer in the rain, sporting a brolly. I nudged my assistant at the time, Michael Cali, seated next to me. And we both nodded approvingly at this nugget of knowing. I recall saying, sotto voce, something like, "Whoa, Cali, write that down. This guy's really onto something!"

I mean, what can you say about shooting in the rain? Uh, use common sense? Don't go? Wear a wet suit and fins? Drop some really good mescaline so the raindrops turn playful colors and actually talk to you?

Bring rain gear for you and the camera. Use the backpack rain protectors—you know, those photo backpack condoms that often come with the higher-end totes? The ones you often stuff in a drawer and don't bother bringing? Bring them. Make sure you have plastic bags for your card wallets, or use the little waterproof containers that are widely available from a variety of manufacturers.

Listen to the weather report, and if the winds aren't egregious, do bring an umbrella. If you are in a fixed position for, say, an event or a concert, you can get brackets to clip an umbrella right

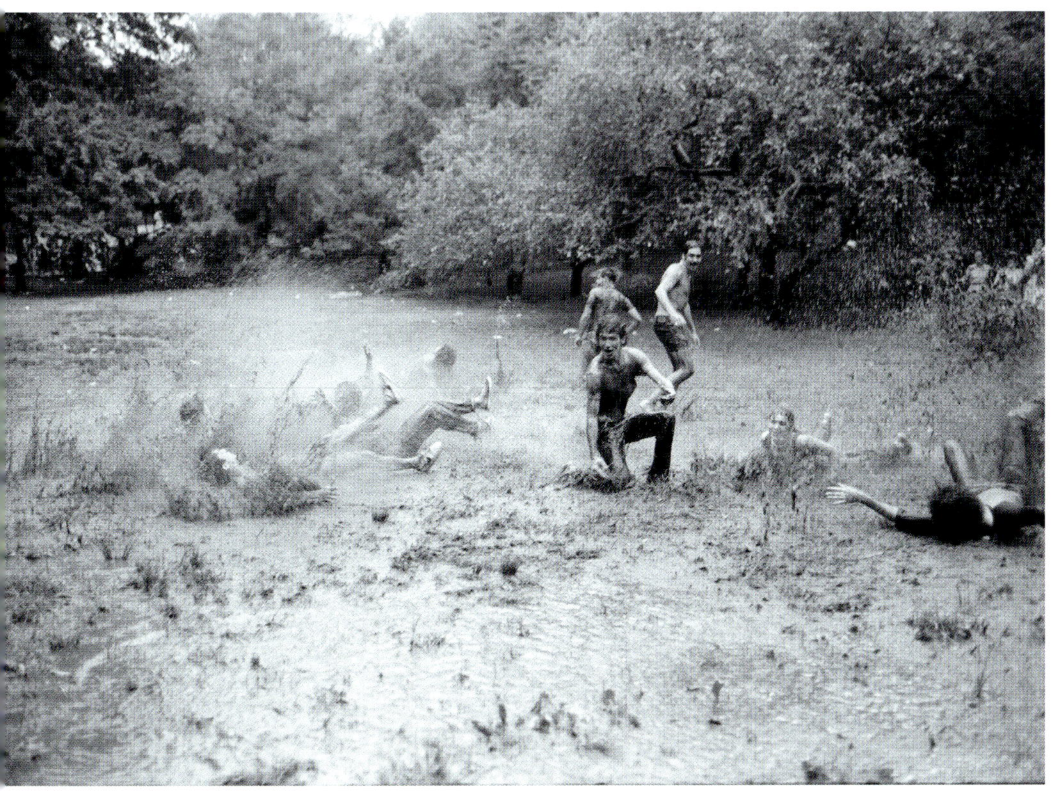

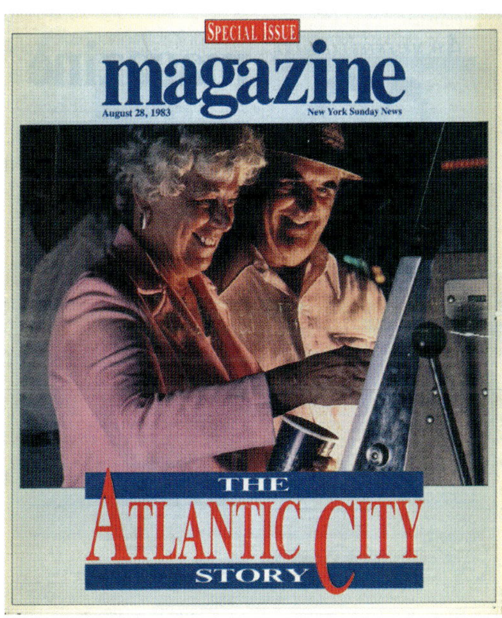

to your tripod, or do a DIY solution on the spot. Careful, though, because if you are in a grandstand position, the sprouting of this umbrella will not be a welcome event for the photographer behind you.

Golf towels with carabiner clips. Clip one to your bag, and one or two to your belt. They have wet/dry towels, with different materials on either side of the towel. Handy.

If you shoot a long lens in a rainstorm, you can enjoy the benefit of still affording a desirable view whilst you are someplace protected, under an awning or something similar. Shooting a wide lens means you wander into the soggy fray. If you do use long glass, remember lens hoods are a good idea. If you have the type of lens hood that either bayonets onto the lens itself or uses a screw to hold it in place once it is seated properly, remember the grafting of the hood onto the glass potentially has a gap, where rainwater can dribble in. Seal that with a couple of swings of gaffer tape or duct tape around the whole barrel. I almost always recommend gaffer tape over duct tape, but in this instance duct tape actually seals better. It might leave some sticky stuff on your lens barrel and hood, but it's easy enough to deal with that later.

And, if possible and affordable, bring internally focusing and zooming lenses into the field on rainy days. The telephotos that physically rotate as you zoom, and get actually longer, expose a part of the barrel that will accumulate moisture. When you retract the zoom factor, that exposed piece of the lens, with all its attendant rainwater, will then telescope back into the interior chambers of that lens, potentially causing havoc and creating a breeding ground for uninvited guests. I once was peering through my old, old school 300mm f/4.5 and actually watched a tiny crawling critter make its way across an element.

I've shot in ridiculous conditions, which might account for the wildlife in that old lens. Such as a rainstorm, at night, with trail bikers. When it's pouring this hard, there's very little to be done. Here is where you need to be prepared and carry one of those raincoats for your camera and lens. They make them for both

short and long glass. I didn't have one on this night, and truth be told, I don't think they even made them around the time I shot this (opposite, top). I just popped long glass on a tripod and did my best. Fierce rain plus nighttime conditions made for a sheet-like effect, which was handy. I told them to look at each other, using their headlamps to illuminate the scene. Even I'm not stupid enough to bring out a flash when there's literally a waterfall coming from the clouds.

There exists a ton of wisdom out there about using silica gel and bags of uncooked rice as an aftermath solution for rain-exposed lenses. Cool. Good stuff. But a 600mm will require a big-ass bag of rice.

I have advocated for shooting rainstorms with long glass, in hopefully persuasive fashion. Now, just to be contrary and confusing about it, remember you can always shoot wide angle and do quite well, too (opposite, bottom).

For the most part, there is never a "never" or an "always" in photography. I have been asked many times, do you always do such and such? My standard reply is that I don't always do, or never do, anything photographically, in the broadest of terms. This remains an utterly situational art and craft, demanding improvisational responses on the part of the photographer. It's vexing in its capricious demands, and wonderfully rewarding (occasionally) when you accede to those demands, despite the murmurings of common sense burbling in the back of your brain, and the practical mandate of needing to get home in time

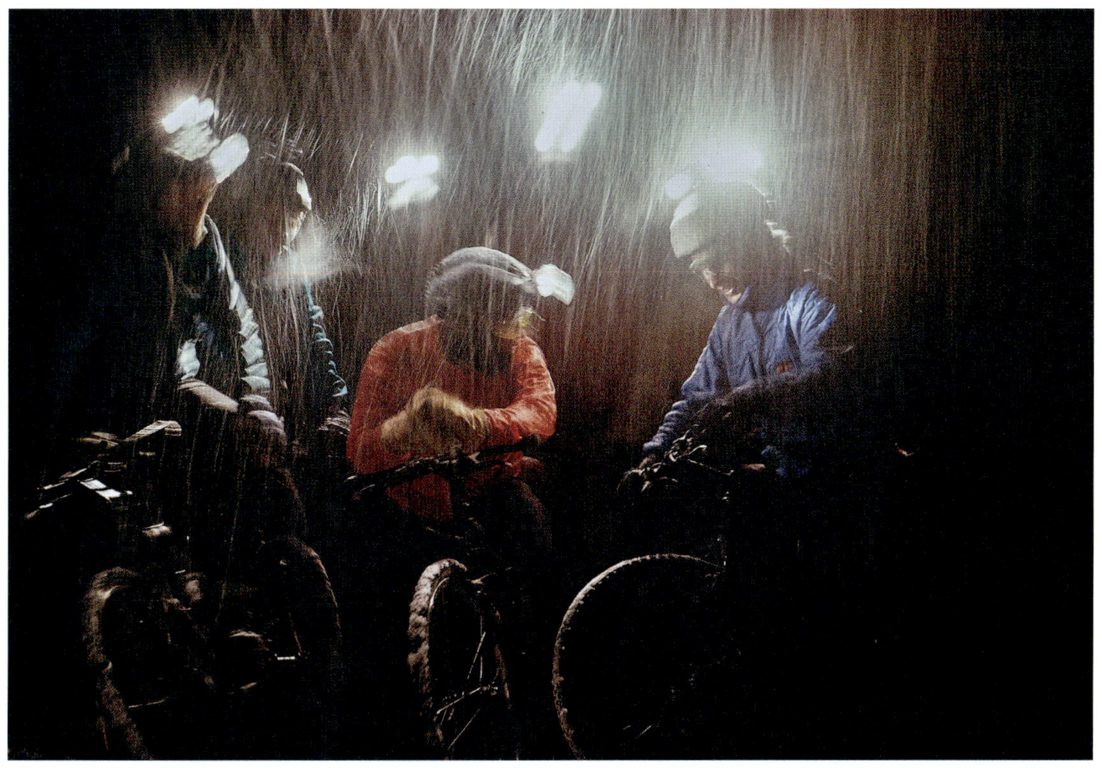

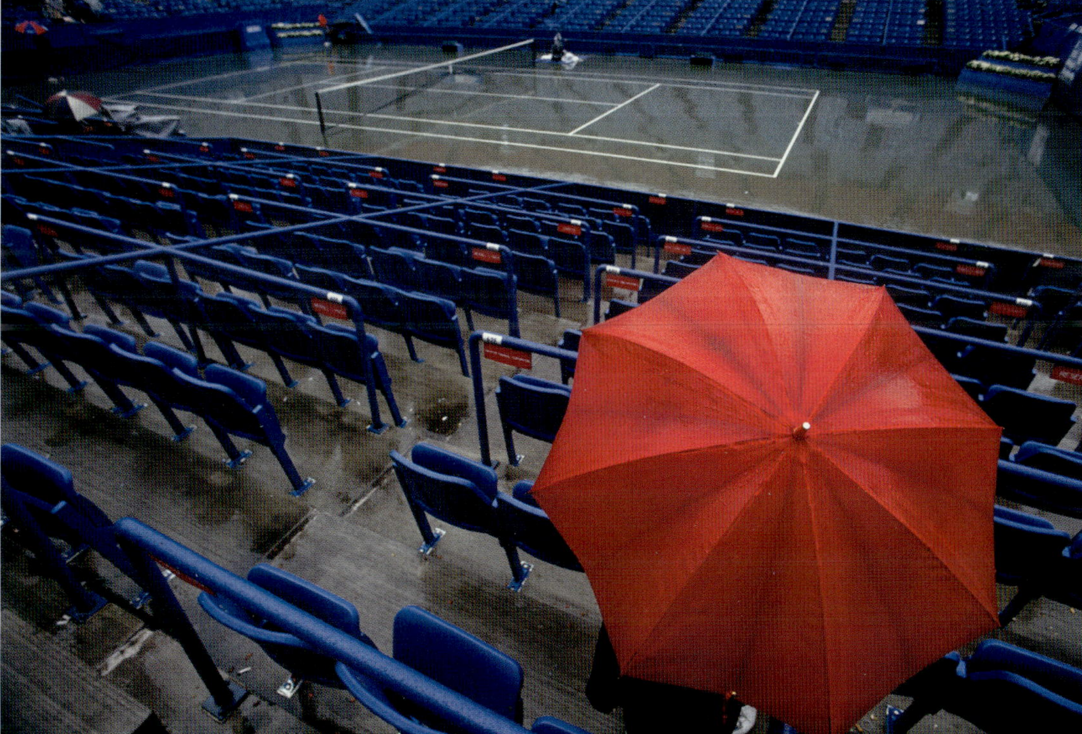

to make dinner. You follow the picture. You react in real time. Where you end up on a job may be miles from where you thought the destination of the day might have been, physically or photographically. And, maybe you shoot rain with a wide angle.

The promise of "the" frame of the day is quite the Pied Piper, beckoning you with its irresistible tune. It can lead you on a merry chase, one where you throw caution and any sense of your more humdrum responsibilities to others in your life to the wind. Perhaps it's best to remember that the legend of the Pied Piper is not a particularly merry one. It is closer to the sirens from Greek mythology, beckoning you, enchanting your camera, but ultimately dashing your photographic hopes on the hard rocks of something you hadn't thought of or prepared for.

Terrible thinking on my part! Let's instead imagine those good pictures in your future are the lyrical lilt of music you hear from an Irish pub down the block, beckoning you indoors to the warmth. Yeah, that's better. Let's sling those cameras with great hope and an enduring sense of excitement.

So, go for it. Follow the picture, even if it leads you into a storm of some kind or other. Pray for rain, and shoot it with any lens that seems right at that moment. Oh, and yeah, maybe bring an umbrella.

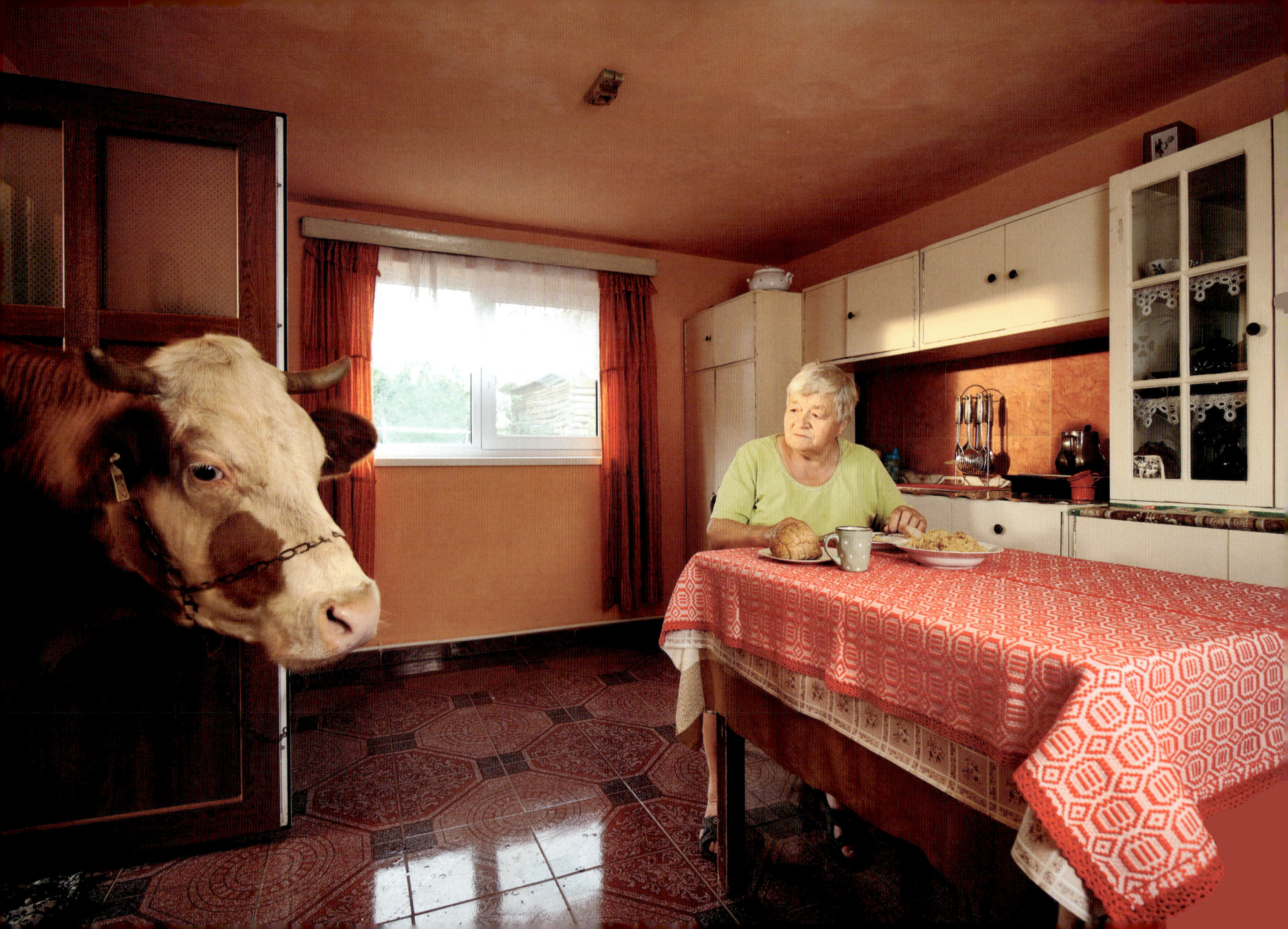

Your Imagination Is the Cow in the Kitchen

And that cow won't leave.

Face it, your imagination is a pain in the ass. As awkward as a cow peering in the door, as incessant as a yipping puppy demanding attention. It can be fun, painful, embarrassing, expansive, expensive, revealing, ennobling, splendidly grand, or deviant in nature. Explaining what you are imagining is a bit like disrobing. You're revealing parts of yourself, parts that many seek to keep private.

It takes guts to reveal the way your mind works. Like throwing down a challenge coin in the bar, it is an act of confidence, or misplaced confidence. If it works, and you're the guy with the coin, you're beaming at the bar, and everybody buys you a round. But if everybody's got a coin and slaps back, you are eating humble pie, and reaching for your credit card.

My mother used the expression "until the cows come home" relatively frequently. It was her version, perhaps, of "until hell freezes over," meaning, of course, a long time, put in polite, folksy fashion. As in, "You'll stay at that kitchen table and finish your homework, and I don't care if it takes you until the cows

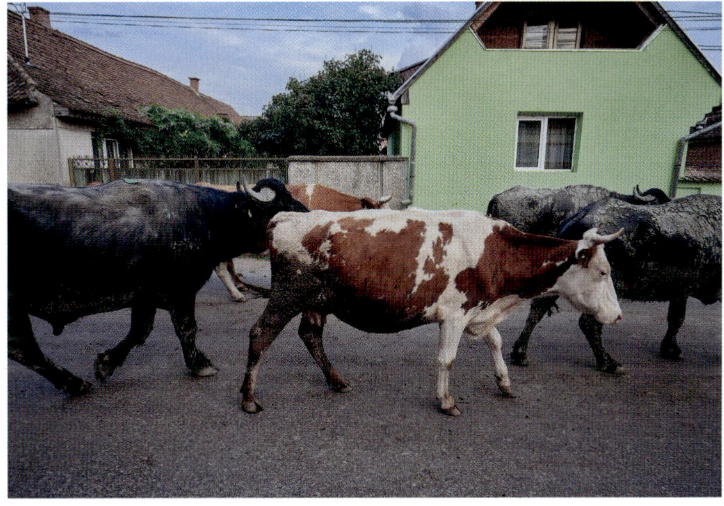

come home!" I knew nothing about cows and had no idea if they ever came home or what might prompt them to do so, but I did know that phrase meant, no matter the task at hand, I was in for the long haul.

Then I went to Romania, where the cows really do come home. Observing this rang a bell for me. (So, so sorry for that.)

In small Romanian farming villages, at the end of the day, the cows leave the fields and come home. As dependably as a shift change signaled by a factory whistle, the cows quit their day-long munching of grass and walk down the main street of the village, turning into their home driveways without guidance or prompting. I was amazed and energized to see this. Mom was right! I imagined secret, wordless cow dialogue: "See ya, Mort!" and "Tomorrow, Harry!" as they parted company for the evening, lumbered up their respective walkways and got ready for dinner and their favorite sitcom.

I never knew I would turn an eye-rolling phrase my mother wielded throughout my childhood into an impulse to photograph, but there you are. What drives the direction of anyone's photography is an amalgam of who we are as people, how we were raised, and the things we were exposed to, fell in love with, or got distressed by.

Hence the cow in the kitchen. First and foremost, I thought it would be fun, a pictorial spin on an old phrase, fallen into disuse. (Wiktionary cites it as "obsolete." I can relate.) I'm also acutely aware, most of the time, of my strengths and weaknesses as a photographer. I enjoyed making snaps of the cows processing down the main drag of the tiny town of Bradut, Romania, but my efforts were half-hearted at best. Everybody else with a camera on that street—and there were numerous photogs along the way—made pretty much the same photos. At this point in my career, I'm really more comfortable dreaming things up than documenting them, so my mind hopelessly, helplessly spins into the realm of "What if?" How do I put a spin on this that no one else would be stupid enough to attempt? The chance to create something even marginally unique is always (well, almost always) worth the risk of failure and ridicule.

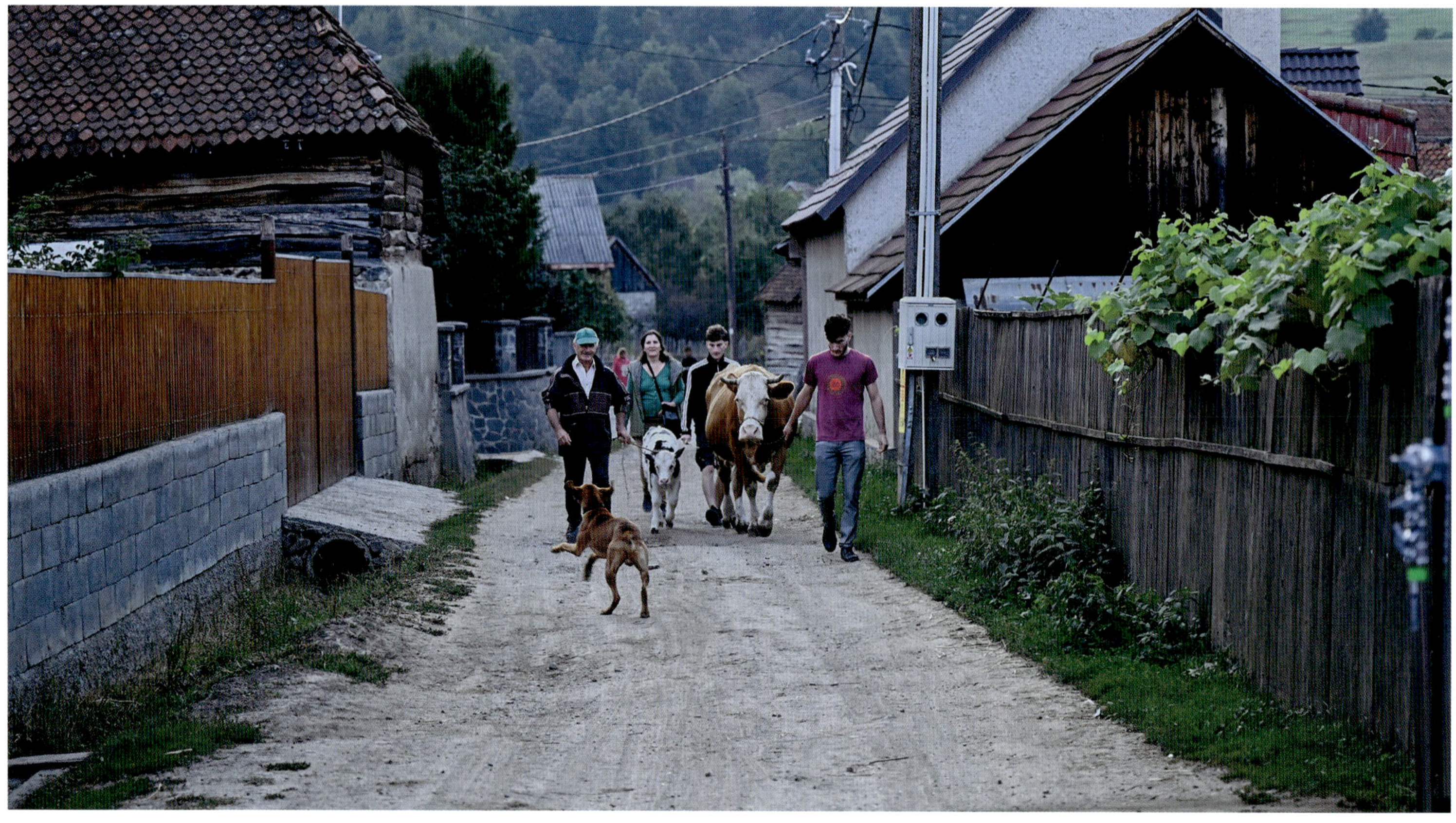

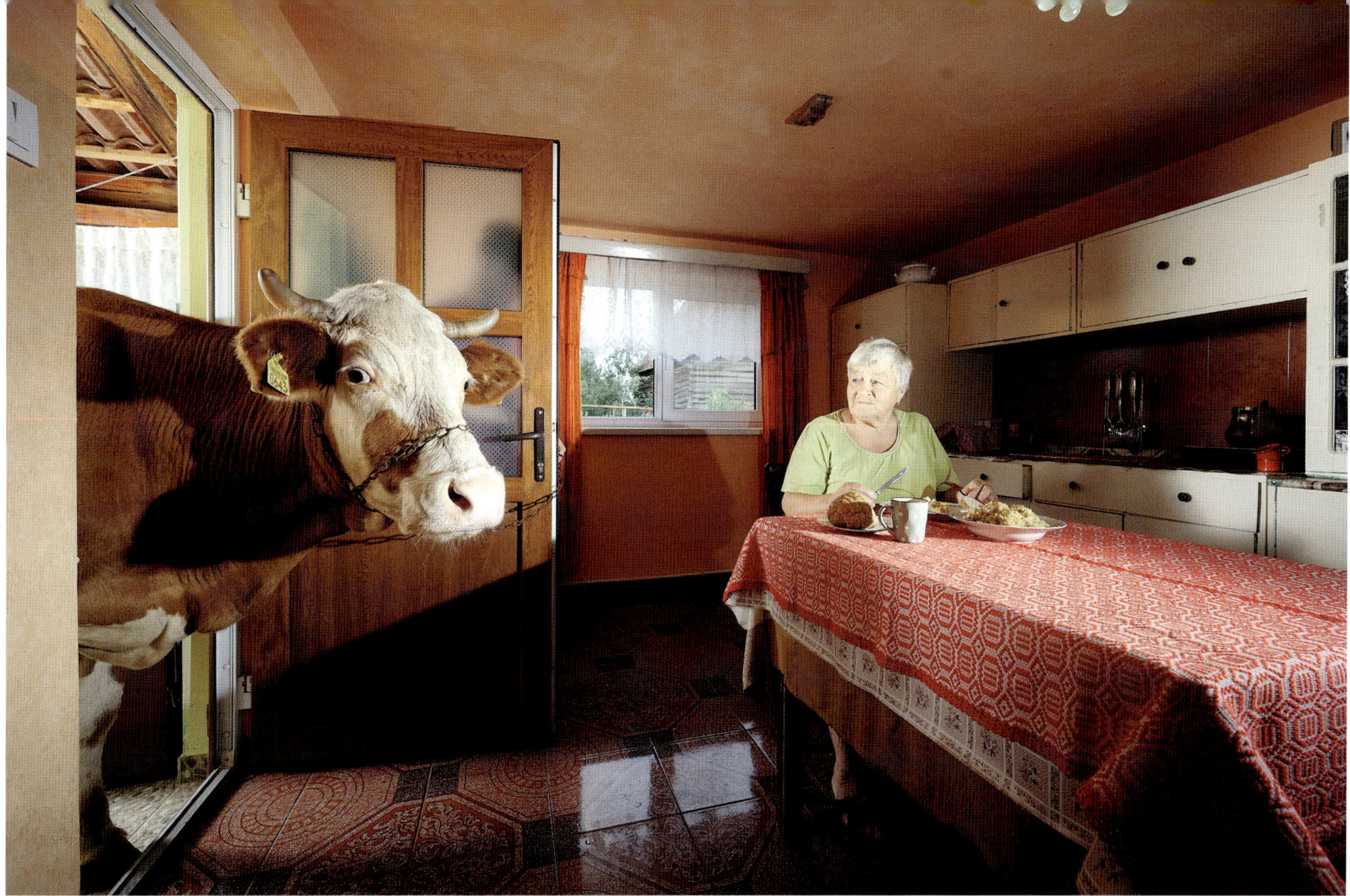

To do stuff like this, you have to explain yourself and your idea, and try not to sound completely nuts. I'm sure my Romanian interpreter chose her words carefully when we approached a lovely family and asked if they would allow their cow in the kitchen. They were the ideal subjects, possessed of all the components required: They had a kitchen, a cow, and a beautifully bemused grandmother who consented to be eating breakfast when Bessie poked her head in the doorway. City kid that I am, I had no idea how difficult it would be to get a cow to do this, but this is where country wisdom took over.

The cow in the picture is a mama cow, and she is very attentive to her calf, as moms tend to be. So, what the farmer and his sons did was bring her baby cow inside the kitchen so that mom, curious and concerned, would peer in to make sure all was well.

A quick note: Try to get your flash exposures as tight as you can before trying something like this. For one of my first strobed exposures (above), which was definitely a new experience for my bovine friend, I don't know whether the flash was just too hot or I had stupidly dialed in TTL and it missed its mark. But the obvious explosion of light in the kitchen got the cow somewhat alarmed, and . . . interested in me.

Cows are very strong, and big. She made her way toward the camera. Dumbass here (that's me) reached out to pet her like a dog, being utterly unaware of the length and dexterous capabilities of a cow's tongue. Perhaps thinking I might have a snack, she slimily, luxuriantly wrapped her tongue around my entire hand and wrist, seeking sustenance or, perhaps, a relationship. The farmers had a good laugh as they came to my rescue. I dangled my hand in the air, dripping with cow saliva, looking at it like it had just done a cameo in *Ghostbusters*.

You've got to have faith in your ideas and do your best to see them through, even though most of the time it would be infinitely easier to just let them slumber. It was not convenient for this family to wrangle a cow into their kitchen! You see them struggling with this very large animal, feeding her snacks and trying to get her to stand still, and there's a baby cow making a racket because this definitely isn't business as usual for her and mom, and you're struggling with the lights and the balance of the scene, trying to make it look natural, even though there's nothing natural about it, and well, it definitely would've been easier for all concerned to have just shut up and left town.

But you can't do that. At least not all the time. All photographers have unfulfilled picture notions and projects they never get to or never turn the corner on. Unfed, uncompleted whimsies that never become pictures. Those can fly through your dreams in restive fashion, or they can outright gnaw on you, like a much less serious version of a police officer who dwells on a cold case that's never been solved. We all got those "if only's" and "I shoulda's."

Which is completely understandable and utterly blameless. Time and life often conspire against ambitious picture aspirations. Sometimes we just have to let the idea go. Budget, too, can be a big enemy. And failure, always an option when you reach, can also be excruciating, embarrassing, and, depending on the scale and cost, career damaging.

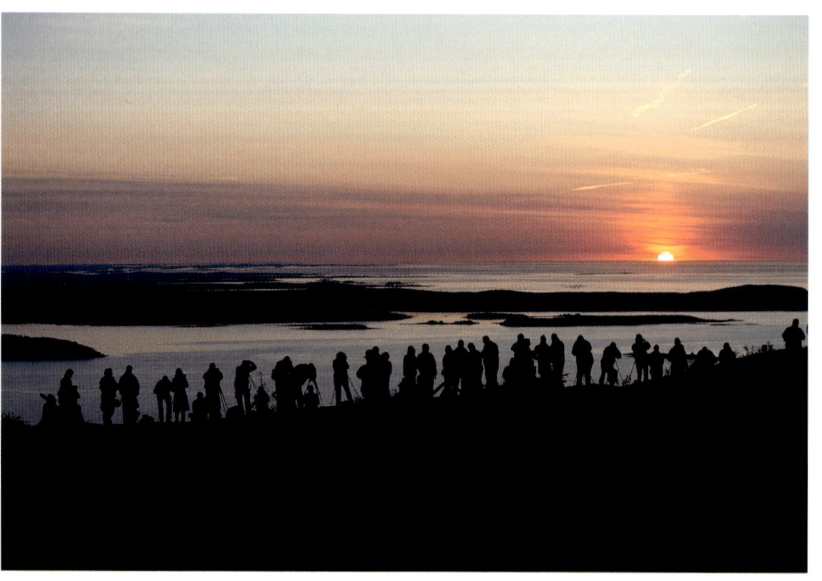

Frankly, it's easier not to risk. It's far easier to pull up at the overlook at dawn, the one everybody goes to, get out of the warm car, set up a tripod, wait for sunrise, hope for a good one, and rattle through lots of frames and exposures so that Photoshop has ample material to chew on later. Apart from the initial pain of your alarm going off at 3:00 a.m., there's no real discomfiture on anyone's part. The rocks and trees are not inconvenienced at all. Pending the uniqueness of the sunrise, which you can make more unique at your computer, you pretty much know you'll get a picture on this morning, and you don't need to do or risk too much. Hell, you barely need to be at the tripod. Once you frame up, and the sun starts cooking, and the colors start blossoming, set up a six-stop bracket, lock up the mirror (or not, depending on the camera), and cue the intervalometer. You've got gloves, hand warmers, foot warmers, thermal underwear, a head lamp, hot cocoa in an insulated cup, and the latest in boot technology. Geez, not even your tripod's cold 'cause you got it draped in LensCoat foam protection sleeves, in your choice of camo colors. Digital camo? Flat black? Forest green?

All this gear and safety and comfort and familiarity most likely produces a photo … we've all seen before. There is nothing wrong with this! It's fun, yea, even bracing, to greet the sunrise with a camera in hand. Win, lose, or draw out there, witnessing the rising glory of the sun or the brightening grayness of "You're screwed," it makes breakfast taste better, knowing you made the effort.

But when the lineup of tripod-lugging photogs is the size of the line outside an Apple store when they launch a new iPhone, well, it's hard to lay claim to that coveted photo turf known as "exclusive."

Think of acting on a wild-ass picture idea, a leap where the landing is uncertain, as a necessary shock to the system, like those ice swimmers in the Nordics who cut a hole in the sea ice in February and jump in. It's really good for you, if it doesn't flat-out kill you. And sometimes, those crazy ideas, as luminously promising as they seem, glowing like embers in your inflamed noodle, can, in fact, damn near kill you, at least professionally. Following your imagination is not risk free.

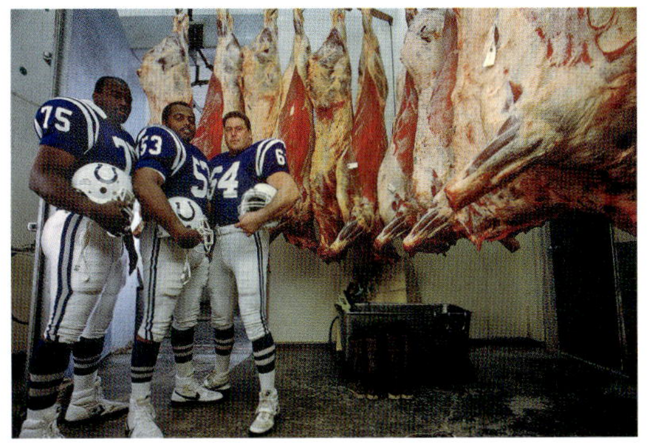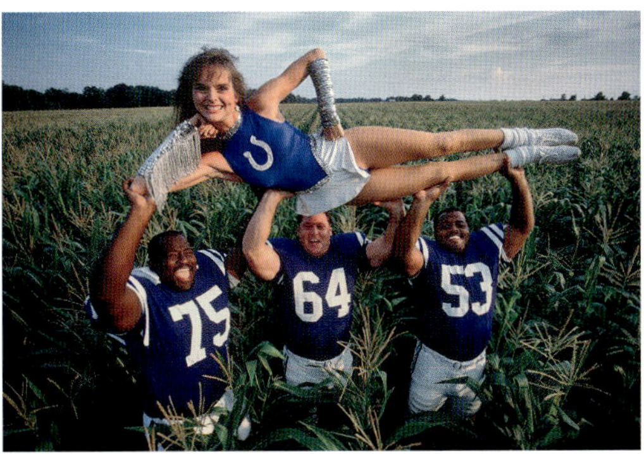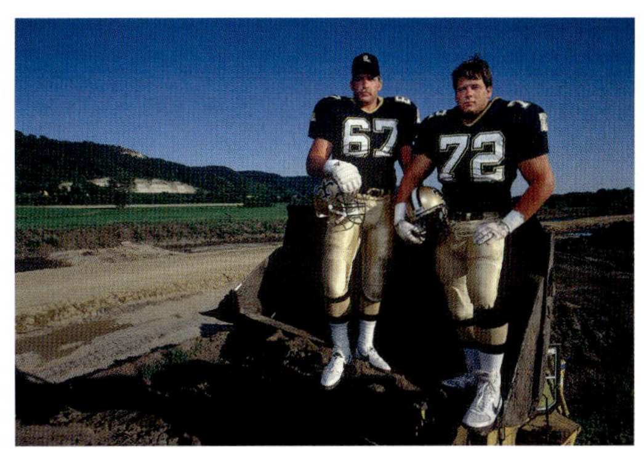

Sports Illustrated once assigned me to photograph the biggest guys in the NFL. Great job, right? The type of project that makes your photo juices run hot as a lava flow. I jumped for joy and started conjuring, making calls to NFL teams, arranging dates and times. Everybody was cooperative, as *SI* at that time was in the catbird seat of sports journalism, and every team and athlete wanted to be in those hallowed pages. Also, the biggest guys on an NFL team are basically all offensive linemen, and nobody ever pays attention to them unless they screw up. They were down for a photo session.

And I went out there with all my harebrained ideas and made some of the worst pictures of my career. I didn't completely understand the impossibility of showing how big somebody is. Big relative to what, or who? The guys they play with are all pretty big, too. Put 'em next to something that suggests size? I tried that, in futile fashion. As I kept shooting and traveling, my interior "bad picture" warning kept going off, like that computer voice in the cockpit. "Terrain, terrain, pull up!"

When you are in the field, having sashayed out there at the beginning of the day with such hubristic, shiny confidence, and you finish that day with nothing but the dread of failure as your companion, it's rough. And, if you're honest with yourself, you know it immediately, while still at the camera. Failure taps you on the shoulder right then and there, grinning at you like the Joker. Remember me? It's your old friend, Failure, back for a visit. You pack up the camera, fold the tripod, and conduct a resigned, interior shrug, thinking, hoping, "Well, maybe they'll like it." It's a bad, bad sign.

And *SI* didn't like it. My editor for that project was not hesitant and deadly honest on the phone. He had all the pictures in hand and I recall him saying he "didn't like them so well." I easily spent about $25,000 of the magazine's dough and not a single picture was published.

I took the offensive line of the Colts to a meat locker with sides of beef. I guess I saw *Rocky* too many times.

Then I had them lift a cheerleader. Can anybody here spell "cheeseball"?

To use football parlance, every idea I acted on moved the chains toward a goal line called failure. To make matters worse, in this instance I caused these guys to miss their training camp meal and had to buy them all dinner. Each of them ordered two main dishes, multiple sodas, and desserts. I didn't know you could spend that much dough in a Red Lobster.

I put a couple guys in the maw of an earth mover. The guy driving the earth mover went to sleep, most likely.

> *I went out there with all my harebrained ideas and made some of the worst pictures of my career.*

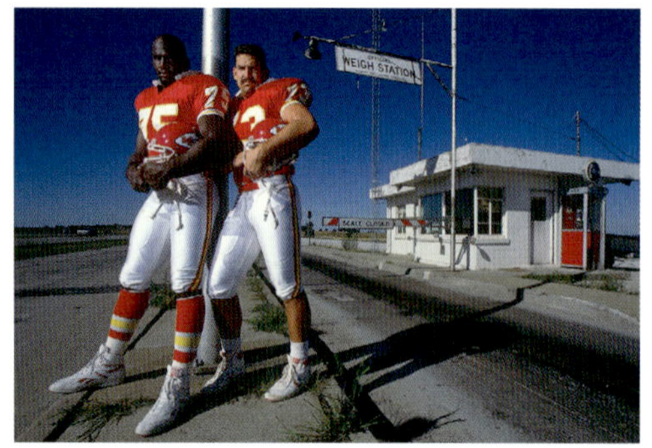

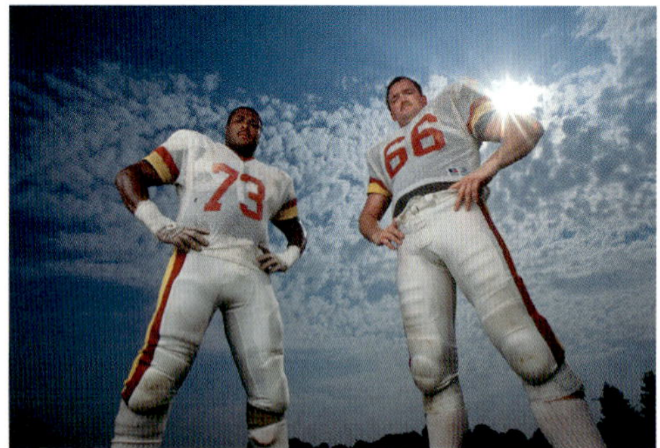

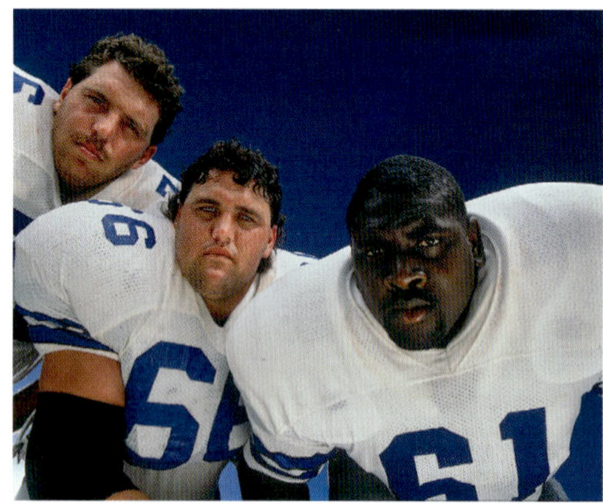

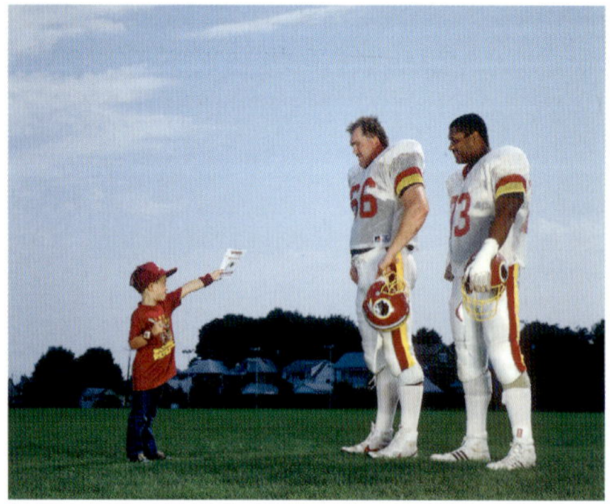

I took a couple Kansas City Chiefs to a truck weigh station. That idea was as lonely as that highway.

I got on the ground and looked up at them. Big deal. As my editor pointed out, nothing from that angle actually showed how big they really were.

I asked a little kid to approach for an autograph. Okay. Cute but still unsuccessful.

I made a couple of cool-looking pictures, but nothing addressed the "bigness" factor, really, and *SI* just trashed the whole thing. The one photo that has stuck with me, sort of, is of Nate Newton, 330 pounds, then of the Dallas Cowboys. I asked him to fly off a diving board, which he did with unusual aplomb. But, again, the bigness factor is not, well, huge in this photo. "Big" got expressed when Nate hit the water and this relatively small pool became a wave machine, which took me by surprise and nearly destroyed my camera.

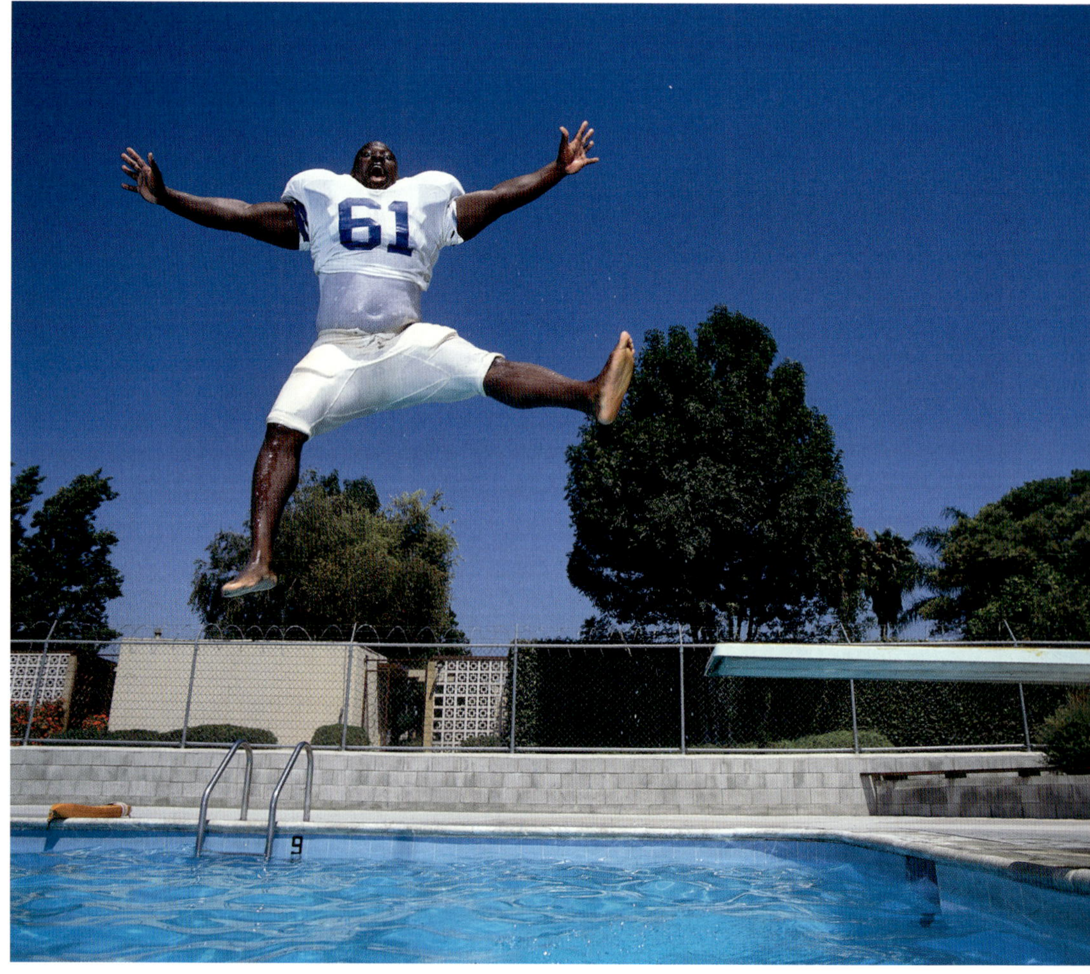

A couple pix were fun, but not big. Joe, we wanted big, remember? This whole thing dented my reputation and my relationship with the magazine, and it caused me great interior despair. I shot this assignment in 1988, which was the year of the big stupid for me. I crossed some boundaries, took some chances, and screwed the pooch more than once. Oh, and I lost my contract with *Sports Illustrated*, which did not hire me again until 2000.

But you have to remain unafraid of your imagination. Let it rip. Try, at least every once in a while, to follow it with a camera, regardless of the potentially foolhardy nature of it or the looming possibility of failure. Remember earlier, when I mentioned that all of our life experience is present at the camera? It's very true.

I grew up on comic books, and as I was the new kid in school on a routine basis, I always had the handy trap door of my fantasy life to jump through and hide away. My imagination would roam places far from the schoolyard or my kitchen table. Still does. I still get wired up by the extraordinarily cool-looking object or fad of the moment, any zeitgeist-y trend that might ignite a picture idea.

Like lasers. Good grief.

Luckily, I had worked with Jackie Joyner-Kersee before. She's a lovely person and a multi-dimensional, astonishingly skilled Olympic athlete. Given her medal haul (three gold, one silver, two bronze) garnered over four Olympic Games, she could legitimately claim to be the best female athlete, ever. Period. I photographed her a number of times, including her in a portfolio of nude Olympians, which I shot for *LIFE* magazine. I shot her from the back, and we tussled a bit about it. She was concerned that somehow the camera would see her chest and record more nudity than she was prepared to accommodate. We talked it out, and I shared Polaroids with her. That put her at ease, and I'm glad it did, as this picture (following page) is now in the collection of the National Portrait Gallery in Washington, D.C.

These next couple of photos (below) of Jackie are not in the National Portrait Gallery. They are in a file cabinet, in my basement, and have been for over 30 years. Deservedly so.

Given her power and stature, and the fact that she gives freely of her time to kids, *Sports Illustrated for Kids* approached me to photograph her for a cover. I thought it would be cool to do sort of an "I Sing the Body Electric," an ode to her physicality, literally translating that Walt Whitman poem's title into some form of electricity. So, on location, somewhat impromptu, I laced Jackie's imposing physique with unjacketed fiber optic cable and made laser beams into track lanes. She was very patient with all this, gracious person that she is.

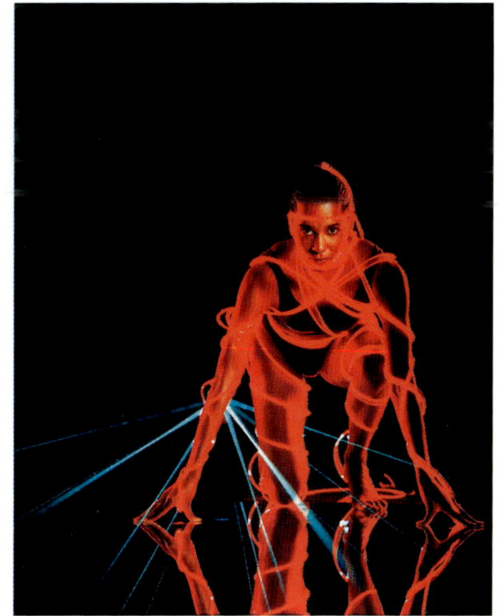 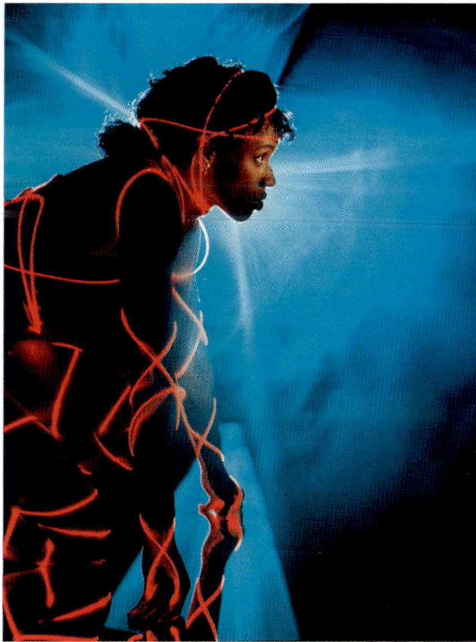

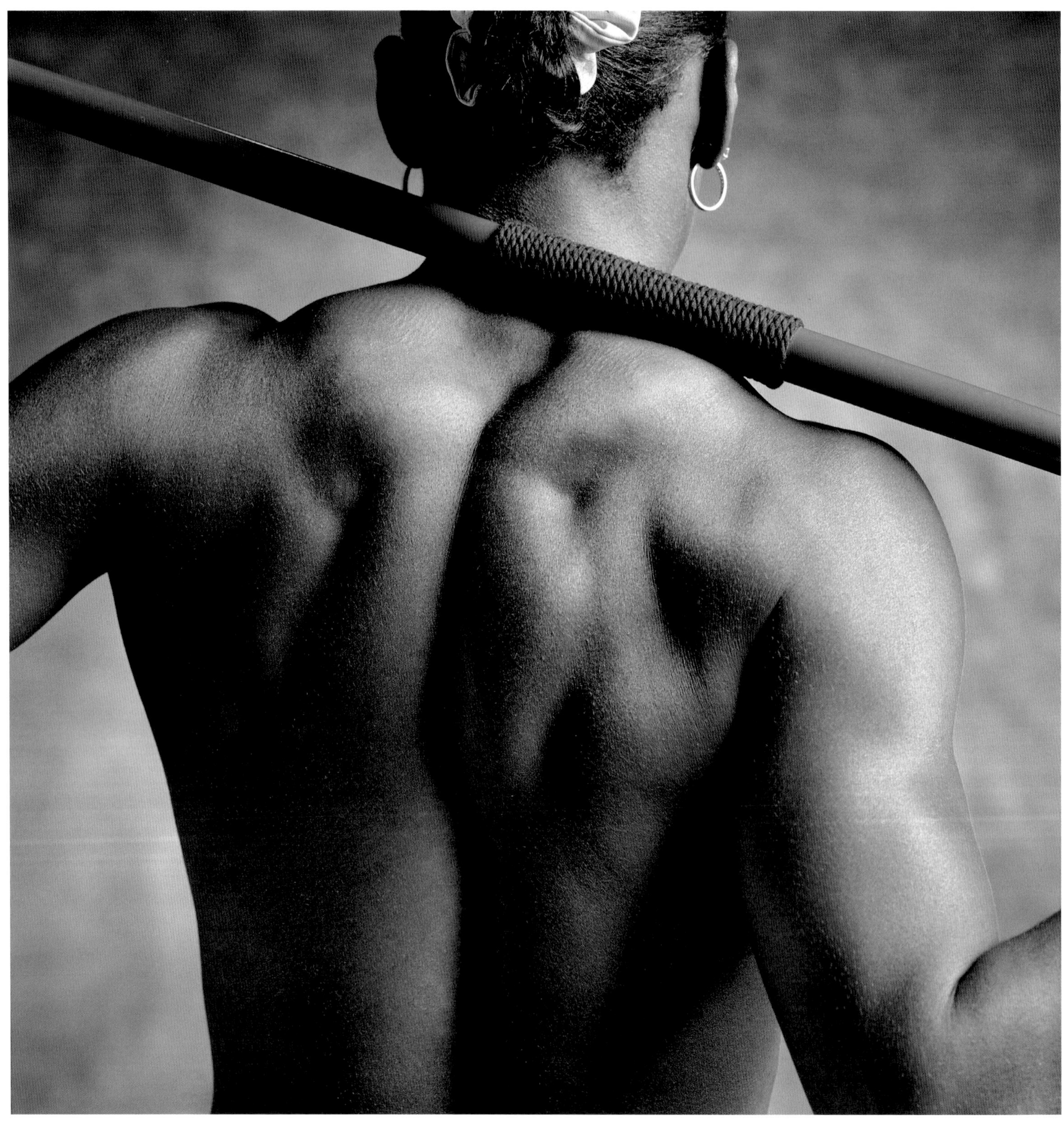

I wish the photos matched the excellence of her patience and presence. Given that the magazine's readership was kids, I kind of gave myself a bit of a pass on this overblown, overwrought flameout of my imagination. The magazine ran it, and the editors were relatively pleased with the results. The kids probably liked it; after all, an adolescent shot it. But these pictures have remained in a dark drawer, as most pictures from most photographers should.

Failures such as these don't cause me to stop and play it safe. No matter how badly scraped your knees and elbows are, you have to get back up on the bicycle. Risk more, risk greater. Your imagination won't ever stop, and neither should you. The photographer has a necessarily restless soul, one that keeps striving for the haphazardly beautiful and keeps looking for those odd, off-kilter things that others pass by without a glance. The phrase "That'll never work" or the even simpler reply of "No" is a red flag to the photographer, a dare that accelerates determination.

So, as disheveled as I have been by these and many other jobs that have gone awry—far too numerous to mention here—I'm still in the ring. And my imagination is a faucet that won't stop running. Some of my ideas are full of bravado and majesty, like sailing ships on a beautiful sea. Others are more devilish and concerning, like storm clouds through my brain that make me afraid of the dark of my soul. But they won't stop, and I've grown comfortable with the notion that the time I spend at my workstation not typing but staring out the window with a vacant expression is the most valuable thing I do.

Let it roll. Dream in unafraid fashion. You might as well. Imagination won't stop. Pictures rise up in your head. The cows just keep coming home. Let them in the door.

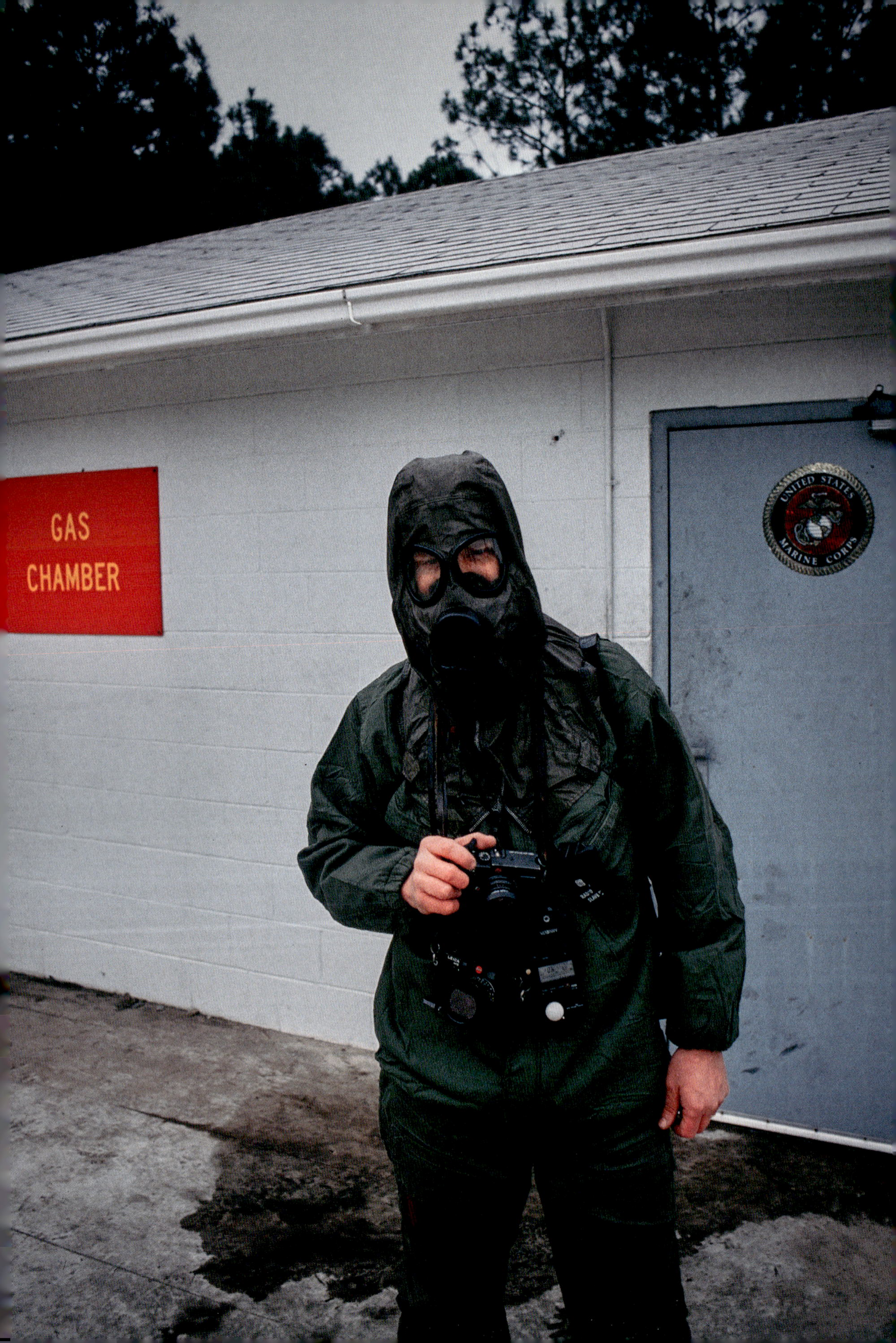

GAS
CHAMBER
UNITED STATES
MARINE CORPS

The Tools of the Trade

As photographers, we adapt continuously, using what is available to us, even if it means, as it often has, concocting some sort of Rube Goldberg, spit-and-glue, seat-of-the-pants, wing-and-a-prayer type of arrangement. When the US Marines permitted me to put a Norman 200B flash up in the interior roof supports of the gas chamber, it was an allowance based on a necessary request. I was shooting Kodachrome for *National Geographic*, and Kodachrome generally liked some measure of light, which was desperately unavailable inside that cinder block house of gas.

I was wearing a full protection suit and, of course, a gas mask. Which meant I could not focus an SLR camera, such as a Nikon F3. Too much gas, too many scratches on the already dim lenses of the protective mask. I used my Leica M6's split-screen focus. It was the only way to have a hope of being ballpark sharp.

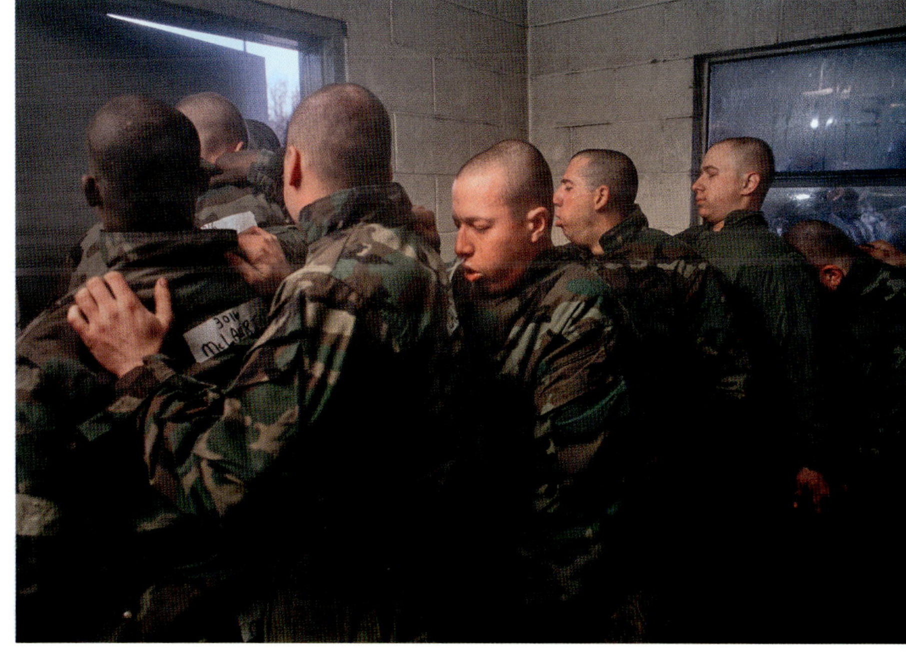

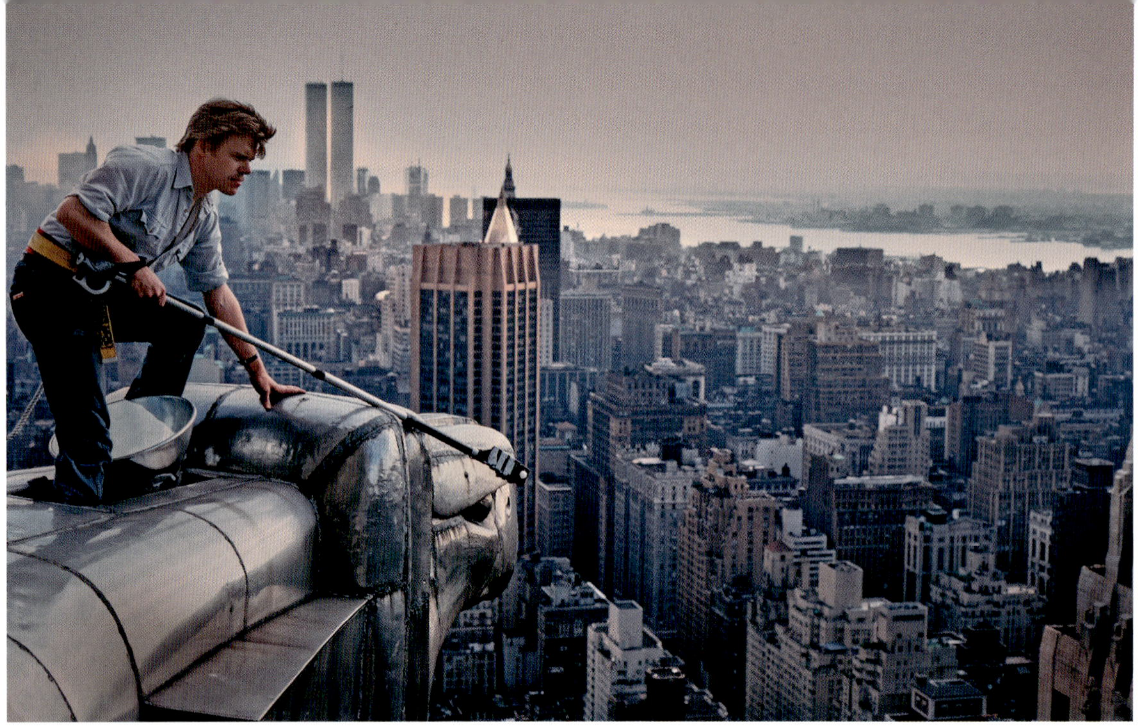

Atop a Chrysler Building gargoyle, the one made famous by Margaret Bourke-White, I naturally brought large flash. I positioned several 2400 watt-second Speedotrons on an outdoor portico a few floors down from the gargoyle. I figured a huge pop of light from several of these units would travel the multiple stories and eventually reach the gargoyle. How to meter such a beast? Monopod, safety wired to my wrist, and a flash meter gaffered to said metal stick. Poke it out there, flash the lights. Bingo. F-stop. To this day, I hope no one was working late that night, on that side of the building, because they would've needed sunglasses. Boom! You could hear those Speedotrons pop at full power, several stories up, over the distant hum of traffic noise below.

Those lights allowed me to extend my working time, as the beautiful daylight faded and the sun worked its unparalleled magic.

I was able to render the client, *Geo* magazine, a different look as the evening progressed—making use of natural light, and then, as darkness closed in, flash. Cool.

Meters on a stick and split-screen manual focus. You use what you have, at that moment. The miracle of the pixels hadn't occurred yet. I thought I would be shooting Kodachrome forever.

Oh, for an LCD! Or accurate in-camera spot metering. Or dynamic AF. With confirmation! Or on-the-fly, adjustable white balance. Maybe amazing high ISO? Too much to ask? It indeed was, and not that long ago.

As a photographer, you take what is given, and nowadays, that's a lot. Even a moderately priced DSLR is a monster, technically speaking. We live in a golden age of photography, driven by technology that is continuously in the passing lane, zooming past us, sucking the wind out of our lungs whilst we stare in bovine wonder at its rapidly receding taillights. "Hey, wait a minute!" is our utterly ineffective cry, unheard, lost in the slipstream. This isn't going to slow down. If we wanted it to, we'd just be spitting in the digital wind.

The tough part now is keeping up. We buy a camera and it's ready for a museum in a couple of years. A four- or five-year-old camera possessed of modest millions of pixels is considered quaint. The cameras coming off the line next year have been in development for years, and they keep coming. You have to place your bets wisely now, as a digital photog, balancing on the tightrope of budget, and facing off with the quality of your deliverables vis-à-vis your client's expectations.

When new cameras come out, my question is always the same: How much better is this going to get?

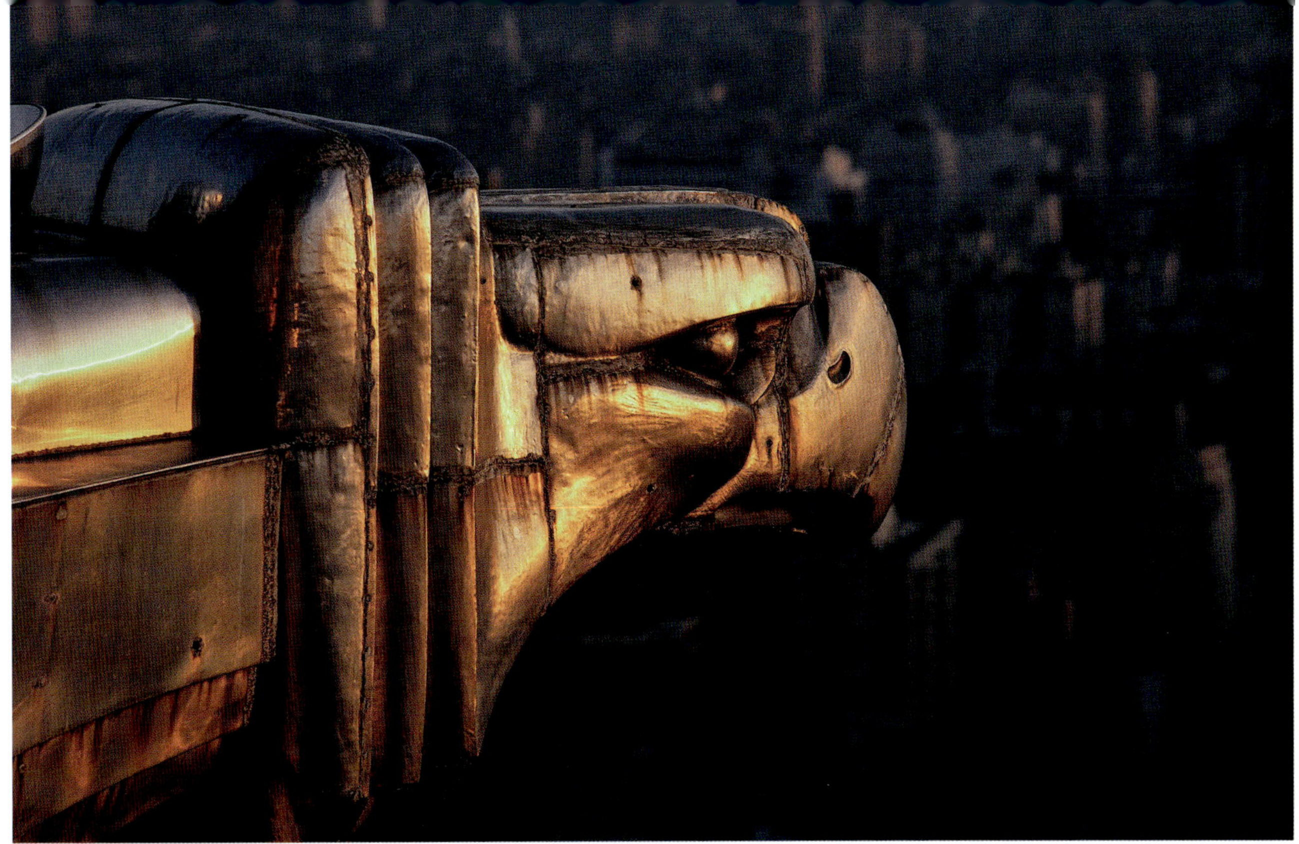

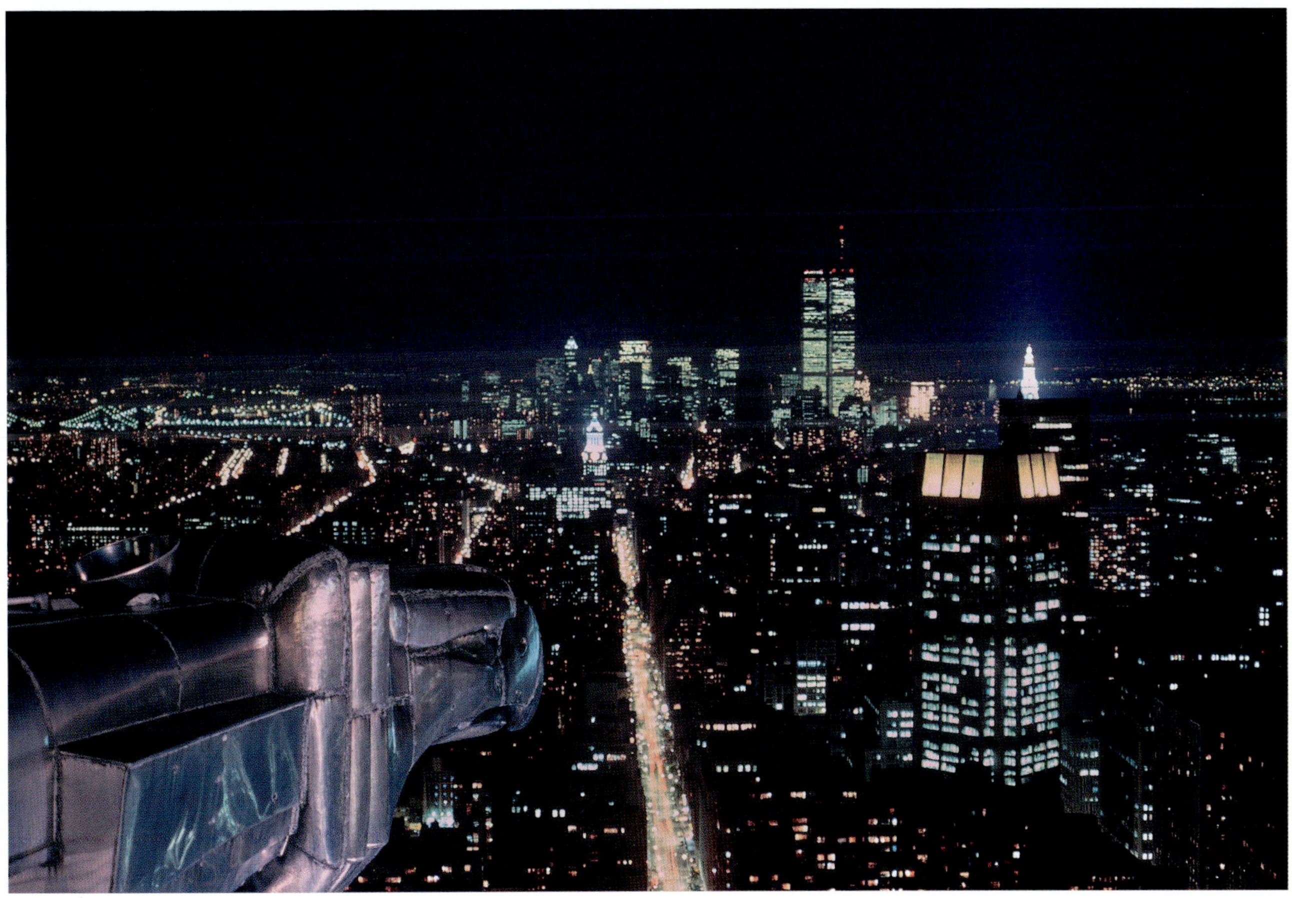

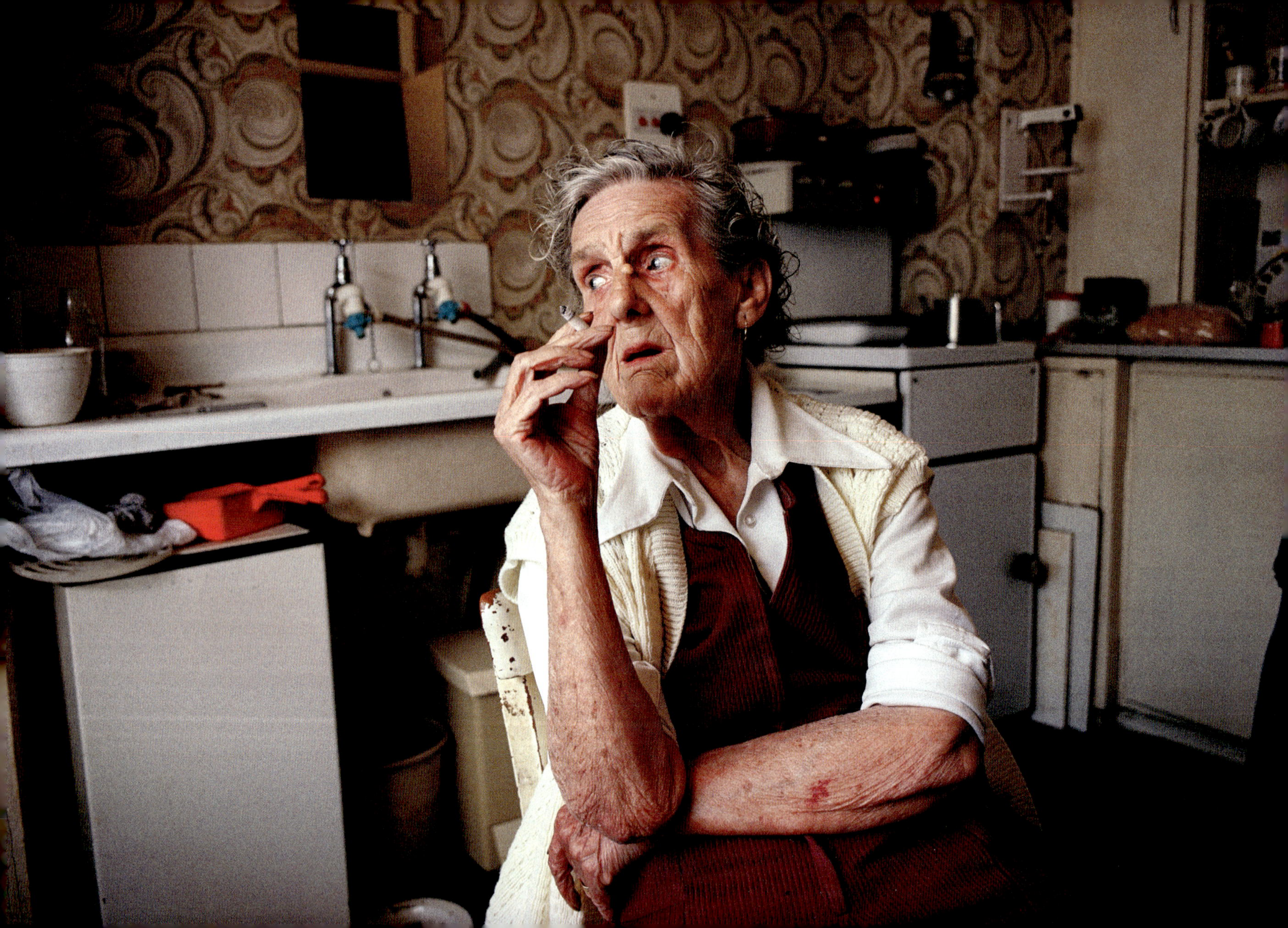

Seeing Window Light, Making Window Light

Naturally occurring, beautiful window light is a gift, occasionally given. It can help you tell the story of a place and its people. It is, after all, part of the scene. That window will remain, and give light to that location, on the other 364 days of the year when you are not there. Properly observed and used, it can be very telling. This lady, a lifelong, old school resident of the East End of London, looks toward the window of her kitchen, which she must have done for many years, even though she was blind and the window just a highlight. But the light draping on the battered kitchen, as lined and worn as her face, speaks beautifully. I could not have approached its inherent eloquence.

It reaches all corners of the kitchen. I can be simply there, shooting quietly as an observer, not a frenetic exclamation point announcing my presence with a series of 200-watt-second calling cards. Sister Christine, a Catholic nun who visited those in need as part of her ministry, guides her hand to her cup of tea. As best I can, shooting a Leica rangefinder, I stay as quiet as the moment. The wordless window behind me lets me do that.

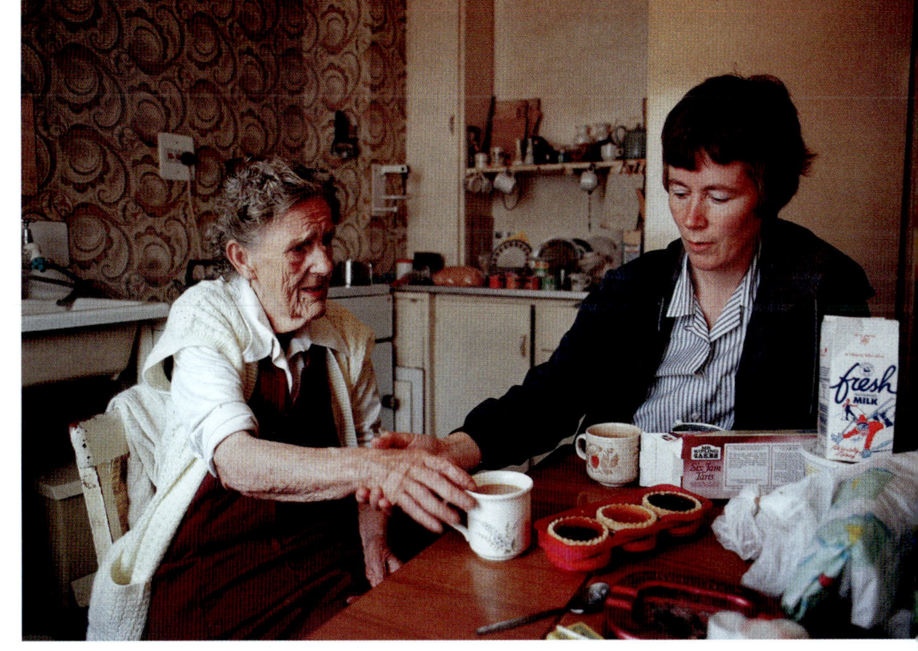

These sleepy Irish schoolchildren sit on the sofa, buttoning up for school in a dappled, lovely, irregular splash of morning light that has a quality I could never mimic or approach with flash. It falls off beautifully but includes the storytelling detail of their artwork on the wall. We have all been here, getting ready for school, half awake, and more than happy to go back under the covers. It's a moment that begs not to be interfered with, and that lucky piece of light behind me allows me to just be at the camera, wordless and (mostly) unnoticed.

Window light speaks volumes, often very quietly. Years ago, on assignment in London's Docklands, I lived on the Isle of Dogs for seventeen weeks. (Back in the day, time on location was a gift *National Geographic* readily gave to photographers.) The story was a local interest story, about how Docklands, long a rough-hewn, working-class neighborhood, and not the most tolerant of places, was being changed overnight by money, investment, construction, and gentrification, perpetrated by a well-heeled group, not so affectionately known as "yuppies."

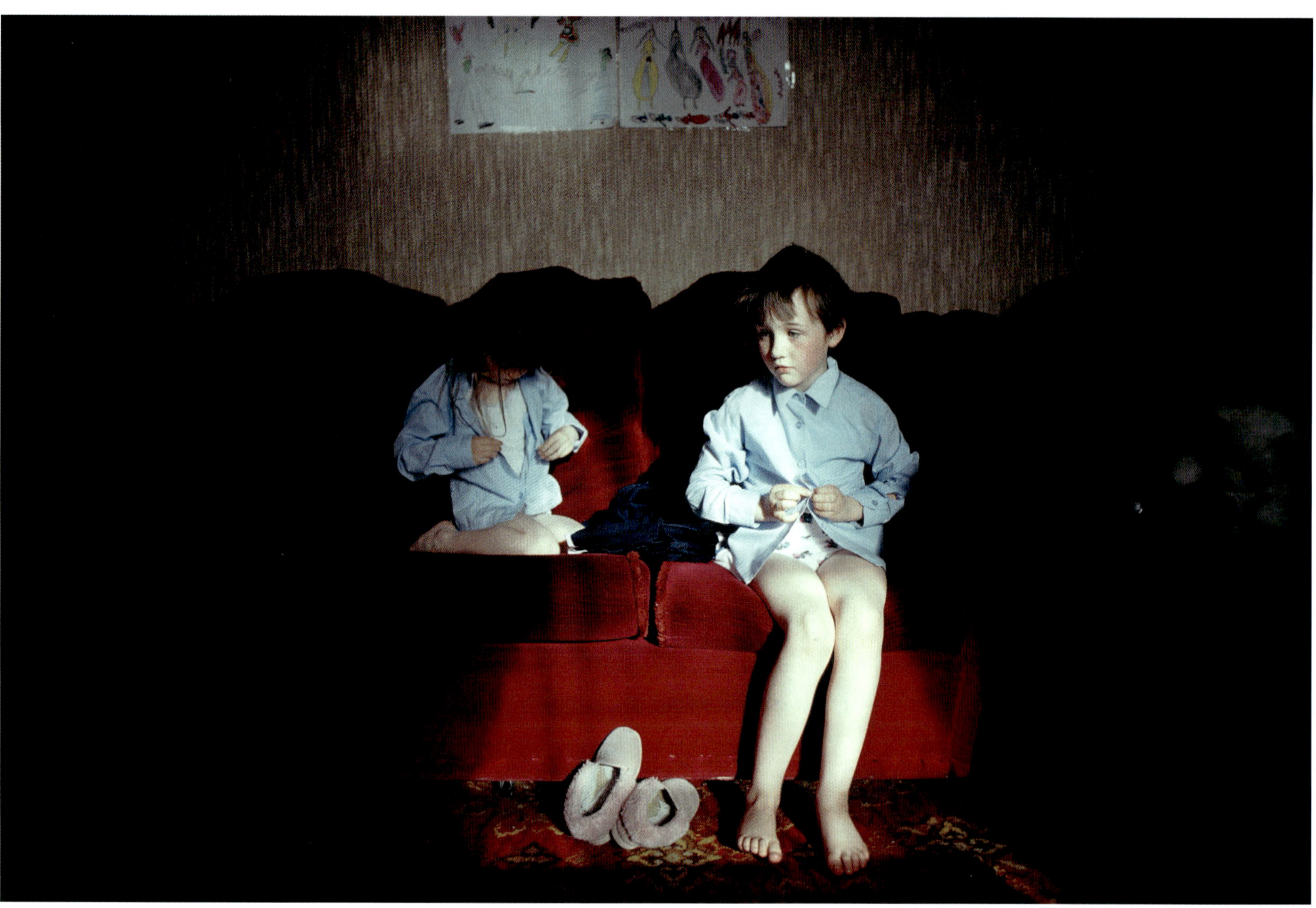

As money poured in, resentment grew. The local attitudes were belligerent, understandably so. One woman I talked with in a local pub jabbed the air with her finger, her other hand wrapped around a pint. "I was born here, my family survived the Blitz here, and by God I'm gonna die here."

George, by the window here, was typical. He was being uprooted out of his lifelong apartment, which was scheduled to be razed, and being given a new one. An arguably better one. But it wasn't home. He told me of his large family, growing up in the East End without means. "When it came to fishes and loaves, and feeding the masses, me mum had Jesus Christ well and truly beat."

I photographed him as he tentatively toured his new, empty digs. The loss of roots, the sense of being lost, the strange aloneness he is engulfed by are emotions given voice by the soft, draped light. George peers out, an alien in a world he wanted nothing to do with. To light this would be like cursing in church.

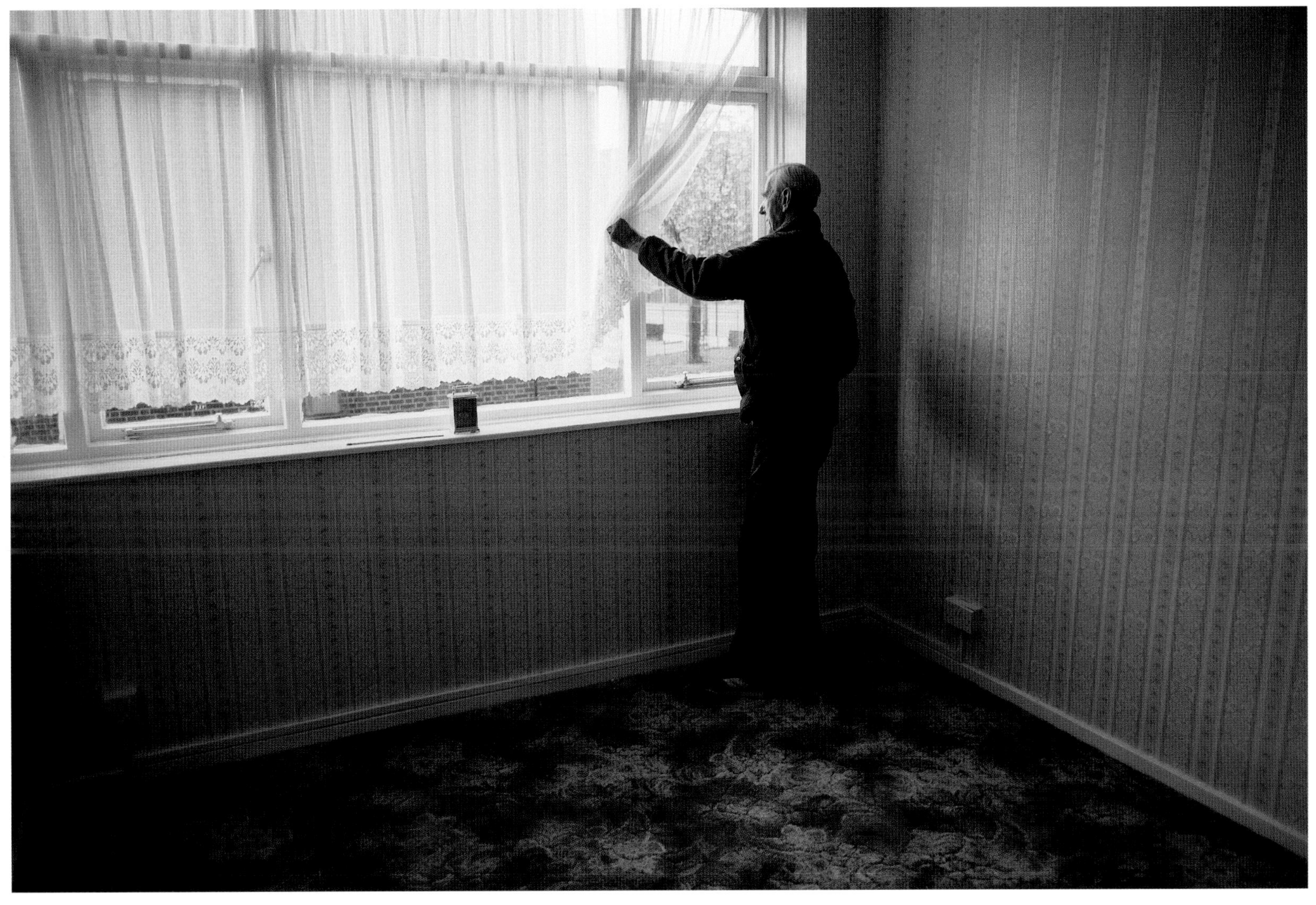

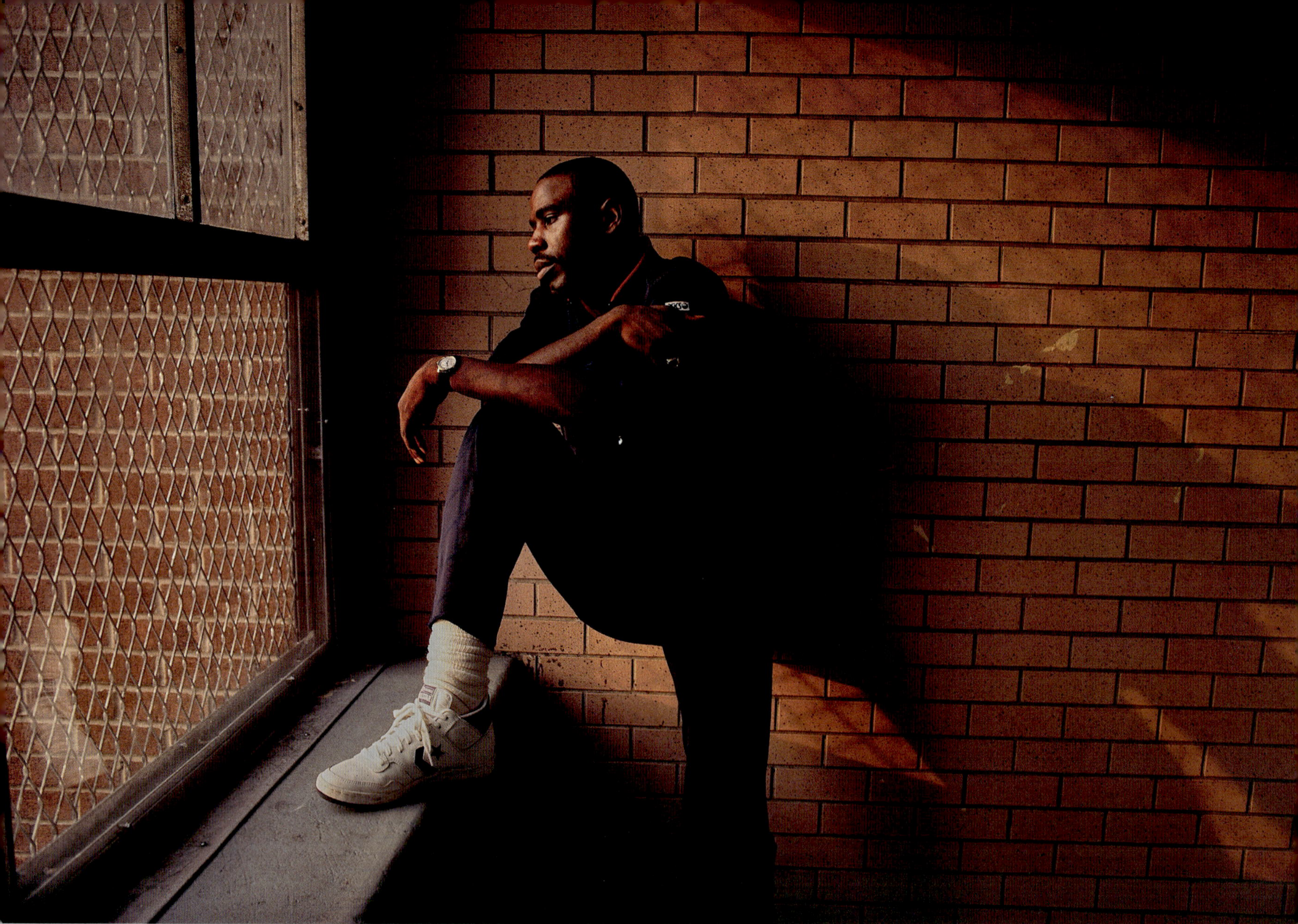

I've mentioned quiet light a number of times, but it doesn't have to be. It does not always require rumination and breathless, reverential silence at the camera. You can turn a corner in an apartment building in NYC, and there it is, screaming through the screens, shouting at you to stop and use it. No ceremony required. Put your subject in it. Shoot like mad as it fades (above). Be insistent about this, as the light demands your attention right now, then withdraws the opportunity quickly.

My friend George Divoky lives three or more months of the year on a deserted, forbidding island, called Cooper Island, in the Beaufort Sea, east of Utqiagvik, Alaska. He has done so for 40 years, spending those months largely alone, in the ongoing observance of a colony of Black Guillemots, a species of Arctic sea bird. His initial intent as a zoologist was to study these remarkable birds, but his long-term, painstakingly detailed observance of the birds has in fact become one of the largest repositories of experiential, irrefutable climate change data on the planet. His perseverance and tenacity are remarkable.

His shack on the island is his home for 90 to 120 days of the year. It's tough to fit a light in there, first off. Any source you might bring is likely to create some sort of lopsided highlights or shadows or tilt the beautiful balance of this stuff-laden environment in an undesired way. In other words, you would work hard to make it look natural. You don't want to interrupt the heartbeat of the place. So why bother? Feel the light that is there. It's lovely, and enough.

Luckily, I did have the good sense to walk in and not try to arm wrestle with the place. All I did was pull the red curtain all the way over the only window. Small move, but essential, and perfectly permissible, as my intent at that moment was to shoot a portrait of George. When I put my camera to my eye, as he was grinding his coffee, the window curtain was swept back (right, bottom).

Where does your eye go? Certainly not to George. I pulled the curtain over the highlight, but not enough.

That screaming sliver doesn't work either. It competes. Begs for attention and gives nothing in return. Keep pulling the damn curtain. All the way. This is not a business for halfway measures. The camera and the pixels will not forgive. They will record the reality you point your camera at in relentlessly faithful fashion. If you see it in the field, through the lens, and it's bothersome, you will see it on your computer, back home, and it will be more so. It won't magically disappear or become less annoying. Leaving that sliver of hot light forces a crop. Now, the crop tool is a necessary and highly effective post-production move. I use it and I'm glad it's there. But it's also a tool with the voice of a stern schoolmarm—for me, anyways.

"Should have moved closer, shouldn't we have?"

"Maybe changed the lens? Taken the time to be more careful?"

"Maybe should have found another place to shoot the picture? Done more research? Not been so lazy?"

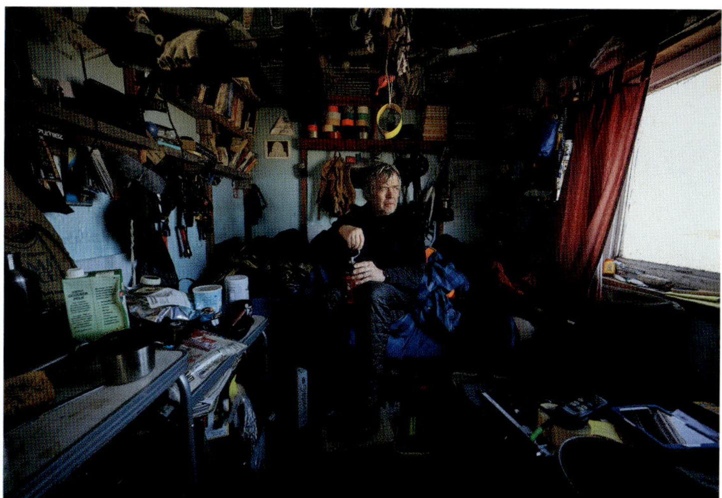

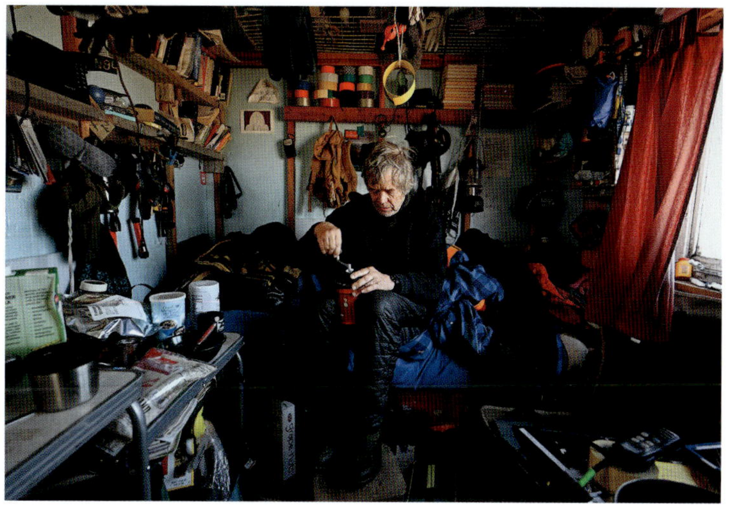

"If you continue on this careless path, you will come to no good, Mr. McNally."

Those reading this book who might have gone to Catholic high school might remember, back in the day, being shown clownish videos highlighting the dangers of drugs, jerking off, promiscuity, teenage pregnancy, and really, almost everything your lack of experience, sense of adventure, hormones, and the general, frenetic idiocy of the teenage years might impel you to do. I remember one film in particular, revolving around the dangers of unprotected sex and the potential result of a child being

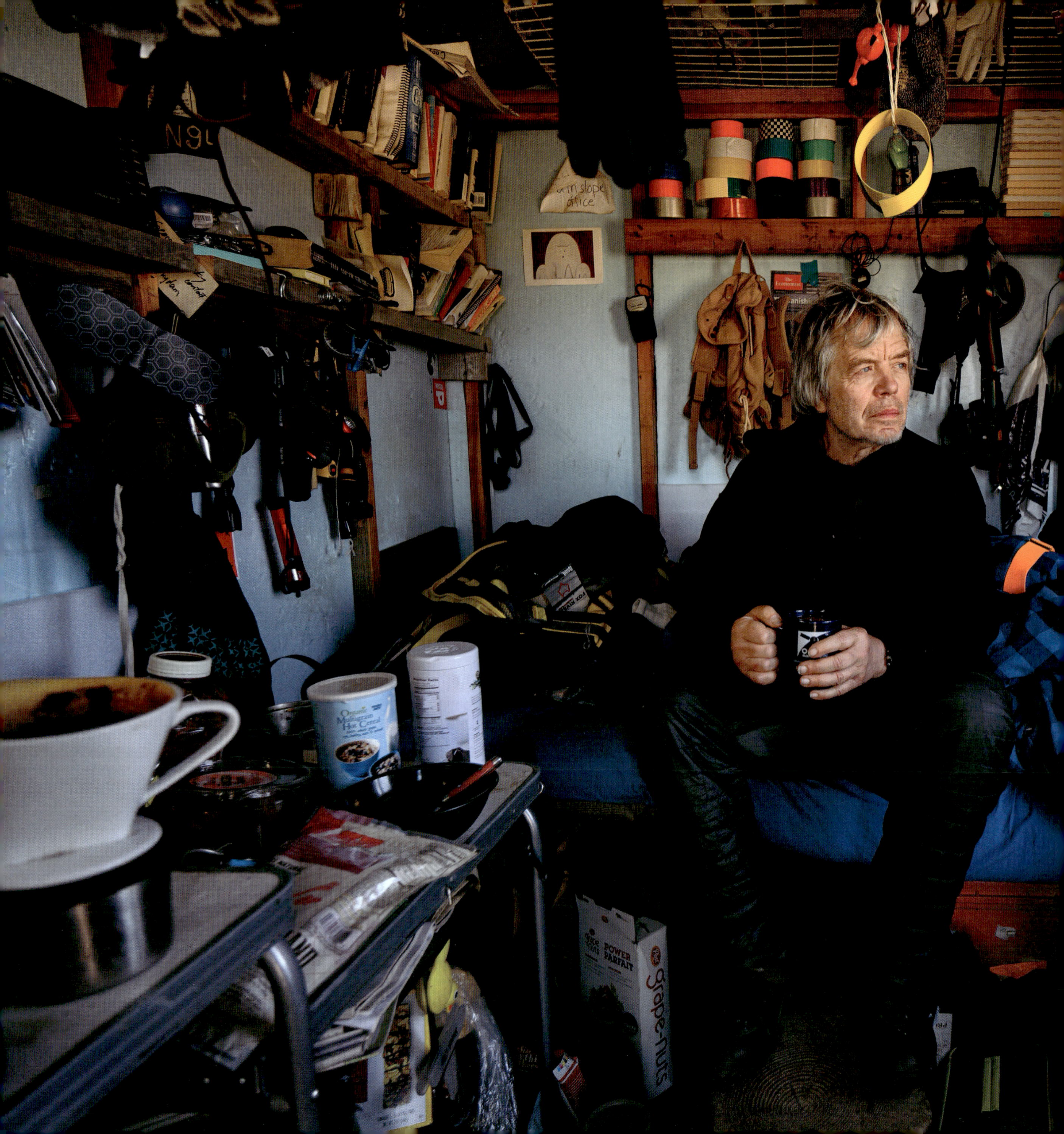

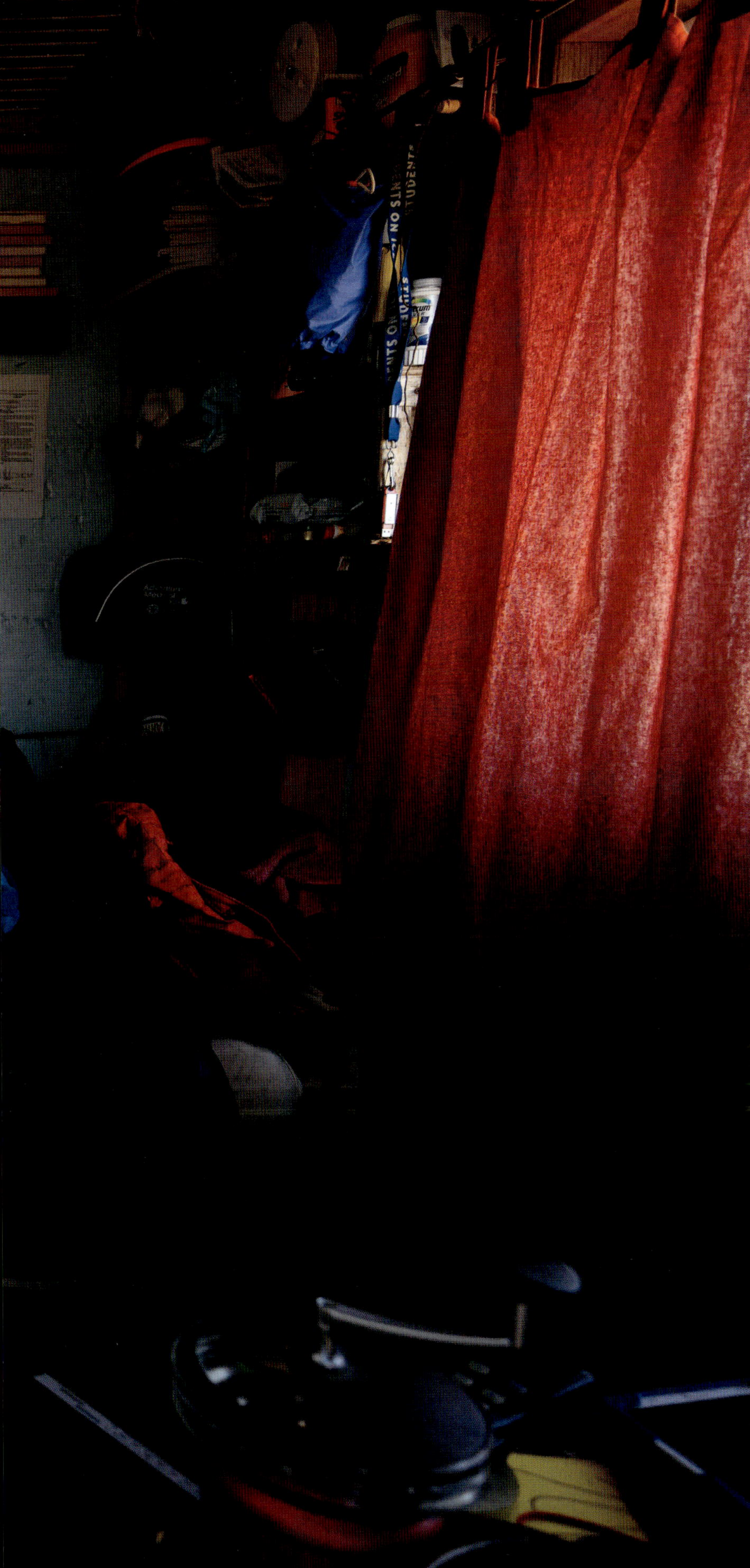

produced from said activity. The title of the film was "Hope Is Not a Method."

Same thing with photography. Look with clear intent. Lock it down.

Pull the curtain all the way. Check the image floating up to your eyes in the LCD to be sure nothing interrupts or stymies the story. It's guaranteed, really, that this picture of George's cabin will be the viewer's only experience of its beautifully picturesque, chock-a-block wonderfulness. Nobody goes to Cooper Island. You have to take the journey for them. Make them feel it. Make them shake their heads in amazement and embrace this scientist's story. Get them involved. Which means not coming back with pictures that are half-baked, seeking the crop tool or the hope-this-makes-it-better slider. The work occurs at the viewfinder, in this shack, on this desolate island.

This picture in George's cabin, by the way, was shot at ISO 1000. What a marvel! Growing up photographically, I often heard the phrase, "If I can see it, I can shoot it." Yeah, you know . . . kinda, sorta, a little bit, maybe. With older transparency films, forgiveness was slight, and high ISO was definitely north of the wall. The higher the numbers of your ISO, the more you had to turn the darkroom into a microwave oven to deep fry your chromes. The result was that you obliterated detail. I learned from listening to the masterful photographer Greg Heisler, who accurately stipulated that if you saw something pleasing, say, indoors, in subdued light, like a theater or the interior of a subject's home, and then attempted to simply snap a photo of that scene with the tools of the day, the resulting photo would've looked nothing like what your human eye—that magnificently adaptable instrument—was effortlessly displaying to your brain. Your eye, effectively, was showing you what it *could* look like on film, if you worked really hard.

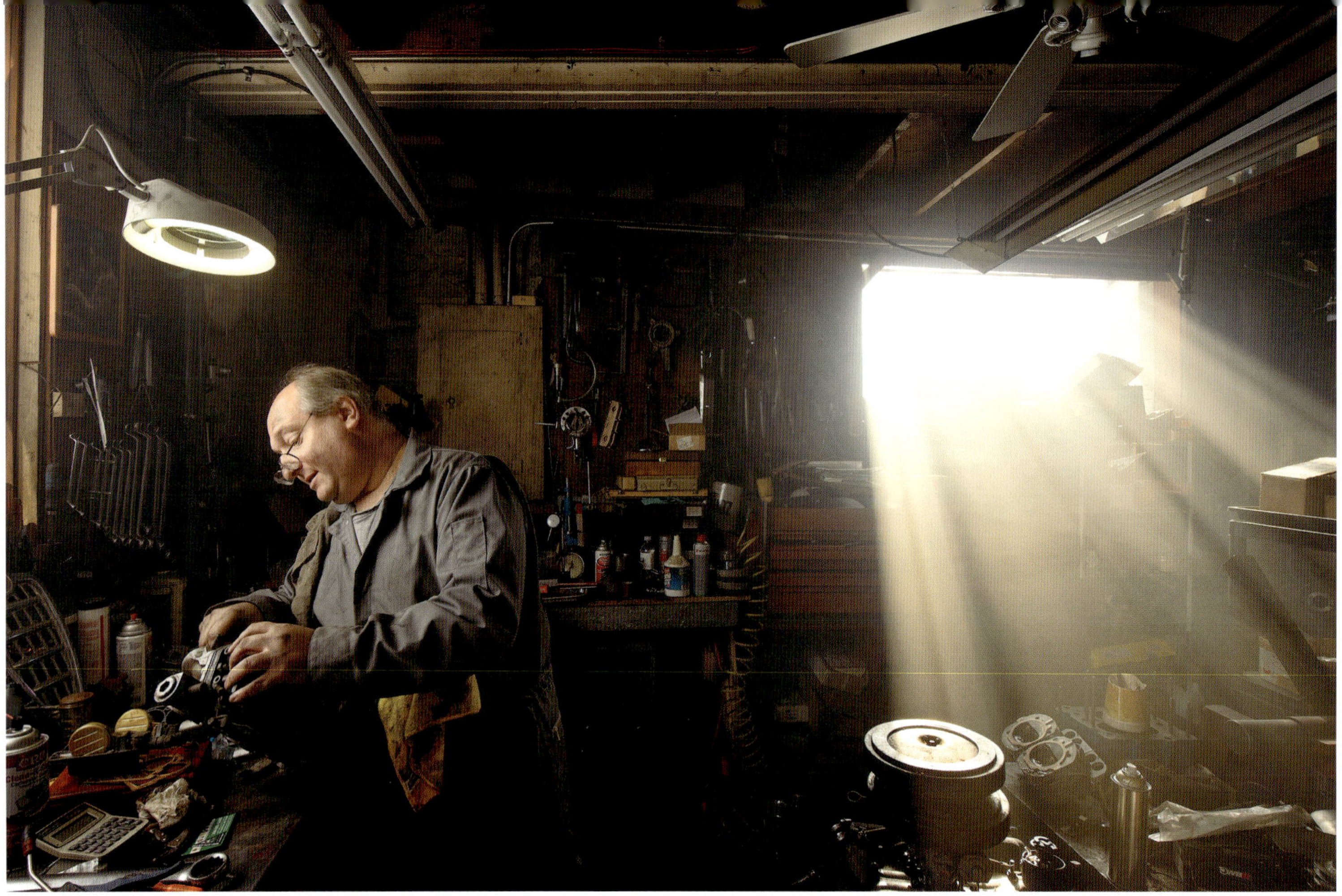

You'd often have to drag out lights, stands, gels. Sometimes a lot of them. Now, though, with the magnificent tools of today's digital cameras, fast lenses, and the ever-on-call emergency room of post, we are finally, really, just about there. If we see it, we can in fact shoot it.

You might notice something similar about the tone and tenor of the natural light photos we've looked at so far. They were all shot editorially, which carries a mandate, as a photographer, to be more of an observer and less of an instigator of the action.

But when the mission of the job at hand crosses the boundary into the realm of commercial work, or marketing, all bets are off. See window light, but also *make* window light.

The light pouring in the window behind this faux repairman is natural sunlight. A gift of bright sunshine flying through the glass and catching the smoke I put in the air. His main light is a simulated window light, created by three Speedlights and a

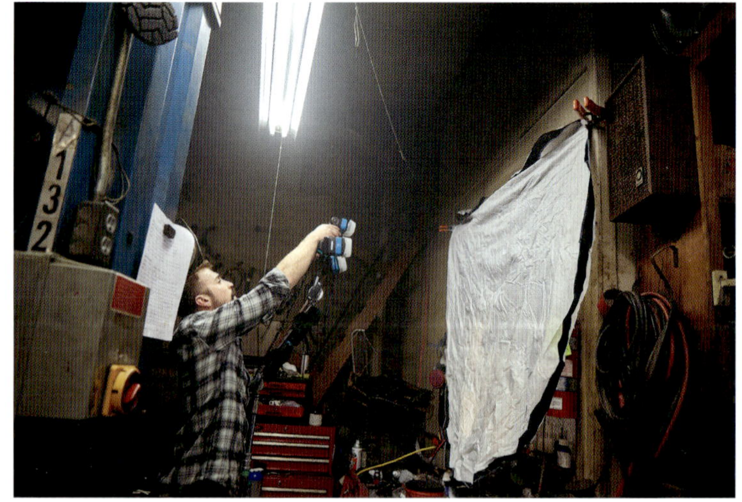

diffuser sheet pinned over the workroom interior window. This window never sees the sun, as it's in the middle of the garage. I made a soft window light through this portal, while letting the sun rage through the smoke.

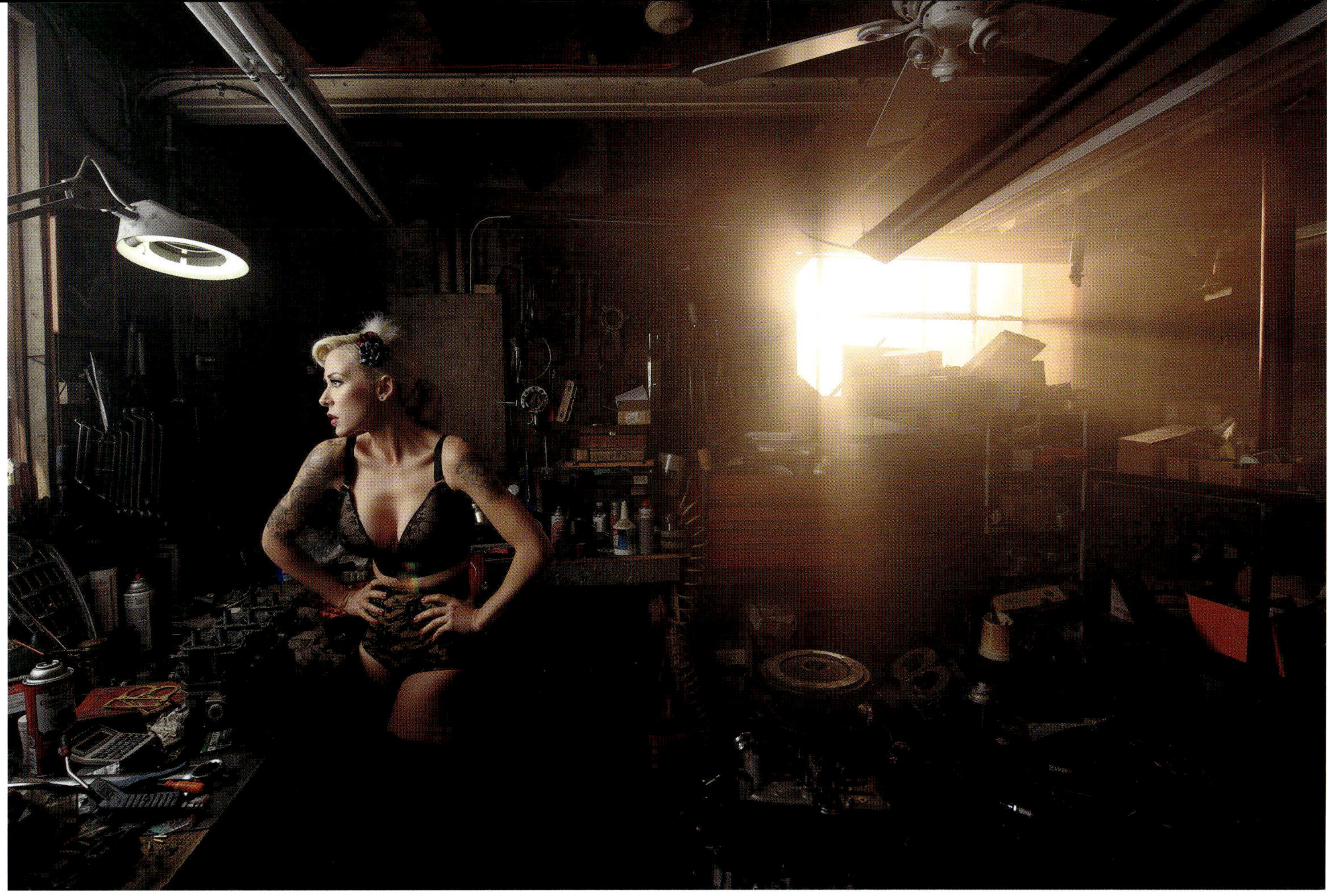

Later that day, for no reason other than we had a combination of Sam Brown, a great stylist, lots of wardrobe, and Laeticia De Valer, who otherwise goes by the name Misfit Dior, or DJ Devaler (pick one), we did a theatrical lingerie pic. It's a picture without a destination, but fun to do. By that time of the day, though, the sun had transported elsewhere. Undeterred, we replaced the sun with a Profoto B4 unit, gelled warm. Luckily, there was a stretch of vacant turf just outside the garage, and an overlarge stand called a "high roller" got the flash head just high enough. The upfront light on the subject remained exactly the same. Speedlights and a broadsheet diffuser.

I gelled the Profoto not simply because the warmth looks nice. Light at that low angle, occurring in nature, definitely has a warm color. To make your flash behave according to the patterns and colors of the sun, take into consideration the angle. High, hard sun is colorless or even slightly cool. Angled light means low to the horizon, which speaks to the golden glow of sunrise or sunset.

These garage pictures are total setups, created, styled, designed, and lit with a marketing purpose in mind. On this day, subtlety was not my main mission, and I designed the light to be an exclamation point, a piece of the picture you definitely notice. That beamy window is blazing its way through my pixels.

To make your flash behave according to the patterns and colors of the sun, take into consideration the angle.

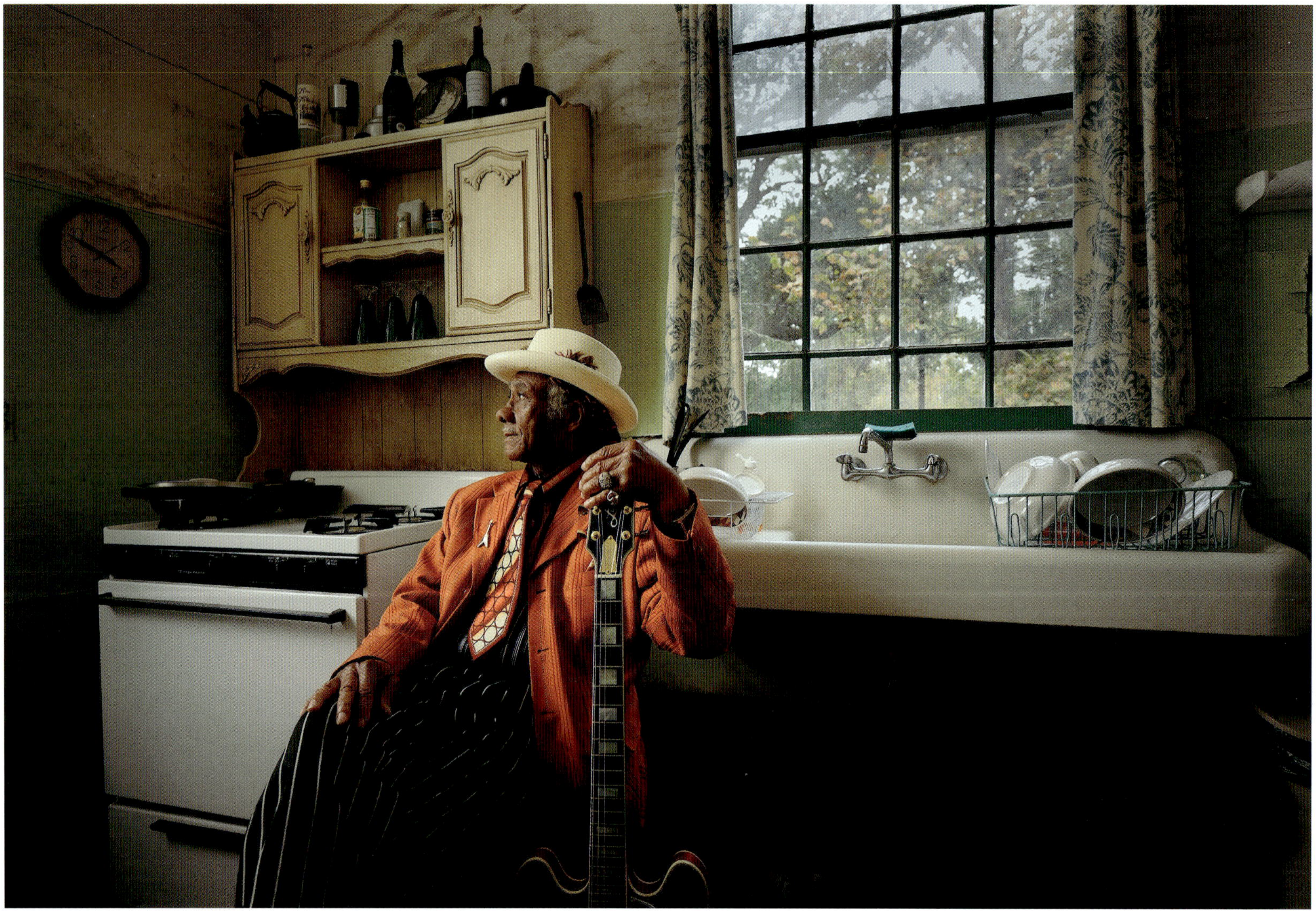

If an unnoticed approach is desired, you can hit the mute button on your flash and make it as quiet and simple as soft daylight. Little Freddie King, the "King of the Blues" of the New Orleans music scene, sits contemplatively in an old-style kitchen, which I fell in love with immediately when I saw it. The window you see in the final photo (below) is exactly reproduced on camera left (as shown at right), where Little Freddie is looking. Same size, same tenor, same exposure as its twin in the photo. Here's where you have to think about the human eye and its biological imperative to be drawn to the brightest aspect of a scene or picture. A natural light

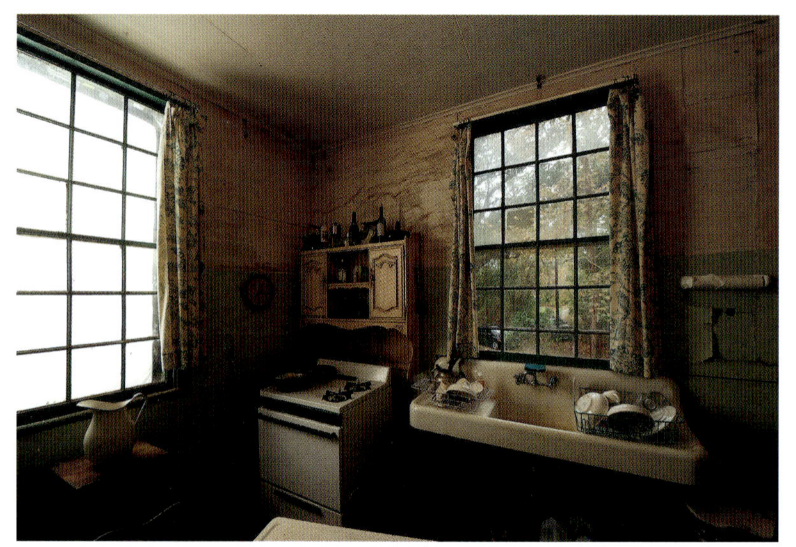

approach here is possible, but in exposing for the left-hand window as it graces Little Freddie, the other, in-the-picture window becomes a raging beast. It will eat your viewer's eyeballs. They will struggle to even see your subject.

You need to tame it by goosing the brightness of the unseen window. With flash. Luckily, Lasto-lite makes diffuser panels in big rectangles that match a window's shape. I hoisted one of these up to the left-hand window, cranked up a flash on another stand, about six feet from the diffuser panel, and went back to camera and dialed it in, just enough (opposite, top). Too much, it's noticed. Too little, the window in the picture takes over. You thread the needle in situations like this. Your flash should leave no fingerprints.

By the way, the windows don't necessarily need to be big. You can make effective use of a small, filthy window in a blacksmith's shop and do just fine. Of course, it helps to have a blacksmith right out of the storybooks, as my subject was (following page). He filled his tiny workroom with his smile, his ebullience, and his obvious love of craft. He was the kind of subject, in the kind of space, that you simply cannot bypass. If you do, it will haunt your days.

The work of the picture was simple. There was a smallish window to camera left. We threw a sheet of diffusion up. Speedlights are on a stand outside, under radio control and gelled warm to mimic the low sun. Here, you have to bow to the reality of the room and the existing light sources. If you pumped that forge hard enough, as this man could, the fire could light up the room a bit. But then the blaze itself would turn into an exposure blast zone. Better to take the time to rig another Speedlight, warmed to the color of fire,

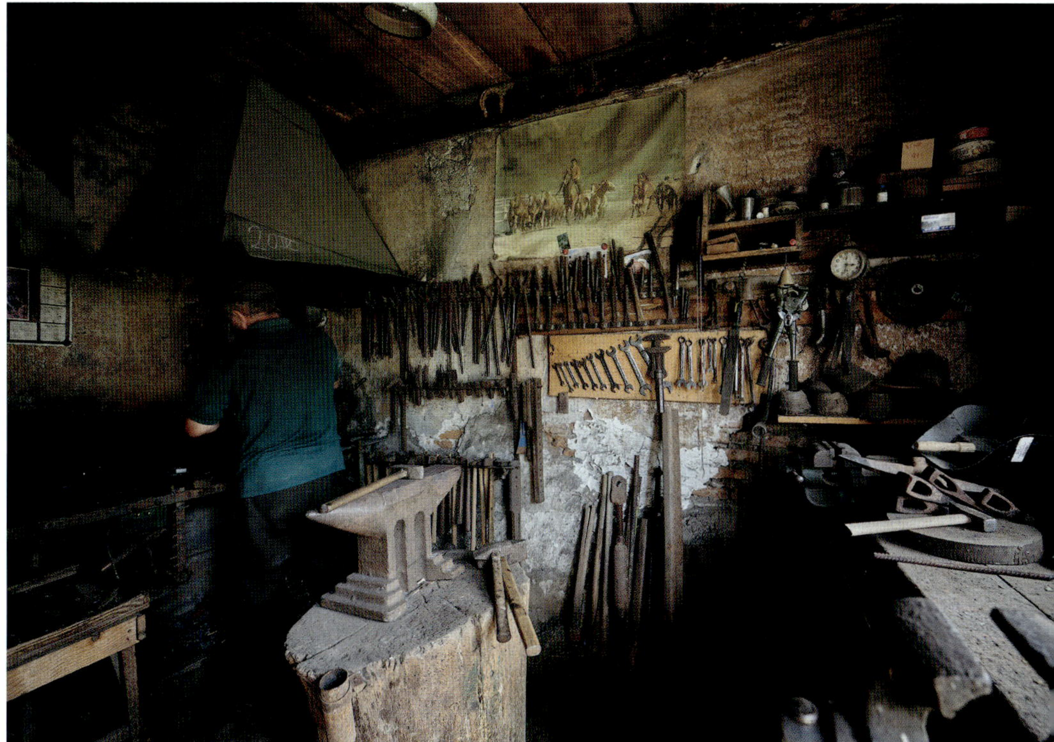

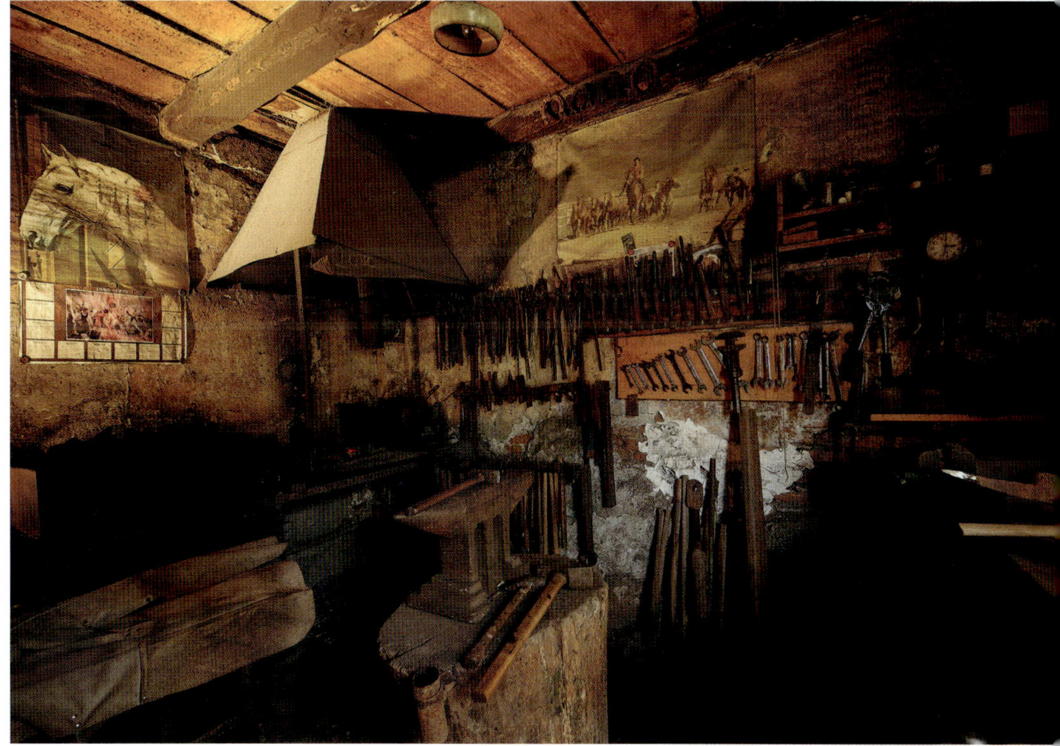

and bounce that up into the ceiling of the room. It is just out of camera view, on the left. That way, the room *looks* like the fire is lighting it up. Then the blacksmith can simply tune the forge to a beautifully picturesque intensity without tasking that very imprecise, variable light source with the additional duty of lighting the room for you. It just has to look nice.

Bringing a naked, ungelled flash in here or, worse, a broad-source umbrella (which wouldn't fit anyway) will get you 3 to 5 for aggravated misuse of light. Go with the flow of the direction and color of the minimal light that exists. Augment, tweak, subtly coax it along with the assist of your applied flash. Don't blow away what exists.

On the previous page, you can see what the room looks like, naked (top), and with the room light overplayed (bottom).

Find the balance.

Light through a window. See it and embrace it. Or make it and work it. All part of the dance photographers must do on location. Sometimes it's a serene waltz. Sometimes you gotta boogie.

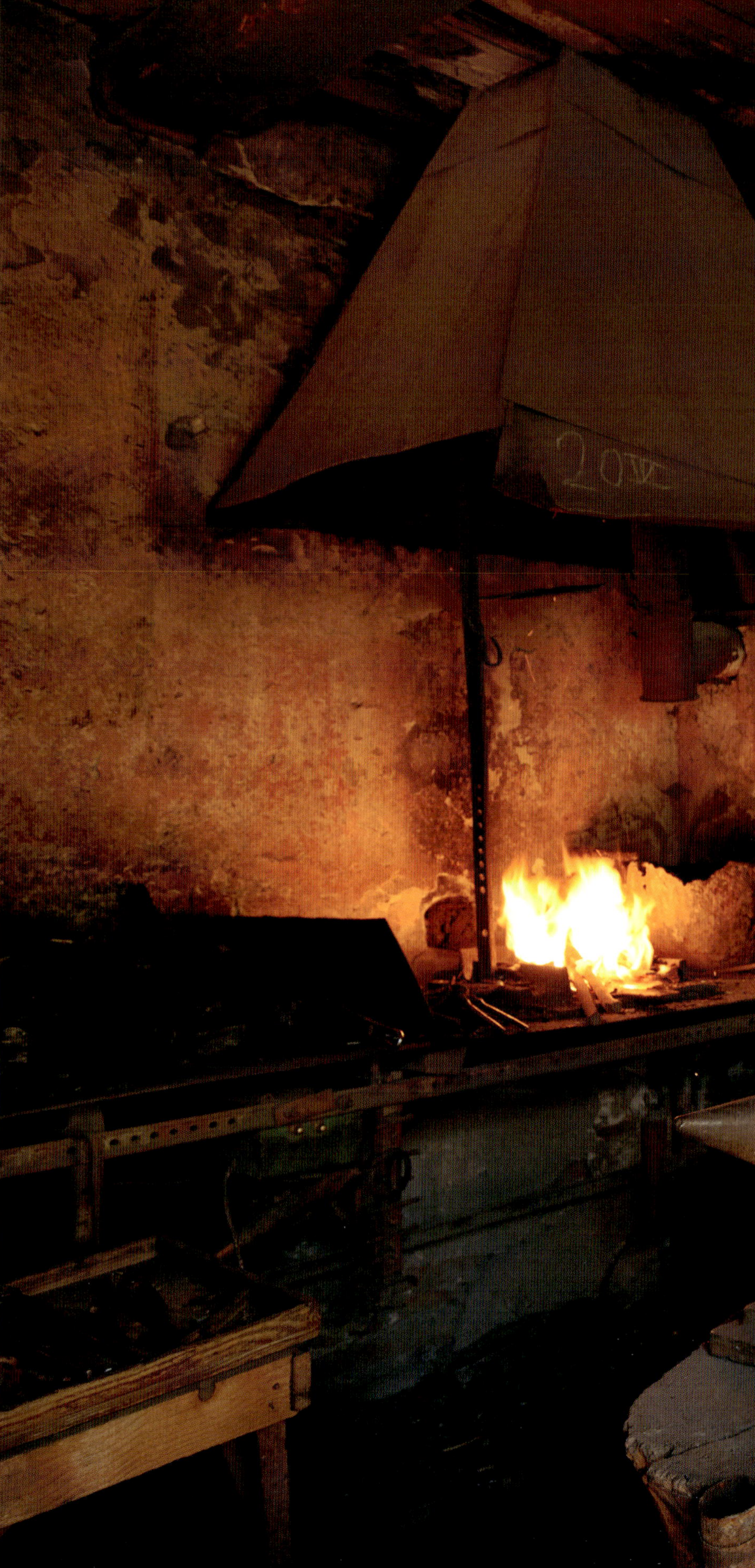

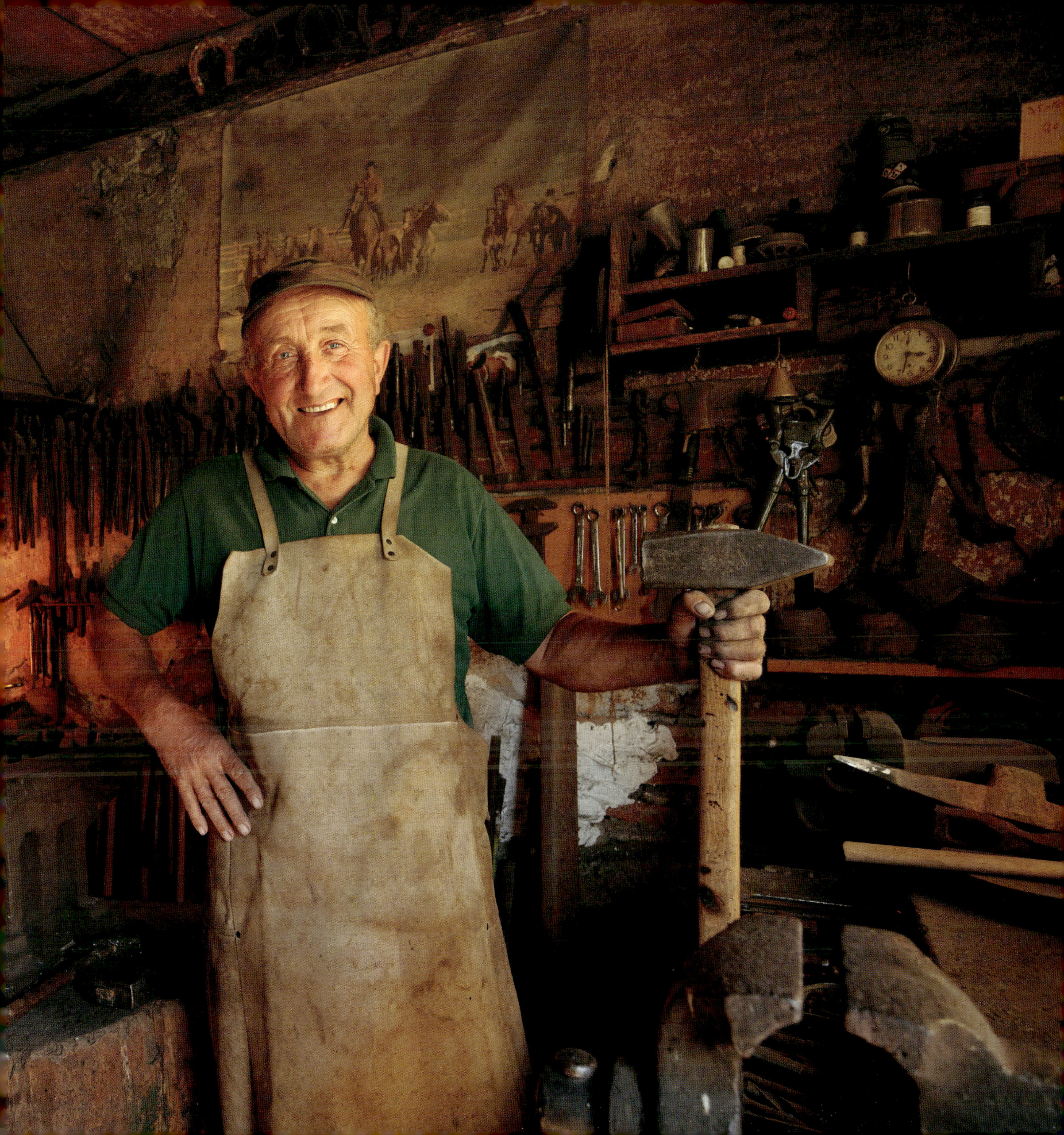

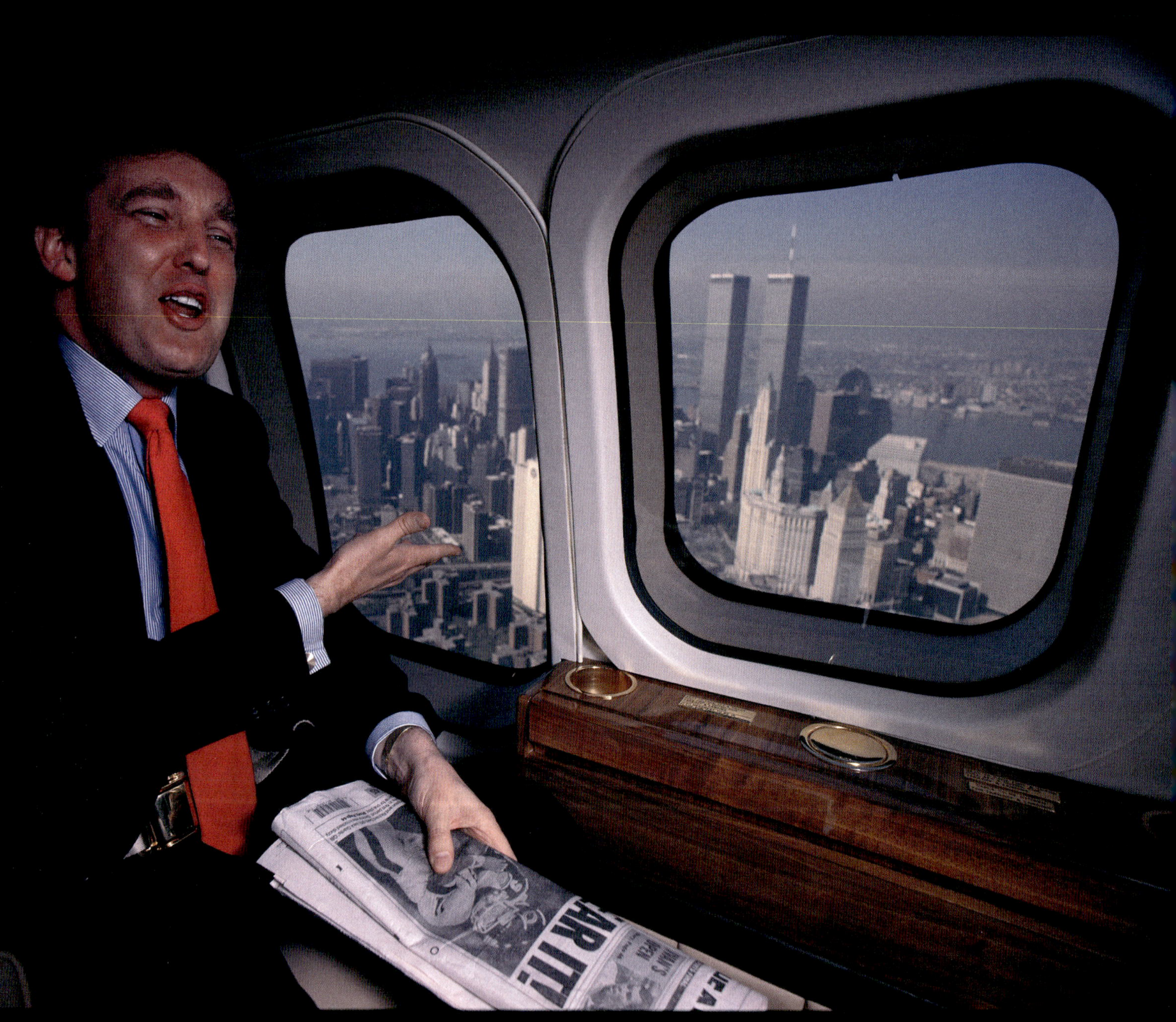
AR IT

How's That for Random? Part Two

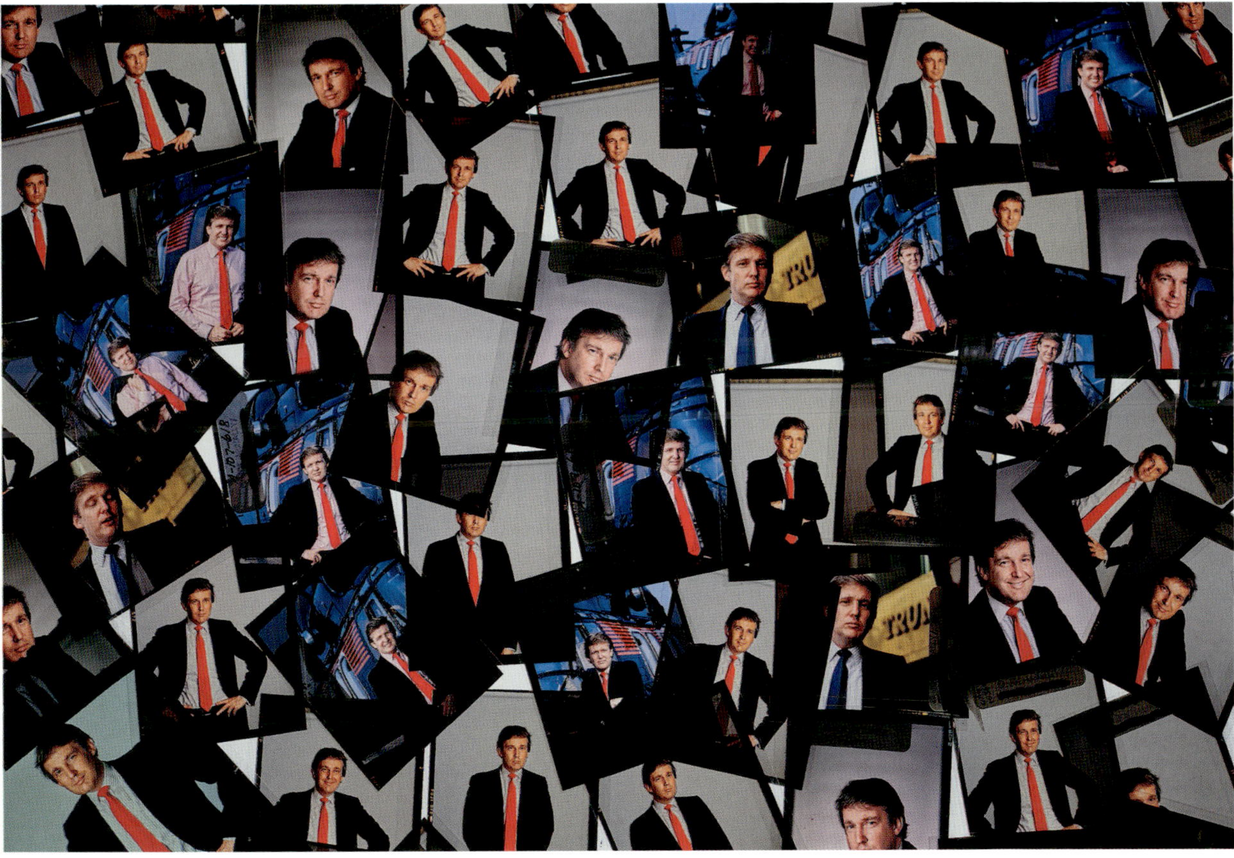

Medium format outtakes on the light table for *Newsweek* cover story on Donald Trump.

In a helicopter, September 1987 (opposite).

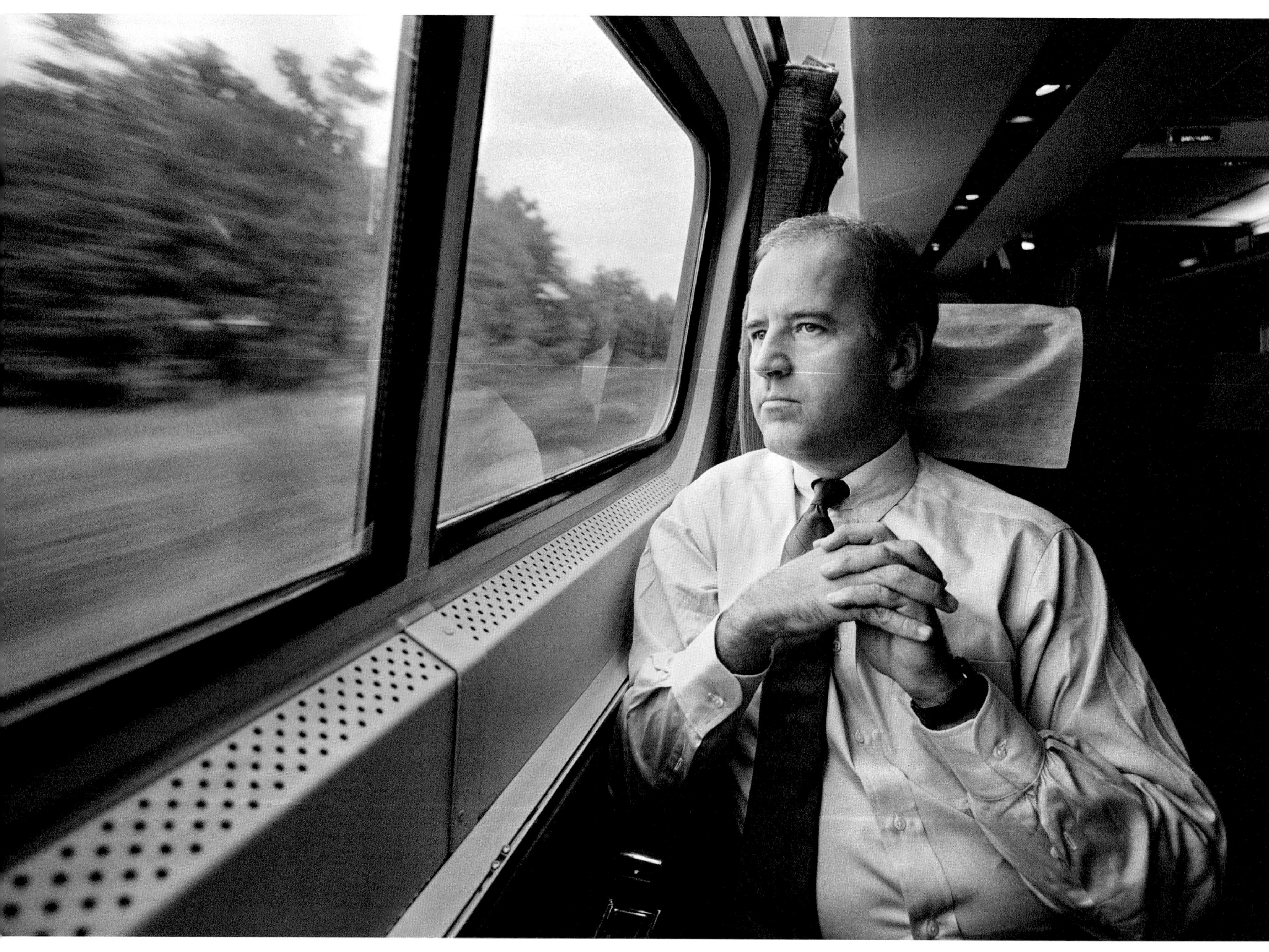

On a train, September 1988.

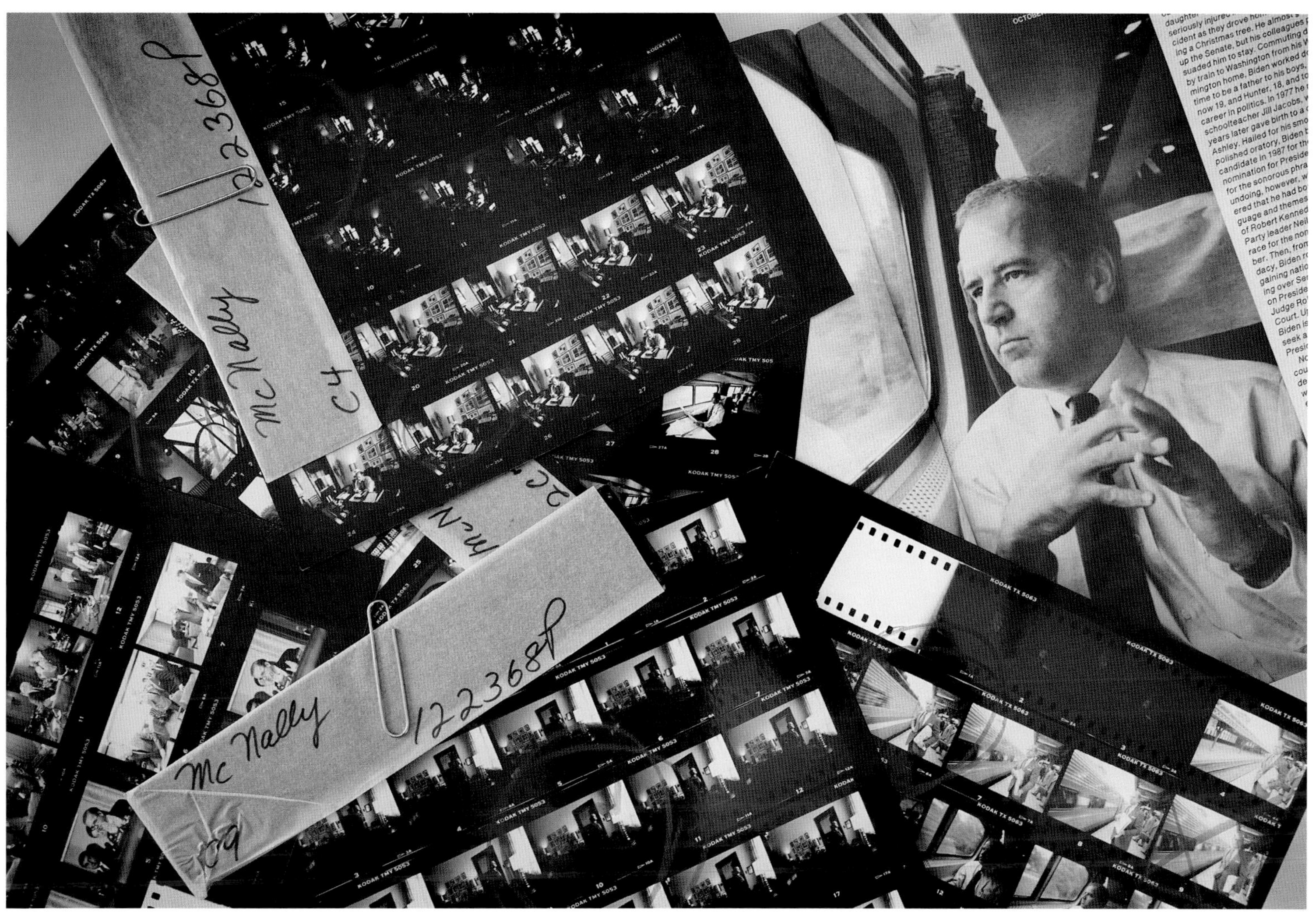

Black and white contacts from a *People* magazine story on Joe Biden.

Blow Smoke!

After all, it's what we do anyway.

A long time ago, I was assigned to photograph famed novelist Joyce Carol Oates—with a Ferrari. The magazine's title was "Quality," and it featured stories of luxe dispatches from the world of the unaffordable. They assigned Oates, a brilliant writer with an inclination to observe the darker aspects of existence, to drive the Ferrari and write up the experience. Which she did, though the safety driver with her, as I recall, mentioned her top speed clocked in around 50 or 60 mph. Okay, cool.

I needed to find a place to shoot this, and I settled on an old garage facility out in Jersey, attempting to contrast the garage, which was the kind of place you most likely might bring a mid-range Chevy or Honda to for service, with the sleek set of wheels she was tootling around in. The garage also had the advantage, as I recall, of being decommissioned. It was destined for renovation, or perhaps to be torn down altogether. We were shooting

at night, which added to . . . I don't know . . . the mystery, the allure, the sexiness of the vehicle? Or, you know, it might have been just the time of day we had to do it, per everyone's schedule. No matter.

I didn't do great with this. I mean, she was a nice enough lady, but she had moon-sized glasses and a tight schedule. And it wasn't like I had the car all day to pre-light the set. She rolled up and I started throwing lights at it. The one thing I was able to do, during the day, was to cut out the metal on the backside of the Garden State sign. The sign was electrically dead, and nobody cared what I did to it. So, I hired a guy with a torch, and he blasted out an opening for my strobes. Hence, the sign looks like it's on.

The rest of it was a mess. I had never really lit a car before. But on this shoot I did discover something important. Smoke. What a wonderful thing. Smoke makes your light look sexy. It gives it

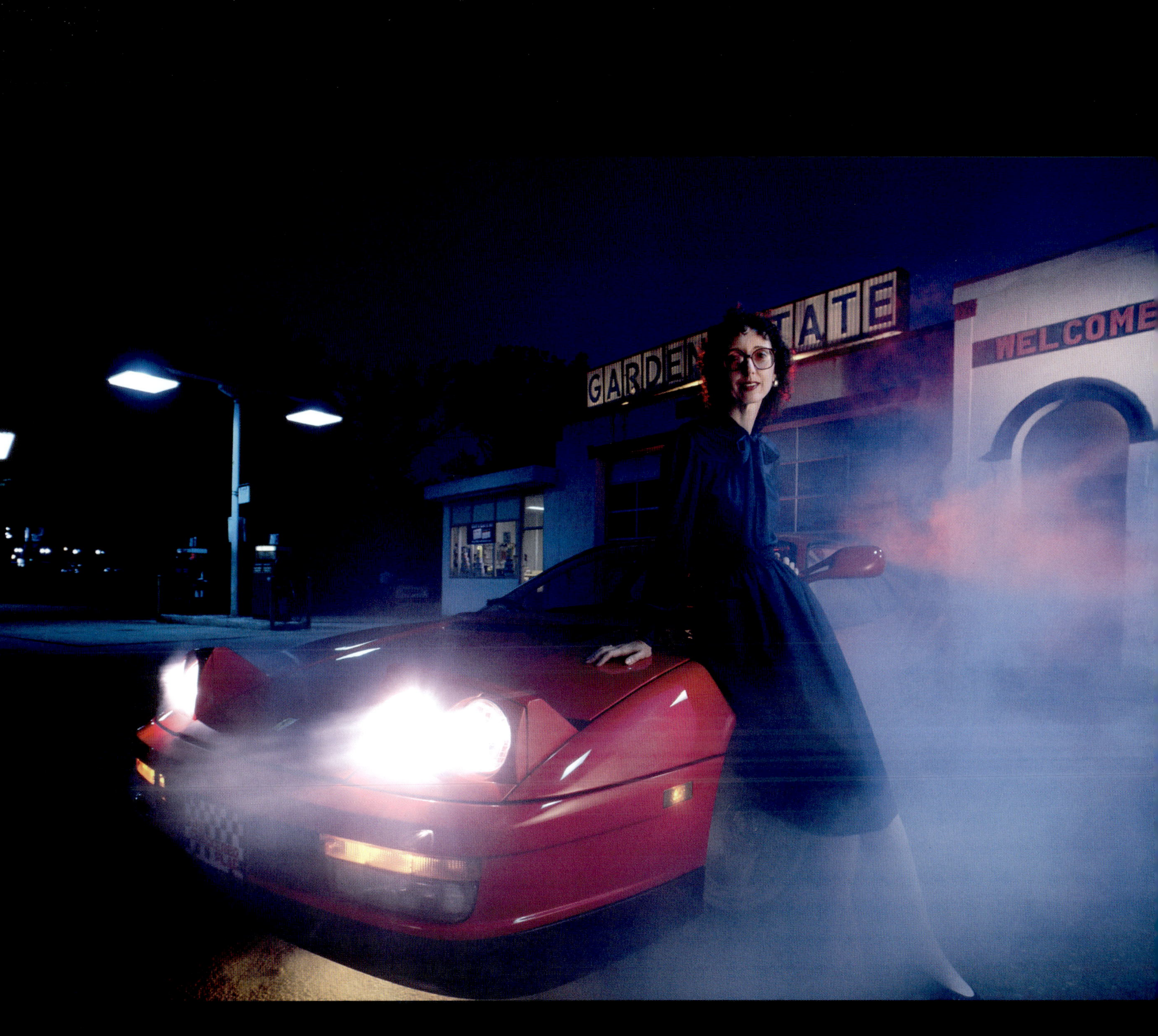

GARDEN STATE
WELCOME

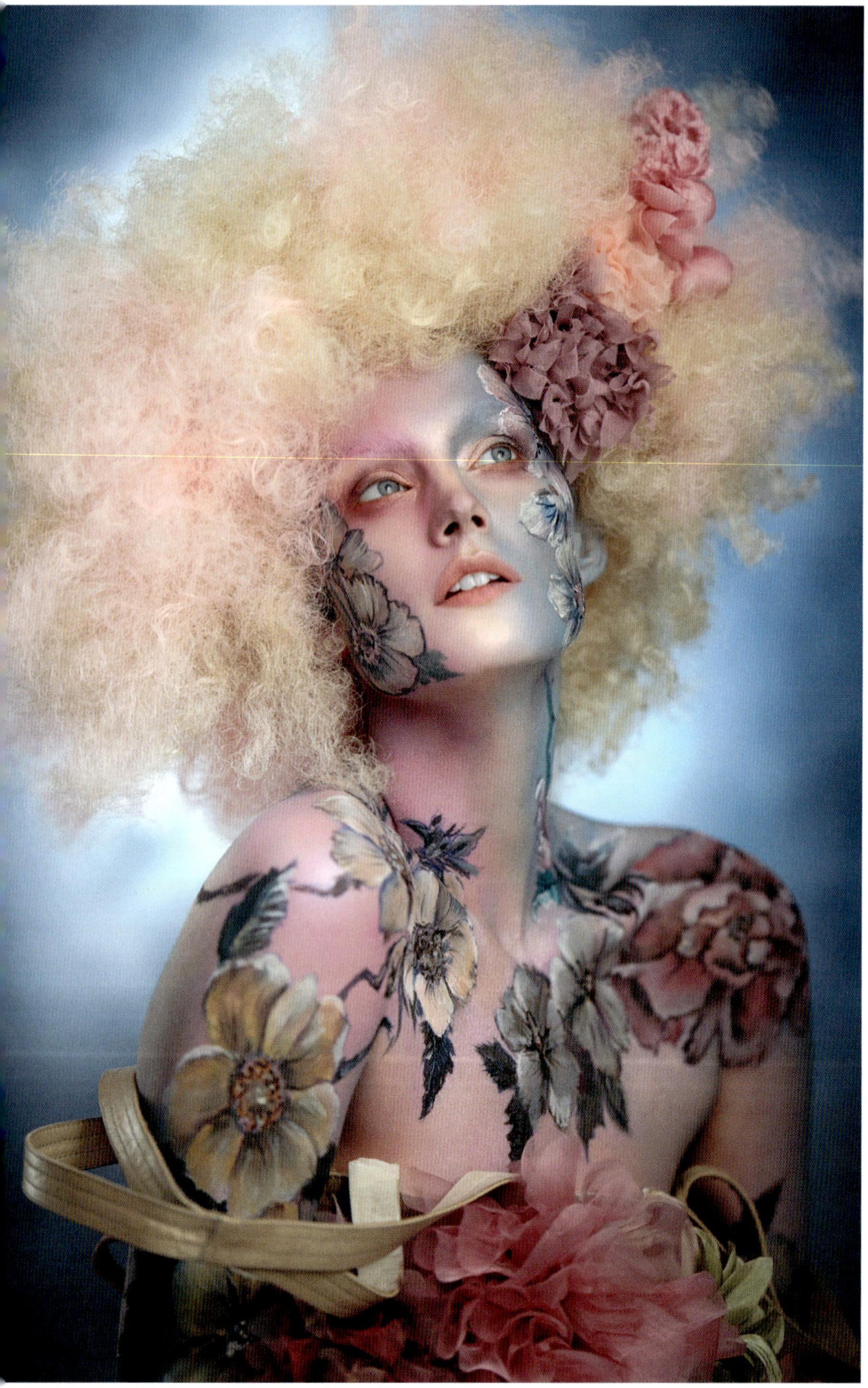

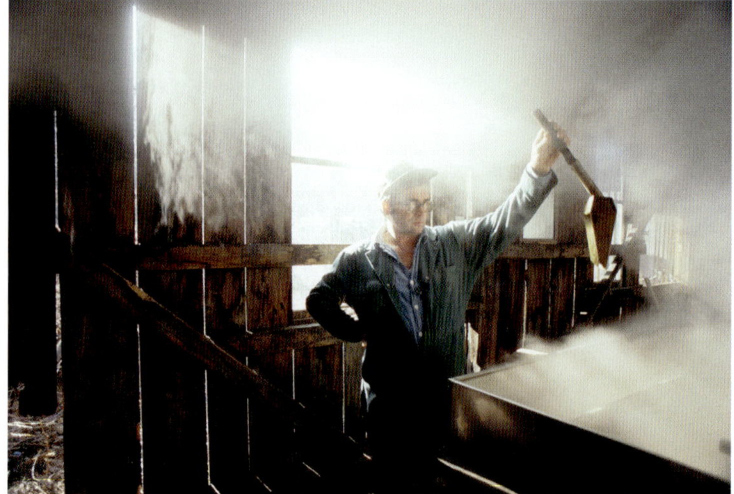

texture and shape. In sinuous and undulating fashion, it curls around in the beams of daylight or flash, dancing in strange and unpredictable ways. It also *covers up a lot of sins.*

I became a big fan of smoke machines. I've owned several over the years, from Roscoe Halloween Party foggers to something more professional, such as I have now, which is called a Fog Fury. Handy. I've also hired smoke professionals. Yes, there are such people who can command the smoke. They can make it flow, hug the ground, drift lightly like a fanciful dream, or totally envelop your subject (left).

I mean, it's great when it's just, you know, there, like at a maple syrup farm (above).

And it's wonderful in spotlights (opposite, top left).

And it can make a forest creepy (opposite, bottom).

And it's pretty much necessary to see a laser beam (opposite, top right).

And it's a cool way to add texture and interest to an otherwise dark background (page 210).

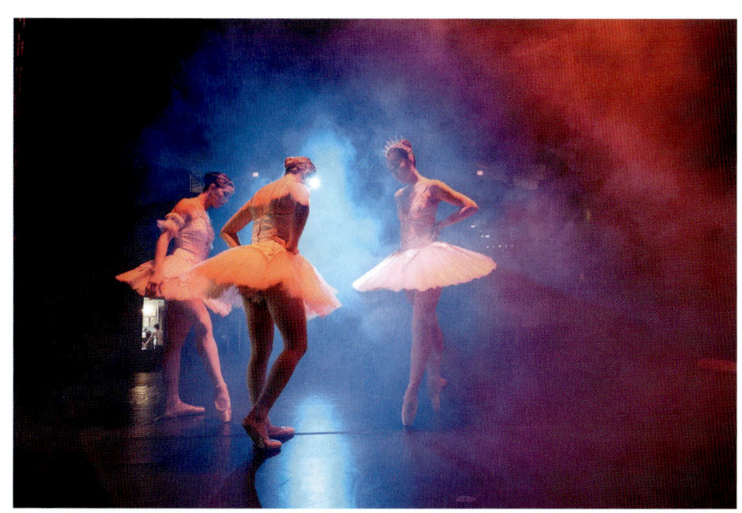
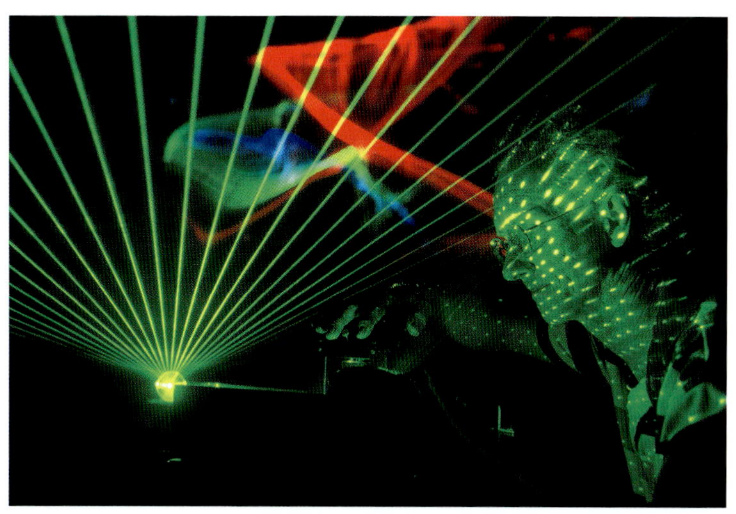

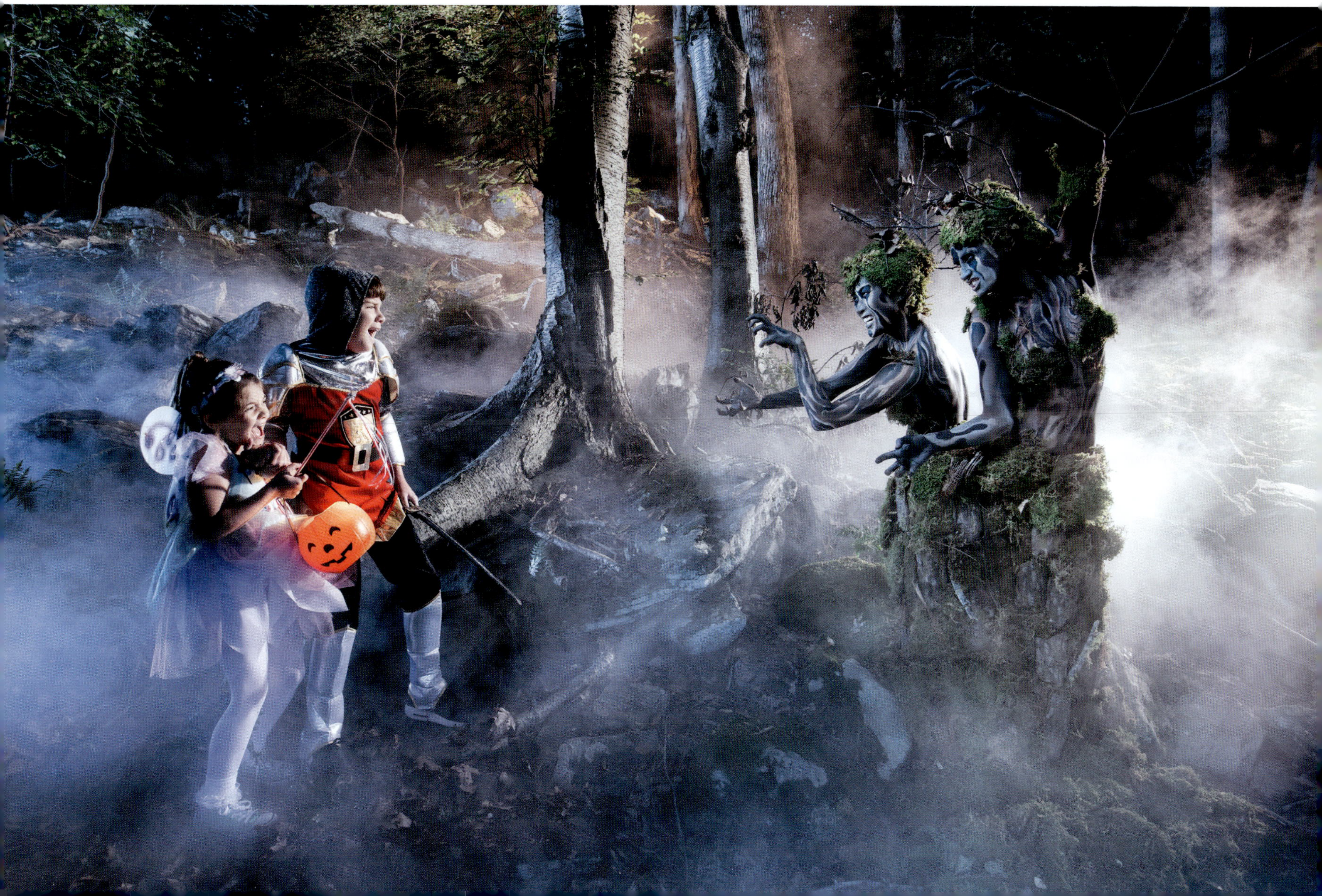

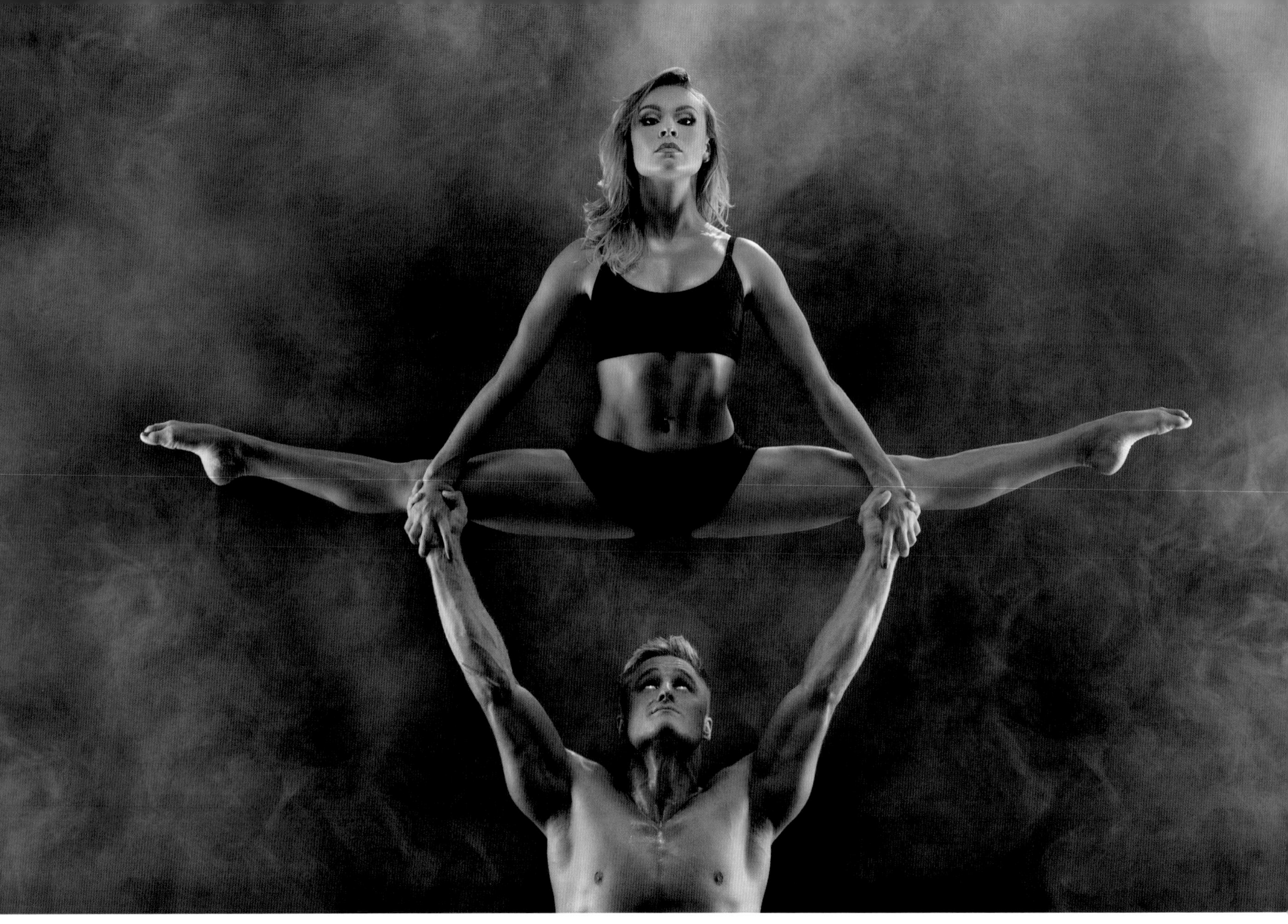

It can be beautiful, mysterious, and wonderful. It can also be seductive, as in, it looks so cool, let's make some more smoke!

Which leads me to what the real title of this story is—*Things Seemed to be Going Well, and Then the Fire Department Showed Up!*

You know, I've been doing this for a long time, and I still get seized by the spells that induce you, as the photographer, to do something stupid in the feverish pursuit of a photo. How many times have I counseled all photographers to do their homework, get the permits, dot the i's and cross the t's? Lots. And it's what we do here at our studio, as Lynn, our studio manager, is a thoroughly by-the-book, tighten-it-up-so-there-are-no-surprises producer. Do it right. No shortcuts. I actually say that somewhere in this very book!

Well, for this final shoot (opposite), we let this theater know we would be using smoke effects, and they okayed it, and they shut off the fire alarms. We have used smoke there before. No worries. But this time I brought smoke bombs. We told them about a smoke . . . machine. Vastly different animals.

We started with the smoke machine. And the aerosol stuff, the very popular "smoke in a can." It was not the stuff of my imagination. The picture was flat. I looked at the smoke bombs in the box.

You know that little voice we all have, the one that is wise, and discerning, and says, "Don't do it, jerkbrain! This will go terribly wrong!"? You know that one? I ignored it.

We ripped open a few smoke bombs, which are essentially pyrotechnics, and kept working. (I say "we," but this one is entirely on me. I directed it, and the crew followed my lead. My name is on the door. End of story.) We tested one, and it seemed benign enough, hand-holdable, not overly hot. We had a big plastic bin to discard them, and fire extinguishers around the set. But, unlike a smoke machine, which you can turn off, these smoke grenades spew. And spew. And spew. Until they're done.

Smoke filled the theater and, as smoke does, found all manner of open portals, i.e., windows and doors to waft out of. *Waft* is too mild a term. Colored smoke was billowing from the theater, and the fire department, including the Fire Marshall, responded.

Were it not for his benevolence—he used the opportunity to teach us, issue a mild reprimand, and take it upon himself to pictorially record all of our smoking devices and do some research on them himself—we could have easily been arrested, fined, sued . . . oh my . . . the stuff of bad dreams.

From now on, if I ever use those devices again, I will hire a professional, check in with the fire department, get the permits required, and, if necessary, hire people to referee the proceedings. We have done this my whole career. We've had fire personnel, medics, child safety observers (required in some states when working with a minor), and even, in the middle of a pandemic, COVID compliance officers, temperature gauge in hand.

I fudged it. Took a shortcut. Convinced myself it would be okay. Didn't listen to the voice. My bad.

Smoke is fun. Sometimes, too much fun. Do the homework. Listen to the voice.

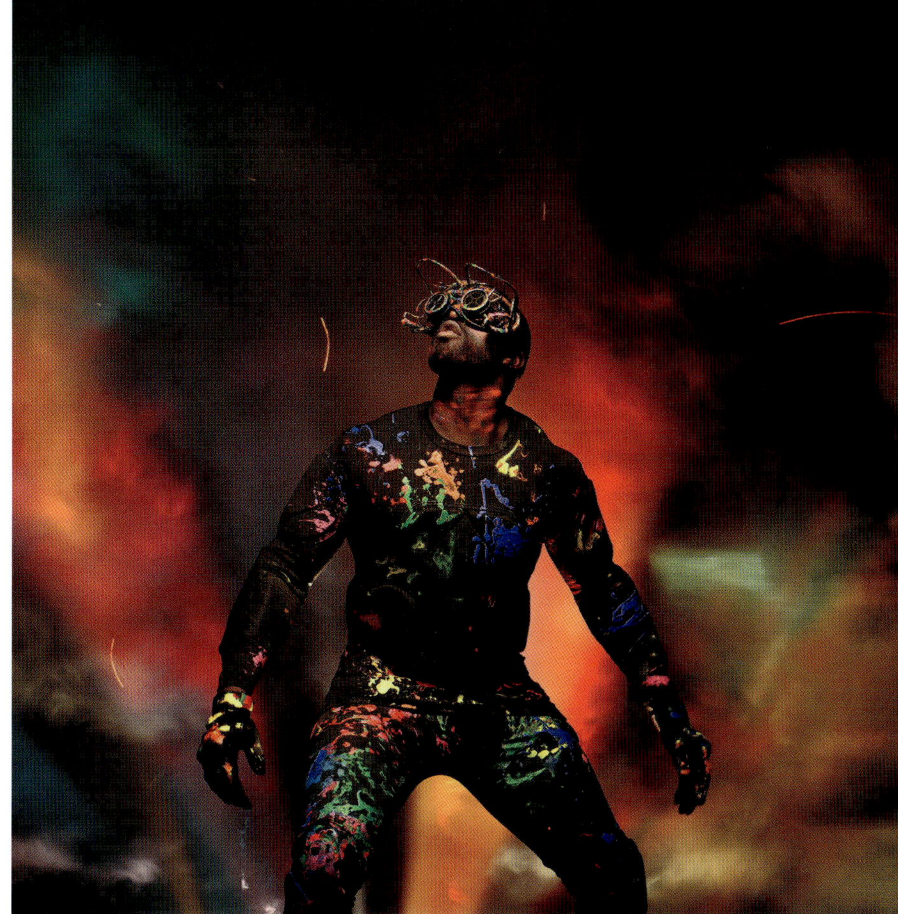

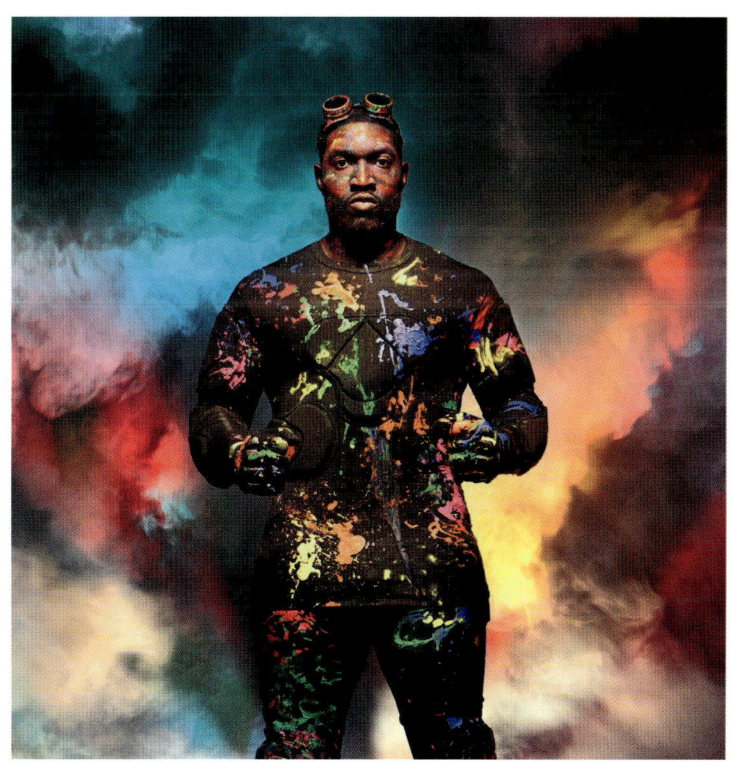

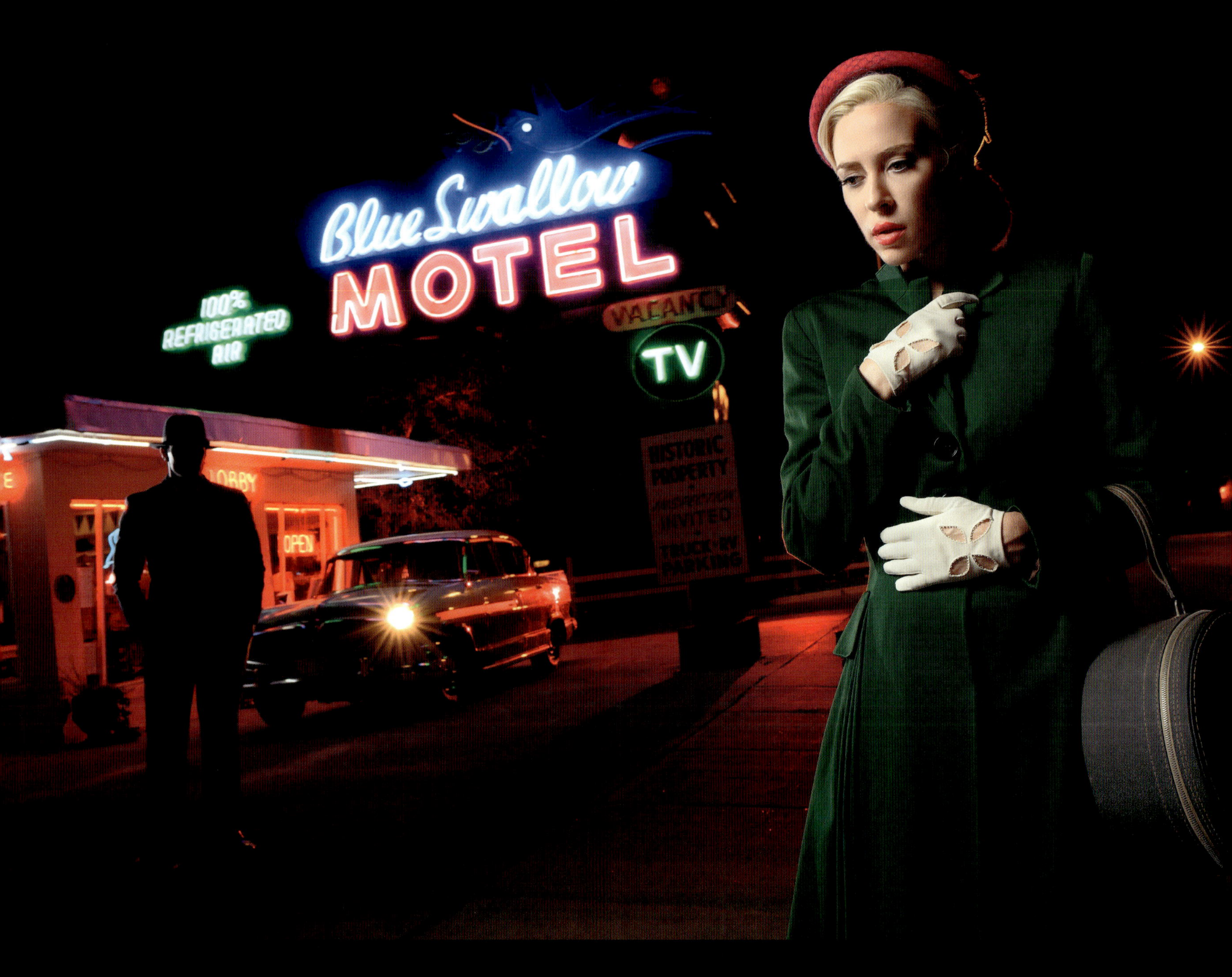

Blue Swallow
MOTEL
100% REFRIGERATED AIR
VACANCY
TV
LOBBY
OPEN
HISTORIC PROPERTY

When the Light Is the Story…but the Story Isn't Just the Light

I went to school to be a writer, so perhaps it's not strange that, having wandered off long ago into the photographic woods, I think of light as language. This is something that has been said for many years, by many photogs. Light is our language, plain and simple. It is rapt, elegant, steeped in drama, rhapsodic, giddy, melancholy, vibrant, poignant, or brash. It can shift the attitude of a scene more quickly than a moody teenager. At the camera, we look for beautiful, apt, lovely light the way a writer seeks to turn a deft phrase and string together words that hook the reader's heart and mind.

Sometimes we work with the light that exists, and it's a worthwhile collaboration, a partnership. The existing light gives you gifts, and you use those gifts well. Sometimes, though, we battle the light. High-noon light? Merciless in its brass-knuckle, cloudless nature, it doesn't seek negotiation. Sometimes we can surrender and walk away, and make arrangements for later, or for another setting, if we blessedly have that option. Often, though, poor bastards that we occasionally are, our editors/clients have assigned us to photographically dig 30 yards of trench on that

day, no matter the cost or conditions. (You had to get married outdoors at noon, huh? Or … you really need to have 100 headshots done in an hour?) Mandated thusly, we pound out desultory frames because we must, and making that 30-yard quota means we get an extra ration of rum at chow tonight. (Or, hopefully, a paycheck.)

On jobs such as these, we become like the faithful Hodor. We hold that door, and do what we must, even though we are doomed.

Other times we are stupefied by the sheer magnificence of a scene, infused with light that is perfection itself, and the camera gobbles up the utter beauty of it. Oh, those wondrous days!

Oftentimes, we have to make the light ourselves, and that light we make actually is the real work. It's the heart of the matter, and the resonant, repeating, feeling nature of the light is the true reason the pictures have any measure of relationship or coherence. When we conjure an adventure such as this, we draw the pictures in our head, and then go illuminate them.

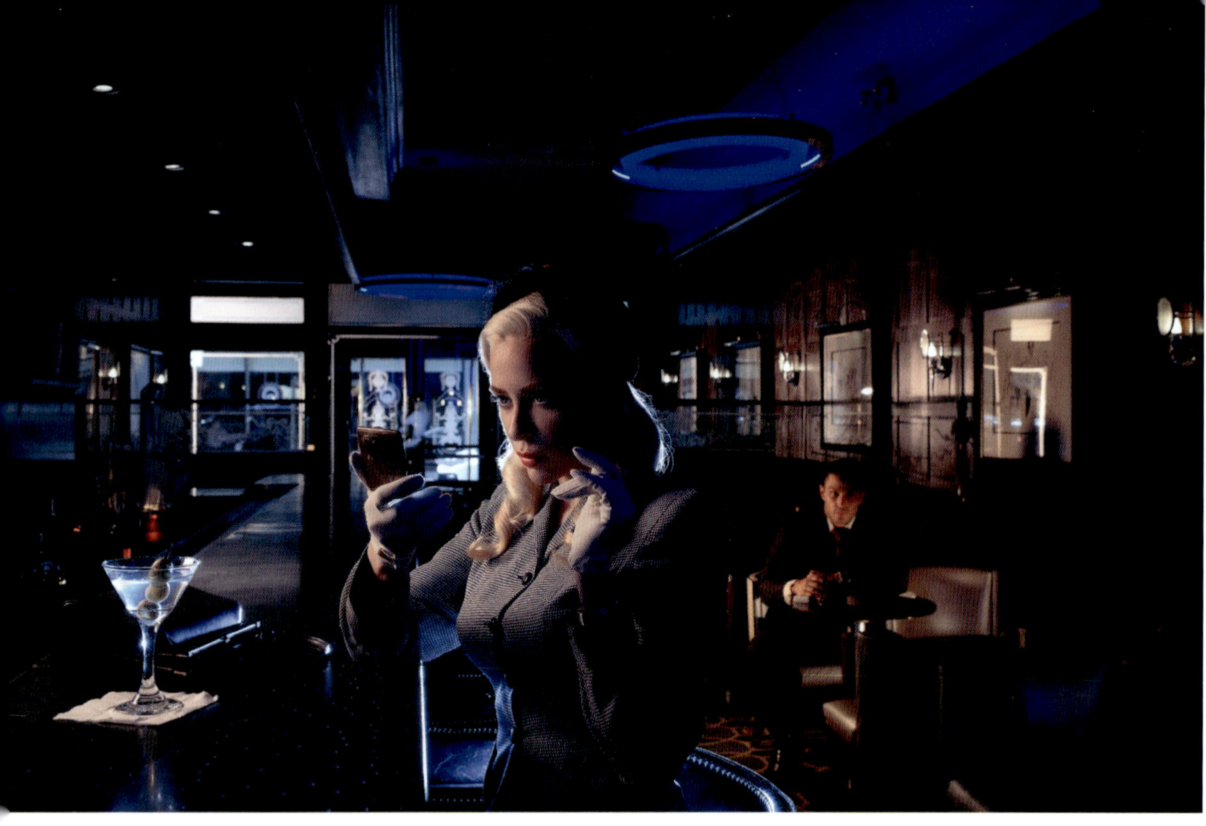

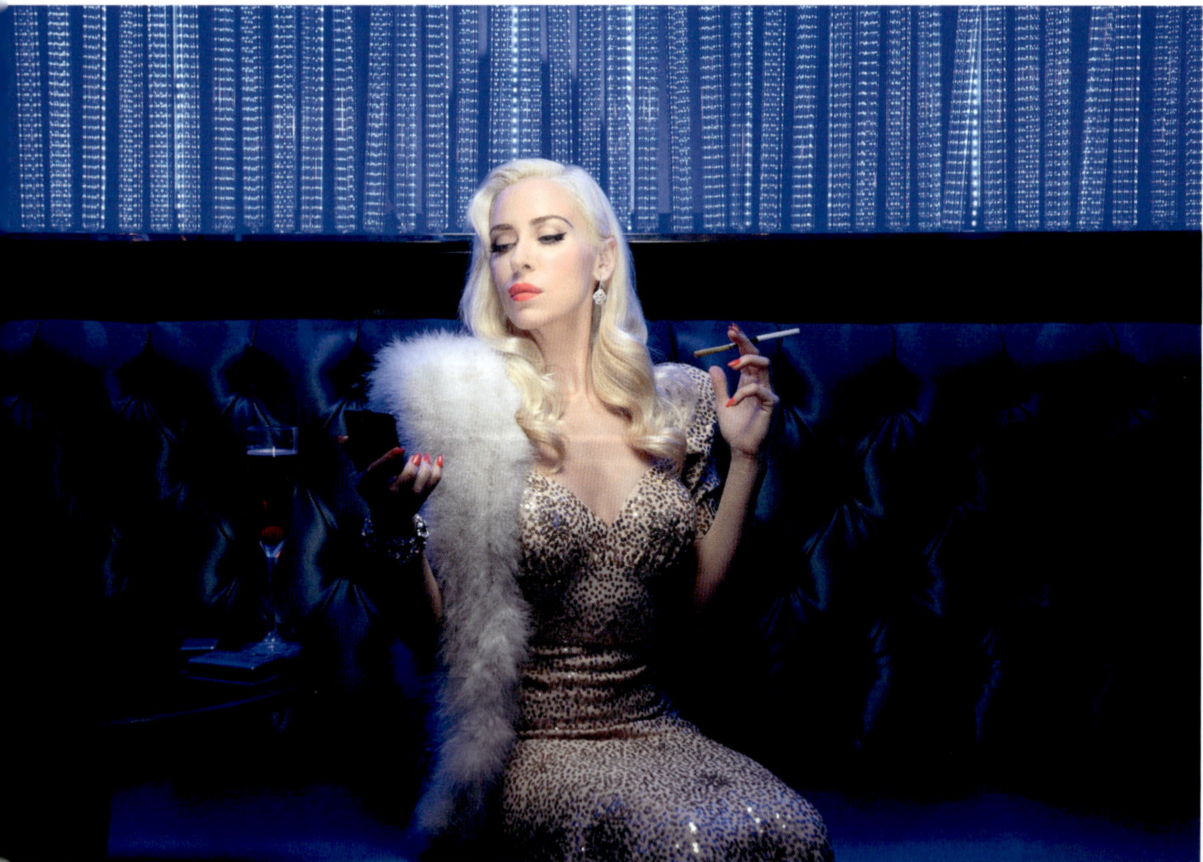

This next collection of images was my response when Nikon assigned me to showcase their entry into the radio TTL flash fracas. "Take our new flash and make pictures with it that could only be done using radio wireless connectivity!" That was the sole directive. Nikon was by no means the first manufacturer to go wireless, by the way. Radio-controlled TTL exposure had been around for a while, during which time the Nikon Speedlight system remained entrenched in line-of-sight misery. But then the SB-5000 came out, and all was forgiven. It knocked me silly with how good it was.

Given my history of burying flashes in unlikely places, this new tech made a perfect partner for the darker side of my imagination. I conjured a storyline based on noir novels and films. The dastardly doings in this mayhem-minded genre of storytelling have certain continuums that are often repeated. Murder, motels, bad guys, good girls gone wrong or in some sort of trouble, mean streets or deserted industrial settings, bars—all pictured in late day, or flat-out night. Which means shadows, moody or angled light, drama, and, if working in the color realm, a saturation verging on lurid. Making light like this, with murderous inflection, a nice, cuddly umbrella stays in the bag; it's about as welcome as a curious cop

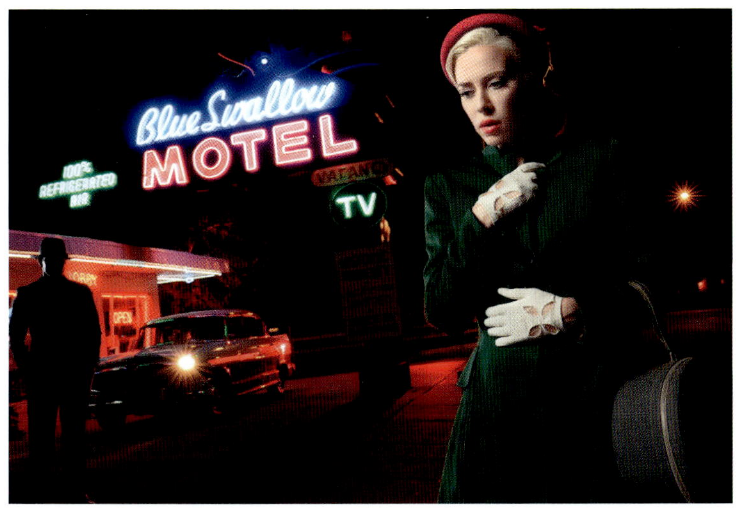

with a flashlight, checking out the noises in the dark, rainy alley while the boss's henchmen are stuffing the body in the trunk of a car.

Illuminating such a storyline meant that often my Speedlights would be well apart from one another, hidden in some way, and thus blind to line-of-sight triggering. I won't go into mechanics here. They are time worn and well known. Lots of information out there about *how to do it*, offered by lots of sources, some more qualified than others. I mean, flash tutorials are now so ubiquitous that we've heard, "The bigger the source, the more diffuse the feel of the light," so bloody often it's like hearing, "Insert the metal tip into the buckle and pull it tightly across your waist."

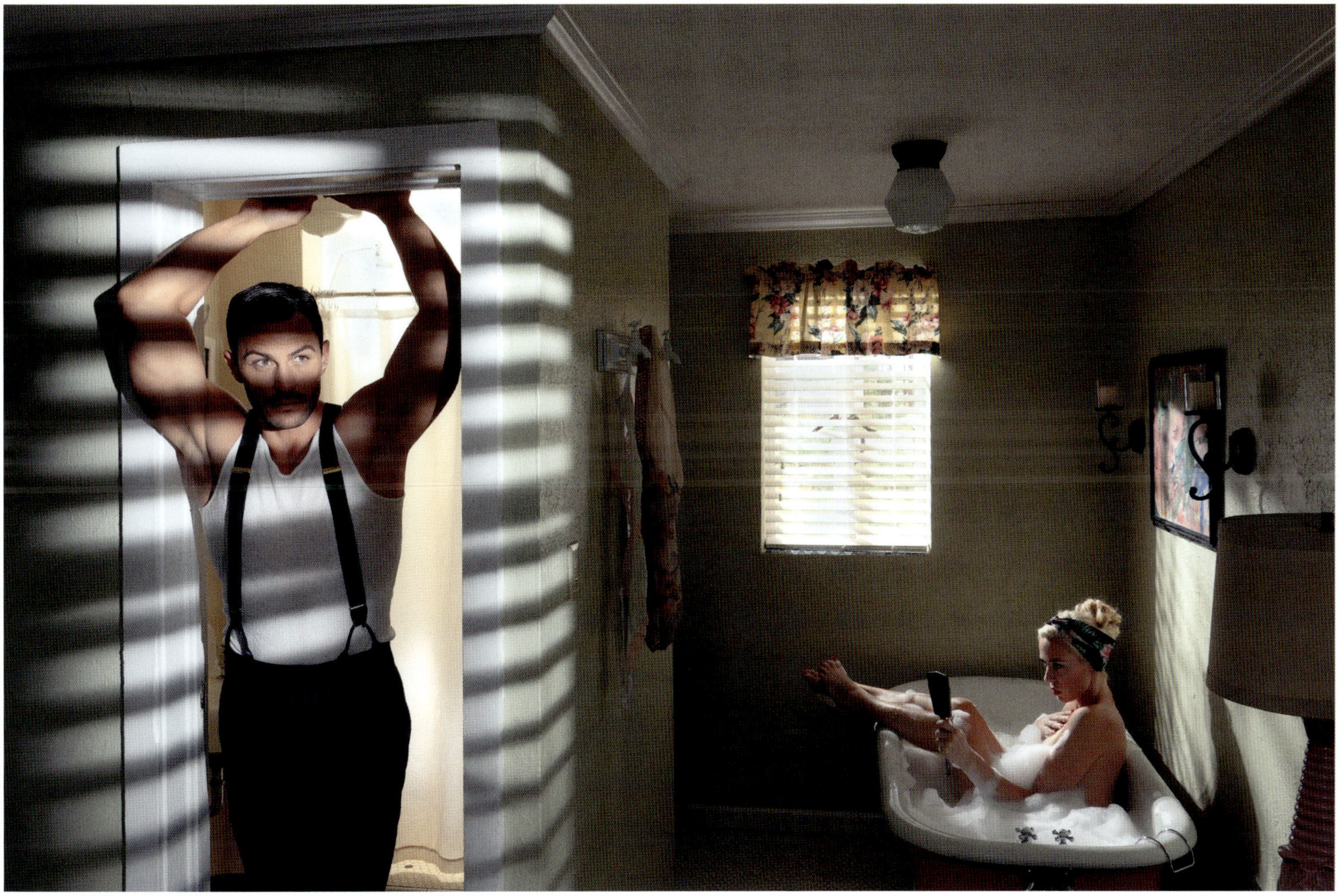

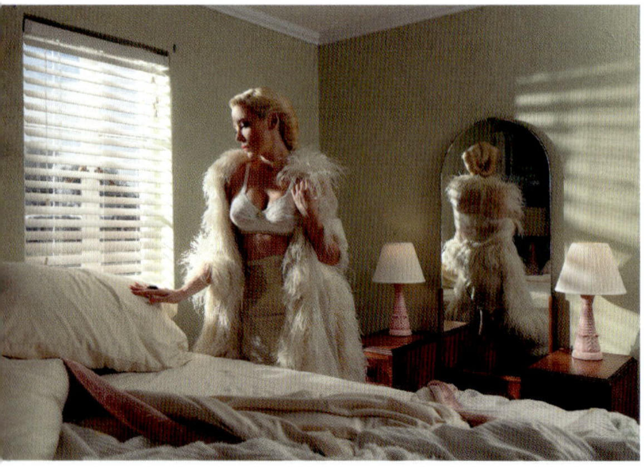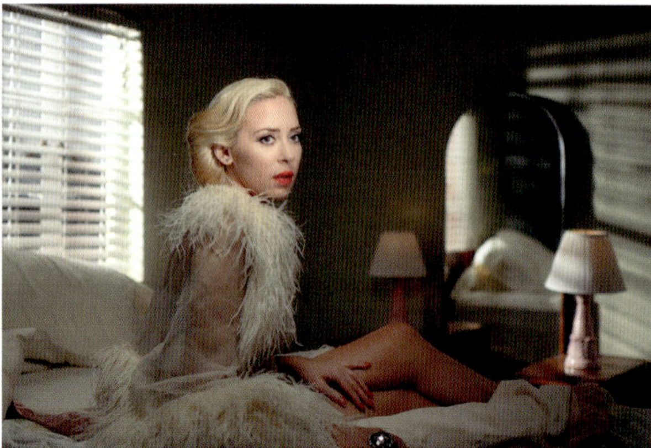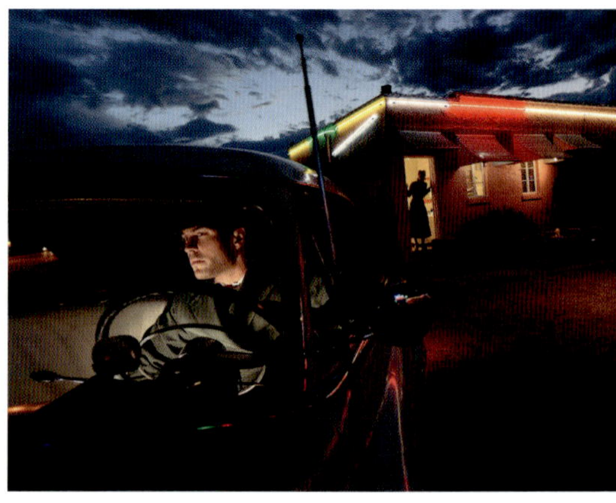

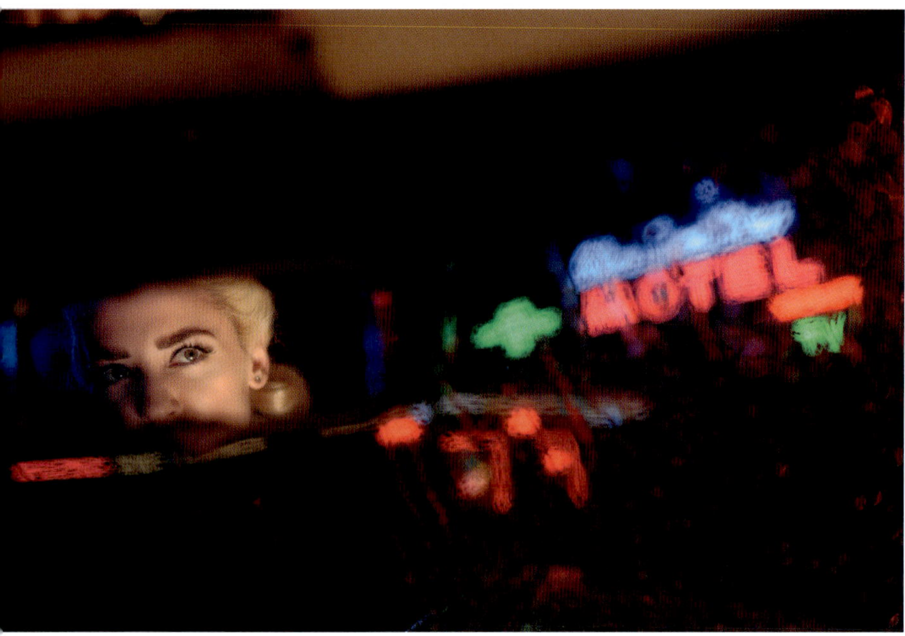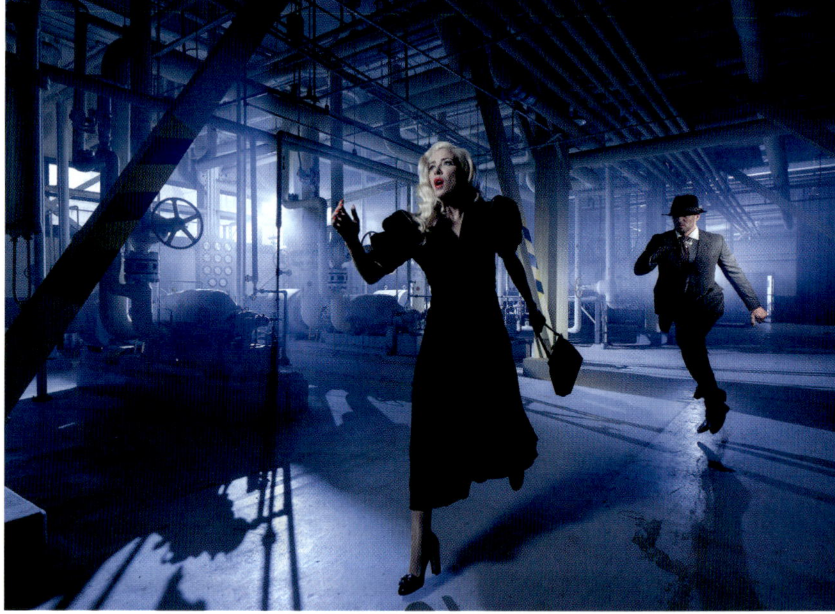

Thank you. I know I should use a big light source. And I know how to put on my seatbelt.

The techniques I used here are available at your local camera store or photo website. Gels: warm, cool, some reds. Raw light, governed by grids or snoots. Occasionally a smallish softbox. F-stop choice was driven by the sense of the scene, and how much or how little needed to be sharp. In short, the tools are simple and familiar. What determines their success is not the exposure or the f-stop or even those newfangled (at that time) wireless TTL communicators that allowed me the leeway to hide flashes.

The raison d'etre of these pictures is the shared camaraderie of the light. It's like they are all gathered around the glow from the same fire. The light informs each scene or vignette and is, hopefully, appropriate for each. A beauty light. A light that throws a shadow and conceals an identity. A red-gelled, gridded light to simulate a taillight. Warm light to play off the cooling blue of twilight. Low light for a face filled with menace.

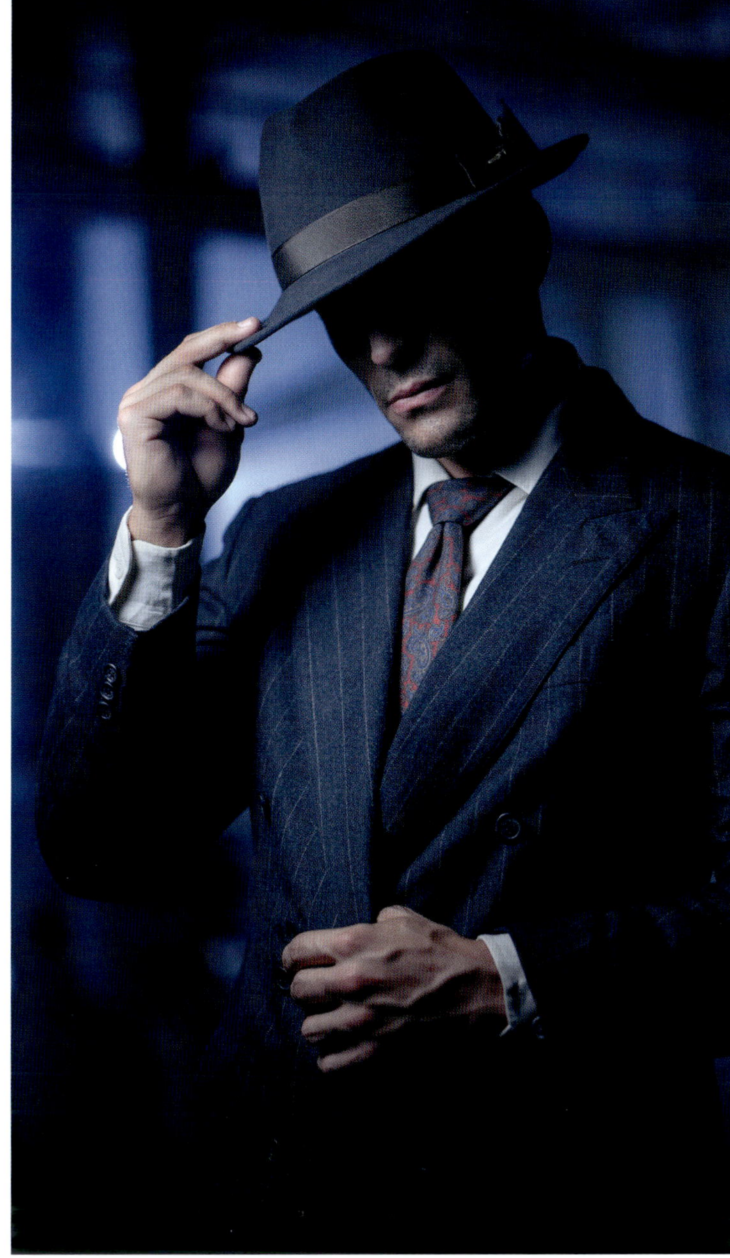

This Speedlight-saturated journey starts in New York City, at The Blue Bar in the Algonquin Hotel (page 214). The lady in question is alone, with her thoughts and a martini, unaware she is being observed. In the Blue Bar, go figure, all the lights are blue. (Sir John Barrymore, the legendary actor, stayed at the Algonquin when performing on Broadway. He suggested blue lighting for the bar, positing that it makes people look good. Every light in there is blue, to this day.)

Hence, my accent lights are blue. A blue-gelled, snooted Speedlight pops her drink, and a light behind her frosts her hair. In

retrospect, I might have tried to boom a warmish light over the top of her, to highlight her hat, but . . . I didn't. Time and money might have implicated themselves in this decision, as I was moving quickly. As locations go, The Blue Bar was costly, and we had a hard stop time, after which they would start admitting patrons. That's a logical, coherent explanation. Or I could be honest and say it was likely that I just didn't see it.

Later, in a more evening look, she again is alone—just her, the champagne, her impeccable fingernails, and a gown to die for. Retro glamour. As they used to say in these movies, "What a dame!"

This is where my imagination really starts driving the train. I conjured her as a government agent, hoarding atomic secrets, or perhaps photos proving Area 51 exists. (The styling is retro, '40s or '50s, so "the dawn of the atomic era" ramblings in my head made sense, at least to me.)

We headed to the classic Blue Swallow Motel in New Mexico, the state that has the dubious honor of hosting the first nuclear explosion in human history. This roadside wonder of a motel was the perfect setting to travel back in time. Neon. Surrounded by open skies. Old prop vehicles, and classically tiny motel rooms where, no doubt, many desperate deeds of sublime, sweaty surrender have taken place. Our lady is followed by the man in the bar from NYC, now lurking in the shadows of the parking lot. A connection is made. An illicit liaison occurs. She bathes, temporarily oblivious to the impending danger. He is framed in a doorway, his eyes seething with menace.

The tryst was obviously a mistake, as she caresses the pillow the next morning, her face limned with remorse and regret. She lays low during daylight hours, then peeks out of her motel door in the twilight. She is being watched. Late at night, under the hopeful cover of a storm, she flees to a pre-ordained meeting place in, of course, a deserted power plant. The G-man she was to meet is not there. But the man in the shadows is. She runs in terror as he springs from behind the machinery. Face cloaked in darkness, he adjusts his fedora. Fade to black.

What do you need to do this? A few lights, some gels, clamps, gaffer tape, a few small, simple light shapers, stands, tripod, camera, and lenses. The kit is not overlarge, complex, or necessarily expensive. Some of the pictures are made with one light. A couple needed two. For a limited number of frames, I went to four, five, or six lights, and admittedly that does require some management.

But the application of these tools is simple, really. It's not about how many lights are used. If deployed, the light is deployed for a reason. *It has a job to do.* It's not an exercise in how many you use. All they do is become the agents of your imagination, and help you make it real. Keep it sparse and to the point. If it helps tell the story, use it. If not, leave it in the bag, and be thankful, as not using it will save you time when you have to strike the set. Remember when I said the use of light is akin to writing? Too many lights are like an out-of-control, run-on sentence, and to be avoided.

Imagination. The truly salient piece of kit you must have on a job like this is your imagination, which drives the storyline. Mix in a healthy dose of pre-visualization. Do a storyboard. Know where you are going before you get there. Accept that the location, the weather, and the physical realities of time and space out there in the field will spin you out a surprise or two, forcing adjustments, but have your visual path mapped out. You may have to take an exit ramp here and there, but do your best to stay on the picture highway of your head.

Confidence. Know you can create the feel of the light you seek, and that you can reproduce that light in a number of frames. None of these pictures is an accident. Confidence allows you to move efficiently, and to keep moving. Timeline is important relative to budget. All these pictures were shot in three days on location. One day in the NYC bar. Then travel. One full day and night at the motel. The next day, drive to the power plant and shoot the same day. Done.

Crew. I am not a one-man band on a job like this. Production, pre-arrangements, permits, fees, and releases all need to be done prior to arrival on location, and that is the job of a good,

detail-oriented producer. You can produce the job yourself, but you don't want to. (I mean, with an overhead mirror and a sharp knife you can take out your own spleen, but a good doc is money well spent.) Producing the job yourself adds infinitely to your workload and fractures your attention at the camera. You want to be responsible for the pictures, not the catering. For production details, it's best to hire a pro. Styling is also crucial. If the look and setting are specific to an era, as they are with these pictures, the styling must be impeccable. This doesn't work if the talent wears cutoff shorts and a Pearl Jam t-shirt.

Talent! Good people in front of the camera. People who fill out the roles you have for them in your head and collaborate with you. Their particular skills enhance and enrich your vision, giving you back something you hadn't completely anticipated. Their own gift for creation sparks with yours.

The gear, while obviously needed, is the least of it. What comes first is the idea, and then amassing the support that idea needs to meet the pixels.

But then, yes, enter the flashes. The light you bring, however much or little, is the shock to the system, jolting the story awake. Without the right light, all those fevered, wonderful picture dreams are dead on the table. The flashes are the lightning bolts animating Frankenstein's lifeless creature. When you hit the light right, though, try not to scream *"It's alive!"* at the camera. It might be disconcerting for the crew.

Of course, as I write this I can sense that you, dear reader, might want to scream at me, "You asshole, big-time photographer with your crew and your catering! I don't have that kind of budget!"

Indeed. Understood. I was blessed on this job, which was a figment of my imagination, that Nikon got behind it, and funded the job. I could hire people who are excellent at what they do, and it became, as it always does, a team effort.

So. Budget. I face off with minimalist budgets on an unfortunately frequent basis. Here, I offer a few caveats and a smattering of advice that can turn a threadbare budget into a nice suit of pictures.

It's a lot of work but you *can* do the production stuff yourself. Work the phones and hammer out your own details. Remember, details are the stitching that hold together the larger bones of your idea. If you neglect the details, the house of cards of location photography will fall down around your troubled head. And you can only identify those details if you have *thought this through.*

Pursuant to details: Nothing on location ever "works itself out." When going into the field, nothing "will probably be okay." A flawed image on the LCD won't audaciously get better when you go full screen on the computer. Pictures don't self-heal, do Pilates, or take the 12 steps to a better version of themselves. If your inner voice is squawking at you to fix something while you are in the field, listen to it, even if the fix requires time and attention that you most likely don't have yards of while out there directing the whole shebang.

Work local. No travel allowed.

Work small cities, or out-of-the-way places. Stay away from metro environments, as they will be costly. A smaller venue might limit the reach of your visual imagination, but access to small-scale stuff is better than no place to work at all. The path of least resistance in terms of logistics is often worth the visual giveback you might have to make. You can judge the ease of this work early, just by how long it takes people to call you back. If you have to chase them, you could be in for a hard road to no.

In terms of production work and prep for a shoot, here's a beautiful phrase to hear: "Well, I'm retired, so it'll be fun to have something to do."

For a different adventure, and one that was much, much constrained by budget, I needed a cemetery. I'm close to New York City, home to acres and acres of the dead. I'm also a (grave) stone's throw (ouch!) from Sleepy Hollow Cemetery, that legendary home of the headless horseman. Didn't even think about ringing these places up. Never bothered making even a tentative inquiry. The bigger the place, the greater the reputation, the more difficult and expensive it all becomes. These places were immediately out of my league, and my budget.

But there's a cemetery literally down the block in my sleepy hometown. I checked with the town clerk and got the name and number for the Graveyard Commission. Who knew? The cemetery needs tending, and reverence, and there's a group of lovely, retired folks who pitch in, and honor those who have passed. The gentleman who's nominally in charge of the commission was the voice on the phone, happy to engage, and he offered to meet me that very day, in the graveyard. When I got there, it was not just him, it was the entire commission, like seven people. We sorted where we could work, and I offered an account of my intent.

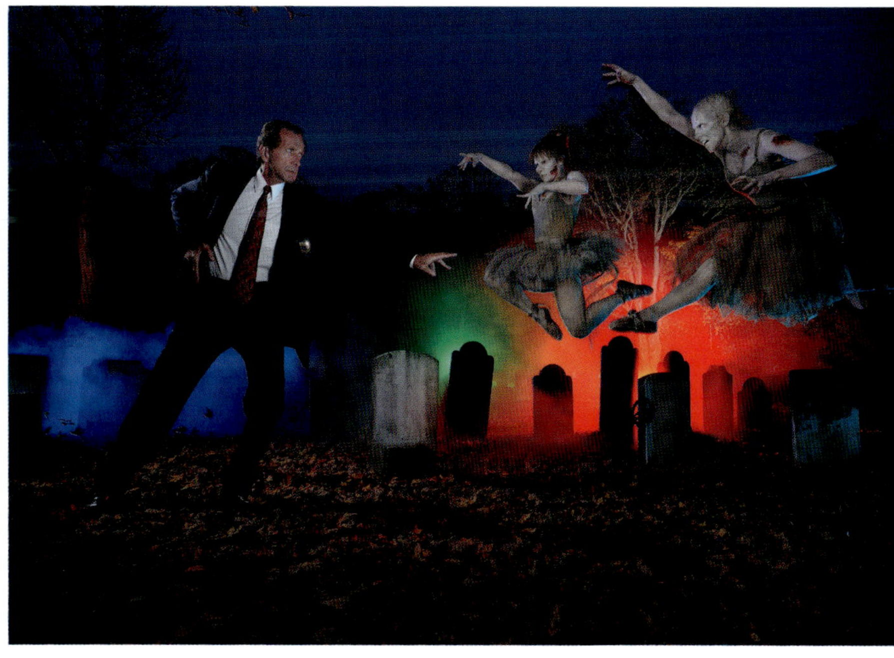

The picture idea was off the wall. I had to look at this group of sensible, down-to-earth folks, overcome my embarrassment, and then confidently spin my tale of a Halloween picture featuring zombie ballerinas.

They were totally hooked. Loved it. The permission process included our town selectman, who signed off immediately. We were home free. I gave the commission a very modest sum as a thank you. They will use the money to do yardwork and clear out the occasional fallen tree. Good deal all around.

Always remember, when doing location work, the operative piece of that phrase is the word location. It's the biggest chip to fall. You could have all the talent in the world banging on your door, begging to be in front of the camera, and no place to put them. Location is the driver. Access. Permission. A place to work that is arranged, buttoned up, and paid for. Permit issued and printed. Nobody to come around in random fashion to pull the plug.

Use connections in your local area. You know people who know people. Work the phones, cite the benefits of letting you pursue your craft, the idea of supporting a local artist. Offer a print or credit in social media. Offer to shoot a picture of their restaurant or bakery, or a group shot of the local volunteer fire department as a fair-minded, civically responsible giveback. Let people hear the passion in your voice. They have to hear, and feel, that you need to do this.

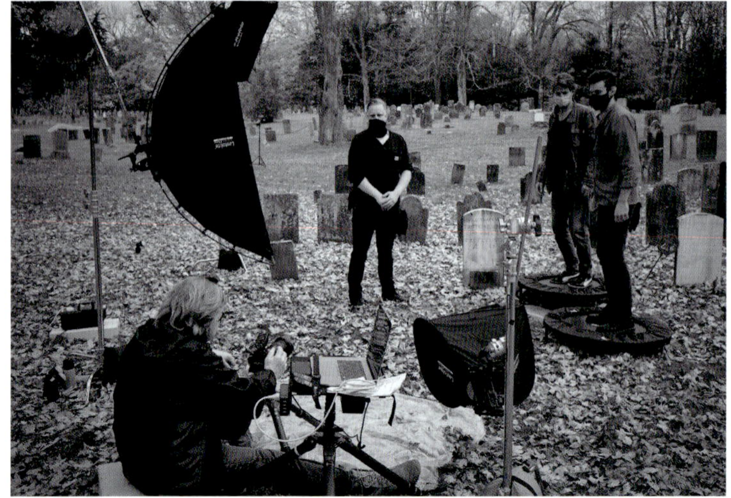

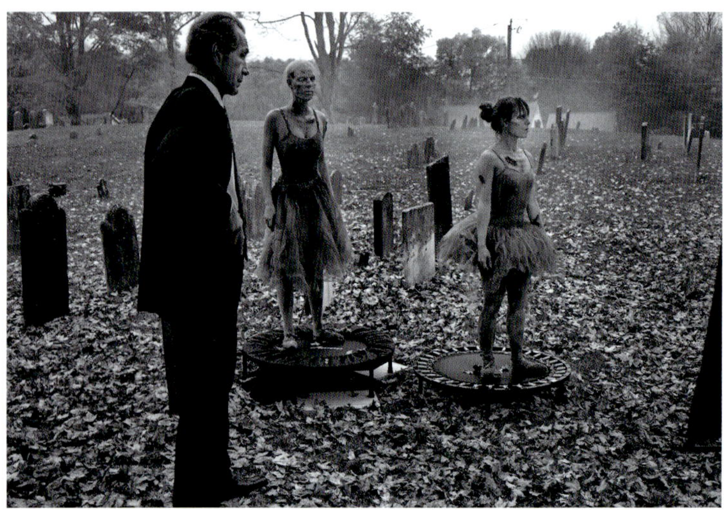

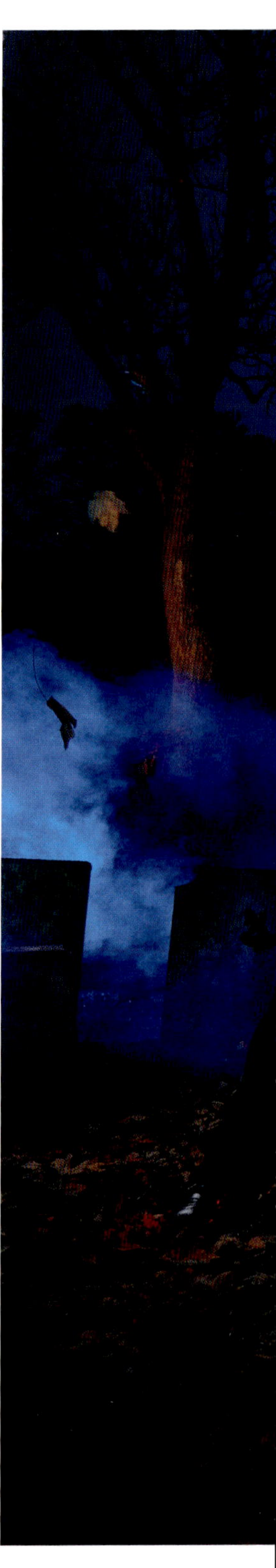

If your inner voice is squawking at you to fix something while you are in the field, listen to it.

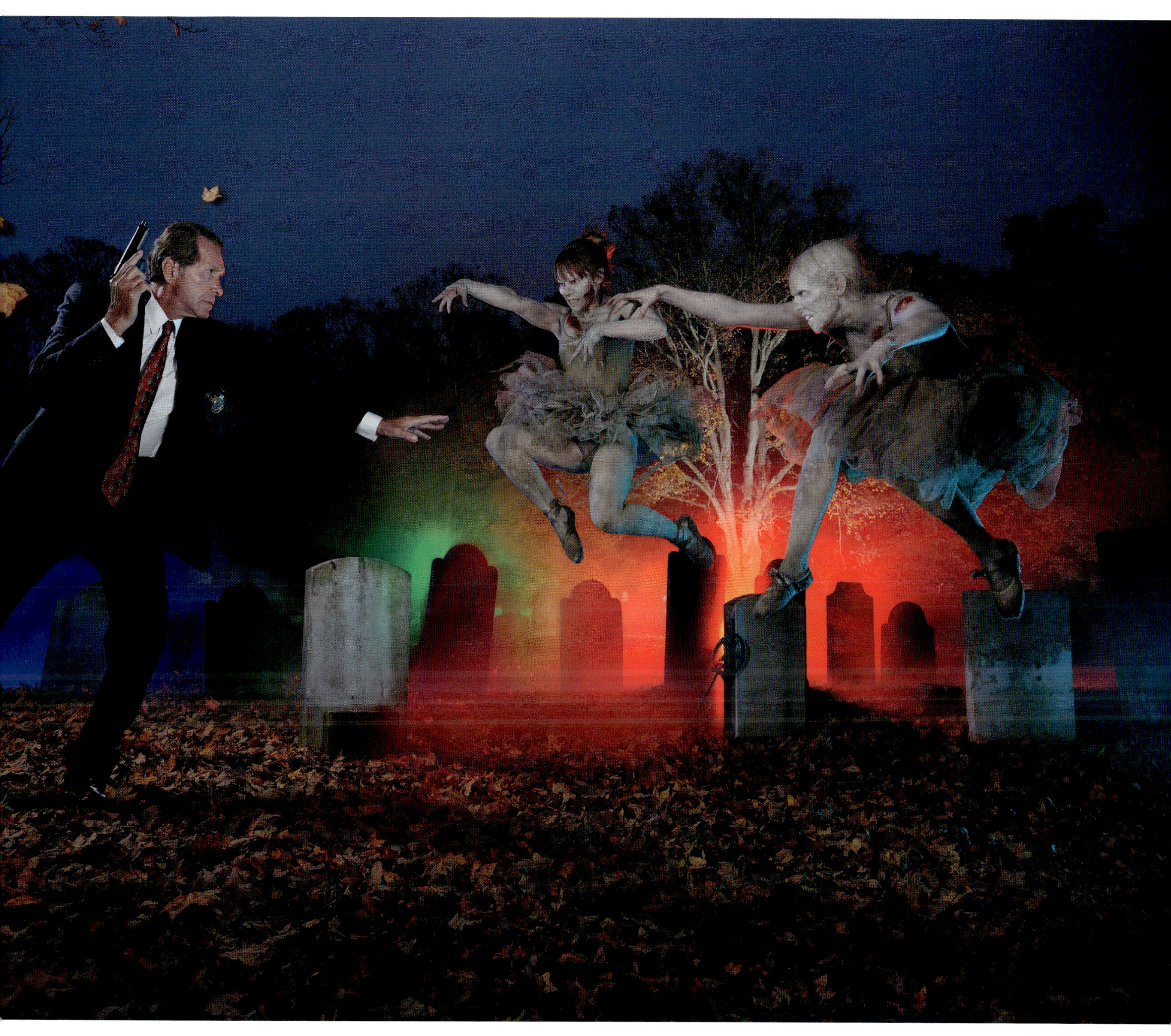

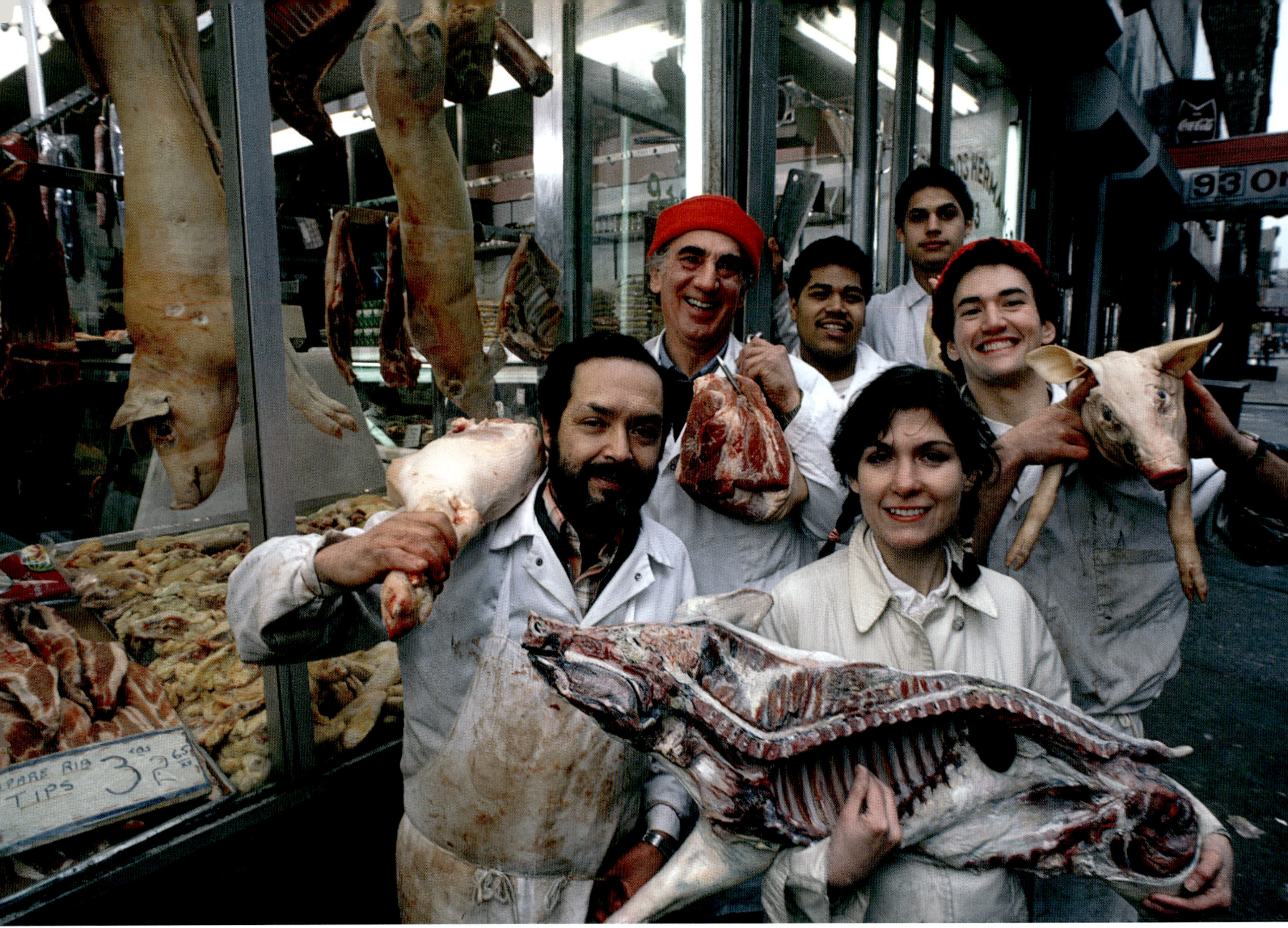

I once photographed an artist on the Lower East Side of New York City who made accurate molds of dead animals and painted them. (They were popular, such was the art scene down there at the time.) She got her "models" from the local butcher shop, who were somewhat head-tilted by the fact that their dead pigs were getting memorialized and hanging on somebody's wall. But they supported her, and her art. So, I made a group photo of her meat supplier outside the shop. Fun pic. It's wonderful when a community or piece thereof rallies behind an artist.

Use young talent, eager for a stint in front of the camera. Or friends. You know people who can inhabit characters, guaranteed. They have to do their own hair and makeup and provide their own wardrobe. Reach out to schools, drama departments, local ballet training institutes, community theater. Sign onto casting networks; they are extremely helpful. We recently put out a casting call for a straightforward modeling stint, male and female, at a very modest rate, $800, considering the rights we stated in the release. We got over a 1,000 replies.

Do the paperwork! Do it prior to arrival on location! Do your best not to present a release on location. It can torpedo the hopefully rosy, "we are all in this together and committed to the sacred act of creation" vibe that should rule on the set. Also, it gives talent a chance to think twice, which is never a good idea.

Be straightforward and present the conditions, the finances, and the paperwork in toto, up front. Then, it's their decision. Once they sign off, it precludes "day of" cold feet and the booby trap of the second guess.

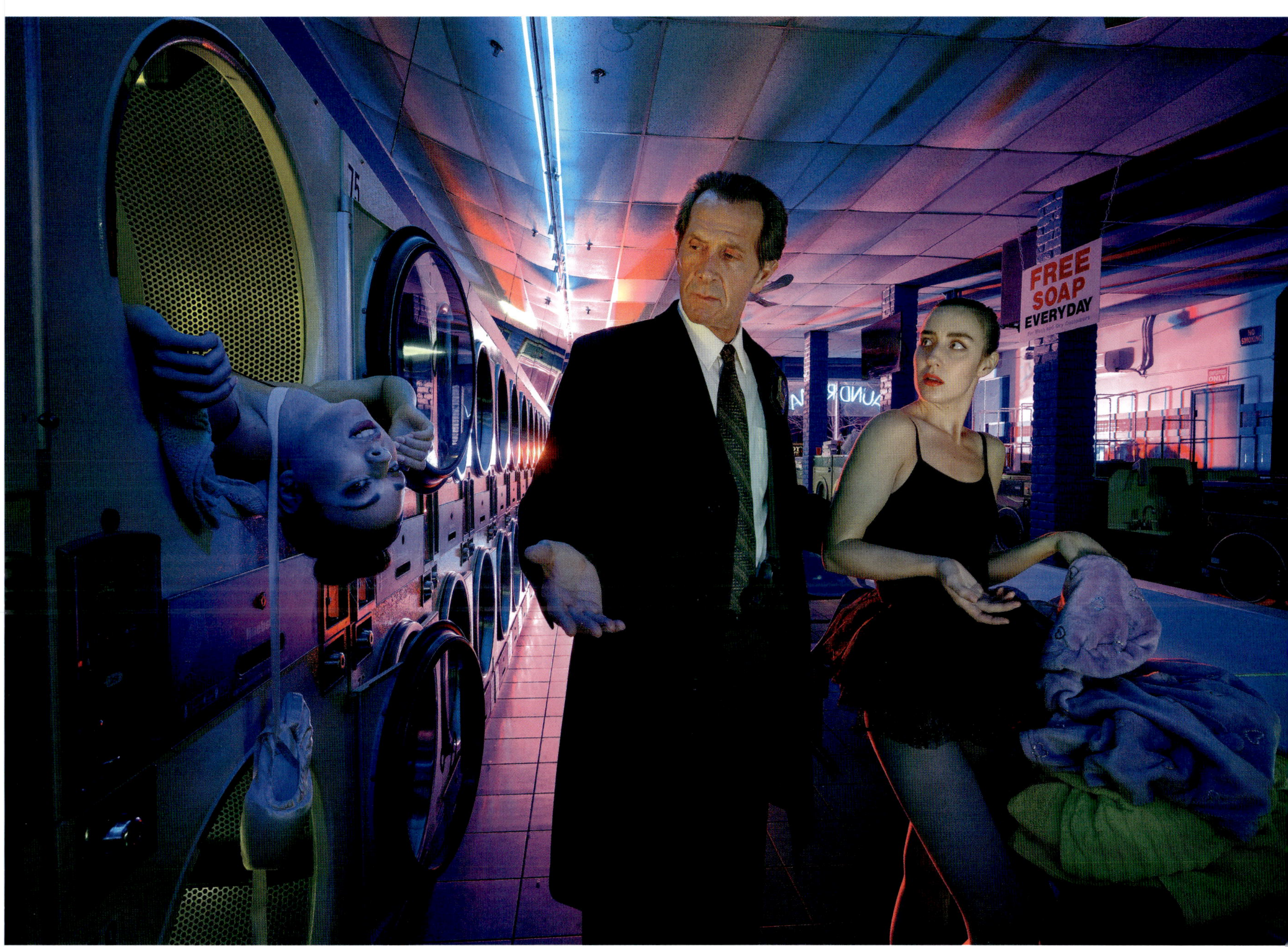

The Call of the
Big Nothing

Backgrounds bedevil us. They are with us, always, and must be on our minds in equivalently ubiquitous fashion. Concrete urban spires and strip mall crawl has blighted reliably unoccupied spaces and replaced, to borrow a phrase, "darkness on the edge of town" with vast parking lots and warehouses. All these utterly unattractive big boxes are buttered in the sickly ochre glow of high-pressure sodium, or worse, the harsh drench of merc vapor, which has the slimy greenish tint of a long-unattended fishbowl. Power lines abound to the point where we feel verily ensnared, Gulliver-like, by wire-wielding Lilliputians, creating busyness and obstruction. From space, the world still presents as a lovely blue marble hanging in the heavens. On the street, it can look like a bedraggled, busy ball of string.

As developers develop, and buildings sprout, and urbanization and gentrification relentlessly proceed, we can feel a bit animal-like, with our natural habitats chewed upon and reduced. Growing up with a camera in New York City, the absolute heart of over-busy urban skew, I knew that, for relief and emptiness, I could reliably drift down to the Meatpacking District on the Lower West Side, to seek cobblestoned streets, dilapidated storefronts, and desperately deserted sidewalks. I rarely applied for a permit. Just went and shot.

It was a refuge, especially if it was raining, as all the overhead racks where they would hang and slide the sides of beef still existed. It was lonely during the day, after the meat markets closed, and barren at night, save for the furtive denizens of the dark who worked those streets, but they were colorful and conversational, and absolutely uninterested in being filmed.

I was photographing a fitness trainer long ago (page 228), and we had a "fashion on the sidewalks" thing planned when the heavens opened, and torrents of rain nixed the idea of working out on the streets. At her suggestion, we pivoted and headed to a radical lingerie shop, of which she was a frequent patron. As she shopped, I turned to my assistant and said something like, "The shoot is about to take on an entirely different look."

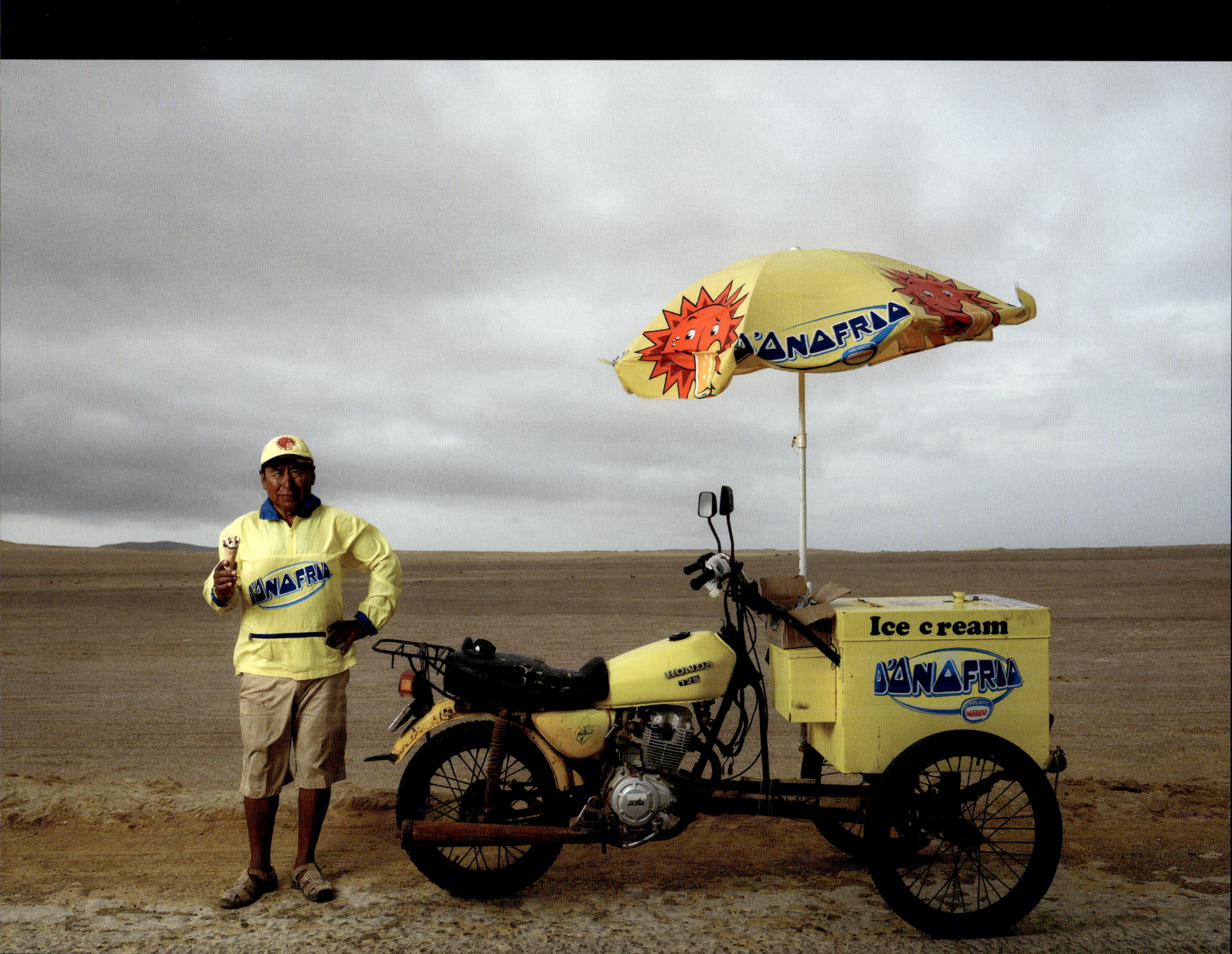
D'ONOFRIO
Ice cream
D'ONOFRIO
HONDA
125

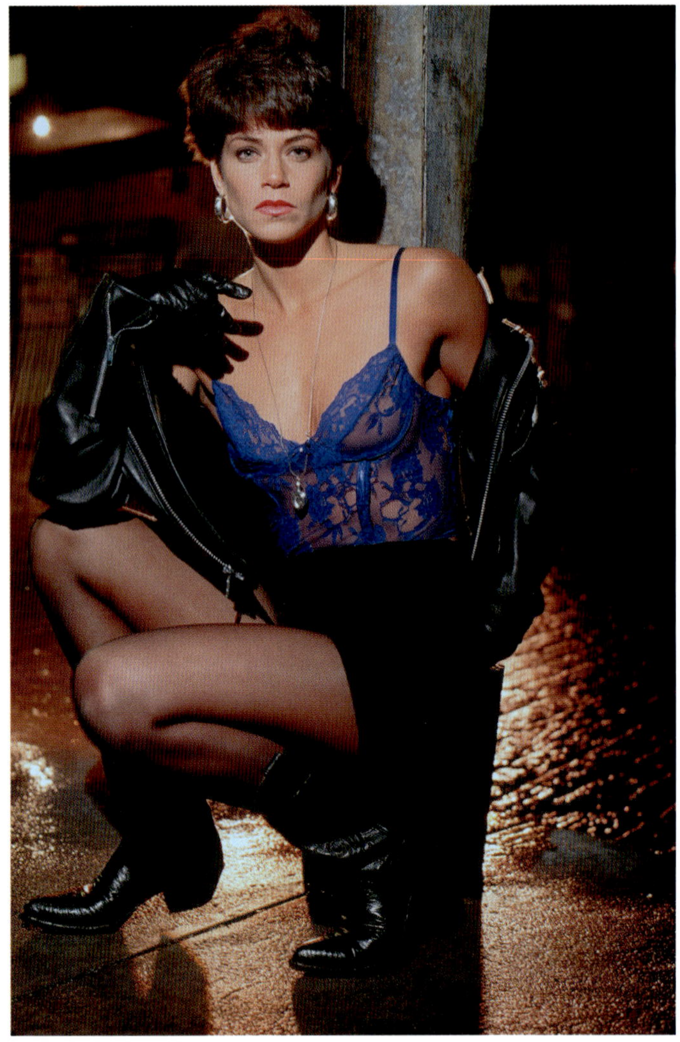

We rolled with it. Went to the Meatpacking District, out of the rain, and started working with one hard-edged flash. Terrific, energetic model. We were pushing the look when an NYPD cruiser rolled up in the rain-soaked darkness and parked 20 or 30 feet downstream of where we were shooting. I exhaled. My reliable, anything-goes neighborhood was about to go poof! I had no permit! They were about to demand documentation, or question my purpose out here, or my morals.

But no such thing happened. The cops stayed in their car, warm and dry, and enjoyed the shoot. I looked at Garth and said, "Very cool. We now have our own security detail."

It was good they were enjoying it because I had my vehicle parked at a 45-degree angle, front wheels up on the sidewalk, raking my headlights off the shiny brick background in an "angle of incidence, angle of reflection" fashion. That's the backlight. No flash, just high beams. The cops didn't bust me on that one, either.

But that version of the Meatpacking District has faded away. The compelling and seductively dangerous darkness, the hard empty streets that once beckoned spur-of-the-moment photo shoots, along with the forlorn or the desperate, on the hunt for strange love, is gone. It's been replaced by a bustling, expensively shiny version of the city, complete with its own Apple store, fer chrissakes.

Clean backgrounds! Unencumbered places to shoot and work! Someplace physically and graphically unbusy. Someplace where unpermitted spontaneity is possible. Harder to find nowadays, as the big cities and the bright lights continue to look under every rock.

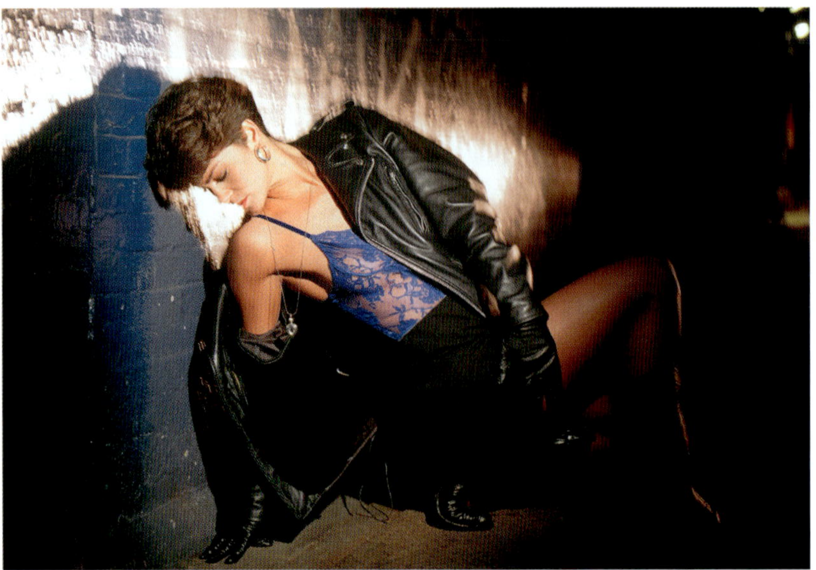

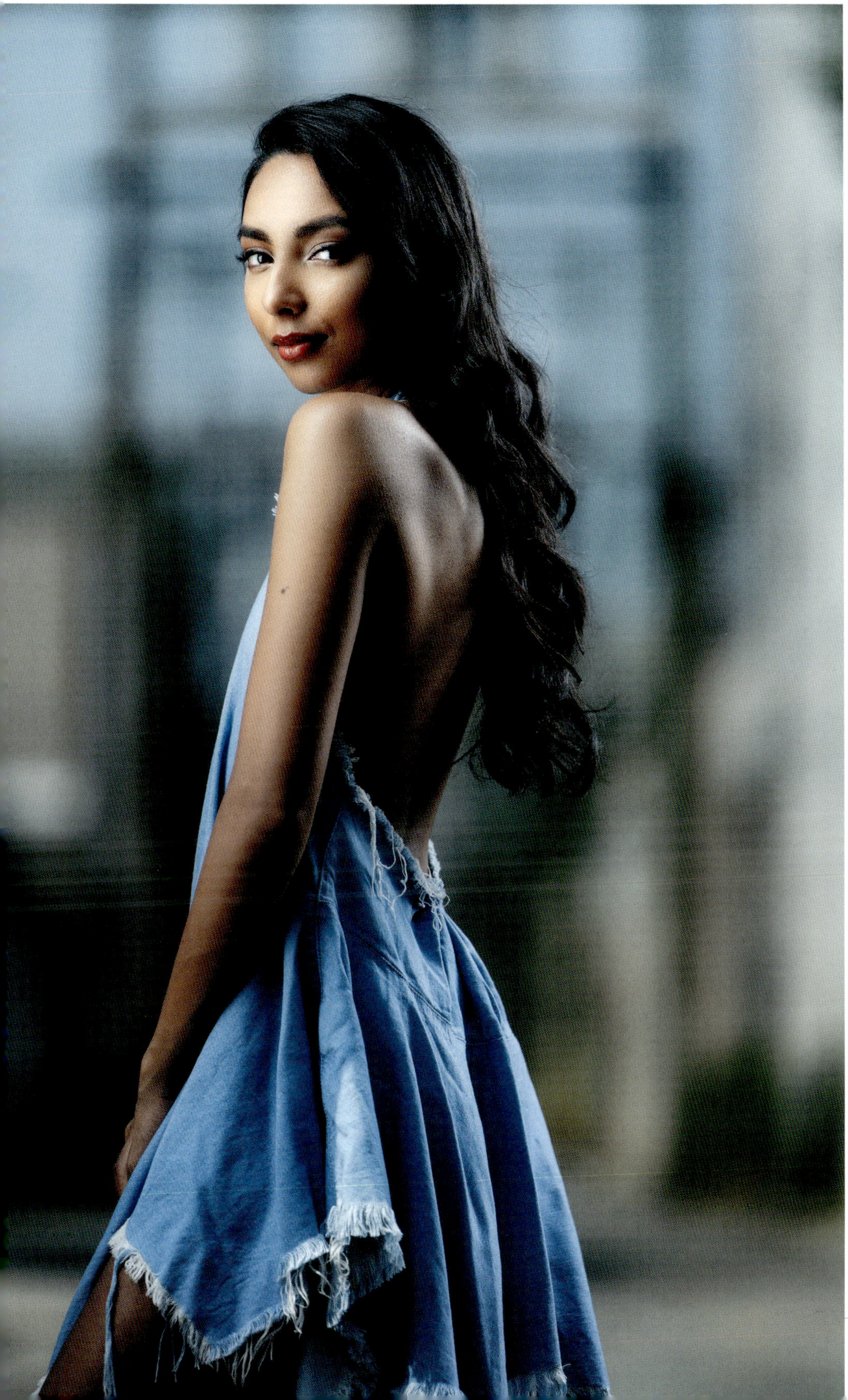

We can use the photo tools at our disposal to minimize and eradicate. A 200mm lens, wide open at f/2.8, turns a Vancouver alleyway, possessed of so many power poles that I thought I had walked into a box of toothpicks, into something geometrically pleasing (left). Speedlights through 1x6 strip softboxes, used in up and down fashion. Vertical lines, vertical shapes, vertical framing . . . vertical flash. Flash follows form.

Even Times Square in NYC can be dropped like a hot rock, via an 85mm lens shot at f/2 (below).

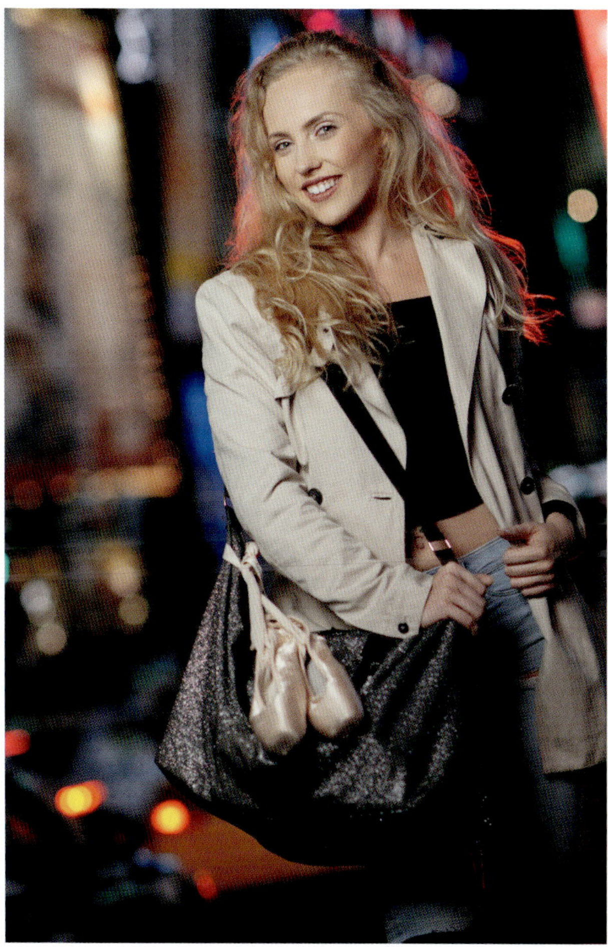

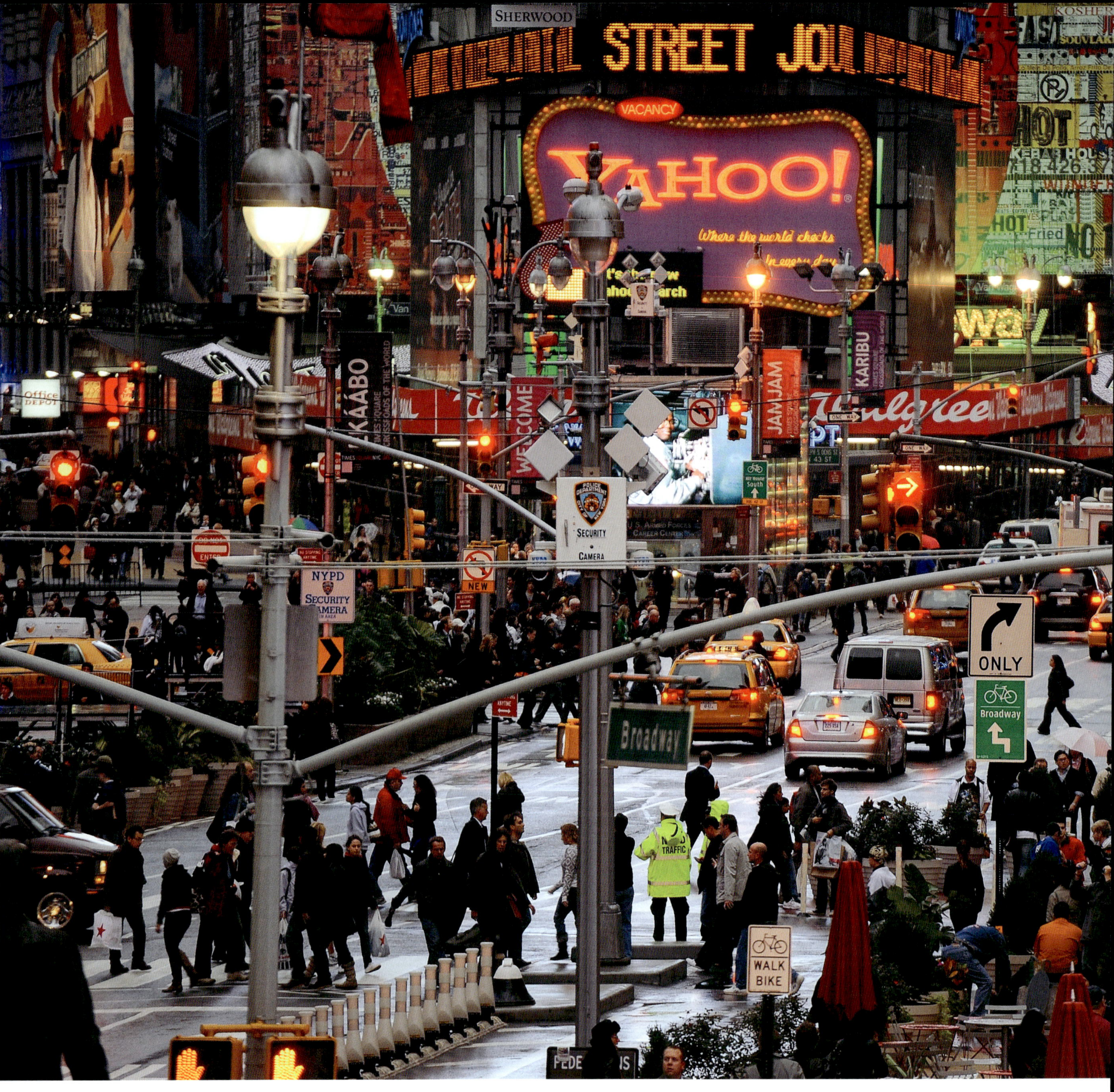

SHERWOOD
STREET
VACANCY
YAHOO!
Where the world checks
Office DEPOT
KAABO
WELCOME
JAMJAM
KARIBU
Walgreens
POLICE DEPARTMENT
SECURITY CAMERA
NYPD SECURITY CAMERA IN AREA
NEW
Broadway
ONLY
Broadway
TRAFFIC
WALK BIKE

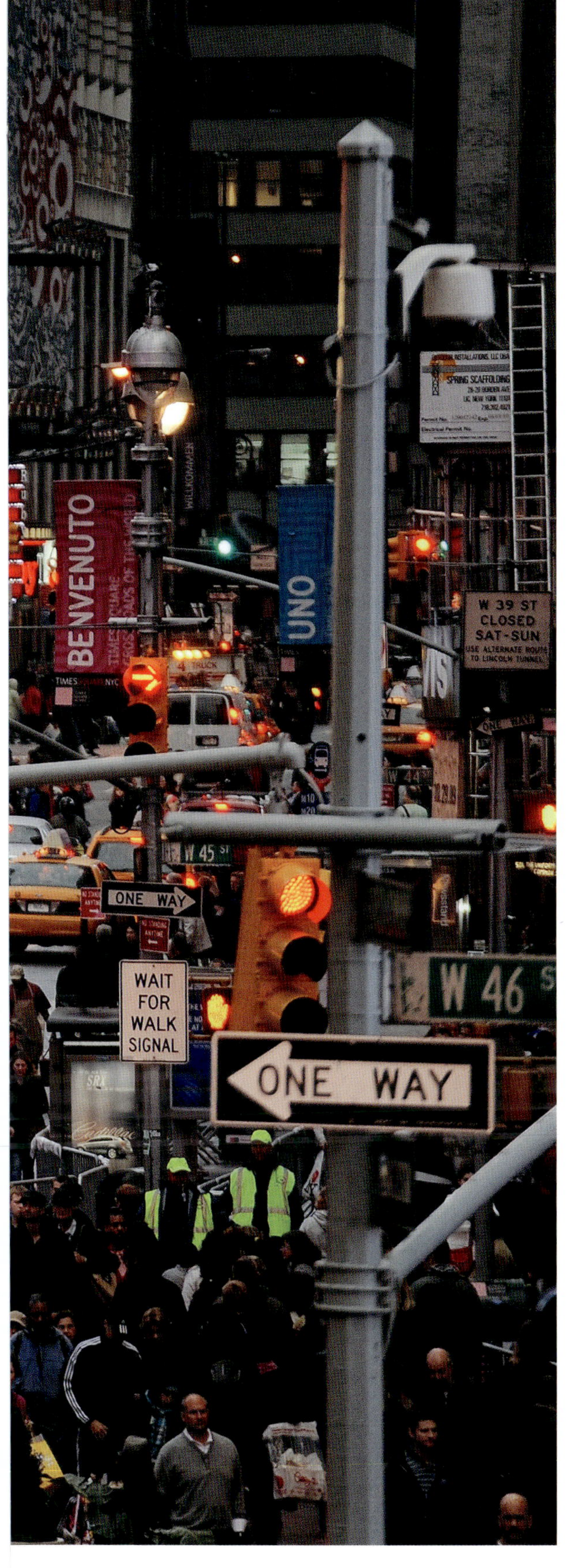

That out-of-focus mix in the background is this scene (left). And truth be told, the explosive riot of color and light that is Times Square is there to be embraced, not ignored or minimized.

At f/1.4, you can even go with wider glass, in this case a 35mm (below, top).

But your approach is limited for this to work. You must get close, work wide open, and accept that the tip of your subject's nose will most likely be a bit out of critical sharpness, sacrificed on the altar of background management.

If you back off, even wide open, with wider glass, then the results are as precarious as Natalie's pose, perched on pointe amidst gawkers and traffic (below, bottom). What a mess!

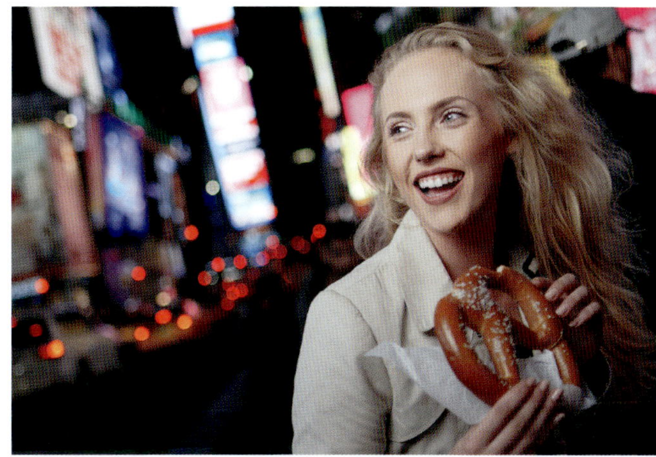

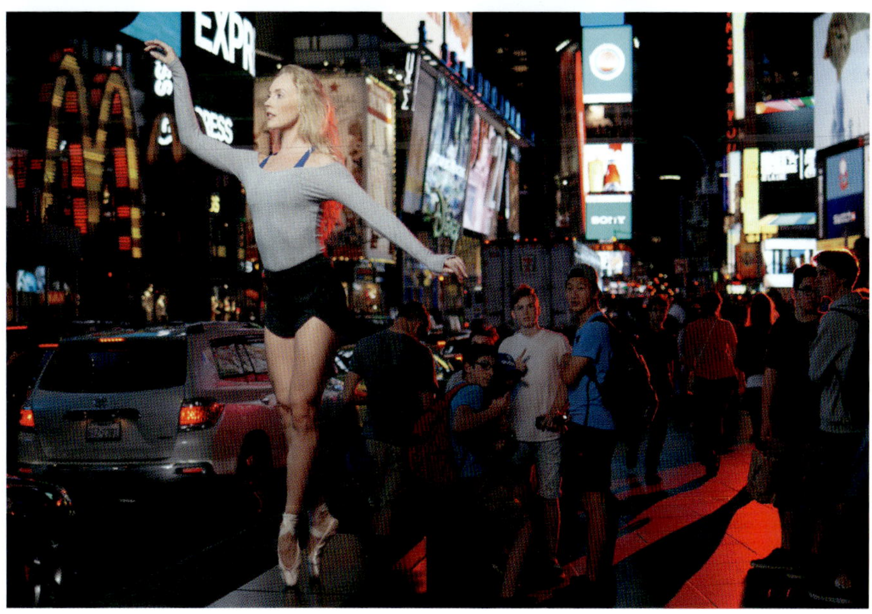

An elegantly clad model walks an endless road. Going to a fancy dinner, out there in the great beyond?

Not having to editorially tether your subject to information—such as "Here's the shopkeeper, and here's the shop"—is very liberating. Referring to photo studios, I've always maintained that they are nothing more than large, sterile rooms with high ceilings and white walls: empty boxes the photographer fills with their imagination.

Well, a dry lake is a really, really big empty box. Clarity of horizon line can lend itself to clarity of thought. Empty spaces. Sadly, like truly dark skies, they are getting hard to find.

Go where there is nothing.

Then, put something in front of nothing.

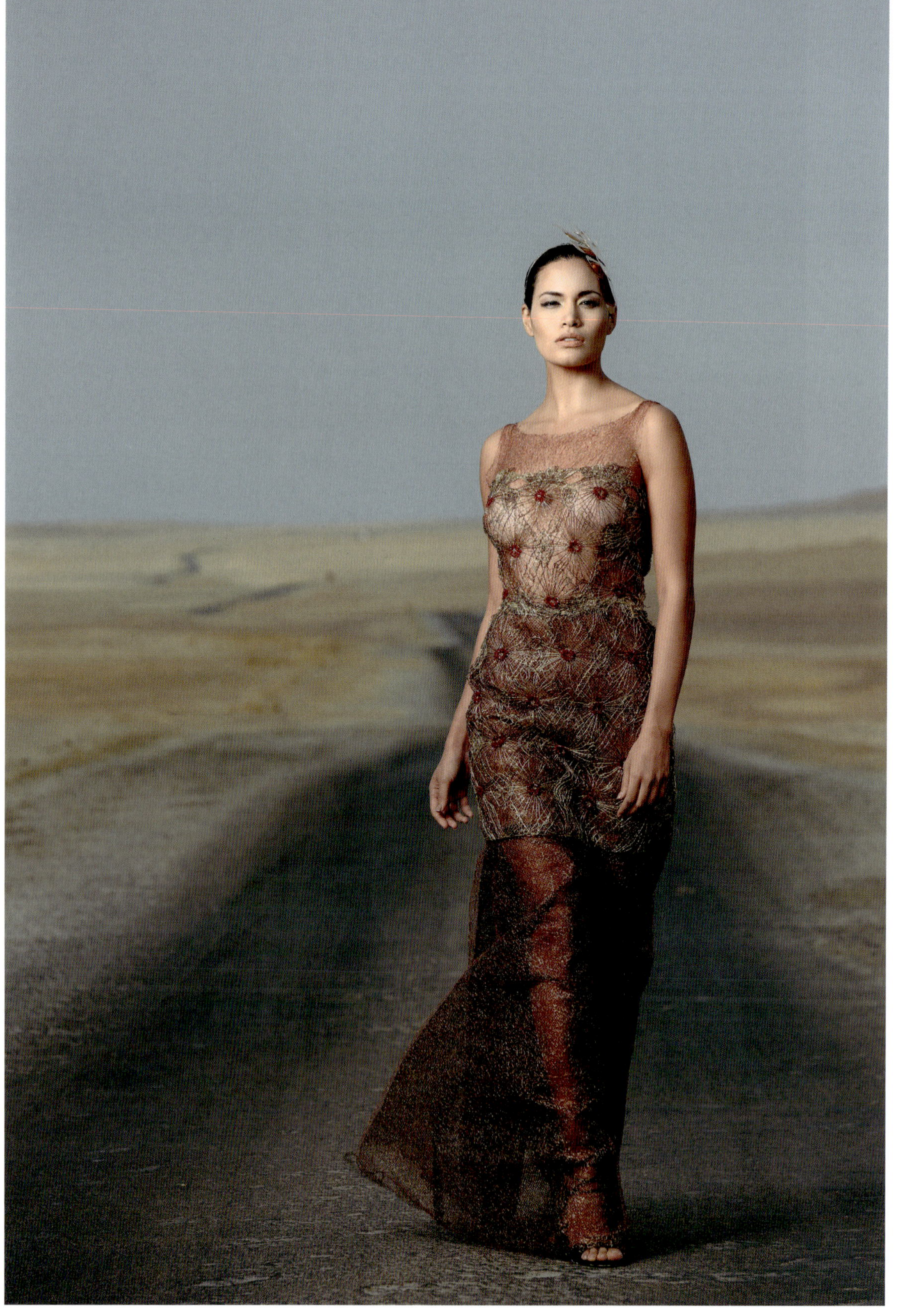

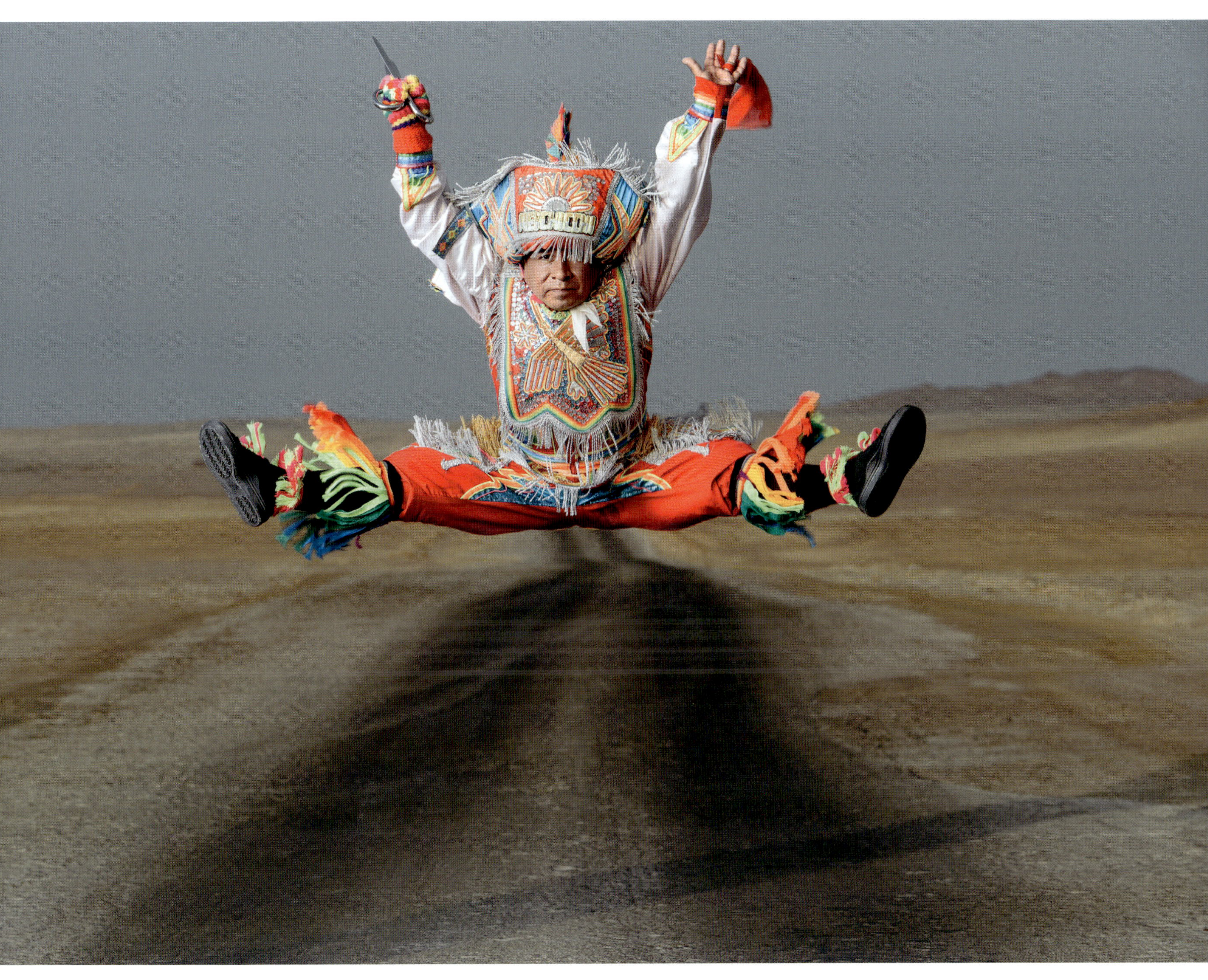

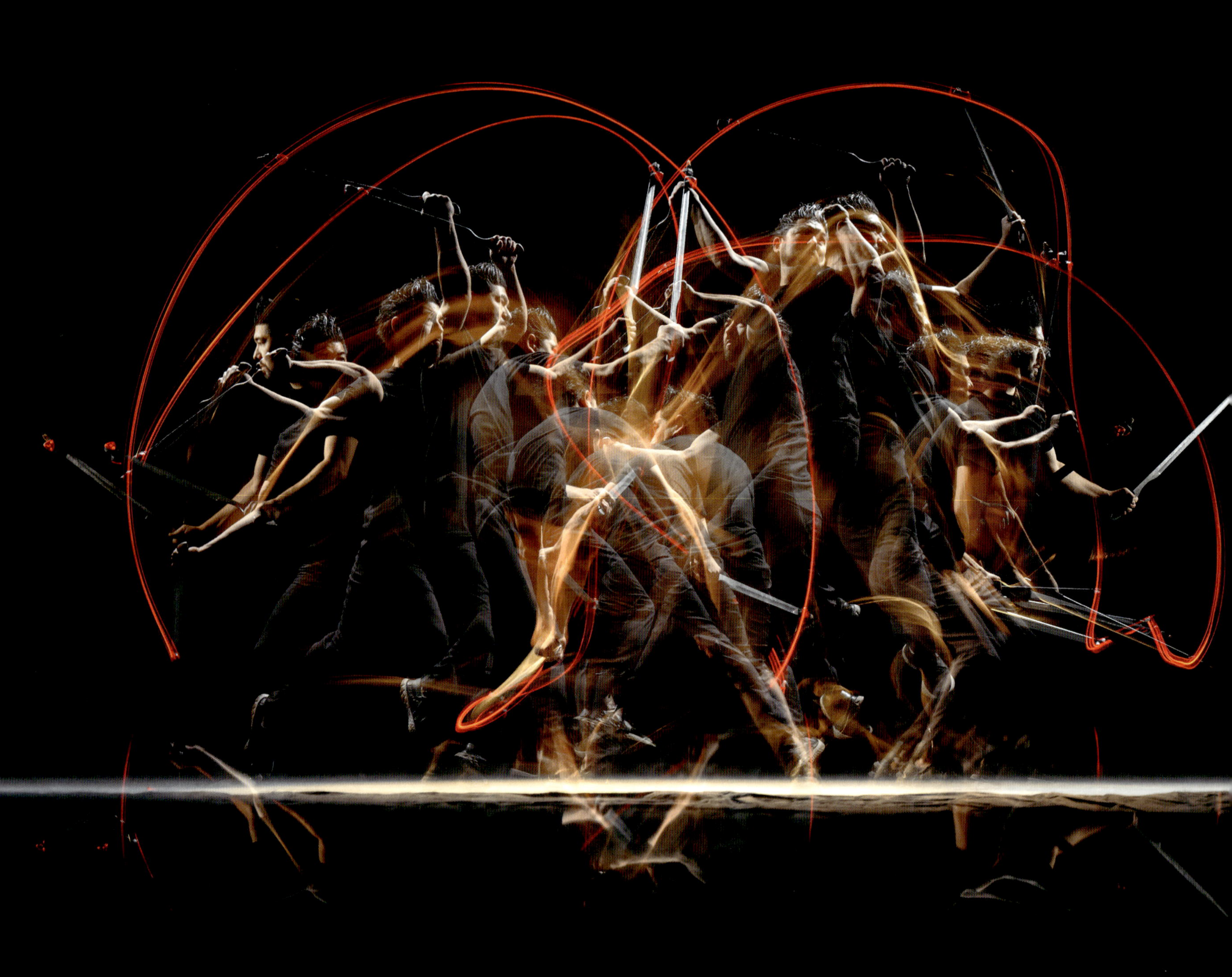

A Visit to the Camera Buffet

Fancy photos!

Updated camera tech has taken so much guesswork out of many of the more complex picture equations, it's now "easier" than it has even been to take a leap of faith and fancy at the lens. Automated flashes and exposures systems sync with each other, talk their way through problems, and work it out automatically, all while we're feverishly pushing the shutter button. The cameras solve so many problems for us, dramatically expanding the range of our imaginations and what's possible at the lens. It's a wonderful evolution. You couldn't drag me kicking and screaming back to the world of 36-exposure canisters and Kodachrome.

But be aware. There is no camera algorithm more astute than the mix of common sense and experience right there in your own noodle. Accumulated picture-making wisdom. The rolodex of survival.

The current and ever-evolving photo technology and options in digital cameras are like a Vegas hotel breakfast buffet. Yards of sumptuous temptation, rolling out before you in heart-stopping, artery-clogging wonder. Eggs Benedict. Buttermilk pancakes, bursting with blueberries. Cinnamon buns, fairly bubbling with lava flows of icing.

When I started in the picture game, your menu options were shutter speed and f-stop. Definitely more like the breakfast service at the Budget Motor Inn out on the interstate than the spread at a richly appointed casino hotel. Shutter speed, f-stop. Rice Krispies with skim milk in a Styrofoam bowl. Oh, and by the way, you gotta focus the camera on your own, too.

Things are blessedly different in our techno-driven digital world. Cameras nowadays stop just short of giving you a shoulder rub and making astute stock picks for your portfolio. It's feverishly exciting, especially for a newcomer, to simply pick up a camera, place it to your eye, and have it factor the world for you. And, of course, the first few reasonable frames are indeed sharp enough, with good color and punch. Wow! This is easy! This camera takes really great pictures! I should do this, you know, professionally!

Stay calm. The machine in your hands is fully capable of automating the picture process in remarkable ways, should you choose to let that happen. Camera menus are deep and broad, and they offer many solutions, options, and checkoffs. The back of the camera you face off with has so many buttons and dials you might as well be looking at the steering wheel of a Formula One race car. The LCD/EVF is so laden with the notifications of the programmable features and what you have turned on, or could turn on, or adjust, or have adjusted, that it's tough (sort of) to actually see your subject in totality. Does that tree in the distance actually have a plus sign on it? No, okay, I get it, it's my camera viewfinder. You are peering at the world through a heads-up display of camera information.

So, what do you do when confronted with all this technological largesse? Be selective. In other words, don't try everything at the buffet. You'll get sick.

I'm talking about knowing when to roll on full Auto and let the camera take charge of the scene (which it can do, quite capably, as noted), or take the information the camera gives you, weigh it, sort it, and then manage that monster. Your own camera brain needs to be the ultimate arbiter regarding placement of the camera and matters of exposure, framing, composition, and the power of a flash. You need to drive the machine, not the reverse. And remember, the reason you picked up the camera in the first place is you imagined pictures. You had visual ideas, notions, or fantasies. The camera doesn't have a dream state. It has a cold heart.

So let's take a situation that, in the days of yore, would have definitely been done on a wing and a prayer.

A flash in a flying machine! Two other planes fly tight on the lead's six. Smoke! Sunset! Figure out the available light. Figure out the flash. Rig and trigger the camera. Where do I start?

Let's take it in pieces and discuss where my fevered brain intersected with the calculating mind of the camera. We are at speed, in the air, so the camera has to fire at a fast shutter speed. I utilized Shutter Priority mode, which is a rarity in terms of my approach, being much more inclined to Aperture Priority, or flat out manual. But here, to ensure sharpness, I needed to know I had a floor for the shutter speed. Those old biplanes are marvelous machines, but they can be a bit of an eggbeater with wings. My camera was clamped above me, on the overhead wing, but up front, just behind the engine and the furious prop, and it was going to get battered by wind and plane rattle no matter how firmly it was clamped. I didn't want my shutter potentially drifting to a slow speed, as it might be inclined to do in Aperture Priority mode. I slammed the camera into Shutter Priority and set 1/500th as my floor.

Focus is manual! The camera and the pilot are static, relative to one another, and with a 14mm throw on the lens, best to drop the focus point on the pilot as he is sitting there, get a confirmation, then shift to manual focus and tape down the lens barrel. Autofocus is a wonderful thing, but it can have a mind of its own, especially when confronted with backlight. You don't want to frame the scene, fly the mission, and have AF

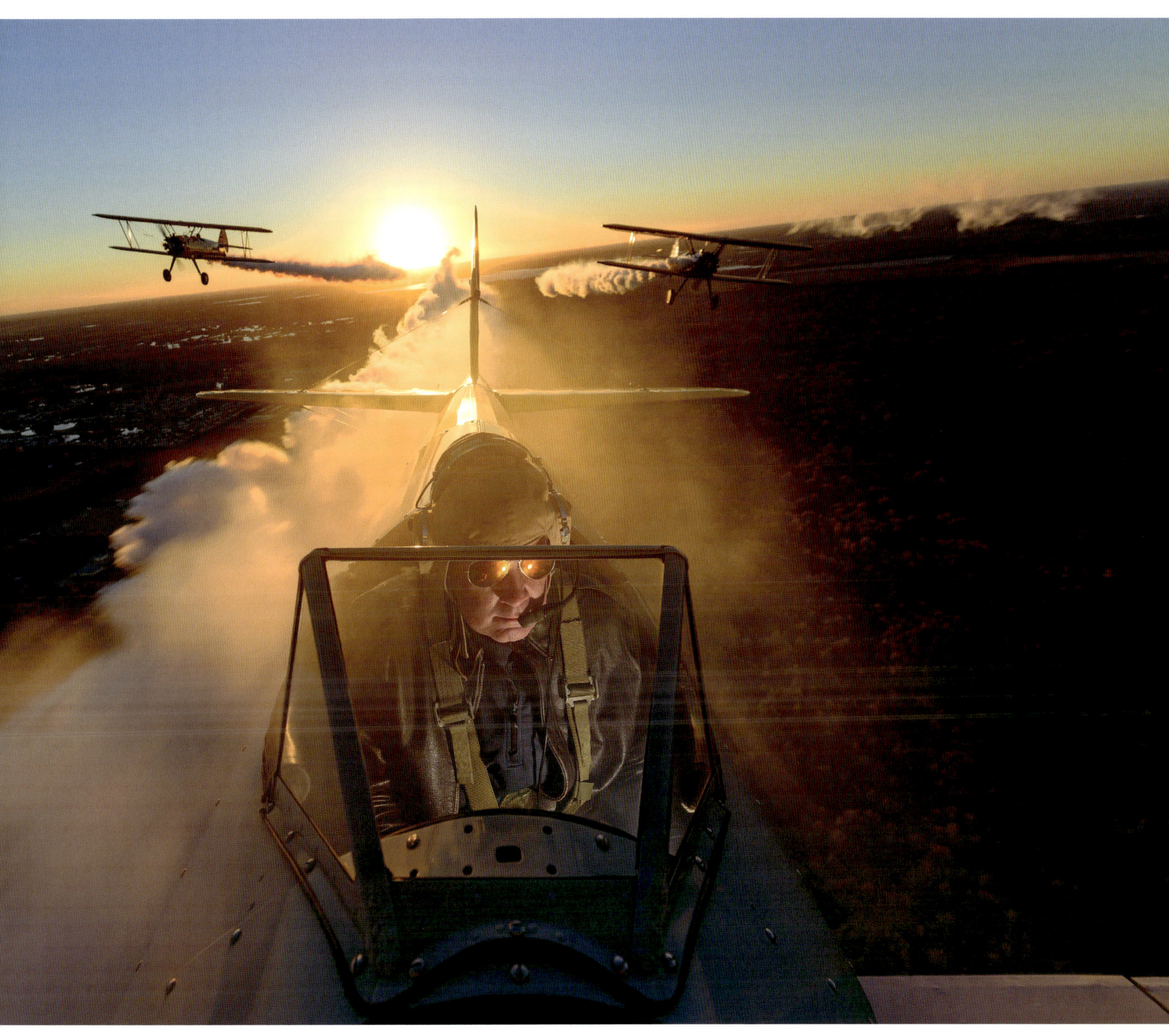

wandering on you. Like the human eye—and certainly my brain—it can be attracted to the bright shiny object, no matter the location of the cursor. I can imagine it going, "Oh, look at the pretty sunset, so deserving of sharpness! I think I'll go there!" Lock it down. Don't let AF go walkabout.

The flash is flying on manual mode, which might sound nuts. But hear me out. In Shutter Priority, the aperture will float to accommodate the perceived exposure, leading one to think this is an ideal opportunity for TTL flash operation to accommodate the f-stop as it potentially shifts up and down. But factoring exposure compensation into a TTL flash, working with a camera racked out to 14mm, looking at backlight, while the flash itself is popping off partly into the sky and partly off a dark jacket, was as big or bigger a guess as taking a stab at the f-stop drift when the plane was aloft. I locked the flashes down at 1/8th power. Eliminate a variable. I tested on the ground, and the flash exposure was hot (below). Which was good news. I knew the aperture would start to close down in the air when the camera would look directly into the sun, and I hoped my seat-of-the-pants guess at flash power would line up. Some of that hot,

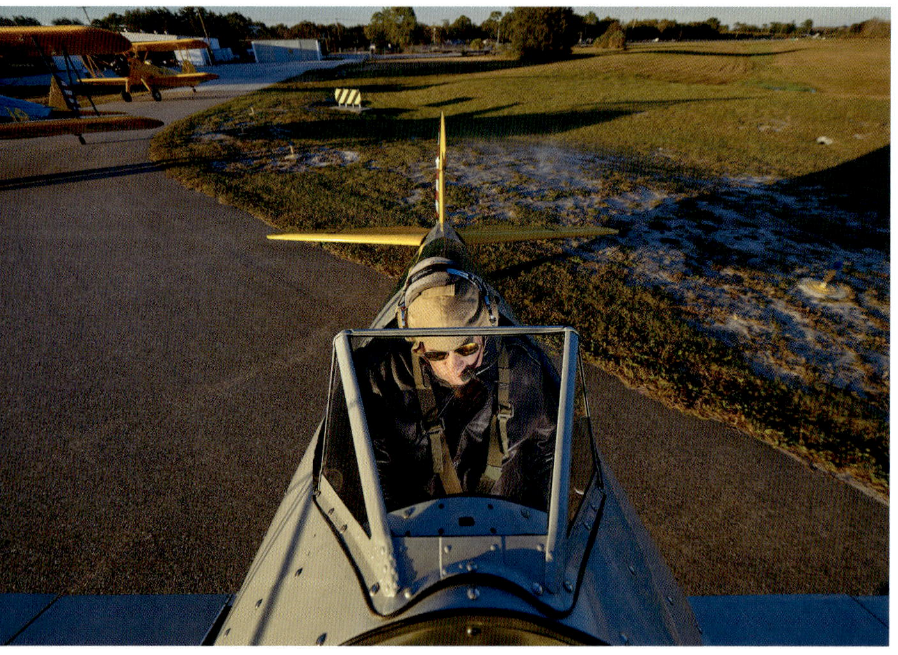

ground-based test exposure would dim down with the fading of daylight as well. It felt a bit like factoring gain for an in-camera double exposure, prior to the tools of today. Definitely a WAG (wild-ass guess).

I gelled the Speedlight warm, clamped it safely, and zip-tied the living daylights out of it. (Zip ties always go on location with us, as they really are essential for making things safe.)

As you might pick up from the far wing camera angle (opposite), I've got an SC-29 cord hot shoed to the camera, running through the guts of the airplane, to the flash, operating on camera right. This is an SB-910 flash! No radio TTL here. Line of sight only, which forced the hardwire option. Thank goodness for the old school interior of the Stearman. The guts of those planes have crevices, openings, seams, and handles galore. You can thread wires all over the place, stem to stern, and not interfere with the flight controls.

I was sitting in the front seat, under my camera, and intently watching the rear-view mirrors for the approaching chase planes. When they got big in the mirrors, I shouted "Smoke on!" into my headset. All three planes let loose with a smoke stream. And I clicked like crazy. That was another reason for the manual, low-power flash approach: 1/8th power meant I could burn frames, a necessary thing as the pilots let fly with smoke for short bursts. If TTL glitched and dumped at high power, it would have meant a few seconds of wasted smoke and sunset. Then another circle in the air, and a drive to a new picture run, coming out of the sun. Precious time burned.

I was selective at the high-tech camera menu buffet. Let's look for a second. On the "thank goodness we can do this now" side:

Shutter Priority mode. Good news. F-stop slides with the light level. Aperture Priority is the mirror of this mode and, conversely, allows shutter speeds to slide around with the variance of the light. Both modes have been with us for a long time now, and are still amongst the biggest, most powerful day-to-day tools we employ.

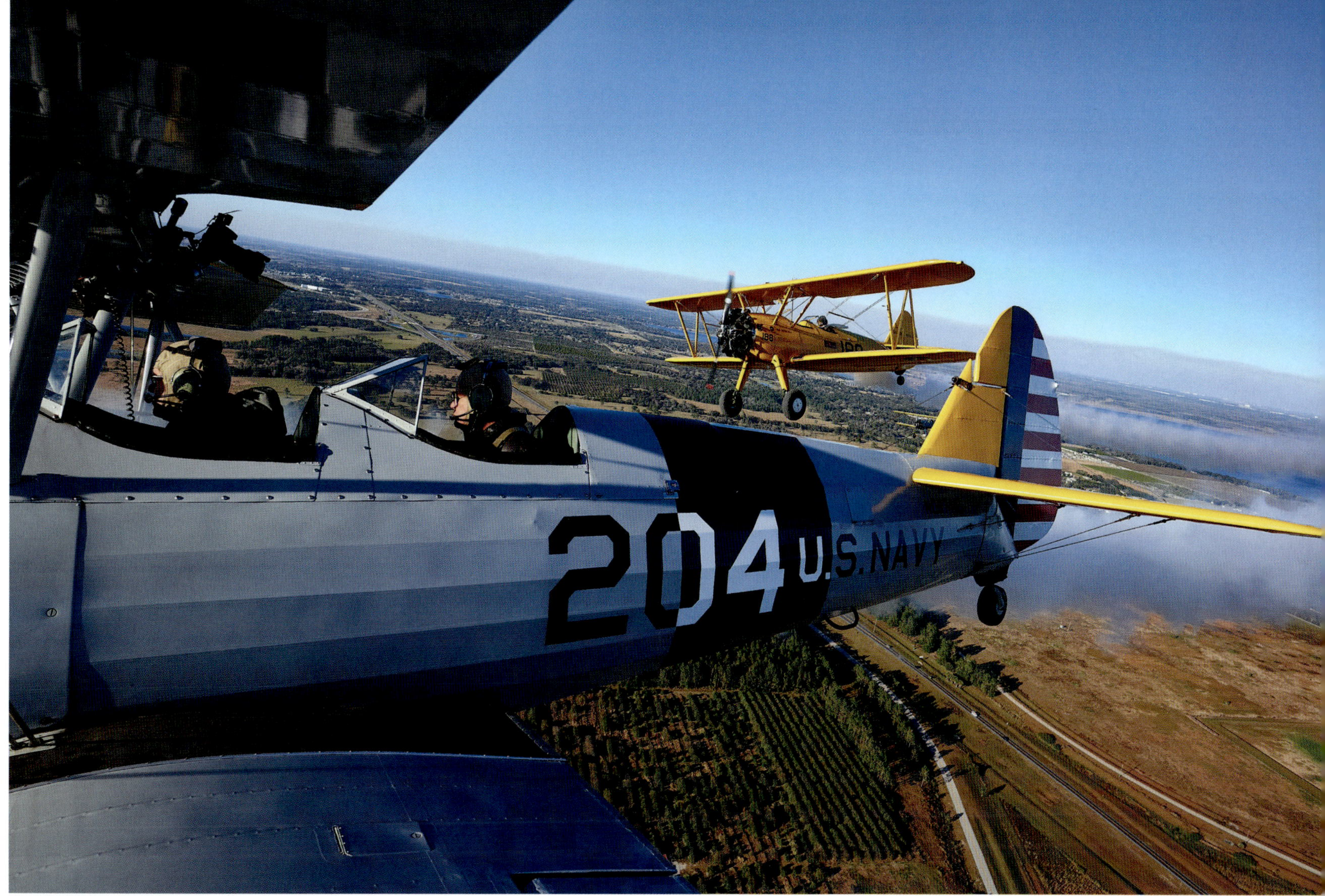

High Speed Sync. Fantastic. When I picked up a camera many years ago, the shutter speed/flash tango was done at a max of 1/60th of a second, which posed serious limitations on all manner of coverage. It was a happy day when we graduated to 1/250th. Now, we have leeway to 1/8000th, which makes for, as they say, a whole new ball game.

Updated, coated wide glass. I was shooting a current 14–24mm f/2.8 zoom up there. Super sharp, and it has all the fixings of modern glass tech. The old school equivalent in terms of field of view would have perhaps been the manual focus Nikkor 15mm f/3.5 lens. Looking directly at the sun, that puppy would have returned one big-ass flare. Modern lens tech rocks.

Card slots! Huge digital storage, fast processing, boffo buffer. Think about doing this and needing to land the plane after every 36 exposures.

Resolution! More and more pixels, more and more range, more and more file depth, enough to hold the sunset brightness and the dark leather jacket all at once.

On the "well, not this time" side:

TTL. Too big a guess factor. Know what your flash is doing. It will replicate the result, frame after frame.

Autofocus. Nope. Still has its distractions and foibles. Nobody's going anywhere, so frame it, focus it, lock it up.

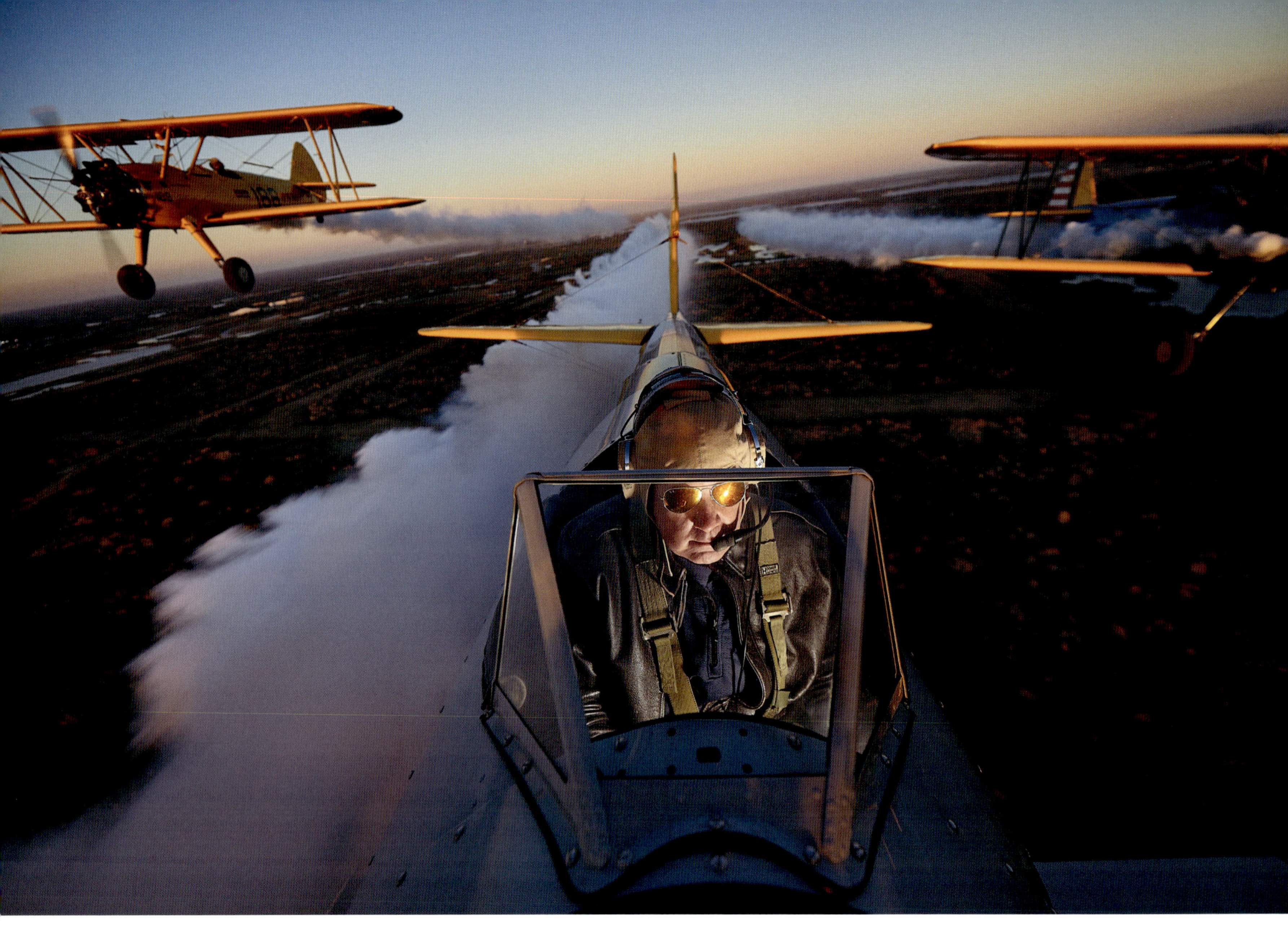

High ISO range. In this instance, lower is better, so I didn't access the new, obvious strengths of higher ranges of modern digital ISO. I had the sun, the sky, and the flash. No need to go to pixel heaven on this one.

I had, of course, complete control of the setup for these air views. Get there way early! I placed the flash, did testing and factoring. I figured predictable and unpredictable wobbles would occur in the air, with the planes moving fast and the sun dropping. The point is, though, I entered into that airspace as prepared as I could be.

One thing I was not prepared for, by the way, was the orange-tinted, mirror sunglasses our pilot, Rob Lock, sported when he angled himself into the cockpit of the Stearman. (He's 6'6" and a former pro basketball player.) They were totally Mad Max cool, and those glasses, coupled with the warm-gelled Speedlight? Bingo! The photo gods smiled on me right there.

The faces of the photo gods tend to be more stern at an Olympics. You have no control and have to do what the officials say and what your credential allows. You sit where you are told. You are on the sidelines with hundreds of other photogs, all looking for an edge, a slice of a second that distinguishes their picture from the thousands of others simultaneously shot. Hard to do, especially when we're all basically sitting in each other's laps and shooting the same glass. Here's where the range of new tech in the cameras really can help you wrap your arms around an event over which you have zero control.

For Usain Bolt's gold medal 200-meter run, I drifted, position-wise. The prime photog spots were even more jammed than usual, given the fact that Bolt was going for his third consecutive Olympic gold in the 200. I went down by the turn, where he and the other runners would come barreling through, sweeping past my lens. I also had a clear view of the start, which, frankly, no one cares about unless there's a slip or a disqualification. Clearly, it was not a prime position. I was pretty alone down there.

Here's where dynamic AF came into play and did far better than I ever could on manual focus. Take a look at this grid (below).

This camera technology is in the "where would I be without it?" category. Here we go:

Dynamic AF. I mentioned earlier how AF can take a wander when confronted with bright backlight, for instance. Here, in an absolutely essential, "never gonna get it again" moment, it performed flawlessly. The Olympics are geared to a light level that appeals to TV, and the athletes generally have colorful uniforms. The AF here, set to a small array of points I kept relentlessly on Bolt's chest, behaved like a pit bull. It clamped down on him and didn't let go.

ISO 2000. Crazy fast, with crazy good quality return.

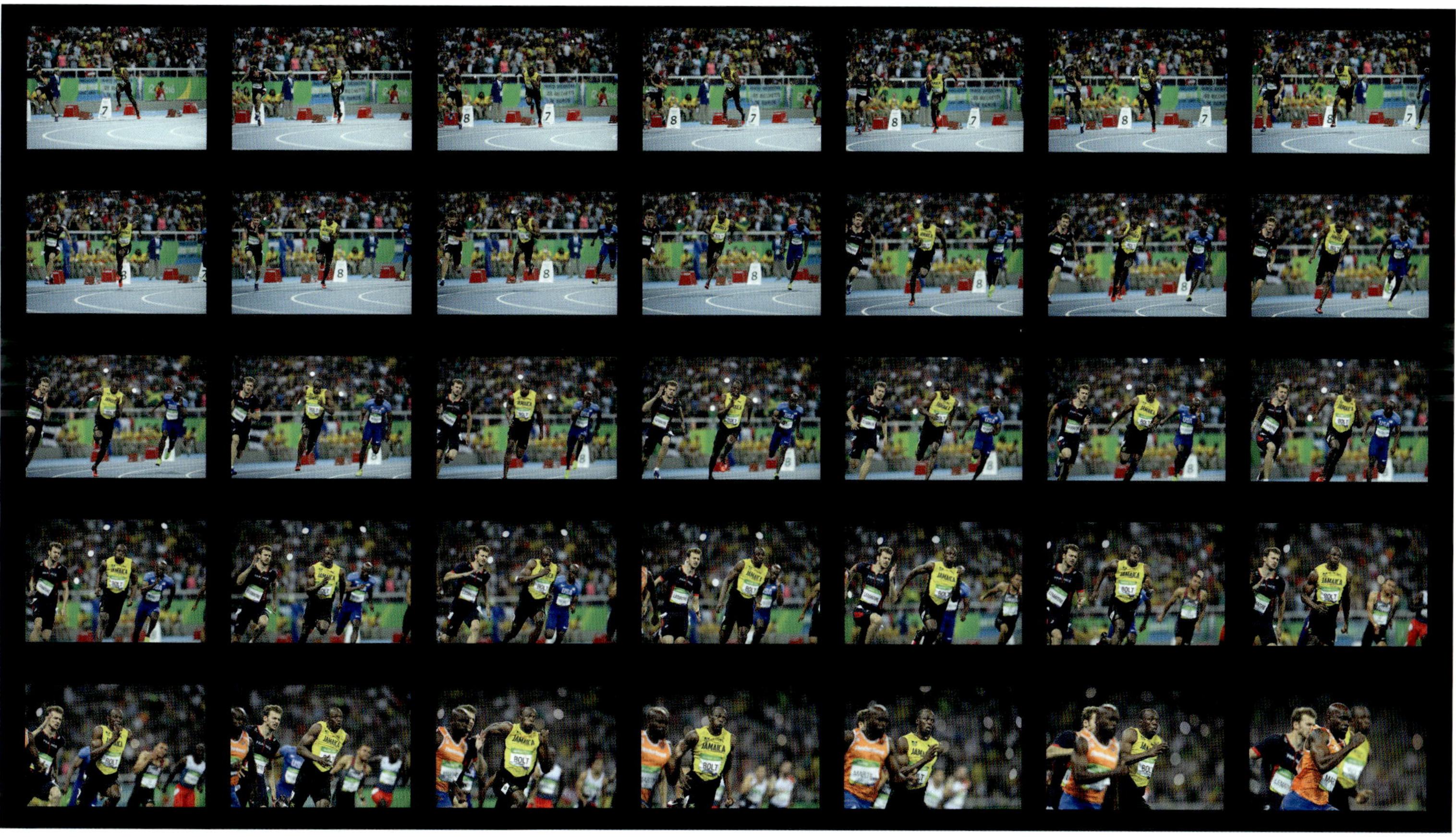

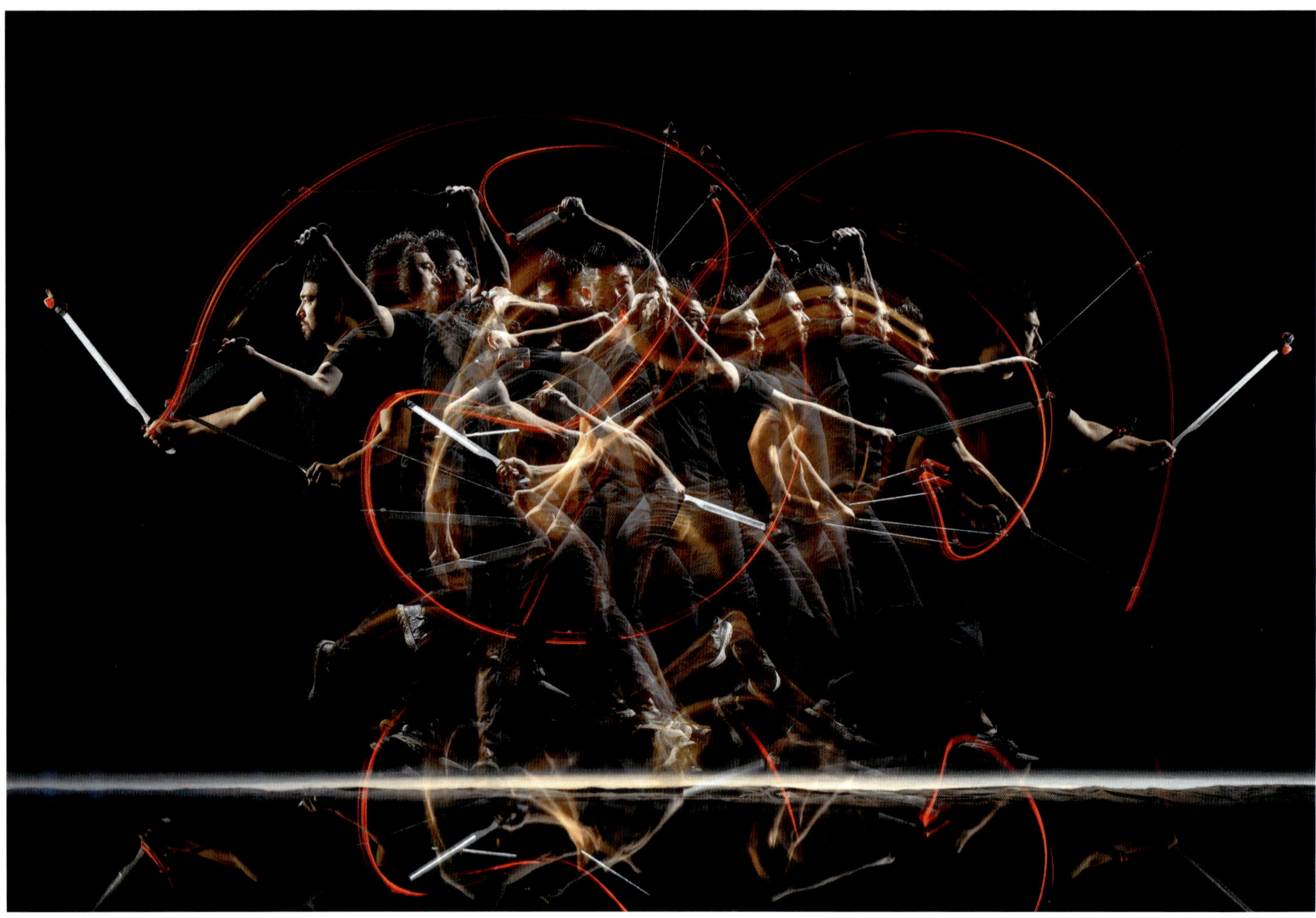

Program three exposures in the Multiple Exposure option. I put the Overlay option into Average mode, feeling that the exposures wouldn't be living at the extremes of exposure range, and could comfortably be merged without dealing with extreme highlights or shadows. I opted to retain the raw files as individual, independent exposures, giving me great leeway in post. I also opted for "overlay shooting," which allows me to see the exposure I just made as I'm about to place the next one. And I programmed "series." In other words, the Multiple Exposure command doesn't evaporate at the end of each multiple exposure, as was the case for many years. For every multiple you would create and finish, you'd then have go back into the menu and tee it up again. Now, you can mandate a multiple, and the camera stays there until you are done with the job. Fantastic. So much guesswork gone with this one menu item.

On to flash. There are three exposures, hence three zones of flash. Group A governs his start position (first exposure) and Group C governs his finish position (third exposure). (Dan Anderson, the martial artist in the photo, is amazingly skilled and fluid, and was able to adjust positions as I needed at camera.)

Start picture (right, top): Single flash, Group A. Radio controlled, from the camera. Lastolite Pro Strip softbox, with a fabric grid to control spread.

Finish picture (right, middle): Group C, same deal as Group A. And I never left the camera.

Cool. These are just tests, and I was able to craft these bookends of the threesome of exposures fairly easily.

Ahh, but the middle (right, bottom). Talk to us, Obi Wan.

The middle is Group B, also radio controlled at camera, programmed into "repeating flash mode" or, as is widely known, stroboscopic. Stroboscopic is useful when parsing out a panning subject, such as a dancer, ice skater, or martial artist, who is potentially moving in such a quick, intricate way that the eye has trouble keeping up. These repeated lightning strikes of flash freeze the spins, twirls, and strikes that are occurring, and depending on the frequency of those bolts of light, can create vastly interesting patterns that detail athletic movement. The moves are sliced and frozen by flash. When you do this, and the lights are going, you can feel you're not on a photo set but back in an '80s disco. I mean, if the '80s serve as a frame of reference for anyone out there. Moving on.

All programmed at the camera! When you opt for repeating flash mode, you are given three interrelated elements to program, all laid out very simply in the LCD: You program the power of the flash, the hertz (Hz), and the total number of times the flashes will fire. (Hertz refers to the number of times something occurs within one second.) They all have to play nicely together and relate well to the speed and movements of your subject.

Things to remember:

Power. You cannot dial a high level of power into the flashes and expect them to repeat furiously. For this, my flashes were set at 1/8th power. Keep your power rating low. Depending on the situation, this might require the use of multiple flashes to double up on the power front.

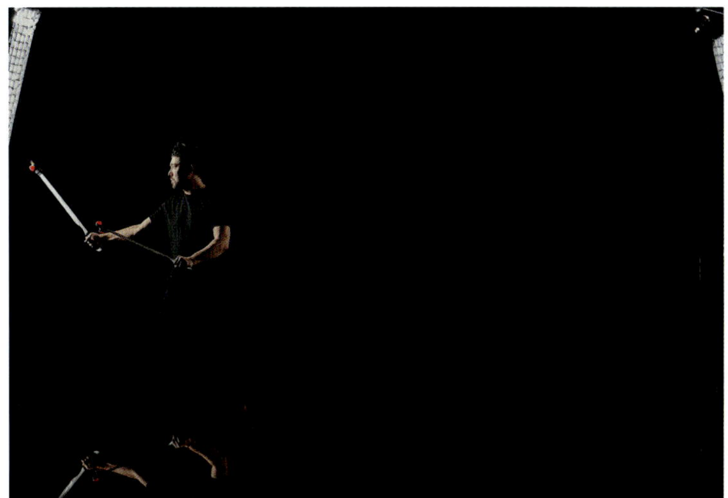

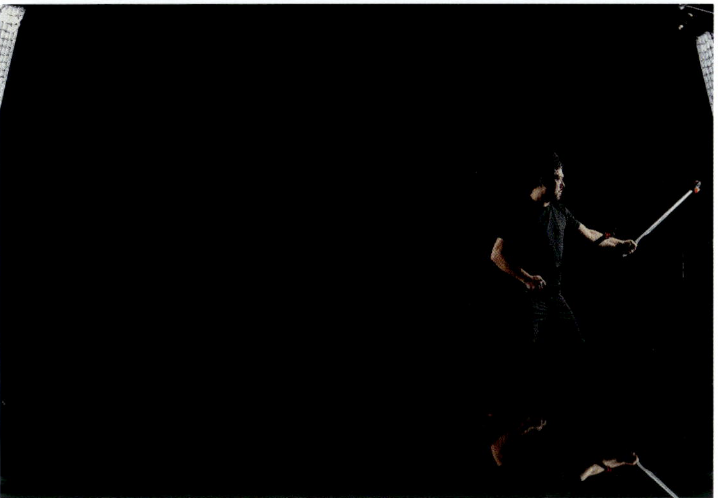

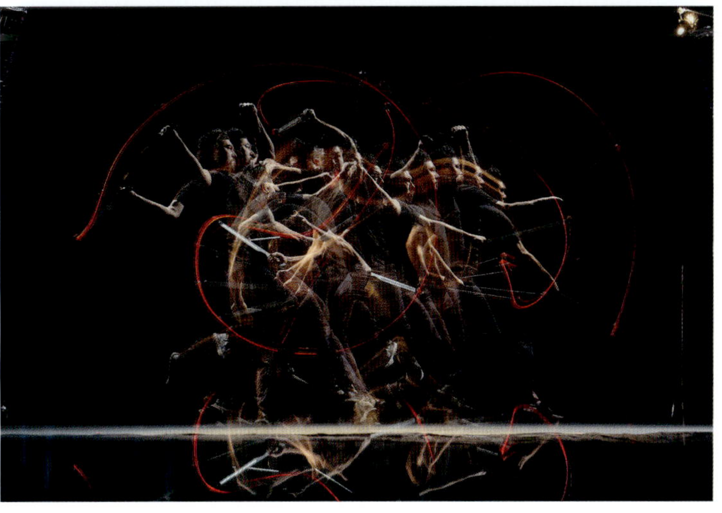

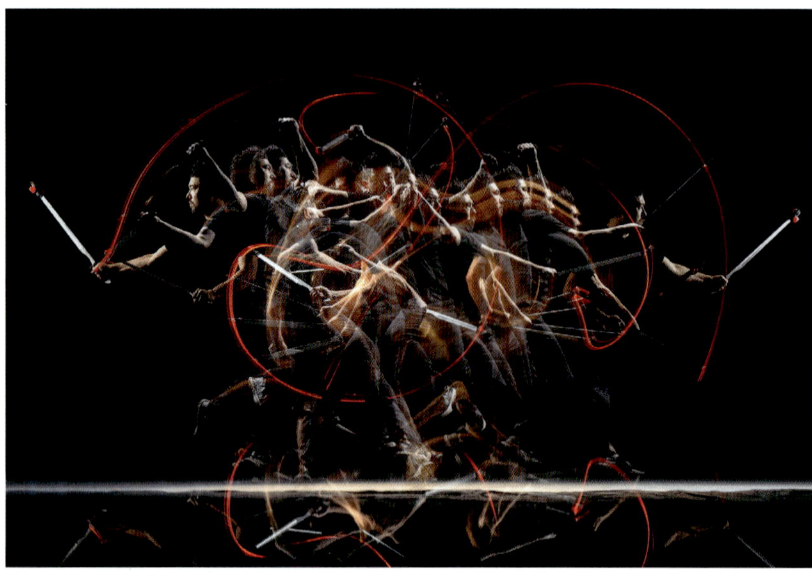

Hertz, and total flash pops. Hertz and the sum total of times the flashes will fire are related. Don't panic! Stick with it!

The classic way to do this is to take your Hertz, which you could program, for instance, to ten. Your choice. The frequency of the flash really determines the look of the photo.

Those flashes, programmed in the LCD to 10 Hertz, will thus fire 10 times in one second, producing the disco effect I alluded to earlier. Given that rating, to keep the math simple, you could program your total number of flashes to be twenty. Your Hz divided into your overall total number of flashes gives you your shutter speed: 10 Hertz divided into 20 times gives you a shutter speed of two seconds. Simple!

> *You don't want to bring someone phenomenally skilled onto the set and then constrain them.*

Well, not really. You can't program an athlete like Dan to go from start point to finish point in exactly two seconds. Just not going to happen. You have to relinquish control to them and accommodate the speed of their movements. They are the star of the show. All this tech stands in service to their excellence, not the other way around. You don't want to bring someone phenomenally skilled onto the set and then constrain them.

Enter shutter speed. For the first and third exposures, using one pop of a flash on a static subject, I simply programmed in a reasonable flash shutter speed.

But for the stroboscopic adventure, i.e., the second exposure, I shifted the shutter speed all the way to Bulb. In other words, the shutter stays open as long as I trigger that button. I have complete control, which I then use to give the athlete leeway to do their thing, at their pace. I watch them, and when they are done, I simply release the shutter. Done.

They then hold that final position, and at camera I reprogram to Group C, the ending single pop of flash. And we are done.

But all the techno-wizardry the camera brings to bear will not work without your proper preparation and pre-visualization. Without the right conditions on location, all the raging technical ability the camera offers will end up being like bringing a bucket of water to a four-alarm fire. To wit, a list:

Complete control of the environment. In other words, darkness. The only thing the camera sees is what you light. You shoot into a straight-up deep black background. No competing elements back there to catch light and interrupt the beautifully orchestrated motions of the athlete.

Bike lights. With blades or other athletic implements, I often attach bike lights. They give you the tracer lines of light that can add visual panache to the photo. Gaffer tape them, glue them, and clip them to feet, sticks, you name it. I once kept taping bike lights to a hammer to show an Olympic hammer thrower's spinning motion (opposite). She spun and let it fly. I went through a lot of bike lights that night.

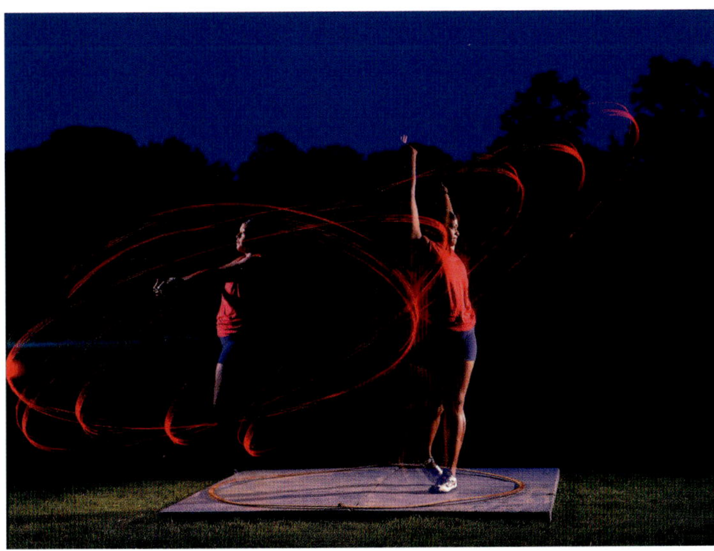

Darkness allows for lengthy shutter speeds, all the way down to Bulb. When you open a camera shutter in a completely dark room, what happens? Nothing. Blackness reigns. You have control. Multiple exposures, long shutter speeds, and stroboscopic are all a trip to the dark side.

The Multiple Exposure mode, along with the aforementioned darkness, gives you a chance to regroup in between the three exposures, and reprogram at camera to shift the flash modes and shutter speeds. First and third exposures are anywhere from 1/60th to 1/250th of a second. (It's not that crucial a choice, because your subject is holding steady, and you both are in a *dark room*.) The second exposure is done on Bulb, varying from, say, 1.5 to 2.5 seconds. (Again, it's not a huge concern, because you and your subject are in a *dark room*.) F-stop remains the same for all three scenarios. For the martial artist image, it was f/6.3.

When each of the three exposures is complete, the shutter closes and literally nothing happens. You are at the camera, reprogramming it for the next exposure. Calmly, quickly, but without a sense of panic because you are not fighting adverse elements that are constraining your options. You have complete control. Did I mention you are in a *dark room*? Moreover, your shutter is closed. The camera is mute.

Auto focus. I made adjustments in AF as well, in between the three exposures. For the bookends, i.e., the static poses, I went with AF-C (Autofocus Continuous), small group, and dropped it directly on Dan. No worries. Standard operating procedure. There are those who might ask, "Why not AF-S and single point? He's not moving." Fair enough. But I chose the dynamic, continuous focus and a small group of activation points because I could not move the camera. It was fixed. He was about to pursue an activity that I had measured, observed, and gauged at camera. And once I've done that work, the machinery remains locked. No more camera movement.

The small group covers an area of his body where there are break points in the contrast levels. He is wearing black and standing on black, so my cursors embrace his face, a highlighted shoulder, a piece of his arm. The camera, set at f/6.3, grabbed this information and was infallibly sharp. And yes, I could have dropped a single AF-S cursor on his face, but that would have required pushing that point and finding the face. With the camera fixed, I might not get that point to be precisely where I would want it. In the interests of moving quickly, the small group AF worked quite well.

But the second exposure, where he is transiting and swinging blades, and flashes are going—here, manual focus is advisable. From his starting point to his finish line, I gave him a strip of brightly colored gaffer tape to follow and keep centered on. I know he's sharp at his starting pose, so I simply switch off AF. Done. For the third exposure, relocate the cursors, turn AF back on. Easy. Buttons at the camera. A beautiful thing.

The reflections. I take no credit here. It's simply a swiped idea from the preeminent photographer Gregory Heisler. Greg would try to liven an otherwise dead foreground in situations like this and insert a small mirror just under his lens, at camera. He would then swing and tilt that mirror until partial reflections occurred. That's what's happening here at the bottom of the frame. A 12" x 12" mirror is levered just under my 70–200mm. Fun to play with. No formula, all situational. Angle it, test it, mess around until you like what it's doing. Or don't.

So, how about everyone grab a scotch, neat, or a toke, or a luxuriant sip of red wine, and take a look at something simpler? No stroboscopic, no third exposure, no bike lights, no mirrors. Just the simple one-two punch of a double exposure, done in camera. No muss, no fuss, no swinging blades or fancy footwork. Just a senior athlete, doing a lift, looking into one light, and then marginally shifting position and looking into another.

The Overlay command in the Multiple Exposure menu option lets you view your first exposure, while you figure out where to place your second. It's crazy simple. This was done on a Nikon Z 7II with a 70–200mm lens for both images. 83mm for the first one, the exercise pic; 195mm for the second, the profile portrait. A two-exposure multiple. Speedlights commanded at camera.

Experiments await your kind attention, dear reader. There's magic and power inside that little box with the lens on it. But remember, all that alchemy lies dumb and dormant, awaiting your commands. You must pull the sword from the stone.

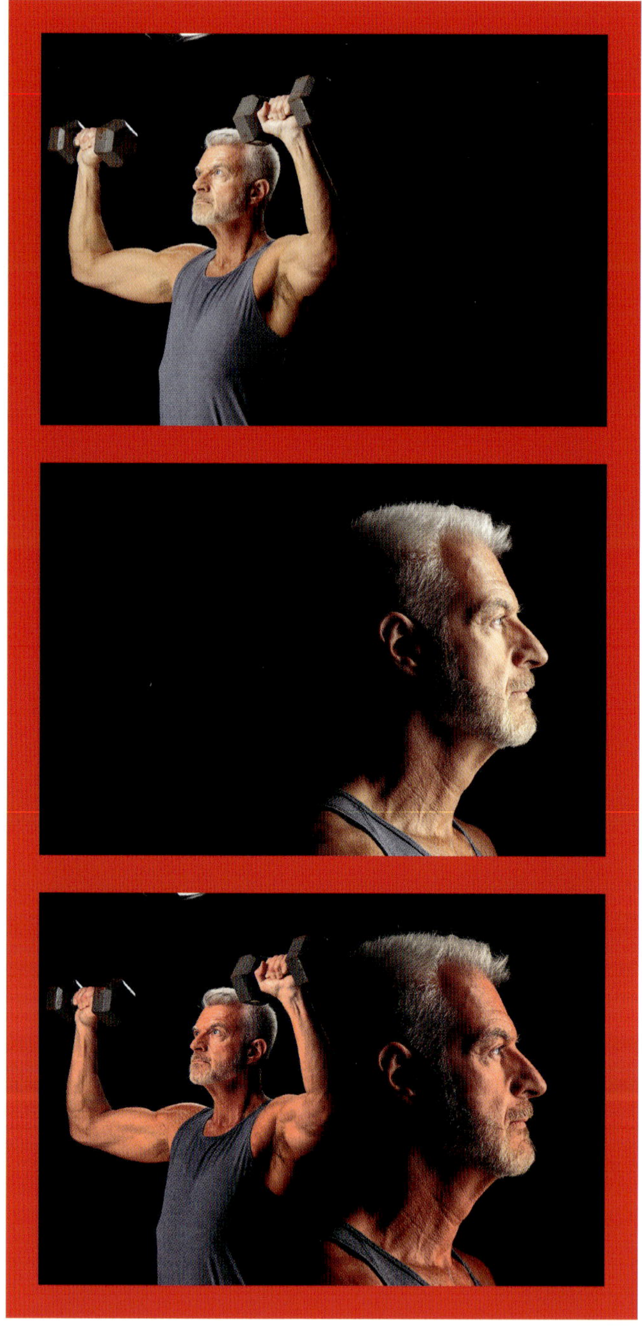

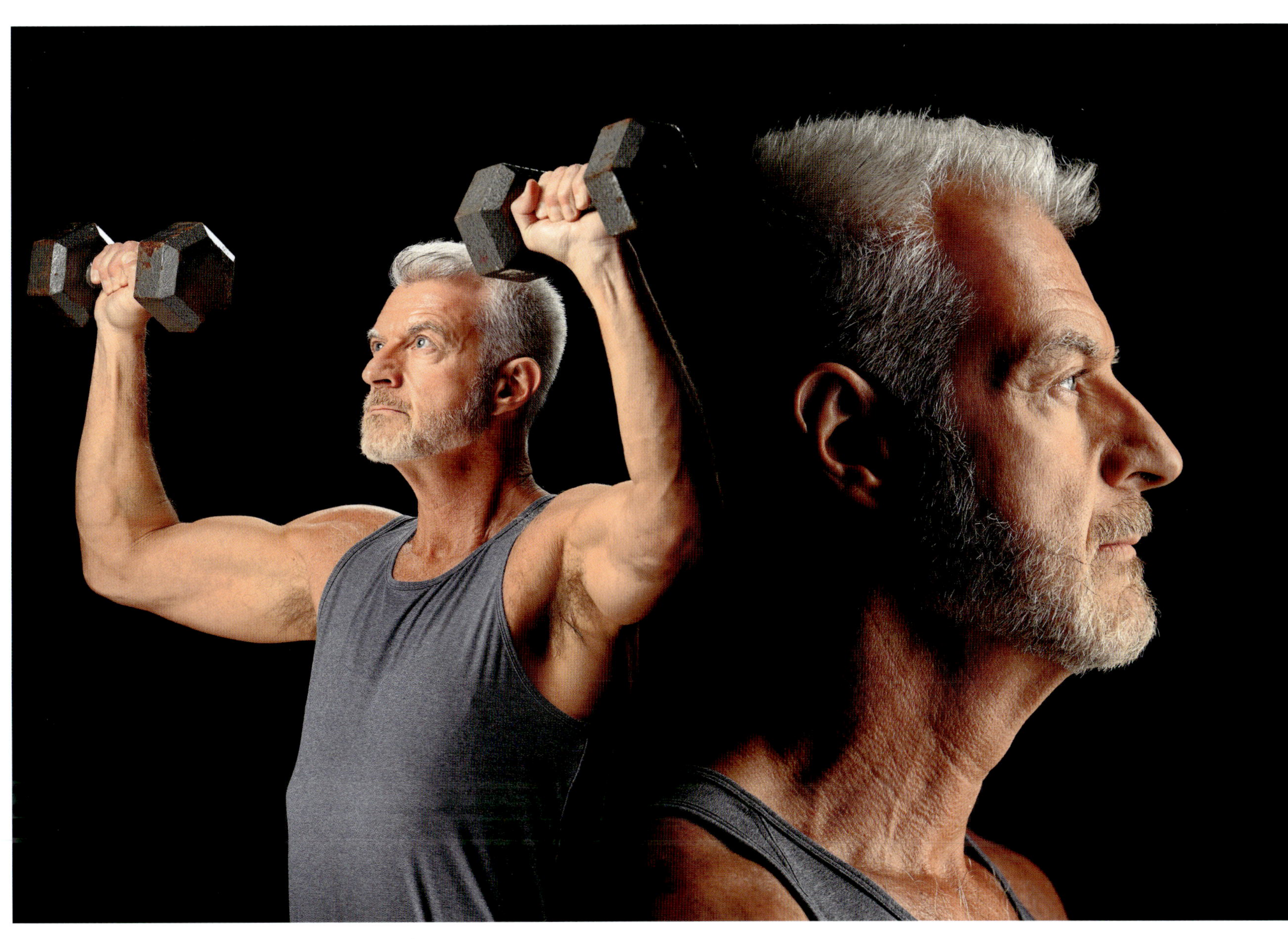

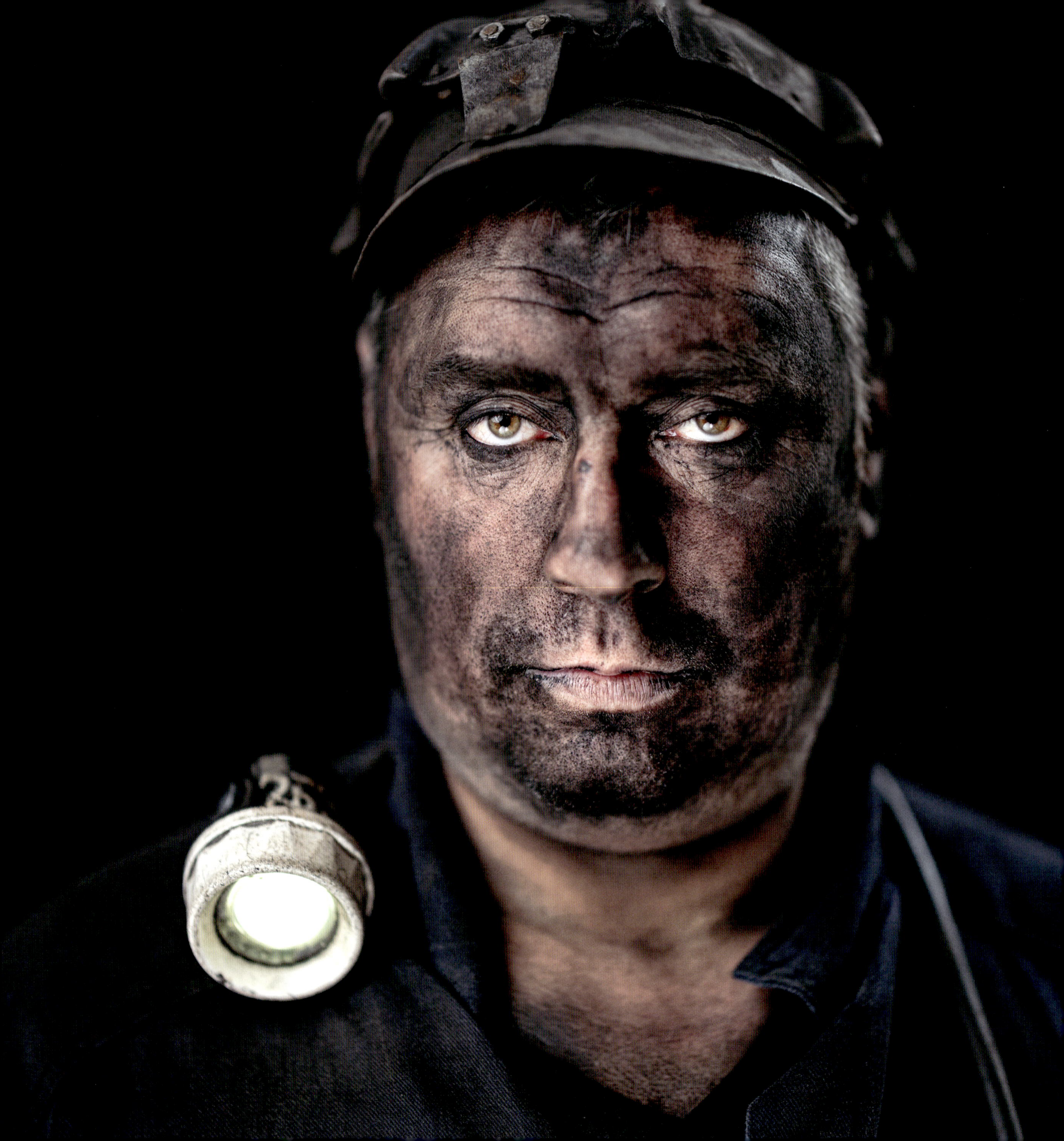

In Pursuit of Darkness

You might not think it's hard, really, to find an environment where it's inherently, resolutely dark, but also interesting. A coal mine fits the bill. And you wouldn't think it all that difficult to find a mine. I mean, it's not like they move around or anything. They're holes in the ground. Don't have to worry about the weather or the light; it's always the same, 7,500 feet under the earth's surface.

The trick is getting down into a coal mine.

Given the tenor of our times, I knew access to a coal mine wouldn't be all that easy, but I had a lucky break and got introduced to a small private mine in southeastern Kentucky. I got vouched for, which you need in coal country, especially when you're from New York. Made portraits of the miners, didn't ask for releases or paperwork. Just a handshake. Made sure all the miners got beautiful prints. I stayed in touch a little bit, from afar, keeping a relationship going for about two years, always with the intent of returning. It's what we do as photographers.

Treat people well. Make sure when they remember your visit, it expresses as a positive thought and not "that asshole from New York with a camera." Then, maybe, you just might be invited back.

The prompt to return came from the Nikon Corporation. They had just developed an ultra-fast lens, the 58mm NOCT, which pretty much breaks the f-stop scale, weighing in at f/0.95. Faster than f/1.0. An engineering feat. A gorgeous set of elements. King of Mount Bokeh. I'll leave the question of needing f/0.95 for the reader to decide. I mean, I get it. It's an accomplishment. Bragging rights for a historic camera brand. Engineers in heat, looking at an alluringly pornographic set of algorithmic possibilities, glowing on the screen like the golden doohickey Indiana Jones swipes at the beginning of *Raiders of the Lost Ark*. You don't need it. It's really not necessary. It would be safer to leave right now. "No one who has gone in there has come out alive!"

But you want it, and f/0.95 demands darkness. I called the mine.

It was blasting away at full production, running three shifts, and I got a date to return. Told the client. I was gearing up to go, and … the mine closed. Shut down. No explanation. Everybody tight-lipped. I had a deadline, and expectations I had created. Foolishly, I even had pictures in my head, already made on the fairy pixels of my imagination. Always a bad idea, kind of like counting on the return from your ill-advised investment in bull semen futures.

To say I was crushed would be to overstate the case. How do you further crush a can that's been laying on the picture highway for 40 years?

One overlooked component of assignment photography goes beyond the knowledge of lighting or camera work and can be described as simple, bullheaded tenacity. I had a mandate to bring the NOCT lens under the earth, and I was determined to do it. No need to call the big corporate mines. Last thing they want around is a photographer. The wildcat mines are dangerous, and illegal, so they don't return your calls. The coal mining industry is under duress and facing extinction. The only way to get this job done, really, at that point, was to leave the United States.

You can get things done abroad that are simply no longer possible here, given the welter of restrictions, insurance policies, the necessity of full-blown releases and permissions from literally everyone in the town, and so forth. Working editorially for a publication, you still can turn the corner, but working this as a commercial job, with money changing hands, intent to promote a product, "in perpetuity" usage clauses, reproduction rights clearances for all known and yet to be discovered solar systems … the easier and ultimately cheaper thing to do is to buy a plane ticket to someplace a little out of the way.

Like Transylvania.

The Jiu Valley in Romania was a legendary coal production area, one of the main economic engines of the entire country. Faded now, Lupeni, at one time a thriving metropolis framed by smokestacks belching black soot into the sky, still has one open mine. It once employed 2,000 men. Now: 160. They said I could come. I packed the NOCT and headed for this gray Transylvanian town.

I have worked in many formerly Communist countries, and the first meetings at Lupeni were an immediate echo back to those times. Blank, faceless buildings. Paneled rooms with huge tables and antiquated phones, where party officials once chain-smoked and demanded higher yields from the blackness of the deep earth. Through the windows of these administrative rooms, in plain view was broken, rusted equipment and savaged earth. Even now, traditions persist, and my arrival prompted a gathering of officials. I smiled and nodded while my fate was determined. A very familiar routine for a photographer: to stand and appear positive, pleasant, and sane while you don't understand a single word being said.

Then, progress. A uniformed lady came in and took my blood pressure. To even get close to the depths of this mine, they want to know your heart is solid and pumping. She nodded and smiled at me. My blood pressure was evidently just fine to go down into one of the most dangerous places I could ever go.

I stripped off my own clothes and suited up, using clothes provided for me from the company washing machines. Crusty and coarse, layer upon layer. Ill-fitting boots. Dented, ancient helmet, which I was ultimately very thankful for, given the uneven, rough-hewn, blasted-rock ceilings I was about to encounter. Headlamp hooked up. Ready.

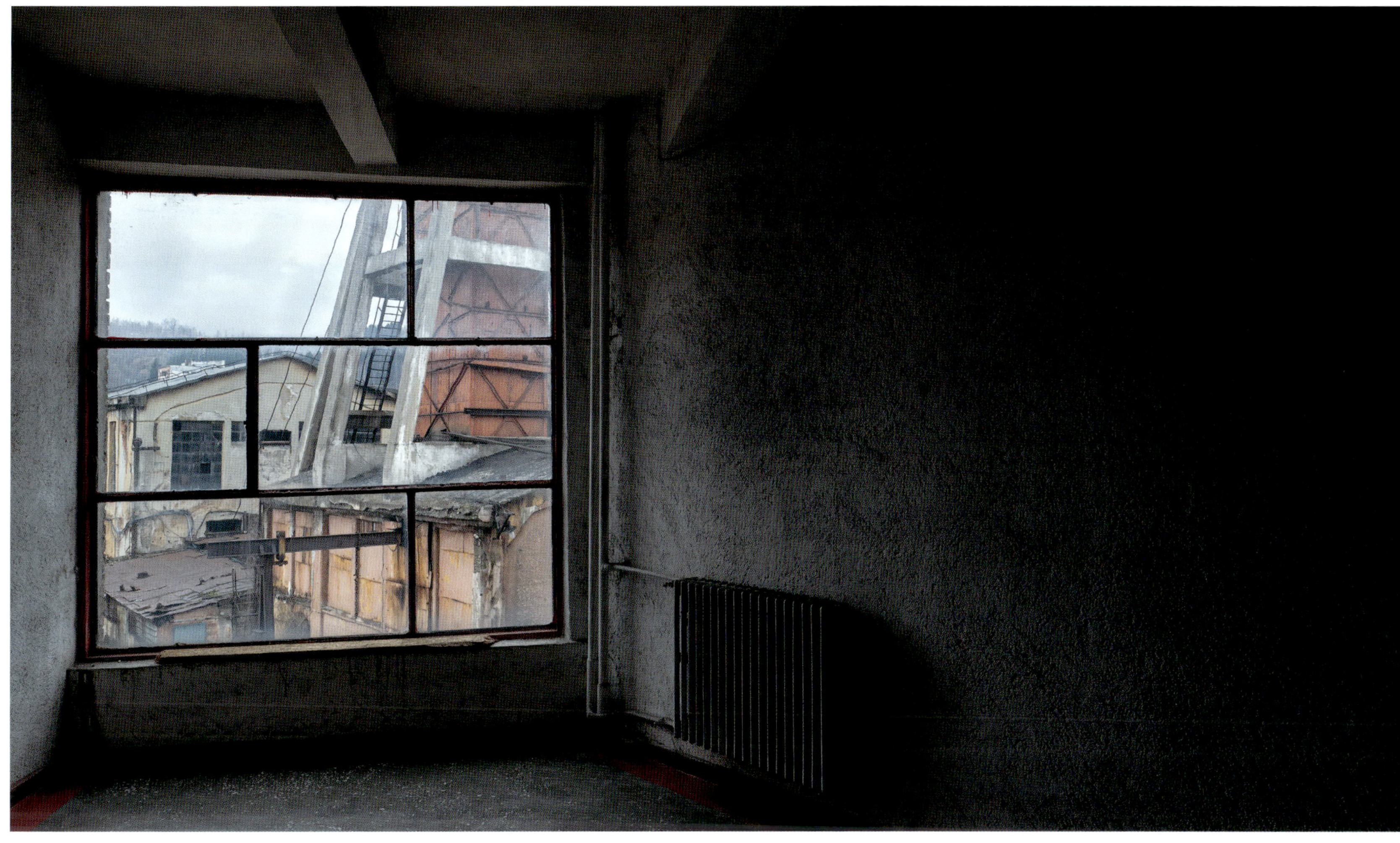

Then, shoulder the gear and walk to where there was no light.

The elevator that brought me down was a rusted, narrow box of iron, not unlike four or five coffins stacked upon one another. Two hundred fifty meters down in a contraption that rumbled and shook. You had the sense of the blackness closing over you, like a night dive in the ocean. I've read too many comics, so I had darkly fanciful notions of the creature in the depths, pulling the levers on this cable-driven sarcophagus.

You know how, when you get into an elevator in your average office building, and right there, next to the Otis brand sign, there's an elevator inspector's schedule, with the latest inspection date and signoff? I didn't see one of those.

(By the way, I used to amuse myself in NYC elevators by checking those inspection cards to look for my namesake, Joseph McNally, an elevator inspector who seemed positively ubiquitous. As a lark, I would point out to fellow passengers that we

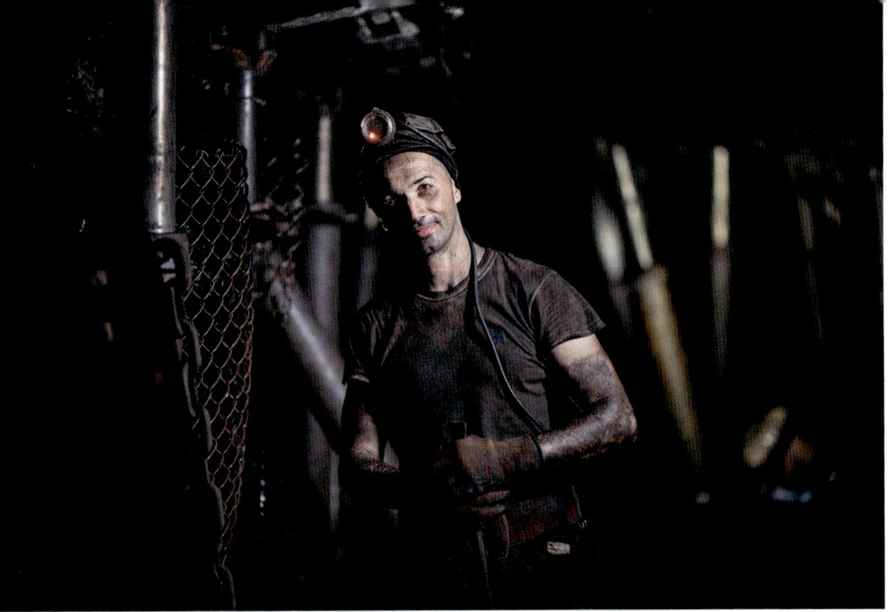

were safe, as my uncle [wink, wink] had checked out the elevator we were riding. I used to think about reaching out to him, wondering if indeed there were family connections. He was indicted in 1997 on federal bribery charges for taking payments to speed up, falsify, or overlook infractions. The indictments swept up just about half of the Big Apple's elevator inspectors, who referred to the payments as "birthday" or "Christmas" presents. During the investigation, one contractor was quoted as saying to one of the inspectors—not Uncle Joe—"You got so many birthdays, you must be 150 years old!")

After the descent, a walk through a leaking tunnel, muck up to your shins, broken rails and hopper cars strewn about, makeshift supports of splintered wood. Two kilometers straight into the heart of the mountain. Sometimes the passage was broad, but often it was cramped and required you to nearly double over while scuffling forward. It took two hours to reach the men. With every step, I pushed my fear back down my throat.

But there, at the rock face, improbably, there were smiles and banter. Exhausted and muddy, I had to relax and revel once again at the resilience of the human spirit. And understand how easy this day was for me. I was just a tourist. These men work in the blackness every day. Three shifts, 24 hours, the digging never stops. No mechanized gear except a couple of drills. Pickaxes, shovels, and strong backs constitute the earth-moving machinery. Yet there was laughter and joking. I shook my head. To paraphrase an old, famous movie poster slogan—a mile under the ground no one can hear you laugh. And, amid the laughs, quiet courage.

I set up a tripod, planted the four-pound NOCT and a Z mirrorless camera. No light down there, just the miner's lamps. I brought an LED panel, and Bogdan, a wonderful Romanian photog who elected to help me, held it aloft. The miners were happy for the break, and I can only imagine the commentary to each other as they posed in turn. The folks who accompanied me down there were literally my VALs (voice activated light stands), and I positioned them where their headlamps could do me some good.

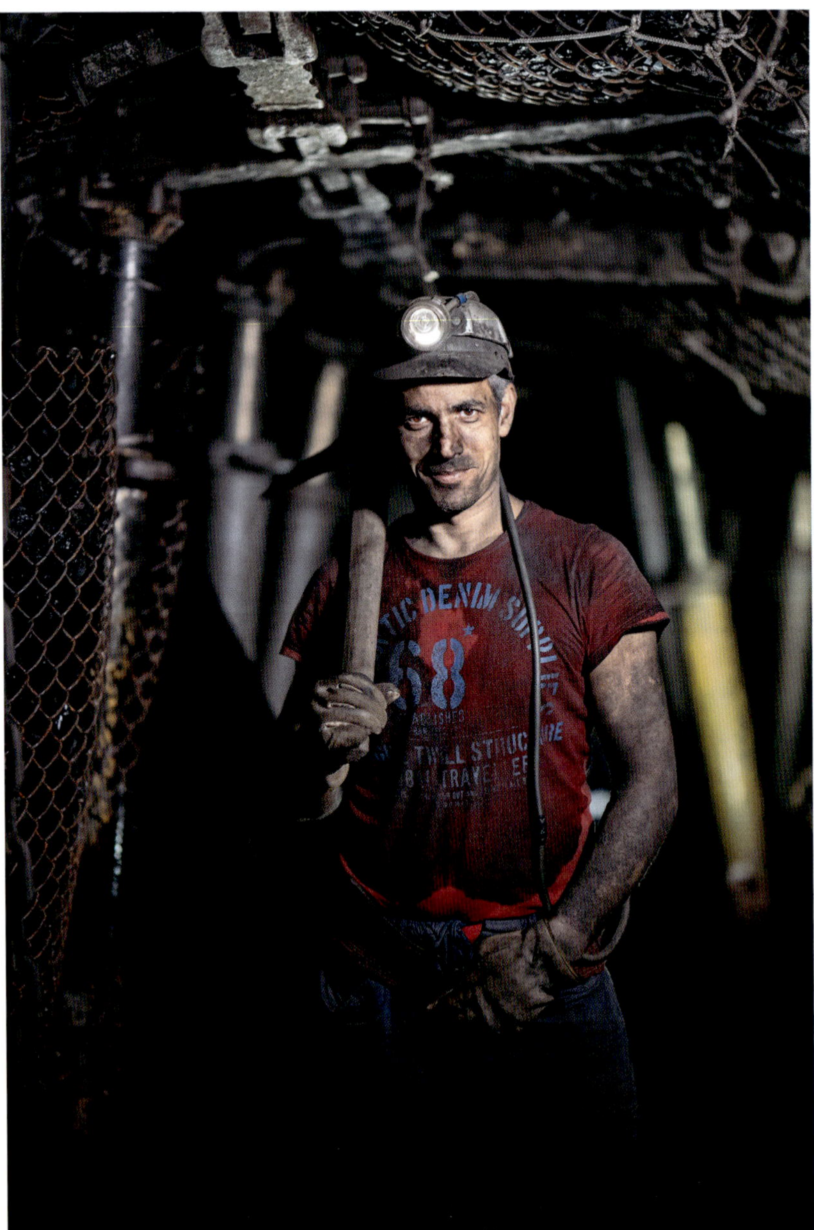

Exhausted and muddy, I had to relax and revel once again at the resilience of the human spirit.

I worked until nearly the end of the shift, and then, drenched in sweat and mud, headed back to the elevator. Two hours once again, back through the muck-laden tunnel. Stumbling—limping, really—on the way back, we were easily overtaken by the miners as their shift broke. They strode with speed and ease through the blasted ruins. Underground gazelles, seemingly more nimble with every step closer to the surface. They were done and heading eagerly back to the light. It's what they do. They trade their daylight hours, their health, and sometimes their lives to bring home a salary that is twice the local level back to their families. And, after 20 years in the mine, a guaranteed pension.

The next day, I set up a studio in the headlamp room, and the shifts came by for their portraits. Knowing what they had just come back from, I was determined at camera to make pictures that honored them, to somehow acknowledge the choice they had no choice but to make, to work in the all-consuming

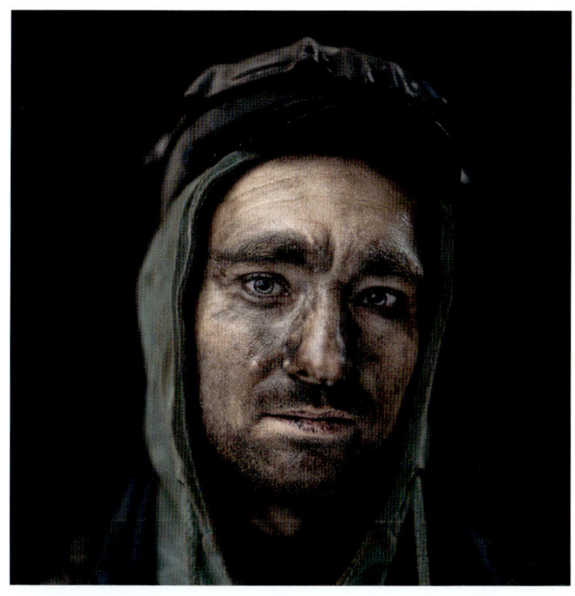

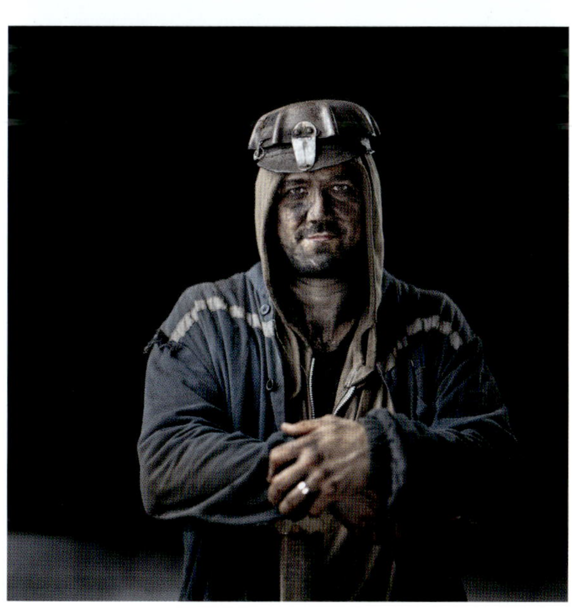

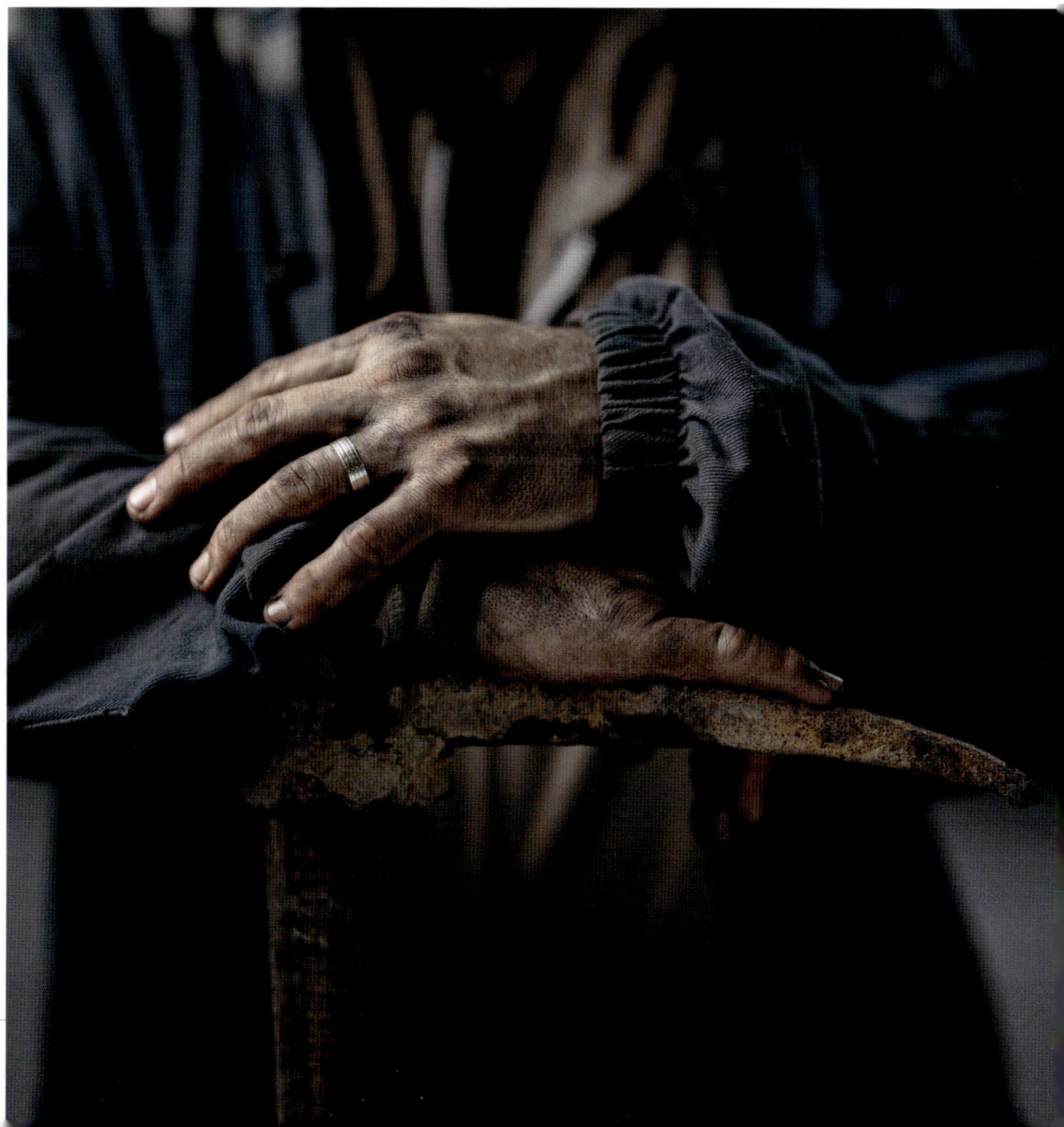

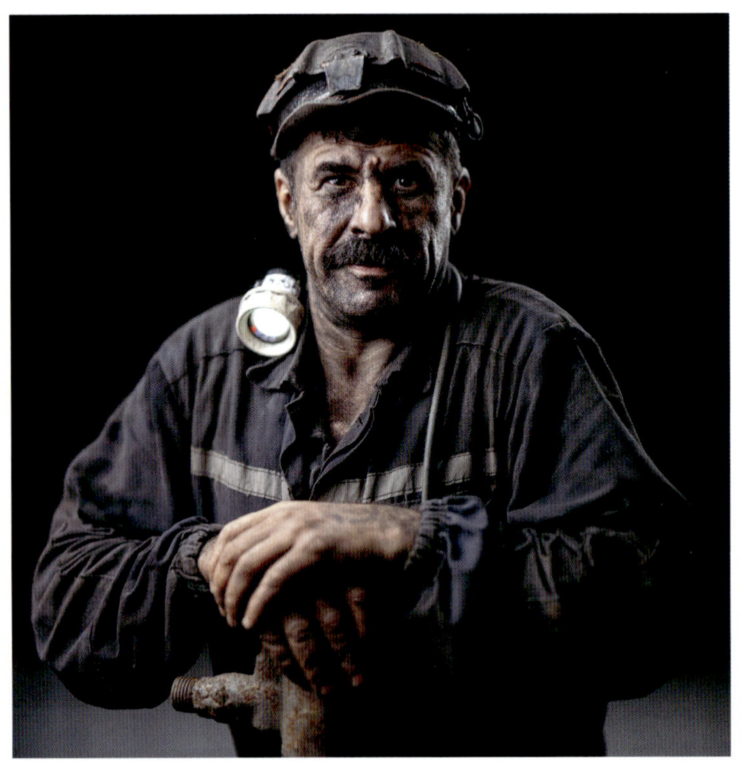
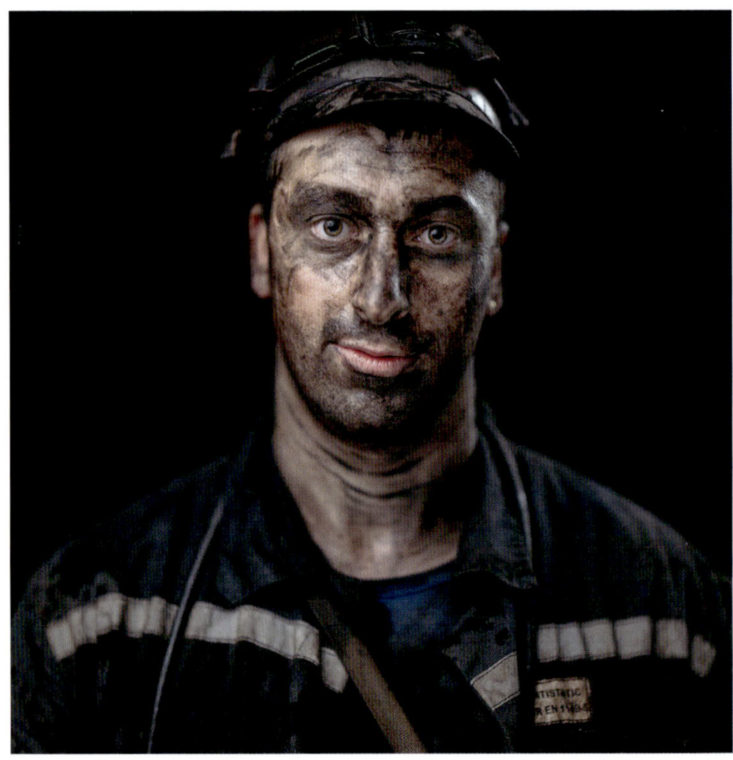
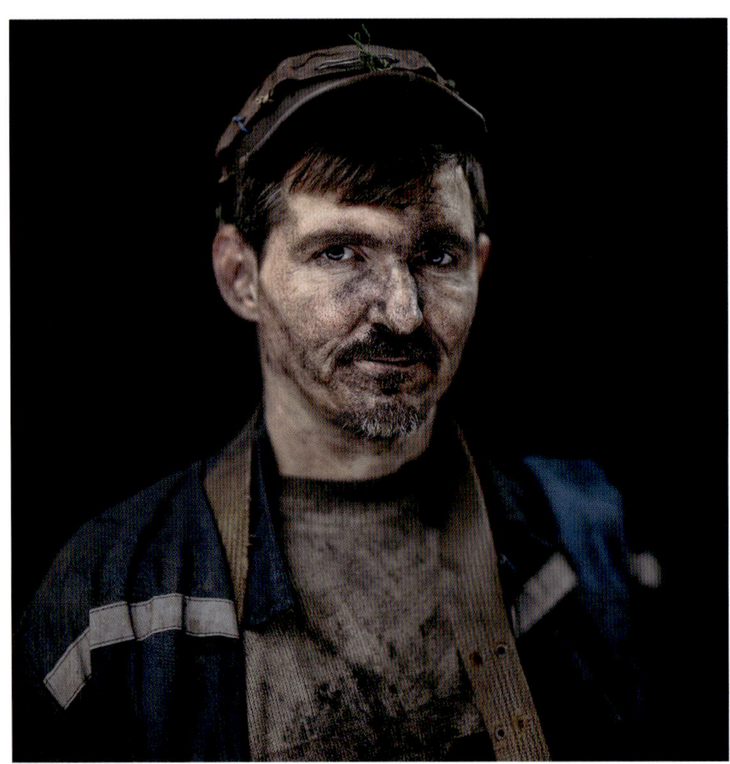
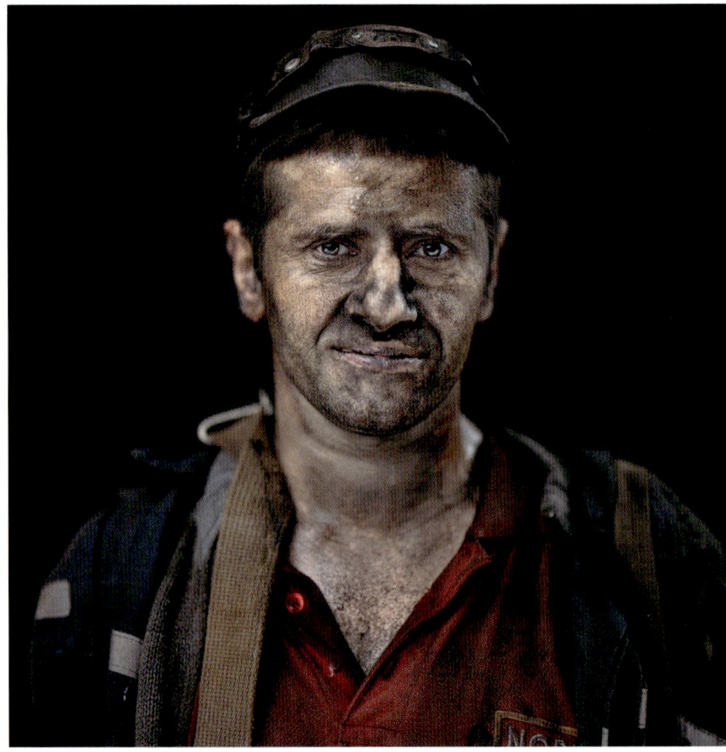

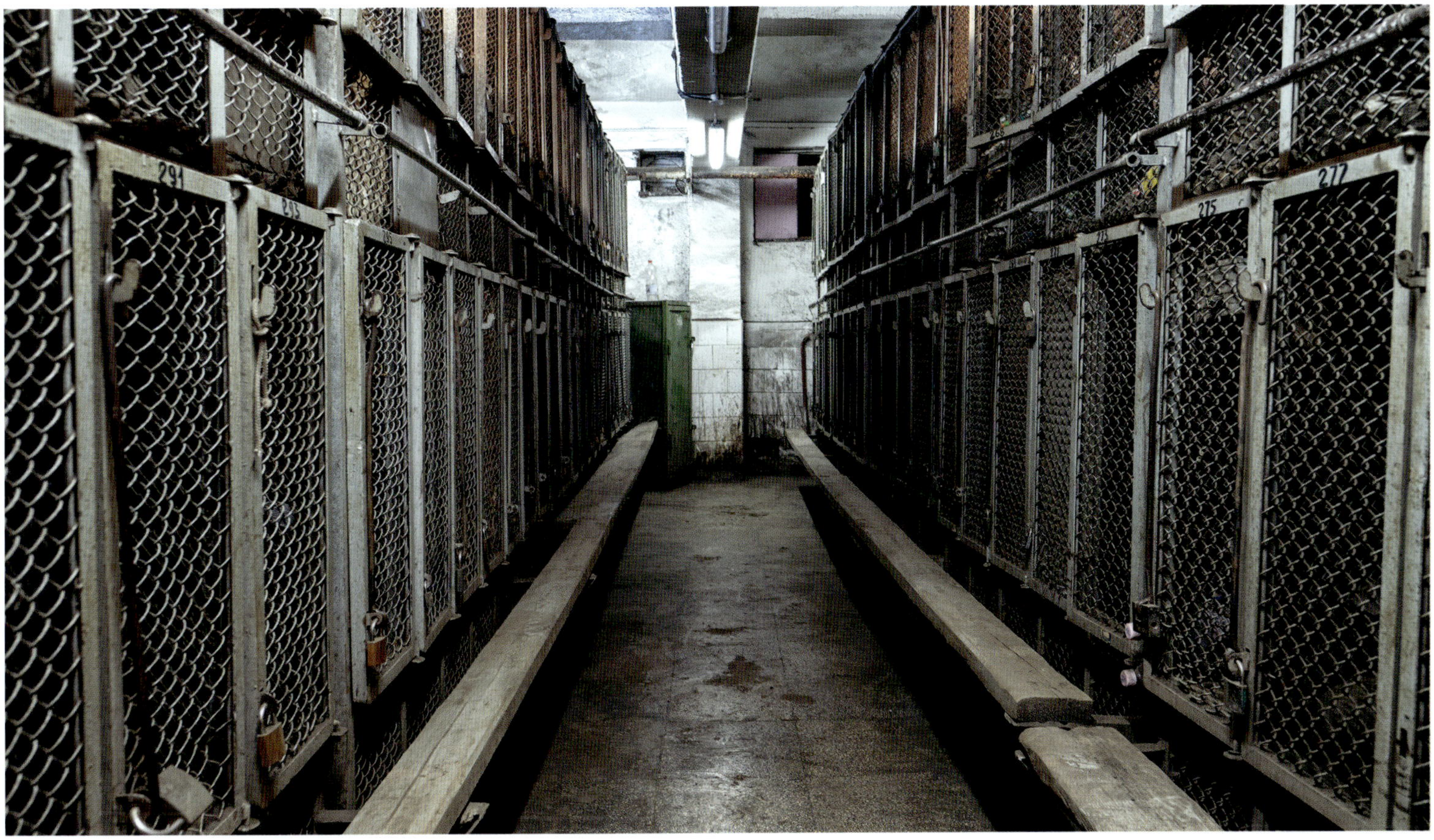

darkness. I wanted to show simple human determination, and how this endeavor of carving coal out of deep rock had also carved itself into their faces and bodies, surely as a quill and ink would have scratched out words on parchment.

Later, as I photographed the battered symmetrical rows of metal lockers in their changing room, the supervisor saw the image on my LCD. He tapped me on the shoulder and gestured toward the lines of locked cabinets. "Like a jail, yes?"

The miners have a tradition. When the shifts trade places, the outgoing men shake the hands of the incoming workers. They say, simply, "Noroc bun," to each other. It means *good luck*.

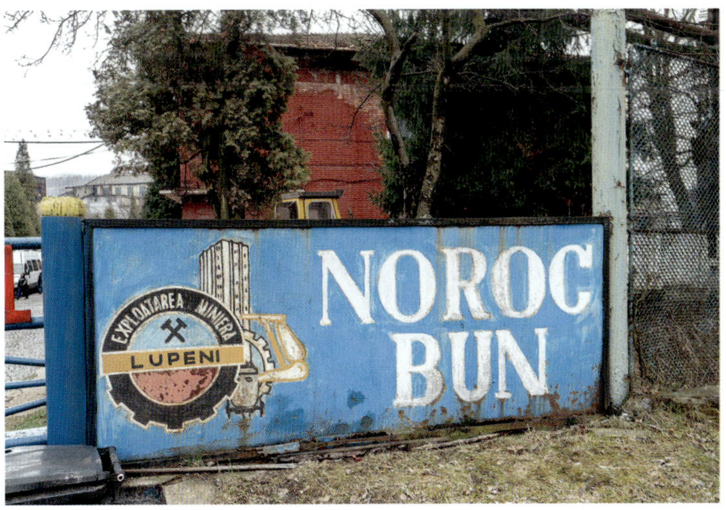

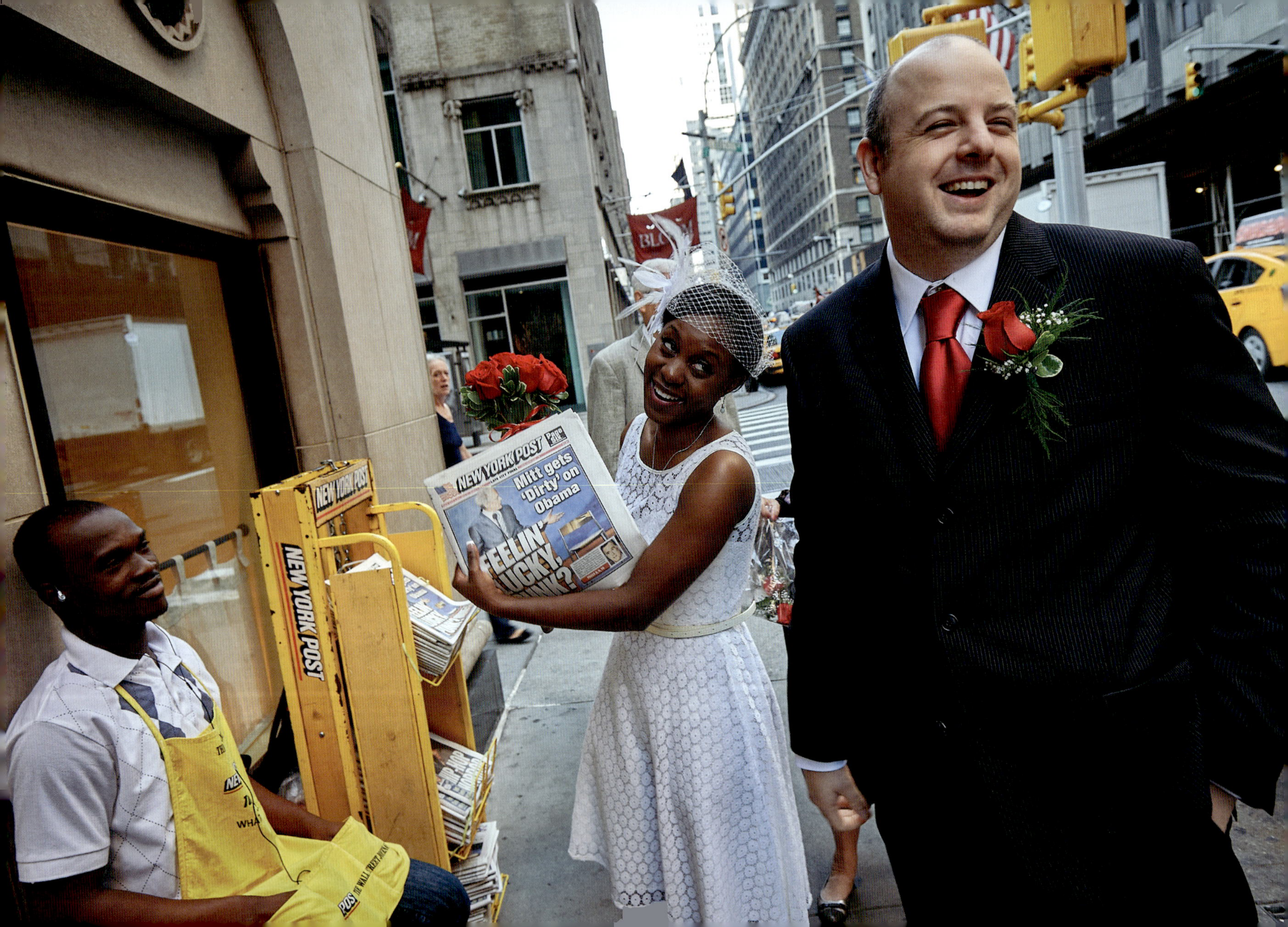

NEW YORK POST
Page Six
Mitt gets 'Dirty' on Obama
FEELIN' LUCKY, PUNK?

On Weddings

I've always loved covering weddings, editorially. Notice I didn't say "shooting weddings," or "being a wedding photographer," which is something I'm most assuredly not. But the emotional adventure of a wedding is always, to me, a great opportunity for picture making. The joy is real, and the pictures flow as easily as the wine.

Such was the case for the vows of my dear friends Gene and Olivia. The emotions were so effortlessly ebullient, the photos made themselves. Their love was powerful, and a joy to witness. They jumped on the NYC subway, went to City Hall, and got hitched. I shot it alone, a camera bag job. The assignment equivalent of breathing sea air with sand between my toes.

I have tremendous respect for wedding photographers. They work unbelievably hard, so much so, in my opinion, there's almost no amount of money that can be charged that is truly

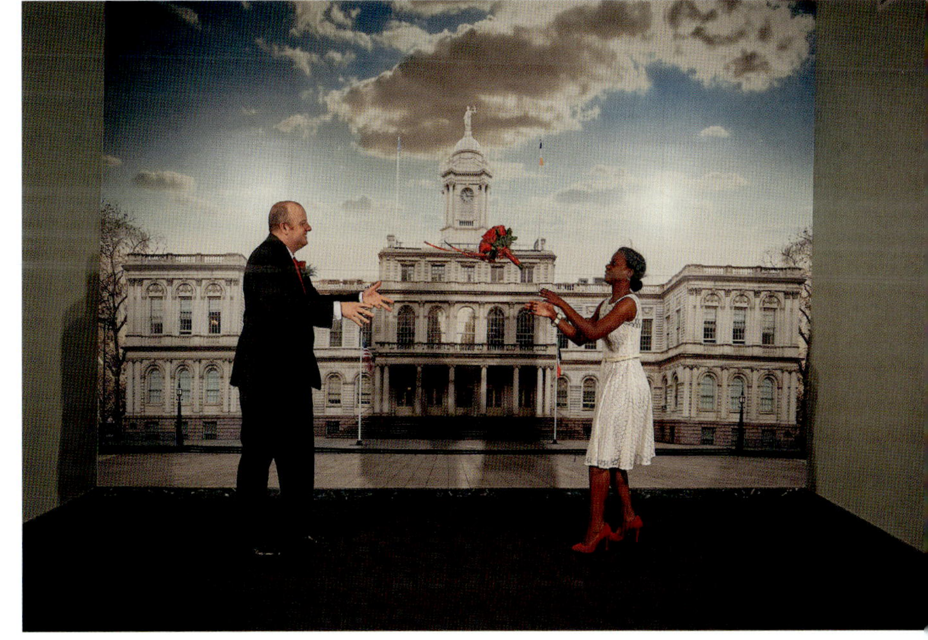

commensurate with their efforts. And, if they risk, and infuse their work with personal style and approach at camera, the ante ratchets upward. They are not just shooting flash-on-camera "safe." They are stamping each wedding with the imprimatur of their flair, their finesse, their dash of sophistication. The couple trusts the photographer's eye to speak with eloquence to their love.

Pressure!

I've shot weddings throughout my career, from a simple subway-to-city-hall marriage to elaborate affairs propelled by a virtual firehose of money. The "lots of money" variety was always a monster for me. I would overprepare, bring too much gear, and worry it to death. I didn't do enough weddings to really have a system, a go-to approach. I would just plug in and work like mad, and often, depending on the size of the gala, have a whole team with me. At the end of the day, I would be a dishrag. Which is being quite kind.

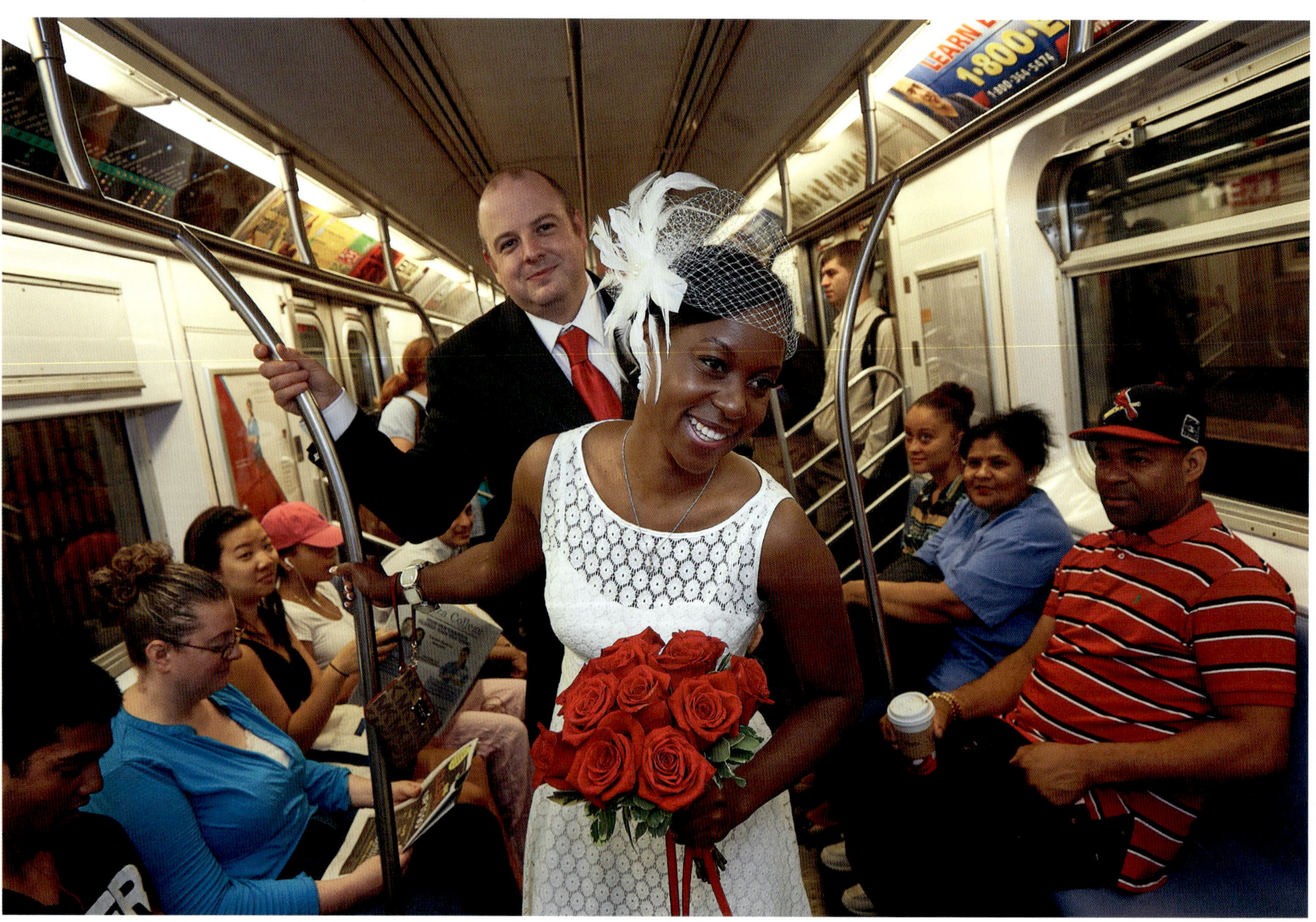

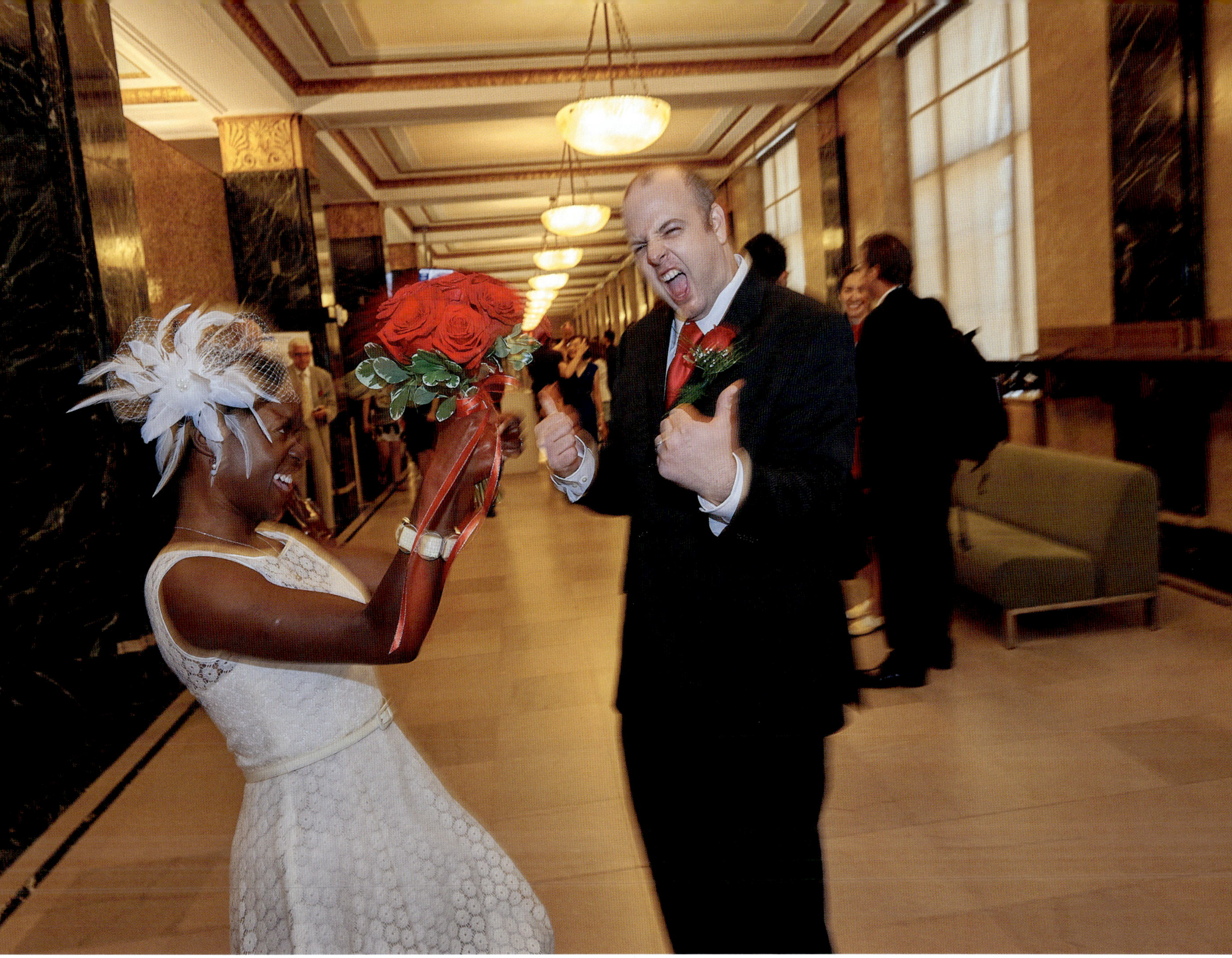

Certainly kinder than my first assistant, Drew Gurian, once was to me on the sidewalks of New York at 3 a.m., after a sumptuously grueling mega-bash, an over-the-top nuptial-on-steroids which had mercifully, finally concluded. We had been covering this rolling, gilded joining of lives since, like, 8 a.m. the previous morning. I was more played than the end of a day of Olympic Games coverage.

As I limped down the block to the studio truck, the crew was gathered, equally exhausted. I approached, looking for all the world like I had just done a triathlon in a tux. The ever-honest Drew looked at me and said, "You look like an old, sad, tired, injured rodeo clown." I never shot another wedding.

Which I miss. Sorta.

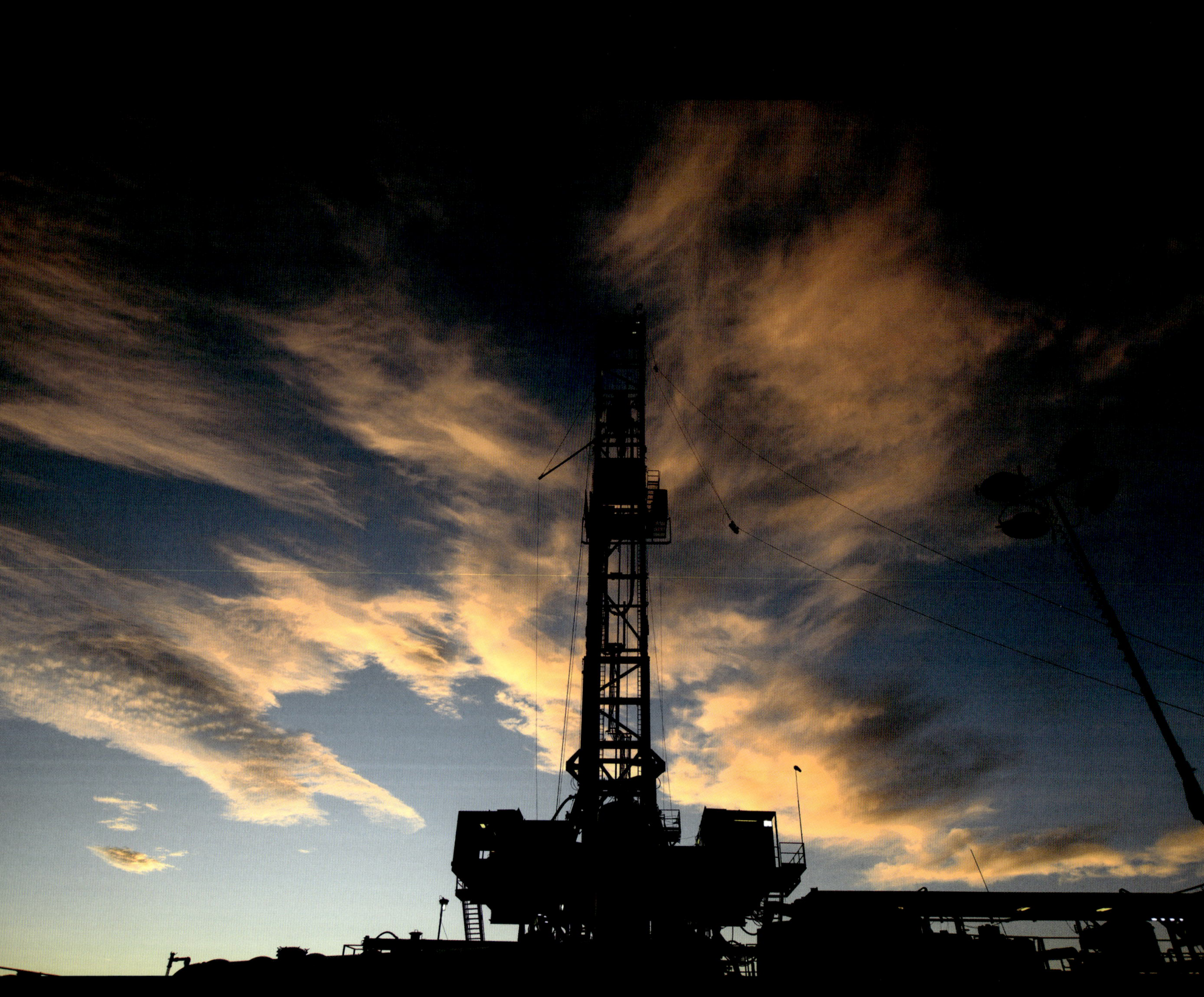

Wildcatter!

Photographers are storytellers, an apt and accurate appellation one hears all the time. We are also prospectors, and opportunists. We see a face, a place, the potential of a story, the interesting confluence of personalities, or the chance for conflict, harm, or heroism, and our antennas go up. Likewise, if we "discover" the previously unreported (at least by us) phenomenon, we dial in. We always have our eyes on the horizon and our ears on the listening post, wondering, observing, seeking. We are on the hunt, collecting shards of experience and encounters, thinking and hoping that they ultimately might make for or lead to good pictures. The stranger, the better. The more out of the way, the greater the chance that place or this person might not already have been reported on. Does it sound crazy, fascinating, remote, off kilter, colorful, rare? Grab the camera! Let's go!

Writers are much the same. They write about the people and scenes that have populated their lives. Noted writer Nora Ephron famously espoused the notion that "everything is copy." Depending on the genre of writing they engage in, they can report, as for a newspaper, or interpret, as they infuse a piece of writing with their own opinions while making an account of others' activities or the news of the day.

Or they can spin characters out of their head, characters who are, in fact, an amalgam of traits, peccadillos, personalities, prejudices, accents, and mannerisms of an array of folks they have encountered. Taken as a whole, the totality of Fred, the somewhat odd neighbor who lives down the block, might not warrant a write-up all on his own, but there's a piece of him (that profoundly odd and unique piece) that's damn interesting, and that piece gets filed in the observant writer's brain, to be ultimately grafted onto someone else's bits and pieces. A character that populates a work of fiction may well be a mosaic of different people met along the way. I recall on my freshman year dorm floor, we had a guy who could fart 60 times in a minute. His innards were piston-like, and his sphincter as dependable as a metronome. We would time him, and occasionally win some beer money off somebody who refused to believe it was possible. He was otherwise completely nondescript. I don't even remember his name. But that one thing . . . well, here I am writing about it 50 years later, so it must have left an impression and got filed away.

Years ago I photographed a young novelist for *People* magazine. We got along, and in conversation we recounted some of our upbringing. I mentioned I rarely drank beer. Historically, in particular, I would never drink a beer in front of my mother. My dad was an alcoholic, and it was the source of bitter infighting between him and my mom. But, as was the tradition of the time, they were locked in an Irish Catholic marriage, a wedded version of *No Exit*. Based on their battered, dented love for each other, they enacted enabling schemes that got them through the day, as people do. Beer was the culprit, especially on weekends. As much as she hated it, though, mom would never deny him the source. She would buy six packs and hide them. In the same place, all the time. She wanted him to find it, you see, 'cause if he didn't, he'd get behind the wheel and go get it himself, which was a bad idea.

I was complicit, too! At the age of three or so, my dad had me trained. Carling Black Label was a popular beer back then, and the commercial for it had a jingle involving "Mabel." As in "Mabel, Black Label, Carling Black Label!" The boys at the bar

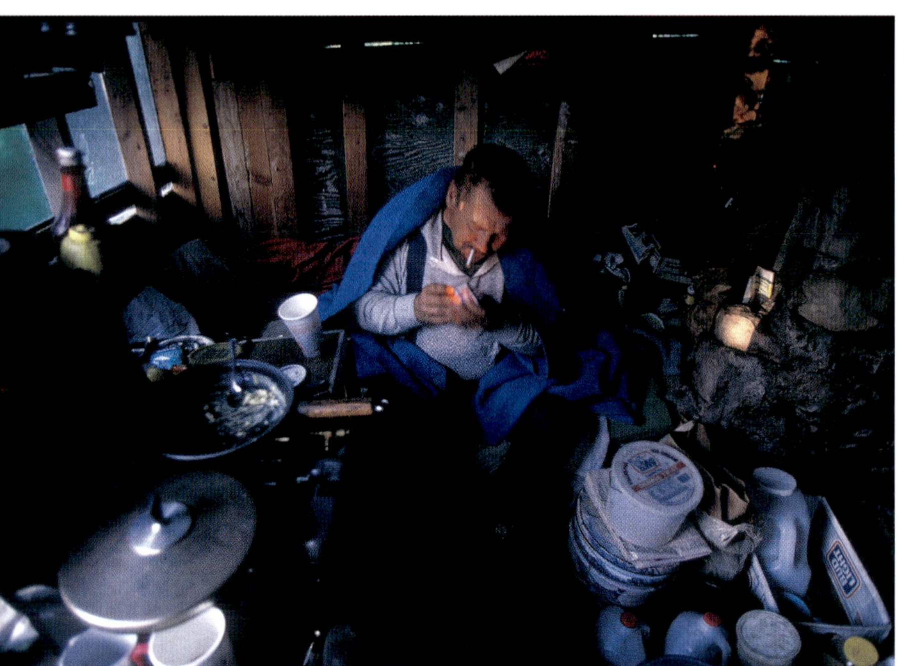

would sing the jingle with a wink and a whistle, and "Mabel," the barmaid, would oblige. Sad but true. This commercial was on TV often enough that I became Mabel. Watching football on the weekends, dad didn't want to get out of the recliner, so he would look at me, raise his finger, and go, "Mabel," with a nod and a smile in my direction. I would hit the fridge and grab him a beer. Started doing it for him as a toddler and was still doing it in high school.

As I was relating this, I became aware the young writer was making mental notes. She was candid. She said, "You know, I'm going to use that at some point." Writers are like folks who collect rocks on the shoreline, scrubbed and smoothed by the ocean. One odd rock, who gives a shit? But collect a whole bunch and put them in a jar, and well, that might be interesting.

It is much the same with photographers. We hear about something or pick up on a news development, and an almost audible thrumming sound starts in our heads. How can I get an assignment? Should I go? Make some calls? What to do? Pack the gear? Jump on the plane? Do I know somebody who knows somebody who can get me in? Of course, a client, a spouse, or literally anybody with some common sense might be compelled to ask questions like, "What assurance do you have that there will be pictures out there waiting for you? This sounds like a wild-ass hunch! How do you know this will work out?"

You don't. You're prospecting, propelled by instinct, hope, and passion, not to mention the almost desperate yearning to make pictures that have power and substance. It's risky, plunging after pictures. We can't sit at a computer terminal and conjure them from bits and pieces of personal history and imagination, as a novelist can. The writer can blue sky and write about the rough-hewn cabin where Harry the oddball hermit lives, perched on the side of a desperately remote ravine. They can spin a fascinating account of someone such as this and never leave their head. Harry, that cabin, and his odd ways might stem from separate elements of utterly disconnected experiences in that writer's life, coalescing into a fascinating account, replete with details and nuance. Fiction, in a word.

But we photogs have to get up off the sofa and go and find a real Harry! We have to pursue, research, and find those odd, fascinating, horrible, wonderful, intriguing, story-worthy people out there in the real world.

Which is alternately a wonderful and vexing task. For photographers, the mantra can be "Make it happen!" Well, often, it doesn't just happen.

I did a story for the *National Geographic* on the human brain. As part of that story, I had to address the critical issue of mentally ill homeless people. I managed to find a sympathetic social services group in Kansas City, and they introduced me to Hobo Ron, who lived in a shanty shack off the highway. He was, when medicated, relatively easy to hang around with.

I spent a few days with him, observing his routines and his difficulties. The pictures came relatively easily, as he was, quintessentially, an odd guy who lived apart from what most folks consider normal. Pictorial interest was therefore pretty much baked into the equation. The hard part was finding him— meeting and working with social services to gain their acknowledgement and let them size me up before bringing me to one of their clients. Then, getting an introduction to Ron. Explaining to him that the magazine would identify him as having cognitive difficulties, and the photos would show his home and lifestyle. It was also crucial to ascertain that he understood these things and that I would be his companion for a bit. All of this necessarily had to happen before I ever put a camera to my eye.

Then, I had to coordinate with him. He didn't exactly observe a timetable or keep a calendar. There was no guarantee being with Ron for a couple days was going to work out or yield pictures pertinent to the story. There was no guarantee he would even be at his shack when I showed up. I went anyway because that's what you do as a photog.

We have to go and see.

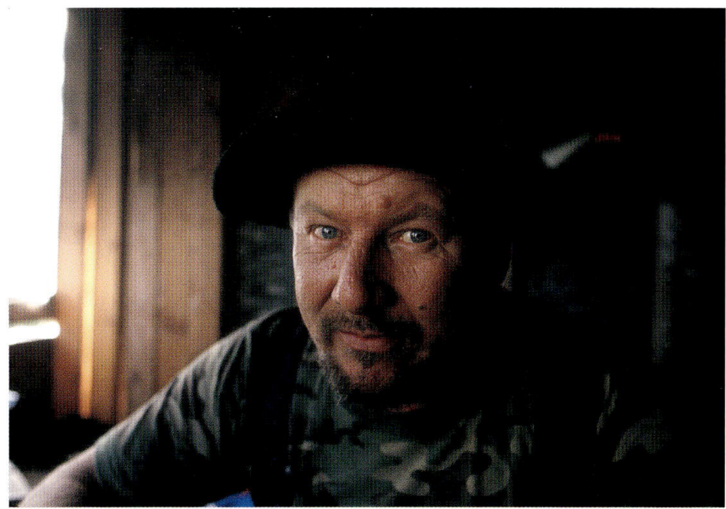

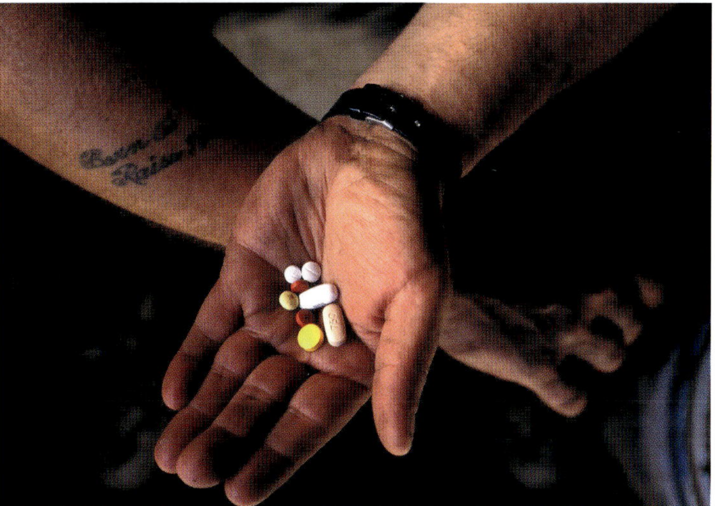

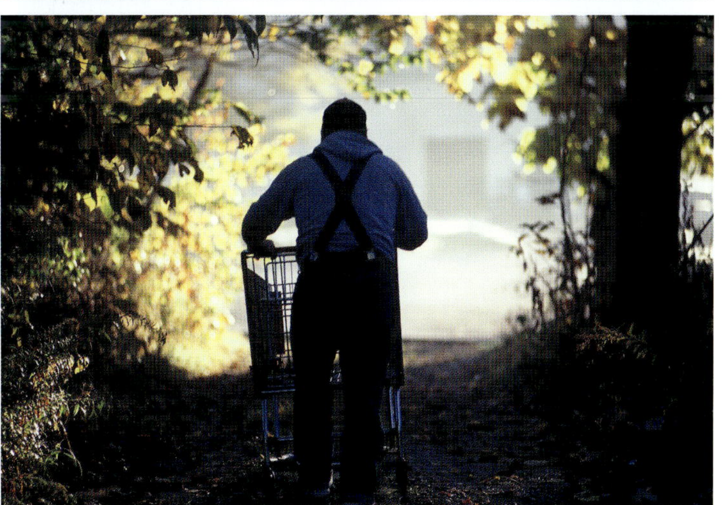

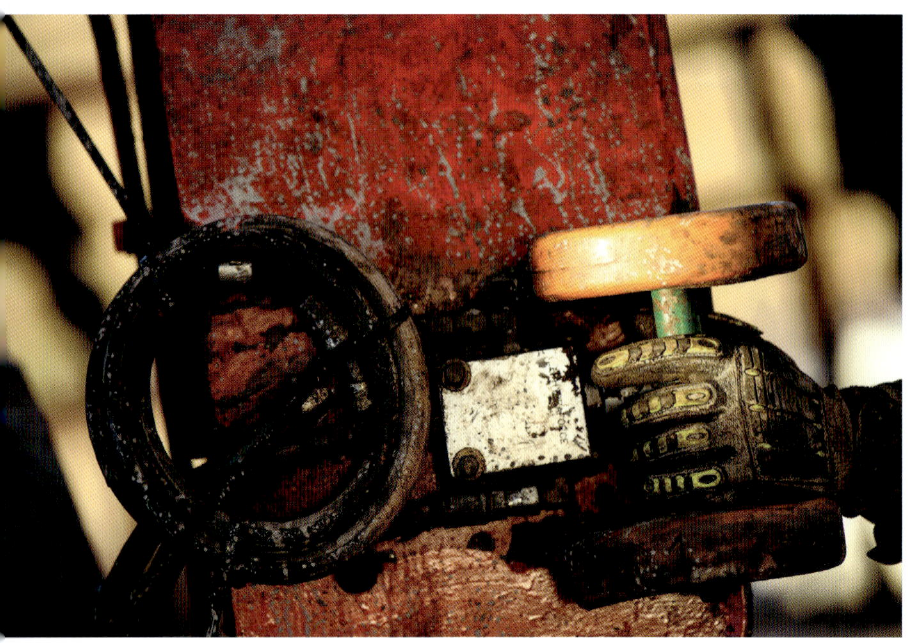

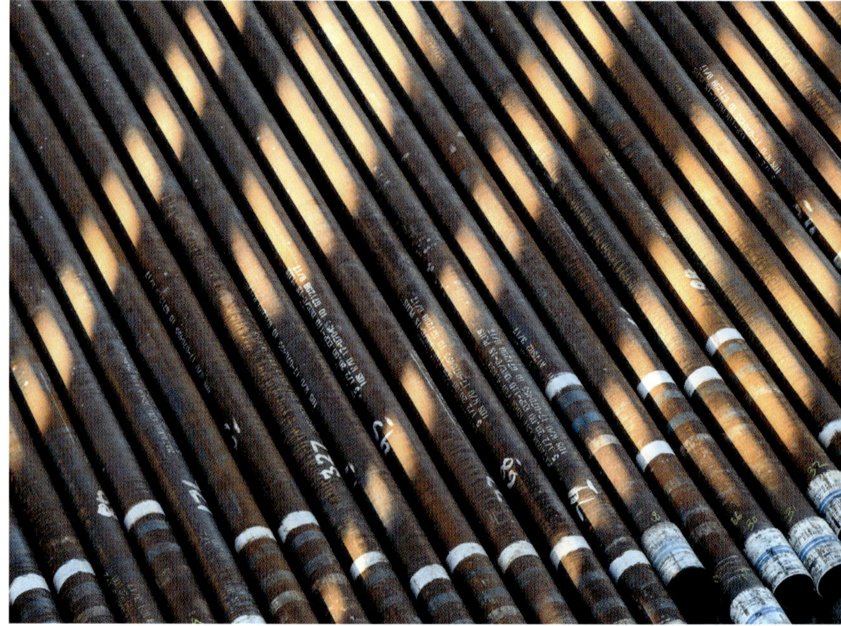

Occasionally, a glimmer, a conversation, or a relationship does present a viable chance to get out there and do some work. I have a dear friend, and we have collaborated on many a picture adventure. She is not a pro but has quite a lovely eye. She's also connected in a big way in the Texas oil business, emotionally via family, and also business-wise. She talked often of doing a project in the oil fields, given her access, but struggled with how to get her arms around it. I suggested that, instead of my offering advice and editing from afar, we go after it together and create a book for this one particular company that appeared to be on the cusp of major leaps into a bigger future.

My suggestion was that we engage in a mutually shot project, which could become a book, a library of photos available for the company to release as slide shows, explanatory videos, large prints for their offices, annual report visuals, and on and on.

(Pictures from corporate assignments get used in fascinating and innumerable ways. I was once commissioned by Malcolm Forbes to shoot helicopter views of his famous yacht, The Highlander [right]. The images were used on the backs of playing cards aboard the boat.)

I wrote up a proposal and a budget. There was interest. Off to Texas. Three times. Meetings, research, orientation, and then an actual scouting trip, which turned into a brief shooting trip. All was well. I reserved my entire month of March for the boots-on-the-ground, camera-in-hand work. Lynn, my ever-cautious studio manager, actually started dialing it in as a real asset in our overall budget planning for the year. Thirty days of work. Tough to come by.

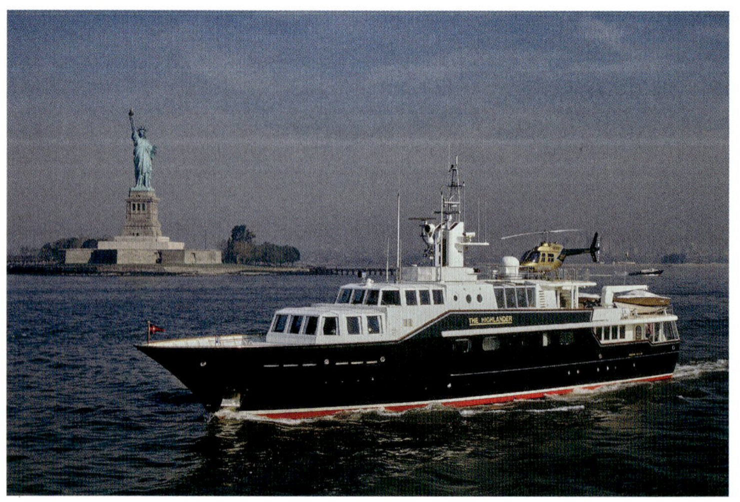

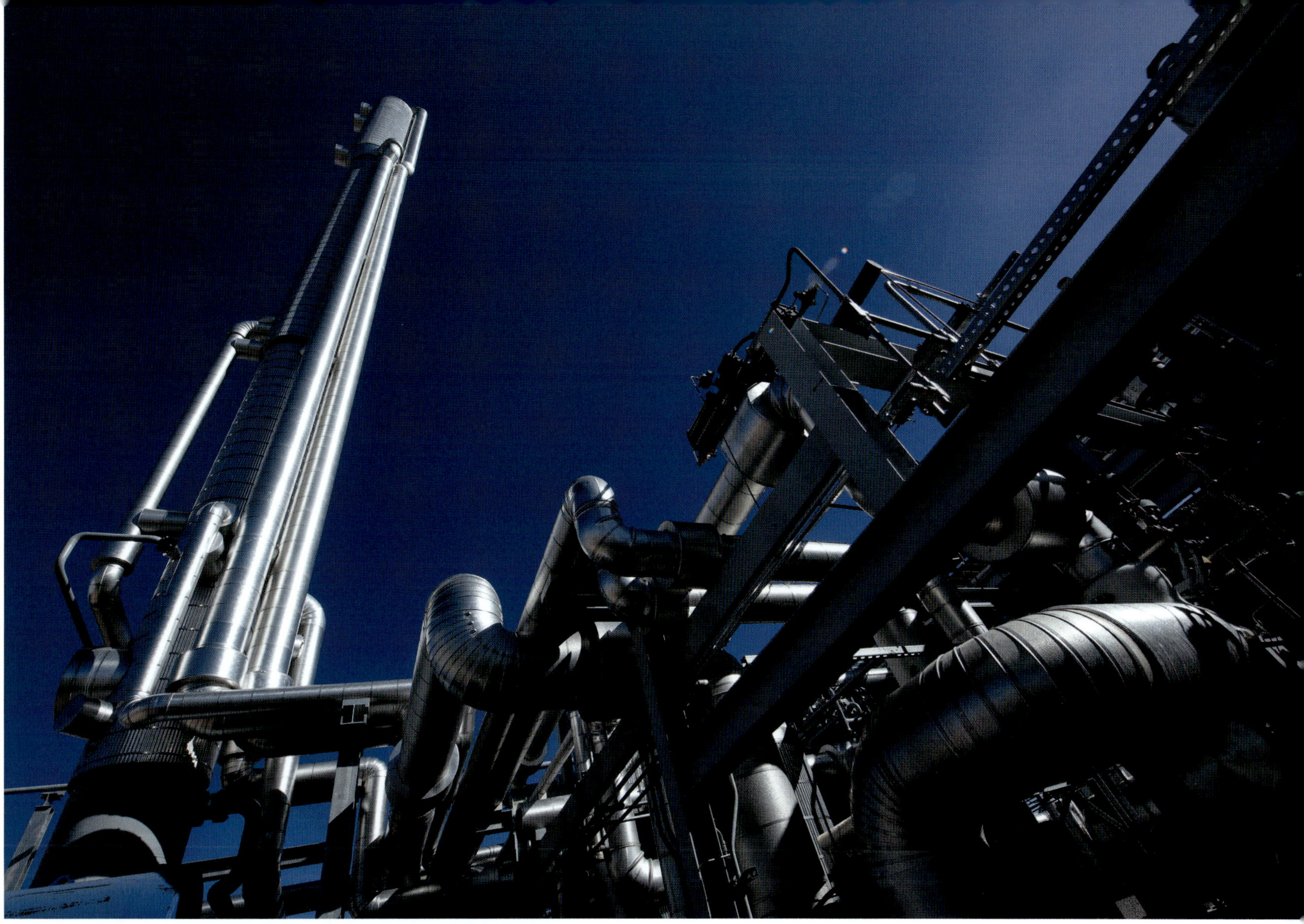

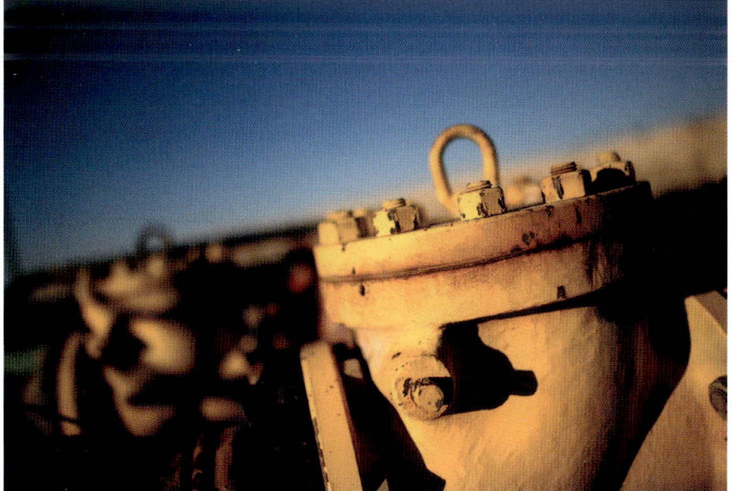

Then, on January 18 of that year, I got a two-line email from the owner of the company:

Since this project began, I have had—and continue to have—serious doubts that this project is right for us . . .

With the wave of an iPhone and a few thumb taps, the project was gone. In its place was a gaping hole in my calendar called March. He might as well have been wielding a rocket launcher instead of a cell phone, as that little electronic missive blew a month-wide crater in my first quarter planning. It presented to me a tough rebound in the working environment of nowadays, where every client assesses every picture assignment

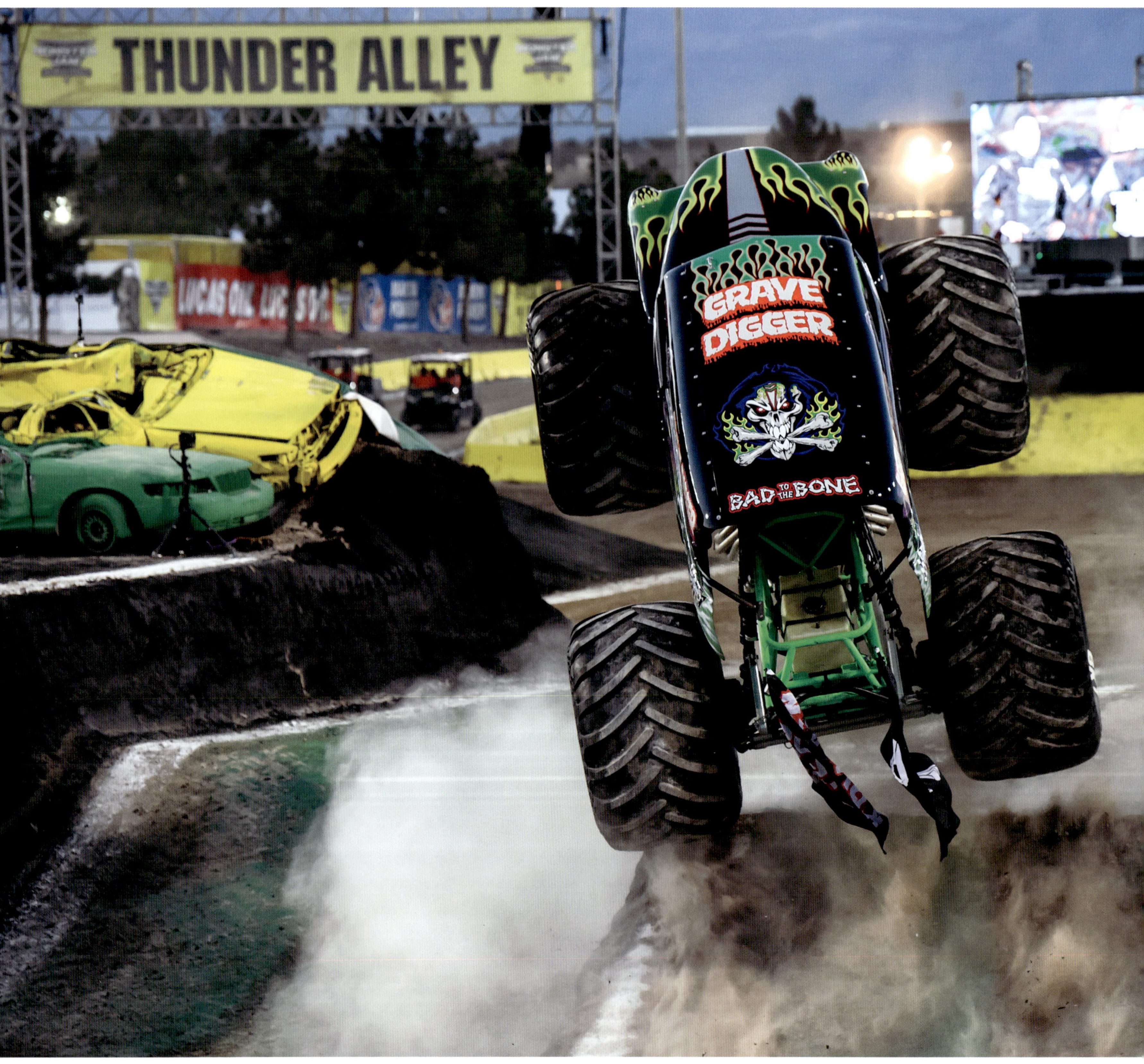

THUNDER ALLEY
LUCAS OIL
GRAVE DIGGER
BAD TO THE BONE

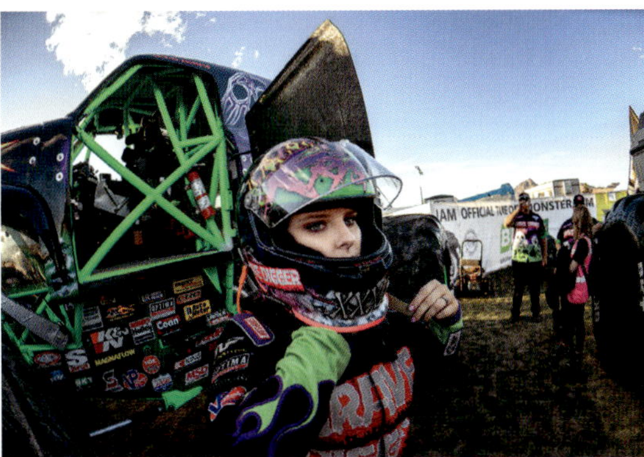

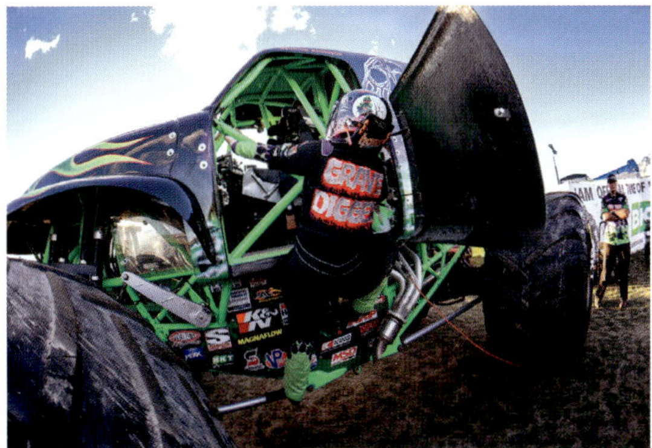

expenditure from all angles, just about to the last minute, before pushing the go button and sending a check.

I sent a stoic "I understand" email in reply. What else to do? The gentleman was gracious enough to offer to cover some expenses, but I demurred, and walked away. Didn't cajole, wheedle, whine, or threaten. It's generally been my mantra, in these circumstances, to simply take the hit and move on. It didn't feel like it would be seemly on my part to get nitpicky and itemize my disappointment in line items and an invoice. I had a measure of consternation about my predicament, to be sure, but also calmness. This wasn't my first rodeo. One door closes, another opens, as they say. Very true in the photographic industry.

Thankfully, ESPN came calling, and that March I was off to Vegas for the Monster Jam World Finals. It wasn't a month's worth of work, but it was fun.

That's the way it goes. Things rise and fall for a photographer, sometimes quite precipitously. You've got to be comfortable with it. The risk. The doubt that invades your sleep. You've got to love this enough that you remain unflinching when the next potential boon/disaster looms. You've got to keep prospecting.

In my Texas travels, I grew very fond of an older oilman, a brilliant geologist with an illustrious history in worldwide oil exploration and drilling. He was a font of country wisdom. He looked at me at one point, his eyes twinkling, and said, "You know something, Joe? You and I are a lot alike. You're just like an oil prospector. You don't know if there's gonna be a picture out there, but you gotta go find out! You're a wildcatter!"

There are numerous definitions of "wildcatter," but the bottom line is that you're a prospector who routinely faces off against very uncertain returns. To draw an analogy here, if you were, say, a professional parachutist, and the odds your chute would open were about the same odds that a photog gets about whether a job will work out . . . you would never jump out of an airplane again.

But as a photographer, you listen to the wind, breathe in a draught of air, go with your gut, and jump. Sometimes the chute opens beautifully, sometimes . . . not so much.

Sometimes you hit oil, sometimes you pound sand. Or get a two-line email.

The State of Things

I got a job a few years ago to photograph four of the astounding women who made up the core of the perennially formidable UConn women's basketball team. The client was *ESPN The Magazine*. Wonderful!

I remember looking around the UConn practice gym and thinking, this is cool. This is what I was raised up doing, photographically speaking. Move in with gear, sort the place out, work under a time pressure, come up with different, graphically pleasing options that actually have some measure of storytelling merit. Punch the ticket, knock it out, move with confidence, direct the action, light people well, get a little goofy here and there. Have fun. It was a day on assignment, which, for a freelance photographer, is like a strawberry sundae at the beach.

I was with people I love. Great team, with Cali, who was our crew chief for many years, and Andrew, a fine young photog who helps out our studio. Annie, my wife, was also on the job, running the behind-the-scenes (BTS) efforts, shooting stills, creating GIFs, wrapping her head around the veritable cornucopia of demands that editorial clients present to the shooter of record, checking in with me, and making sure no piece of the puzzle went missing. We were working for Tim Rasmussen, a terrific editor, a great presence in the industry, and a dear friend.

I did well with the job. Not a whooping, hollering, shoot-the-chandelier-right-off-the-ceiling feeling of "doing well," but a solid, efficient, relax-in-the-car-when-you-leave-knowing-you-have-a-picture kind of feeling. The you-deserve-a-nice-glass-of-Merlot-tonight kind of aura. If I were a photography professor assessing this assignment, I would give me a B, maybe B+, grade.

I had one hour with the athletes who, just to ramp up the wonder of the day, were some of the sweetest, most talented kids I have run into in recent times. These four young women had just won 100 games in a row, setting an NCAA record and basically chewing through all manner of competition with the steely resolve and glint-in-the-eye assuredness of veteran gunslingers. They were the Seal Team Six of women's college basketball.

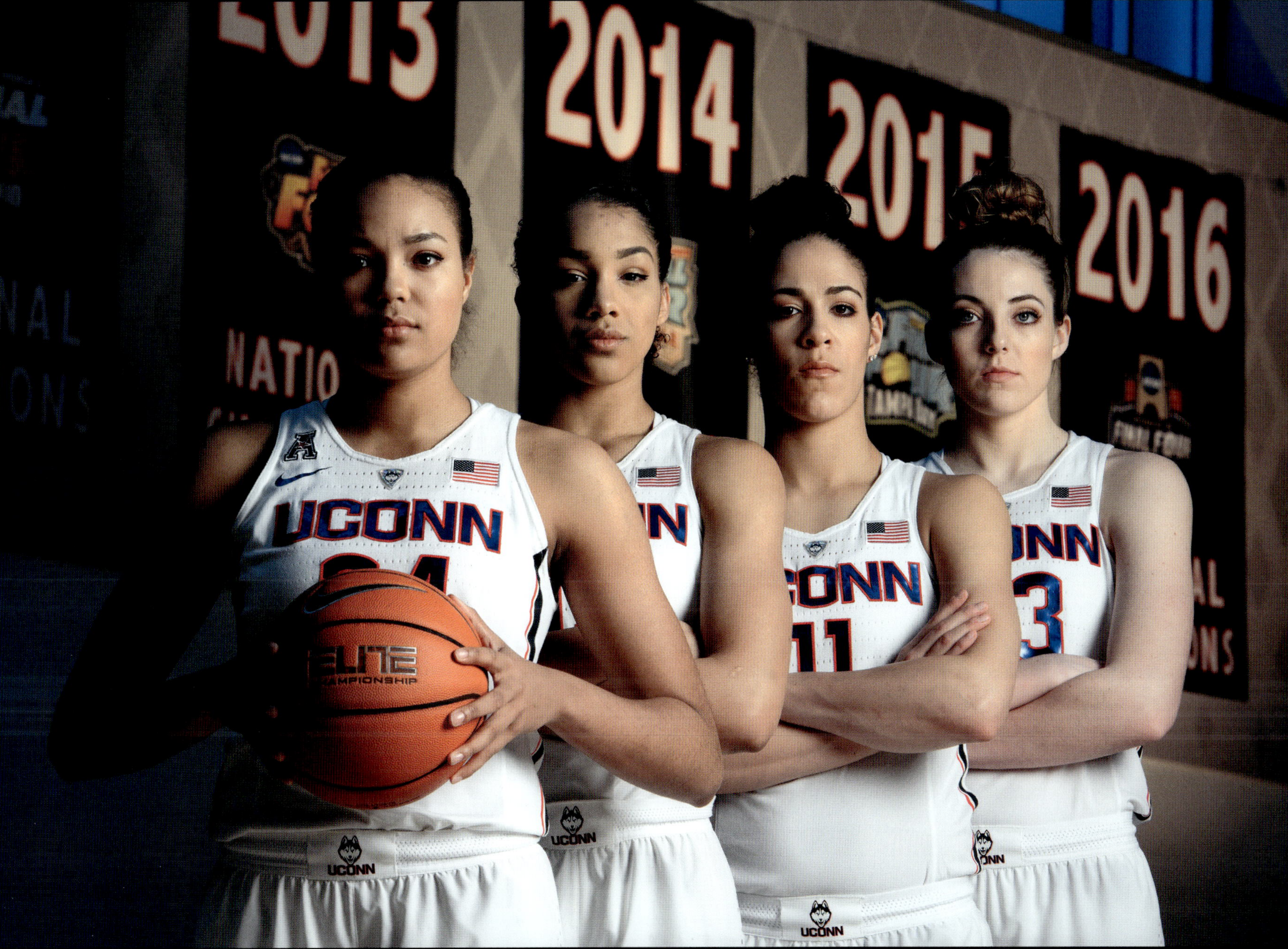

I created four setups for the hour, and wheeled the athletes through them in rapid succession. I had no props except a couple basketballs and the fairly unadorned walls of the practice gym. Which was okay. There was, thank goodness, an array of UConn championship banners on one wall, and a big-ass Husky painting on the floor. Enough to make a picture work and have some sort of reference point, or impactful angle. Actually, it was more than enough. Compared to some locations I've been sent to, which are akin to a photographic gulag, this gym was a graphical garden of delights, a boon to the senses, a rhapsody of pictorial elements. Okay, not really. But I did have a couple things to work with. And the wonderful youngsters.

> *I heard that inner voice again—and ignored it.*

The editor Tim assigned to this job was lovely to work with, responsive and encouraging. We had a fair bit of chatter prior to the job, which was cool, and, of course, she was concerned about the budget, like all editors nowadays. At the end of the day, she liked the job! Only question she had was about one setup, where I stupidly got the athletes to mug aggressively for the camera, and neglected to do so much as one frame from that angle where they had calmer expressions. Sigh.

I've talked previously about the inner voice that murmurs to you on location. Well, I heard that inner voice again—and ignored it. Went with the fierce looks, and moved on quickly. And, of course, it was the one area of the take the editor zeroed in on and asked, "Quick question: Do you have this setup, with the player's mouths closed by chance?"

Uh, I have them with their mouths even more wide open? Aaargh! Of course I didn't have their mouths pleasantly closed. That would have been too smart! I should have made a few frames with the young women quietly gazing at the camera. That's the glitch that keeps this take out of the "A" realm in terms of grade.

Wonderful day, really. Local job, and I was with Annie, and home that night in my own bed. Simple job to edit. We shipped it in, a picture got picked, we tweaked the file a tiny bit, and we were done. So what's wrong?

Nothing, really. Once you say yes to the job, and indicate a willingness to shoot in this vein and genre—that being magazine editorial work—you sign on to the whole damn program. Four of us went to that gym in a loaded Chevy Suburban. Rolled in with a four-wheeled hand truck and a couple other two-wheeled hand carts. Spread the gear out and got to work. As I looked around, though, I shook my head. I've got a lot of stuff, and this was the job for a lot of stuff. On the floor, I had deployed, ultimately, five Profoto B4 generators, each with its own head. Five of these sets, all told, is an investment of about $45K. Then there were Profoto B1 units, four of them, clocking in at just shy of $10K. Then the light shapers and grip, maybe $5–8K.

And we're not even at the cameras yet. Throw the camera package in, at say, $40K, and well, I had about $100K of my own invested dough spread around that practice hall. I didn't rent the stuff to the magazine. That was not possible. My fee for the day was $600. Assistants were billed at $300 each. Hair-and-makeup person was $300. Annie, for all her excellence, was billed as a "GIF Videographer" at a token rate of $200. Mileage was billed, as was a digital capture package of $850. Whole deal came to $3,521.14.

The fee structure was incorporated into a much larger, six-page agreement that gave the Disney-owned ESPN a pretty much unfettered run of usage of any image I might have produced on said assignment day. Case closed. As contracts go these days, this one was relatively benign. They still had a scale in there indicating the traditional "day rate against space" payment structure; in other words, if on this day, for a named fee of $600, the angels sat on my shutter button and I produced a two-page spread and a cover, I would get the larger fees associated with that usage. That didn't happen on this day. And many, many contracts with publications have done away with this potential upside for the freelancer. As in, sometime in the future you may get a phone

CREATIVE LICENSING FEES		
	JMP will be compensated a day rate, as established by CLIENT, against space.	
	TOTAL CREATIVE FEES (not including space, which is TBD):	**$600.00**
PRODUCTION EXPENSES		
FIRST ASSISTANT #1	1 pack, 1 shoot, 1 wrap day @ 300 per day:	$900.00
FIRST ASSISTANT #1	1 shoot day @ 300 + mileage:	$413.94
GIF VIDEOGRAPHER:	1 shoot day (for the purpose of social media) @ 200:	$200.00
HAIR-M/U ARTIST:	1 shoot day @ 300 + mileage:	$343.20
MILEAGE:	2 vehicles @ 200 RT miles each: 400 miles @ 53.5 per mile:	$214.00
DIGITAL CAPTURE:	Creation of digital image files:	$850.00
	CLIENT will receive an edit of JMP's top selects, toned and optimized for reproduction. If additional retouching is requested, JMP will do so at the rate of $150 per hour.	
	TOTAL PRODUCTION EXPENSES:	**$2,921.14**
TOTAL CREATIVE FEES & PRODUCTION EXPENSES:	$600 + $2,921.14:	**$3,521.14**

call and hear, "We can print billboards along the highways of the moons of Jupiter and you still only get the flat fee, bub!" Fierce cackling ensues at the other end of the line.

You will notice in the behind-the-scenes photos (page 277, top right) the presence of an ESPN video crew, filming us and photographing the hoopsters. That goes along with the $600 rate: You and your crew sign off on releases for them to put you on ESPN television should we be deemed entertaining.

I glitched during the day and remembered I really should have had a bigger boom to slide a light out and over the talented foursome, so the intrepid Lynda, a local freelancer who works with our studio, got into her car in the morning and followed me up after we had departed. Her day rate for that delivery was $250. My bad. Always a danger on local jobs, right? You start thinking in the car, well, maybe I should have this, or that, or, well, this additional item I did not bring might provide a different look … and there goes part of your day rate. You can't bill the client additionally for your own idiocy or insecurities.

I took the crew out for dinner that night at a nice local restaurant, which was not part of the assignment agreement, obviously. It's just a good thing to do. Keep a crew happy. Treat them well. They work hard to make the job succeed. That dinner put me into negative numbers for the day, but that's okay. It was a job that had a bit of pressure associated with it, and we did well. We had ventured once again into the uncertain wilderness of photographic endeavor and had returned. Mission accomplished.

But, obviously, the scenario described here ain't a living. Not even close. Even take away the extra assistant and the post-job dinner, and there's still not enough dough left to run a studio, or run a life, or to buy gear, pay a mortgage or a school bill, or even feed a healthy rabbit.

The editor and I had some budgetary back and forth during this job, and she basically said she deals with two camps of photogs. One group accepts the fact that editorial work is, at this point, simply a calling card, bragging rights on social media, an attention-getting bid for commercial clients to possibly notice. And then there's the other group, who adamantly try to stick to the notion that they can make a living shooting in this style and genre. Which historically, back in the day, was thoroughly possible.

No longer. It becomes now more of a choice, based on business and branding considerations. How much can I afford to lose today, financially speaking? It is worth it? Do I make it back in PR or social media buzz? Is it portfolio-worthy? Does it lead to more work for this client, like covers, or pieces of a big picture act? In this case, the client being ESPN, I took a gamble that continuing a relationship might lead me to be chosen for one piece, just one, of *ESPN The Magazine*'s The Body Issue, which had become their vehicle of record for the year, much akin to the way *Sports Illustrated*'s Swimsuit Issue had been for many years.

That didn't happen. It turns out The Body Issue—again, much like the *SI* swimsuit juggernaut of yore—actually had its own crew and editors, and the selection of photogs was heavily freighted with politics, long-standing relationships, and, of course, who might be the hot shooter at that moment and have a certain zeitgeist-y feel for the subject at hand. Also, ESPN is a vehicle for Disney to make money, further relationships with high-profile athletes, and draw attention to a movie, or a theme park, or whatever corporate synergy strategy is deemed to be the watchword of the day. In other words, the higher profile the job, the more likely the choice of photog and the style and conduct and even the location can be impacted by lots of different types of pressure, from a variety of quarters, virtually all of them driven by some sort of economic or marketing metric.

> *How much can I afford to lose today, financially speaking?*

The way money impacts what magazines do or don't do is nothing new. For years, many magazines have done focus group research for their potential cover images and layouts prior to publication. Whatever cover image those folks around the conference table say they like and might buy, well, there's your cover.

As noted earlier, it was a hectic but very fun day in the field, the kind of day I really enjoy. A job like this pings on a wide variety of your photo and survival skills. And, again, the fact of an assignment means you're putting your eye to the camera with purpose, and I've always found that exhilarating. It makes the math disappear. I shed the weight of the distressing numbers, and simply shoot pictures.

Here we go with a timeline of pictures and events.

Call sheet:

<table>
<tr><td colspan="2" align="center">SCHEDULE</td></tr>
<tr><td>NOON</td><td>ALL PHOTO CREW ARRIVES AT LOCATION</td></tr>
<tr><td>12:30 PM</td><td>HMUA ARRIVES AT LOCATION</td></tr>
<tr><td>1:00 PM</td><td>APPROX ARRIVAL FOR TALENT</td></tr>
<tr><td>2:30 PM</td><td>SHOOT BEGINS</td></tr>
<tr><td>3:30 PM</td><td>SHOOT ENDS, CREW WRAPS AND DEPARTS LOCATION</td></tr>
</table>

First setup (below and opposite). One big light source, radically pitched to the side to give my subjects an edge. Fill skip off a large Tri-Grip on the floor, silver side up. Incandescent white balance. One raw light in the way back lighting the posters.

First test, using the crew (below). The hoopsters are in makeup. Flash, but not enough control of the environment. Auto WB. Cali is bemused. Annie is trying to somehow get her 5'3" frame closer to the dimensions of the ballplayers, and doing an amazing job of it.

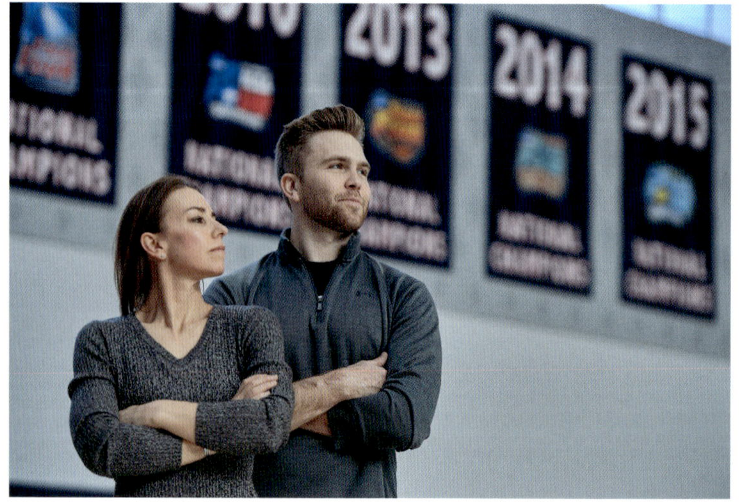

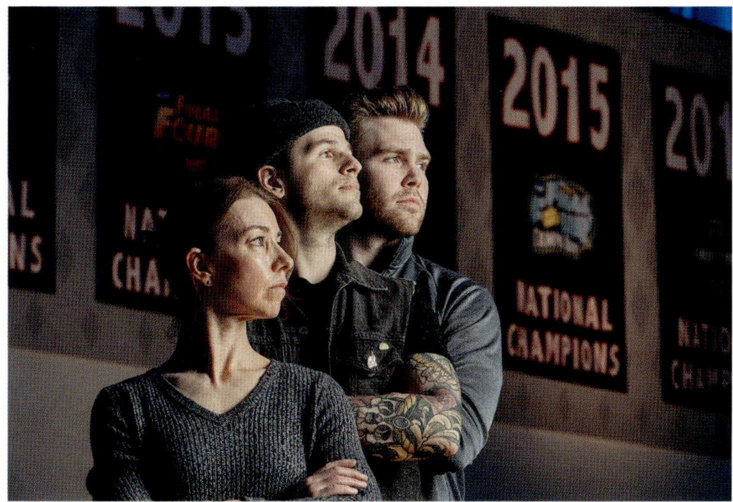
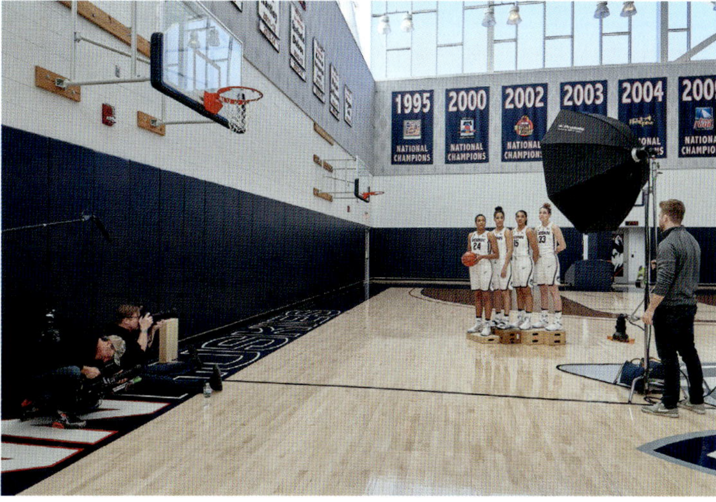

Create backlight, switch white balance, shutter speed goes from 1/80th to 1/200th. Lots of light, hence the Profoto B4 units. Long lens on this. Need f/16 for sharpness from front to back. ISO 400.

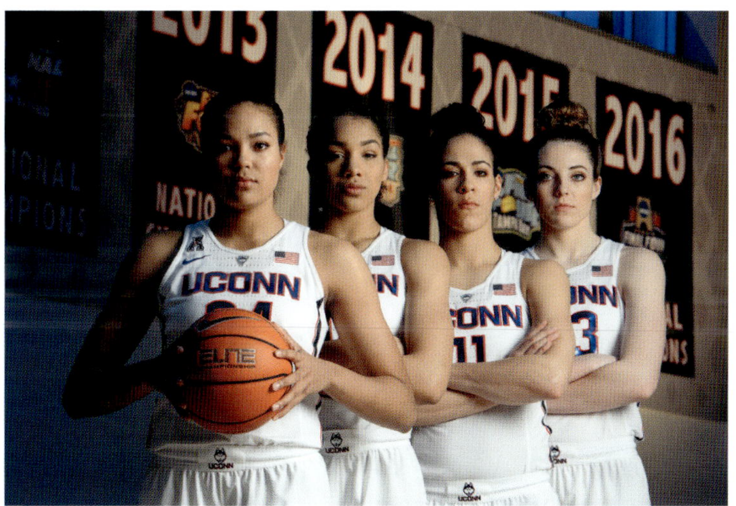

Good setup. Work it. Look at the camera, and at the light.

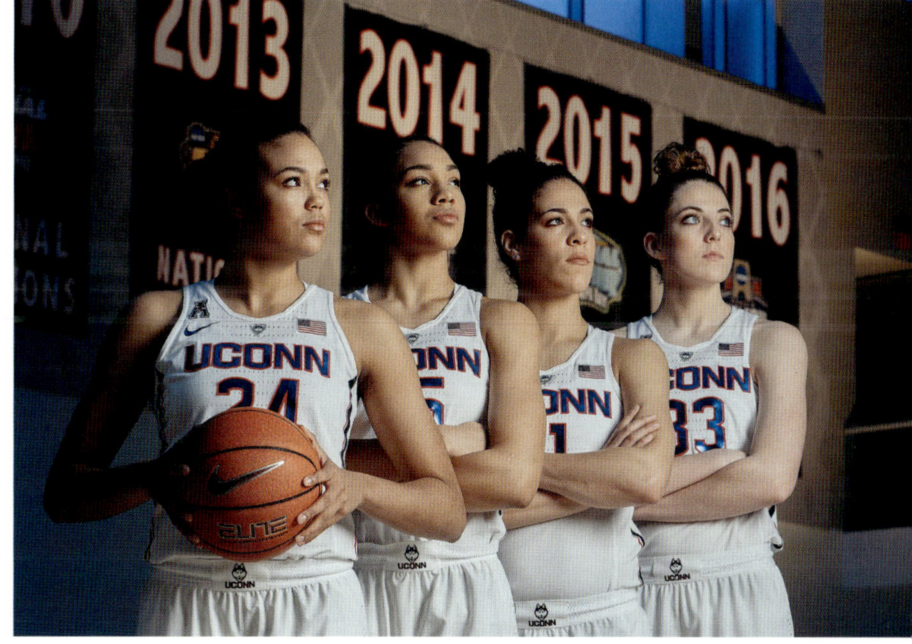

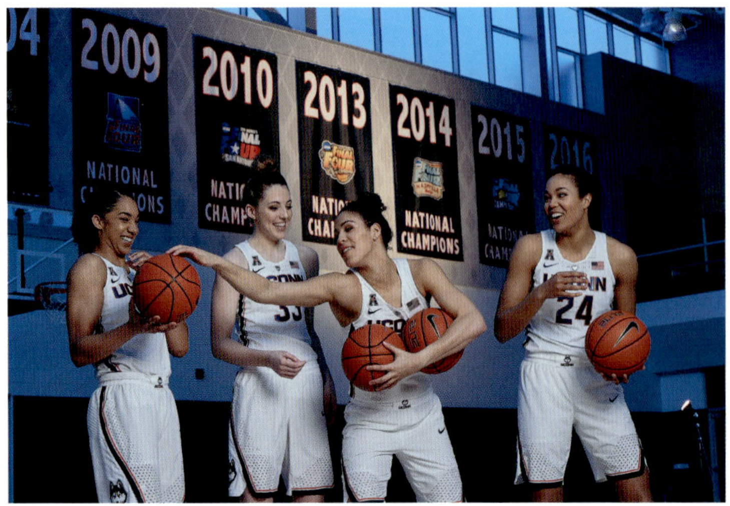

Have some fun.

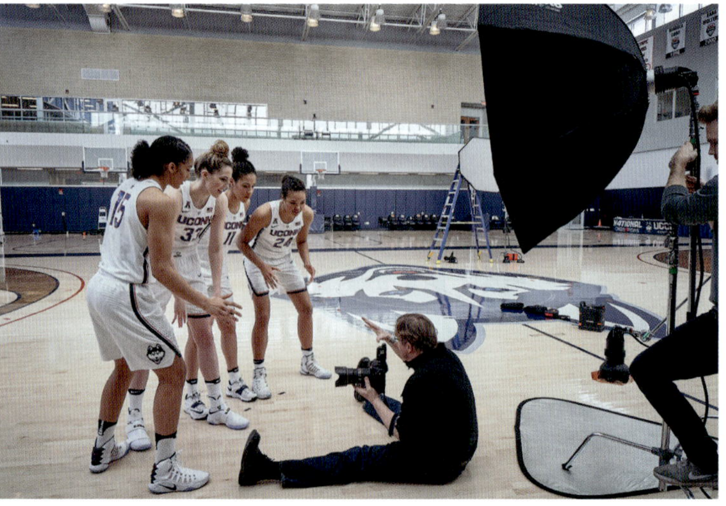

Move on. Clock's ticking. Second set, with same light pattern, just much closer. Notice another set in the background, with the ladder, prepped and ready. Great to have a couple basketball courts to spread out the setups.

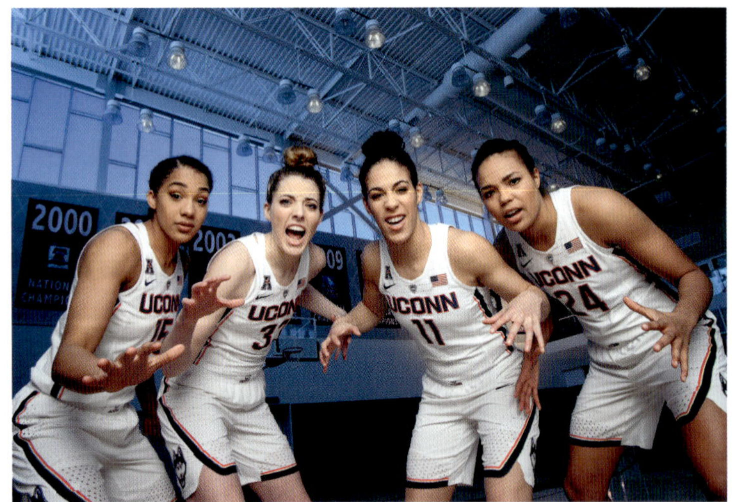

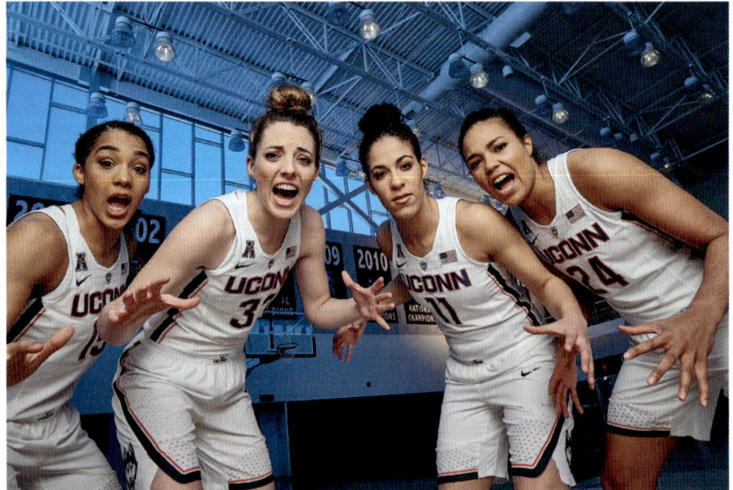

Nice light but the expressions don't cut it, as noted earlier. Not their fault. Mine. Should have had them relax and be themselves. Would have taken less than a minute.

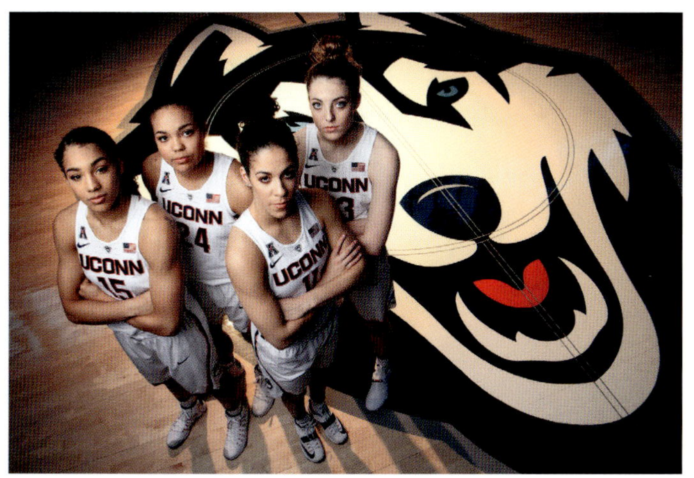

Next setup, and my favorite pic of the day (below). Overhead angle, with the Husky mascot on the floor. One big main light, and a warmed-up spot for the background, in this case, the floor.

Did the serious, bad-ass, we-own-the-paint look, and then, blessedly, let them have some fun.

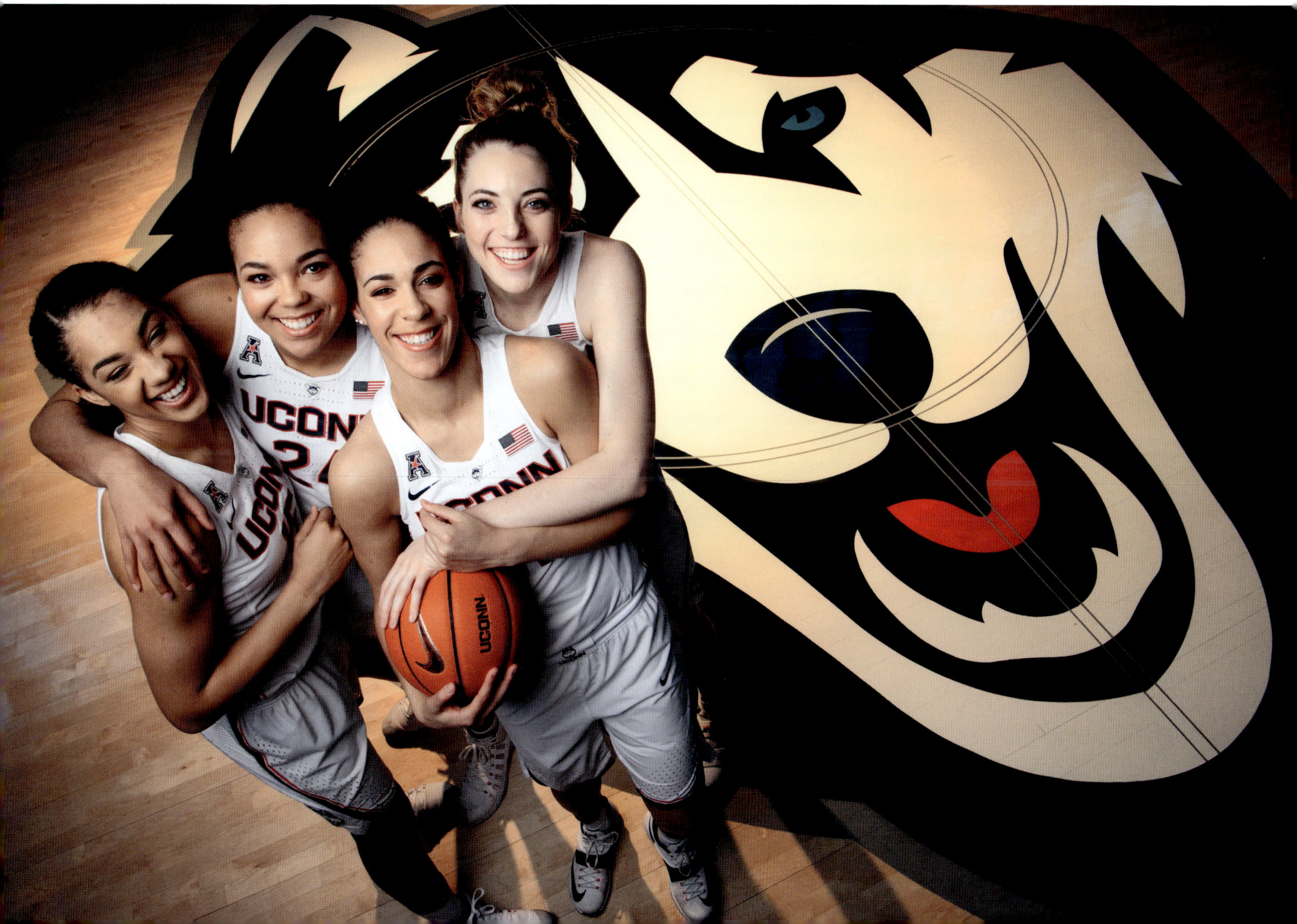

And the last setup of the day. Kind of lame, but I shot it. Here's me directing (right), and the young women trying not to laugh too hard at me.

Then, closing with a moment or two of goofiness. I loved these kids.

And . . . I loved the work. Win, lose, or draw. I have always loved the work.

ESPN The Magazine, in print, is gone. I'm still here.

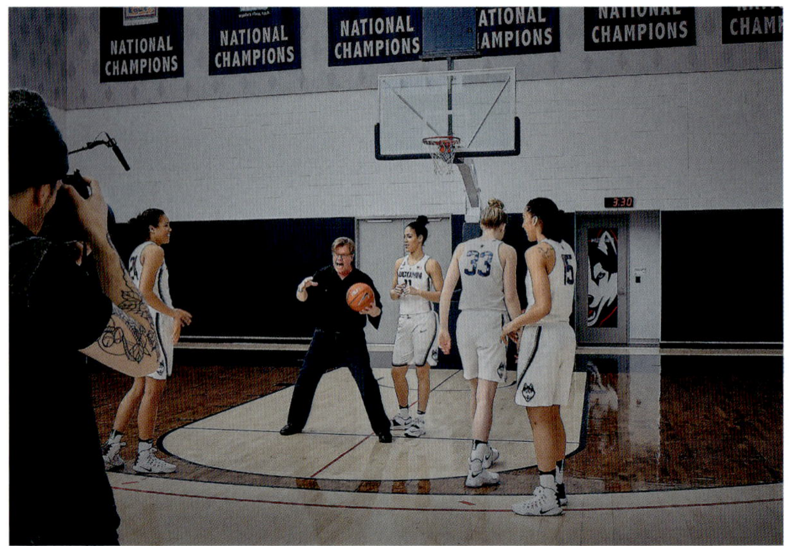

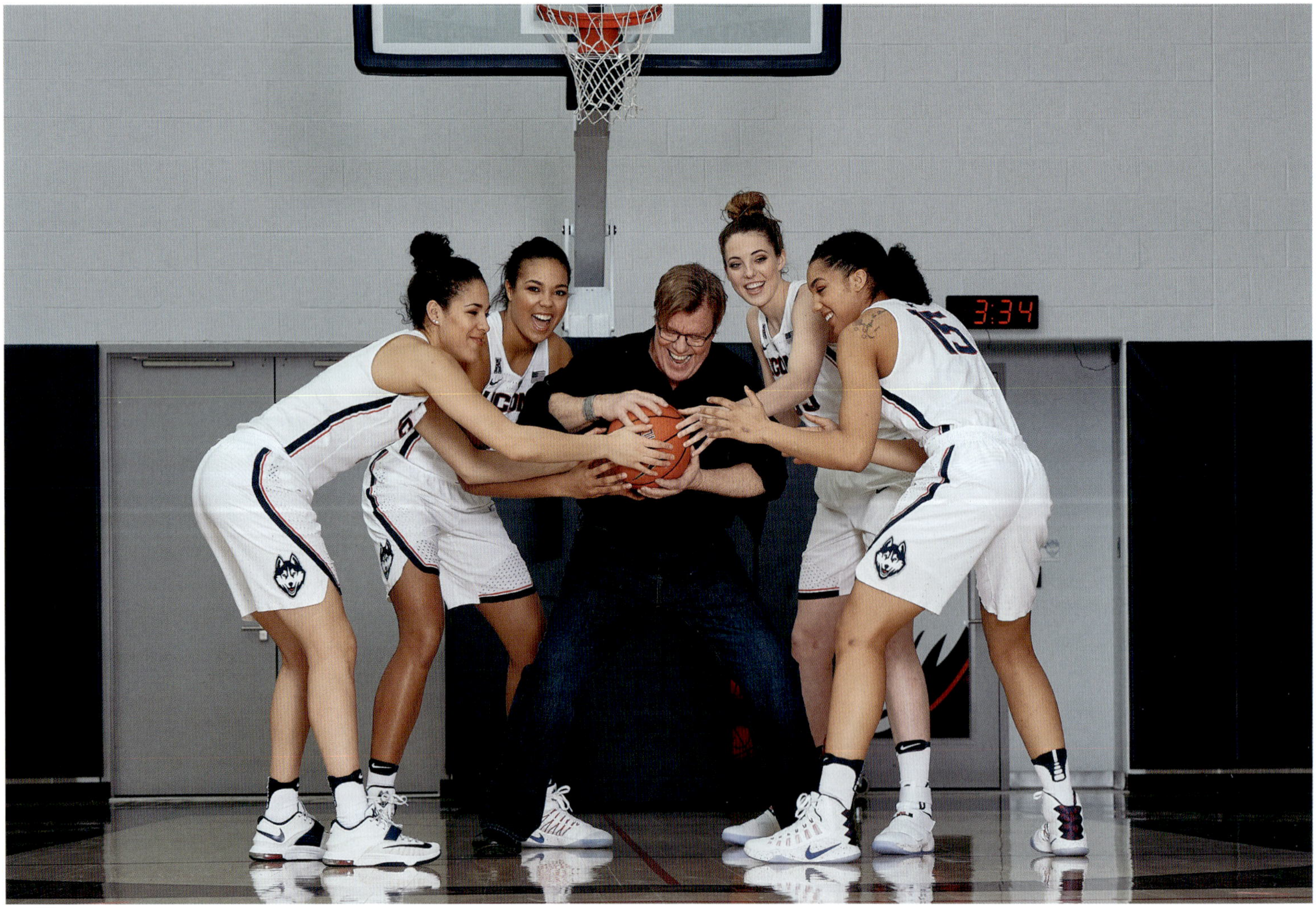

From a Taxi

At this point, when engaged in a casual conversation, you have to sort of push me a little bit to admit I'm a photographer. When you open that door, a wonderful exchange can occur, no doubt. But, if another door opens, it can get exhausting, real quick. When you admit to your profession, it can unleash a torrent of how the person speaking to you "could have been a photographer, but they just didn't have the time." Or they have a relative or close associate who's doing "professional photography."

"Oh, hey cool, you're a photographer! Yeah, my brother is a photographer, too! He retired from his office job and now he takes pictures, you know, like this picture he's got of an old cabin with a thatched roof in this pretty field with flowers and it's really beautiful, you know? He went to Ireland last year and because he's a photographer now he was able to write off a bunch of the trip. I wanted a big print of that picture but he told me, 'Hey, if I give it away I can't make money on it, you know,' so he eventually sold me one, but smaller than I wanted. He sells the bigger ones for, you know, like 60 bucks each."

The person describing his tax-scamming, skinflint brother was the driver of the taxi I was at that moment imprisoned in. We were on the highway, and the speed which we were traveling precluded me from opening my door and pitching myself into traffic. Smile plastered on my face, I just nodded through this whole soliloquy, and the dark part of my brain overtook me. I found myself asking the driver, in inside words, "Sir, can you please drive the car into the oncoming lane of traffic, and do it at speed, so the result

is certain? Stuck as I am in the back seat here, I'm thrilled to reflect on the lifetime of effort I've made to get good at something that is now evidently a tax deduction for your cheap-ass brother who won't even give you a print of what is almost certainly a horrendous landscape photo."

"Let's die together, shall we?"

The above description is pretty much what happened, and I wrote it up on a whim and sent it to the editor of this book, not expecting a serious reply, really, but he actually came back with this:

"Joe, I think maybe you're glamorizing 'the life' just a bit here. This is utterly dripping with romance and, as Cartier-Bresson once called it, the 'joie de vivre of the photographer.' Actually . . . now that I'm thinking about it . . . perhaps the 'decisive moment' has always been misunderstood. Perhaps it's the moment when you realize you're about to kill a cab driver, look up his brother (start with the cabbie's wallet), kill him, find the file of the thatched-roof Ireland scene, examine the GPS data (then destroy the file 'for the good of humanity'), go to that location, set it ablaze, and then, as the Irish police descend on the scene and unleash a hailstorm of slugs into your back, you, in Willem Dafoe–*Platoon* style, fall to your knees and reach both hands upward, heavenward, in a final gesture of redemption, forgiveness, and surrender."

I think Ted, the editor of this book, is onto something. And of course, this is why you need a good editor, who really commits to the spirit of the project.

Photography: To Write with Light. But First, Write on Paper.

It is nighttime at the museum. At the base of a grand, ornate staircase, a lone security guard is asleep at a simple desk with a lamp. The plain, battered desk is out of place in the voluptuously arty venue, where the walls are adorned with magnificent paintings and the gilded ceilings give off a golden glow, even at night. The overall hue of the scene is twilight blue, and the shafts from the outdoor streetlights flood through the huge windows.

Sweeping down the staircase in rapid but silent fashion is a beautiful, mysterious lady, tresses and gown aloft and flying, given the speed of her exit. She has just stolen a copious amount of precious gems!

But, disaster looms. Her gown, blowing behind her, is in the process of toppling a bust atop a display column, which is halfway crashing to the floor. Alarms are starting in the background, and obviously, the police are responding out on the street, as the red flashes from their warning lights are slicing through the windows. Adding to her woes, the satchel she carries, filled to the brim with precious stones, has opened in her haste, and gems and pearls are dropping out of it, bouncing on the floor.

Will she escape?

I'm often asked, in a teaching scenario, what advice I might give to get started in this field, especially for young, aspiring photographers, contemplating the great void faced after leaving the convivial, supportive halls of learning and attempting to scale the Cliffs of Insanity, otherwise known as professional photography.

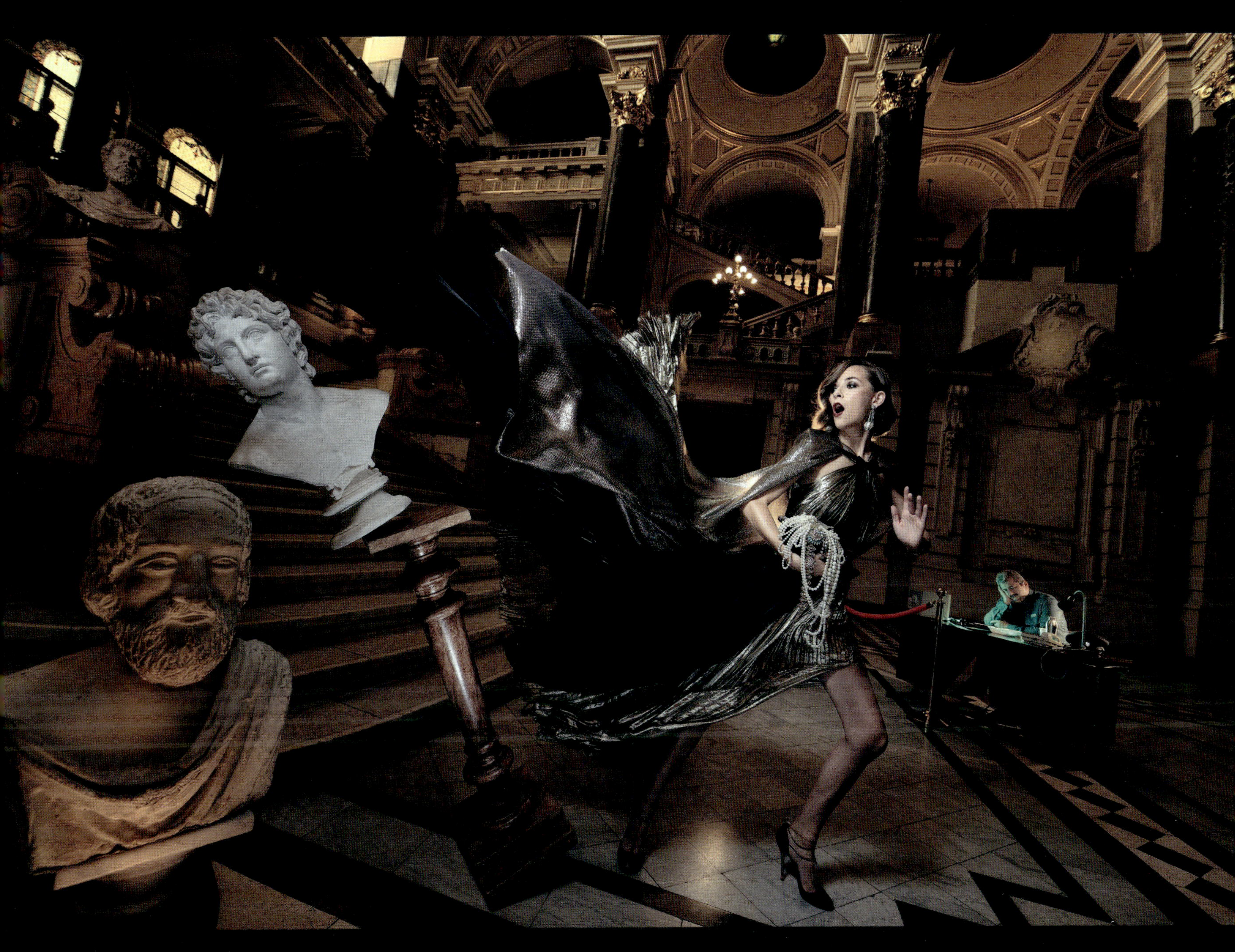

I always respond in helpful and serious fashion, as it's a serious question they face. But I also am intensely aware that, most of the time, what I'm offering is just so much platitudinous bullshit.

"Work hard."

"It's a marathon, not a sprint."

"Wear sunblock."

"Always use a tripod."

"Bring spare batteries."

"Work entire to detail."

"Don't use HDR as it reflects an utter failure of will, talent, perspective, and imagination."

"Except when it's a commercial job and you have to make plates and combine them afterwards and it's what the client wants."

"Observe the rule of thirds."

"Rules are meant to be broken."

"Always remember: When you take a camera in hand, and sally forth into the world, absolutely convinced of the worth of your vision and the importance of your about-to-be-created visual messaging, nobody cares."

And so forth.

The one very serious and worthwhile piece of advice I do offer in terms of counsel is, to a degree, unexpected.

"Write well."

Huh? I thought I had to shoot pictures well!

Remember how, way back in the opening chapter ("A Leap of Faith"), I mentioned that the general operating hypothesis at the newspaper was that if you were bright, energetic, and could carry on a conversation, they made you a reporter? And if you had a driver's license, they made you a photog?

It was a continuation of what I had experienced in school. At the Newhouse School of Journalism at Syracuse University, in order to successfully complete your master's degree in photo-journalism, you had to, at that time, write a well-researched, voluminous thesis. Photographs were allowed, to be sure, but the bulk of the thesis had to be written. The headmasters and headmistresses of the school obviously imagined that those possessed of the arcane mastery of the dark art of the picture were somehow without words, and communicated in a form of patois, known only to the robed brothers and sisters of the lens.

In other words, we had to prove we could write a coherent sentence. In all the other curriculum sequences, such as news-papering, magazine writing, public relations, or advertising, command of language was presumed, so those folks could just take a test and get out of Dodge with the parchment proclaim-ing their master's degree. But we of the photo sequence had to create a learned document, consisting of many words, to demonstrate familiarity and competence with language.

I importune those young people who seek advice to read a great deal, and to be aware of the world and the trends going on in our life and times. I also counsel an awareness of the history of this field, knowing those who have gone before, and to be voracious in their ongoing visual rummaging, examining all manner of styles and genres. All of this would greatly contribute to an ability to sit at a keyboard and write something marginally compelling.

I also urge upon them a sponge-like quality, an ability to absorb influences from the 360-degree experience of life, and let it shape the way they see. These inflections could come from literature, movies, music, childhood traumas, or delightful memories. Things internalized at an early age could bubble to the surface and find their way into a manner of photographing. These things could be subtle and lovely, or outrageous and inap-propriate. They constitute the emotional mosaic we essentially are when we look through a lens.

In college, I got a summer job as a director of a program where high school students could come to Syracuse University and take college classes. I ran the dormitories and was, theoretically, responsible for their extracurricular activities, as well as corralling their more hormonally driven antics, such as confiscating the ladders the boys would buy or swipe from the physical plant to access the dorm windows of the girls. I invited Dr. Sol Gordon to come and lecture these heavy-breathing young people. He was a noted (and controversial) sexologist who had authored a comic book called *Ten Heavy Facts About Sex*. The lecture was well attended.

The first thing he said after stepping to the podium was, "All thoughts are normal!" I heard him say that in the summer of 1974, and it has stayed with me to this day. It's very calming.

Embrace your imagination, even if it veers into strange territory, outside the wire. Be aware and responsive to the kaleidoscope of the world around you. And write it down. And, when necessary, be able to write something, on demand, cool and compelling about something that interests you, which in turn will prompt someone else's interest, a someone else who potentially has money to award to you, so you can stoke the fires of your photographic intent.

Be it a client, an editor, a grant giver, or a patron, all photographers, to get off the dime and into the field, must first present a convincing case, in words—and perhaps supported by pictures, if some exist—on the prospective project. Often, though, it's just words. A proposal. Something lucidly presented, well-articulated, and either forceful enough in its logic or fanciful enough in its lyrical power to literally demand that it be done. Your words need to engage the client, or entity, often before your pictures do, because the pictures are not done yet. They live in your head, and need to be done, by your lights. You need to convince somebody else, often somebody with a tight budget and very little time to dwell on what you need to do, to give you money and go. It's a tough throw. "Your project" burns brightly in your breast, but you must give coherent, eloquent voice to

this flame, and not just stand there with glassy eyes and a heaving bosom.

Reality check. The venerable *National Geographic* magazine, keeper of the keys of photojournalism, long a defender and funder of long-form photo projects, has, in very recent memory, been purchased—lock, stock, and pixel—by Rupert Murdoch, of Fox fame, a publisher whose entire reputation and fortune has been built on hysterical and often false reporting. *Nat Geo* was then packaged with other bits and sold off to the Walt Disney Corporation, which currently has stewardship of the famed yellow border. How important do you think your picture project is to the lords of Disney, compared to the next attack of the mutants of the Marvel Universe?

It's harder now than it ever was. I remember when magazines were comparatively awash in money. So much so that John Whelan, a notable, take-no-prisoners type of photo editor at *Newsweek*, got called into the managing editor's office to explain why a particular photographer on assignment for the magazine had gotten arrested in a foreign and somewhat dodgy place. The magazine had to go to bat for this freelancer's release, incurring complications that needed time and money to solve. Hence the visit to the boss.

Whelan looked at me and rhetorically asked, "What am I going to say? How do I explain that I gave this guy a $2,000 guarantee and a plane ticket just to get him out of my cubicle, 'cause he was so goddam annoying?"

It was like that, a bit, in the '80s. You could be nudgy, persistent, and pesky, and simply hang around long enough that somebody would give you some dough just to get you out of the office and out of their hair. That doesn't happen anymore. Every penny is looked at. And the need to put people out there, to fund projects, to place people in the field, is assessed from every angle. Details indicating the depth of your research are crucial. France, for instance, is neither a project nor a story. It's a country. However, a pictorially driven piece about the effects of climate change on the French wine industry, an industry that constitutes a huge psychological, emotional, financial, and physical aspect of the French identity as a nation—now that's a story. Supported by facts, the impact of warmer weather, the changes in the grapes, the lessening of the value of exports, the resultant impact on trucking, shipping, and the overall devaluation of the prestige of French wine, along with the concomitant and rueful, saddening cultural haymaker to the gut of French pride . . . well, that's intriguing indeed. And valid. And pictorial. And timely. Editors check boxes when assessing the creation of potential content, and this one has some very potent boxes checked off.

The scrutiny of the proposal, and of you, can be intense. You must remain confident in your ideas, even amongst a sea of naysayers. You need to defend and explain the positives of doing it your way. And explaining a picture idea to folks sitting around a conference table, who are perhaps not the most creatively inclined, can be excruciating. You can feel like you're in that room and everybody there is wearing clothes, except you. But you do it because you just want the pictures so badly.

To create business, and to stay in business, you need to move and convince people with words, even before you do that with your pictures.

I was asked to be one of four photographers, worldwide, to pictorially inaugurate the Nikon D850, at that point a brand-new digital camera that would take its place in the annals of some of the best digital imaging machines ever made. My arena was to

be fashion. The creatives, based in Singapore, asked for treatments, as in proposals. Their mandate:

TASK
- You need to come up with 2–3 ideas that represent the combination of high-res and high speed.
- Write your own "I am" line that will accompany the visual.

DELIVERABLES
- A comprehensive written and visual description of 2–3 ideas (they repeat what they state under "Task").
- 1 Key Visual including post-production (portrait and landscape format).
- 1 Profile Image of you and your signature.
- 5 "Side Shots" (not BTS [behind the scenes], but outtakes of the key visual).

I created three scenarios: one in the desert, one on rooftops, and the one they chose, which came to be called the "High Fashion Heist." The simple text that launched all the shenanigans starts this story.

No matter that the fantasy cat burglar on the stairs took all of 10 minutes to conjure and write up. No matter that early readings of Ian Fleming's accounts of 007, "license to kill," were a staple of my youthful imagination and sparked my brain in this direction. Or that the subsequent graduate course in James Bond films I embarked on, starting back when Sean Connery was the debonair, conflicted assassin, gave me a sense of the moody staging and lighting I might need to bring to bear. Mysteries! Elegance! Deadly deeds in the dark of night!

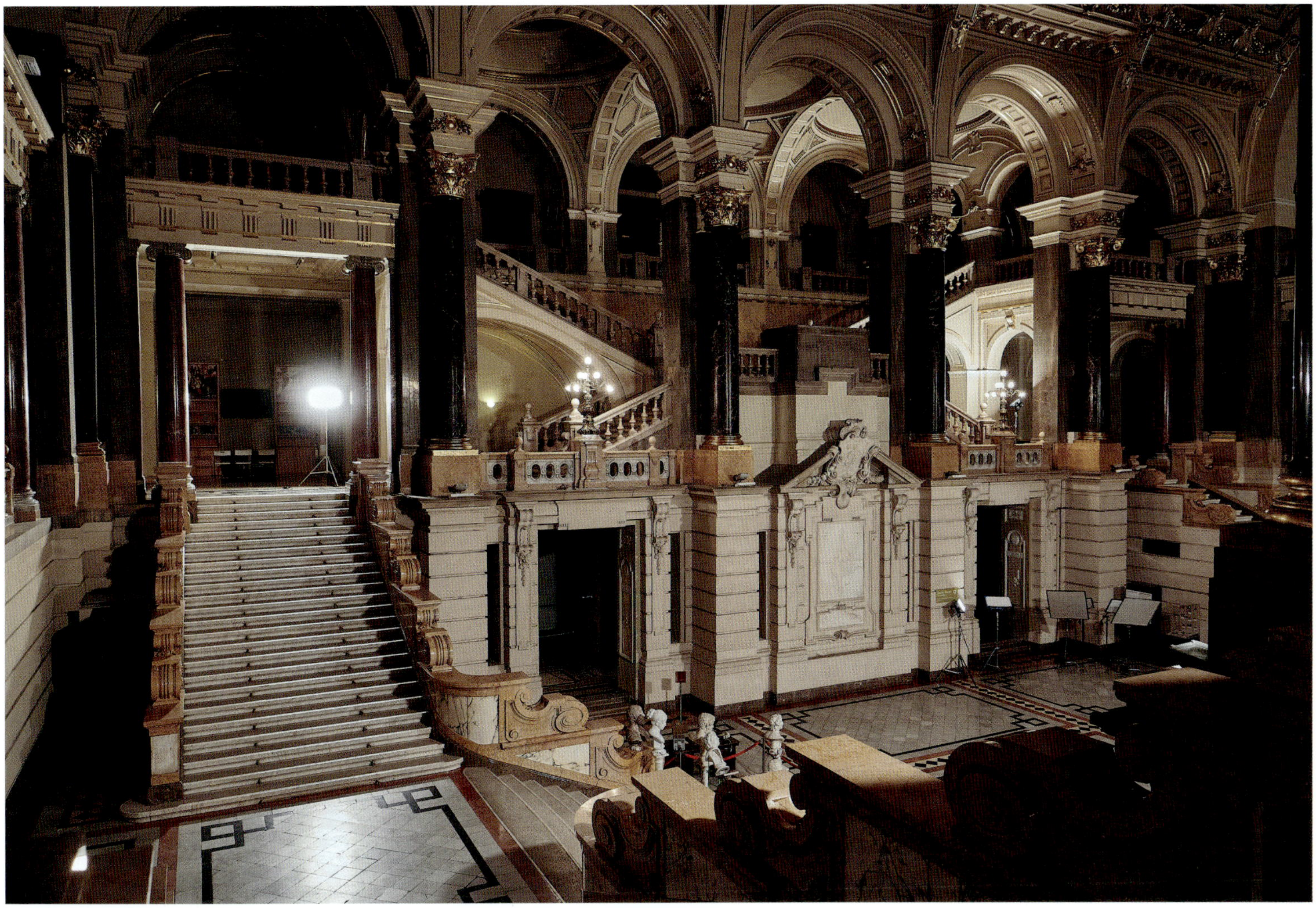

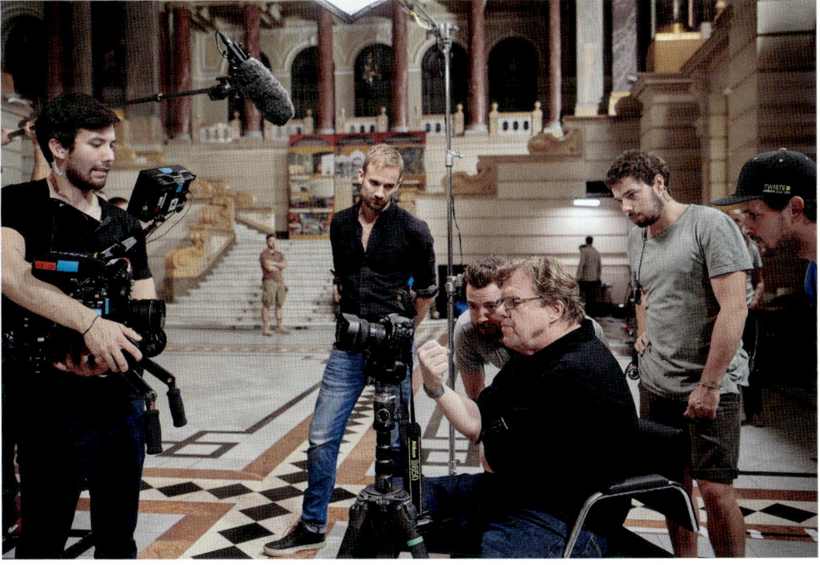

Those trifling few paragraphs started the ball rolling for one of the biggest jobs of my life. The creatives in Singapore approved the concept and hired me, a U.S.-based photographer, then liaised with a German agency, which in turn hired a Canadian film crew. Location scouts offered numerous options, mostly in Europe, home to any number of grand museums. We are a small world now, digitally bound together. In short order, all these disparate talents and puzzle pieces were bound for Budapest. I now had to light an entire museum. In front of the client, the crew, and multiple video cameras. We used so much light we had to have the flash and grip trucked in from Munich.

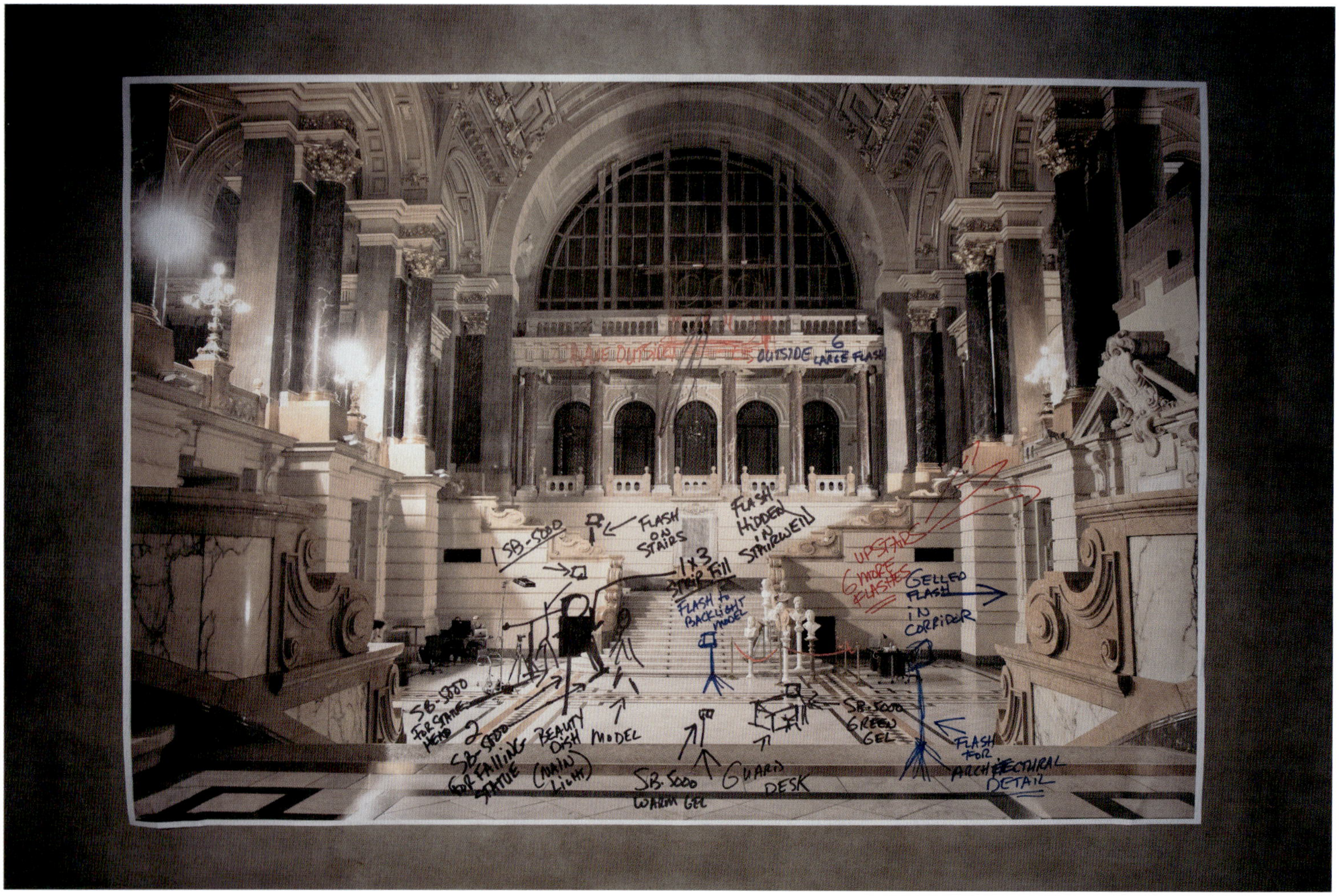

OUTSIDE
OUTSIDE 6 LARGE FLASH
SB-5000
FLASH ON STAIRS
FLASH HIDDEN IN STAIRWELL
1 x 3 STRIP FILL
FLASH TO BACKLIGHT MODEL
UPSTAIRS 6 MORE FLASHES
GELLED FLASH IN CORRIDOR
SB-5000 FOR STATUE HEAD
SB-5000 FOR FALLING STATUE
2 BEAUTY DISH (MAIN LIGHT)
MODEL
SB-5000 WARM GEL
GUARD DESK
SB-5000 GREEN GEL
FLASH FOR ARCHITECTURAL DETAIL

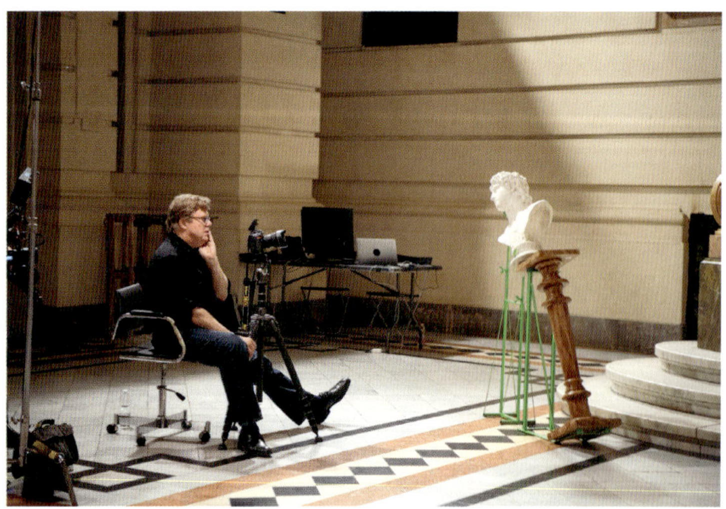

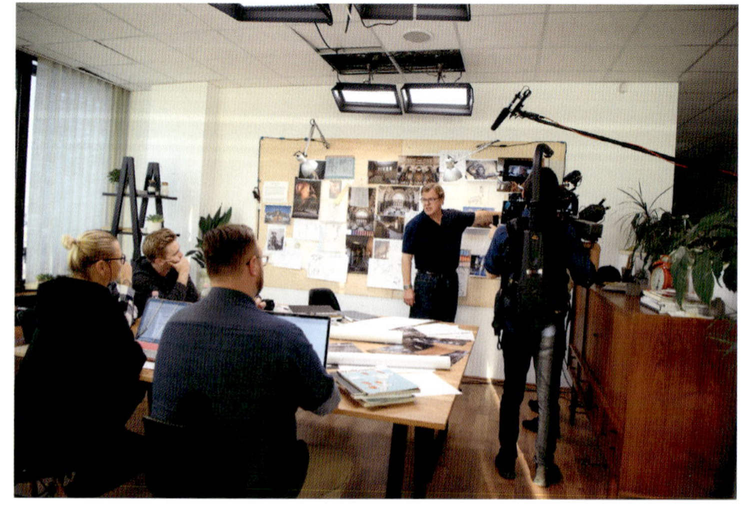

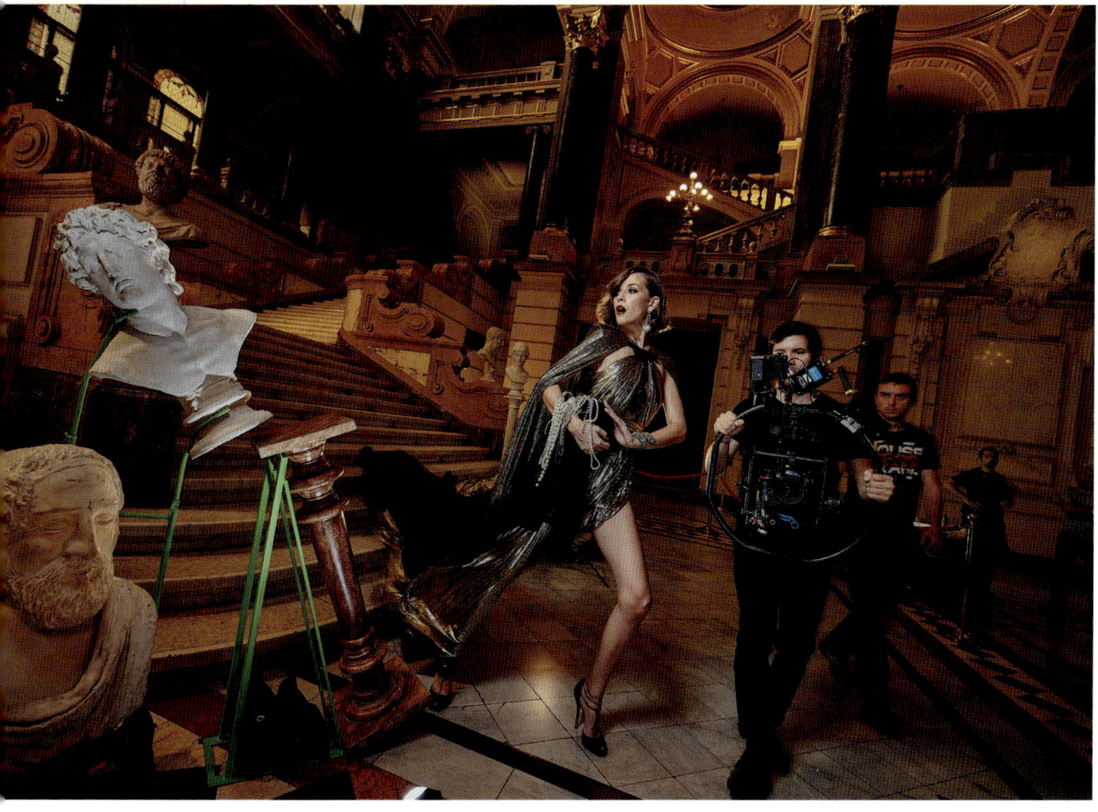

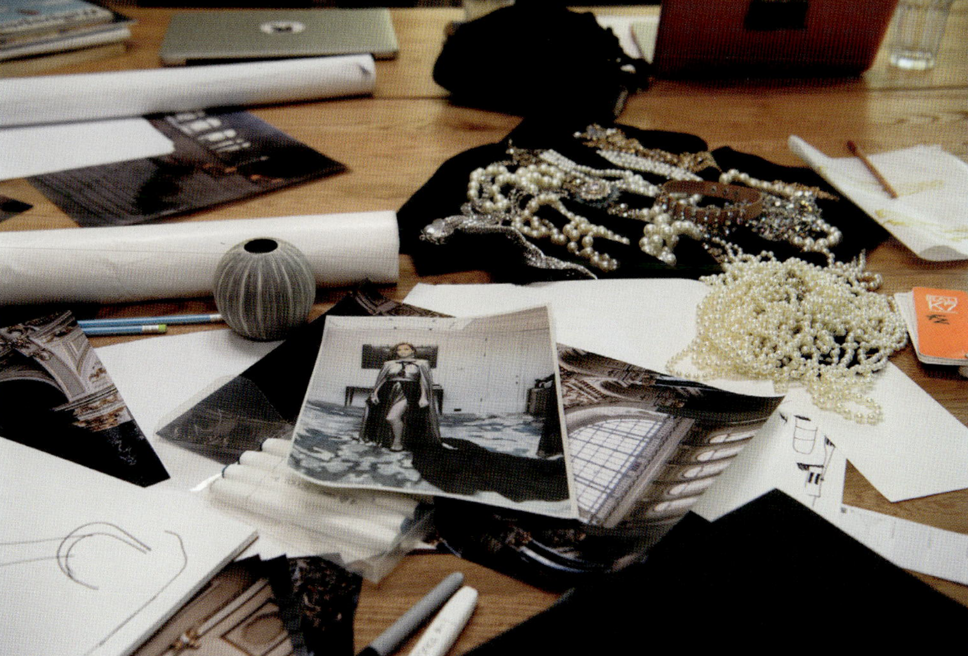

On a big job like this, you are the eye of the storm. You're directing the light, the action, and the staging. Everything from where to put the tripod to the final choice on the wardrobe is on your shoulders. You assemble a great team, and you have tremendous and talented help, but as is always true, it's your name on the door. Final responsibility for the shot remains with you. It's a pressurized swirl, for several days.

Sketches, directives, prepping, and assembling all come to a head eventually. You have to actually do the shot, the classic "Okay, put your pixels where your mouth is" moment. It's daunting. A gateway to go through. Another door to force open just because you have to keep risking, and keep working at the boundaries of whatever talents you might possess. The jackhammers of doubt are rattling your skull. Outwardly, you don't betray lack of confidence, guts, or solutions. Build the picture. Drive through the problems. There's not a moment you can't be "on" because you are shooting the shot, and you are also the subject of the all-important BTS: You are mic'd for the entire week, cameras are pointing at you constantly, and people are asking if you could do that again, or rephrase that directive. If you sneeze, fart, weep, or curse, it's recorded.

Being able to effectively describe how important and necessary it is that someone give you an assignment, or some funding, is just as important as the pixels.

What came out of my imagination on this job, as silly and ephemeral as it was, led to one of the biggest shoots of my career. I was unabashed to write it down and submit it, thankfully. A few minutes of florid, fevered conjuring ultimately kept more than 30 people busy and employed for about a week.

It called on all my experience and skills at the camera. Stressful, but wonderful. Another page of the adventure book. Eye in the camera. And words on a page.

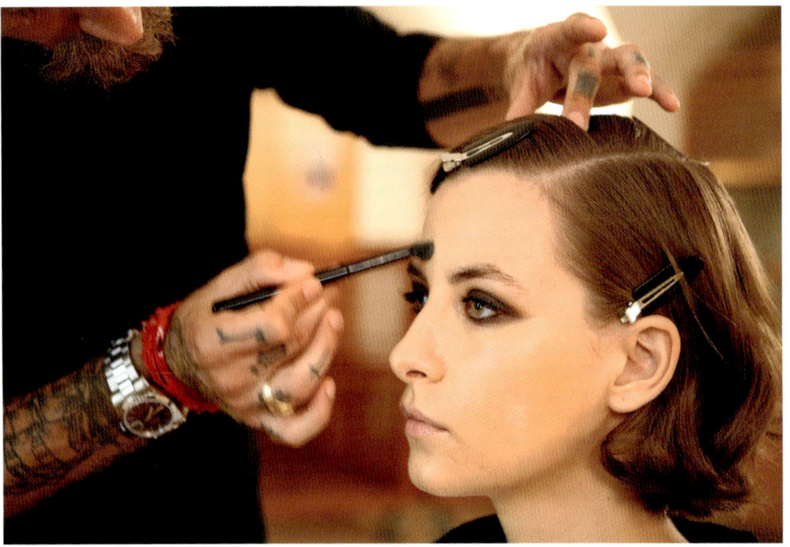

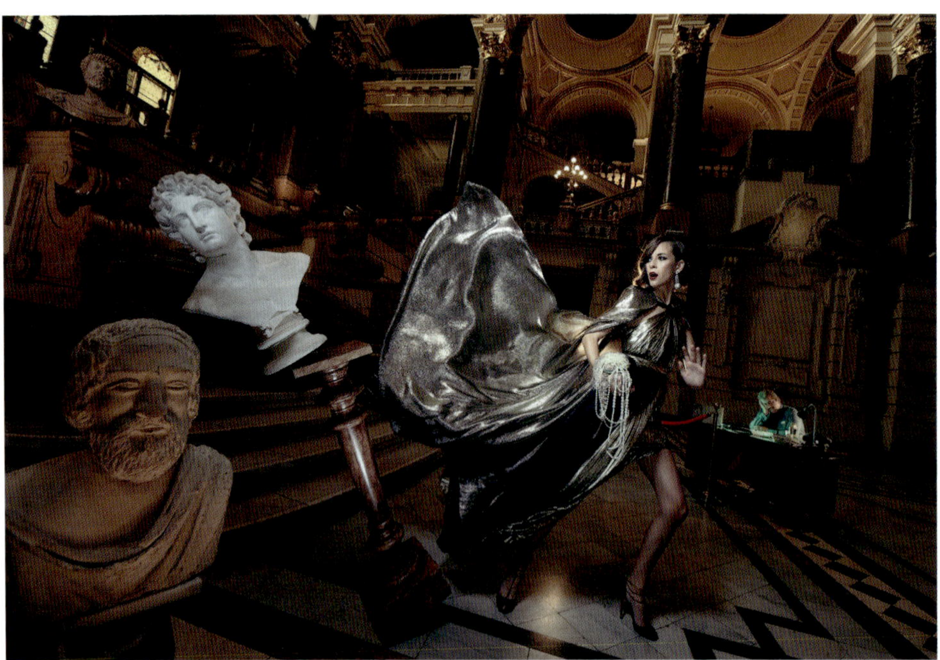

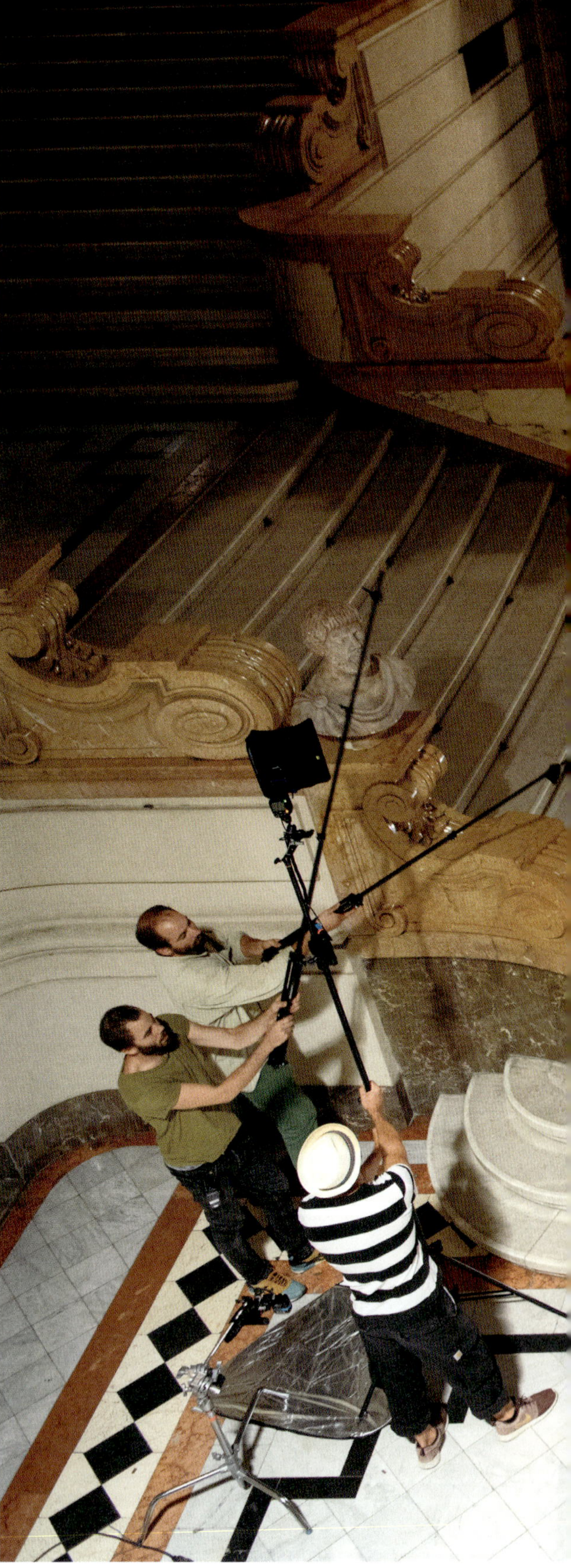

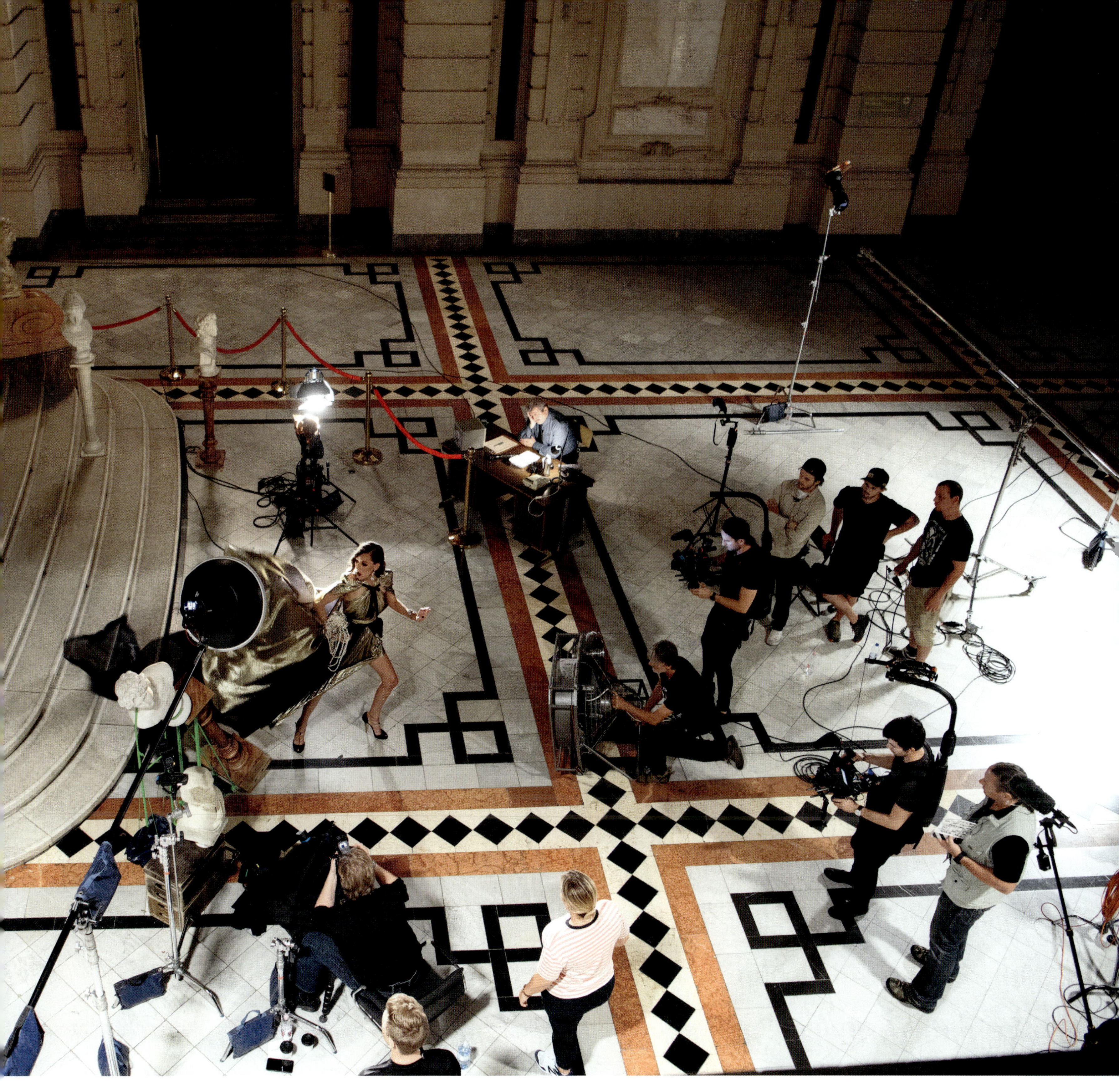

The Fixer

I worked in Rwanda for a brief period, just after the 100-day genocide that occurred there in 1994. On my last day in the country, I was due to fly from Kigali to Nairobi, but early in the day the flight was canceled. Tom, my fixer, a Ugandan, told me I could get the nightly flight from Entebbe Airport, near Kampala, the capital of Uganda. We could drive across the border and get there in plenty of time. As often occurs on a job, this was easier to talk about than actually do.

It was a horrendous day. On the drive north we were stopped at three checkpoints by the various armies, and at the last one, they literally tore my bag apart, throwing my gear and clothing all over the tarmac. This was in the days of film, and of course, I had been shooting panorama 617 cameras, which meant nearly all of the assignment coverage was on overlarge 120 film cassettes.

I had done my best, wrapping some film in thoroughly filthy underwear, some in a shave kit, and taking some of the rest and sequestering them in the actual cavities of the Fujica pano cameras, which were quite large. The shutter was in the lens of that style of camera, so those bodies had, comparatively, a fair bit of empty space in the interior chambers.

But film being a physical object—and in the case of a photographer on assignment, there were numerous, numerous of those physical objects—you are naked in the face of scrutiny, without a shred of power over your own fate, desperately looking for luck or grace or reason to transport you

across a border of what at the time was a very unreasonable place in the world. It was a day when I kept repeating my own personal mantra about the act of being a photographer: The Lord looks after a fool.

Tom was cool during the whole trek, continually negotiating and explaining. I stayed quiet, nodding, presenting documents and a face I hoped didn't portray my inner anguish and dread. We got through to the airport, parked, and went in. I purchased a one-way ticket and sat with Tom and paid him for his excellent services and thanked him for his kindly demeanor and hard work. I was just another journalist to him, and certainly he had his own interior opinions about the numbers of international press that had convened to report on the convulsive horror that had rent this small country in the heart of Africa. But he was a companion to me. He was the only person I had really talked with very much while I was in Rwanda.

Understand, this was before the ubiquity of English as a more and more common universal language, before the serious onslaught of computers, and when email and cell phones were, comparatively, in their infancy. I traveled with a notepad and a pen, not a laptop. There was no FaceTime or unlimited texting. Just some creaky, expensive, rotary dial landlines at the hotel. I had no contact with anyone at home. Nobody back there knew anything about what I was doing, day to day. In terms of the normal back and forth of a day—car chats, observations—Tom was it.

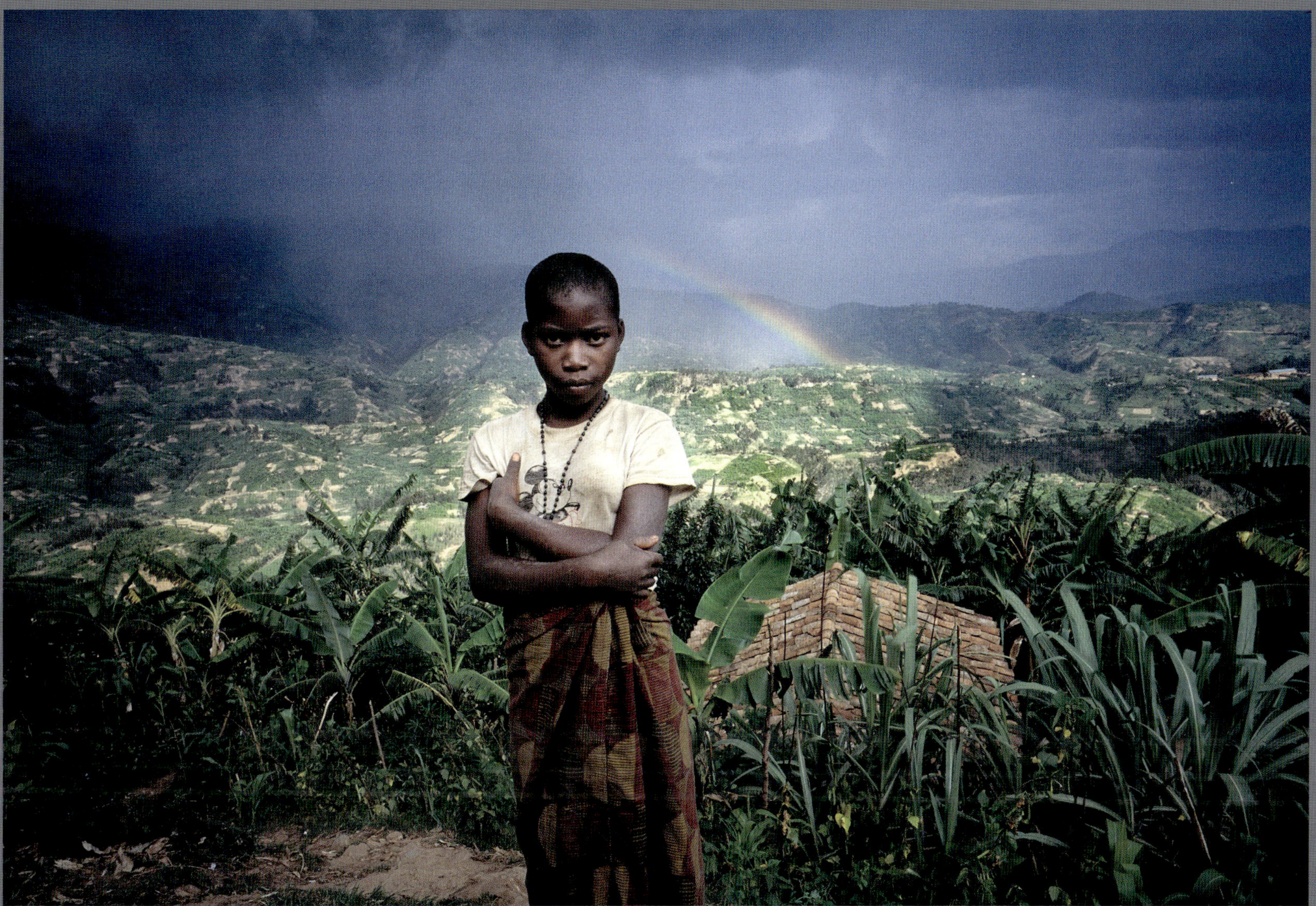

We shook hands, and he walked down the hallway of the airport. There were big windows at the end of the hall, and in that bright backlight, he quickly became a silhouette, and then just a shimmer. I sat back down on the cracked plastic chair near my gate and realized I had just said goodbye to the one person in the world who actually knew where I was.

It was December. On the Muzak system, holiday melodies piped in. Bing Crosby, perhaps. It might have been "White Christmas." I stared ahead. And I never felt more alone.

In Pursuit of Heroes

Every year I tell myself I'll go to *National Geographic's* annual get-together, which is still called the National Geographic Seminar. Historically, it was comprised of photo lectures and programs, speakers, "works in progress," cash bars, get-togethers amongst the photogs, and punctuated by "the prom," a photo community bash with music and dancing. It's changed and diminished over time, but they resolutely have continued to stage some version of the original event every January.

Every year, I do fancy going. And every year, I pretty much don't go. Except one year, somewhat recently. I noticed that Danny Lyon, a Magnum photographer, was speaking, along with Julian Bond, who was one of my early political and social activist heroes. He helped found the Student Nonviolent Coordinating Committee (SNCC, referred to in conversation as "SNICK") and the Southern Poverty Law Center. He also served in the Georgia House of Representatives and the Georgia State Senate. He remained active his whole life in politics and policy, constantly advocating for racial justice, fair housing, and LGBTQ rights. He was also involved in the anti-Vietnam War movement.

As was Danny Lyon. Danny became the official photog of SNCC and covered the tumult of the civil rights movement in a truly present and effective way. He went on to do noteworthy books on bikers and on the Texas State Department of Corrections, among others. He photographed six prisons in Texas, spending over a year on the project, and it resulted in a book called *Conversations with the Dead*. It's an astonishing tome, and one of the early books I bought while a photo student as inspiration for my yet-to-be-embarked-upon career. I have kept it for many years.

Danny and Julian remained friends, and they were paired onstage at the Geographic seminar. I decided to go down to Washington, D.C. I brought my book.

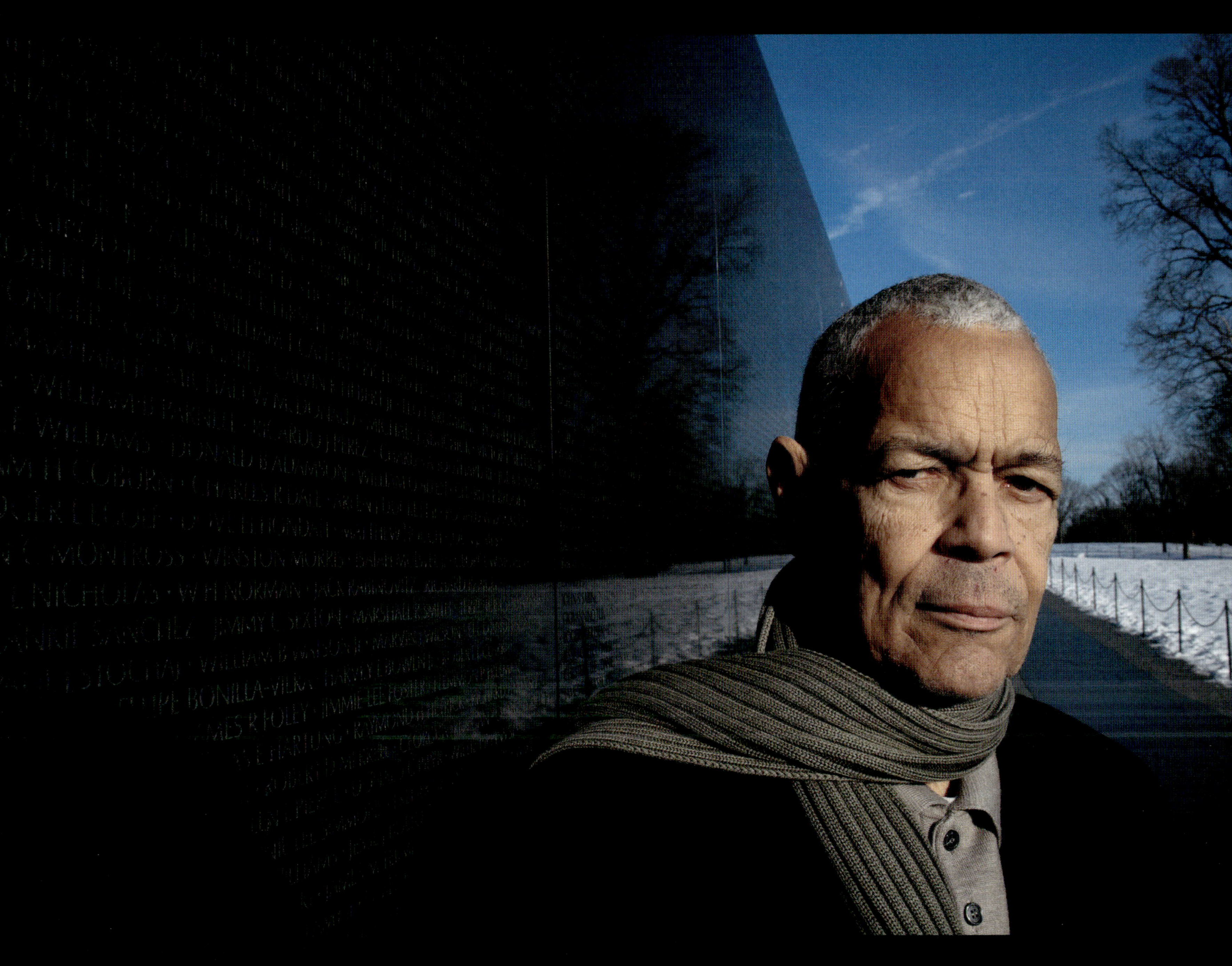

They recounted their adventures for the crowd. Mr. Bond was effervescently cerebral, dignified, and regal. Danny . . . was not. I winced a couple times. Gamely, though, I approached him after the talk, and politely told him he was a huge influence on me and asked him to sign my book. He did, but, well, let's just say he wasn't gracious about it. That's okay. My long-held treasure of a book is now signed by the creator. He's done formidable work, and well, maybe he was just having a bad day.

But Julian Bond! Hearing him speak, I admired him even more than I already had, historically speaking. I started spinning possibilities in my head. One of the reasons I was in D.C. for the seminar, truth be told, was that I was on assignment for LIFE Books. They were publishing a book about the Vietnam War— the war on the ground there, and the war here in the U.S., as the country tore itself apart with protests. I was assigned to photograph a group of vets who agreed to come to the Vietnam Veterans Memorial Wall to share thoughts with our writer and to be photographed. I also had to photograph those who opposed the war. Mr. Bond qualified on that front, for sure. I communicated to my editor, asking permission to approach him, and got a green light.

I got this email in response:

I would very much like to be included in this project.
I am flattered to be considered.

I can be reached most easily at this email address.

—Julian Bond

So, the back of the hand and utter indifference from a photographic hero, but gracious acceptance from someone who could have easily not bothered to reply. We made a date.

He had a lovely home and a study that was a history lesson in his lifelong fight for racial justice. I knew his time was tight, so I began working in the dim, cool window light of the winter, just barely eking its feeble way through his study window. It was not preferable light. But that is the way of it, as a photographer. You assess, sometimes quite quickly, and begin to work, because you have to. It's about making a commitment and putting your camera to your eye. The job has started, and just like a boat about to leave the dock, you have to step on board or be left behind.

He began to show me memorabilia from the history of segregation, and I began to photograph. I knew none of these pictures worked and would never see the light of day, but I plunged ahead anyway. I was intensely curious about the artifacts, and he was equally happy to show me. It got us off to a good start. In this situation, explaining that you were waiting for some sort of as yet unseen light to be set up without starting to shoot would make for the very definition of an awkward pause.

That unseen light was outside, making unsteady progress toward his window. My assistant had a large softbox on a Profoto B4 light, and he was relentlessly pushing it through shrubbery and snowbanks to get that light by the study window. In this way, via a remote trigger on my camera, when he got it into position, I would have "natural window light" at my beck and call. I could also migrate the color from the cold of winter shade to something more welcoming. Cool is off-putting. Warm invites you in.

You can see the progress in this sequence of unretouched images (opposite). His bookshelf is warmed by the artificial tungsten lights in his ceiling fixtures. But that light is pooled on the memorabilia, and rapidly gives way to absolutely glacial light coming through the window. I'm able to handle it better when I ask him to bring a book by the window, but the feel of the light has no spark. The background of his office, which is important for the reader to see, fades to black.

Enter the softbox! Now I have soft, warm light at my command, and it wraps up both the office and the man, and gives me a fighting chance at establishing him and his work environment. The space he works in provides lovely and viable context, and is therefore essential editorial information. Leaving it unattended would rob the viewer of both information and enjoyment, and it's your job at the camera to provide both, when possible.

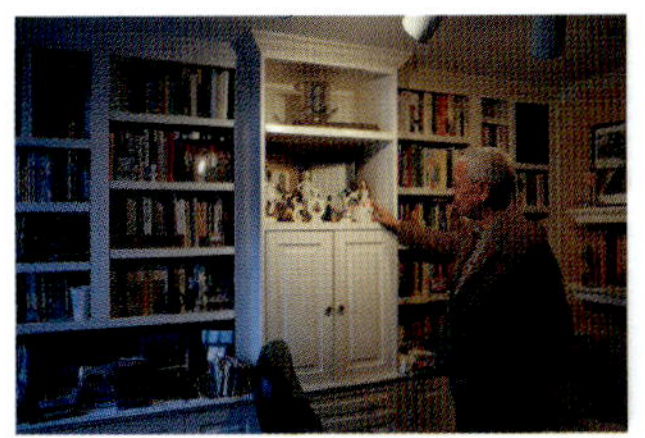 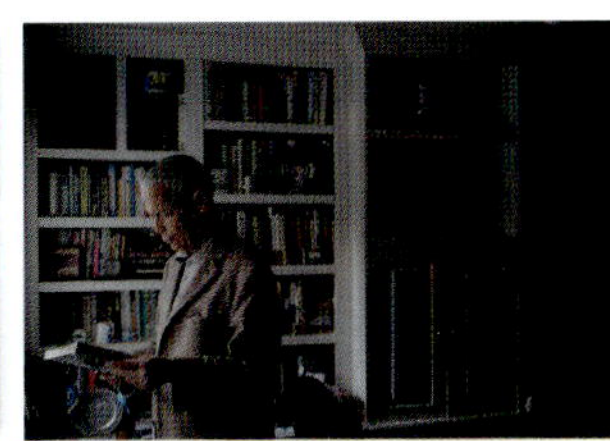 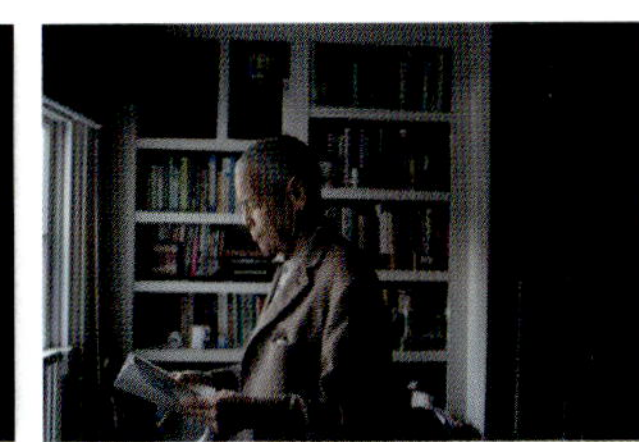 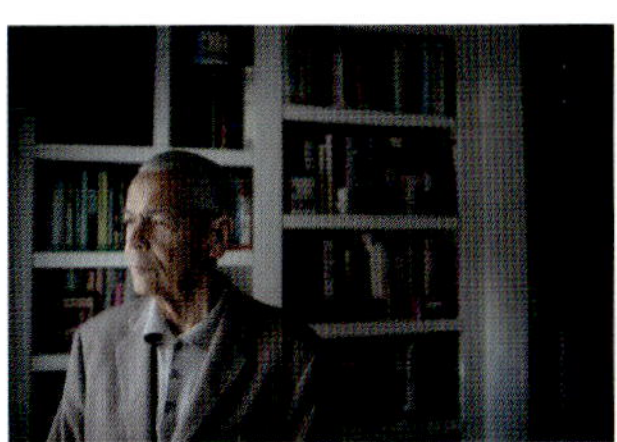 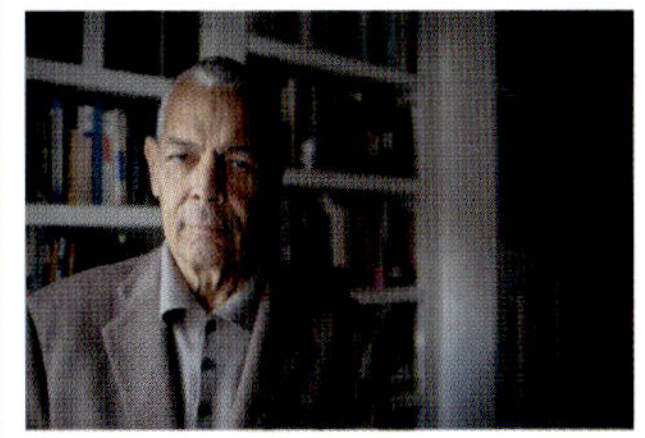

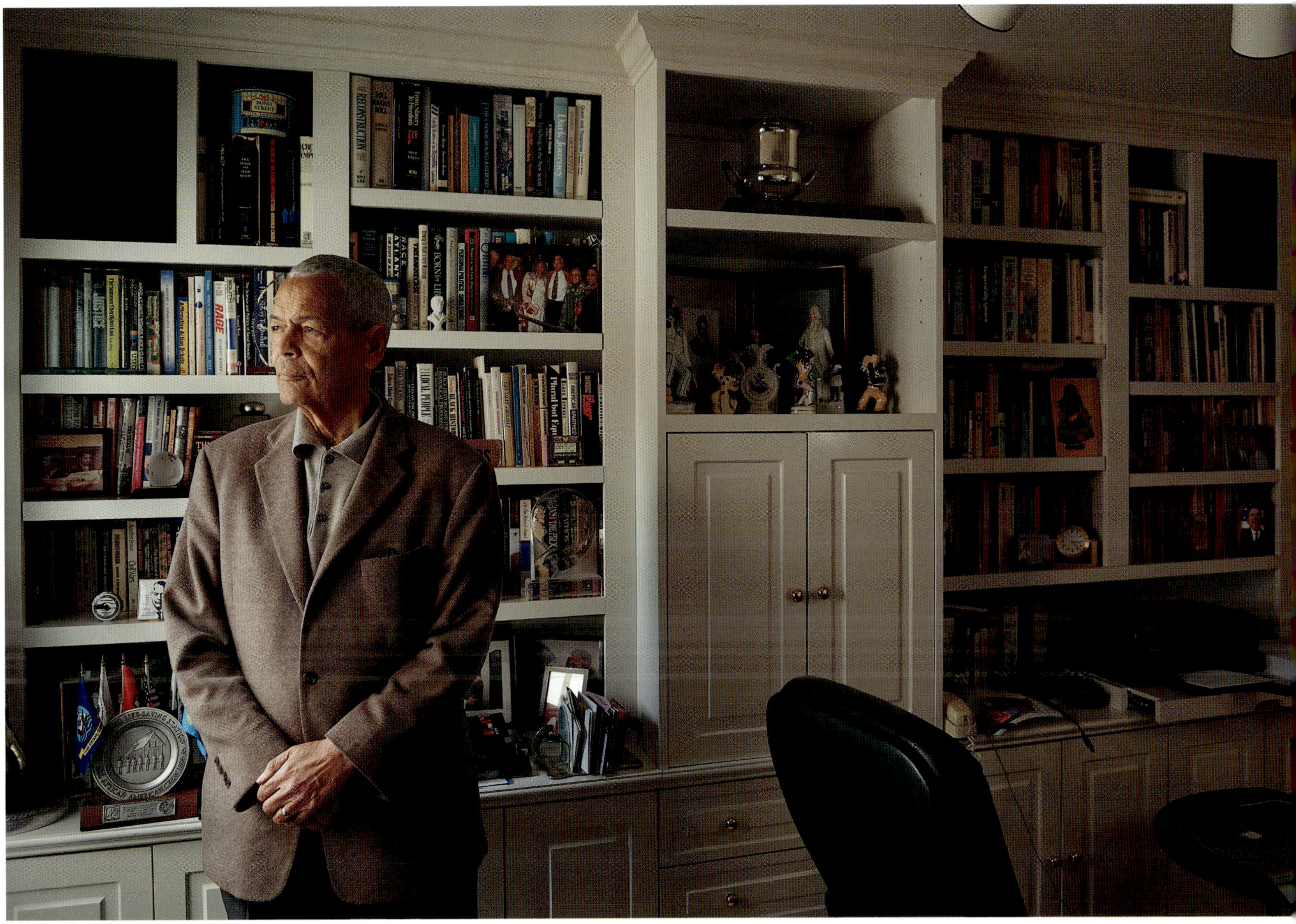

As important as these pictures were, though, and necessary to shoot (you always want to photograph at your subject's home, no matter what), I needed a reference to Vietnam. His involvement in the anti-war movement was the reason I got a thumbs-up to shoot this in the first place. Without placing him in a context that spoke to the war, my efforts would never see ink. Thankfully, he had allowed time for us to go to the Vietnam Veterans Memorial Wall, those poignant, piercing black slabs of granite bearing the names of the war dead.

As photographers, we often hear phrases like, "Oh, man, you shoulda been here last week, it was beautiful!" or, "Wow, it's usually much busier than this, I don't know what's going on." And, in my case especially, "Geez, it usually doesn't rain so much this time of year!" I hear that one a lot.

Not this day. Julian Bond and I arrived at the Vietnam Memorial at a perfect time of day, with perfect light to match. My first frame of him at the wall was shot at 5:14 p.m. My last frame was 5:29. In 15 minutes, the job was done. The home pictures would go into the file. The pictures at the memorial immediately became the pictorial hook I hung the whole effort on.

During the shoot, I worked quickly from wide lens to telephoto.

A quick frame, out of the gate (top).

Then my personal select, the photo leading this story (middle).

Backing off a bit. Remaining mobile (bottom).

Then telephoto, minimum depth of field. 200mm lens at f/2 (opposite, top).

I worked minimum DOF and then amplified DOF via f-stop and lens choice. His expressions were not mobile. I didn't need him to smile. It would have been out of place for him, especially with that serious, emotionally somber background. He was who he was, and it was plenty.

One of the beautiful things about being a photog is that you do, on occasion, get to meet and photograph your heroes. In the case of Mr. Bond, it was not a disappointment. And Danny, well, I came home and put the book back on my shelf.

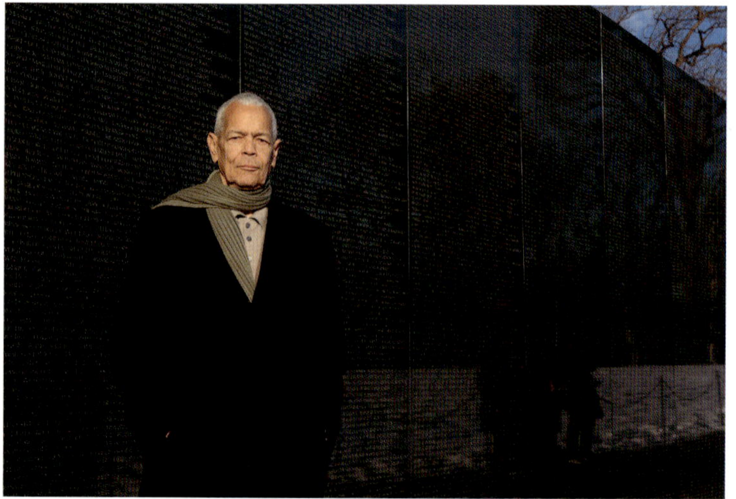

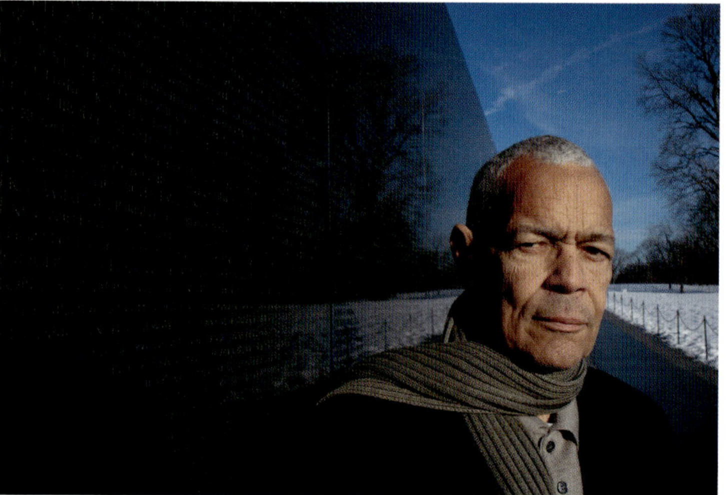

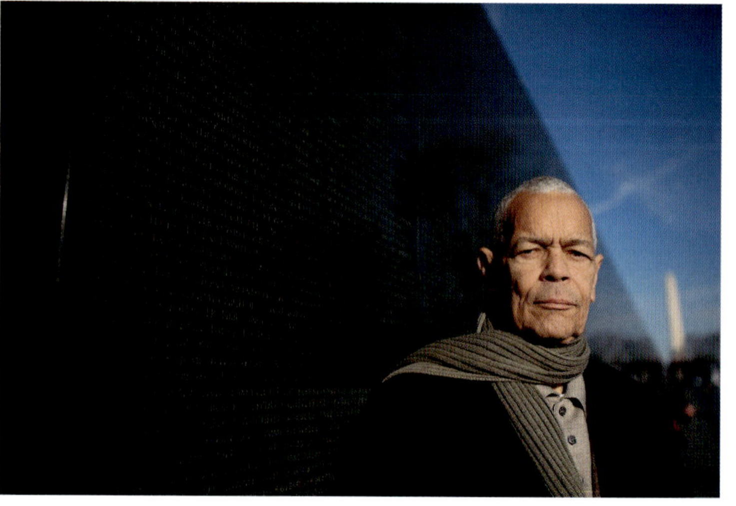

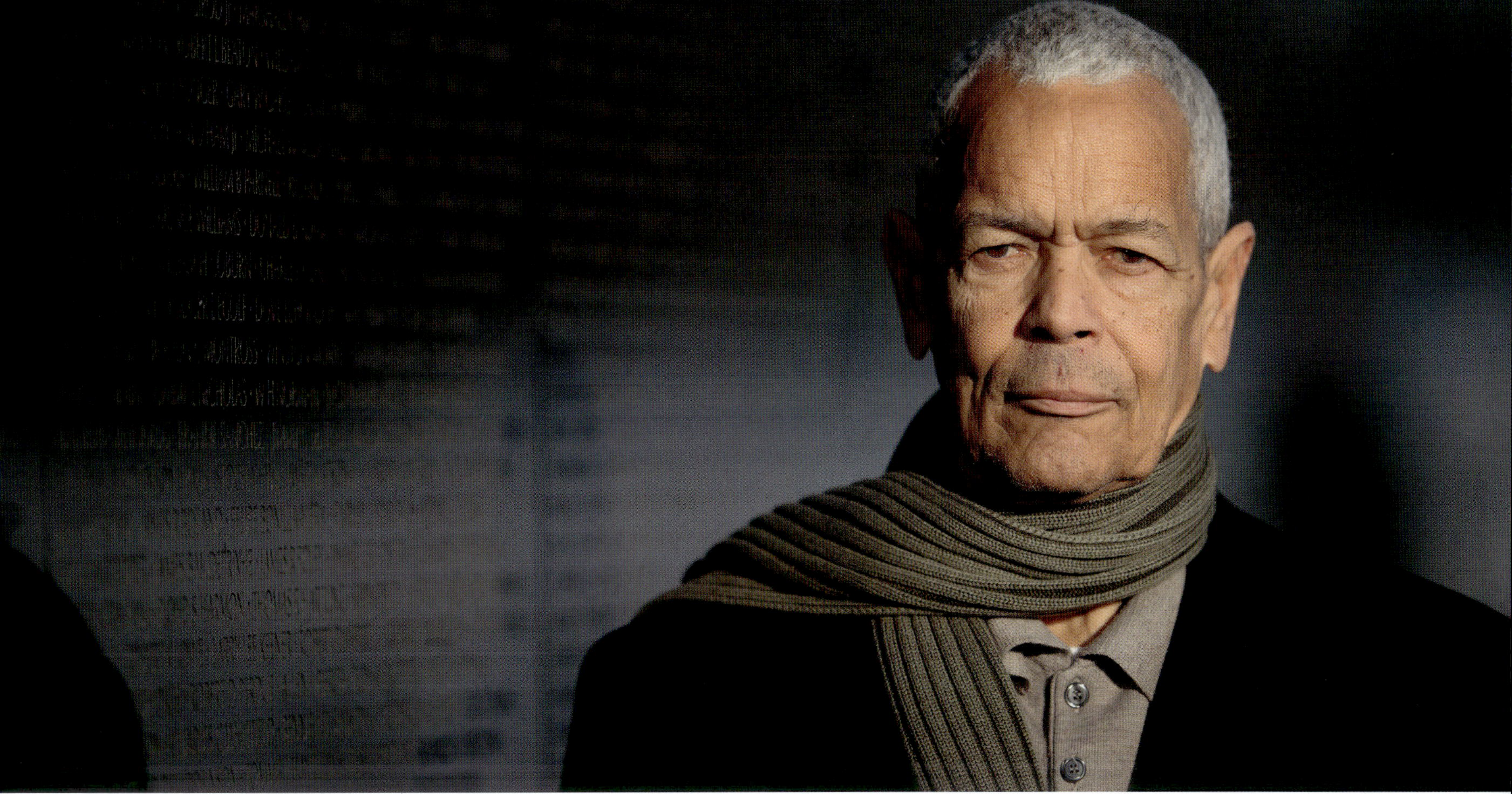

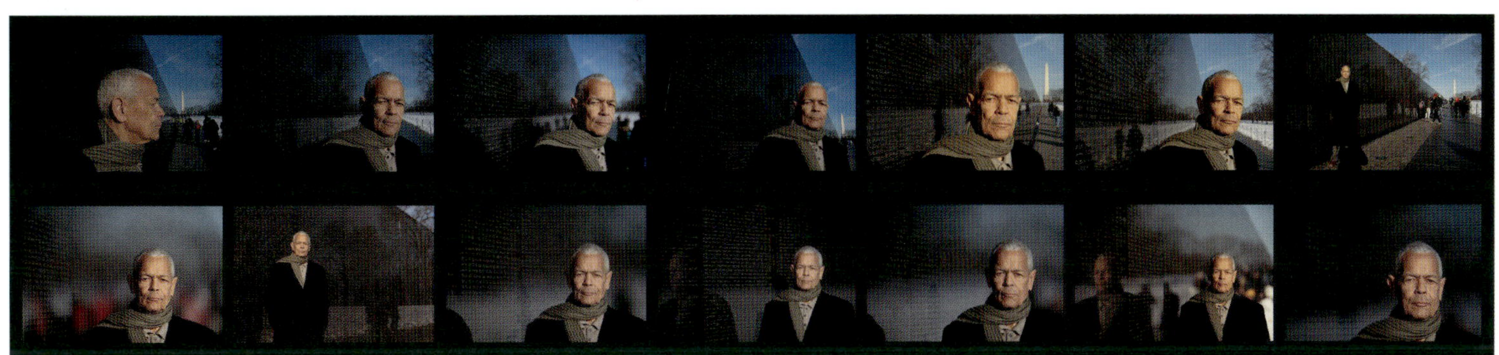

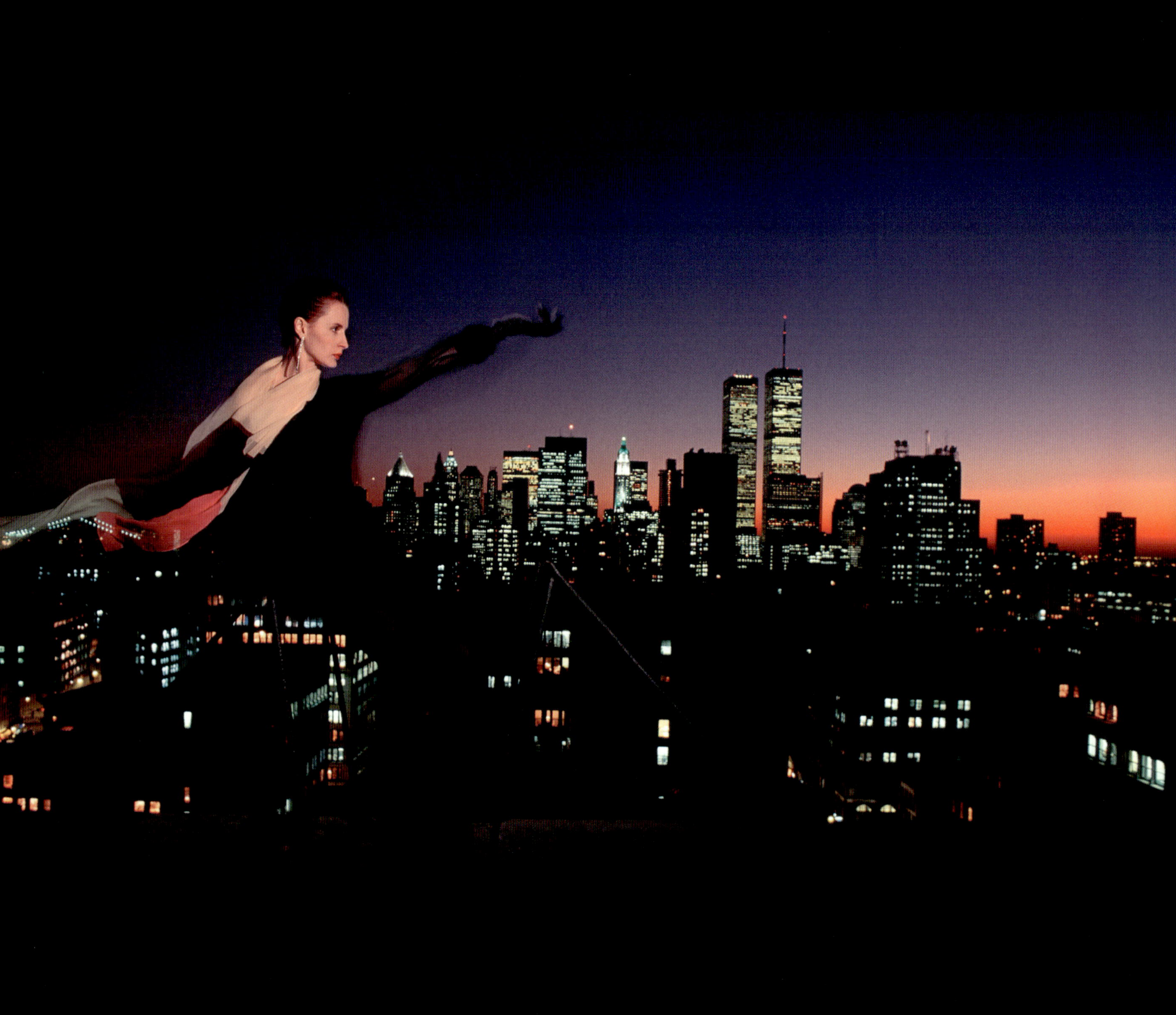

Making Pictures,
Making Friends

I have written of this picture before (opposite). I discussed it in *The Hot Shoe Diaries* as a lesson in filtration, and how a green gel over the Speedlight and a corresponding magenta gel on the camera lens would render a normal skin tone and, simultaneously, clean up a fluorescent-laden cityscape and take a pleasing but average sunset and make it seem like end of day on Tatooine. Full green gel = 30 points of magenta (roughly, to your taste). It was a two-step that we did religiously back in the film days, but which we have largely abandoned after the dawn of digital, pixels, Photoshop, plugins, selective color, and who knows what else. At the time I shot this, I was dealing with the physical, relatively immutable reality of Kodachrome, so it behooved me to sort out color issues right there at the camera.

There's no need to rehash the technique of this picture. I bring it to the fore again for a couple of reasons, quite apart from the lingo of "place the light 10 feet from your subject and understand this source of light will produce a poppy, hard light effect, with contrast and shadows, given its small size relative to the subject."

No need to go there. What this picture is really about is trust.

Hey, wait a minute, I thought this was about the color! Or the pixels! Or the lens!

No, it's about trust.

I picked Rita from her headshot sheet long ago. I didn't know her, she didn't know me. She was luminously beautiful in her disseminated modeling photo, but you have to cross your fingers when casting from cards. The photos that models and agencies put out there, while not misleading, are often highly retouched and obviously calculated to put the best pictorial foot forward. As an analogy, we've all seen those hotel brochures, where a luxurious room, shot for the brochure with pretty, open light and a 14mm

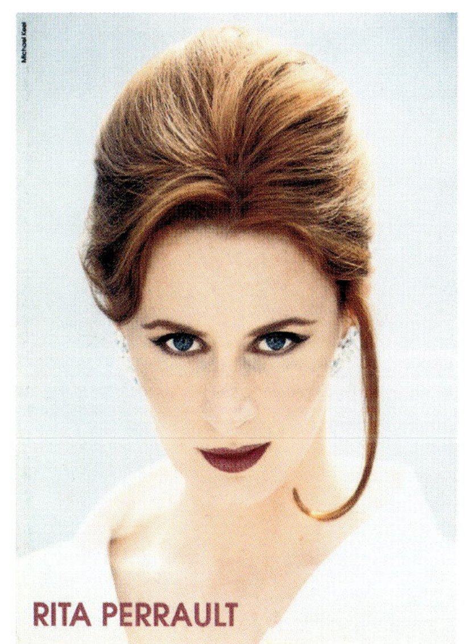

lens, makes it seem like you could stage a soccer match in it, when in reality it turns out to be something of a broom closet with a view of the dumpster. Just saying.

A tip when casting: ask the model you are thinking of casting to send a few current snaps. Easy, given the wonders of cell phones.

That was not possible in 1988. I loved Rita's headshot, so I booked her. She showed up, game and beautiful, went to the

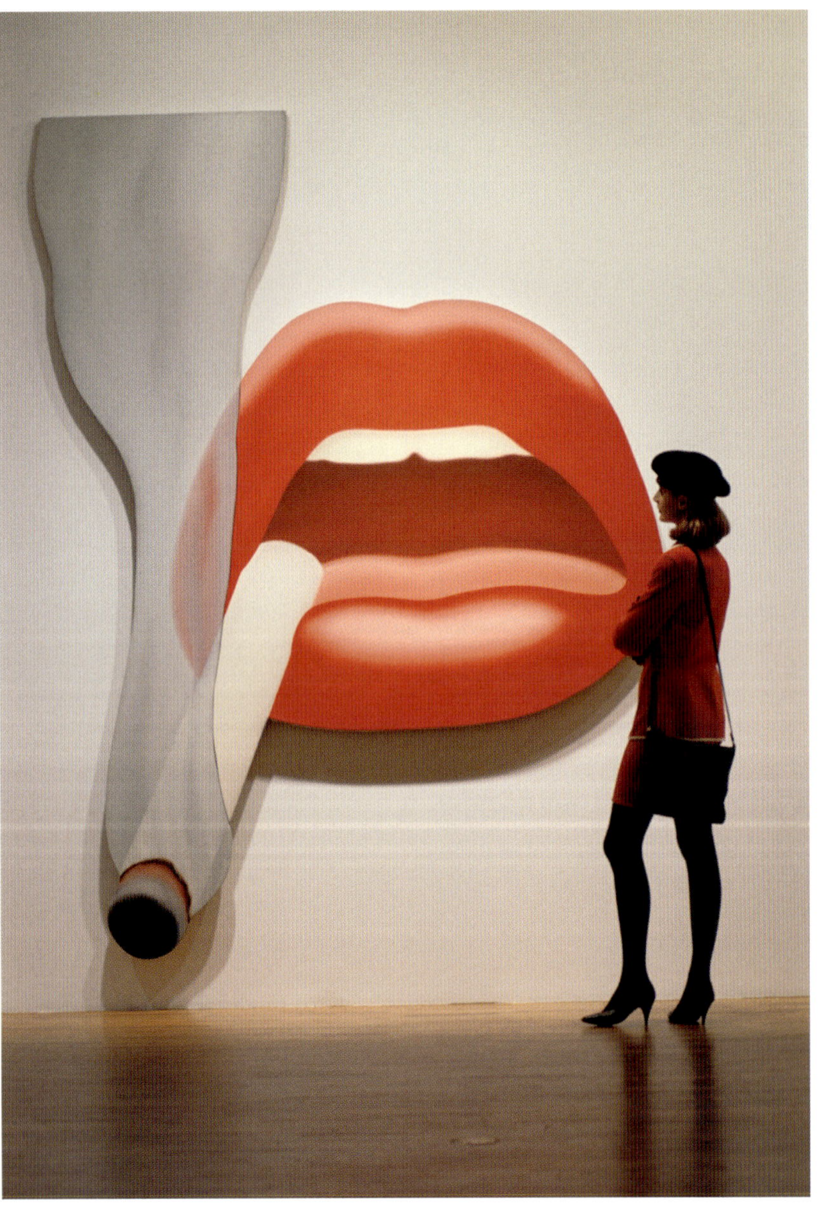

roof, and got out on that fire escape. She gave me look after look, working hard, hanging on in the wind, 15 stories up. How can you not appreciate that at camera?

That's the amazing, unexpected joy of photography. I went to that roof to make a picture, not a lifelong friend. That didn't even cross my mind. One and done. Great job, thank you very much. But Rita and I, perhaps because of the banter pertaining to the precarious perch she was on, became dear friends, and remain so to this day. She ran her own shop, a small agency called REP Management, and for a number of years she was my go-to call when I needed to cast a model. We got to know each other so well that she would tease me when I called, and give me a tsk-tsk on the phone. "Joe, all these years now, and you're still calling me, asking me to find you a girl."

After she grew away from the modeling business—running a restaurant for a time called Rita's Burgers—I would still importune her with requests for picture favors, as she was always classically elegant in front of the camera. For instance, I photographed her for *National Geographic Traveler* on a story about the great museums of New York. She got kitted out as only she can, and came to MOMA and helped me, perusing the artwork. Shooting a story like this for a magazine like *Traveler*, it was handy to have a ringer for a couple hours that day.

And we have gone through life's journeys, supporting each other, as friends do. Through Rita I met Ronnie, who became her husband, and Rita, Ronnie, Annie, and I would double-date. When I was courting Annie, we all went to dinner in Greenwich Village, and after, walking north on Sixth Avenue, Annie and Rita were walking arm in arm. Walking behind them, Ronnie linked arms with me and gave me that eternal, time-honored guy's advice: "This Annie's a keeper. Try not to screw it up."

As Rita always says, I'm her favorite photographer, so it was natural of her to ask me to shoot her wedding, which I was happy to do. She wanted all B&W, natural light. A Tri-X wedding.

She was an exquisite bride, to be sure, and it was an easy wedding to shoot. Given their outsized roles in the image and hospitality world (Ronnie is a well-known caterer and a chef),

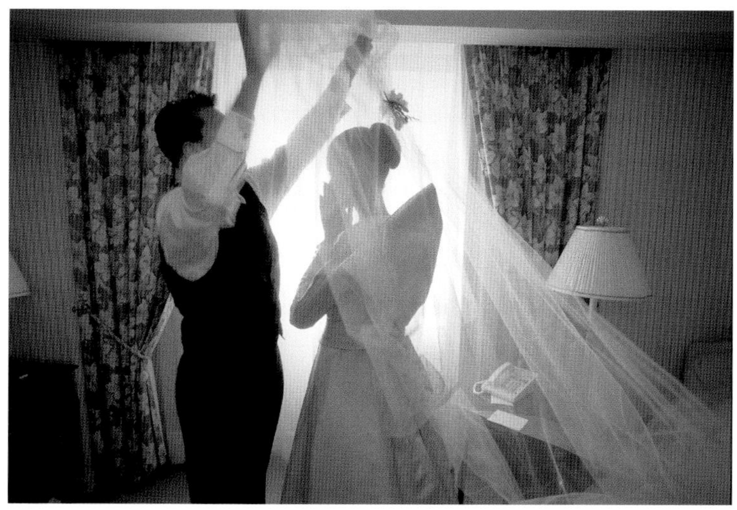

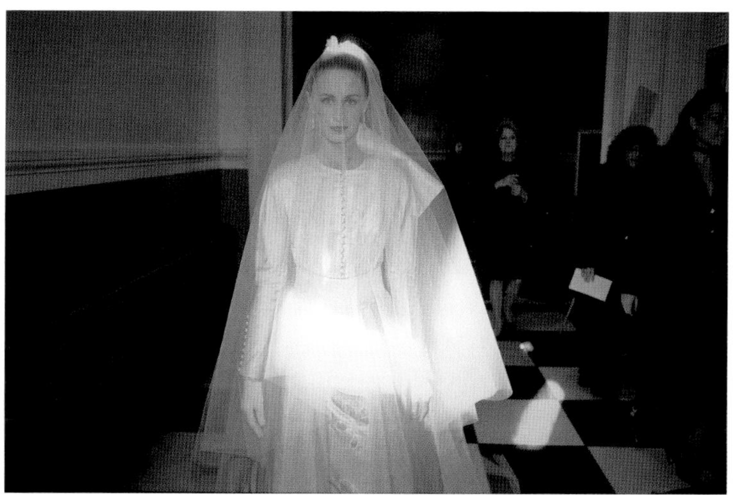

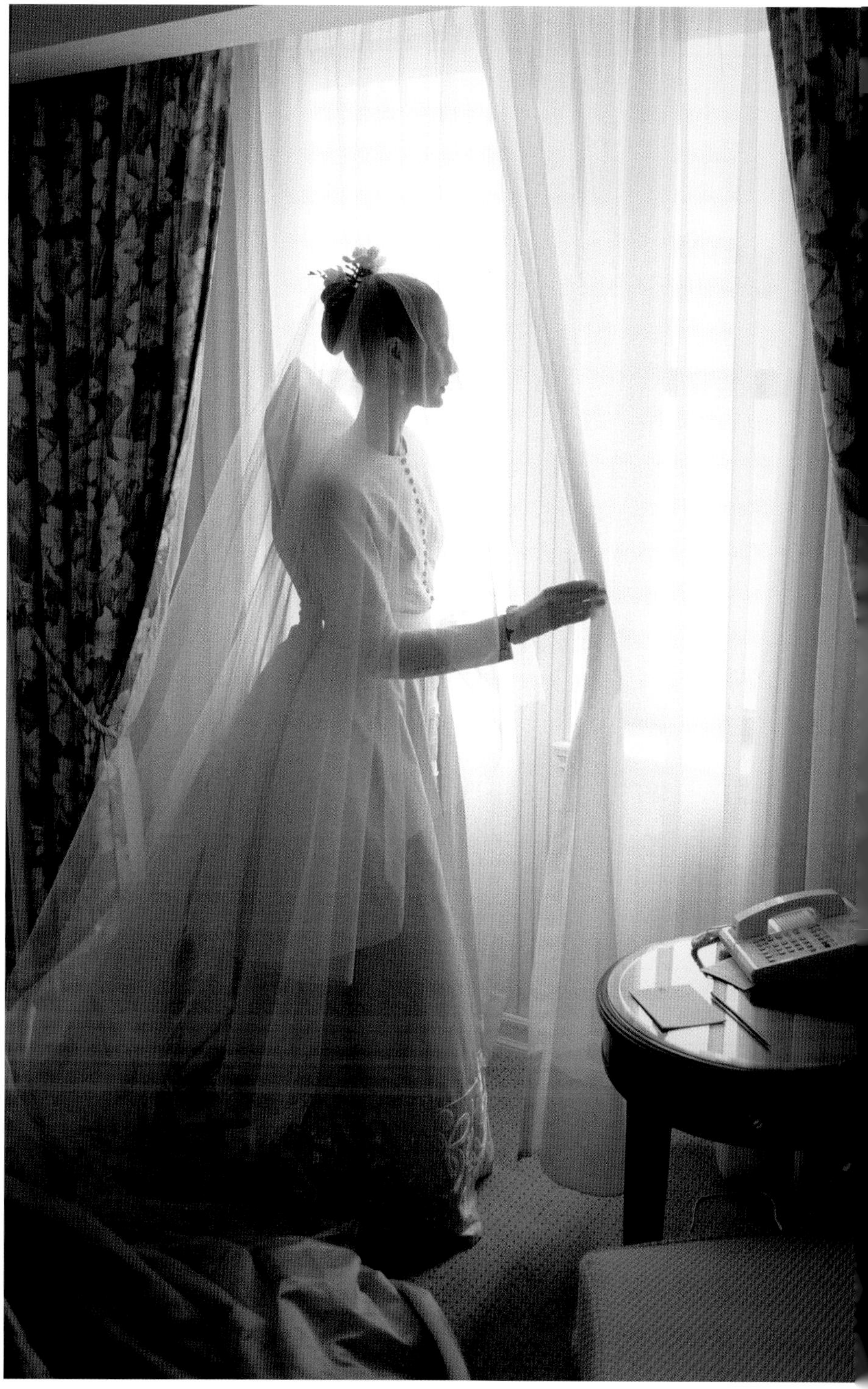

they naturally picked an amazing venue for their reception—
Industria SuperStudios, one of the premiere sound stages in
the city. This place had all the grip and lighting gear you could
imagine. (And trust me, I can imagine a lot.) I commandeered a
cyc and six 2400ws Speedotrons, firing shoot-through umbrellas into a 12-foot silk, making a massive light cube, and went
to town shooting big groups and portraits. I had thought this
through, of course, and brought my Fujica 617 Pano camera
with me, loaded with medium format black and white film. Lots
of f-stop. Lots of sharpness. Corner of the cyc. And a favorite
wedding photograph of an amazing couple who have been my
friends for years (following page, top).

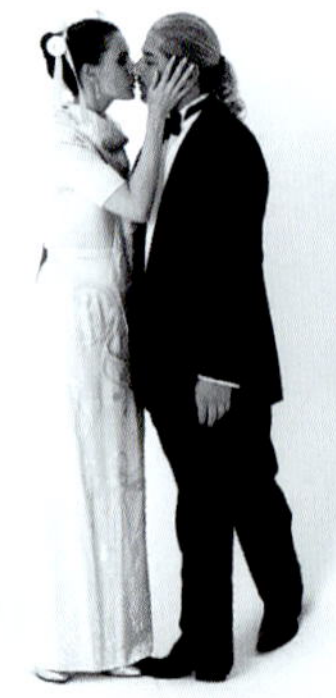

And we are still friends, all these years later, surviving the bumps and vicissitudes of life. I asked her to pose for me once more, for this book (opposite), and of course, she sorted out a classy place.

Again, a rooftop. (This time a terrace, blessedly, not a funky fire escape.)

Again, a beautiful scarf. (Though not quite as big as the first time, that wind whipped adventure of long ago.)

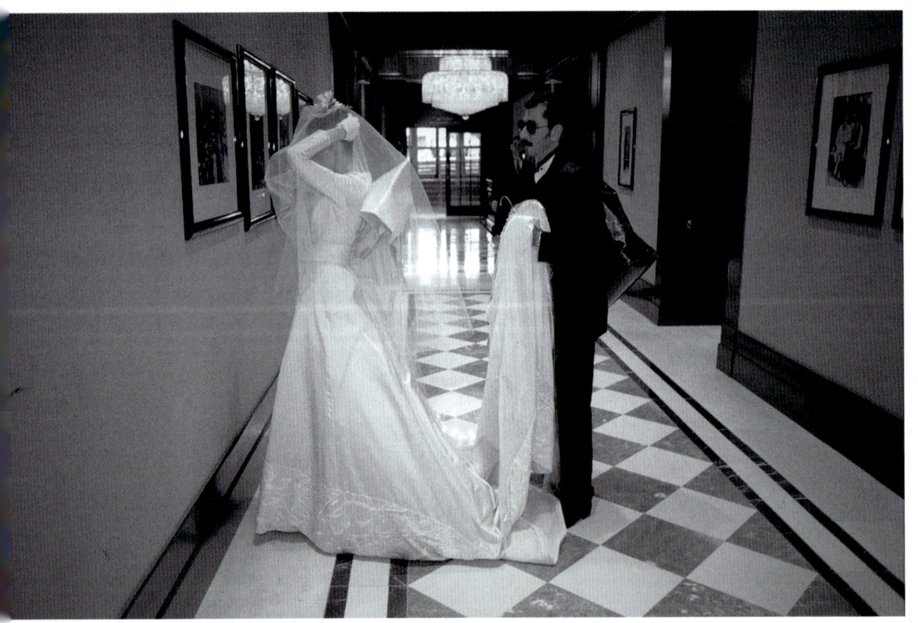

Do you ever reflect on the luck of being a photographer? Time does not stop, except for us. We have that shutter in our hands, a time freezer. Everyone takes pictures, especially now. Lives are being recorded relentlessly, regardless of their note, wit, or momentous occasion. Here's what I had for breakfast! I confess I care not.

But when you get good with that camera and point it at significant things in effective fashion, oh what a story you write! You photograph the life around you, the people around you, becoming part of the tapestry of their lives. Photographs are the rings on the human tree, marking time and life and growth. Thoughts, feelings, and moments would have slipped away, were it not for . . . that picture. Your subjects. You write their name down, forever. Photos are not emails, fleeting and fragile, bound to be discarded. (Unless you've engaged in misdeeds and they're retained for evidence.)

No, photos are much more akin to cave paintings. An illustrated thought or moment or occasion. Telling people about it is one thing. Showing them is a whole different ball game.

Photographs are the rings on the human tree, marking time and life and growth.

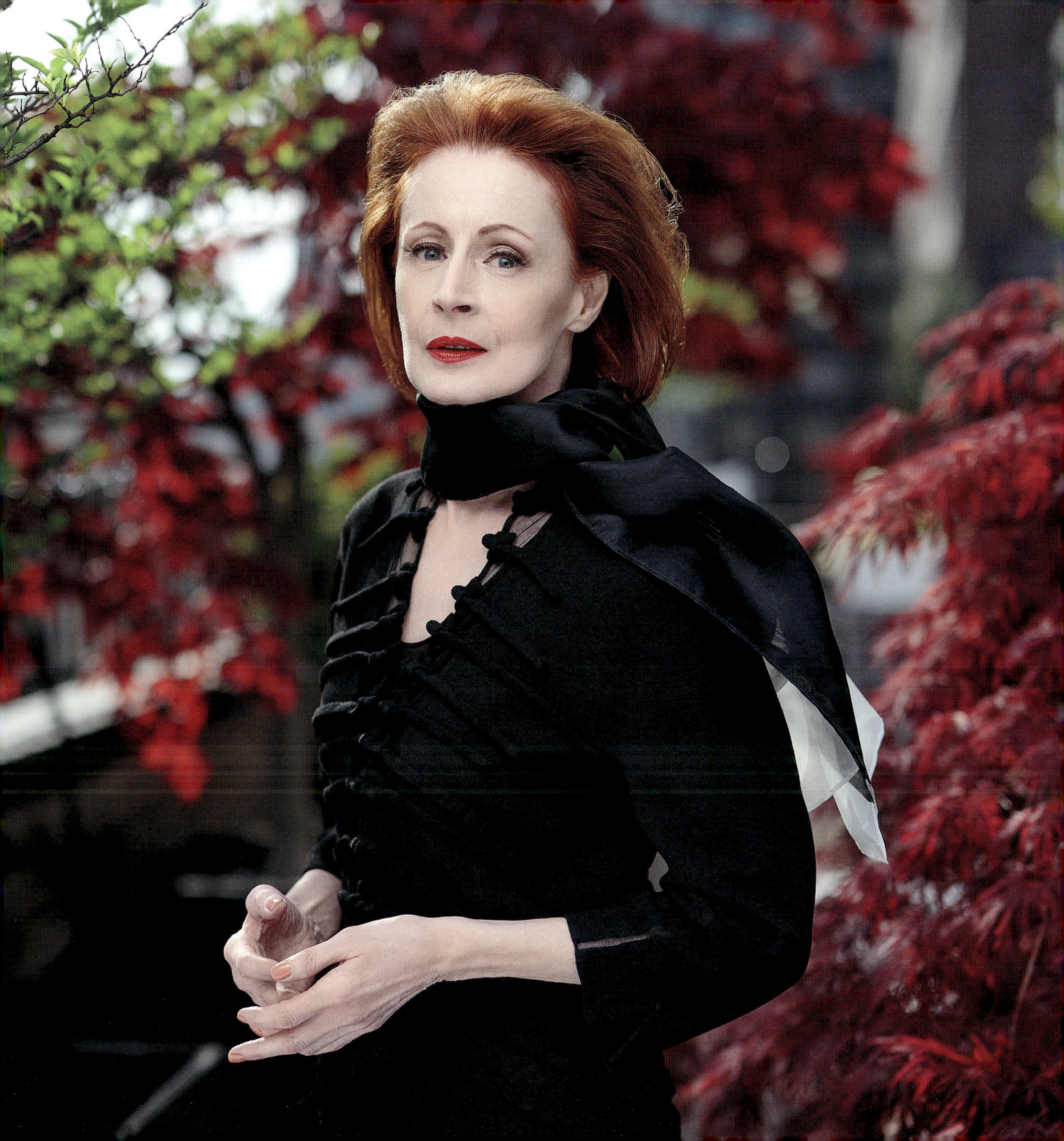

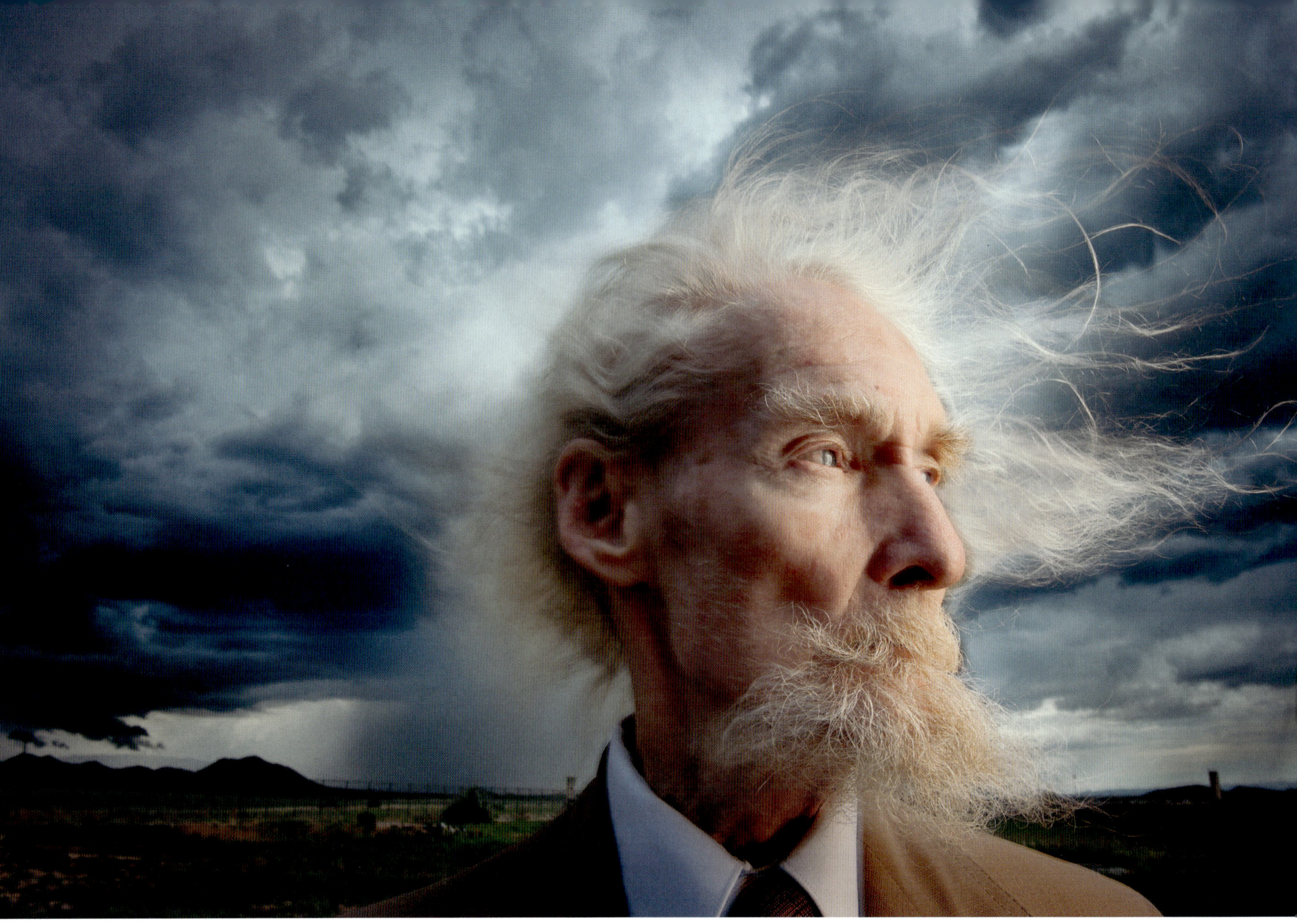

Tell me, when you look at a photo of an important day, or time, or outing in your life, that you cannot once again feel the same breeze, smell the food, hear the rush of the waves, relive the wonder, the fear, the angst of that day, that moment.

That conversation that so often starts amongst friends, "Remember when we used to . . . ."

Well, you do remember, because you made a picture of it.

So many people I looked at through the lens became so dear, and enriched my life, and illustrated the attic of my memory.

My dear friend Donald (above) is amongst the clouds now. I photographed him many times over the years, and we became close. Donald always told me, "Joe, the day they put me down, all the music in the world's gonna stop." I look at this picture, and I can hear that music, all over again. Friday nights at Tiny's, spinning his honey on the dance floor. The aroma of Cuervo in his "coffee cup." The raspy twang of his voice.

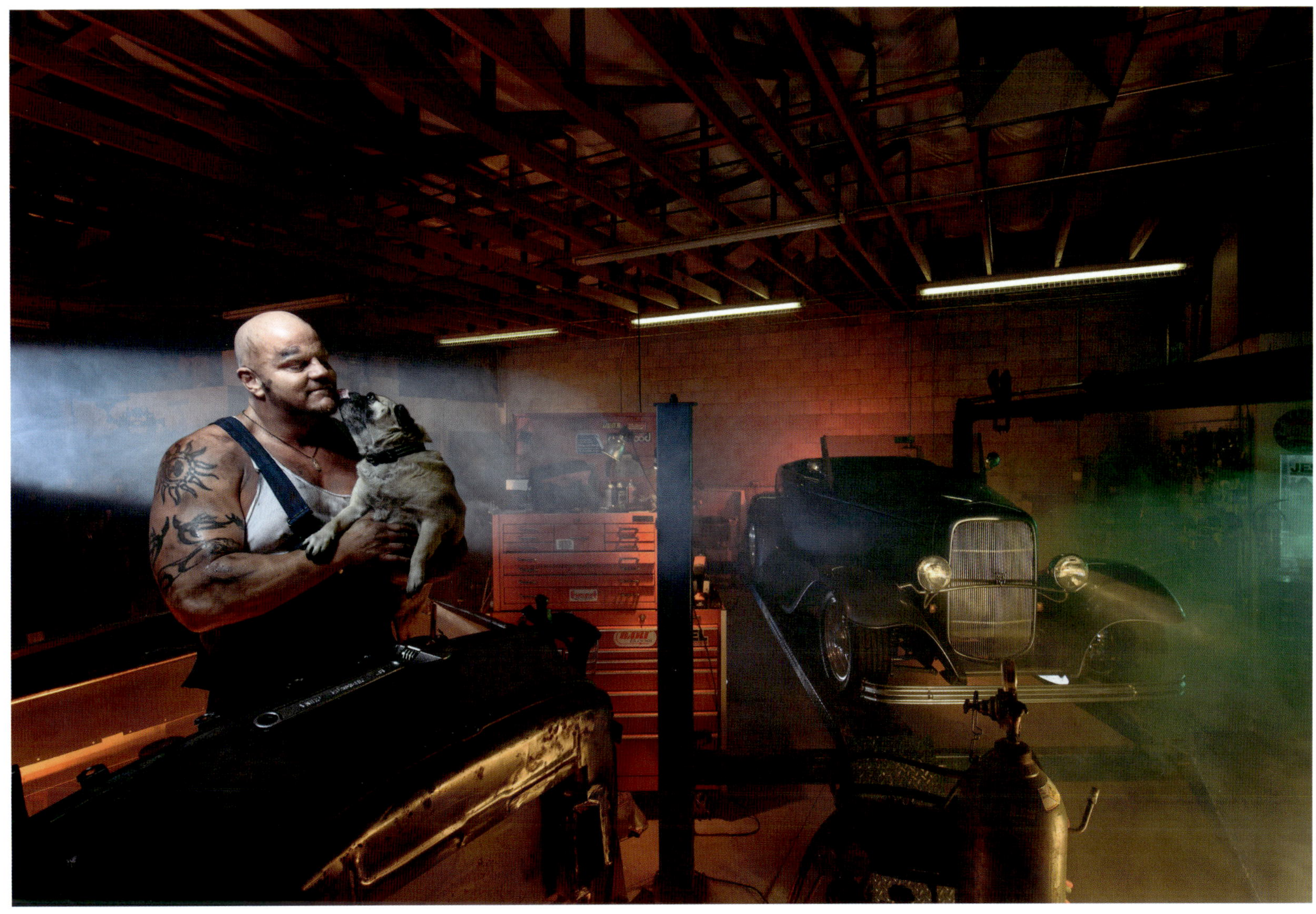

Drew Moore (above), who played for many NFL teams, and always called me coach, is gone. But his ebullient good nature resonates in this frame. Big guy, big heart. When he passed, I had a shoot in my head, destined for him. It'll have to wait.

The first time I ever photographed Sharon (following page), I asked her to take all her clothes off. I mean, she knew about this beforehand. I didn't spring it on her at the studio, as in, "Hey, wanna shoot some nudes?" No.

She was my first subject for a '96 *LIFE* magazine portfolio, depicting Olympic athletes in the nude. I wasn't after erotic content (hey, it was *LIFE*, fer chrissakes) but more so the beauty of the Olympic body, the aspirational, astonishing physical architecture of these magnificently tuned competitors. I was also after how training at grueling, arduous sports leaves its mark on the body.

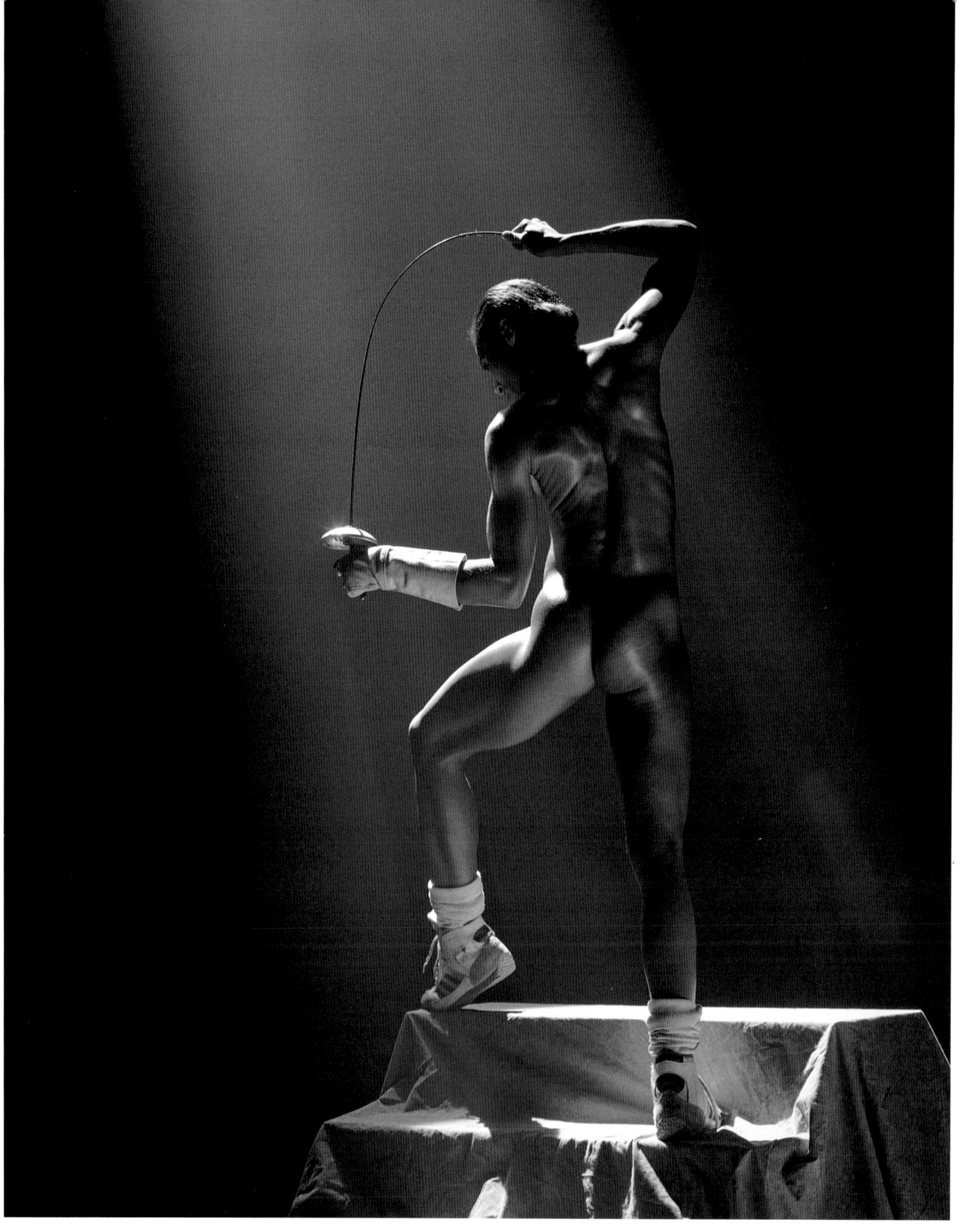

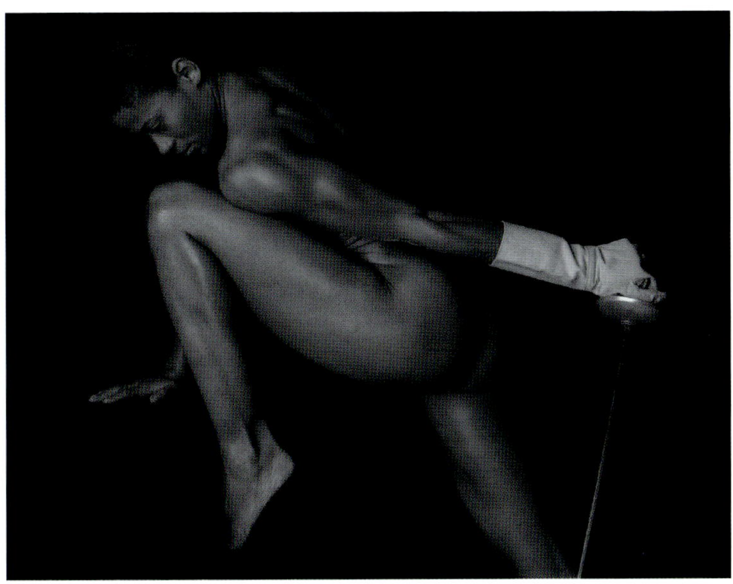

Sharon trusted me, right out of the gate, and I'm forever in her debt. It was not an easy set, as I quixotically thought I could shoot the whole project on an 8x10 camera. Which is what I used to shoot some of the take of Sharon. Thankfully, after this session, seeing how the 8x10 extended the time for the shoot, and made it overly exacting for focus and flash power to produce f-stop, I abandoned that large format notion. But there's no doubt about the grace and loveliness of 8x10 film.

And Sharon, talking of grace and loveliness. She is such an ebullient spirit, with a smile that embraces all, that I knew I would work with her again. On a *National Geographic* story on human performance, I rented a studio in New York, unbeknownst to my editors, and commissioned a few days to create poster-like photos of beautiful, powerful humans. I photographed dancers, and then I photographed Sharon. As a three-time Olympian in fencing, she perfectly personified the chiseled, warrior woman I was seeking to depict.

I've been asked over time, "Hey Joe, the set's a mess, why don't you clean that up?" Which of course is eminently doable. But I don't do it. This is the way I framed it. This was the set on

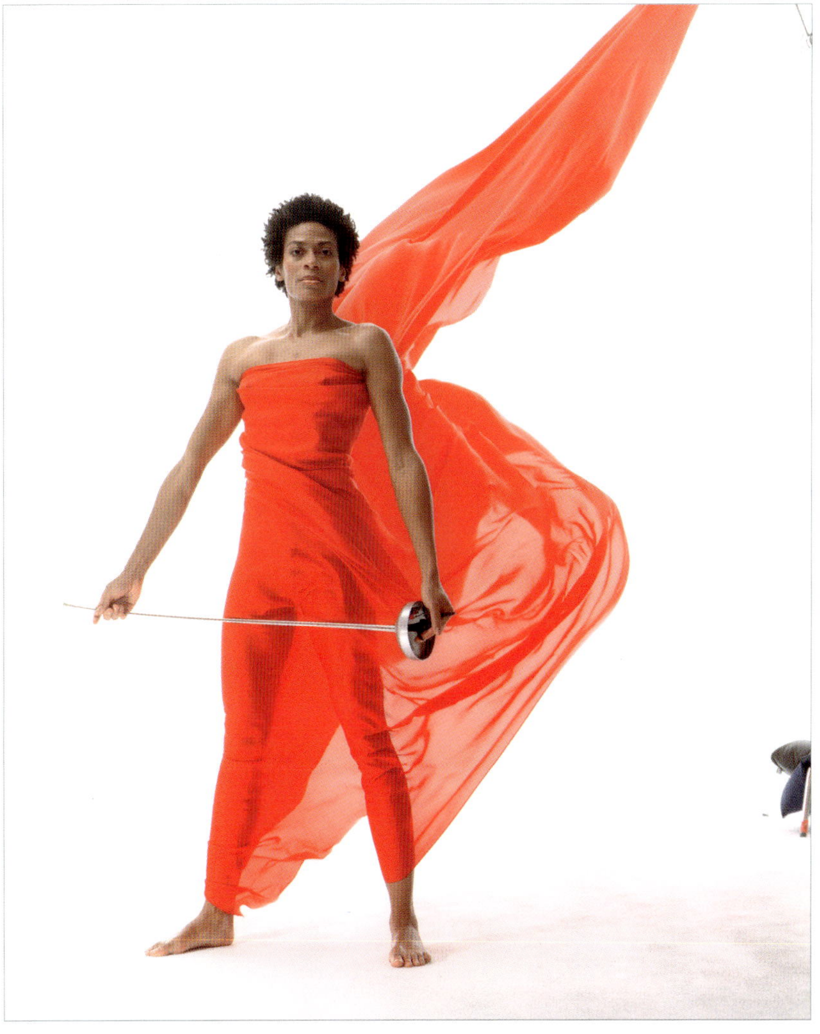

that day when Sharon looked at the camera and commanded it. When you frame someone like this through the viewfinder, do you feel the thrill? Do you feel the utter privilege of driving a camera in the direction of perfection? I simply became the conduit, clicking frame after frame as she looked at the camera as if from Olympus itself. It was also, honestly, the second time I photographed her, and the second time I asked her to take her clothes off. She simply shook her head at her photographer friend.

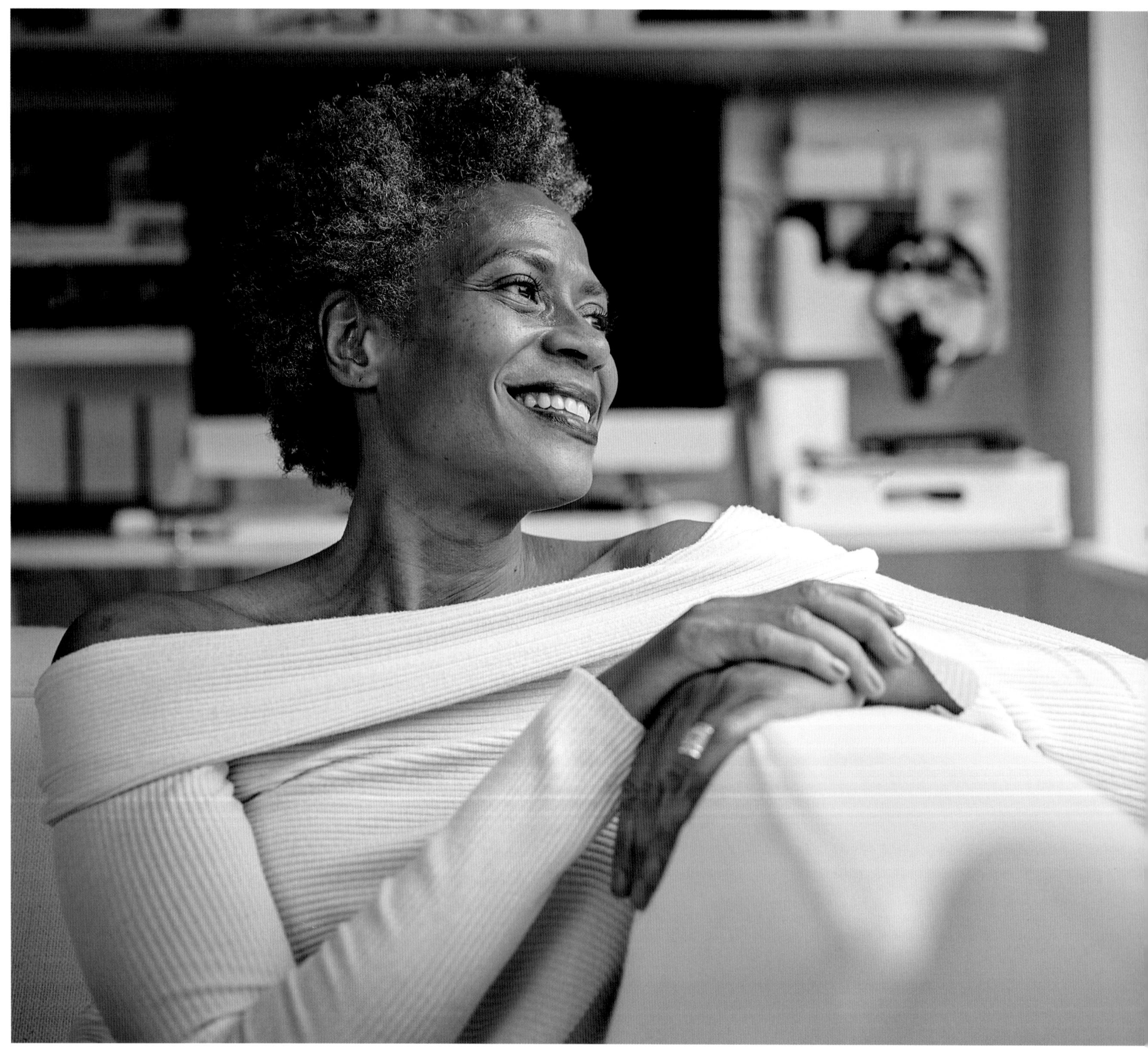

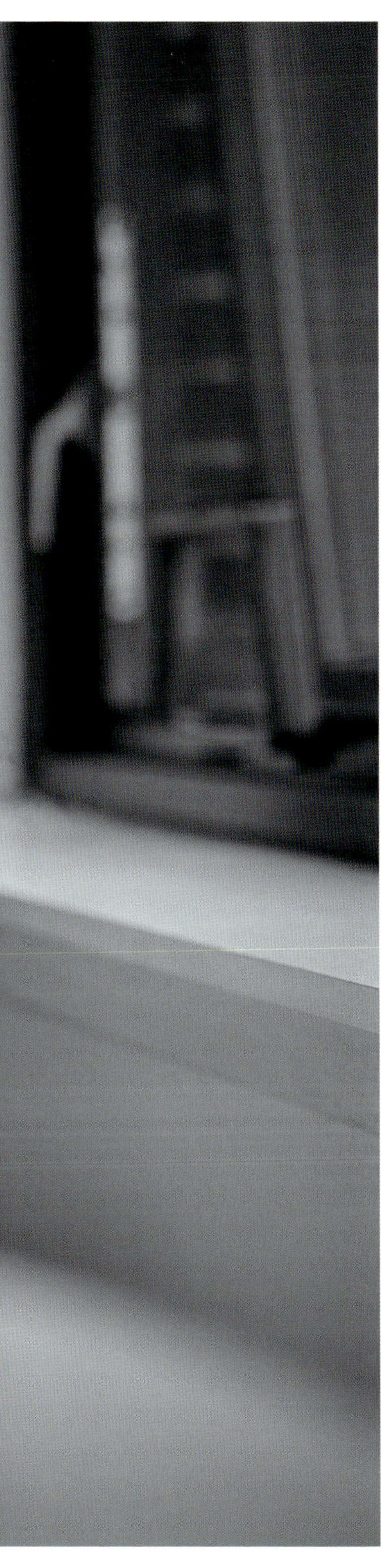

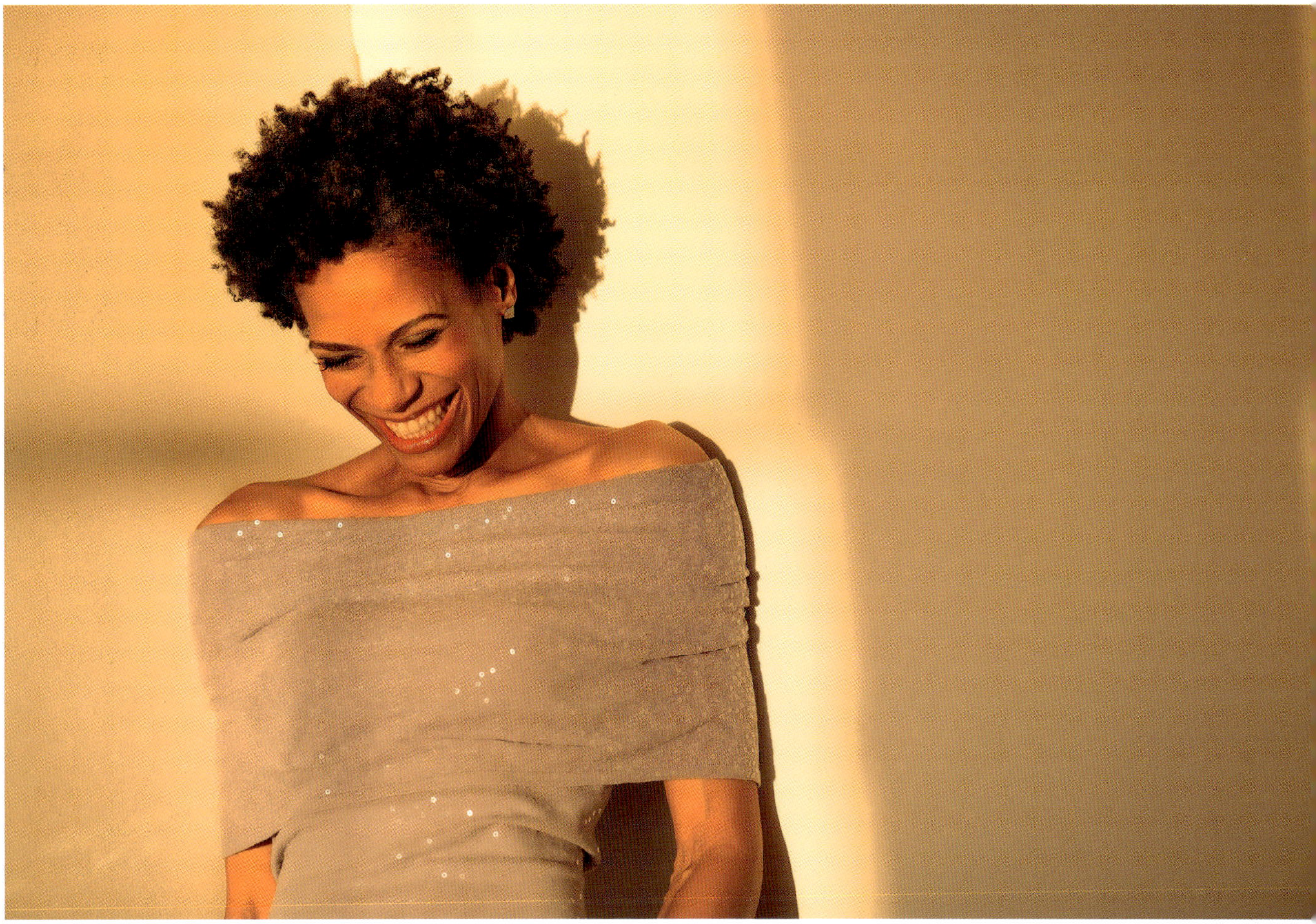

And then, she was perfect for a simple shoot where her smile rightly became the star (above), instead of her fencing foil.

She told me after this shoot that I must be slipping, 'cause she kept her clothes on.

I reached out to her to be part of this book (opposite), and again she was as gracious and beautiful as ever.

Time passes. Friendships deepen. Memory remains, contained in a rectangle. Pictures as the mile markers of life's travels.

Think about it . . . feel it. The camera is not just a machine, dry and lifeless. Gears and wires. Glass and bits. It's supple as a muscle, fluid as a feeling. On the best of days, it doesn't just depict exterior form and function. It sees and feels the beating heart of your subject.

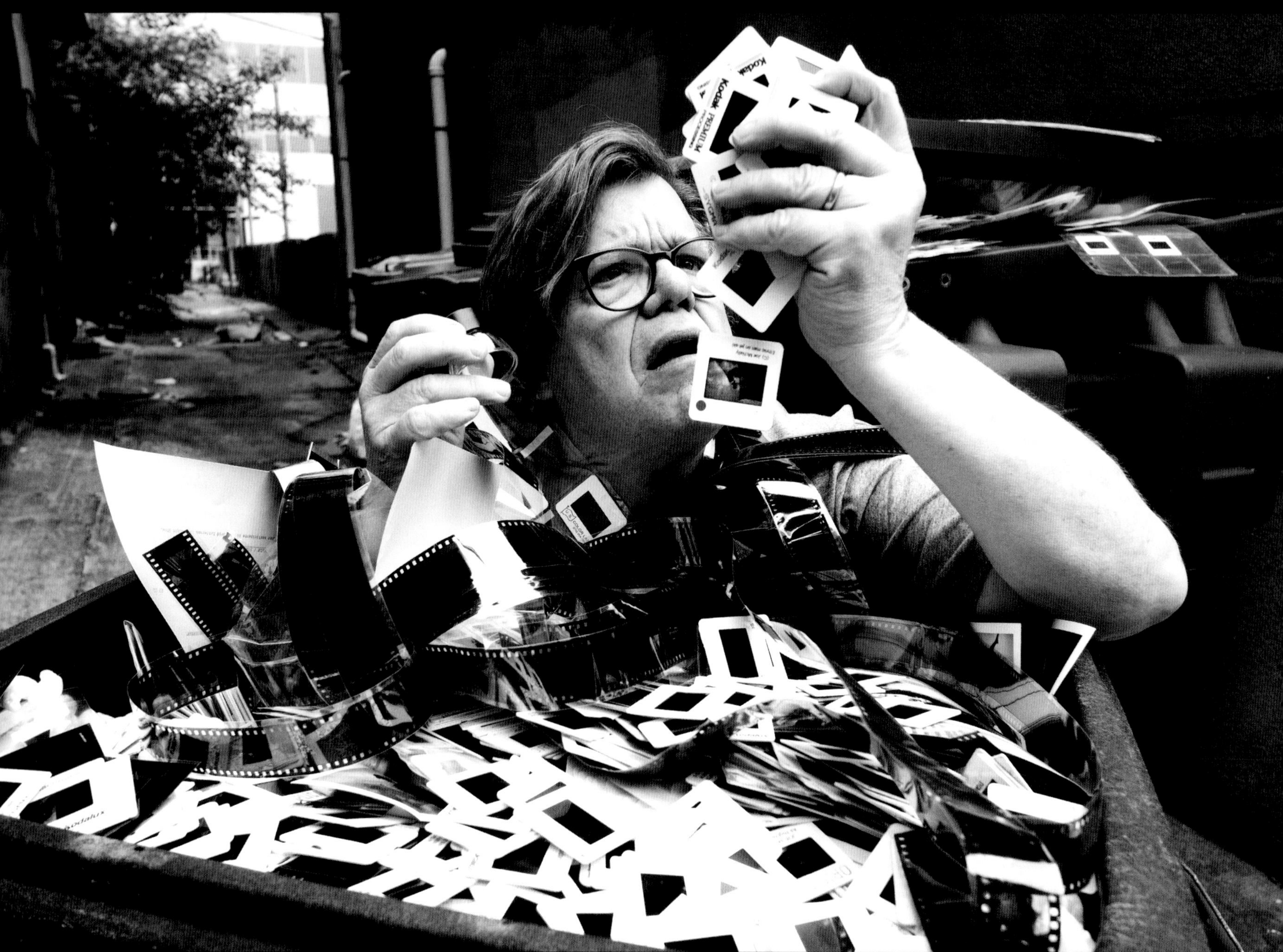

What Was I Thinking?

The recent pandemic introduced time for many reveries, reflections, and ruminations. And time, at long last, to confront the hundreds and hundreds of pounds of transparencies, negatives, and prints loosely collected in the strewn about Lego boxes of file cabinets in our downstairs conference room at the studio. Beige, drab cabinets fairly bursting with misfortune. Slide pages stuffed with Kodachromes: some revelatory, some cringeworthy, some prompting a rueful smile, some surprising and heartwarming. Some only retained because I started at tabloid newspapers, where the rule of retention was, "Keep everything on file. This guy might kill somebody someday and we'll need a picture."

But, finally, time to do it. The pandemic was awful, but amongst the small, varied personal silver linings we all experienced, one, for me, was time at home. Time to write a book, time to look at some pictures. Time to be astonished and confounded. Time to be tilt-of-the-head pleased, as in, "Wow, that's pretty good. Never got published. Too bad." Time to be absolutely mystified as to why I kept getting assignments, as in, "Geez, that's awful."

Time to think about legacy. Time to think about pictures, and how all this seemed so important at the time. Time to wonder about that moment when I finally put a camera down. Will anyone remember I ever picked one up?

Place in the universe. A rumination. Turn the page, and read on . . .

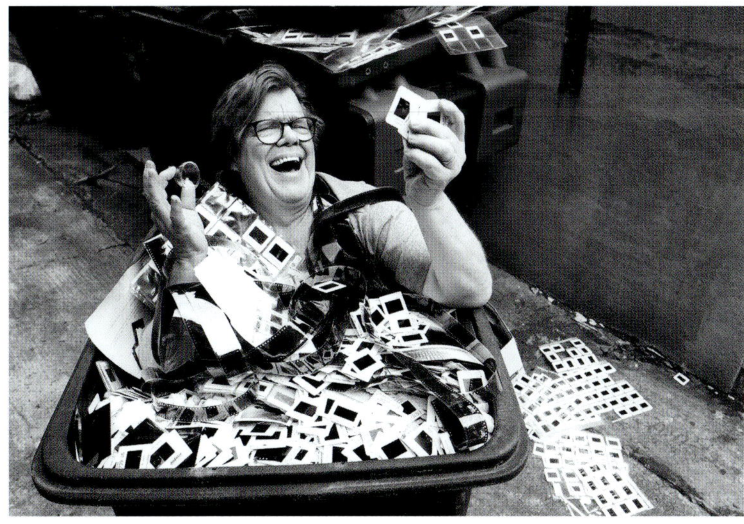

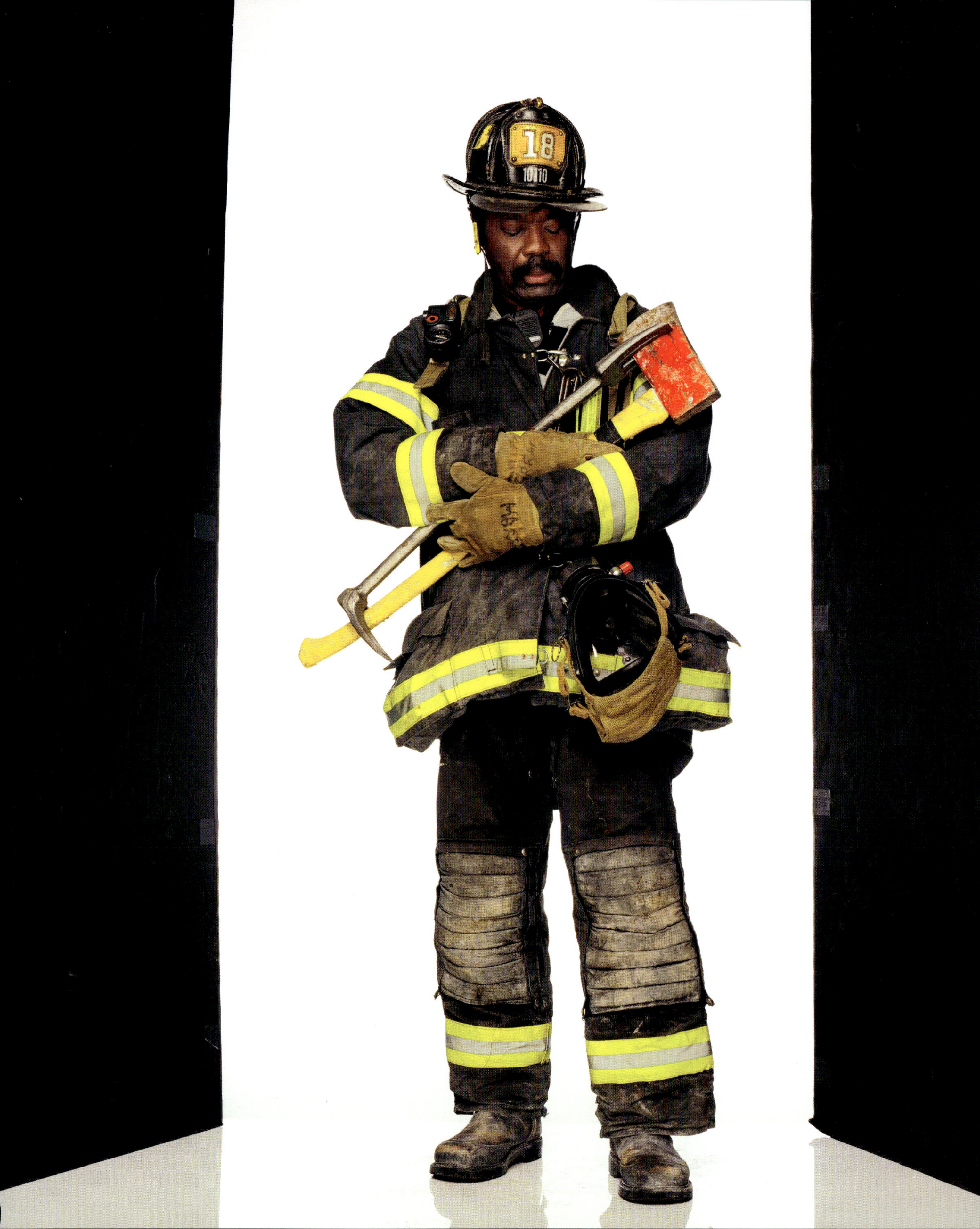

On Being Iconic, Important, and Remembered

Be at peace. It's not up to you.

In the dictionary, *iconic* is described as something "resembling an icon." No surprise there. Further, this adjectival extension of *icon* is generally construed in everyday language as "widely recognized and well established," or being of "distinctive excellence." It is, regrettably, a descriptor used quite often in reference to photographs. Even more regrettably, I've heard some photographers refer to their own work as iconic. I've read blogs where the photog author has actually said something along the lines of believing that one or more of their photos would probably be remembered as one of their "most iconic."

Okay, hold the phone.

Let's play the *iconic* game, shall we? I'll offer a description of a photo, and you conjure it in your head. There are no prizes in this game, sorry. It is, however, a brief, painless exercise, and potentially illuminating.

Young girl horribly burned, running down the road in Vietnam, after a napalm attack.

Got it, right? No picture necessary.

A Depression-era migrant mother, her children clinging to her desperately, worry and pain etched in her face, stares bleakly.

Know it immediately. The pain of that mother's face is burned into our brains.

Sailor kisses a nurse in Times Square at the conclusion of WWII.

A picture everyone can draw from their memory.

Gandhi and his spinning wheel.

The essence of Gandhi, in a photo. You have seen it, and you know it.

A lovely young lady, on the rocks by the shore, with a sunset sky and two flashes being used, TTL, one through a softbox up front, camera left, and one set at −1 EV, with a warming gel, to backlight her shoulder and hair.

This one. I know I've seen it, I know this one … yep, ummm … well, I think, you know, I've seen this one … *everywhere.*

This is all true, yes? In our heads, we know those famous images immediately. We don't have to have them shown to us. They are burned into our collective consciousness, our shared visual history. They are emotional touchstones, triggering joy, sadness, and reflection, a viscerally immediate connection to a moment in time that is so staggeringly human and important we cannot look away. These photos slice life with such power that they stay alive in our heads and hearts, even though they were made years ago. We look at them now, and we know them. People will still be looking at them, and knowing them, a hundred years from now. And the reaction will be the same. A punch to the gut. A slap in the face. A ping in the heart. A knowing smile.

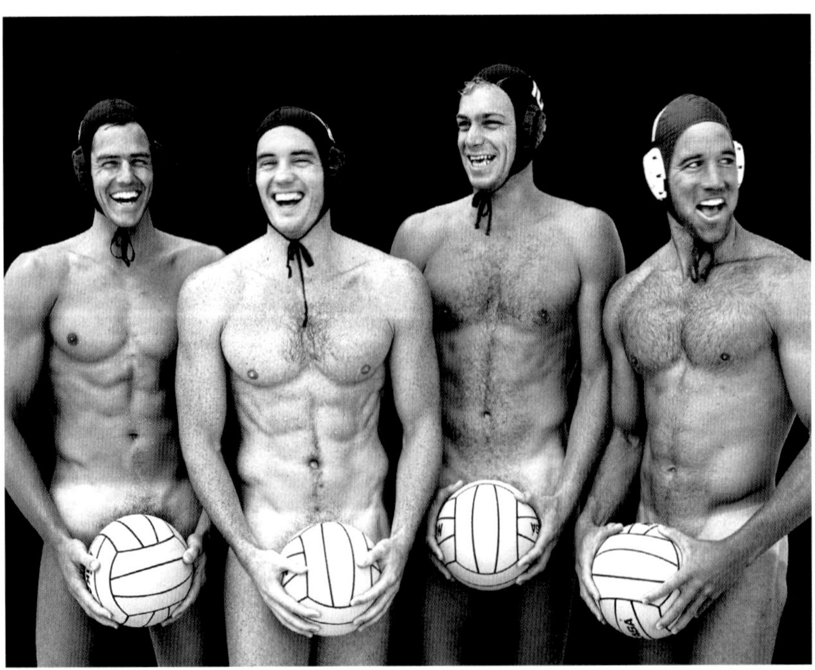

But you're having trouble placing that last one. You're puzzled. Let's see: young lady, rocks on the shore, nice flash technique … hmmm … did I see that one on Flickr, or 500px, or Instagram? Or that photography website, or the photo flash guide I read once? Actually, you've seen it in all those places, perhaps even simultaneously.

But you can't really pinpoint it because you've seen 10,000 photos just like it. I've shot a bunch of these myself. They're pretty, and that, in and of itself, is important. They represent knowledge of craft—again, important. They have good color, tone, saturation, excellent skin work, and flawless post-production. Nicely done. Bravo. I never thought of putting the light there. Cool.

But does it stick with you? Or is it like a meal of tofu and sprouts, where you're hungry an hour later? These kinds of pictures are like the mantelpiece decorations you buy on sale at Pier One. They look nice from a distance and add mood or ambience to the room. But if you knock one of them off the mantel and it breaks into a bunch of pieces, it ain't worth the time to glue it back together. You just order another one out of the catalog.

In other words, it's not grandma's crystal.

Grandma's crystal is irreplaceable. It's not only visually beautiful, but it has the power of memory, of transport in time. When you hold it, you can hear her voice and feel the skin of her cheek as she kissed you and tousled your hair. Rife with feeling, and beauty, it becomes part of your heart.

It's the same with a truly iconic photo. It's here to stay. Like an important and imposing rock, out there in the fast-moving stream, but one that is impervious to erosion. No matter how many years and how much life rushes around it, it remains, still flinty, never smoothed down or subdued, edges sharp as ever. It has staying power. It is not a consumable. It endures.

When a photographer lays claim to "iconic" turf on behalf of their own photos, you immediately know at least a couple of things.

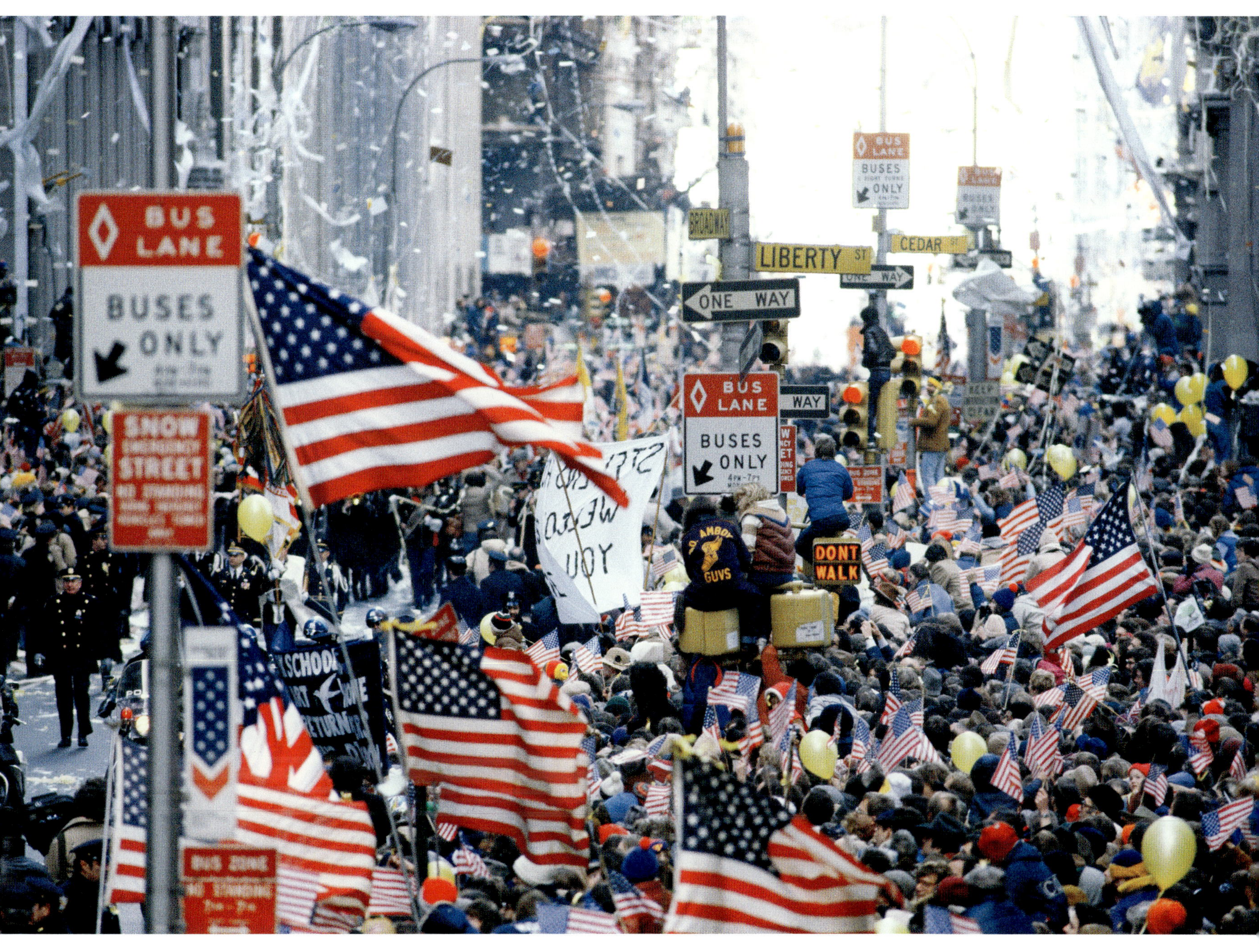

BUS LANE
BUSES ONLY
SNOW STREET
BROADWAY
LIBERTY ST
CEDAR ST
ONE WAY
BUS LANE
BUSES ONLY
4PM-7PM MON
WAY
ONE WAY
DONT WALK
SO. AMBOY GUYS
BUS ZONE

First and foremost, the photos in question are most likely not iconic.

And second, the photographer doing the spouting knows this.

Because here's the thing. If you've shot an iconic picture, you don't have to say it. The photo says it, loudly and clearly, all on its own. The picture will pound its own chest, thank you very much. Just shut up and get out of the way of the clarity of its impact. Anything you say will just muddy the waters. When it comes to the utter, essential nature of an iconic image, wordlessly and deeply connecting to our souls, florid verbiage becomes unnecessary, useless weight on the drag strip.

Photographers have a natural and understandable fear of their work being forgotten, or not reckoned with. We fear being inconsequential and forgotten as much as many people fear death and dismemberment. It can make us chatty sons of guns. I'm sure you've heard that description of a conversation with a photographer: "But that's enough about me, let's talk about what you think of my work." All photographers who have

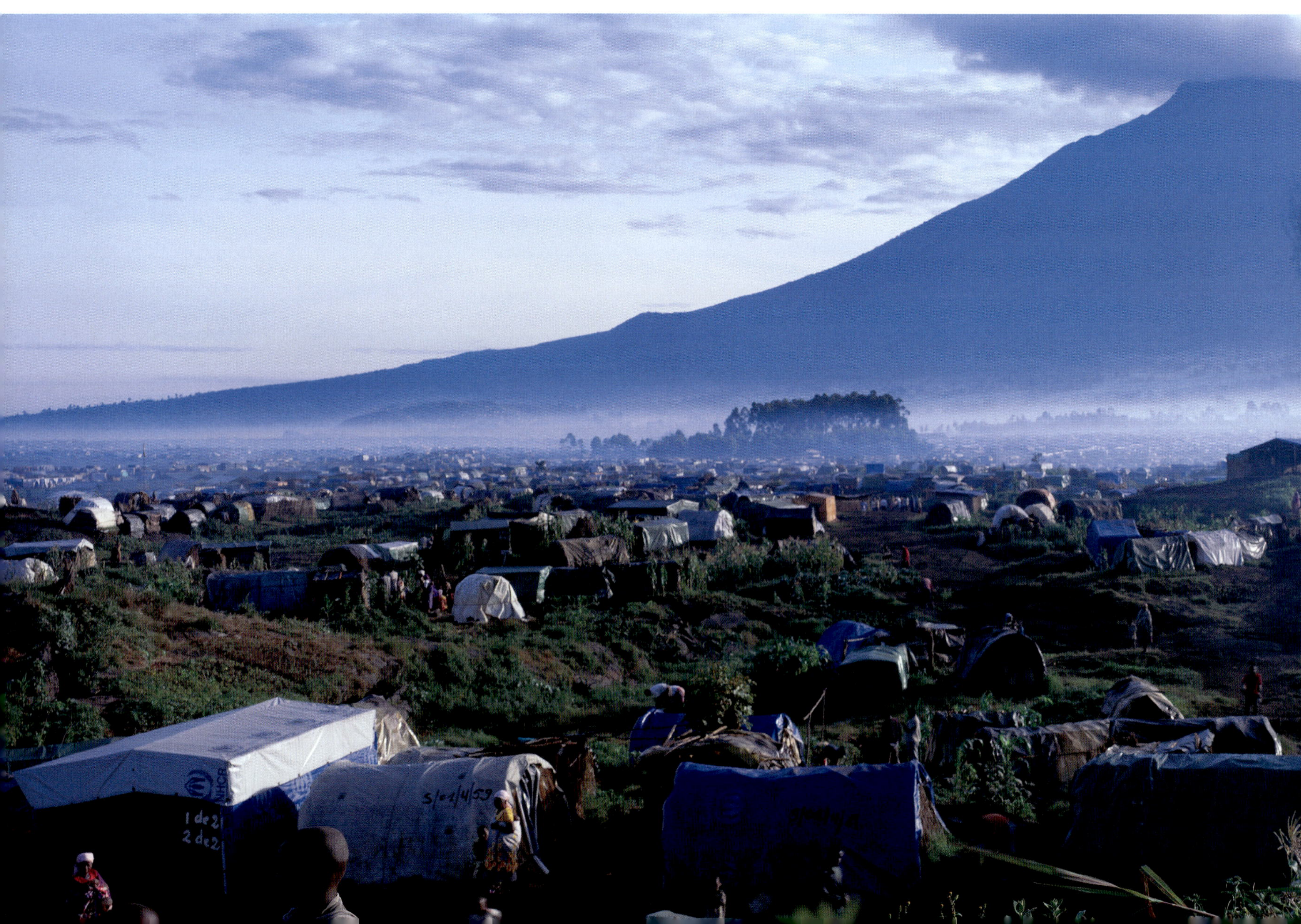

picked up a camera with serious intent want to check the box called memory. It's natural. After all this furious clicking, we'd love it if somebody outside of our family actually remembered a picture or two. But that, like so many things we face off against as photographers, is beyond our control.

I had a show a few years ago at the prestigious Monroe Gallery in Santa Fe. I'm old enough and have been shooting long enough to call it a retrospective. Sid and Michelle Monroe are incredible people, completely versed in the history of photography, and well aware of its worth and importance in our lives. For them to award me their precious walls to hang my photos on was one of the honors of my career.

But I do remember standing there in the gallery, surrounded by a well-curated sample of the best of my work, and thinking, "That's it?" There were about 50 pictures on the wall, representing 40 years in the field, and well, that was that. I was happy and proud, for sure. But I was also, well, maybe confounded is a good word. My smile was not completely rueful at that moment, but

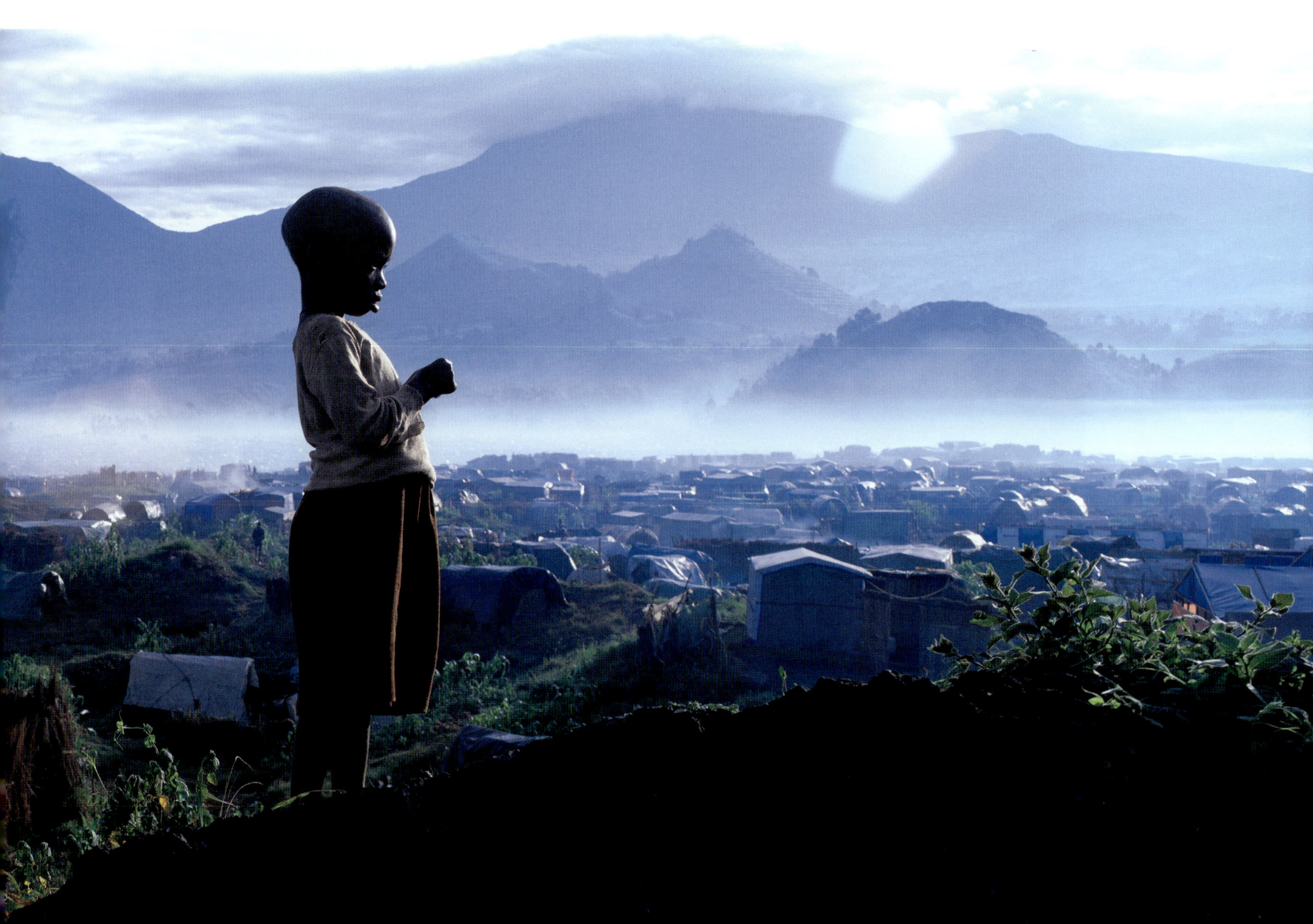

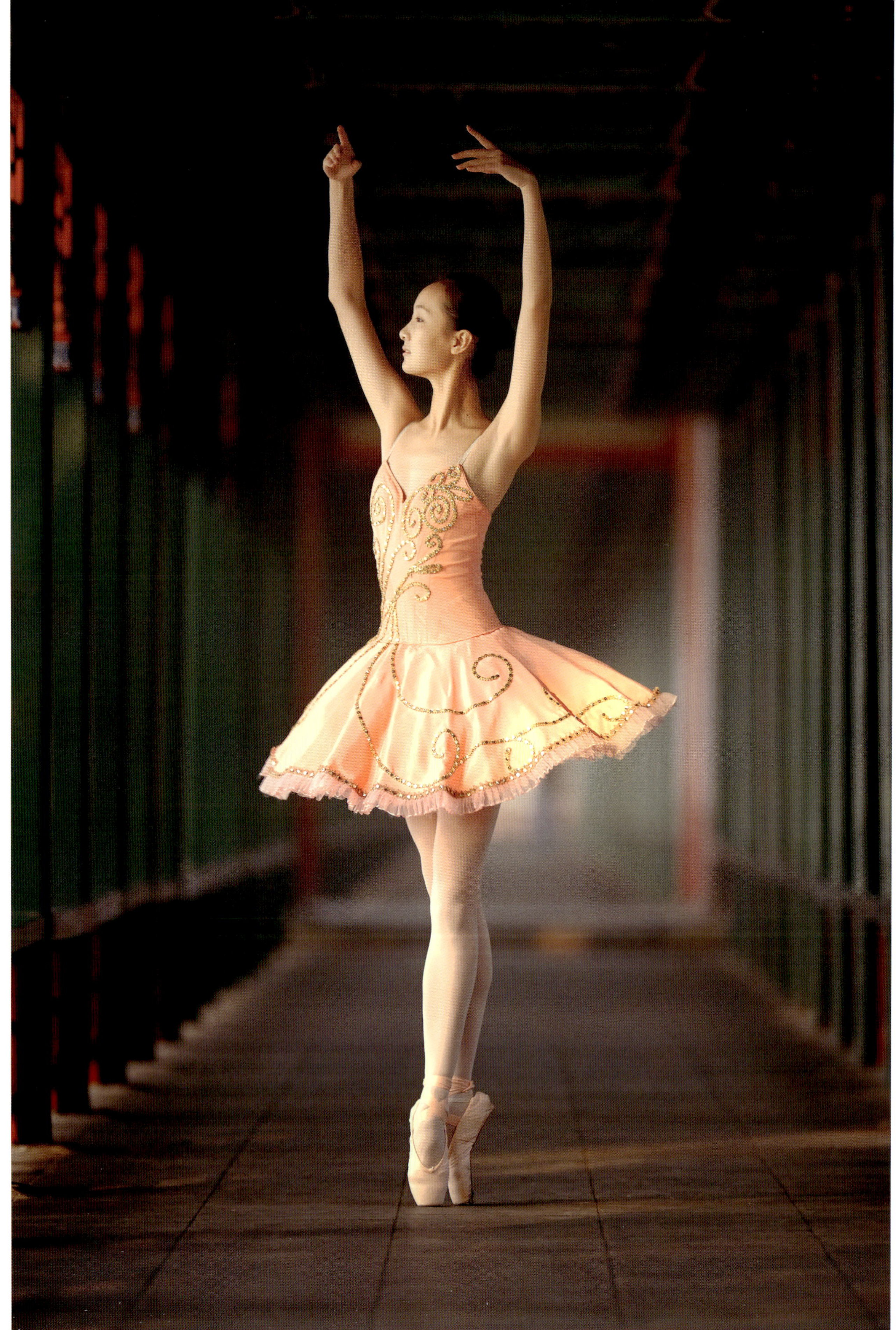

it stopped way short of beaming. There was a fair amount of regret on those walls. Those good pictures, beautifully printed, were also reminders of better pictures I missed. Of people encountered and then gone. Of times I was so intent on witnessing someone else's life I forgot to show up for my own. Printed echoes on the walls, faintly heard still, in the chambers of my head and heart.

The show was well reviewed. I'm not much up on the art world but there are small, powerful journals where reviewers can praise or scorch an artist, to great effect. My show was reviewed in one of them, and the Monroes were thrilled. It was a very positive review in a prominent art publication that really carried some weight. I read it, and always remember the reviewer's very perceptive judgement. He said, "These photos are memorable but not iconic."

And he was right.

Which actually warmed my heart. Memorable pictures. That's great. It means, on the day I shot that image, in that instant, I did my job with uncommon verve and panache, or intensity, or that I was so involved, so committed, that my finger didn't trip the shutter, my heart did. Those moments are thrilling indeed, even now, still after all these years. When you get what you came for. When the frame is filled with your imagination, writ large and made real. I've dropped a few of those memorable moments here on these pages, accompanying this ramble.

The iconic pictures I described earlier are an impossibly high bar, truth be told. Very few photographers ever climb those heights. That doesn't mean a career is wasted, or

inconsequential. This is a lifetime of striving, this photographic life. Much of that striving goes toward the essential issue of making a living. Which sounds quite mundane, this being a profession that is often bound up with such hyperbole and mythmaking that it seems lighter than air, shrouded in mysteries known to only a few. "I spent some time with my subjects, and they trusted me utterly, enabling me to become invisible, and touch nothing except with my eyes, and the photos of that day will live on as shouted affirmations of essential truths that will echo down the corridors of time forever." Or, "She turned, and gave the camera a look that froze time and space, a look of legendary beauty, and my camera became her partner in recording the passion of that fleeting moment, now everlasting via my artistry at the lens."

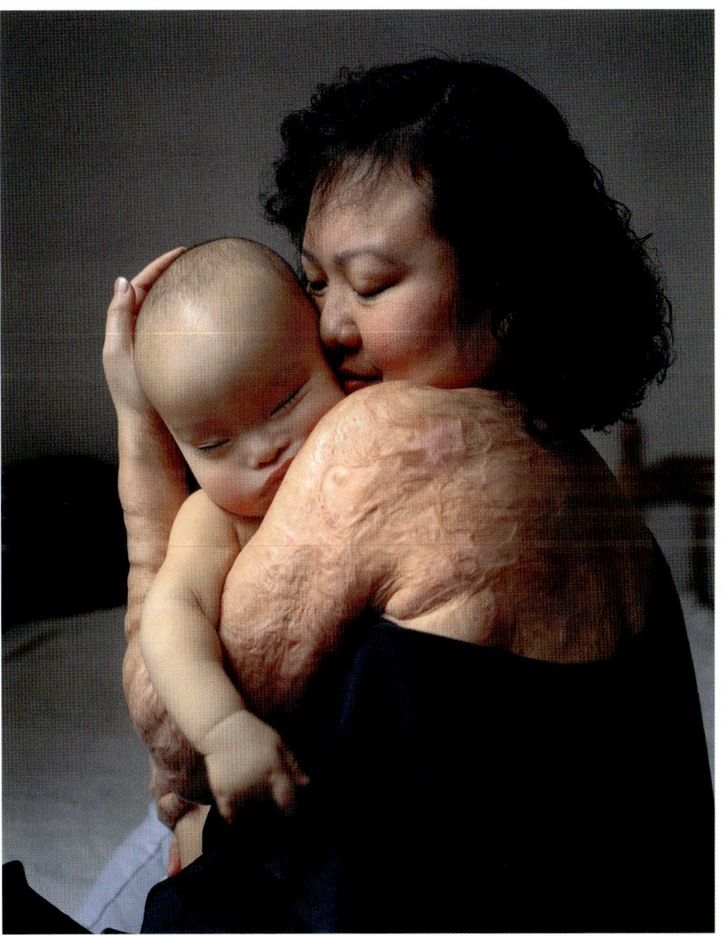

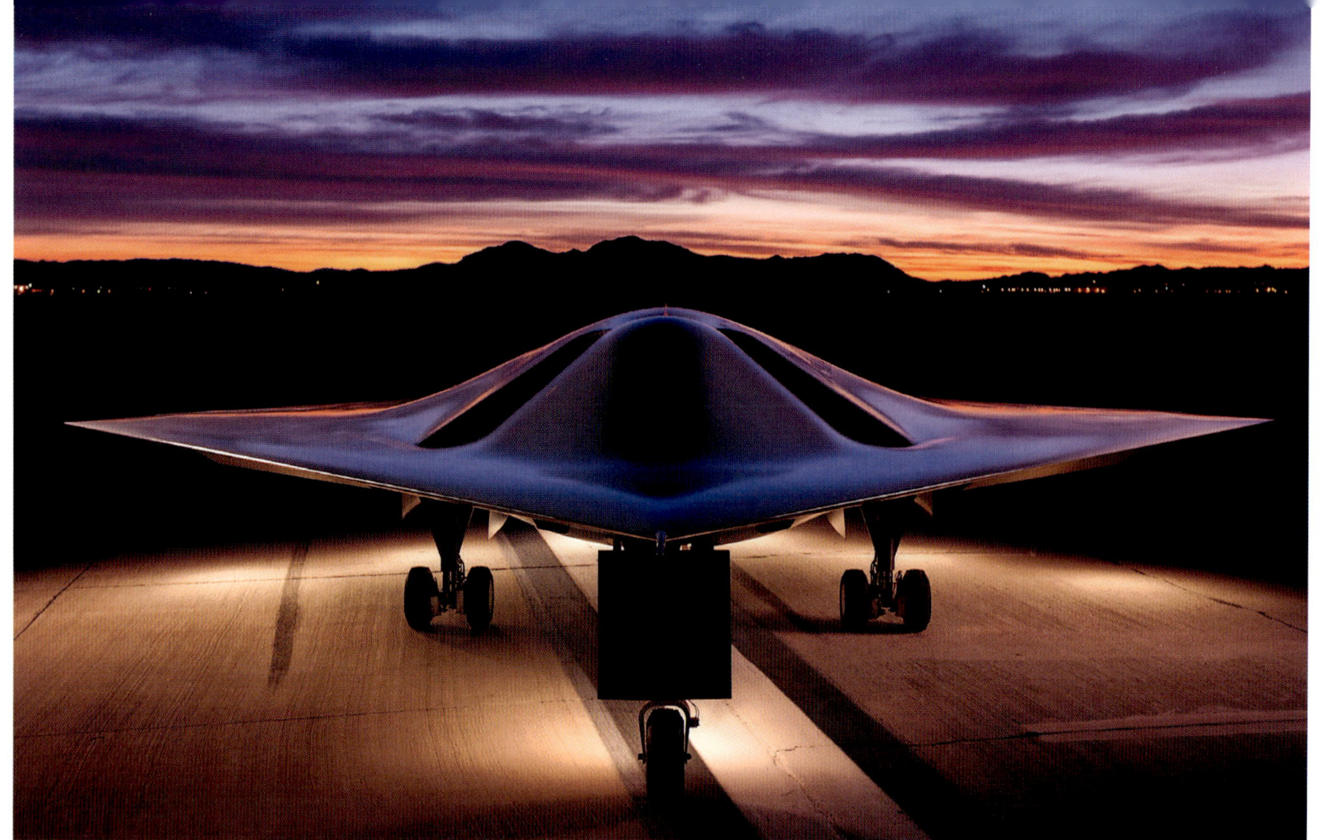

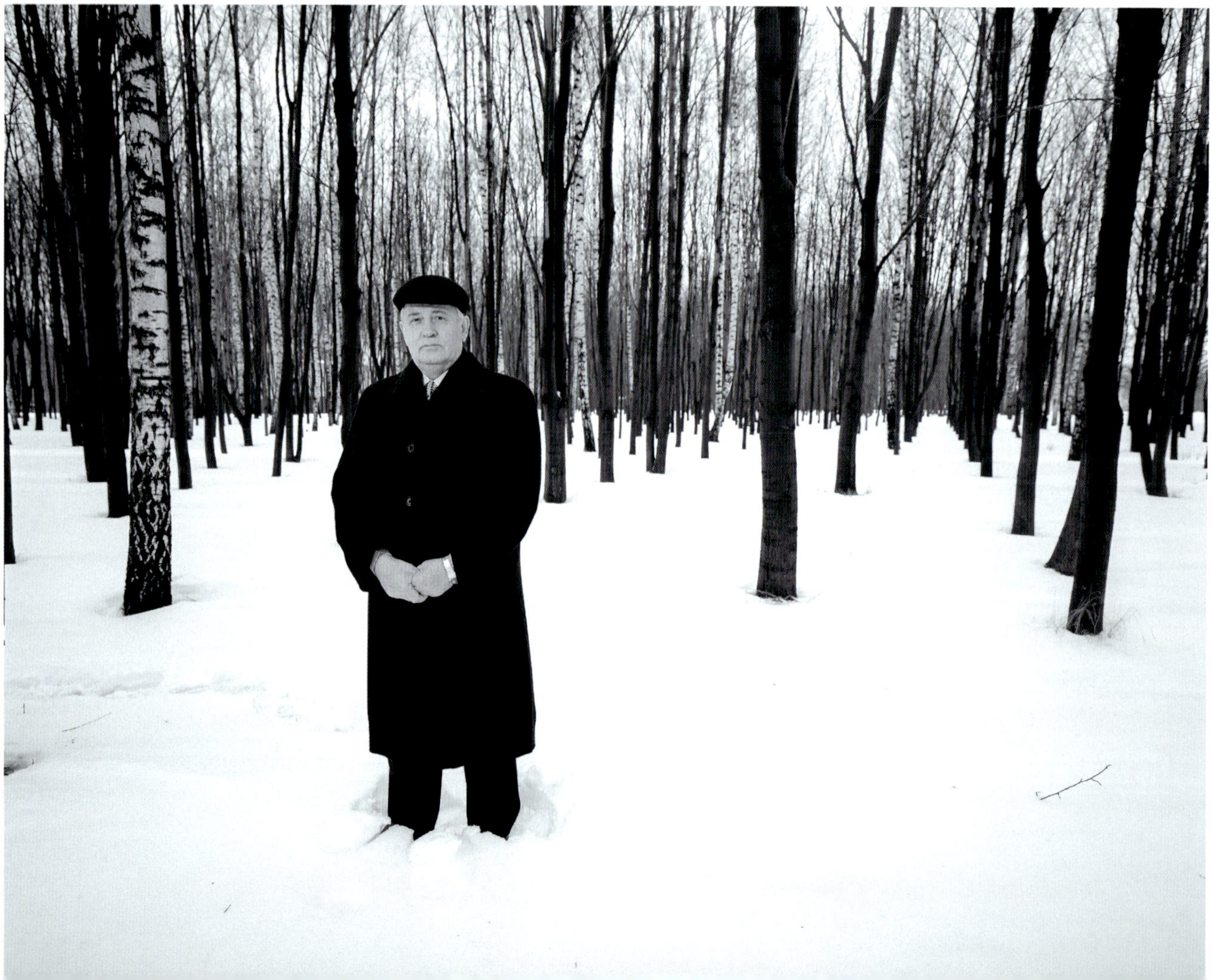

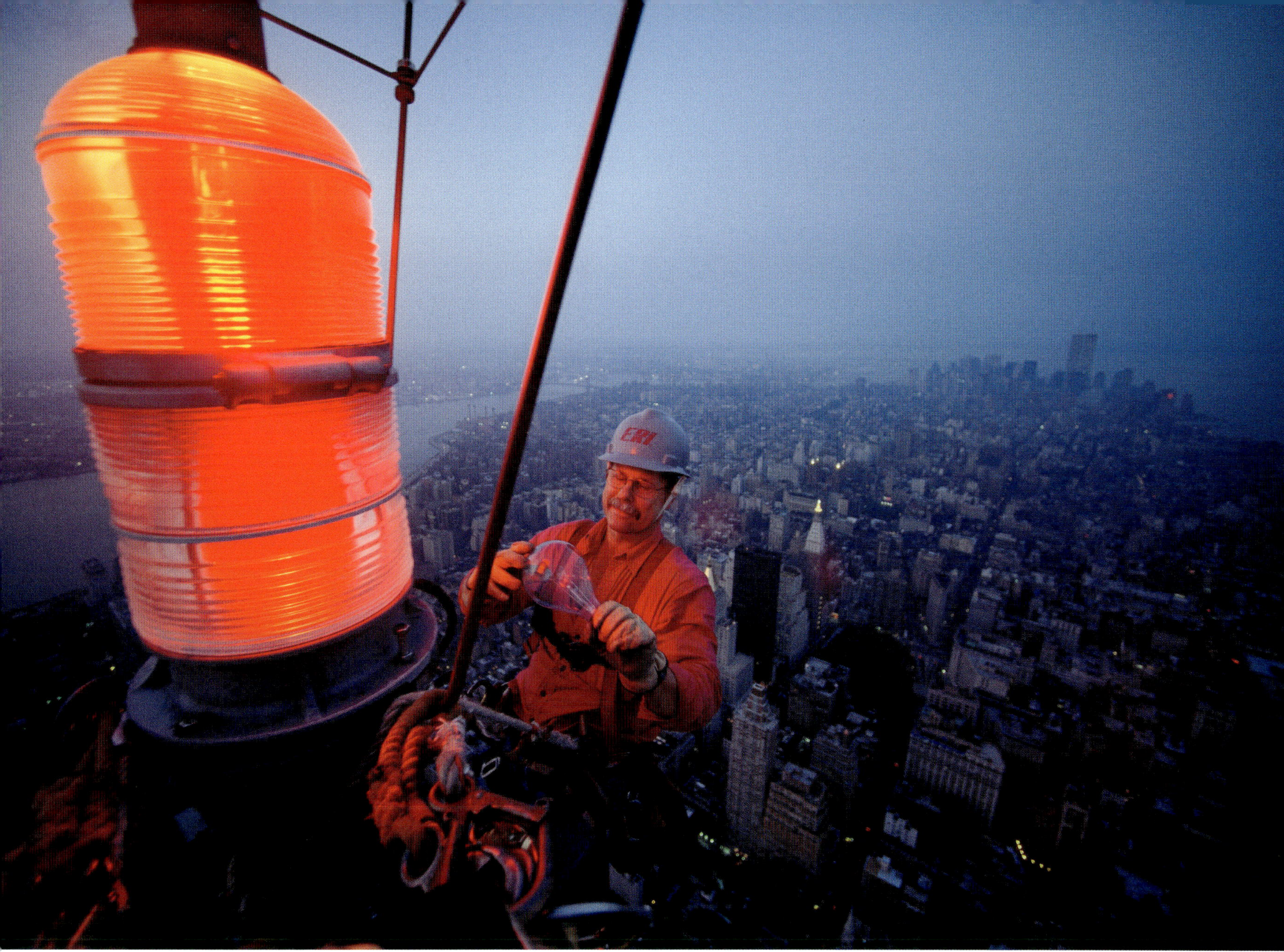

Boy, some photogs sure can spin it. One of my friends, a long-time editor at *Nat Geo*, would occasionally tell me of working with an enormously talented photographer, and his images would come up on the editing screen, and he would tee off in Shakespearean terms, describing how his pictures, when closely examined by those with a higher understanding of his intent, had massive import, not immediately recognized, of course. They required serious study to see the intricate connections to art, science, literature, and the essence of human nature. He would invariably snip off discussion or comeback with a punctilious, "Do you see my point?" During these overlong dissertations, my editor friend, who is possessed of a dark imagination and has read far too many spy novels, would imagine himself cocking his head, and looking at this imperious photog with a maniacally evil smile and devilish twinkle in his eye while he slowly slipped a length of piano wire from his belt. Do you see my point?

Great stuff can happen at the camera, for sure. But for most of us, myself included, going to work with a camera is much like … going to work. We have a job. We do it well, hopefully. We act with professionalism and dispatch. We satisfy the client's needs, we please our subjects, who are happy with the result. We go home, download the images, have dinner with our families. Do some post-production work, and send over the images, along with a bill. Case closed on that less than memorable day.

Which are most of our days.

Even in the life of truly great photographers, the angels only sat on their shoulders sporadically, at best. It is why, as I always point out, when you go to a retrospective showing of one of the greats of our industry, you tend to see the same 30–40 pictures. That's because, in their lifetime, they witnessed the truly astonishing just a sprinkling of times and had the guts, the acumen, and the presence of mind to put the camera to their eye. Good pictures, purposeful pictures, useful pictures—these happen all the time. Noticeable, eye-popping, heart-stopping pictures—well, we all hope for those a few times in our career with a camera. The truly great, iconic pictures, the ones on which our visual memory is built, the ones that need no explanation or public relations person to explain why they are good for your eyes, well, those are like finding the one, true ark.

Ease up on yourself. Remember, what is iconic to no one else is potentially iconic to you. A picture charged with meaning and import, if only personally. A corner turned, or a client won. A memory of a split second when everything worked, and you were through the door and in an entirely new space, with a camera. An image of a loved one. Here's an iconic picture, for me (below).

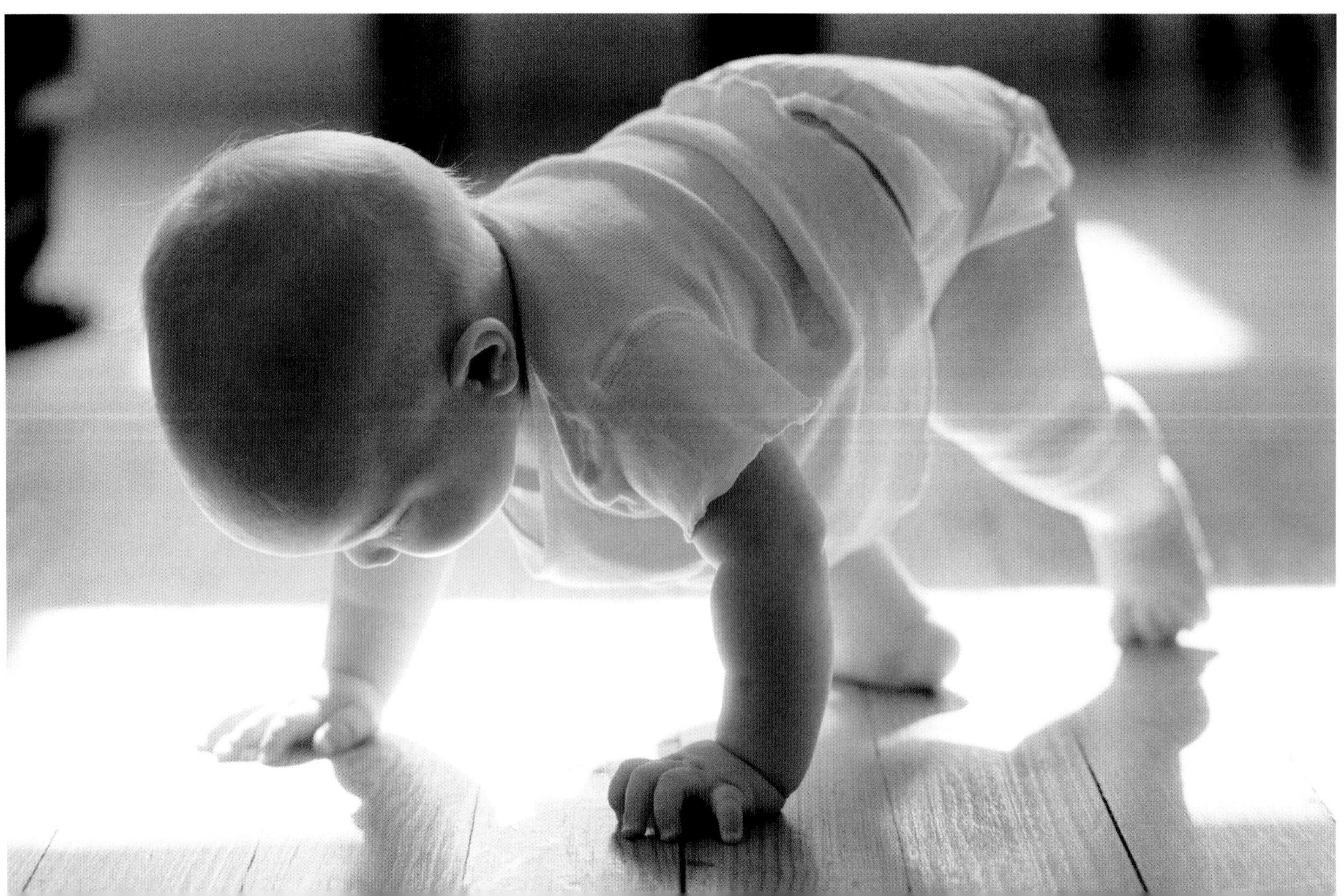

It's iconic to no one else, though everyone likes it. (They better, it's my kid.) It's my oldest daughter, Caitlin, trying to stand and walk at, maybe, six months. She couldn't do it, but she was trying. Intuitively, she knew walking was where it was at, and her early determination spoke to my heart, as a new father and a photographer. The light, the little t-shirt and diaper combo, the glow on her face. This picture also glows in my heart. If someone really pushes me to come up with "my favorite picture" after all the hundreds of thousands I've shot, well, this is certainly one of them. Deeply personal. Iconic, for me, though I never speak of it as such.

Likewise, when I made this picture of Annie (right), now long ago, striding with beautiful purpose across the deck of the USS Truman naval aircraft carrier, I was already hopelessly in love with her. I think I had been in love with her since I first remember seeing her, across the Nikon Professional Services counter at the Olympics in Sydney, Australia. I'm a visual person (go figure) and I have a snapshot of her profile in my head and heart since seeing her there. I remember thinking to myself that the very idea of ever asking such a beautiful lady to go out with me was hopeless, and I would be punching way out of my weight class.

Turns out, she did say yes to having a coffee, and thence, improbably, wonderfully, to spending her life with me. We've had many adventures, and an unlikely one we share as a couple has been to be "trapped" and then catapulted off an aircraft carrier. I remember sitting with her onboard the COD (Cargo Onboard Delivery) plane and as the crew chief sounded the alarm and shouted, "Ready, ready, ready!" doing a happy dance together. And boom! We were off into the sky.

She's smart and beautiful, carrying in her heart a raucous, unquenchable spirit of adventure. That spirit has enriched and deepened our love over time, as I have admired it, stood in awe of it, and shared it with her. And this photo, which is really a personal snap, captures Annie—hair in the wind, camera at the ready, thriving in the different, drinking it in, reveling in it. Iconic to no one but me. My true love, captured at a shutter speed almost as fast as she drives.

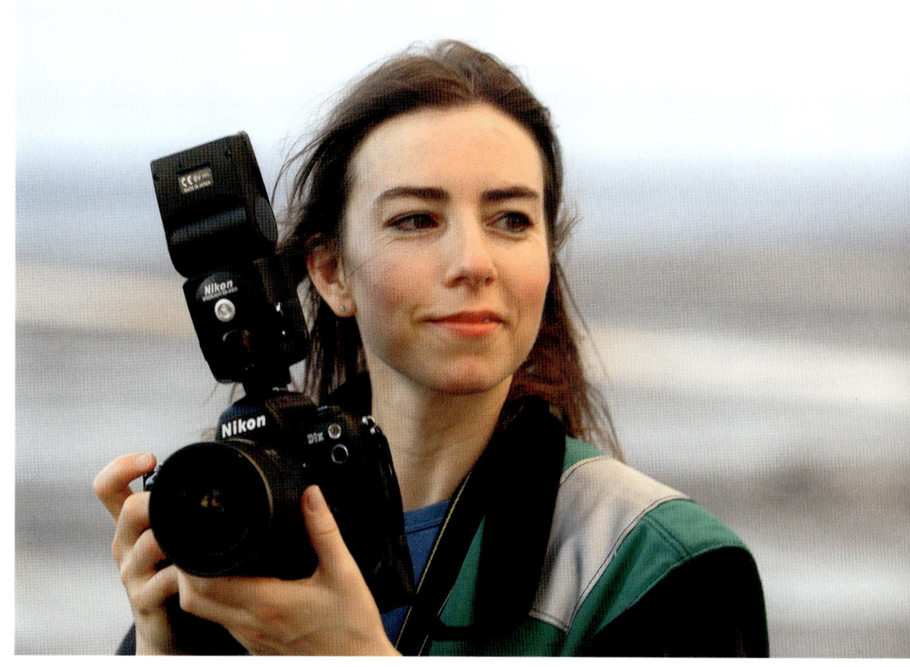

Not long ago a photo publication asked me to write a letter to the young photographer I once was. Back when I was entering the fray, caught up in the ego-driven spin cycle of comparison with other photogs, wondering who got what job and why I didn't, worrying about the bills and my place in the whole photographic enterprise, desperate to make an impression, build a career, impress an editor, get a cover, waiting breathlessly for *the* phone call, the job for the ages that would let everyone know I'd arrived. The assignment, you know, that was the ticket to the land of "iconic." It's a wonder I wasn't so exhausted by all of this angst and yearning that I still had the strength to occasionally push the shutter button.

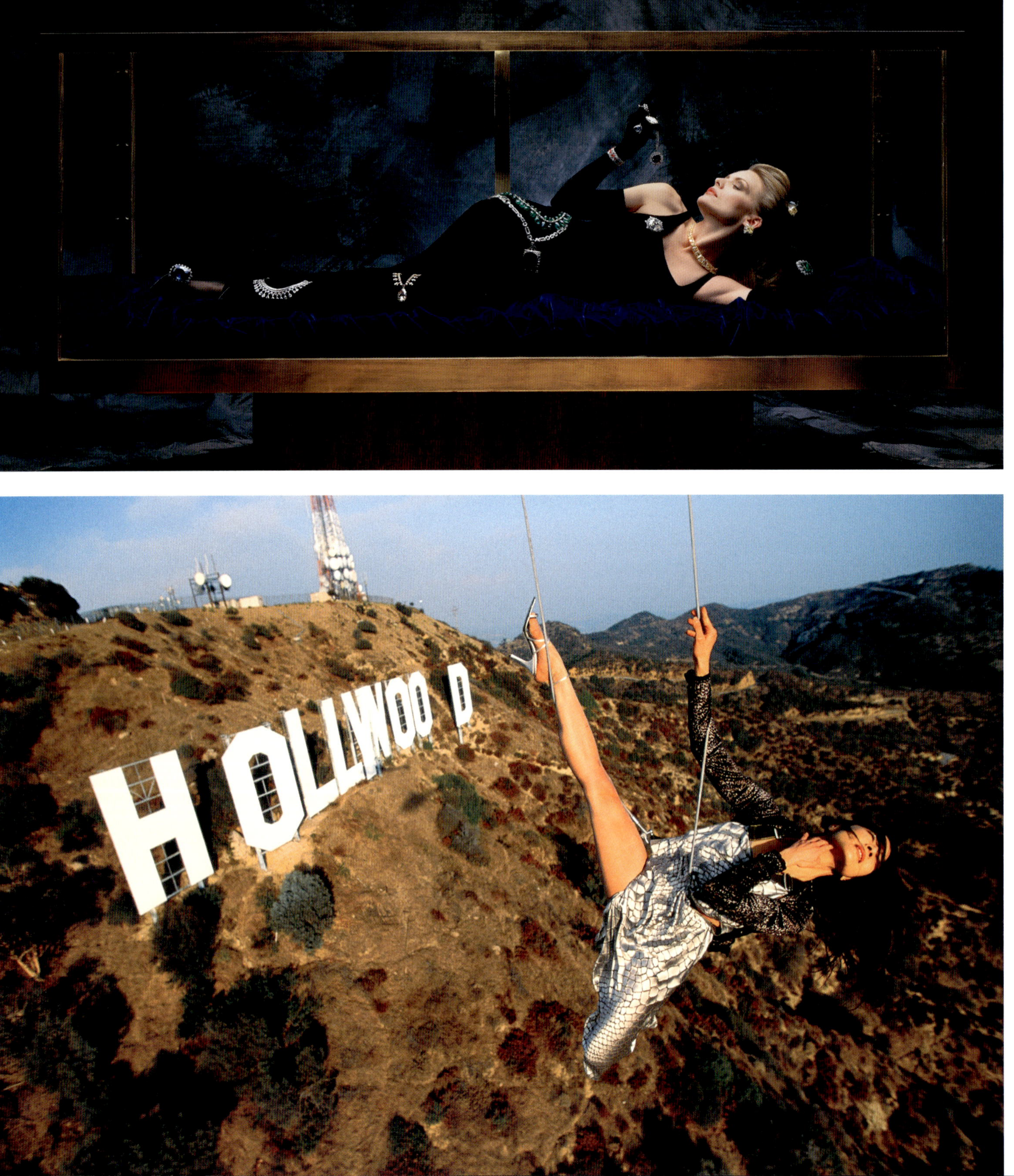

HOLLWOO D

The letter went something like this:

So, what would I say to my younger self, all these exposures later?

Oh, you know, the usual. Try not to worry, even though this is a worrisome thing to do. Be frugal and conservative on the money side of things, even though this business requires a degree of entrepreneurial risk that practitioners of more sober-sided endeavors would look upon as positively quixotic, yea, even downright foolhardy.

Try to relax! I would say. Even though the slightest quiver in the weather patterns can dash your hopes for a picture, thus imparting to this profession a certain level of ambient anxiety that is not generally present in, say, the world of office jobs. Be comfortable with uncertainty! I would counsel. There are many unseen dangers out there lurking in the pixel forest.

Ah, but the biggest dangers lurk within yourself.

So get over yourself! That's a good and important one, and one that many a shooter simply cannot seem to manage, even when faced with insurmountable evidence that being more light-hearted and less self-involved would be a good idea. Remember that lip service about your pictures and how fantastic they are is in abundance. Serious support is scarce. It's tough out there.

I have been to many gatherings of prominent photographers, both real and self-appointed, and one hears a generally intoned mantra mumbled in between cocktails and an increasingly disappointing and economically minded offering of hors d'oeuvres about what we do as being "important."

(Upon my first cover story for *National Geographic*, I hosted such a gathering. I honored the long-time tradition photographers upheld there by throwing a cover story party. It was de rigueur at that time. I went over the top, so giddy was I about my first *Nat Geo* cover that I spent about $1,000 on shrimp and vodka-soaked sardines. Over time, those cover parties rapidly receded into the realm of boxed wine and Ritz crackers, and thence to no observance at all.)

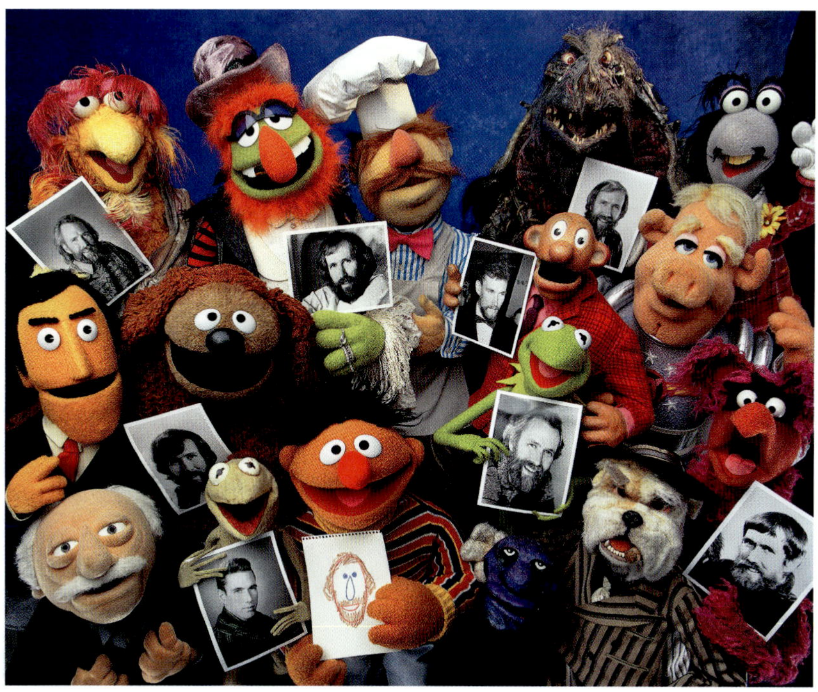

And, of course, what we do is important, massively so. We document visual history, small and large. But then, a cautionary note always creeps into my head: If what we do is so important, why do the people we do it for treat us so poorly? Those increasingly drab cover parties marched in lockstep with the downgrading of contracts, predatory rights grabs, layoffs, and a variety of indignities manifesting themselves in restrictions in field expenses. Why are we so beset, as a group? So downgraded, in terms of value, with great consistency? Why is the first phrase of the assigning phone call, "We have virtually no budget"? This business has always been tough, and it gets tougher all the time.

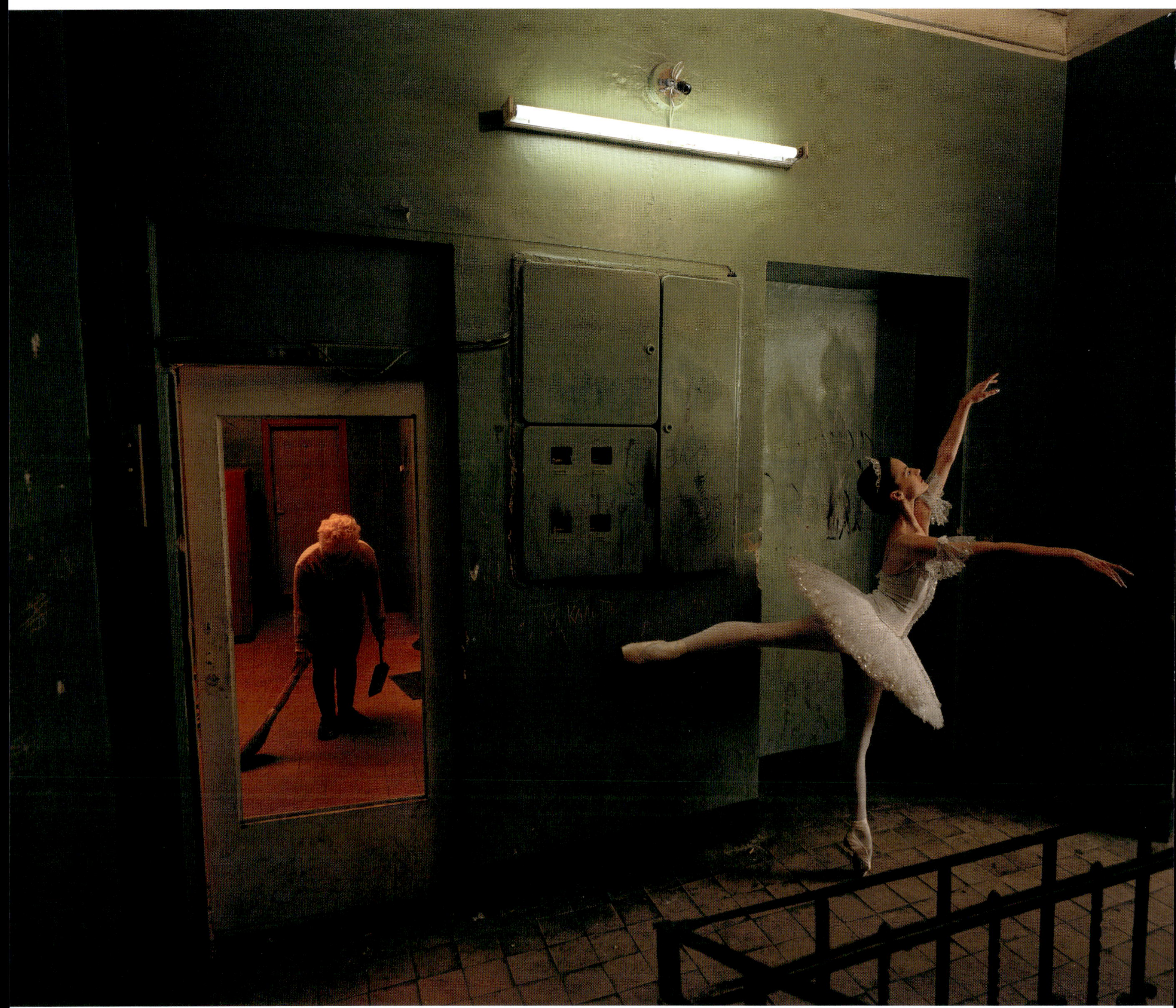

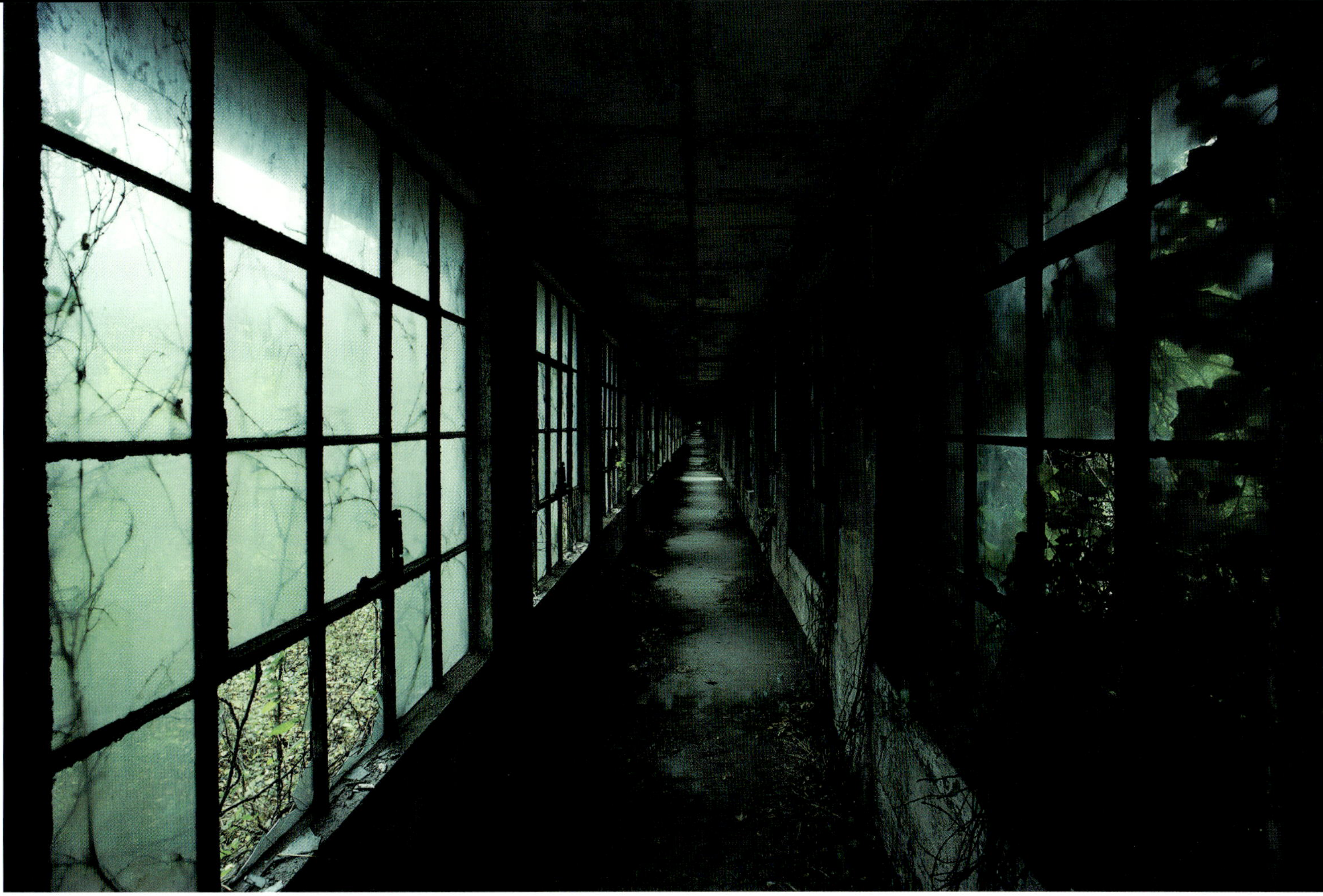

So, how do you weather this long-term, never-ending storm? How do you armor up and protect your photographic soul from being essentially drained out of you? This business is like Imhotep, the mummy, who just keeps sucking your organs out of your inner cavities. As Beni, the mummy's ill-fated assistant, says, "Prince Imhotep thanks you for your hospitality . . . and for your eyes . . . and for your tongue . . . but I'm afraid more is needed." Where does it stop?

Here's a thought. Let go. Be happy. Realize the trappings of photographic ego are heavy indeed, like toting a massive tripod around with you on a shoot. When accolades are offered, be gracious, but deflect. Don't take to heart the press clippings that say you are an amazing photographer. This should be easy for you to do, as you are the only one who has seen your outtakes and what a friggin' mess they are.

And, to a reasonable degree, care not about the fee, or the deadline, or the unrealistic expectations. Those realities will embitter your attitude and blight your pixels. Be lighter of heart about all this, for photography itself is not designed to always be ponderous and dark of mood. Revel in the sound of the shutter—it is the exclamation point at the end of the sentence, "I am a photographer!" Understand that being a photographer still requires you to take a walk, whilst others labor seated at computers. Accept the glorious fact that what you do today with a camera will almost certainly be inconsequential, but that sliver of hope still gleams in your head and heart that the next frame is the one.

And the beautiful thing is, whenever you pick up a camera, there will be a next frame. And it might just be . . . iconic.

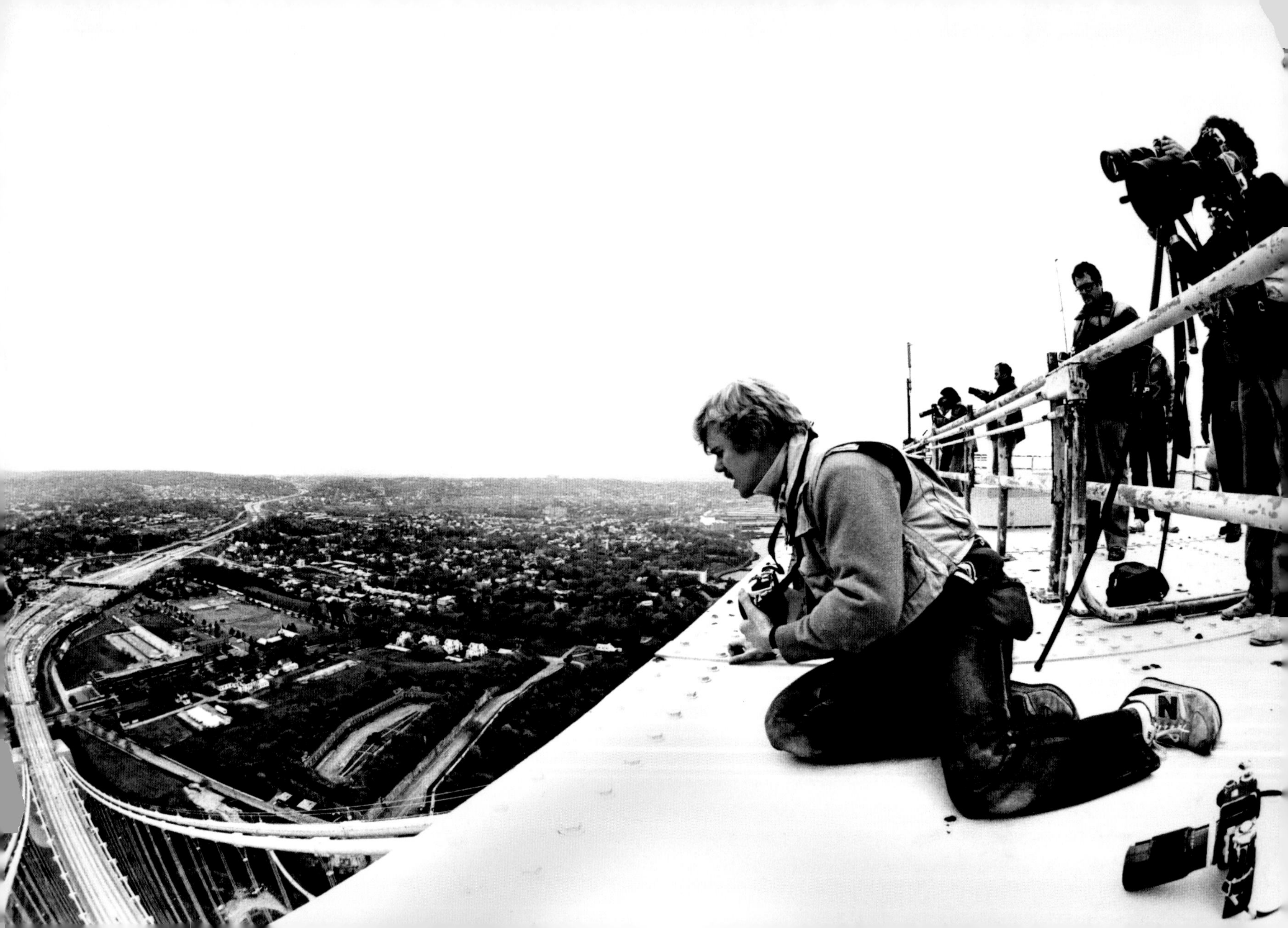

In Closing

I've been writing this book for the last two years, and I've been thinking about it for the last five, and living it for the last forty.

The life of a photographer is largely about climbing over the safety rail and peering out, and over, and beyond. And we keep doing it, ill-advisedly, despite the fact that there is often nothing there to see, or what is seen is disappointing, irrelevant, drab, and hardly worth the effort, much less the risk to ourselves.

But we keep doing it. Over and over, with no assurances of success, safety, or remuneration. Because there may be a picture there. Unlikely, but possible. And that tantalizing possibility is the endless fuel that animates the photographic spirit, and makes you climb over the rail, even when logic says stay put.

The Irish poet laureate Seamus Heaney, possessed of a deep eloquence and understanding of the human condition, may have unwittingly penned the best description of a photographic career. It is, in fact, carved on his gravestone in the north of Ireland.

"Walk on air against your better judgement."

Love and light to all.

-30-

Index